PRIME

Dedication

I dedicate this book to the late, great Joshua Ozersky, my friend and partner in Meatopia, who inspired me to write, and wrote the foreword to the resulting book *Hog*. He is profoundly missed.

It turns out writing is not as easy as I once thought; it really is a craft, and Josh's prose is where I turn when I need to be inspired in my own stumbling efforts. He wrote this:

"As a food writer, I am handicapped by gross deficiencies. I've never worked in a restaurant or gone to cooking school, and am utterly ignorant of whole cuisines, but no man feels food more deeply. It's my whole life, and my connection to it is wildly, shamefully emotional: I live it, and that bone-deep obsession powers my work. That honesty, unwholesome though it may be, fixes my view and grants me the kind of zeal and rancor that makes writing about roast beef meaningful.

When I started to write about food my voice led me through my dark places. It makes my work good, or at least honest, and honest is enough."

Joshua Ozersky 1967–2015

Mitchell Beazley

RICHARD H. TURNER

PRIME

The Beef Cookbook

An Hachette UK Company

www.hachette.co.uk

First published in Great Britain in 2017 by Mitchell Beazley,
a division of Octopus Publishing Group Ltd
Carmelite House, 50 Victoria Embankment
London EC4Y 0DZ

www.octopusbooks.co.uk

Photography copyright © Paul Winch-Furness 2017
Text copyright © Richard H Turner 2017
Design and layout copyright © Octopus Publishing Group Ltd

Distributed in the US by Hachette Book Group
1290 Avenue of the Americas, 4th and 5th Floors
New York, NY 10020

www.octopusbooksusa.com

Distributed in Canada by Canadian Manda Group
664 Annette St., Toronto, Ontario, Canada M6S 2C8

ISBN 978 178472 101 5

A CIP catalogue record for this book is available
from the British Library.

Printed and bound in China

10 9 8 7 6 5 4 3 2 1

All recipes have been tested in metric. Both imperial and
metric measurements have been given in all recipes. Use
one set of measurements only and not a mixture of both.

Eggs should be medium unless otherwise stated. This book
contains dishes made with raw or lightly cooked eggs, and raw
or cured beef. It is prudent for more vulnerable people such as
pregnant and nursing mothers, invalids, the elderly, babies and
young children to avoid uncooked or lightly cooked dishes.

Ovens should be preheated to the specific temperature – if
using a fan-assisted oven, follow manufacturer's instructions
for adjusting the time and the temperature.

Publishing Director Stephanie Jackson
Managing Editor Sybella Stephens
Copy Editor Annie Lee
Art Director Juliette Norsworthy
Photographer Paul Winch-Furness
Illustrators Grace Helmer, Ella Mclean
Food Stylist Richard H Turner
Home Economists Emily Kydd,
Matthew Brown
Prop Stylist Linda Berlin
Assistant Production Manager
Lucy Carter

Contents

Foreword by Mark Schatzker

Eating is a funny thing. The desire for food to be at its most delicious is universal. And yet, the food we often eat is far from that ideal. It's all thanks to the human mouth.

On the one hand, you need a mouth in order to eat – that much is obvious. But when meals end, we begin using our mouths for something else: talking. This is where things often go wrong.

We get hung up on words. For example, we get obsessed with places. Every ten years or so, some new place pops into vogue, and within a week it seems every chef is doing his own take on some obscure regional recipe, particularly, it seems, chefs who have never visited that area. We also become fixated on techniques. A few years ago, there was a spell of several months where no one who knew anything about food wanted to eat anything that wasn't cooked in a plastic bag.

There's nothing inherently wrong with places or techniques. But they are not, in themselves, a silver bullet conferring deliciousness on a sauce, a dish, or a meal. In our enthusiasm for good food, we get lost in concepts and very often end up making food bad. There are, however, a vanguard of chefs who measure food by a simple but all important metric: the way it tastes. Richard Turner is one. He's not a traditionalist – there are recipes in this book for Kimchi Hash, West African Suya and Burmese Beef Curry. But he's not taken in by the food world's frequent bouts of silliness. He just loves food. And he wants other people to love the food he loves, and for the same reason.

Which brings us to beef, the king of all meats. The bedrock protein. The eternal object of our primordial meat hunger. When a boneless breast of chicken looks in the mirror, it wishes it was beef. All of which makes today's sorry state of beef all the more perplexing.

Over the past several decades, we have engineered our agricultural system to produce beef at the lowest possible price. Beef today is cheap. It's amazing to consider that you can walk into a supermarket and buy a rib eye steak – a vanishingly scarce piece of carcass – for a few pounds or dollars.

But it's lost the one thing that made it so desirable in the first place: flavour. So we do to beef what we do to boneless chicken breast – we smother it in sauces and rubs and marinades.

To any beef lover, loving beef has become inordinately difficult. It's as though red meat has lost its voice.

I wrote an entire book about what happened to beef. When it came out, I started hearing from all sorts of chefs, most of whom would write to tell me that they had cracked the mystery of the perfect rub (it would invariably involve powdered soup mix), or magical marinade (which was actually a salad dressing), or the perfect ratio of brisket to chuck in a burger grind (which makes no sense, because no two briskets and chucks are alike). And then I heard from Richard Turner, who worshipped at the same altar of simplicity. A good steak, he said, needed two things: fire and salt.

If you love beef, listen to Richard Turner. Listen to what he says about what kind of cows you should eat, what those cows should eat, the kinds of lives they should live, how they should be killed, cut, and, finally, cooked. Take a morsel of that beef – that Smoked Prime Rib, that scrap of Pickled Tripe, that slug of Beef Heart Tea – and put it in the place it was destined for: your mouth. More eating, less talking. It's the way food was meant to be.

Mark Schatzker, 2017

Introduction

When meat cravings hit, more often than not what springs to mind is beef... and specifically steak. It's the embodiment of premium meat, the most expensive thing on the menu. There are restaurants devoted solely to beef – dimly lit and decorated in leather and dark wood, steakhouses are temples to our carnivorous voracity. As well as its own restaurant genre, beef has its own piece of cutlery: the steak knife, large, imposing and Ramboesque. Steakhouses might show you the meat raw, carried out to diners on a tray with various chunks of dark red flesh for us to point at. "That one" we might say; it's all very primal. *Prime* is about beef and steak: why it's special and what it takes to make this king of meat great.

In this book, I've explained what it takes to grill the perfect steak, roast the perfect joint and make the perfect burger, as well as the different ways to get the best out of the cuts and – in some cases – breeds. These are guidelines rather than rules. If you have read the book, you will hopefully be using a nice piece of extensively farmed pure-bred native beef, and you'll understand that uniformity is not one of its many excellent qualities. I've put together some 160 or so recipes, some classics from around the world and some unique recipes from my notebook. As a rule of thumb, 1kg (about 2lb) of beef feeds four to six people, but I'm not the meat police, so I am really leaving it up to you.

Between the recipe chapters, I will also highlight the shortcuts most farmers are pressurized into taking, at great cost to our palates and even to our health. In a destructive cycle, our meat lust fuels intensive farming, which in turn makes it cheap to buy and encourages excessive meat consumption. It is a cycle that benefits no one, including the farmers forced to sell meat so cheaply that their sales barely cover their costs. It's not good for our own health, nor for the health of the animals we farm.

There is a lot of scaremongering in the media about meat eating, and consumption of meat has been linked to obesity, diabetes, heart disease and certain cancers. Since much of the meat eaten around the world is intensively farmed, and since these scare stories don't differentiate between intensively farmed and naturally reared meat, this is an understandable mistake. In the chapter on health I make the case for judicious consumption of naturally reared, high-quality beef, as part of a healthy, balanced diet.

Elsewhere in the book, I outline the differences between intensive and extensive farming and why they are important. There is a vast difference between the meat from animals raised with pride and the meat from animals bred for profit, and this is why they taste so different. Much of this difference is down to feed, which is one of the most important factors in beef flavour and health.

I also discuss slaughter, which is as important as how you rear the animals, and I explore the hanging of beef and the pros and cons of extended ageing. Finally, I'll tell you a bit about butchery techniques and give some rough bovine myology (where all the bits come from).

In *Prime* I want to make the case for sensible shopping, buying less beef but of a better quality – meat that's been reared by farmers who care. One way to avoid intensively farmed beef is to be much choosier about where we buy it. Few supermarkets sell good, extensively farmed meat, and labels can be misleading, so I give an honest and truthful opinion of what they actually mean.

As with my previous book, *Hog*, there is a whole chapter on breeds and why the breed informs flavour. I've stuck to the important beef breeds, as I'm reasonably certain a description of breeds such as Ankole-Watusi is beyond the remit of this book (though it is a fine-looking animal).

Prime is a celebratory story running from Angus to White Park, with a little zealous drum banging along the way, and if I've climbed on my soapbox a little too much, I apologize. I hope to give good reasons to source, buy and cook beef with respect for the farmer, the animal and your stomach. Like any good story, there are villains, but I've tried not to condemn out of hand – we omnivores are all in this together and, collectively, we share responsibility for the beef industry of today. As the beef guru Mark Schatzker opines, it's much better to try to influence from the inside than to cast stones from the outside.

Ingredients

It is difficult to write this section without sounding like a broken record, but I'll try. The general gist is to buy consciously, ask questions and don't settle for second best.

Meat As explained in more detail in the section on Buying Beef (see pages 294–5), buy the very best you can afford, if possible from someone who is knowledgeable on the subject. Ask questions like "How was the animal farmed?" "How old was it?" "What did it eat?" "What breed was it?" and be prepared to spend a little more for a little less quantity. Beef should be an occasional weekly extravagance – yes, you read that right. I'm suggesting we all eat a bit less meat, but of a lot better quality.

Fruit & vegetables Many of those immaculately clean and uniform vegetables you see in the supermarket aisles and in their sterile packaging have been farmed industrially. They are less nutrient-dense than vegetables farmed organically, or those grown by the small band of farmers who farm on a small scale and naturally. The supermarket versions also taste of less: one of the secrets of the great ingredient-led restaurants is their vegetable sourcing. The carrot or squash you eat at St John, the River Café or Chez Panisse is not the same as the one you bought in the supermarket, and if you search out your own supply you absolutely can cook food that is just as tasty as at those restaurants.

It's also important to buy in season. Asparagus bought in winter will have been grown in a different hemisphere from where you live and flown halfway around the world. That means it will have been produced with some serious jiggery-pokery and downright shenanigans so as still to look fresh upon arrival. (And that's not to mention the cost of getting it there.) Buy as much as you can seasonally – for your taste buds, your wallet and the environment.

Salt I use sea salt almost exclusively in my cooking; it contains trace minerals that give it a more complex flavour than ordinary table salt. Table salt also contains anti-caking agents that adversely affect the flavour of your food. Learning how to use salt is perhaps the biggest secret to great cooking – too much makes food taste salty and creates a kind of "seasoning fatigue" when the dish is eaten, while too little means food tastes bland.

Spices All spices should be used fresh, especially pepper, and should be freshly ground. If you're not doing it already, this one small piece of advice is going to improve your cooking immeasurably. When spices are ground, they start to release volatile oils into the air – that's flavour! Buy small amounts from a source with a high turnover, and grind as you cook, using either a mill or a mortar and pestle.

Vinegars & oils Not all vinegars and oils are made equal. With oils it pays to buy small bottles as often as possible: although they might not go off, they certainly deteriorate over time, particularly olive oil. Vinegars keep well, but avoid industrially produced ones. If at all possible, look for live, naturally brewed vinegars – or go one better and make your own.

Dairy Okay, it's soapbox time again: buying ethically farmed grass-fed dairy is as important as buying good grass-fed meat. Good dairy should be consumed in reasonable quantities. Good dairy also tastes better – *quelle surprise*! If you can find cultured cream and butter from grass-fed herds, you are in for a treat. Buy cheeses from experts in the field, who have kept them carefully. Never, ever buy grated cheese: it tastes rank.

Eggs As with meat and dairy, pay close attention to where your eggs come from and how they are produced. It matters that hens are treated well, with room to range and forage. The reason is that if we eat animal products, our consciences should be clear about how those animals lived. It also matters because healthy, happy animals produce tastier, more nutritious, safer food, and nowhere is that clearer than with eggs. Buy free-range and, if you can, buy organic – or if you have the space, keep hens yourself and enjoy their freshly laid eggs.

Fish There's very little fish in this book, so I'll keep this brief. Buy sustainably. Treat fish with the same respect as you do meat – ask questions and avoid factory-farmed fish or endangered species such as tuna.

I use a fair quantity of anchovies and it's not always clear how sustainable they are. As a species, anchovies are near the base of the food chain, and the impact of their large-scale removal on the marine ecosystem is poorly understood. Keep an eye on this and avoid using them if there's any question.

Nuts When buying nuts, we might consider the ethics of production: one of the nut industry's biggest concerns over the years has been labour standards. One issue is home working – where employees process nuts at home – which is difficult to monitor for safety and hours worked. Even in factories, women working in nut production earn meagre wages and are exposed to smoke and the nut's corrosive oil. As a rule, we should assume there are issues with labour unless proved otherwise. Farming all over the world is a low-margin business, with pressure on cost and therefore on labour conditions. Look for the Fairtrade mark, which resembles a person waving over a yin-yang symbol.

Avoid Chinese pine nuts if you can. I once fell foul of something called pine mouth, after eating Chinese pine nuts bought from a supermarket. All I could taste afterwards was an overriding metallic flavour, which made my job extremely difficult, aggravated by my lack of information on it at the time – I didn't know it wasn't permanent! I regained my taste buds after a week, but the only thing I could drink during that time was water, and all food tasted unbearably metallic. Good for weight loss, if nothing else.

1

Steaks

My perfect steak

There is no such thing as a perfect steak, of course – nature doesn't work that way, and the flavour of steak is subjective. However, these are my preferred cooking methods. My perfect steak has a sweet, meaty smell and taste, has a flavour that keeps on going in the mouth, and is moreish and beefy. It has been hung for around five weeks (excessively hung meat can mask inferior meat). When raw, it is not wet or sticky, nor is it soft or mushy. It is a brighter red colour than the well-marbled, intensively grain-fed steak, which is often graded by the amount of white and creamy marbling. In my perfect steak, if the marbling is visible at all, it is a pale yellow intramuscular fat that has been laid down slowly – more often, however, it is invisible to the naked eye.

The science behind cooking a perfect steak

Maillard is the chemical reaction that occurs when meat is browned, and it is one of the main reasons that grilled and roasted meat tastes so delicious. Maillard begins at 140–170°C (284–338°F). Knowing the correct temperature that a grill or pan needs to reach for Maillard to happen, recognizing the right time to season the meat and put it on the grill, and understanding how sugars and amino acids in meat combine at high heat to produce reactions and flavour compounds, can only help us become better cooks.

Different cuts of meat have varying degrees of tenderness, which can largely be attributed to the collagen in each muscle. Collagen is made of naturally occurring proteins and is the main component of connective tissue in muscle. The strength of the collagen varies in different cuts of meat and is also dependent on the age, breed and sex of the animal. Muscles that do very little work have weak collagen. Prime cuts generally have less connective tissue and collagen and are consequently more tender. Less expensive cuts usually have more connective tissue and collagen and so tend to be tougher. Understanding collagen is an important part of understanding cooking. In order to turn a tougher, collagen-rich cut into something delicious, juicy and tender, the muscle must be cooked with a lower, even heat so that the collagen molecules unravel, break down and dissolve into soft gelatine that bastes and moistens the meat.

Preparation Allow the steaks to sit for 30 minutes in order to come up to room temperature; this is known as tempering. Then dry the steaks off, because wet steak will struggle to form a decent crust and can pick up some unpleasant boiled-meat flavours – although once the steaks have been tempered at room temperature, they are already slightly drier than they would be straight from the refrigerator.

Seasoning I like pure Maldon sea salt flakes to season steaks; I never use table salt. This is because, as explained on page 10, table salt is saltier and contains anti-caking agents which are not suited to steak.

I season aggressively, throwing handfuls of salt at the steak, shaking it over the tray before cooking it. During this process, much of the salt falls off, and what's left is the correct amount of seasoning, in theory.

As with everything, there are variables to watch out for: thicker steaks, such as chateaubriands and bone-in ribs,

Medium-rare

Medium

Medium-
well done

require more seasoning than thinner steaks because of their lower ratio of surface area to meat.

Not all steak is hung for the same amount of time, and it's important to note that steaks of different ages take seasoning differently. If you think about it, it's obvious that a younger, wetter steak will absorb more seasoning than an older, drier one.

The amount of salt required also varies according to cooking method. On a grill with bars, much of the salt falls off the steak and onto the charcoal; when cooking in butter, some of the salt dissipates into the butter; and when cooking in a pan with minimal fat, almost all of the salt remains on the steak.

A truly great steak cook understands all these variables and adjusts the seasoning marginally according to the thickness, age, moisture content and cooking method of each steak.

Some say you shouldn't season the steak until after you've cooked it – they're wrong.

When is it cooked? Some say to prod different
parts of your hand or face and compare with the texture of the steak to tell when it is cooked, but this is not a reliable method. There is no particular test that will tell you when a steak is perfectly cooked to your liking, and only with practice and experience you will get used to the "feel" of the correct cooking temperature.

It is also worth bearing in mind that cooking temperatures are subjective and perceptions vary from country to country. My cooking temperatures are perhaps a touch more cooked than those of, for instance, a Frenchman or Spaniard, and this is deliberate. Most of the great steak cuts contain fat and fat needs to be at a certain temperature to be digestible, and do its job of lubrication and flavour transfer. It's for this reason I don't cook steaks rare, except under duress. These are the temperatures I work to, bearing in mind the internal temperature should be at the bottom end of each range at the end of cooking and towards the top end once rested.

Medium-rare: 55–60°C (130–140°F)

Medium: 60–65°C (140–150°F)

Medium-well done: 65–70°C (150–160°F)

Cooking over charcoal

Cooking on a live fire grill is a skill and craft all of its own, made easier by the performance and quality of the material you're burning. Success in cooking over a flame, whether direct or indirect, is down to the ability to control temperature, and while it is possible to give you guidance as to how to do this, the technique can really only be learned through practice. Just keep lighting your grill and cooking on it, and you will begin to understand the hot spots and cool spots, how long it takes for the coals to burn down for the optimum grilling temperature, and how long a full load of charcoal lasts.

Light the grill early enough to allow it to die down before cooking the first piece of meat. Make sure the grill is hot, but not too hot: the charcoal should have burned down and be coated in white ash. It should not be so hot that you can't stand close to it; if it's too hot for you, then it's probably too hot for the steak. The aim is to get a good char on the outside while keeping the meat juicy and tender inside, which is impossible with a thin piece of meat – ideally, the steak should be at least 4cm (1½ inches) thick. Take it out of the refrigerator 30 minutes before cooking, to bring it up to room temperature. At the last second, season the meat well, but don't use any oil on it – if the grill is at the correct temperature, the meat won't stick.

Direct cooking over charcoal or wood

When cooking directly over charcoal, it impacts the meat with high surface temperatures. The heat is not deflected or absorbed by anything during the process and does not affect the meat solely through the convection currents, as it does with indirect cooking. With a little skill, direct live fire cooking is one of the most exciting methods of cooking.

Place the meat on the grill and leave it for a couple of minutes before turning. Then, carry on turning every couple of minutes until you've achieved some enticing Maillard caramelization. If the piece of meat is thick, you'll need to turn it regularly to avoid burning. Move your meat if you see yellow flames from the barbecue – this means that fat has caught fire, which can make the meat taste too smoky. Don't overcrowd the grill; make sure there's plenty of space between each piece of meat.

It's impossible to give exact cooking times, as it all depends on the thickness of the meat, the animal it comes from, the cut and the temperature of the grill. However, as an example, a 600g (21oz) bone-in sirloin takes around 4 minutes on each side over hot charcoal, plus a 10-minute rest at 57°C (135°F), in order to be medium-rare. The key thing to remember is to take the meat off before you think it is ready and then let it rest.

Indirect cooking or charcoal roasting

Indirect live fire cooking is far from an exact science, but as long as you have a meat probe to hand, all should be well. Probes are invaluable tools, but the sense of touch is still important, which becomes apparent through experience. Using both alongside each other will allow you to train your fingertips without too many mistakes. There is no shame at all in using a meat probe, and it is the only way to produce consistent results, particularly if you are in the early part of your journey as a meat cook.

Controlling the temperature of your barbecue using the air vents will enable you to use techniques for taking larger prime cuts to medium-rare. This set-up also provides a safety net if you have a particularly fatty piece of meat and do not want to suffer flare-ups that could ruin something special. Being able to moderate the cooking using two different zones (direct and indirect heat) is particularly helpful in this respect – if the grill is getting a little out of control and larger cuts are at risk of burning before they are properly cooked, just move them to the indirect area, where they can rest until the grill calms down.

To achieve this set-up, you need to light your charcoal and wait until it is ready to use – make sure your coals and wood are really hot and white. Push the coals to the side and put on the lid, keeping the vents open a little to allow air to pass out. This is so that indirect convection currents flow through the barbecue in much the same way as for a convection oven, with the heat being diffused throughout the cooking chamber so that it flows evenly around the meat. The cooking is much more even than over direct heat.

You are now ready to cook indirectly. When the barbecue is used this way, as a charcoal roaster, it means you can cook almost anything that you can in a conventional oven. On the top of your barbecue, you'll probably find a heat gauge, which is there precisely for when you want to use the barbecue for indirect cooking as an oven.

Combining direct and indirect cooking

If a piece of meat is really thick, it can be started using the direct cooking method and finished using the indirect cooking method. Larger cuts of meat such as bone-in ribs and chateaubriands benefit greatly from using indirect heat to finish the cooking.

Clinching or dirty cooking

At the other end of the spectrum is clinching, or dirty cooking, of steak, direct on the wood or charcoal. The technique is awesome in its simplicity: instead of using a grill, meat is cooked directly in or on the hot charcoal or wood. The most important thing is to use good-quality charcoal and wood and to show no fear. While burning is an understandable concern, it is unfounded, as it's actually harder to burn a steak this way than it is if you're new to grilling. When meat gets close to the hot coals, it will burn, but put it right against them, up close and personal, and the coals don't get enough oxygen to create fire, so you're cooking purely on the heat of the charcoal. This process super-heats the fat and allows steam to penetrate the meat more quickly than with direct or indirect cooking.

Cooking in butter

Take the steak out of the refrigerator 30 minutes before you're planning to cook, to allow it to come to room temperature. Heat a heavy-based griddle pan or frying pan over a medium-high heat, then season the steak lightly, bearing in mind that less falls off in a pan than on a grill. Put it flat-side-down in the pan and cook for 90 seconds on each side, pressing down with a spatula, until both sides are well browned. Add the butter, and some garlic and thyme if you are using them. The rapidly melting butter, flavoured with crushed garlic, is then used to baste the steak as it cooks. This gives it a gorgeous richness; the browning butter helps to impart some lovely, savoury flavour to the crust along with the garlic.

In theory, you remove the steak from the pan and leave it somewhere warm to rest for 10–15 minutes, then serve. However, if the steak is thick enough, I've been known to turn the heat off early and allow the steak to rest in its pool of butter in the pan instead.

Frequent flipping is the key to moist steak, as neither side has the time to absorb – or to release – large amounts of heat. The meat cooks faster and its outer layers end up less overdone.

Direct cooking over charcoal

Clinched over charcoal

Serves
4

2 x 500g (1lb 2oz) bone-in steaks such as T-bone or prime rib, cut 3–4mm (about ⅛ inch) thick

50g (1¾oz) beef dripping

125g (4½oz) unsalted butter

4 thyme sprigs

2 garlic bulbs, cloves peeled

1 rosemary sprig

Maldon sea salt flakes and freshly ground black pepper

Butter-fried steak with golden garlic

This is old-school French cookery at its best. If you can find grass-fed butter, then use it – evidence is mounting that grass-fed butter is healthier than intensively farmed butter, and it's certainly better for you than margarine or oil.

Season the steaks all over with salt and pepper.

Heat the dripping in a large cast-iron skillet or frying pan. When it has melted and is foaming, add the steaks and cook over a high heat until crusty on the bottom, about 3–4 minutes. Turn the steaks and add half the butter, the thyme, garlic cloves and rosemary to the skillet.

Cook over a high heat, basting the steaks with the foaming butter, garlic and herbs, turning once more and adding the remaining butter. Cook until the steaks are medium-rare, 3–4 minutes longer. Transfer the steaks to a chopping board or plate and allow to rest for at least 10 minutes, preferably longer.

Remove the herbs and keep frying the garlic until golden and soft. Cut the steaks off the bone, then slice the meat across the grain and serve with the meat resting juices poured over and the fried garlic cloves.

Classic steak garnishes

Place a pile each of Grilled Portobello Mushrooms, Slow-roasted Tomatoes and Onion Rings on the plate with your steak, finishing with watercress.

Grilled Portobello mushrooms Serves 4–6

A great steakhouse menu virtually writes itself, and a mushroom side is a must. I've been cooking my mushrooms with Worcestershire sauce for years, but have recently taken to the sweetness of kecap manis instead. Try it.

12 large Portobello mushrooms

4 garlic cloves, crushed

1 banana shallot, finely chopped

a few thyme leaves

a few tarragon or/and parsley leaves, chopped

1 tablespoon kecap manis (sweet soy sauce)

1 tablespoon Madeira Gravy (see page 114)

1 teaspoon lemon juice

Maldon sea salt flakes and freshly ground black pepper

Grill the mushrooms until just cooked, over charcoal if available or in a nonstick pan if not. Cut each one into quarters.

Toss the mushrooms with the remaining ingredients and correct the seasoning.

Allow to sit for a few minutes, then serve.

Slow-roasted tomatoes

Serves 4–6

These are more slow-dried than roasted, and are intense and tangy.

1kg (2lb 4oz) ripe plum tomatoes

a few thyme sprigs, leaves picked

100ml (3½fl oz) extra virgin olive oil

1–2 garlic cloves, sliced, to taste

Maldon sea salt flakes

Preheat the oven to 110°C (225°F), Gas Mark ¼.

Halve the tomatoes and place on a baking tray, cut side up. Sprinkle with salt, thyme, a little oil and garlic slices.

Place in the preheated oven and leave overnight.

Transfer to sterlized jars (see page 163), cover with olive oil, and keep until needed.

Onion rings Serves 4–6

I've tried dozens of versions of onion rings and these are by far my favourite. Part battered, part breadcrumbed: the best of both worlds.

1 red onion

1 brown onion

100ml (3½fl oz) malt vinegar

vegetable oil, for deep-frying

plain flour seasoned with salt and pepper, for dusting

panko breadcrumbs

For the batter

330ml (11oz) lager

160g (5¾oz) plain flour

a pinch of cayenne pepper

a pinch of English mustard powder

Maldon sea salt flakes and freshly ground white pepper

Peel the onions and cut them into rings 1cm (½ inch) in width. Place in a dish, pour over the vinegar and leave to marinate for 3 hours.

To make the batter, pour the lager into a large mixing bowl and gently whisk in the flour until you get a smooth, silky consistency (you may need more or less flour than specified). Add the cayenne, mustard and seasoning.

Heat the oil to 180°C (350°F) in a deep-fat fryer. Drop the onion rings into the seasoned flour, then into the batter, then into the seasoned breadcrumbs. Fry until golden brown, then remove with tongs and place on kitchen paper to drain. Season and serve.

Watercress

A bunch of fresh watercress is a must-have side for any steak.

Most jerk recipes call for the meat to be marinated before cooking, but not this one – it makes for a fresher, zingier result that I really like. You can, of course, just grill the steak and cauliflower if the direct to coals "dirty" cooking worries you.

Jerked steak & cauliflower

1 tablespoon allspice berries

1 tablespoon cracked black peppercorns

½ teaspoon ground cinnamon

½ teaspoon freshly ground nutmeg

1 tablespoon chopped thyme leaves

4 spring onions, chopped

3 Scotch Bonnet chillies, finely chopped

1 tablespoon dark brown sugar

1 teaspoon Maldon sea salt flakes

30ml (1fl oz) dark soy sauce

finely grated zest and juice of 1 lime

1 cauliflower

2 x 500g (1lb 2oz) rib-eye steaks

thyme sprigs and lime wedges, to garnish

Light your barbecue and allow it to burn down to a smoulder.

Blend all the ingredients together, except the cauliflower and steak, and set aside.

Cut the cauliflower into quarters through the stem, so that it doesn't fall apart. Season the steak with a little salt and place directly on the coals with the cauliflower.

Cook the steak to medium, turning both the meat and the cauliflower all the time – the cauliflower is ready when the stems are soft but it still has a bite.

When the steak and cauliflower are cooked, coat them liberally in the sauce and allow to rest for 10 minutes. To serve, chop or slice the steak and serve with the cauliflower with lime wedges and thyme sprigs scattered over.

Serves

4

The Philly cheese steak began life at a hot dog stand near south Philadelphia's Italian market, and became so popular that it graduated to a restaurant which still operates today – Pat's King of Steaks Since 1930.

Philly cheese steak

extra virgin olive oil

600g (1lb 5oz) rib-eye steak

50g (1¾oz) onions, sliced

50g (1¾oz) green peppers, sliced

50g (1¾oz) mushrooms, sliced

1 garlic clove, crushed and chopped

200g (7oz) American-style provolone cheese, sliced

4 hot dog rolls or "hoagies"

100ml (3½fl oz) ready-made marinara sauce (or any tomato, onion and garlic pasta sauce)

Maldon sea salt flakes and freshly ground black pepper

On a lightly olive-oiled griddle or plancha over a medium heat, grill the steaks until coloured all over but still rare, then remove and set aside to rest. Add the onions, peppers and mushrooms and cook, stirring, for a few minutes, until caramelized. Add the garlic, salt and pepper and cook for another 30 seconds, then push the mixture to one side of the griddle.

Slice the steak thinly and add to the hot part of the griddle, then break into smaller pieces with the end of a flat spatula or slice.

When cooked to your preference, mix the vegetables and meat and divide into 4 portions. Top the portions with the cheese and let it melt.

Cut the rolls open and hollow out some of the soft white bread part from inside. Place the top side of each roll face down on top of a portion of meat and cheese.

When the cheese has melted, flip the piles over, season with pepper, add the marinara sauce, then add the base of the rolls. Serve immediately.

Serves
4

100ml (3½fl oz) natural yogurt

50ml (2fl oz) cider vinegar

50ml (2fl oz) lemon juice

2 garlic cloves, crushed

3–4 tablespoons Middle Eastern Rub (see page 30)

1kg (2lb 4oz) boneless rib of beef, cut into 1–2cm (½–¾ inch) thick slices

For the sauce

200ml (7fl oz) tahini

2 garlic cloves, crushed

50ml (2fl oz) lemon juice

50ml (2fl oz) natural yogurt

You will also need

4 metal skewers

Fillings

4 lavash or flatbreads

Bread & Butter Pickles (see page 31)

Beef Dripping Fries (see page 31)

grilled tomatoes

Middle Eastern Rub (see page 30)

Steak shawarma

While travelling through the Middle East researching shawarma for Condé Nast, I found beef was used almost everywhere – probably, I think, because the more traditional mutton was more expensive than imported beef. It may not be traditional, but steak shawarma is just as tasty.

Mix the yogurt, vinegar, lemon juice, garlic and spice rub together and pour over the sliced beef. Mix well, cover and refrigerate for a few hours.

Remove the meat from the fridge and mix again. Layer the beef on to 4 large metal kebab skewers and wrap tightly in several layers of clingfilm to make a firm roll. Refrigerate overnight.

Combine the sauce ingredients, mix well, cover and set aside.

Remove the steak shawarma from the fridge, take off the clingfilm and cook over charcoal, taking care to keep it turning so that it cooks evenly.

As the steak is cooked, slice layers off from the outside in thin pieces.

Lay one lavash or flatbread on greaseproof paper, and add enough beef to cover a quarter of the surface. Top with some Bread & Butter Pickles, a few Beef Dripping Fries and some grilled tomatoes. Drizzle with the tahini sauce, season with extra steak rub, then tightly roll into a shawarma inside the paper. Repeat with the remaining breads, beef and fillings.

This rub uses a classic combination of redolent spices commonly used throughout the Middle East to season meat. As always, it's only as good as the ingredients, and whole spices trump ground spices every time.

Middle Eastern rub Makes 500g (1lb 2oz)

25g (1oz) hot smoked paprika

25g (1oz) black peppercorns

25g (1oz) cumin seeds

20g (¾oz) coriander seeds

20g (¾oz) whole nutmeg

20g (¾oz) cinnamon sticks

10g (¼oz) cloves

10g (¼oz) cardamom pods

100g (3½oz) palm sugar

250g (9oz) Maldon sea salt flakes

Toast the spices in a hot pan, then blitz with the palm sugar to a rough powder. Combine thoroughly with the salt and keep in a sealed container.

Versions of these pickles are found all over the world – they provide much-needed acidity to cut through the rich meat.

Bread & butter pickles Makes 1 litre (1¾ pints) or serves 20

5 large cucumbers

2 onions

85g (3oz) Maldon sea salt flakes

600ml (1 pint) cider vinegar

400g (14oz) soft brown sugar

2g (¹⁄₁₆oz or about ⅓ teaspoon) ground turmeric

10 whole cloves

1 teaspoon black mustard seeds

1 teaspoon fennel seeds

1 teaspoon coriander seeds

Wash the cucumbers and onions and slice into 4mm (about ⅛ inch) thick pieces. Layer them in a non-reactive container, with the salt distributed in between the layers. Cover with clingfilm and put a heavy weight on top to help extract the water from the vegetables. Leave for at least 4 hours, until limp but crunchy.

When ready, pour away the liquid and rinse the cucumbers and onions under cold running water, tossing constantly for 5 minutes, until no longer salty. Leave to dry.

Put the vinegar, sugar and spices into a saucepan and stir over a medium heat until the sugar has dissolved. Bring to the boil, then add the cucumber and onions to the pan. Cook for 2 minutes, until the cucumber has browned through but not cooked. This is important, as overcooked cucumbers will soften. Remove from the heat and leave to cool.

Transfer the pickles to sterilized jars (see page 163) and store in the refrigerator for up to 2–3 weeks to mature.

Traditionally the Great British fish and chips were cooked in beef dripping, a practice that has sadly fallen by the wayside for reasons beyond my ken. If you are old enough to remember proper fish and chips, these beauties will be a trip down Memory Lane. It's not traditional, but a grating of Parmesan on top after frying makes things interesting.

Beef dripping fries Serves 4

1kg (2lb 4oz) Maris Piper potatoes (or other suitable chipping potatoes)

beef dripping, for deep-frying

malt vinegar

Maldon sea salt flakes

Peel and wash the potatoes and put through a French fry potato cutter, or cut into 1cm (½ inch) chips using a knife.

Put them into a pan, cover with cold water, salt and bring to the boil. Cook for 8 minutes, then drain and allow to steam-dry. Set aside until cool.

Heat the beef dripping in your fryer to 140°C (285°F). Put the sliced potatoes into the dripping and fry for 4–5 minutes, ensuring they are completely submerged all the time. Remove the fries from the dripping and allow to drain completely on kitchen paper, then chill until completely cooled.

When needed, reheat the dripping to 190°C (375°F). Return the chips to the fryer and fry for 4–5 minutes, or until golden brown. Drain on kitchen paper, then place in a bowl, season with sea salt flakes and a spray of malt vinegar, and serve.

Serves 4

Fajitas are a modern Tex-Mex creation. The first culinary evidence of them – the cut of meat, the cooking style (directly on a campfire or on a grill), and the Spanish nickname – goes back as far as the 1930s, to the ranchlands of south and west Texas. During cattle round-ups, cows were butchered regularly to feed the hands. Hearty border dishes like *barbacoa de cabeza* (head barbecue), *menudo* (tripe stew), and fajitas or *arracheras* (grilled skirt steak) have their roots in this practice.

Steak fajitas

4 limes

2 tablespoons olive oil

4 garlic cloves, crushed

4 teaspoons ground cumin

2 teaspoons dried oregano

2 teaspoons freshly ground black pepper

1kg (2lb 4oz) skirt steak, cut in half

1 red pepper

1 green pepper

1 onion, peeled and cut in half

8 large flour tortillas

400g (14oz) can black beans, drained and mashed

pico de gallo or Salsa Mexicana (see page 210)

Guacamole (see page 210)

150ml (¼ pint) soured cream

Maldon sea salt flakes

small bunch (about 30g/1oz) of coriander, finely chopped, to garnish

Squeeze the juice from the limes and mix with the olive oil, garlic, cumin, oregano, black pepper and Maldon salt. Lay the steaks in a shallow dish or tray and pour over the marinade. Turn to coat the steaks all over in the mix, then cover, chill and allow to stand for a few hours.

Light your barbecue and allow the coals to burn down to ash white. Wipe any excess marinade from the steaks and cook them for 5 minutes on each side. Remove from the grill and leave to rest for 10 minutes. While the meat is resting, grill the whole peppers and the halved onion, turning regularly. When cooked and the pepper skins are blackened, remove from the grill and skin the peppers. Chop or slice the peppers and onion.

To assemble the fajitas, warm the flour tortillas on the barbecue and spread with mashed black beans. Top with thick slices of steak, chopped roast peppers and onions, pico de gallo or Salsa Mexicana, Guacamole, some soured cream and garnish with coriander.

Makes
1

A steak sandwich should be a very simple affair, but the permutations are legion and are not always successful. This is my favourite after years of making them. Don't over-grill the sourdough – it should be just warmed through, singed and still chewy.

Steak sandwich

175g (6oz) rib-eye steak

2 slices of fresh sourdough

30g (1oz) Hollandaise: Anchovy, Horseradish or Stilton variations all work well (see page 36–7)

5g (⅛oz) fresh horseradish

a handful of watercress

10g (¼oz) red onion, peeled and shaved very, very thin

Maldon sea salt flakes and freshly ground black pepper

Season and chargrill the rib-eye steak, then remove from the heat and leave to rest for 5 minutes.

Lightly grill the sourdough slices on the grill – they should be barely toasted.

Slice the steak into 1cm (½ inch) strips.

Spread your Hollandaise of choice on one piece of grilled sourdough toast. Pile the sliced rib eye over the Hollandaise, and grate fresh horseradish on top. Pile watercress on top of the steak, then top with shaved red onion and place the other slice of toast on top. Serve warm.

Makes
300ml
(½ pint)

Hollandaise is one of the five sauces in the "mother sauce" repertoire of French cookery. It is so named because it was believed to have mimicked a Dutch sauce for the King of Holland's state visit to France. Made with egg yolks and butter, it is a phenomenally versatile sauce that carries strong flavours well. From this basic preparation, much deliciousness can be derived.

The magic of hollandaise

Base sauce

250g (9oz) unsalted butter

3 large free-range egg yolks

1 tablespoon water

1 tablespoon lemon juice, plus extra to taste

dash of Tabasco

Warm the butter gently until almost melted.

Whisk the yolks, water and lemon juice in a medium–small saucepan for a few moments, until thick, pale and mousse-like.

Set the pan over a medium-low heat and continue to whisk at a reasonable speed, reaching all over the bottom and edges of the pan, where the eggs tend to overcook.

To moderate the heat, frequently move the pan off the burner for a few seconds, and then back on. (If, by chance, the eggs seem to be cooking too fast, set the pan in a bowl of cold water to cool the bottom, then continue.)

As they cook, the eggs will become frothy and increase in volume, and then thicken. When you can see the pan bottom through the streaks of the whisk and the eggs are thick and smooth, remove from the heat.

Very slowly and gradually add the warm butter, at little at a time, whisking constantly to incorporate each addition. As the emulsion forms, you may add the butter in slightly larger amounts, always whisking until it has been fully absorbed. Continue adding butter until the sauce has thickened to the consistency you want and all of the butter has been incorporated.

Add a dash of Tabasco and a dash more lemon juice to taste, whisking in well. Season as the individual variation calls for (see right).

Variations that go well with steak

Béarnaise Finely slice 3 shallots and place in a pan with 100ml (3½fl oz) of white wine vinegar, 100ml (3½fl oz) of water, ½ teaspoon of crushed black peppercorns and the stalks from 2 large tarragon sprigs and a large chervil sprig, reserving the leaves to finish the sauce. Reduce this mixture by half, then pour into a suitable container (a squeezy bottle or glass jar) and leave to infuse overnight in the refrigerator.

Finish the Hollandaise recipe with 1 tablespoon of the strained reduction, salt and pepper, 1 teaspoon of chopped chervil and 1 teaspoon of chopped tarragon.

Beurre noisette Heat the butter to a foam and allow it to subside, then repeat and use to make the sauce as usual.

Choron sauce Blanch, peel and deseed 3 ripe plum tomatoes and chop the flesh well. Warm through and fold into the Hollandaise sauce, adjusting the seasoning with salt and pepper.

Anchovy hollandaise In a mortar and pestle grind 50g (1¾oz) of good anchovy fillets in oil, ½ a small garlic clove, ½ a small deseeded red chilli, a few thyme leaves, a couple of basil leaves, 1 teaspoon of Dijon mustard, 1 teaspoon of red wine vinegar and a few grinds of black pepper. When smooth, fold into the Hollandaise and serve.

Bone marrow hollandaise Replace half the butter with diced bone marrow and season with salt and pepper and a teaspoon of the Béarnaise reduction above.

Garlic hollandaise Wrap 1 garlic bulb in foil and bake in a low oven for 1 hour. Cut the top off the foil parcel and squeeze all the baked garlic purée out into a dish. Fold this garlic purée into the Hollandaise sauce, season to taste with salt, then serve.

Horseradish hollandaise Finish the Hollandaise with plenty of fresh grated horseradish folded in, and season to taste with salt.

Kimchi hollandaise Blend or chop 100g (3½oz) of Kimchi (see page 89) to a paste and fold into the Hollandaise.

Mustard hollandaise Finish the Hollandaise with 1 tablespoon of Dijon and 1 tablespoon of wholegrain mustard, then season to taste with salt.

Orange hollandaise Make the Hollandaise using blood orange juice instead of lemon juice, finish with finely grated blood orange zest and season to taste with salt.

Sherry hollandaise Replace the water and lemon juice with 2 tablespoons of very good sherry (I use Oloroso or Amontillado – the better the sherry, the better the sauce) then season to taste with salt.

Stilton hollandaise Crumble 125g (4½oz) of Stilton into chunks and allow to warm, then gently fold into the sauce, keeping the small chunks intact.

Serves 4

While the origin of the taco is a mystery, its history dates back to the eighteenth century, with an early written reference calling them *tacos de minero*, or "miner's tacos". It's believed that this was because they were a common food in the Mexican silver mines. During the 19th century, tacos arrived in America with the influx of Mexican immigrants. A group of female street vendors known as the Chili Queens sold tacos on the streets of Los Angeles, and when tourists began to swarm to the city, they would seek them out. This became a core part of the LA experience, and as the next generation of these original Mexican immigrants climbed the social ladder, the taco gained in popularity. Slowly but surely the taco became part of wider American culture.

Steak tacos

600g (1lb 5oz) rib-eye steak

1 tablespoon Basic Beef Rub (see page 40)

¼ white cabbage

juice of 1 lime

12 mini soft flour tortillas

2 avocados, chopped

4–5 tablespoons Chipotle Ketchup (see page 41)

24 coriander sprigs

Season the steaks liberally with the steak rub and chargrill to medium, the best temperature for this rib-eye. Remove from the heat and allow to rest for at least 10 minutes.

Very finely shred the white cabbage and toss with the lime juice.

Warm the flour tortillas, wrapped in foil, over a griddle or in a medium oven.

Slice the steak, then place a little cabbage, some avocado, a thick slice of steak and 1 teaspoon of Chipotle Ketchup on each tortilla and garnish each one with 2 sprigs of coriander. Serve 3 tortillas per portion.

Rubs are an essential part of a barbecue. They can be little more than salt and pepper, sometimes called a "dalmatian rub" and used for the simple seasoning of a joint of beef, or they can be big sugary rubs that create the thick bark on competition-level briskets (see page 211 for my simple version). Sugar and salt play a fundamental part in both the development of bark when smoking and in the retention of moisture in the meat.

Basic beef rub Makes 450g (1lb)

250g (9oz) Maldon sea salt flakes

100g (3½oz) maple sugar

25g (1oz) English mustard powder

25g (1oz) hot smoked paprika

25g (1oz) freshly ground black pepper

25g (1oz) fennel pollen (or toasted fennel seeds if unavailable)

Simply blend all the ingredients together and use as directed in your chosen recipe.

This is a very simple sauce that's served me well over the years.
In winter I use canned tomatoes rather than fresh.

Chipotle ketchup Makes 600ml (1 pint)

200g (7oz) ripe tomatoes, chopped

200g (7oz) onions, peeled and chopped

200g (7oz) apples, peeled,
cored and chopped

200g (7oz) smoked chipotle peppers

200ml (7fl oz) cider vinegar

4 teaspoons Maldon sea salt flakes

20g (¾oz) hot smoked paprika

2 tablespoons clear honey

Place all the ingredients except the honey in a stainless steel pan and bring to a gentle simmer. Continue to simmer for 2 hours, then add the honey and return to a simmer before passing through a vegetable mouli or sieve.

Decant into sterilized bottles (see page 163) or jars and seal. When cool, refrigerate for a few days before using. It will keep for a few weeks in the fridge.

Serves
1

Deckle is the juiciest, tastiest bit of the rib-eye, also known as the *Latissimus dorsi* in bovine myology. Served with my interpretation of the classic rocket and Parmesan salad, it makes a rather lovely light lunch. This is the steak salad to end all steak salads, restraint and simplicity being – as usual – the thing.

Steak salad

For the dressing

30g (1oz) Parmesan cheese, finely grated, plus extra to serve

1½ tablespoons white balsamic vinegar

2 teaspoons lemon juice

1 teaspoon Dijon mustard

4 tablespoons extra virgin olive oil

Maldon sea salt flakes and freshly ground black pepper

For the salad

200g (7oz) deckle steak (see recipe introduction)

100g (3½oz) wild rocket leaves

First make the dressing. Blend the Parmesan, vinegar, lemon juice, mustard, salt and pepper with a mortar and pestle until smooth. With the machine running, gradually add the oil and blend until emulsified and well incorporated.

Season the deckle, then grill to medium-rare and set aside to rest for 10 minutes.

Meanwhile, pick and wash the wild rocket.

Slice the deckle and arrange neatly on plates. Toss the rocket leaves in the dressing and arrange next to the grilled deckle.

Grate extra Parmesan over the top and eat.

Side dishes for steak

2 live native lobsters

150g (5½oz) Maldon sea salt flakes

100g (3½oz) Garlic Butter (see page 113)

Grilled lobster with garlic butter Serves 4 as a side dish

I have included this because I like to serve it alongside grilled steak, as an homage to the classic surf 'n' turf. Served in steakhouses since the 1960s, surf 'n' turf has had a chequered history, falling in and out of favour. Chef Alain Chapel served lobster with pigeon, and temples of gastronomy such as London's Le Gavroche (where this recipe is from) have followed suit. I see nothing wrong with it, and indeed a cut such as fillet positively needs a little help.

Kill your lobsters by piercing the head behind the cross mark with a knife.

Bring 5 litres (about 9 pints) of water to the boil in a large pan with the sea salt flakes – this is roughly the salinity of seawater. Plunge your lobster into the boiling salted water and cook for 8 minutes, then remove the pan from the heat and allow to cool for 8 minutes with the lobsters still in the water.

Remove the claws, crack with a hammer and extract the meat, keeping the pieces whole. Cut the body of each lobster in half lengthways and remove the meat, again in large chunks. Remove the tail meat. Remove the intestinal tract and the grit sac and discard. Spread the shells generously with the garlic butter, then season the lobster meat and replace neatly in the shell halves. Spread over more garlic butter.

Grill over medium hot charcoal until the butter is bubbling. Serve with grilled steak, of course.

For the stock

(Makes 1 litre/1¾ pints)

500g (1lb 2oz) lobster shells

½ carrot, chopped

½ fennel bulb, chopped

½ onion, peeled and chopped

4 garlic cloves, chopped

1 celery stick, chopped

olive oil, for frying

1 litre (1¾ pints) fish stock

faggot of herbs (bay leaf, fennel and thyme)

½ lemon, sliced

For the fideuá

250g (9oz) fideuá noodles

2 tablespoons olive oil

2 large garlic cloves

2 good-sized ripe tomatoes, halved, deseeded and grated (discarding the skin)

1½ teaspoons sweet paprika (pimentón dulce)

0.4g packet (large pinch) saffron threads, crumbled

1 whole lobster, blanched and shelled (use the shells to make the stock)

Maldon sea salt flakes

aïoli (garlic mayonnaise), to serve

Lobster fideuá   Serves 4

In the spirit of surf 'n' turf, this is a more refined lobster pasta dish, based on a seafood dish originally from the coast of Valencia. It is similar to paella, but with noodles instead of rice.

Roast the lobster shells in the oven at 220°C (425°F), Gas Mark 7 until just caramelized.

Meanwhile, fry the stock vegetables in a little olive oil until golden brown.

When the lobster shells are roasted, pound them using a mortar and pestle (or bash them with a rolling pin), then place them in a large saucepan with the fish stock and cooked vegetables. Bring to a gentle simmer and cook for 30 minutes.

Remove from the heat and add the faggot of herbs and the sliced lemon. Leave to infuse for 10 minutes, then pass through a fine sieve, taking care to extract all the juice from the solids. Discard the solids and pour the stock into a saucepan over a very low heat and hold just below simmering, ready for adding to the fideuá.

In a large frying pan, toast the fideuá noodles until they turn a light golden brown colour – about 10 minutes – turning them during cooking so that they are toasted on all sides. Remove from the pan and set aside.

Heat the olive oil in the frying pan over a medium-low heat, then add the garlic cloves and cook slowly to give some flavour to the oil. When the garlic cloves are golden brown, remove from the oil, crush and return them to the pan.

Add the fideuá and stir well to coat, then add the warmed stock. Add the grated tomatoes and cook for 3–4 minutes until thickened. Stir in the paprika and crumbled saffron and cook for 1 minute. Bring to a gentle rolling boil and cook for 5 minutes (try the stock now to check if the amount of salt is right and, if not, amend accordingly).

Add the lobster meat and cook for a further 4 minutes. Remove from the heat, cover, and leave to stand for 3 minutes. Serve with aïoli as a side dish to the steak.

Wild mushroom orzotto

Serves 4

A splendid side dish for braised beef dishes, this orzotto will soak up the gravy and become all the more flavoursome for it.

25g (1oz) dried porcini mushrooms

1 banana shallot, finely chopped

2 garlic cloves, chopped

60g (2¼oz) unsalted butter

300g (10½oz) wild mushrooms, cleaned and chopped

200g (7oz) pearl barley

750ml (1¼ pints) Basic Beef Broth (see page 112)

50ml (2fl oz) extra virgin olive oil

100ml (3½fl oz) good Italian red wine, such as Chianti

50g (1¾oz) Parmesan cheese, finely grated

1 tablespoon chopped flat leaf parsley leaves

Maldon sea salt flakes and freshly ground black pepper

Soak the dried porcini in boiling water for 20 minutes.

In a large frying pan gently cook the chopped shallot and garlic in 40g (1½oz) of butter until soft but not coloured. Drain the porcini, reserving the soaking liquid, then roughly chop and add to the pan with the chopped wild mushrooms. Season and continue to cook until tender.

Put the pearl barley in a sieve and wash thoroughly in cold running water. Cook in a pan of salted boiling water for 15 minutes, until just tender. Drain the barley and cool slightly.

In a medium saucepan, bring the beef broth to a boil, reduce the heat to low and keep warm.

In a large saucepan, heat the olive oil, add the mushroom mixture and barley and stir to coat. Add the red wine, followed by the broth a ladle at a time, and cook over a moderately low heat, stirring constantly, until nearly absorbed. Keep stirring until the barley is al dente and suspended in a creamy sauce, about 25 minutes. Stir in the grated Parmesan, the remaining butter and the parsley, season with salt and pepper and serve.

Wild mushroom fricassee

Serves 4

This is my go-to mushroom fricassee from Harvey's, chef Marco Pierre White's first restaurant, which existed years ago in Wandsworth Common, London. Nowadays, I might leave out the tomatoes in the depths of winter.

600g (1lb 5oz) small wild mushrooms

50ml (2fl oz) light olive oil

50g (1¾oz) unsalted butter

1 tablespoon finely chopped shallots

1 teaspoon crushed garlic

1 teaspoon thyme leaves

splash of red wine vinegar

5 tomatoes, peeled, deseeded and finely chopped

1 tablespoon chopped chives

Maldon sea salt flakes and freshly ground black pepper

Pick over and clean the mushrooms carefully. Ideally brush them to remove any dirt, but a quick rinse won't harm them too much if they are dried immediately. If large, slice them – if small leave them whole.

Heat the oil in a large non-stick pan and fry the mushrooms in batches, setting them aside on a plate.

Return the pan to the heat and add the butter, shallots, garlic, thyme leaves and finally the fried mushrooms. Toss to mix and continue frying until the garlic is cooked out and turns translucent.

Season to taste with salt, pepper and a splash of vinegar, then toss in the tomatoes and chives and serve.

Braised shallots & garlic with bone marrow Serves 4

I wrote this recipe after a late-night conversation with the inimitable chef Marco Pierre White in Margaret River, Australia. We'd just finished cooking a dinner in a winery there and he was regaling me with a list of his favourite steak garnishes. This is my interpretation of one he described having eaten in France. It's really just a very posh onion gravy.

500g (1lb 2oz) whole button shallots

250g (9oz) garlic cloves

1 tablespoon good beef dripping

1 small faggot of herbs (thyme, rosemary and bay leaf)

300ml (½ pint) Madeira Gravy (see page 114)

200g (7oz) bone marrow, cut into medallions

chopped flat leaf parsley leaves

Maldon sea salt flakes and freshly ground black pepper

Peel the shallots, down to taking off one white layer of skin, and peel the garlic cloves.

Heat the dripping in a pan and fry the shallots and garlic in batches until golden brown.

Place the shallots in a small lidded casserole with the faggot of herbs and the Madeira gravy, and place in the oven for 1 hour, or until the shallots are easily pierced with a knife. Add the garlic and return to the oven for 20 minutes, then add the bone marrow medallions and chopped parsley. Remove the faggot of herbs and allow to heat through.

Season and serve with grilled steak, or use in Collard Greens & Gravy (see page 331, where you can also see a photo of this dish).

Creamed spinach with shirred eggs Serves 4

I've been making this for some years now, having first tasted its inspiration at Henry Harris's brilliant restaurant Racine. His version contained foie gras rather than anchovy and egg, which is certainly no bad thing.

500ml (18fl oz) double cream

5 anchovies, chopped

1 large rosemary sprig

4 garlic cloves, crushed

¼ nutmeg, grated

1kg (2lb 4oz) spinach

a little unsalted butter

¼ teaspoon cayenne pepper

4 free-range eggs

Maldon sea salt flakes and freshly ground black pepper

Place the cream, anchovies, rosemary, garlic, nutmeg, salt and pepper in a pan and bring to a gentle simmer, then remove from the heat and leave to infuse for 20 minutes.

Remove the stalks from the spinach, then wash thoroughly and blanch in boiling salted water. Drain, then squeeze the spinach dry and roughly chop into 5mm (¼ inch) pieces.

Pass the hot cream through a sieve over the chopped spinach and reheat, then correct the seasoning, adding the cayenne pepper.

Lightly butter a serving dish and pour in the hot creamed spinach. Make 4 wells in the spinach and crack the eggs into the wells. Bake in a preheated oven at 170°C (340°F), Gas Mark 3½ for 4 minutes, until the eggs are just set, and serve immediately.

Blue cheese gnocchi gratin

Serves 4–6

These delicious dumplings would normally be eaten as a first course in Italy, but they also make a great accompaniment to steak.

400g (14oz) russet potatoes, peeled

250ml (9fl oz) double cream

1 rosemary sprig

½ teaspoon freshly grated nutmeg

1 large free-range egg, lightly beaten

150g (5½oz) Parmesan cheese, finely grated

120g (4¼oz) plain flour, plus extra for dusting

50g (1¾oz) unsalted butter, at room temperature, plus extra for greasing

10g (¼oz) dried breadcrumbs

120g (4¼oz) Gorgonzola Dolce

Maldon sea salt flakes and freshly ground black pepper

Place the potatoes in a large pot, cover with water and add a pinch of salt. Bring to the boil, then reduce the heat and simmer for 20 minutes or until tender. Drain, set aside and allow to steam-dry.

Preheat the oven to 180°C (350°F), Gas Mark 4.

Bring the cream, rosemary, and half the nutmeg to the boil in a small saucepan, then remove from the heat and allow to sit until needed.

Pass the potatoes through a potato ricer into a large bowl. Add the egg, half the Parmesan, the flour and the remaining nutmeg and season well with salt, then, using your hands, gently mix to a dough. Transfer to a floured surface and cut into quarters. Roll each quarter into a thick rope about 2cm (¾ inch) in diameter, then cut into 3cm (1¼ inch) pieces.

Bring a large pot of salted water to the boil. Lightly butter a baking dish. Working in batches, cook the gnocchi for 2–3 minutes or until they float to the surface. Using a slotted spoon, transfer the gnocchi to the baking dish.

Mix the remaining Parmesan, the butter and the breadcrumbs together in a small bowl.

Strain the cream mixture over the gnocchi. Break off small pieces of Gorgonzola and scatter them over the top, then sprinkle over the breadcrumb mixture and bake in the preheated oven until bubbling and golden brown, 15–20 minutes.

Tomato salad Serves 4

Heritage or heirloom tomatoes are old varieties grown for historical interest as well as for their flavours, which are widely perceived to be better than that of modern cultivars. They often have a shorter shelf life, but can be more disease-resistant than commercial tomatoes. Many heirloom tomatoes lack a genetic mutation that gives modern tomatoes an appealing uniform red colour. Varieties bearing this mutation, which have been favoured by the industry since the 1940s, have a decreased ability to make sugar within the fruit. If you are used to eating mass-market modern varieties from a supermarket, a heritage tomato can be a revelation.

800g (1lb 12oz) mixed heritage tomatoes, some cut into chunks and some into slices

1 banana shallot, finely sliced into rings

10g (¼oz) flat leaf parsley leaves

juice of 1 lemon

100g (3½oz) Creamed Horseradish (see page 227)

a large glug (I leave this to your personal taste) of extra virgin olive oil

Maldon sea salt flakes and freshly ground black pepper

Make sure your tomatoes are at room temperature – if possible they should never have seen the inside of a fridge.

In a bowl toss together the tomatoes, shallot rings and parsley leaves, and season to taste with salt, pepper and lemon juice.

Spread the Creamed Horseradish in a serving dish and top with the tomato salad, making sure to leave some of the cream visible underneath.

Finish with a glug of extra virgin olive oil over the top and serve.

Watercress salad Serves 4

Not all watercress is created equal. It takes time to develop its distinctive, deep peppery taste, so search out lush, dark green leaves with some body.

100g (3½oz) watercress

50g (1¾oz) cucumber slices, skin on

50g (1¾oz) gherkins, cut in julienne strips

10g (¼oz) lilliput (tiny) capers, washed

50ml (2fl oz) Mustard Dressing (see page 328)

Maldon sea salt flakes and freshly ground black pepper

Wash the watercress thoroughly.

Toss the cucumber, gherkins, capers and watercress in a bowl with the dressing, then season to taste.

Roast corn grits with bone marrow & truffle Serves 4

Usually eaten at breakfast, grits have their origin in Native American corn preparation. Traditionally, the hominy (dried corn) for grits was ground on a stone mill, then passed through screens, the finer sifted material used as grit meal, and the coarser as grits. Many American communities used these mills until the mid-20th century, farmers bringing their corn to be ground and the miller keeping a portion as his fee.

2 sweetcorn cobs

50g (1¾oz) unsalted butter

1 onion, peeled and finely chopped

2 garlic cloves, crushed

100g (3½oz) corn grits

500ml (18fl oz) hot Basic Beef Broth (see page 112)

250ml (9fl oz) double cream

50g (1¾oz) bone marrow, chopped

1 small black truffle or ½ bunch of spring onions

Maldon sea salt flakes and freshly ground black pepper

Remove the husks from the corn and roast the cobs on a hot charcoal grill or griddle pan until slightly blackened. Slice the corn kernels from the cobs and roughly chop.

Melt the butter in a large skillet or saucepan, then add the chopped onion and sauté until slightly soft. Add the garlic and cook until both are softened. Stirring constantly, add the grits, followed by the hot beef broth. Continue to cook over a low heat, stirring almost constantly, until the grits are creamy.

When the grits are almost done, add the corn kernels and the cream. Simmer, stirring constantly, for about 5 minutes or longer, until thickened. Season with salt and pepper.

Fold in the bone marrow and serve with shaved black truffle over the top in winter, or sliced spring onions the rest of the year.

Green beans Serves 4

A classic steakhouse side. Wait until summer before buying these, and if you can avoid using beans flown in from another continent, do so. We have forgone the beauty of seasonality in favour of convenience and are all the poorer for it. Summer vegetables in winter are sad.

50g (1¾oz) smoked streaky bacon lardons

1 banana shallot, finely chopped

1 garlic clove, crushed

50g (1¾oz) unsalted butter

500g (1lb 2oz) fine green beans, topped and tailed

250ml (9fl oz) water

4 ripe plum tomatoes, blanched, peeled and chopped

Maldon sea salt flakes and freshly ground black pepper

Cook the bacon in a pan over a medium-high heat until the fat begins to render, then stir in the shallot and garlic and cook for 1 minute.

Add the butter, beans and water and cook until the water has evaporated and the beans are tender, tossing from time to time.

If the beans are not tender once the water has evaporated, add a small amount more water and let them cook for a bit longer.

Season with salt and pepper, toss in the tomato and serve.

Creamed corn Serves 4–6

Creamed corn is a part of Midwestern and Southern American cuisine, made by pulping corn kernels and collecting the milky residue. This is my interpretation.

400ml (14fl oz) double cream

4 garlic cloves, bashed

1 large basil sprig

2 small red chillies, split

1kg (2lb 4oz) sweetcorn cobs (about 4 large cobs)

50g (1¾oz) quick cook or instant grits or polenta

50g (1¾oz) unsalted butter

Maldon sea salt flakes and freshly ground black pepper

Place the cream, garlic, basil and chillies in a pan. Season with salt and pepper and bring to a gentle simmer, then remove from the heat and leave to infuse for 20 minutes.

Cut the tip off each cob. Using a small knife, cut the kernels from the cob and place in a large bowl. Using the back of the blade, scrape against the cob to press out the milky liquid and add to the kernels.

Pass the hot infused cream through a sieve over the sweetcorn and place back over a low heat. Stir in the polenta and butter and allow to thicken and cook for a few minutes. Correct the seasoning and serve.

Pennybun & bone marrow sauce Makes 500g (1lb 2oz)

A delicious beef sauce that goes well with fish or veal, and can also be used as a stuffing. Pennybun is the English name for porcini or cep mushrooms.

10 dried porcini mushrooms

50g (1¾oz) unsalted butter

50g (1¾oz) Preserved Bone Marrow (see page 163) or fresh bone marrow, chopped

1 garlic clove, crushed

150g (5½oz) sourdough breadcrumbs

250ml (9fl oz) Basic Beef Broth (see page 112)

50g (1¾oz) Parmesan cheese, finely grated

½ bunch of flat leaf parsley, leaves picked and chopped

finely grated zest and juice of 1 unwaxed lemon

Maldon sea salt flakes and freshly ground black pepper

Soak the porcini in warm water for at least 1 hour, then drain and chop, reserving the soaking liquid.

Melt half the butter with the bone marrow in a pan. Add the chopped porcini and crushed garlic and cook for a few minutes. Add the breadcrumbs and season, then increase the heat a little.

Add half the porcini liquor and the remaining ingredients and stir to bring together (discard the remaining mushroom liquor, which could contain grit). Remove from the heat and serve.

Marchand de vin butter

Makes 300g (10½oz)

The name of this classic red wine butter sauce for grilled steak translates as "Wine merchant's butter". Use the best red wine you can: it would be a shame to source great steak, cook it carefully and judiciously, only to chuck a bit of cheap plonk into this butter.

300ml (½ pint) red wine

30g (1oz) finely chopped shallot

300ml (½ pint) Basic Beef Broth (see page 112)

100g (3½oz) grass-fed unsalted butter

100g (3½oz) bone marrow

1 tablespoon chopped flat leaf parsley leaves

1 teaspoon lemon juice

Maldon sea salt flakes and freshly ground black pepper

Put the wine and shallot into a pan over a medium heat and simmer until the wine has reduced by half. Add the beef broth and simmer until reduced to a glaze.

Cream the butter with the bone marrow, then fold in the parsley and lemon juice and the reduced wine mixture, then season to taste.

Roll the butter into a sausage shape and chill to firm up.

Slice into discs and serve on top of grilled steak.

Caviar butter Makes 200g (7oz)

Serve this with grilled steak.

125g (4½oz) salted butter

1 soft-boiled free-range egg, grated

1 tablespoon chopped flat leaf parsley leaves

1 tablespoon chopped shallots

1 tablespoon chopped capers

56g (2oz) can caviar

Beat the butter until light and fluffy, then fold in the remaining ingredients, the caviar last of all.

The butter can then be either spooned out, or rolled in clingfilm to form a sausage, then chilled. When firm, remove the clingfilm and slice.

Creamed spinach on toast

Serves 4–6

Another creamed spinach side dish (for the other see page 49) – this one having the benefit of toast to soak up steak or roast beef juices. Spinach and steak are an age-old classic steakhouse combo and if it ain't broke, don't fix it.

20g (¾oz) unsalted butter

1kg (2lb 4oz) young spinach, picked and washed

1 large garlic clove

100ml (3½fl oz) double cream

100ml (3½fl oz) beef jus, thin gravy or reduced Basic Beef Broth or Madeira Gravy (see pages 112 and 114)

4 slices of sourdough

Maldon sea salt flakes and freshly ground black pepper

Melt the butter and allow it to foam to nut brown. Add the spinach and stir until wilted, using a fork with the garlic clove stuck in the tines.

Continuing over a medium heat, add the double cream in a thin stream, allowing it to reduce as you go. Repeat with the beef broth or gravy and allow it to reduce to a syrupy consistency. Adjust the seasoning and take off the heat.

Grill the sourdough on both sides, so it's toasted but still chewy.

Top the toasts with the creamed spinach and serve.

Fried beets Serves 4–6

Fried beets make a marvellous steak side and are marginally better for you than chips. Possibly.

1kg (2lb 4oz) cooked mixed beetroots, either oven-baked or ember-baked

beef dripping, for frying

rice flour, for dusting

Maldon sea salt flakes

Creamed Horseradish (see page 227), to serve

Peel the cooked beetroots and cut them into large chips.

Heat some beef dripping either in a deep-fat fryer or in a large pan to the depth of 10cm (4 inches).

Liberally dust the beetroot chips with rice flour, then fry in the hot beef dripping until golden and crisp.

Drain on kitchen paper, then season with salt and serve with Creamed Horseradish.

Exploding onions Serves 1

This American steakhouse side is really a showboat version of onion rings. It's very tasty nonetheless, and is worth a try.

oil, for frying

1 large sweet onion, such as Vidalia

300g (10½oz) plain flour

1 teaspoon cayenne pepper

2 tablespoons paprika

½ teaspoon dried thyme

½ teaspoon dried oregano

½ teaspoon ground cumin

2 large free-range eggs

250ml (9fl oz) milk

225ml (8fl oz) water

Maldon sea salt flakes and freshly ground black pepper

Preheat the oil in a deep-fat fryer to 180°C (350°F).

Cut off 1cm (½ inch) from the top of the onion and peel. Place the onion cut side down on a board. Starting 1cm (½ inch) from the root, make a downward cut perpendicular to the root, all the way through to the board, stopping 1cm (½ inch) from the root, so the onion stays intact. Repeat three times, to make 4 evenly spaced cuts around the onion.

Continue slicing between each section until you have 16 evenly spaced cuts.

Turn the onion over and use your fingers to gently separate the outer layers, keeping the onion in one piece.

Mix together the flour, cayenne, paprika, thyme, oregano, cumin and ½ teaspoon of black pepper. In a small deep bowl, whisk the eggs, milk and the water.

Place the onion in a separate bowl, cut side up, and pour all the seasoned flour mixture on top. Cover the bowl with a plate, then shake back and forth to distribute the flour. Make sure the onion is fully coated, especially between the "petals". Lift the onion and pat off the excess flour; set the bowl of seasoned flour aside.

Coat the onion in the egg mixture, making sure to coat all the layers completely. Remove, letting the excess egg drip off, then repeat the flouring process.

Carefully lower the onion into the oil, cut side down. Fry for about 3 minutes, then turn the onion over and cook until golden, about 3 more minutes. Drain on kitchen paper.

Season with salt and serve.

Mashed potato with bone marrow & onion gravy

Serves 4

There's not much that can improve a great mash with gravy, but this has a damn good go.

200g (7oz) Preserved Bone Marrow (see page 163)

1kg (2lb 4oz) Maris Piper potatoes

200ml (7fl oz) milk

200ml (7fl oz) Onion Gravy (see page 115)

Maldon sea salt flakes

Whip the preserved bone marrow using a stand mixer until light and fluffy, then pass through a fine sieve and set aside.

Peel and chop the potatoes and put them into a pan. Cover with cold water, season with salt and bring to the boil, then reduce the heat to a simmer and cook for 20 minutes. Use a sharp knife to check they are cooked, then drain in a colander and allow to steam-dry.

Bring the milk to the boil, then remove from the heat.

Pass the potatoes through a vegetable mill or potato ricer, then fold in the milk and correct the seasoning.

Heat the onion gravy. Put the mash into a serving dish and pipe the whipped bone marrow into the centre. Pour the hot gravy over the top, to cover, and serve.

Mashed potato with extra virgin olive oil Serves 4

Typical of the Mediterranean, mashed potatoes soaked in extra virgin olive oil makes a delicious and simple side to rich meat and offal. Try sprinkling chopped green peppers on top for extra freshness.

500g (1lb 2oz) Maris Piper potatoes

4 garlic cloves, peeled

1 teaspoon Maldon sea salt flakes

125ml (4fl oz) extra virgin olive oil, plus extra to serve

chopped green pepper, to garnish (optional)

Peel and chop the potatoes and put them into a pan with the garlic. Cover with cold water, season with the salt and bring to the boil, then reduce the heat to a simmer and cook for 20 minutes. Use a sharp knife to check they are cooked, then drain in a colander and allow to steam-dry.

While still hot, pass the potatoes and garlic through a potato ricer or vegetable mouli into a bowl. Fold in the olive oil, then season with salt to taste. Serve in a deep dish garnished with chopped green pepper and more olive oil poured over the top.

Potato, Parmesan & anchovy gratin Serves 4–6

Loosely based on Jansson's Temptation, but using salted Spanish anchovies instead of Abba Grebbestad ansjovis – which are actually cured sprats – this potato garnish is one of my favourite side dishes of all time. If you have access to the Scandinavian cured sprats you could use them – the dish will be more authentic, although I'm not convinced much improved.

1 litre (1¾ pints) single cream

1 large rosemary sprig

1kg (2lb 4oz) waxy potatoes, peeled

2 large garlic cloves, crushed to a purée

100g (3½oz) salted anchovies, chopped

100g (3½oz) Parmesan cheese, finely grated

50g (1¾oz) fresh breadcrumbs

Maldon sea salt flakes and freshly ground black pepper

Put the single cream and the rosemary sprig into a pot. Bring to the boil, season to taste, then remove from the heat and set aside for 20 minutes to infuse.

Preheat the oven to 160°C (325°F), Gas Mark 3.

Slice the potatoes using a mandolin and tip them into a large bowl. Pour the cream though a fine sieve into the bowl of potatoes. Spread the garlic purée in a large (2 litre/3½ pint) gratin dish and layer up the potatoes and anchovies. Cover with foil and bake in the oven for about 1 hour, or until cooked through and the potatoes are tender when tested with a knife.

Remove from the oven, sprinkle with Parmesan and breadcrumbs, then return to the oven, uncovered, and bake for a further 20 minutes, or until golden and bubbling.

Macaroni cheese Serves 4–6

Swap the macaroni for par-cooked cauliflower to make the ultimate cauliflower cheese, or mix the two for a cauliflower macaroni cheese.

1 garlic clove

360g (12oz) dried elbow macaroni

500ml (18fl oz) milk

50g (1¾oz) butter

50g (1¾oz) plain flour

80g (2¾oz) Stilton cheese, crumbled

80g (2¾oz) Cheddar cheese, grated

80g (2¾oz) Ogleshield or other washed rind cheese, grated

a pinch of grated nutmeg

125g (4½oz) mozzarella, chopped

3 tablespoons finely grated Parmesan cheese

3 tablespoons panko breadcrumbs

Maldon sea salt flakes and freshly ground white pepper

Preheat the oven to 200°C (400°F), Gas Mark 6. Rub a 20 x 20 x 5cm (8 x 8 x 2 inch) baking dish with the cut side of the garlic clove.

Cook the pasta in a large pan of boiling salted water until al dente or according to the packet instructions.

In a small pan bring the milk to a foamy boil, then reduce the heat to low and keep warm. In another saucepan, melt the butter over a medium heat, whisk in the flour and continue to cook till smooth and a pale "roux" has formed. Whisking constantly, slowly add the hot milk to the roux, then continue to whisk until the sauce thickens and bubbles gently, about 2 minutes. Add the Stilton, Cheddar and Ogleshield, season with a pinch of salt and white pepper and the freshly grated nutmeg, and stir until the cheeses have completely melted and the sauce is smooth.

Drain the pasta and return it to the pan. Add the cheese sauce and mix to combine. Fold in the mozzarella and quickly pour into the baking dish before the mozzarella melts. Bake for 8 minutes, then remove and sprinkle the mixed Parmesan and panko crumbs on top. Put back into the oven and bake for a further 8 minutes, or until golden brown.

Ash-baked sweet potatoes with caramelized onion

Serves 4

This recipe calls for burning the skin of the sweet potato to an unappetizing black, but don't be put off as it's actually delicious. Should the prospect of burnt skin not appeal, you can always eat only the flesh – but that would be a shame.

4 large orange-fleshed sweet potatoes

1 tablespoon butter

2 large onions, peeled and finely sliced

50g (1¾oz) clear honey

50ml (2fl oz) cider vinegar

1 tablespoon thyme leaves

1 tablespoon rosemary leaves, chopped

Maldon sea salt flakes and freshly ground black pepper

Place the sweet potatoes in the dying embers of a charcoal grill or barbecue, then pile the embers up around the potatoes and allow them to cook through. The skin will burn, but that's OK.

While the potatoes are cooking, heat the butter in a large heavy-based pan and fry the onions for 20 minutes over a medium heat until softened and golden in colour.

Add the honey and cider vinegar and simmer for a further 20 minutes until most of the liquid has evaporated, stirring constantly.

Add the herbs and season with plenty of salt and pepper.

Remove the sweet potatoes from the ashes and dust them off, then split them and fill with the hot onion mixture. Serve with grilled steak or roast beef.

Truffled Tunworth

Serves 4–6

Tunworth is my favourite cheese – it cannot be improved upon. It can, however, be mixed up a bit with the addition of a little truffle and cow's curd, then used as a steak garnish. Buy your truffle fresh online – if you pick up one of those sad little jars in a supermarket, you'll wonder why I bothered with this recipe.

1 whole Tunworth cheese

100g (3½oz) cow's curd or curd cheese

1 whole small fresh black truffle

Slice the top off the Tunworth cheese and reserve. Scoop out the soft cheese from the inside, leaving at least 1cm (½ inch) of cheese around all the edges – this is to avoid it from collapsing.

In a bowl, mix the soft Tunworth with the cow's curd, blending it to a smooth consistency, then grate in the whole black truffle through the large holes of your grater.

Pipe this mixture back inside the cheese until it's full, and place the reserved lid on top. Cover and keep in a cool, cheese-friendly place until needed.

When your steak is cooked, slice the Tunworth in wedges and lay 1 wedge on top of each steak, allowing it to melt gently. You're welcome.

Semi-cured foie gras garnish Serves 4-6

Originally an Egyptian ingredient of fattened goose or duck liver, that has quite rightly garnered a bad reputation among ethical carnivores and animal rights activists alike. There are, however, natural occurrences of foie gras in birds migrating south for the winter, which is probably how the Egyptians discovered it. In Spain there is a chap farming seasonal and ethical foie gras without *gavage* or forced feeding of any kind, and it's this that I would urge you to use if you can source it.

1 x 600g (1lb 5oz) whole ethically reared raw duck foie gras, cleaned and deveined (see recipe introduction)

20g (¾oz) Basic Beef Rub (see page 40)

50ml (2fl oz) Madeira

Maldon sea salt flakes

Lay the cleaned foie gras on a piece of baking parchment. Lightly season with the steak rub and splash over the Madeira.

Using a sheet of clingfilm, roll the foie gras into a tight cylinder. Secure the clingfilm at both ends, then refrigerate for 1 hour.

Remove the clingfilm and wrap the foie gras in a layer of cheesecloth. Tie the ends of the cheesecloth, squeezing the foie gras to create a tight cylinder. Place in a plastic container and bury it completely in salt. Refrigerate for 12 hours.

Remove the foie gras cylinder from the salt and unwrap the cheesecloth.

Shave the foie gras into thin slivers and let it melt on top of hot steak.

Oyster sauce

Makes about 200ml (7fl oz)

One day in 1888, Lee Kum Sheung was cooking oyster soup as usual, but lost track of time. Smelling a strong savoury aroma, he lifted the lid of the pot and noticed that the normally clear oyster soup had turned into a thick, brownish sauce that astonished him with the most fragrant smell and unique, delicious taste. This oyster sauce went on to be particularly popular with beef.

200g (7oz) shucked oysters, juices reserved

50ml (2fl oz) water

50ml (2fl oz) light soy sauce

50ml (2fl oz) dark soy sauce

50g (1¾oz) sugar

Drain the shucked oysters, reserving the liquid. Use a sharp kitchen knife to roughly chop them.

Place the chopped oysters in a small saucepan with the reserved oyster juices and the water. Bring to a simmer, stirring the contents of the saucepan occasionally to prevent the oysters from sticking to the pan. Reduce the heat to low, allow the liquid to drop to a gentle simmer, and cook for 10 minutes or until thickened, stirring from time to time.

Add the soy sauces and the sugar and simmer for a further 5 minutes until the sugar dissolves, then pour the contents of the saucepan, through a sieve or strainer. Save the liquid and discard the solid ingredients.

Breeds

A breed is defined as a type of cattle, carefully selected over time, that reliably reproduces its qualities and appearance in its progeny. Each breed has its own particular merits and characteristics, and it takes generations to create and fix a new breed.

Today's cattle breeds were developed through selective breeding to enhance characteristics that were suited to their local environments. Cattle in cold, mountainous areas were small, hardy beasts, with a thick coat of long hair and a knack for surviving in harsh conditions. Cattle in lowlands with a temperate climate were less hardy and adapted to flatter grazing pasture, while those in cooler lowlands were somewhere in between.

What's more, in the days when rural settlements often comprised a single wealthy landowner and many tenant-farming families, each family would keep a milking cow, which needed to be in calf to produce. Not being able to afford their own bull, they used the services of the lord of the manor's bull, which attended to the entire settlement's cows. The bull imprinted its genes on every calf, and these characteristics strengthened with each generation, forming local traits that eventually became breeds.

Cattle breeding continued in this haphazard manner until the mid-18th century, when the famous agriculturalist Robert Bakewell, from Leicestershire in England, pioneered selective breeding by keeping the sexes separate, choosing traits to fix and deliberately in-breeding.

Many of these British and Continental European breeds then went on to cross the Atlantic, taken by explorers and settlers to North America, where they continued to develop into other breeds. Later some were exported around the world, as far afield as Australia and New Zealand.

In the second half of the 20th century, native heritage breeds went into decline as post-war farming techniques favoured hybrid animals (which grow faster due to something called hybrid vigour – see page 98), and as modern practices were introduced, in order to produce larger quantities of cheaper meat. Recently, however, we have seen a return to favour of many of these old breeds, as butchers, chefs and consumers are voting with their stomachs and searching them out.

Included here are the breeds that I know and use, or that are famous. It's by no means a comprehensive roll call – there are breeds I have never encountered, so am loathe to write about – but the list does, in my opinion, include all the great beef breeds. As previously explained, breed is only part of the equation. If you are in Africa eating the most amazing Ankole-Watusi steak, and wondering why on earth it wasn't included in the book, let me hazard a guess that your animal led a good and happy life, fed on a variety of grasses, herbs and clovers, and died a stress-free death, which made it such a righteous feast. While finding specific breeds is an important issue when searching for the best meat, any animal can only fulfil its genetic potential with the right feed, husbandry and slaughter. Only when all four things combine do we get meat as it really should be eaten.

Aberdeen Angus

This is a truly famous, if much abused, breed name, and much of today's beef contains some Angus genes. Developed from cattle native to the Scottish counties of Aberdeenshire and Angus, it has been recorded since the 16th century. Hornless cattle in Aberdeenshire and Angus had been locally called Angus doddies or Buchan humlies, but in 1824 William McCombie, of Tillyfour, Aberdeenshire, began to improve the stock, and he is regarded today as the father of the breed. The first herd book was created in 1862, and the breed society was established in Scotland in 1879. By the mid-20th century the cattle were commonplace throughout the British Isles, and today their genes are used the world over to grow prime beef.

In Europe, meat can be sold as Aberdeen Angus if it has at least 50 per cent Angus genes, which means that almost all meat sold as such is actually a cross. Because of commercial factors, such as rate of weight gain, 100 per cent pure Aberdeen Angus beef is quite rare and rather special.

Pure Angus typically mature earlier than other native British breeds. They are hardy, making them able to survive the harsh Scottish winters. They are naturally polled (hornless) and usually black, although more recently red colours have emerged. The UK registers both in the same herd book, but despite their being genetically identical, they are regarded in the US as two separate breeds – Red Angus and Black Angus. Black Angus is the most common breed of beef cattle in the US.

In 1883 the American Angus Association was founded in Chicago, and the first herd book was published in 1885, when both red and black animals were registered without distinction. However, in 1917, in an effort to promote a solid black breed, the association barred the registering of red and other coloured animals.

The American Angus Association created the "Certified Angus Beef" standard in 1978 to promote the idea that the meat was of higher quality than beef from other breeds of cattle. All cattle are eligible for this evaluation if they are at least 51 per cent black and exhibit Angus influence, which includes crossbreds. However, they must meet all ten of the following criteria:

- Modest or higher degree of marbling
- Medium or fine marbling texture
- "A" maturity
- 64.5–103.2cm^2 (10–16 inch^2) rib-eye area
- Less than 453.6kg (1,000lb) hot carcass weight
- Less than 2.5cm (1in) fat thickness
- Moderately thick or thicker muscling
- No hump on the neck exceeding 5cm (2in)
- Practically free of capillary rupture
- No dark cutting characteristics
- Usually black or red in colour

Unfortunately, this means the name Angus is somewhat devalued unless you can verify it is 100 per cent pure, which is a rarity.

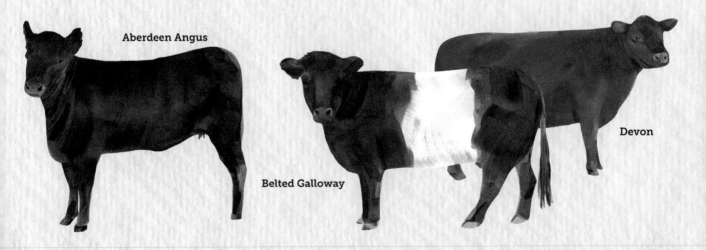

Aberdeen Angus

Belted Galloway

Devon

Belted Galloway

Also known as "belties" in the UK and "Oreo cows" in the US, this breed originated in Galloway, southwest Scotland. Well suited to rough grazing land and adapted to living on the poor upland pastures and windswept moorlands of the region, Belted Galloways are able to maintain good condition on this less than ideal pasture, and can produce quality marbled beef on pure grass without finishing (altering their diet before slaughter, see page 128).

Galloway breeders acquired their own herd book in 1878, and in 1921 the Dun and Belted Galloway Association was formed in Scotland. The name was changed to the Belted Galloway Society 30 years later, as Dun cattle were no longer registered. The Society keeps and records pedigrees for Belted Galloways and it oversees the registration of White and Red Galloways.

Galloway cattle are naturally polled. The most visible characteristics of the Belted Galloway are the long hair coat and the broad white belt that completely encircles the body. The coarse outer coat helps shed the rain, while the soft undercoat provides both insulation and waterproofing, enabling the breed to spend winter outdoors.

Riggit Galloway cattle are an archaic strain, easily identifiable by the white stripe, running down the spine. (The term "riggit" is a Scottish vernacular reference to this stripe.) The main body colour can be black, blue/black, red, brown or dun, and the white coloration may include a widening of the stripe to cover much of the back (particularly on the hindquarters), white under the keel of the animal, and white flashes among the solid colour.

British White

This is a naturally polled, large and hardy native breed exhibiting the dual characteristics of beef and milking ability. It is white with black or red points – that is, muzzle, ears, eye rims, horn tips and feet. The modern breed of cattle known as British Whites can claim direct links with the ancient indigenous wild white cattle of Great Britain, notably those from the park at Whalley Abbey, Lancashire.

Charolais

White, cream or pale straw-coloured, these large animals are long-bodied, heavily muscled and late-maturing. Most Charolais have short horns and pink muzzles. Charolais is the most common beef breed in France and was introduced to the southern US in 1946 and the northern US in 1965.

British White

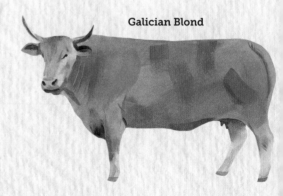

Galician Blond

Devon

This is one of several breeds derived from the traditional red cattle of southern England, the others being the Hereford, Sussex, Lincoln Red and Red Poll. They vary in shade from a rich deep red to a light red or chestnut colour. A bright ruby-red colour is preferred and accounts for the breed's nickname, the "Red Ruby". The hair, which is of medium thickness, is often long and curly during the winter but short and sleek in summer. The switch of the tail is creamy white.

Although the Devon was originally a horned breed, American stockmen have developed a polled strain of pure-bred Devons.

The Devon was previously classified as a dual-purpose breed. Over the past half-century, however, it has been developed as a beef-type breed. Its ability to utilize grass and other forages efficiently has heightened its popularity in areas such as southern Brazil, Australia and New Zealand.

Dexter

The smallest of the European cattle breeds, the Dexter originated in southwestern Ireland and was brought to England in 1882. Dexters come in three colours – black, red and dun – and should have no white markings except for some very minor white ones on the belly/udder behind the navel, and some white hairs in the tail switch.

Originally, Dexters were typically horned, with small, thick horns growing outwards with a forward curve on the male, and upwards on the female. However, a naturally polled strain was developed in the 1990s.

The breed virtually disappeared in Ireland, but was still maintained as a pure breed in a number of small herds in England and also in the US. The Dexter's small size notwithstanding, the body is wide and deep, with well-rounded hindquarters.

The beef produced by Dexters is well marbled and tends to be darker than most, with an intense beefy flavour. Good Dexter beef is some of the best I've tasted and right up there with that of Highland.

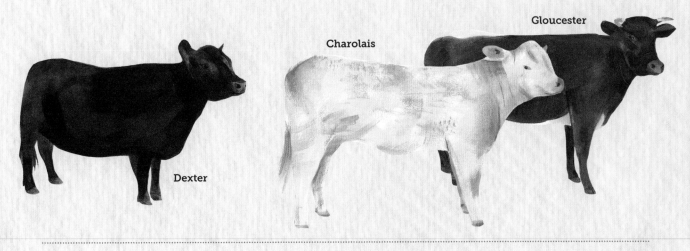

Dexter

Charolais

Gloucester

Galician Blond

Also known as Rubia Galega, this is a breed native to Galicia in northwestern Spain. It is raised mainly for meat and is distributed throughout Galicia, with about 75 per cent of the population concentrated in the province of Lugo. It is found particularly at altitudes above about 550m (1,800ft) in mountainous areas in the northern part of Lugo. The coat may be red-blond, wheaten or cinnamon-coloured. A herd book was established in 1933.

Gloucester

These are large cattle, coloured a rich dark brown in the cows, calves and steers, and almost black in the bulls. They have a white belly and a white stripe (known as a finching stripe) along the spine and continuing over the tail. They normally have well-developed white horns with black tips.

Cattle of a similar type were numerous in England's Cotswold Hills and Severn Valley as early as the 13th century. They were valued for their milk, for providing strong and docile draft oxen and eventually for their beef. By 1972 only one significant herd remained and the breed was in danger of dying out. The next year, the Gloucester Cattle Society was revived and the breed has moved from near extinction to a rating by the Rare Breeds Survival Trust of being "At Risk", as there are still fewer than 750 registered breeding females.

Hereford

Red and white in colour, with varying shades from deep cherry to a light orange, Herefords have white running from the face to behind the ears and down the chest. They are stocky and square in appearance, with obvious muscle mass in the shoulders. Their hair ranges from slick and smooth to short and curly, thickening in winter. Herefords are widely used in both intemperate and temperate areas for meat production, and more than five million pedigree Hereford cattle now exist in more than fifty countries. The Hereford cattle export trade was begun in 1817 in the UK by the politician Henry Clay, who exported them to the American state of Kentucky. In the 1840s the breed began to be exported across the Atlantic more extensively, spreading across the US and Canada through Mexico to the great beef-raising countries of South America. Hereford cattle are now found all over the temperate parts of the world.

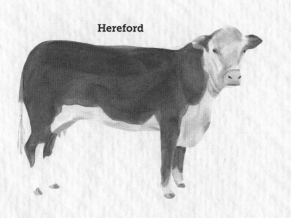

Hereford

Highland

Longhorn

Highland

These cattle are tough and hairy, and one of Britain's purest breeds, having been improved by selection rather than cross-breeding. They have long horns and long, wavy coats that are coloured black, brindle, red, yellow, white, silver or dun. They are raised primarily for their meat. They originated in the Highlands and Western Isles of Scotland and were first mentioned in the 6th century. They have an unusual double coat of hair. On the outside is the oily outer hair – the longest of any cattle breed – covering a downy undercoat. This makes them well suited to conditions in the Scottish Highlands, a region with a high annual rainfall and sometimes very strong winds, and it gives the breed the ability to overwinter outside. Their skill in foraging for food allows them to survive in steep mountain areas where they both graze and eat plants that many other cattle avoid. They can also dig through the snow with their horns to find buried plants. A herd of Highland cattle is known as a "fold".

The meat of Highland cattle is tender and leaner than most beef because the cattle are largely insulated by their thick, shaggy hair rather than by subcutaneous fat. Unfortunately, they are slow-growing, and animals are few and far between. Highland cattle can produce beef at a reasonable profit from land that would otherwise normally be unsuitable for agriculture. At the festival Meatopia UK 2016, I had the good fortune to taste a seven-year-old Angus Mackay Highland from the Isle of Mull, hung for a couple of weeks – it may be the best beef I have ever tasted. The beef guru Mark Schatzker agrees: in his book *Steak* he found Highland beef to be the best he had encountered on his global search.

Limousin

The Limousin is naturally horned and has a distinctive light wheat to dark golden-red colouring, although international breeders have now bred polled and black versions. These highly muscled cattle originate from the Limousin and Marche regions of France. Having been first exported in significant numbers in the 1960s, they are now found in around 70 countries. Limousins became popular because of their low birth weights (which means ease of calving), higher than average dressing percentage (ratio of carcass to live weight) and yield (ratio of meat to carcass), high feed conversion efficiency and ability to produce lean, tender meat.

Lincoln Red

Large cattle that are a dark red in colour, this breed was originally called the Lincoln Red Shorthorn. Now they may be polled or horned. "Shorthorn" was consequently dropped from the name in the 1960s. They are noted for their docility and ability to thrive under all conditions. They originate from Lincolnshire in eastern England where they were selectively bred from the indigenous draught cattle of the region by crossing with red Shorthorns to produce a dual-purpose breed. They are now exclusively a beef breed. First exported more than a century ago, they are now found in a dozen or so countries around the world.

Limousin

Lincoln Red

Red Angus

Longhorn

This breed is not to be confused with the Texas Longhorn (see page 74) which is also often called "Longhorn cattle" or "Longhorns". English Longhorns are a brown and white breed of beef cattle originating from Craven, in the north of the country. They have curved horns that tend to grow down around the face, framing it. The notable horns that distinguish this breed from others can make them appear aggressive, although they are, in fact, quite docile. Longhorns live longer than other breeds of cattle and are also known for calving with ease. They have a white patch along the line of their spine and under their bellies.

Though long-horned oxen were already predominant in Craven in the 16th and 17th centuries, the English Longhorn breed was much improved for beef by Sir Robert Bakewell, at a time when large amounts of meat were needed to feed people who had moved to towns and cities in the Industrial Revolution.

Red Angus

These cattle are a dark golden red in colour but otherwise identical to Aberdeen Angus, and they produce beef of a similar quality. Naturally polled like their black relatives, they are one of the world's top beef breeds. The Red Angus Association of America was founded in 1954 by breeders, in response to having their cattle struck off from the herd book for not conforming to a changing breed standard regarding colour.

Red Poll

A deep red with white only on the tail switch and udder, and polled, the Red Poll evolved in the 19th century from a cross of the Norfolk Red beef cattle and Suffolk Dun dairy cattle breeds, both of which are now extinct. Red Poll cattle were exported around the world in the mid-19th century for beef production, although they are considered a dual-purpose breed. Consequently the Red Poll has been used to create several new breeds across Latin America and the Caribbean.

Santa Gertrudis

Red in colour, the Santa Gertrudis may be polled or horned. This is a hardy breed that is good for beef production, with excellent mothering ability, ease of calving, heat tolerance and parasite resistance. Santa Gertrudis cattle are known the world over for their ability to adapt to harsh climates.

Developed on the King Ranch in southern Texas, by mating Brahman bulls with Shorthorn cows, they were named for the Spanish land grant where Captain Richard King originally established the King Ranch. The breed was officially recognized by the USDA in 1940, becoming the first beef breed formed in the US. In 1950, the Santa Gertrudis Breeders International Association was formed at Kingsville, Texas.

Red Poll

Santa Gertrudis

Shorthorn

These cattle are coloured red, white, roan, red and white, or roan and white, and the rare Whitebred Shorthorn has been bred to be consistently white. Shorthorn cattle originated in the northeast of England in the late 18th century and were developed as dual-purpose – suitable for both dairy and beef production. However, certain bloodlines within the breed always emphasized one quality or the other. Over time, these different lines diverged, and by the second half of the 20th century, two separate breeds had developed – the sturdy Beef Shorthorn and the Dairy Shorthorn. As an archetypal British beef breed, the Beef Shorthorn has spread in huge numbers all over the world, where it has adapted to tropical and subtropical climates.

Simmental

The defining characteristic of a Simmental is the white face, with coat colours ranging from yellow to dun red, marked with white on the legs and tail. No other breed in the world has such a large within-breed type variation as Simmental. American Simmentals are mainly black or dark red. Most Simmental cattle are solid in colouring. From the late 1960s to the 1980s, traditionally coloured (spotted red and white) Simmental were deemed most desirable by Simmental breeders, as well as the industry. It is among the oldest and most widely distributed of all breeds of cattle in the world, and was recorded as having originated in the valley of the Simme River, in the Bernese Oberland of western Switzerland, in the Middle Ages.

Shorthorn

Sussex

Simmental

South Devon

This breed is a rich, medium red to golden sand with copper tints, though it varies in shade and can even appear slightly mottled. The breed today is predominately used for beef production, although it has been milked in the past.

These large cattle evolved from the large red cattle of Normandy which were imported into England at the time of the Norman invasion (11th century). The South Devon of today originated in southwest England, in an area of Devon known as the South Hams, from where the breed spread across the counties of Devon and Cornwall. Geographical isolation caused the North and South Devon to become physically distinct types, though occasional crossing between the two breeds occurred until the mid-19th century. South Devons are now farmed all over the world on five continents.

Sussex

This breed has a deep red-brown coat, with a white switch to the tail. It is a medium-sized, long-bodied animal, and traditionally it has white horns, although naturally polled strains have also been developed. They hail from the Weald of Sussex, Surrey and Kent in southeast England and are descended from the draught oxen long used in this area. From the late 18th century, they were selectively bred to form a modern beef breed, which is now used in many countries around the world. The Sussex has a placid temperament but can be very stubborn. It is one of several similarly coloured breeds of southern England – the others include the North Devon, the Hereford, the Lincoln Red and the Red Poll. All these breeds derive originally from the traditional multipurpose red indigenous cattle of the region.

Texas Longhorn

This breed is known for its characteristic handlebar horns, which extend, tip to tip, 1m (39in) and often over 1.5m (58in)! Their coloration ranges from red to black with assorted white spots, speckles and splotches. They are completely distinct from the British Longhorn, having descended from the first cattle in the New World, an Iberian hybrid of two ancient cattle lineages: "taurine" descending from the domestication of the wild aurochs in the Middle East, and "indicine" (Indian). They were brought by Christopher Columbus and the Spanish colonists, and have a high drought-stress tolerance.

South Devon

Texas Longhorn

Wagyu

Wagyu

This refers to any of four mostly black breeds. The Japanese Black makes up 90 per cent of all fattened cattle in Japan. Strains of Japanese Black include Tottori, Tajima, Shimane and Okayama. The Japanese Brown, or Japanese Red, is the other main breed; strains include Kochi and Kumamoto. They are genetically predisposed to intense marbling and to producing a high percentage of oleaginous unsaturated fat. The meat from such Wagyu cattle is known for its quality and is judged on four different criteria: the marbling intensity; the colour of the fat; the colour of the muscle tissue itself (the meat); and the shape of the muscle.

Originating in the second century, primarily as a work animal for the rice paddies, they have come to be known as the most highly marbled and most expensive beef produced in the world today. Different breeding and feeding techniques were once used, such as massaging or adding beer or sake to their feeding regimen to aid digestion and induce hunger during humid seasons; the massaging also prevented muscle cramping on small farms in Japan where the animals did not have sufficient room to use their muscles. Neither of these techniques affect the flavour, and they are no longer widely used.

Welsh Black

As the name suggests, these are naturally black, and they generally have white horns with black tips; some are also naturally polled or hornless. The occasional Red individual occurs, having once been more common. The Welsh Black was a dual-purpose breed until the 1970s, but is now mainly used for beef.

Its hardy nature, coupled with its habit of browsing as well as grazing, makes it ideal for rough pasture such as heathland and moorland, and for conservation grazing. Welsh Blacks are found throughout the UK and although small numbers exist around the world they have not been extensively exported.

White Park

Also known as the Ancient White Park, the White Forest, the White Horned, the Wild White or simply "the Park", the White Park is porcelain-white with black or red coloured points. The teats and horn tips usually are black but may lack pigment. Its horns are long or medium-long. In cows they normally grow sideways, curving forwards and upwards. In bulls they are stronger and less curved. White Park is a rare breed, with ancient herds preserved in Great Britain. It includes two very rare types that are often regarded as distinct: the Chillingham and the Vaynol.

Welsh Black

White Park

Burgers

My perfect burger

While America is considered the home of the hamburger, patties of chopped beef have, in fact, been part of Eastern European cuisines for centuries. Russian traders brought them to Hamburg in the 15th century, and then four centuries later, when most German immigrants to America travelled from the port of Hamburg, they brought their taste for "Hamburg-style beef" with them. By the 1830s, a New York City restaurant was serving Hamburg Steak, and in 1873 the *New York Times* wrote that it was "simply a beefsteak redeemed from its original toughness by being mashed into mincemeat, then formed into a conglomerate mass. This is very appetizing, but conscience compels us to state that it is inferior to the genuine article". Oh, how things have changed.

The state of Wisconsin claims to have come up with the modern burger, when in 1885 Charles Nagreen made sandwiches from his homemade meatballs and sold these "hamburgers" at his local county fair. By the 1920s, the first hamburger joints had appeared, followed by Wimpy in the 1930s. In 1948 the McDonald brothers turned their barbecue restaurant into a drive-in that sold hamburgers, fries and milkshakes.

It may not be the world's healthiest sandwich, but a classic burger still hits the spot like nothing else. Its diversity is mind-boggling. To get an idea of how many variations on the burger there are in the US alone, read George Motz's compendious *Hamburger America*, a riveting joy for any fellow burger geek.

A feast for the senses

Eating a burger is a multisensory experience – taste is only one component of the perfect patty. Sight, smell, feeling and even sound also contribute to our perception of how it tastes. Good presentation combines with the aroma of first-rate ingredients and of the fat in the beef to whet the appetite. The feeling of the soft, warm bun in the hand adds to the anticipation – a perfect burger should never be eaten with cutlery.

Sound is often the forgotten sense; a burger would be disappointing without hearing the crunch of lettuce.

Essential components

My perfect burger is 10cm (4 inches) tall, 10cm (4 inches) wide and boasts eight layers:

- warm toasted bun top
- tomato ketchup
- juicy beef tomato
- slice of melted cheese
- seasoned patty of beef
- crunchy salad and fresh onion
- mustard-mayonnaise sauce
- warm toasted bun base

The patty

The star of this chapter is the patty. All the other components – bun, lettuce, cheese, sauce – are part of the delivery system and so are supporting acts. The way the meat is minced and the cuts that are used in the grind are the most important factors in producing a truly great burger. It is important to start with fresh beef mince – the fresher the better – so if you can mince your own on the day of cooking, you'll get to eat restaurant-quality burgers. (By fresh I mean freshly minced. The beef should, of course, have been hung according to your preference; (see pages 194–5).) Failing that, ask your butcher to mince your beef for you on the morning of cooking.

A lot of thought is given to meat blends in the burger world, and different cuts do give their own qualities to a burger. Fat is imperative to a great burger, providing moistness and flavour. As a rule, most burger aficionados incorporate around 20 per cent fat in their blend, but I know of at least one successful purveyor that prefers 30 per cent, and damned fine burgers they are, too. If you like your burger pink, spare a thought for the type of fat you use; different beef fats have different melting points, so I favour bone marrow. My favourite blends are:

• A simple 90 per cent chuck with 10 per cent bone marrow, the chuck naturally containing over 10 per cent fat and the bone marrow topping it up to over 20 per cent.

• 80 per cent offcuts left from butchering prime steaks with 20 per cent aged cod fat (soft beef fat taken from the hindquarter, not from a fish). This blend has the benefit of aged steak flavour.

• 60 per cent chuck, 20 per cent heart and 20 per cent bone marrow. Heart is often used in cheap burgers pertaining to be 100 per cent beef as it is cheap and is hard to sell on its own. It does, however, have an interesting flavour that I'm quite fond of.

Decide on your chosen meat blend, and chop the various cuts into 2cm (¾ inch) cubes, then refrigerate until very cold. It doesn't hurt to also chill the meat grinder attachment, just to be on the safe side. Heat is the enemy of good burger patty preparation. Using a meat grinder fitted with a 4mm (about ⅛ inch) plate, grind the meat, then refrigerate once more until very cold. Change the grinding plate to a 6mm (¼ inch) plate and refrigerate the whole attachment again.

When cold, pass the meat mixture through the grinder and lay out the strands of meat, trying to keep the grain of the individual strands running lengthways, in the same direction, without getting tangled together.

Divide the minced beef into 200g (7oz) piles, taking care not to handle or mix them too much. With your hands cupped, gently form them into balls, then loosely press each ball into an even patty, around 12cm (4½ inch) wide and 2cm (¾ inch) thick. Lay the patties between squares of greaseproof paper and refrigerate them for an hour before cooking. Note that at no point has any form of seasoning, filling or flavouring been added: burger patties should be 100 per cent pure beef. Anything else is a beef sausage or stuffing.

The bun

The next most important element is the bun. The very best buns are, of course, homemade, and I've included my current favourite recipe on page 84. A burger bun should be firm enough to hold the filling without getting immediately soaked and disintegrating in a soggy mess. It should be innocuous in flavour, with no herbs or spices. A burger is about the beef, the whole beef, and nothing but the beef. The bun should be the same size when toasted as the burger is when cooked.

The extras

Sauces, pickles and salads are important, but should be kept to a minimum. Their role is to insulate the bun from the juicy burger, to complement the star of the show and to offer texture, crunch and freshness. It goes without saying that all these accompaniments should be of the best possible quality. You might even consider omitting sliced tomato in the depths of winter, in favour of a perfect sliced raw Portobello mushroom.

Having talked about keeping things simple and the roles each part of the perfect burger plays, I'm going to suggest an optional "pimp" of the classic burger. Serving a side dish of thin but tasty beef jus with a burger might horrify my slightly fanatical burger associates, but it certainly adds something to my perfect burger.

Serves
4

800g (1lb 12oz) burger mince,
made with 90 per cent chuck steak,
10 per cent fat (see page 80)

85g (3oz) bone marrow, chopped

4 thin slices of cheese, Ogleshield
if at all possible, Cheddar if not

4 tablespoons mustard mayonnaise
(50:50 mix of mustard and mayonnaise)

4 Burger Buns (see page 84), slightly
smaller than each patty

4 tablespoons tomato ketchup

4 leaves of Bibb (Butterhead) lettuce

4 thin slices of red onion

4 thin slices of beef tomato

2 Half Sours (pickled cucumbers),
halved (see page 85)

Maldon sea salt flakes and freshly
ground black pepper

Cheeseburger

Opinions vary on the perfect cheeseburger, but for me it's all about
the beef – whatever you add should support and not overwhelm that
beefiness. These are garnishes that have proven themselves in every
burger dive up and down the country, and are now considered classic.

Mix the minced chuck steak into the fat and bone marrow, and form 4 loose patties
(see page 80). Season and grill on one side, then flip to grill the other side. Top with
the cheese and cook until pink or cooked, however you like them.

Split and toast the buns directly over the hot side of the grill until browned, about 30 seconds.

Spread the mustard mayonnaise on the bases of the toasted buns and the ketchup
on the tops.

Place a lettuce leaf and a slice of onion on top of the mayonnaise side of the buns
and a tomato slice on the ketchup side. Stack the sandwich with the patty in the
middle and serve with a Half Sour spear half on the side.

Burger buns Makes 8 large buns

125ml (4fl oz) warm milk

200ml (7fl oz) warm water

2 teaspoons active dry yeast

20g (¾oz) sugar

500–525g (1lb 2oz–1lb 3oz) strong
white flour, plus extra for kneading

2 teaspoons fine sea salt

1 teaspoon vitamin C powder

3 large free-range eggs

40g (1½oz) unsalted butter, softened

1 tablespoon water

Combine the milk, water, yeast and sugar in a small bowl, whisk well and leave to stand for 5 minutes until foamy.

Mix the flour, salt and vitamin C powder in the bowl of a stand mixer fitted with a dough hook. Add the water/milk mixture and mix on medium-low speed until just combined. With the mixer still running, add 2 of the eggs, separately, waiting for the first egg to be fully incorporated before adding the next. Add the butter 1 tablespoon at a time until fully incorporated.

Continue to mix on medium-low speed for 2–3 minutes. If the dough appears too sticky, add more flour, 1 tablespoon at a time, until it pulls away from the sides of the mixer (it will still stick to the base). Continue kneading until the dough is smooth and elastic, 5–6 minutes longer.

Loosely cover the bowl with clingfilm or a clean tea towel and let it rise until doubled in volume (about 1 hour at room temperature, or 6 hours in the fridge).

Turn the dough out on to a lightly floured surface and, using a bench scraper or sharp knife, cut it into 8 equal pieces, each about 120g (4½oz).

Line 2 baking sheets with nonstick baking paper. Form each piece of dough into a ball and place on the baking sheets, 4 per sheet, about 10cm (4 inches) apart. Spray with nonstick cooking spray (or brush with oil), cover loosely with clingfilm, and allow to rise for about 1 hour at room temperature, until about doubled in size.

Adjust the oven racks to lower-middle and upper-middle positions and preheat the oven to 200°C (400°F), Gas Mark 6. Gently press the dough balls down until 10–12cm (4–4½ inches) wide and 4cm (1½ inches) high. Beat the remaining egg with 1 tablespoon water and brush the entire exposed surface of the buns. Bake them for 7 minutes, then remove from the oven, brush with the remaining egg wash, and bake for 10–15 minutes longer, until a deep, shiny, golden brown, rotating the baking sheets from top to bottom and front to back halfway through baking. Transfer the buns to a wire rack and allow to cool completely.

Half sours
Makes 3 x 1 litre (1¾ pint) jars

Half sours are half-pickled gherkins, or wallies.

20 small cucumbers

5 garlic cloves

small bunch of dill

500ml (18fl oz) white wine vinegar

500ml (18fl oz) water

125g (4½oz) Maldon sea salt flakes

125g (4½oz) caster sugar

5 hot red chillies, split

15g (½oz) mustard seeds

15g (½oz) black peppercorns

Wash the cucumbers and drain well, then place them in sterilized Kilner jars (see page 163) with the garlic and dill sprigs. Mix the remaining ingredients together and stir until the salt and sugar dissolve. Pour over the cucumbers.

Close the jars and leave to pickle for 1 week. At the end of the week they will be half sours, or half-pickled.

Pickled shiitake mushrooms
Makes 50ml (2fl oz)

30g (about 1oz) dried shiitake mushrooms

60g (2¼ oz) sugar

70ml (about 5 tablespoons) light soy sauce

70ml (about 5 tablespoons) cider vinegar

20g (about ¾oz) piece of fresh root ginger, peeled

Steep the shiitakes in boiling water until softened, about 3–5 hours. Lift the shiitakes from the steeping liquid (reserve the liquid), discard the stalks and cut the caps into 3mm (⅛ inch) slices.

Strain and reserve 50ml (2fl oz) of the steeping liquid and pour into a saucepan.

Add the mushroom caps, sugar, soy sauce, cider vinegar and ginger. Bring to a gentle simmer and cook for 30 minutes, stirring occasionally, then remove from the heat and leave to cool. Strain into a sterilized jar (see page 163), discarding the ginger, seal and leave for 1 week to pickle before use.

Serves
4

1 beef tomato

200g (7oz) Parmesan cheese, grated

4 tablespoons American mustard,
French's for preference

4 tablespoons tomato ketchup

4 tablespoons mayonnaise

4 tablespoons soy sauce

800g (1lb 12oz) burger mince, made
with 80 per cent chuck steak,
10 per cent fat, 10 per cent bone
marrow (see page 80)

40g (1½oz) fried chopped onion

40g (1½oz) chopped Pickled Shiitake
Mushrooms (see page 85)

4 thin slices of Gentleman's Relish,
around 40g (1½oz) (see page 88)

4 thin slices of Ogleshield
or Cheddar cheese

4 Burger Buns (see page 84)

4 leaves of Bibb (Butterhead) lettuce

smoked Maldon sea salt flakes
and cracked black pepper

Umami cheeseburger

It is of course impossible to improve upon the simple perfection of the
classic cheeseburger. There is, however, a Californian company in LA
that comes close, and this is my take on their creation. There are a lot
of ingredients, but I promise it'll be worth it.

First make the oven-dried beef tomato: slice the tomato into rounds 1cm (½ inch) thick.
Place on a baking tray and place in a preheated oven at 110°C (225°F), Gas Mark ¼, for
a minimum of 4 hours to dry out, turning halfway.

Next, make some Parmesan tuiles: take a nonstick baking sheet and divide the grated
Parmesan into 4 equal-sized round piles. Bake in a preheated oven at 180°C (350°F), Gas
Mark 4 for about 5 minutes until the cheese has melted and is golden. Remove and leave
to cool on the sheet.

Mix together the mustard, ketchup, mayo and soy sauce to make your umami sauce.

Mix the minced chuck steak into the fat and bone marrow and form 4 loose patties
(see page 80). Lightly season the burger patties with smoked Maldon sea salt flakes
and cracked black pepper, then grill until charred and cooked medium-rare.

While hot, top with the fried onion, Pickled Mushrooms and Gentleman's Relish, followed
by a thin slice of Ogleshield or Cheddar (the residual heat will melt the cheese).

Split and toast the Burger Buns. Spread both sides of the toasted buns with the umami
sauce, then place a lettuce leaf and some dried tomato slices on the base. Transfer
a stacked patty on top, followed by a Parmesan tuile and finally the bun top.

Gentleman's relish is a Victorian spiced anchovy butter often eaten on toast by the well-to-do as a post-dinner savoury. It's also good to have on hand for serving with a steak, or in fact with any grilled meat. Use the very best-quality anchovies – Spanish if possible – and don't worry, they won't make your steak taste fishy; anchovies are full of umami, which helps to amplify the meatiness of the steak.

Gentleman's relish Makes 450g (1lb)

125g (4½oz) anchovy fillets in oil

250g (9oz) unsalted butter, chopped

small pinch of cayenne pepper

small pinch of ground nutmeg

small pinch of freshly ground black pepper

small pinch of ground cinnamon

25ml (1fl oz) lemon juice

25ml (1fl oz) Worcestershire sauce

25ml (1fl oz) water

Put all the ingredients into a blender and blend until smooth.

The mixture can then be beaten until fluffy and piped through a piping bag if using immediately, or it can be rolled into a log, wrapped in clingfilm and chilled until needed. Keep in the fridge for up to 1 week, or freeze.

When required, just cut a thick slice, remove the clingfilm and serve on top of your steak or burger.

Koreans are fanatical about kimchi: they have more than 200 kinds. For centuries they have believed that eating kimchi reduces cholesterol, promotes brain health and protects against obesity, cancer, digestive and colorectal disease. They believe it has anti-ageing properties, that it's good for your skin and immune system, and that it's antioxidative and probiotic. In short, Koreans believe kimchi is the elixir of life. It turns out they might be right, as Western science is beginning to confirm what they have long known: fermented foods are incredibly good for you, and as luck would have it they are also extremely tasty.

Kimchi Makes approximately 2 x 1 litre (1¾ pint) jars

2 heads of Chinese leaf cabbage, outer leaves discarded

4 teaspoons Maldon sea salt flakes

4 teaspoons caster sugar

50g (1¾oz) garlic cloves, grated

50g (1¾oz) piece of fresh root ginger, peeled and grated

50g (1¾oz) *gochugaru* (Korean red pepper powder or flakes)

50g (1¾oz) anchovy fillets in oil

50ml (1¾fl oz) light soy sauce

50g (1¾oz) salted shrimp, from a jar

4 teaspoons rice flour

50ml (2fl oz) water

100g (3½oz) spring onions, cut into 2cm (¾ inch) pieces

100g (3½oz) daikon, cut in julienne strips

100g (3½oz) carrots, cut in julienne strips

Cut the root off each of the Chinese leaf cabbages, but ensure they are in sections joined together, then cut them in half lengthways. Toss the cabbage leaves in a bowl with the sea salt and sugar, taking care to season in between every leaf, then leave overnight at room temperature.

The following day, rinse the leaves in cold water and gently squeeze dry.

Put the garlic, ginger, *gochugaru*, anchovies, soy sauce, shrimp, rice flour and water into a blender and blend until smooth. Remove from the blender and stir in the spring onions, daikon and carrots.

Layer the leaves with the paste mixture, making sure every part of every leaf is coated. Fold each half cabbage in 3 to make a parcel, then pack into airtight plastic containers and leave at room temperature for another 24 hours before chilling.

The kimchi will be tasty after 1 week and really zingy after a couple of weeks. Sealed, it will keep in the fridge for a few months, however, its character will change over time and after 1 month it will become funky and fizzy.

It can also be layered on to clingfilm, rolled into a neat sausage and sliced, if serving as a garnish.

Serves
4

800g (1lb 12oz) burger mince, blend of your choice (see page 80)

4 Burger Buns (see page 84)

50ml (2fl oz) mustard mayonnaise (50:50 mix of mustard and mayonnaise)

4 leaves of Bibb (Butterhead) lettuce

4 large dessertspoons Kimchi (see page 89)

100g (3½oz) Braised Short Ribs (see page 265), shredded

4 thin slices of Ogleshield or Cheddar cheese

Maldon sea salt flakes and freshly ground black pepper

Kimchi burger

Kimchi and beef go together like ham and eggs, so inevitably someone in Korea came up with the kimchi burger, and just as inevitably I came across it on the internet one evening and fell in love. I spent months developing my version – from the kimchi to the addition of braised beef and cheese, it's the Marmite of burgers, either loved or loathed.

Blend together your choice of minced chuck steak, fat and bone marrow and form 4 loose patties (see page 80). Season with salt and pepper.

Grill the patties until charred and cooked pink, or done.

Split and toast the buns directly over the hot side of the grill until browned, about 30 seconds.

Spread the mustard mayonnaise on the bottom half of each toasted bun. Add a lettuce leaf to each one, followed by a spoonful of Kimchi.

Top each grilled burger patty with some of the hot shredded Braised Short Ribs, top this with the sliced cheese and let it melt in the residual heat.

Stack a burger patty on top of the kimchi, followed by a toasted bun lid to finish.

Serves
4

This started life as an ode to the famous Green Chilli Cheeseburger at the Bobcat Bite restaurant in Santa Fe, but as it developed I added more and more chillies. It might seem like a competitive attempt to burn your tastebuds into submission, but the combination of chillies provides complex flavour that can still be appreciated above the heat. Where chilli quantities are concerned, this recipe is merely a guide...

Green chilli cheeseburgers

2–4 whole green chillies

2–4 teaspoons Adobo Chilli Sauce (see below)

4 tablespoons mayonnaise

800g (1lb 12oz) burger mince, blend of your choice (see page 80)

8 slices of Ogleshield or Cheddar cheese

4 large Burger Buns (see page 84)

4 leaves of Bibb (Butterhead) lettuce

2–4 tablespoons sliced pickled green jalapeños

Maldon sea salt and freshly ground black pepper

Grill the fresh chillies, or place them directly over a gas burner, turning occasionally, until charred and blistered all over. Transfer to a sheet of foil and wrap tightly. Set aside for 5 minutes, then remove from the foil and carefully peel off most of the skin. Discard the stems and seeds and roughly chop the chillies.

Combine the Adobo Chilli Sauce and mayonnaise in a small bowl and stir to combine. Set aside.

Blend together your choice of minced chuck steak, fat and bone marrow and form 4 loose patties (see page 80). Season and pan-fry one side of the burger patties, then press the chopped fresh chillies into the raw side.

Flip the patties to fry the other side and top each patty with 2 slices of cheese.

Split and toast the buns directly over the hot side of the grill until browned, about 30 seconds.

Spread the base of each bun with the Adobo Chilli Sauce mayonnaise, then add the lettuce and the burger patties. Top the patties with pickled jalapeños, then close the buns and serve.

Adobo chilli sauce Makes approximately 300ml (½ pint)

8 garlic cloves

5 jalapeno chillies, halved lengthways and deseeded

large bunch of coriander

large bunch of parsley

olive oil

Maldon sea salt flakes

Heat a frying pan over a high heat and char the garlic and chillies. Tip into a food processor or blender and add the herbs and a generous pinch of salt, then blitz. Slowly pour in enough olive oil to achieve a sauce-like consistency and continue to blitz. Taste and correct the seasoning if needed.

Store covered in the fridge in a sterilized container (see page 163) with a layer of olive oil on top.

Serves **4**

I came across mustard frying at In-N-Out Burger in Los Angeles and tried it out in London. It must be done on a griddle or a plancha, so it's the one burger I don't charcoal grill. If you ever make it to an In-N-Out, it's called "Animal Style" and is off-menu, though everyone orders it.

Mustard fried onion burger

200g (7oz) sliced onions

small knob of bone marrow

800g (1lb 12oz) burger mince, blend of your choice (see page 80)

100g (3½oz) American mustard, French's for preference

4 leaves of Bibb (Butterhead) lettuce

4 Burger Buns, split and toasted (see page 84)

Maldon sea salt flakes and freshly ground black pepper

1 whole Half Sour (pickled cucumber, see page 85)

On a griddle, a plancha or in a nonstick pan, fry the onions with the small knob of bone marrow until golden, then remove from the pan and reserve.

Blend together your choice of minced chuck steak, fat and bone marrow and form 4 loose patties (see page 80). Season the burger patties with salt and pepper, then spread one side of each raw burger with the mustard.

Heat a nonstick pan without oil until smoking hot and fry the mustard side of each burger patty, then cover the other side of the patty with the fried onions and flip the burger over. Press down on the patty with a slice, pushing the underside hard into the onions so they stick to the patty and start to burn a little. Continue cooking until cooked pink or done, as you like them.

Place a lettuce leaf on each bun base and top with a burger patty and then the lid. Serve with extra mustard and a spear of Half Sour on the side.

In 1900, when Louis' Lunch of New Haven, Connecticut, started making "hamburger sandwiches", there were no burger buns, so they used sliced white bread. In 1970 they broke free of constraint and added cheese. This is based on their sandwich...

Cheeseburger toastie

4 x 150g (5½oz) burger patties, blend of your choice (see page 80), loosely formed

butter

8 slices of white bread

8 slices of Ogleshield or Cheddar cheese

1 red onion, peeled and sliced

4 ripe beef tomatoes, sliced

Maldon sea salt flakes and freshly ground black pepper

Season the burger patties and fry them to your liking.

Butter the outside of the bread. Make sandwiches with bread on the base (butter side on the outside), followed by a slice of cheese, then a patty and a second slice of cheese. Top with sliced onion and tomato and finish the sandwich.

Pan-fry in the burger pan with the burger drippings until golden (you may have to do this in batches unless you have an enormous frying pan).

Remove from the pan and eat, preferably without condiments.

Rearing

Great beef starts with the farmer, and one of the very first choices a farmer makes is between a native pure breed and a modern cross-breed that benefits from hybrid vigour (heterosis). This is the improved or increased function of any biological quality in a hybrid, as a result of mixing the genetic contributions of its parents. Examples of these enhanced traits include the fact that crosses grow faster than pure-bred cattle, thereby gaining weight more cheaply, and are also hardier than pure breeds. There's nothing unethical about all of this, but in my admittedly unpopular opinion, anything that speeds up growth is at the expense of flavour. This initial choice in itself informs the next choice: whether to farm intensively or extensively.

Intensive farming

Over the last 50 years, farming has gone through massive industrialization, and as food has become cheaper, farmers have been forced into ever-higher levels of efficiency including the production of animals that grow at incredible rates. At one end of the spectrum, huge feed lots keep tightly packed animals on dry ground, feeding them grains to fatten them quickly, before slaughtering them on huge production lines. This method of production, which accounts for as much as 75 per cent of all cattle farmed in some countries, is known as intensive farming. As the name indicates, intensive farming is about getting an animal to slaughter weight as quickly and cheaply as possible. Modern intensive farming practices cater to a contemporary beef market that serves a demand for cheap meat at the expense of quality.

Intensively farmed animals are reared using unnatural commercial feed, antibiotics and, in some countries, growth hormones. The animals suffer a miserable life, and the way they are farmed has a negative impact upon the environment. These animals grow fat quickly, but it's the wrong kind of fat. Intensively farmed animals are not free to exercise. They are stressed all the time and they are fed cheap, unnatural food that they are not suited to eating, in order to achieve maximum weight gain in the shortest time achievable. The aim is quantity over quality. The flavour of the meat, as well as the nutritional quality, suffers as a result.

Intensively farmed animals are also prone to disease, which is why they're routinely dosed with antibiotics to keep them alive. The meat, in turn, is thought to cause antibiotic resistance in humans.

Extensive farming

It's not all doom and gloom, however. A small band of ethical farmers ensure that cattle have enough space to roam free and eat a grass-fed diet, and they are taken short distances to small local abattoirs for slaughter. It takes much longer to rear animals this way and consequently it costs more, but on the plus side, meat raised this way tastes completely different to that which is raised intensively.

This slower and more expensive process allows cattle access to pasture or forage, space to move around and social interaction (yes, cattle benefit from this), and they consequently live a much happier life.

Extensively farmed animals graze freely for the majority of their lifetime in pastures that are plentiful with grasses, clover, shrubs, wild plants and insects, in an ecosystem that's biologically natural and untreated. The character of the pastures changes seasonally, and animals are rotated between different pastures, creating a very distinctive flavour profile in the meat, while also recycling nutrients and sequestering carbon in the soil (see page 318). Natural habitats provide sanitary conditions, less stress on animals and natural resistance to disease. Good meat comes from animals that have been raised this way, without hormones, or unnecessary antibiotics. In extensive farming, antibiotics are not part of a feeding protocol; they are used only when an animal is sick, and that animal is then separated from the herd until recovered.

Good animal husbandry and welfare are imperative to producing good beef: happy livestock that is well looked after will taste better. The quality of the meat will be compromised when welfare is neglected, and, unsurprisingly, the best meat will come from those farmers who value its importance. Look for native breeds that have been grown slowly and naturally, fed without the aid of hormones and not pumped full of grain to fuel fast growth. It is only through buying extensively farmed rare-breed meat that extensive farming can grow and these passionate farmers can continue their great work. Recently the intensively farmed market has declined as increasingly savvy shoppers seek assurances about where their meat comes from: perhaps the tide is turning.

Veal

There are, of course, good reasons to eat veal: its lightness, freshness, delicacy and subtlety. These are the hallmarks of young meat, which has its delicious place in the gastronomic world. And times have changed when it comes to veal production. The vilified system of housing veal calves in crates so small they couldn't even turn around was outlawed in the UK in 1990.

Modern veal is mostly called rose veal. It is made from young animals up to about eight months old, raised on some beef feed and then pasture in the summer months. Eating rose veal is actually helping to solve the problem that dairy farmers have in finding something to do with the male calves created by their industry.

Dairy cows are kept constantly pregnant to feed our milk and cheese habit, but while female calves can go on to replace their mothers in the dairy system, there is no market for the male calves of dairy breeds, which aren't considered good for beef. The result is that they don't fetch enough for the farmer to break even on feed and care costs.

Male dairy calves are therefore slaughtered at 24–48 hours old. A small band of committed farmers are rehabilitating the pale, delicate meat which has a long culinary tradition; eating rose veal is utilizing those calves and solving a problem.

In addition, a small number of farmers continue to feed some male calves on a "nurse cow", usually a retired dairy cow, rather than the actual mother. They are fed on a diet of milk along with barley straw for roughage which allows their guts to develop properly. The result is veal that is closer to the traditional, old-fashioned milk-fed veal: delicate and sweet in flavour, and pale in colour, but without any of the welfare issues.

The organization Compassion in World Farming would like us to return to the dual-purpose (good for both beef and dairy) cattle of old, with dairy cows that are impregnated with semen from beef breeds. The resultant dual-purpose offspring could then be reared for beef, while the mother goes back into dairy production. This sounds like a brilliant solution to an uncomfortable issue.

Older beef

Real beef, the kind of beef upon which Britain built its beefy reputation, is pretty unusual in today's profit-driven farming. All meat takes time to develop flavour, but our food industry, driven by economic and political forces, slaughters animals far too early in their natural lifespan. It is a crime against taste – particularly when it comes to beef. Given that cattle might naturally live for up to 20 years, you can see what a truncated life they lead. There is an absolute correlation between age and flavour, but, sadly, few farmers can possibly afford to keep their animals for longer than a couple of years. What we are actually buying and eating is more akin to veal than beef, which becomes glaringly apparent if you've ever been lucky enough to eat beef from an older animal. There are a few Highland cattle slaughtered at over three years old, and occasionally as old as ten years, and, of course, there is the Basque Cider House Steak and the Galician bullock beef of Spain. Look out for beef from these older animals – if you know a great butcher, you might see it. It really is an absolute revelation.

Basque cider house steak

Basque Cider House Steak (or Basque import beef) comes from dairy cows that have reached the end of their useful milking life at about four years and are then given up to four more years' retirement, to improve the meat quality and develop fat. The Basque Country has a long tradition of eating dairy steak in their cider house eateries. The tradition was for the farmers to bring the meat to the cider house in exchange for cider; hence the name Basque Cider House Steak. The beef has the much sought-after heavy marbling that gives flavour and succulence to the meat, as well as that naturally developed flavour from the older animal. Despite being known as Basque, however, this beef is from cows that were raised in countries such as Germany, Austria, Poland or even Ireland. The carcasses are sent to the Basque Country, which until recently was the only market for this relatively expensive steak, and from there are imported into Britain for further ageing, as the Spanish tend not to hang meat for more than three weeks.

It's actually a brilliant idea. All meat takes time to develop flavour, and intensive farmers, driven by economical and political forces, slaughter animals far too early in their natural lifespan. If you think about it, these dairy cows have lived a productive life, they were not hurried to a killing weight and they grew up at a natural pace, developing flavour and fat before being "put out to pasture". No beef farmer could possibly afford to keep his or her animals for so long, and if the grass the cow grazes on during its retirement is of good quality, and if the animal is unstressed at the time of slaughter and then is properly hung and butchered, it can, and in fact does, taste superb. It really is a beautiful solution to another difficult question: what to do with old dairy cattle when their milk dries up.

Galician bullock beef

There has been some confusion between Basque beef and Galician beef, but Galician beef is never from dairy herds. Much of the Galician beef comes from the Galician Blond cows, which have veal as a byproduct, but the prized meat comes from old bullocks, which for obvious reasons would struggle to be dairy cattle. Known as Buey, it is regarded as the best beef from the Galician Blond breed and it's very hard to source. Before tractors the bullocks were used as working animals on the farm. Keeping a castrated bull for 15 years is very expensive, and now there's little reason to do so, except as a pet. The fat is yellow rather than white, from the beta-carotene in the pastures the bullocks graze on. Because they are slow-growing, the fat speckles the meat, unlike the big globules of fat you get from corn-fed animals. Some of the best steak in the world comes from these beasts, because of the amount of time they've had to develop flavour. And, of course, it does raise the question: what might a similarly reared Longhorn or Aberdeen Angus taste like? At the time of writing there are some attempts to find out, as a Yorkshire farmer and a Spanish beef importer are working together to answer this very question. Exciting times.

Grilled

1 small onion

4 garlic cloves

1 thumb-sized piece of fresh root ginger

1 green chilli

1 green pepper

1 spring onion

1 tablespoon powdered kuli-kuli (see below)

2 tablespoons suya pepper mix (see below)

1 tablespoon Maldon sea salt flakes

1kg (2lb 4oz) rump steak, trimmed

16 wooden skewers, soaked in water

For the salad

¼ red cabbage

¼ white cabbage

4 ripe tomatoes

1 cucumber

1 red onion

2 lemons, 1 juiced, 1 cut into wedges

3–4 tablespoons extra virgin olive oil

Maldon sea salt flakes and freshly ground black pepper

West African suya

A spicy West African variant of the shish kebab, introduced to the Hausa people of Cameroon by Arabic traders. Suya kebabs are usually made using short skewers of deeply seasoned meat. The thinly sliced meat is then barbecued and is commonly seen as part of street food menus.

To make the marinade, peel and roughly chop the onion, garlic and ginger. Trim and deseed the chilli and green pepper, then roughly chop. Trim and roughly chop the spring onion. Place all these in a blender and blend until smooth, then add the kuli-kuli powder, suya pepper mix and salt and blend again to combine.

Thinly slice the beef and flatten the slices with the flat side of a knife. Coat the beef in the marinade, then cover and pop into the fridge to marinate for a couple of hours. Thread 4 slices of beef on to each soaked skewer.

To make the salad, trim and finely shred the cabbages, finely slice the tomatoes and cucumber, and peel and finely slice the onion. Combine all the vegetables in a large bowl, adding a good squeeze of lemon juice, the extra virgin olive oil and a pinch of salt and pepper.

Heat a charcoal grill and, when the coals are smouldering and ash-white, cook the beef skewers, turning regularly until golden. Serve with the salad, with the lemon wedges for squeezing over.

Kuli-kuli and suya pepper mix are available in African shops, some larger supermarkets or online. Powdered kuli-kuli can be substituted with ground peanuts.

Serves
4

One of the world's fifty most delicious beef preparations, according to CNN, and claimed by more than one South East Asian country as its own, satay's origins probably lie on the island of Java in Indonesia, despite being common throughout the region.

Beef satay

1 lime

1 tablespoon kecap manis

1 teaspoon crushed garlic

1 teaspoon grated fresh root ginger

1 teaspoon grated fresh root turmeric

½ teaspoon ground coriander

½ teaspoon ground cumin

½ teaspoon freshly ground black pepper

600g (1lb 5oz) rib-eye steak

For the sauce

250ml (9fl oz) coconut water

100g (3½oz) unsalted natural peanut butter

100ml (3½fl oz) kecap manis

50ml (2fl oz) sriracha sauce

2 teaspoons crushed garlic

1 teaspoon grated fresh root ginger

finely grated zest and juice of 1 unwaxed lime

For the garnish

1 small cucumber

1 large banana shallot

½ small bunch of coriander, leaves picked

50ml (2fl oz) rice vinegar

1 teaspoon caster sugar

pinch of Maldon sea salt flakes

8 wooden or bamboo skewers, soaked in water

Finely grate the zest from the lime and combine in a bowl with the lime juice, kecap manis, garlic, ginger, turmeric, coriander, cumin and pepper. Cut the steak across the grain into thin strips and add to this marinade. Toss to coat, cover and refrigerate overnight.

Mix all the sauce ingredients together in a small pan and bring to a gentle simmer. Cook for 1 minute, then remove from the heat and allow to cool.

Cut the cucumber in half lengthways, then slice each half into thin slices and tip into a bowl. Cut the shallot lengthways into thin slices and add to the cucumber with the coriander leaves, vinegar, sugar and salt.

Remove the steak from the marinade and thread on to wooden or bamboo skewers, allowing 1 strip of beef per skewer (see photo, left).

Cook the satays either on a preheated barbecue or on a hot, ridged griddle pan for 2–3 minutes per side, turning once, until medium.

Serve the satays with the sauce and the cucumber and shallot garnish on the side.

Serves
4

You often hear the refrain that "fat is flavour", and this simple but delicious garnish helps leaner cuts of grilled steak along by providing a little tasty fat in the form of bone marrow. If fillet is your thing – and who am I to judge – then this will make it all the better.

Charcoal-grilled bone marrow with horseradish snow & toast

8 x 5cm (2 inch) cut bone marrow shafts

sourdough loaf, sliced

1 small piece of fresh horseradish, peeled

Maldon sea salt flakes and freshly ground black pepper

Lightly season the cut sides of the bones and grill cut side down, over charcoal if possible, for 3 minutes.

Grill the sourdough.

Using a fine grater, grate fresh horseradish over the top of the split bone marrow shafts and serve with the sourdough toast.

Serves
4

Another iteration of grilled bone marrow, this time using split marrow shafts and slow-cooked, sweet confit of onion.

Charcoal-grilled bone marrow with onions & toast

200g (7oz) Onion Confit (5 x recipe on page 162)

4 x 10cm (4 inch) bone marrow shafts, split lengthways (ask your butcher to split them for you)

sourdough loaf, sliced

smoked Maldon sea salt flakes and freshly ground black pepper

Prepare the Onion Confit as in recipe on page 162, adding 2 teaspoons of bone marrow at the start. Cook over a low heat for 1 hour, stirring constantly, until the onions are honey-coloured, sweet and soft.

Lightly season the split sides of the bones and grill cut side down, over charcoal if possible, for 3 minutes.

Grill the sourdough.

Top the grilled sides of the bones with the hot onions and serve with the sourdough toast.

Tripe is tricky, and is either loved or loathed. If you don't like this preparation you are in the latter camp, since it's as vanilla as tripe is ever likely to get.

Charcoal-grilled honeycomb tripe

400g (14oz) honeycomb tripe

800ml (1½ pints) Basic Beef Broth (see page 112)

200g (7oz) Garlic Butter (see page 113)

100g (3½oz) fresh breadcrumbs

bamboo skewers, soaked in water

For the citrus dressing

finely grated zest of 1 small unwaxed orange

finely grated zest of 1 unwaxed lemon

finely grated zest of 1 unwaxed lime

100g (3½oz) Garlic Butter, melted (see page 113)

Cut the honeycomb tripe into 4cm (1½ inch) square pieces and leave under running cold water for 30 minutes.

Preheat the oven to 140°C (275°F), Gas Mark 1.

Place the tripe in a cocotte dish (or small casserole) and cover with the beef broth and the lid, then braise in the preheated oven for 2 hours, or until tender.

Drain the tripe and place in a bowl. While it's still hot, add half the Garlic Butter and toss to combine, making sure to coat every piece of tripe in the butter. Finally, coat each piece generously with breadcrumbs.

Thread the tripe on to bamboo skewers, about 3–4 pieces per skewer, and charcoal-grill over a high heat, making sure the breadcrumbs are well scorched.

Mix all the ingredients for the citrus dressing together, and serve in a bowl on the side.

Serves
4

Liver and onions is proper English café fare, but is sometimes served in posh restaurants with the ingredients refined somewhat. This is my version, which sits bang in between greasy spoon and posh nosh.

Calves' liver & onions

600g (1lb 5oz) calves' liver, cut into 1cm (½ inch) slices

200ml (7fl oz) milk

8 smoked streaky bacon rashers

8 sage leaves

3 onions, peeled, halved lengthways, then cut lengthways into 5mm (¼ inch) slices

25g (1oz) butter or dripping

100g (3½oz) plain flour seasoned with salt and pepper

600g (1lb 5oz) Mashed Potatoes (see below)

Madeira Gravy, to serve (see page 114)

Maldon sea salt flakes and freshly ground black pepper

Soak the liver in the milk for 20 minutes.

While the liver is soaking, cook the bacon and sage leaves in a large nonstick frying pan over a medium heat, turning over occasionally, until crispy. Transfer the bacon and sage to kitchen paper to drain. Set aside half the fat from the pan.

Season the onions and gently cook them in the bacon fat remaining in the pan, with the butter or dripping, over a medium heat, stirring frequently, until golden brown, around 15 minutes. Remove from the pan and set aside.

Drain the liver and pat dry, discarding the milk. Dredge the liver in the seasoned flour, shaking off any excess.

Add the reserved bacon fat to the frying pan and place over a medium-high heat until hot but not smoking. Add the pieces of liver and fry, turning them over once, until browned but still pink inside, about 4 minutes total.

Serve the liver topped with the onions and bacon, Mashed Potatoes and Madeira Gravy on the side.

Mash and gravy is one of those food marriages that satisfies the soul – great with steak or as part of a roast dinner, and virtually essential with many of the braised dishes in this book.

Mashed potatoes Serves 4

500g (1lb 2oz) potatoes for mashing, peeled and quartered

125g (4½oz) unsalted butter

125ml (4½fl oz) double cream

Maldon sea salt flakes

Place the potatoes in cold salted water and bring to the boil. Reduce to a gentle boil for 20 minutes, or until cooked through. Remove the potatoes from the water and air-dry in a colander. While the potatoes are still hot, pass them through a potato ricer or vegetable mouli.

Put the butter and the cream into a pan and simmer until reduced by half, then fold in the mashed potato and season to taste.

Serve in a deep dish, ideally with Madeira Gravy (see page 114) poured over.

1kg (2lb 4oz) beef bones

1 small beef shank

1 oxtail

2 onions, peeled and halved

2 large carrots, split

2 celery sticks

2 large dried shiitake mushrooms

2 dried porcini mushrooms (20g/¾oz)

1 garlic bulb, broken into cloves but not peeled

1 faggot of herbs (thyme, bay, rosemary and parsley)

1 spice bag (20 fennel seeds, 20 black peppercorns, 1 star anise)

250ml (9fl oz) Madeira

250ml (9fl oz) soy sauce

5 litres (9 pints) water

Basic beef broth Makes about 6 litres (10½ pints)

I was taught to use three basic stocks as the base for sauces – veal, chicken and fish – but I've always had a nagging doubt: if making a sauce for pork or beef, why would you use any other stock than that made from the bones of the meat you are cooking? This is my basic broth (call it stock if it pleases you), and the foundation of many of these recipes. I've shoehorned in as many sources of umami as I can and consequently it's not a subtle stock, but then beef can take it.

Preheat the oven to 200°C (400°F), Gas Mark 6 and lightly roast the bones, beef shank and oxtail for about 30 minutes. Put the onions cut side down into a dry pan over a high heat and leave until very dark brown, almost burnt.

Place all the ingredients in a very large pan and bring to a gentle simmer. If you don't have a pan large enough to hold the full quantity, it can be divided between 2 pans.

Skim off any scum that rises to the surface and cook for 6 hours, skimming every 30 minutes or so. The trick here is to simmer at a bare roll and skim any impurities regularly for a clean, clear master broth.

Without moving the pan, turn off the heat and gently ladle the broth out of the pan through a very fine sieve, taking care not to disturb the base too much.

Cool and reserve until needed. Once chilled, this broth can be frozen in 500ml (18fl oz) or 1 litre (1¾ pint) batches.

For when something lighter than a beef broth is needed, use my Master Vegetable Broth which has bags of flavour (see opposite).

Master vegetable broth

Makes about 6 litres (10½ pints)

This broth can be thickened with a little potato flour, rice flour and grated Twineham Grange vegetarian cheese, to give body to soups or stews.

4 onions, peeled and halved

4 garlic bulbs, split horizontally

4 fennel bulbs, halved

4 large carrots, split lengthways

4 large beetroot, peeled and split lengthways

4 celery sticks

4 leeks, split lengthways

200g (7oz) dried shiitake mushrooms

200g (7oz) dried porcini mushrooms

100g (3½oz) miso paste

4 chillies, split lengthways and deseeded

1 faggot of herbs (thyme, bay, rosemary and parsley)

1 spice bag (20 fennel seeds, 20 black peppercorns, 1 star anise, 1 liquorice stick, 1 cinnamon stick)

250ml (9fl oz) Madeira

250ml (9fl oz) soy sauce

250ml (9fl oz) balsamic vinegar

5 litres (9 pints) water

Put the onions and garlic cut side down into a dry pan over a high heat and leave until very dark brown, almost burnt.

Place all the ingredients in a large pan and bring to a gentle simmer. Skim off any scum, then cook for 2 hours, skimming every 30 minutes or so. The trick here is to simmer at a bare roll and skim any impurities regularly for a clean, clear broth.

Without moving the pan, turn off the heat and gently ladle the broth out of the pan through a very fine sieve, taking care not to disturb the base too much. Cool the broth and reserve until needed. Once chilled, this broth can be frozen in 500ml (18fl oz) or 1 litre (1¾ pint) batches.

Garlic butter Makes 300g (10½oz)

Great with grilled meat, shellfish or for brushing on bread, garlic butter at its most simple is just that – garlic and butter – but it can include anchovies, hazelnuts, herbs, spices, alcohol and even cheese. This is the version that I commonly use.

20g (¾oz) garlic, finely chopped (8–10 cloves)

250g (9oz) salted butter, chopped

2 teaspoons Pernod

1 large banana shallot, finely chopped

½ bunch of flat leaf parsley, leaves picked and chopped

freshly ground black pepper

Blend the garlic with the butter, Pernod and black pepper.

Fold in the chopped shallot and parsley, adjust the seasoning, and serve on top of a freshly grilled hot steak, allowing the butter to melt all over.

Or roll the butter into a sausage shape and chill to firm up. Slice into discs and serve on top of the steak.

Wild garlic butter

Makes 300g (10½oz)

When wild garlic is abundant in spring, replace the garlic in the above recipe with double the quantity (40g/1½oz) of wild garlic, for a fantastically vibrant seasonal variation.

Makes
600ml
(1 pint)

Madeira is for me the king of cooking wines, its rich heady flavour going particularly well with beef. What makes Madeira wine unique is the estufagem ageing/heating process, meant to duplicate the effect of a long sea voyage through tropical climates on wine barrels. In the production of Madeira it occurs while the wine is in cask, with the resulting wine darkening and acquiring that rich character. Outside of Madeira wine this is seen as a problem, but much of the characteristic flavour of Madeira is due to this practice. All these gravies can be frozen in small batches, once made, for future use.

Madeira gravy & some of its possibilities

60g (2¼oz) chopped shallots

100g (3½oz) butter

250ml (9fl oz) Madeira

2 litres (3½ pints) Basic Beef Broth (see page 112)

Maldon sea salt flakes and freshly ground black pepper

Cook the shallots in 20g (¾oz) of the butter until soft, then add the Madeira and cook until reduced to a glaze.

Add the Basic Beef Broth and continue simmering until reduced by three-quarters.

Whisk in the rest of the butter and season to taste.

Mustard gravy

100g (3½oz) English mustard

600ml (1 pint) Madeira Gravy (see opposite)

Whisk the mustard into the finished Madeira Gravy.

Bone marrow gravy

100g (3½oz) bone marrow, chopped

600ml (20fl oz) Madeira Gravy (see opposite)

Stir the bone marrow into the finished Madeira Gravy.

Pepper sauce

250ml (9fl oz) double cream

600ml (1 pint) Mustard Gravy (see above)

100g (3½oz) jarred green peppercorns, with their brine

freshly ground black pepper, to taste

Add the double cream to the Mustard Gravy and bring to a gentle simmer. Stir in the green peppercorns with their brine, and season to taste with plenty of pepper.

Truffle sauce

as many black truffles as your bank balance will allow

600ml (1 pint) Madeira Gravy (see opposite)

Shave or grate fresh black truffle into the Madeira Gravy and stir. Serve in a sauceboat, with a mountain of extra truffle shaved over the top – now is not the time for skimping.

Onion gravy

25g (1oz) butter

8 large onions, peeled, halved and cut into long slices

600ml (1 pint) Mustard Gravy (see left)

Maldon sea salt flakes and freshly ground black pepper

Heat the butter in a large heavy-based saucepan and add the sliced onions. Reduce the heat to low and leave the onions to cook gently for about 30 minutes, checking and stirring occasionally to prevent sticking. The onions should be soft and translucent, and slowly caramelizing to a dark golden brown.

Stir in the Mustard Gravy, season to taste and serve.

Serves
4

2 small banana shallots, thinly sliced lengthways

½ bunch (about 15g/½oz) of mint, leaves picked, very roughly chopped

250g (9oz) fillet steak

250g (9oz) cooked tripe, thinly sliced (see page 110)

2 red bird's-eye chillies, thinly sliced, plus extra to serve

½ teaspoon chilli flakes

20g (¾oz) Thai toasted rice powder (see below)

a few kaffir lime leaves, finely shredded

½ bunch of spring onions, thinly sliced

½ bunch (about 15g/½oz) of coriander, coarsely chopped

½ cucumber, thinly sliced, to serve

1 head of butter lettuce, to serve

For the dressing

finely grated zest and juice of 2 unwaxed limes, plus extra juice to serve

1 tablespoon fish sauce (such as nam pla or nuoc nam), plus extra to serve

20g (¾oz) palm sugar

Tripe laab style

Laab is the national dish of Laos, but it has also migrated to Isan, an area of Thailand where many people are of Laotian descent. It is deliciously hot, spicy and zingy.

First make the dressing: whisk the lime zest and juice, fish sauce and palm sugar in a small bowl. Pour half this dressing into a small plastic container and set aside.

To the remaining dressing add the sliced shallots, half the chopped mint and the beef. Toss to combine, and leave to marinate for a couple of hours.

Remove the beef from the marinade and cook on a charcoal grill, turning regularly, for 8 minutes, or until medium-rare. Remove and allow to stand for 10 minutes, then thinly slice. Place the beef in a large bowl and add the tripe, fresh and dried chillies, toasted rice powder, shredded kaffir lime leaves, spring onions, coriander and remaining mint.

Adjust the seasoning with extra fish sauce and lime juice, and serve with the reserved dressing, cucumber, extra chillies and the lettuce leaves.

Ready-made toasted rice powder is available in Asian food stores, but if you can't find it you can make it at home in a skillet. Place a skillet over a medium-low heat, then add Thai sticky rice grains, stirring and shaking the pan every few seconds to make sure the grains are evenly toasted. After 10 minutes or so, the grains will turn golden brown. Remove the skillet from the heat and let the rice cool completely, then grind it in a mortar or a coffee grinder, 2 tablespoons at a time, until a fine powder is achieved.

Serves
4-6

Also known as galbi, this cut is traditionally filleted away from the bone into a flat, steak-like cut. Another version is the less traditional LA cut (pictured), which is more akin to flanken ribs.

Kalbi ribs

2kg (4lb 8oz) kalbi cut rib meat, flattened out

100g (3½oz) light muscovado sugar

1 small Asian pear, peeled and grated

1 small onion, peeled and grated

1 garlic bulb, cloves crushed

250ml (9fl oz) light soy sauce

125ml (4fl oz) water

60ml (4 tablespoons) mirin

20ml (¾fl oz) dark sesame oil

¼ teaspoon freshly ground black pepper

To serve

Kimchi (see page 89)

cooked sticky rice

4 spring onions, diagonally sliced

Toss the beef in the brown sugar until evenly coated, then toss with all the remaining ingredients. Place in an airtight container and refrigerate overnight.

Light a charcoal grill and allow the flames to burn down and the coals to become ash white.

Drain any excess marinade from the beef, then grill the ribs for 3 minutes on each side, or until cooked to your liking.

Serve with Kimchi, sticky rice and the spring onions.

Makes
8

50g (1¾oz) beef dripping

200g (7oz) Kimchi (see page 89), drained

8 hot dog buns, split

100ml (3½fl oz) mayonnaise

8 Franks, or beef hot dogs (see page 213), scored in a criss-cross fashion

100g (3½oz) Ogleshield or Cheddar cheese, grated

200g (7oz) Kimchi Kraut (see opposite)

sriracha sauce, for drizzling

1 bunch (about 30g/1oz) of coriander, leaves picked, to serve

Kimchi dogs

On a research trip to New York with the Hawksmoor team we visited a cocktail bar called Please Don't Tell, where you have to enter through a phone box. One of the bar snacks was a small kimchi hotdog that was so knock-your-socks-off delicious that it's stuck in my mind. This is my ode to that memory.

Light a charcoal grill and allow the charcoal to burn down to ash white.

Heat the beef dripping in a frying pan, add the kimchi and fry until coloured all over, about 3 minutes.

Brush the insides of the split hot dog buns with dripping and grill, cut sides down, until crisp. Turn and grill the other side. Spread the cut sides with mayonnaise.

Grill the hot dogs until charred all over, about 3 minutes. Tuck the fried kimchi into the buns with the grilled hot dogs and grated cheese.

Top with the Kimchi Kraut, drizzle a little sriracha on top and serve sprinkled with the coriander leaves.

It's not unreasonable to think that the early coleslaws were actually fermented krauts made sour by bacteria and preserved. This kimchi kraut is in that spirit: a kind of hybrid kraut-slaw that's great with grilled meats or in sandwiches.

Kimchi kraut   Makes approximately 1kg (2lb 4oz)

1 small white cabbage

1 bunch of spring onions

2cm (¾ inch) piece of fresh root ginger

3 garlic cloves

1 carrot

1 tablespoon Maldon sea salt flakes

1 teaspoon *gochugaru* (Korean red pepper powder or flakes)

Shred the cabbage and spring onions very finely and put into a bowl. Grate the ginger, garlic and carrots and add to the bowl with the salt and red pepper powder and toss everything together. Massage the vegetables with strong hands until moist, to make the brine. Salt pulls water out of the vegetables to create an environment where the good bacteria (mainly *lactobacillus*) can grow and proliferate and the bad bacteria die off.

Pack the mixture into a sterilized Kilner jar (see page 163), periodically pressing it down tightly with a large spoon so that the brine rises above the top of the mixture and no air pockets remain. Be sure to leave at least 3cm (1¼ inches) of space between the top of the cabbage and the top of the jar. Pour any brine left in your mixing bowl into the jar, and scrape in any loose bits stuck to the sides of the bowl or to the sides of the jar.

Place a sterilized glass weight on top inside the jar, then seal the jar. Place in a cool dark place for 1 week to ferment, making sure the kraut remains covered with liquid. If mould appears, remove it and wash the glass weight.

The longer you ferment it, the greater the number and variety of beneficial bacteria that can be produced. If it smells and tastes good, it has successfully fermented and can be kept preserved in your refrigerator for up to 1 year.

Beet kraut   Makes approximately 1kg (2lb 4oz)

1 head of red cabbage

1 large beetroot

20g (¾oz) fine sea salt

Shred the cabbage finely and grate the beetroot. Mix them thoroughly in a bowl with the salt, then massage with your hands until the brine starts to be released, at least 5 minutes.

Pack very tightly indeed into a sterilized Kilner jar (see page 163), pressing it down until the liquid starts to appear. Place a glass weight on top and seal the jar.

Place in a cool dark place for 1 week to ferment, making sure the kraut remains covered with liquid. If mould appears, remove it and wash the glass weight.

After the week is up, place the jar in the refrigerator and keep for a further 3 weeks. It should now be ready to eat either as it is or – particularly delicious – mixed with a little chopped preserved lemon and natural yogurt.

Serves
4

Flanken cut ribs are cut in sections across the bone. Each piece has three or four pieces of bone, with a generous portion of meat around them. They can be tough, so they must be marinated, and cooked pink or low and slow until falling off the bone.

Grilled flanken cut short ribs

2kg (4lb 8oz) flanken cut short ribs, cut 1cm (½ inch) thick

150ml (¼ pint) cold black coffee

150ml (¼ pint) sweet soy sauce

150ml (¼ pint) Madeira

Maldon sea salt flakes

Put the ribs into a dish. Combine the liquids and pour over the ribs, then refrigerate for 4 hours, turning them over halfway through.

Light the barbecue and allow it to burn down to a smoulder.

Drain the ribs, season with salt, then grill slowly for several minutes each side, or until caramelized all over.

Remove from the grill and serve as a starter, with Shaved Vegetable & Herb Slaw (see below), or even as a meaty side dish.

A fresh vegetable slaw that's great with grilled steaks or as a sandwich filler. Purple asparagus is becoming more and more common and is often eaten raw – it's sweeter than green asparagus and tastes of peas – to me, a good thing.

Shaved vegetable & herb slaw Serves 4

40g (1½oz) pea shoots

60g (2¼oz) baby carrots, shaved

60g (2¼oz) baby fennel, shaved

60g (2¼oz) purple asparagus, shaved

1 bunch of spring onions, shaved

1 bunch (about 30g/1oz) each of mint, flat leaf parsley and coriander, leaves picked

½ teaspoon fennel seeds, toasted

½ teaspoon Maldon sea salt flakes

1 teaspoon freshly ground black pepper

For the dressing

50ml (2fl oz) organic cider vinegar

1 tablespoon extra virgin olive oil

15g (½oz) caster sugar

juice and finely grated zest of ½ unwaxed lemon

Toss the pea shoots and all the shaved vegetables and herbs together.

About 10 minutes before serving, whisk the dressing ingredients together. Add the dressing to the vegetables with the toasted fennel seeds, season and toss together.

Serves
4

"Wash a large beast's heart clean and cut off the deaf ears, and stuff it with forcemeat... Lay a caul of veal... over the top to keep in the stuffing. Roast it either in a cradle spit or hanging one, it will take an hour and a half before a good fire; baste it with red wine. When roasted take the wine out of the dripping pan and skim off the fat and add a glass more of wine. When it is hot put in some lumps of redcurrant jelly and pour it in the dish. Serve it up and send in redcurrant jelly cut in slices on a saucer." From "To make a Mock Hare of a Beast's Heart" by Elizabeth Raffald, *The Experienced English Housekeeper* (1769).

Charcoal grilled calf's heart

1 calf's heart (you can ask your butcher to prepare it if you're squeamish)

50ml (2fl oz) good red wine or sherry vinegar

1 garlic clove, crushed

a few thyme sprigs

Maldon sea salt flakes and freshly ground black pepper

small handful of watercress, to serve

freshly grated horseradish, to serve

For the pickled carrrots

150ml (¼ pint) water

150ml (¼ pint) cider vinegar

70g (2½oz) caster sugar

1 teaspoon Maldon sea salt flakes

4 heritage carrots, finely sliced

First of all prepare the heart. Trim away the large blood vessels as well as the two large flaps from the top of the heart, as well as any obviously sinewy parts. This should leave the heart looking neat, with 2 cavities within. Cut it open, lay it out flat and cut it into 5cm (2 inch) squares, 5mm (¼ inch) thick. Anything thicker, such as the ventricles, will need to be sliced horizontally.

Wash the pieces of heart and toss them into a bowl along with the vinegar, salt and pepper, garlic and thyme, making sure everything gets coated well. Cover and marinate for 24 hours.

To make the picked carrots, put the water, cider vinegar, sugar and salt into a bowl, add the sliced carrots and toss to coat. Leave to pickle for 20 minutes.

To cook the meat, you need a hot barbecue. Place the pieces of heart on the barbecue and turn after 2–3 minutes, then cook for the same time on the other side.

Serve thinly sliced, with the pickled carrots, watercress, freshly grated horseradish and ground black pepper.

Charcoal roasted ox

OK, so since this requires specialist equipment, several hours' preparation and 24 hours' cooking, I realize it's unlikely you will cook this particular recipe, and in truth it's a tad beyond even me, but luckily I know a man for whom this is just another day at the office. When I approached Charlie Carroll, of Flat Iron restaurants in London, to come and cook at my festival, Meatopia, he agreed with one small caveat – he wanted to roast a whole ox over smouldering charcoal. And who am I to refuse such a request...

Charlie took a small ox, about 300kg (660lb), with the well-marbled whole body of carefully reared beef. It had good external fat cover, and a fat score of 4 litres (7 pints). His supplier had removed the fillets, excess cod fat and part of the topside to allow a spit to be mounted close to the spine of the ox.

A custom-built 4.2m (14ft) steel spit stand was made using 2 shin/shank clamp brackets and 2 spine brackets and this was set over a hearth, about 3.3 metres (11ft) wide, 60cm (2ft) deep and 1.5 metres (5ft) high, with a fire bed/grate approximately 30cm (12 inches) from the ground. The ox was then mounted on to the spit and clamped firmly into place.

Two 1.8 metre (6ft) diameter cartwheels were then attached to the ends of the spit and placed on two stands to support the spit (with rollers to adjust the distance from the fire). The balance of the spit could be adjusted by letting it turn freely, hung with the heaviest part down, before adding weights to the top of the cartwheel until the wheel could spin freely and was evenly balanced.

A large fire was lit underneath using well-seasoned oak, with the ox positioned about 1.2 metres (4ft) from the fire edge so that the surface temperature reached no higher than 150°C (300°F) in 15 minutes. The ox was then basted with the drippings using a long ladle, and the spit was turned 90° every 15 minutes with the spit locked into place with a pin in the cartwheel – this was repeated throughout the following 24 hours, each time the surface temperature of the ox was checked using an infrared temperature gun to ensure it was always between 100–150°C (210–300°F), controlled by making small adjustments to the size of the fire or distance from the fire.

Cooking at a higher heat (more than 150°C/300°F at the end of each 15-minute exposure) would risk burning the surface, or the entire animal catching alight, while cooking at a lower heat (less than 100°C (210°F) at the end of each 15-minute exposure) would risk enzymatic over-softening of the core meat and undercooking.

As the end of the 24 hours cooking and basting approached, the core temperature around the aitchbone/core of the silverside, underneath the shoulder blade, was tested to check if it was at the minimum core temperature of 50°C (120°F)– at this point it was ready to carve, season and eat, ideally with Yorkshire Pudding cooked in the ox drippings (see page 304), with gravy and freshly grated horseradish.

Heart is a woefully under-used offal that deserves to be made more of, and this is an easy introduction. The mighty chef Fergus Henderson served this fantastic sandwich at the very first Meatopia festival in the UK.

Grilled ox heart buns with pickled walnuts

400g (14oz) ox heart

4 tablespoons red wine vinegar

1 tablespoon Maldon sea salt flakes

1 teaspoon freshly ground black pepper

1 tablespoon chopped thyme leaves

40g (1½oz) watercress

40g (1½oz) shallots, sliced

40g (1½oz) Pickled Walnuts (see below)

4 Burger Buns (see page 84)

Trim the heart of anything that looks like sinew and remove any blood clots. Slice it open, lay it flat and cut it into 60g (2¼oz) pieces, each about 5mm (¼ inch) thick.

Toss the pieces of heart in the vinegar, salt, pepper and thyme and leave to marinate for 24 hours.

Heat the grill or griddle pan and sear the heart for 3 minutes on each side.

Serve with the watercress, shallots and Pickled Walnuts in the toasted buns.

Pickled walnuts Makes 2 x 1 litre (1¾ pint) jars

1kg (2lb 4oz) freshly picked whole unripe soft walnuts, picked end of June or early July

225g (8oz) fine sea salt

1 litre (1¾ pints) malt vinegar

400g (14oz) dark brown muscovado sugar

1 teaspoon allspice berries

1 teaspoon cloves

½ teaspoon ground cinnamon

½ teaspoon black peppercorns

1 tablespoon grated fresh root ginger

Pickled walnuts are a great accompaniment to beef, either as a garnish or thrown into stews or braises. Quintessentially English, they can of course be bought ready pickled by Opies, should you need them and be unprepared.

Prick the soft walnuts with a fork (the shells won't have formed yet, so pricking is easy) then cover with water and add half the salt.

Leave for 1 week, then drain and repeat with a fresh brine solution, using the other half of the salt, and leave for another week.

Drain the walnuts and lay them out on trays in a dry, airy place for a few days, by which time they will have turned black.

Combine the remaining ingredients in a saucepan. Bring to the boil, then add the walnuts and simmer for 15 minutes. Cool, then spoon the walnuts into large (1 litre/1¾ pint) jars and cover with the liquid. They will take a few weeks to pickle, and will keep for up to 1 year in the fridge.

Feed

Cattle evolved as grazers and ruminants, which means that pasture containing grasses, wild flowers and herbs is their natural diet. Grazing and foraging provide nutrients and minerals and make for a happy and consequently tasty animal. Foraging is an important part of cattle welfare and cannot be adequately replaced by feed. There is a huge difference between cattle principally given compound feed and an animal allowed access to good-quality land upon which to graze.

Grain-fed All cattle start out eating grass soon after weaning, so technically all beef is grass-fed early on, but then it starts to get complicated. Some countries transfer calves at around 350kg (770lb) in weight to feed lots. There they are fed rolled corn, corn byproducts, potato byproducts, barley and other grains, as well as roughage (which may consist of alfalfa, corn stalks, sorghum or other hay), cottonseed meal, and premixes. The premixes are composed of vitamins, minerals, chemical preservatives, antibiotics, fermentation products and other essential ingredients that are purchased from premix companies, usually in sacked form, for blending into commercial rations. In the American northwest and Canada, barley, low-grade durum wheat, chickpeas, oats and occasionally potatoes are used as feed. A beef steer might gain nearly 1kg (2lb 4oz) a day on grass but almost double that on these feeds. So animals are vanishing from fields, and the tasty, healthy, grass-fed meat they produce is hard to find.

In a typical feed lot, a cow's diet is around 60 per cent roughage, 30 per cent grain, 5 per cent supplements and 5 per cent premix. This diet lowers the pH (alkalinity) in the animals' rumen. Because of the stress of their environment and also because of some illnesses, many cattle are routinely dosed with antibiotics.

Cattle going through feed lots are slaughtered at 14–16 months. They grow fatter and faster if they're being fed grain, so they are going into feed lots at younger ages to shorten that time as much as possible. In a feed lot environment, grain gives a feed to weight-gain ratio of 1kg (2.2lb) for every 6kg (13.2lb) of feed they eat. Feed lot diets are high in protein, to encourage growth of muscle mass and the deposition of marbling; this marbling is desirable to consumers, as it contributes to flavour and tenderness. The animal may gain an additional 180kg (400lb) during its 200 days in the feed lot. Once cattle are fattened up to their finished weight, they are slaughtered.

Animals that eat a lot of commercially produced feed produce saturated fat, whereas animals allowed to graze and forage produce more polyunsaturated fat. The double bonds that form the structure of the polyunsaturated fats are softer, making for softer, creamier fat. We know that this matters for texture and mouth feel, but there is strong evidence that feed also directly influences the flavour of meat. And many people who have trouble digesting grain-fed beef find they have no problem eating grass-fed meat.

All of this grain-fed beef is very similar in flavour. It's done that way to guarantee its consistency, but consistency is boring, and if cattle are fed a bland, high-grain diet, they get ultra-marbling, which is so revered but tastes bland and one-dimensional, much like its feed. It doesn't have the subtlety of naturally reared and extensively farmed beef. In French wine-making terms, it doesn't have terroir, or the flavour of the natural environment in which it was produced, including factors such as the soil, topography and climate.

Grass-fed, grain-finished Cattle on a diet of pasture alone take a long time to reach their kill weight, so in Europe farmers "finish" cattle on grain, and sometimes peas and molasses, for five or six weeks before slaughter. This traditional method has stood the beef industry in good stead for hundreds of years. Finishing cattle involves slightly altering their diet for the final month or so before slaughter, in order to ensure that the meat develops the characteristics needed for dry ageing and good eating.

Until this point, at around two years, rare breed extensively farmed cattle have had a diet consisting almost entirely of grass, hay or silage. The grass-fed approach allows for gradual, unhurried maturation, which is essential for depth of flavour and quality. However, because of the relatively low protein value of grass feeds, this does mean that the animals haven't yet developed enough fat to protect the flesh during dry ageing. Providing a higher protein supplement for the final month sees that the animals are fit for dry ageing and can also give the meat a little added sweetness.

The combination of pasture quality and finishing feed is the most important contributing factor to producing good-quality, tasty beef. Getting nutrition right can mean the difference between success and failure – it really is that important. Cattle have the ability to grow at an incredible pace, and during the first few months they will lay down mostly muscle and bone and a little fat. Anything tasty takes time, which is the guiding principle of the Slow Food Movement, and I'm absolutely convinced that extensively reared, grass-fed animals are tastier than intensively reared grain-fed beef.

In the summer of 2016 I was shown around Barnhart Ranch in Oregon, in the American northwest, by Wes Davies of Country Natural Beef, a cooperative of almost 100 ranches across the western US. The cooperative owns and manages more than 100,000 mother cows on millions of acres of private and public lands. It was founded for the purpose of providing customers with healthy and wholesome beef at a price that supports sustainable ranching, and all of its members believe that healthy and productive land is also biologically diverse. Their cattle are treated well and they embrace humane animal-handling practices while remaining economically and environmentally viable. At 350kg (770lb) the animals are transported from the ranches to the feed lot in Oregon, where they are kept very separate from the other cattle and given more space with some forage. No antibiotics, hormones, growth promoters or feed additives are used, and the occasional animal that requires any medical treatment is pulled from their programme and sold on another market. From what I saw, this method of cattle rearing is not that far removed from some of the best in Europe.

Grass-fed

At the other end of the spectrum are purely grass-fed cattle, which are finished on grass and stored hay, never on grains; from an evolutionary standpoint, this is the most natural way of feeding cattle. Grass finishing pre-dates industrialized farming, but takes longer and costs more, and so was largely abandoned when cheap corn and grain became prevalent. Today there is a growing band of enlightened farmers who understand grass finishing and, through proper genetic selection and efficient high-quality pasture management, are producing beautiful natural beef that tastes how beef might have done 100 years ago. Grass-fed cows grow at a slower pace and are slaughtered at 24–36 months. When you keep cattle on grass their whole lives, and truly have them forage for a diet that their bodies have evolved to eat, you allow them to grow slowly.

Not surprisingly, caring for the animals for so long can be expensive for farmers and consumers, and the "grass-fed" label is open to abuse. The Agricultural Marketing Service developed the US Department of Agriculture (USDA) grass-fed standard, but the Food Safety and Inspection Service actually enforces it. The two organizations, even though they're both part of the USDA, don't communicate especially well. Consequently, you see a lot of beef labelled as "grass-fed", but whether or not it actually meets that standard is questionable. The USDA allows producers to determine whether or not their beef meets the grass-fed beef marketing claim standard. Farms "self-certify" their own beef, and the Food Safety and Inspection Service generally goes along with their claim.

The American Grassfed Association has far more stringent standards than the USDA, and hires third-party auditors to inspect the farms across the country each year. According to its standards, grass-fed cows should be given continuous access to rangeland, and they cannot be fed grains or grain byproducts except in times of severe drought when the welfare of the cattle is a concern.

After the Barnhart Ranch I visited the Alderspring Ranch, in Idaho. Here they go a step further – the cattle never see a feed lot and are the epitome of free-range. At this family-owned and operated ranch, Glenn and Caryl Elzinga rear Angus or Angus cross, which are certified organic, with help from their family: Melanie, Abigail, Linnaea and Ethan. Oh, and Konrad the Border Collie, an integral part of their herding in Idaho's stunning Salmon River Mountains. To finish, Alderspring Ranch feeds its beef nothing but green grass and grass/alfalfa hay; so the cattle are strictly 100 per cent grass-fed and grass-finished. The cold summer nights and high soil mineral levels of the Salmon River mountain pastures grow grass like nowhere else, resulting in a uniquely flavourful beef. The Elzingas believe Idaho to be the best grass-fed beef producing area in the US, and because they only sell beef from their ranch, they know each animal's history. Each cut is labelled and traceable to a single steer, and, unusually for the US, they also dry-age their grass-fed beef. Alderspring Beef is processed in a small, USDA-inspected facility, traditionally butchered and hand-cut. The ranch is small enough for intimate care of the land and livestock, but large enough to grow beef on a viable scale. And they have been growing 100 per cent grass-fed beef for discerning patrons for more than 15 years, perfecting their production and processing methods over the years. They clearly know how to manage their pastures and grazing animals for optimal health, growth and – I can testify to this – flavour.

4 Raw & cured

Serves
4

400g (14oz) freshly butchered sirloin steak (aged meat will not work here)

80g (2¾oz) wild rocket salad

100ml (3½fl oz) very good Italian extra virgin olive oil

finely grated zest and juice of 1 unwaxed lemon

30g (1oz) Parmesan cheese, or 20g (¾oz) fresh white truffle in season

Maldon sea salt flakes and freshly ground black pepper

Carpaccio

Carpaccio is based on the Piedmont speciality carne cruda all'Albese, and was famously created by Giuseppe Cipriani of Harry's Bar in Venice. With only five main ingredients, it's more important than ever that every one of them is in tip-top condition and the best that money can buy.

Remove all the fat and any sinew from the sirloin steak and slice as thinly as possible – if this proves tricky, the sliced meat can be beaten out between 2 sheets of clingfilm.

Spread the thin slices of meat over 4 plates, covering them entirely.

Season liberally with salt and pepper and scatter the rocket over the top, then drizzle with the olive oil. Grate over a little lemon zest, then cut the lemon in half and squeeze the juice over as well.

Finally, grate or shave your choice of Parmesan or white truffle over the top and serve.

MOO

Tell your butcher that you are making carpaccio when purchasing your beef, to ensure they give you the freshest cut.

Steak is so often eaten raw that it is no longer a surprise, though it does carry a small risk. But living without danger means you miss out as it can be delicious. Cooking may be the only absolute insurance, but raw is worth a little risk in my book. Buying from a good, busy butcher means the produce is turning over quickly and the meat is fresh. Tell your butcher you will be eating this raw.

Thai beef salad

400g (14oz) fillet steak, un-hung or freshly butchered

12 bird's-eye chillies

2 teaspoons kaffir lime juice (or use regular lime juice)

2 teaspoons lime juice

2 teaspoons palm sugar

½ teaspoon salt

2 teaspoons fish sauce

2 small red shallots, sliced

2 spring onions, sliced

2–3 coriander sprigs, leaves picked

2–3 mint sprigs, leaves picked

3 fresh kaffir lime leaves, finely julienned

4 Little Gem lettuce leaves

¼ cucumber, sliced

10g (¼oz) Thai toasted rice powder (see page 116)

Slice the fillet steak across the grain into 5mm (¼ inch) slices and place in a shallow dish.

Slice the chillies and pound, using a mortar and pestle. Add both the lime juices, sugar and salt. Pour over the steak, mix well, then cover and allow to marinate for 10 minutes to absorb the flavours.

Mix in the fish sauce, shallots, spring onions and herbs and serve on top of the lettuce leaves.

Garnish with sliced cucumber and sprinkle with toasted rice powder.

Serves **4** as a starter

Tataki refers to a Japanese method of preparing fillet of beef, in which the meat is lightly seared, marinated, sliced thinly similar to sashimi, and served with a citrus-soy dipping sauce.

Beef tataki

500g (1lb 2oz) fillet steak

small handful of shiso leaves

small handful of mizuna leaves

1 tablespoon pickled ginger, julienned

1 tablespoon daikon, julienned

½ red chilli, julienned

1 spring onion, finely sliced

sancho berries or sancho pepper, to taste

80ml (2½fl oz) Japanese soy sauce (*ponzu shōyu* sauce)

10g (¼oz) freshly grated wasabi (see below)

Maldon sea salt flakes

Season the fillet steak with salt and leave it to rest for about 10 minutes at room temperature. Heat a flat griddle or a heavy-based frying pan until smoking hot. Sear the beef for 1 minute on each side – it should be rare on the inside.

Slice the steak 5mm (¼ inch) thick and place straight on to a bed of the shiso and mizuna in a circular fashion.

Garnish with the pickled ginger, daikon and red chilli, and finely sliced spring onion. Season lightly with freshly ground sancho berries or sancho pepper.

Mix the Japanese soy sauce (*ponzu shōyu*) sauce with the freshly grated wasabi and serve on the side, for dipping.

MOO

You can buy fresh wasabi from www.thewasabicompany.co.uk – alternatively substitute with fresh horseradish.

All recipes serve **4**

Here are my favourite chopped steak preparations. It's probably clear by now that anchovies and bone marrow are pivotal to my being, and the first two recipes highlight why. A small green salad, toast or potato chips could be served as a side with all five recipes.

Chopped steak tartare

400g (14oz) freshly butchered fillet steak

10g (¼oz) finely chopped banana shallot

10g (¼oz) finely chopped cornichons

10g (¼oz) whole lilliput (tiny) capers

20ml (¾fl oz) tomato ketchup

2 teaspoons Tabasco sauce

2 teaspoons Worcestershire sauce

10g (¼oz) Creamed Horseradish (see page 227)

4 small free-range egg yolks

Maldon sea salt flakes and freshly ground black pepper

4 slices of toasted sourdough, to serve

Finely chop the fillet steak into 4mm (about ⅛ inch) cubes and place in a bowl.

Add the shallot, cornichons, capers, ketchup, Tabasco, Worcestershire sauce and Creamed Horseradish. Taste, then season with salt and pepper and mix well.

To serve, divide the steak tartare mixture between 4 plates and make an indentation in the centre of each 1. Carefully tip a yolk into each indentation, on top of the steak tartare. Serve with toasted sourdough.

Chopped veal with tuna mayonnaise

400g (14oz) rose veal fillet, cut into 4mm (about ⅛ inch) dice

1 banana shallot, very finely chopped

finely grated zest and juice of 1 unwaxed lemon

1 tablespoon finely chopped parsley leaves

50ml (2fl oz) mayonnaise

50g (1¾oz) canned tuna, drained

50g (1¾oz) anchovy fillets, drained

20g (¾oz) capers

50ml (2fl oz) single cream

2 teaspoons Worcestershire sauce

Maldon sea salt flakes and freshly ground white pepper

To serve

mojama (air-dried tuna)

fried potato crisps or toast

Place the chopped veal in a bowl and add the shallot, lemon zest and chopped parsley and stir together.

Blend the mayonnaise to a smooth sauce with the tuna, anchovies, capers, cream, Worcestershire sauce and lemon juice. Mix with the chopped veal and season to taste with salt and white pepper.

To serve, place a pile of the chopped veal mixture in the middle of 4 plates and grate a little mojama over the top. Serve alongside potato crisps or toast.

Chopped steak with anchovy toast

400g (14oz) freshly butchered fillet steak

50ml (2fl oz) extra virgin olive oil

juice of ½ lemon

4 slices of sourdough

Maldon sea salt flakes and freshly ground black pepper

For the anchovy cream

25ml (1fl oz) cider vinegar

1 hard-boiled free-range egg yolk

1 tablespoon Dijon mustard

1 teaspoon caster sugar

½ teaspoon Maldon sea salt flakes

½ teaspoon white pepper

50g (1¾oz) anchovies in olive oil, drained

1 garlic clove

a few thyme leaves

¼ teaspoon unwaxed lemon zest

100ml (3½fl oz) single cream

First make the anchovy cream: put all the ingredients, except the cream, into a blender and blend for 30 seconds. With the machine running, slowly add the single cream in a thin stream until just incorporated, then pass through a fine sieve and refrigerate until needed. Dice the fillet steak into 4mm (about ⅛ inch) cubes, place them in a bowl and season to taste with the olive oil, lemon juice, salt and pepper.

Grill the sourdough and spread the slices with Anchovy Cream.

Pile 100g (3½oz) portions of chopped steak in the middle of 4 plates and serve with the anchovy toasts on the side.

Yukhoe (Korean steak tartare)

10g (¼oz) caster sugar

1 tablespoon water

1 Asian pear

400g (14oz) freshly butchered fillet steak

6 garlic cloves, crushed

3 spring onions, finely chopped

2 teaspoons soy sauce

2 teaspoons honey

2 teaspoons sesame oil

1 teaspoon roasted sesame seeds

5g (⅛oz) roasted pine nuts (not Chinese, see page 11)

Maldon sea salt flakes and freshly ground black pepper

gochujang (Korean chilli paste), to serve

Dissolve the sugar in the water. Peel and core the pear, then cut into julienne and place in the sugar water. Refrigerate until needed.

Julienne the steak and place in a bowl with the garlic, spring onions, soy sauce, honey and sesame oil. Add the sesame seeds, season to taste and mix well.

Drain the pear and place on plates in a nest-like shape. Place the steak mix over the top and garnish with the roasted pine nuts.

Serve with *gochujang*, a spicy and pungent fermented Korean condiment made from red chilli, glutinous rice, fermented soybeans and salt.

Chopped steak with bone marrow toast

1 large bone marrow shaft, cut into 7cm (2¾ inch) lengths (ask your butcher to do this)

400g (14oz) freshly butchered fillet steak

4 slices of sourdough

5cm (2 inch) piece of fresh horseradish, peeled

Maldon sea salt flakes and freshly ground black pepper

Preheat the oven to 200°C (400°F), Gas Mark 6. Season the bone marrow shafts and roast for 15 minutes, until cooked through. Scoop out the marrow.

Dice the fillet steak into 4mm (about ⅛ inch) cubes and place in a bowl. Season the beef to taste with plenty of salt and pepper. Grill the sourdough, spread with warm bone marrow and season lightly.

Pile 100g (3½oz) portions of chopped steak in the middle of 4 plates and place the bone marrow toasts on the side. Using a fine grater, grate fresh horseradish "snow" over the chopped steak and serve.

Serves
10
as a starter

I'm not a great fan of fillet steak: there's not enough texture or flavour for my liking. However, this is a splendid use of fillet that makes a great starter. As always, using the correct ingredients will pay dividends – freshly crushed black peppercorns, for instance.

Cured fillet steak

250g (9oz) Maldon sea salt flakes

250g (9oz) light muscovado sugar

100g (3½oz) freshly grated horseradish

1 garlic clove, crushed

10 rosemary sprigs

1kg (2lb 4oz) fillet steak (barrel or centre cut)

50g (1¾oz) freshly cracked black peppercorns

meat-curing muslin sleeve or stockingette

To serve

Beet Kraut (see page 121)

finely chopped preserved lemon

To make the curing mixture, combine the salt, sugar, horseradish, garlic and rosemary and leave to dry on a tray overnight.

Trim any excess fat and sinew from the beef and rub the meat with the dried ingredients.

Scatter 1cm (½ inch) of the curing mix into a tray and place the beef on top. Cover this with another layer of the mix, then cover the tray, pop it into the fridge and leave to cure for about 36 hours, turning the meat every 12 hours.

When the beef has cured, remove it from the mix and brush off any excess. Roll the fillet in freshly cracked black pepper, then wrap in a muslin sleeve/stockinette and hang up in a cool place to air-dry overnight.

Unwrap, slice thinly and serve with Beet Kraut and finely chopped preserved lemon.

Serves
8-12
as a starter

1kg (2lb 4oz) raw Salt Beef
(see page 148) or brined brisket

¼ teaspoon freshly ground black pepper

¼ teaspoon freshly ground nutmeg

½ teaspoon ground ginger

¼ teaspoon cayenne pepper

25g (1oz) salted anchovies

250ml (9fl oz) Basic Beef Broth
(see page 112)

250ml (9oz) beef dripping,
plus extra to seal the pots

hot toast, to serve

Spiced potted beef

Potting was a method used for extending the shelf life of meat before the advent of refrigeration. The meat is cooked and, while hot, very tightly packed to exclude air, then it is covered with hot fat. As the fat cools, it hardens and forms an airtight seal, retarding spoilage by airborne bacteria. It can then be stored in a cool place, such as a cellar or pantry, until required. For a longer shelf life, sealed jars can be boiled in pots base-lined with cardboard to stop them rattling and breaking, then allowed to cool in the water.

Preheat the oven to 140°C (275°F), Gas Mark 1.

Cut the beef into 5cm (2 inch) chunks and place in a cast-iron pan with all the other ingredients, except the extra dripping. Cover the pan and place in the oven for 4 hours.

Remove from the oven and leave to cool slightly. Flake the meat with your fingers and pack into sterilized ramekins or mini Kilner jars while still warm (see page 163 for how to sterilize jars). Melt some more beef dripping and spoon over the top to seal.

Refrigerate for 36 hours before eating, as it improves with time, and use within 1 week. Serve with hot toast or Yorkshire Pudding and Onion Gravy (see pages 304 and 115).

Serves
6

Another ancient method for preserving beef. And from salt beef (which can be cooked and eaten in its own right) come Pastrami and Corned Beef (see pages 150 and 152).

Salt beef

4 litres (7 pints) water

500g (1lb 2oz) Maldon sea salt flakes

200g (7oz) dark muscovado sugar

20g (¾oz) pink curing salt (93.75% salt, 6.25% nitrate), also called Prague powder No. 1

20g (¾oz) pickling spice

2kg (4lb 8oz) navel-cut beef brisket

5 onions, peeled and chopped

10 garlic cloves, crushed

To serve

6 bagels

butter

hot mustard

sliced pickles

To make the brine, bring 2 litres (3½ pints) of water to the boil with the salt, sugar, curing salt and pickling spice. Stir until the salt and sugar have dissolved, then remove from the heat and add a further 2 litres (3½ pints) of cold water. Pour into a sterile bucket or large plastic food tub and leave to cool completely.

Remove the fat from the exterior of the meat, leaving a 5mm (¼ inch) layer on one side. Add the meat to the curing solution and place a large sterile weight or plate on top to submerge it. Leave it at cool room temperature for a minimum of 7–10 days, until it is well cured and pink in colour – though it can stay in the brine for another week, should you prefer a saltier end product. Move the meat every day or so, just to stir up the cure.

Once cured, drain the beef and soak it overnight in clean water to desalinate it. Then put it into a pan, cover it with fresh water, add the chopped onions and garlic and poach gently for 3 hours.

Once cooked and tender, cut into thick slices and serve on fresh buttered bagels, with hot mustard and pickles.

Makes enough for a large crowd

This was originally made with goose breast, which was inexpensive in Romania, and was known as *pastramă*. When Romanian Jews emigrated to New York in the 1870s, beef navels were cheaper than goose, so they adapted their recipe and began to make beef pastrami.

Pastrami

10g (¼oz) ground coriander

5g (⅛oz) English mustard powder

5g (⅛oz) paprika

10g (¼oz) soft brown sugar

20g (¾oz) freshly ground black pepper

2kg (4lb 8oz) Salt Beef (see page 148)

You will also need

a meat thermometer

Blend together all the spices, sugar and pepper to make a rub. Rinse the meat, pat it dry with kitchen paper, then apply the rub liberally, pressing it into the surface of the meat to help
it adhere. Put into the fridge, unwrapped, for a minimum of 2 days.

Preheat your smoker to 110°C (230°F), according to the manufacturer's instructions. Using a fruit wood, smoke the beef for up to 6 hours, or until an internal temperature of 90°C (195°F) is reached. Leave to cool, then wrap in clingfilm and refrigerate until needed.

To reheat, steam gently until heated through.

Cecina

Cecina is salt-cured, air-dried beef, and is a true delicacy of Spain. For centuries, homes in the Maragara area (in the northwest of Spain) traditionally kept a dried beef leg in the larder to feed the family. The production process contains six steps, which are called *perfilado*, *salado*, *lavado*, *asentamiento*, *ahumado* and *secado* or *curación*.

The cecina produced in the province of León, aptly called cecina de León, is famous for its quality, and has a protected geographical identification under the law. The altitude and dry climate of León is perfect for the production of cecina; however, a passable version can be made at home with practice. Like almost everything beef-related, it comes down to the quality of the meat you start with.

The dry-curing of beef involves a number of biochemical reactions, caused by enzymes, which cause a breakdown of proteins in the muscle tissue, creating large numbers of small peptides and free amino acids, while the lipids in the muscle and connective tissue break down and create free fatty acids. It requires patience, persistence and fastidious kitchen practice. The entire process takes 7 months.

It takes clean hands and plastic gloves (cleanliness is paramount) to begin this process: a piece of beef shank is first rubbed with 1kg (2lb 4oz) Maldon sea salt flakes to cover every exposed part, flesh and bone. The beef is then placed skin side down in an immaculately clean plastic tray or tub and covered with a sheet of clingfilm. Another tray is placed on top and a heavy weight placed on top of that, at least 4kg (9lb) or more.

The beef is then refrigerated for 2 weeks and checked every day, with any liquid poured off, and re-rubbed with fresh salt. When the beef is firm to touch, with little give, it's time to wash it thoroughly in cold water before smoking.

The beef is then ready to be cold-smoked for 2 weeks. It's not an easy process keeping a cold smoker going for 2 weeks, and this is best done outside in winter.

After smoking, the meat is air-dried for around 6 months in a cool room with windows that can be opened and closed to regulate the temperature and humidity, or hung in a walk-in refrigerator at about 5°C (40°F) with 60–70 per cent humidity – much like air-dried ham.

When the beef shank is ready, at around the 6 month mark, it will have lost about one-third of its original weight.

The success of air-curing your own cecina depends in equal parts on the quality of the meat you start with, cleanliness, the environment you hang it in... and a portion of luck.

Serves
8-10

500g (1lb 2oz) leftover cooked Salt Beef
or Pastrami (see pages 148 and 150)

200g (7oz) good beef dripping,
with jelly if possible

Corned or bully beef

This name comes from the treatment of the meat with large grained rock salt, also called "corns". It was popular during the war, when fresh meat was rationed, and it was known as bully beef – "bully" being a corruption of the French *bouilli*, meaning "boiled". Corned beef remains popular in the United Kingdom and in countries with British culinary traditions, and is commonly eaten in sandwiches, as corned beef hash, or with chips and pickles.

Chop the leftover Salt Beef or Pastrami into 1cm (½ inch) cubes and place in a bowl. Warm the beef dripping until liquid, then add the beef and mix well.

Pack into terrine moulds, cover and refrigerate to set.

When needed, cut into slices and serve with pickles, or use for making hash (see page 155).

Serves
1

I grew up on this stuff, and it pleases me to see it still being served in one guise or another in restaurants. Often it's pimped almost beyond recognition with duck or goose or smoked meats, but at its heart it's still hash – or bubble and squeak, if cabbage is included.

Corned beef hash

50g (1¾oz) beef dripping

1 large onion, peeled and finely sliced

1 large potato, such as Maris Piper, peeled and cut into 1cm (½ inch) chunks

300ml (½ pint) Basic Beef Broth (see page 112)

200g (7oz) Corned Beef (see page 152), cut into 1cm (½ inch) chunks

2 free-range eggs

Maldon sea salt flakes and freshly ground black pepper

brown sauce, HP for preference, to serve

Melt half the beef dripping in a skillet or ovenproof frying pan over a medium-high heat. Fry the sliced onion until golden, stirring frequently, then add the potato, toss to mix and pour in the broth. Simmer for 15–20 minutes, until the potatoes are really tender and the broth has all but evaporated.

Heat the grill. Stir the Corned Beef into the pan, then increase the heat and cook, stirring occasionally, for about 5 minutes, until heated through. Now put the pan under the grill for about 5 minutes, until the top is crisp and golden.

Meanwhile, heat the remaining dripping in a small frying pan and fry the eggs to your preference. Personally I like them sunny side up, with crispy edges and a seasoned white. Serve on top of the hash, with brown sauce on the side, of course.

Serves
1

It would not be unreasonable to say that the Reuben served at Katz's Delicatessen in New York City might be THE GREATEST SANDWICH IN THE WORLD. A Reuben is usually made with corned beef, but at Katz's you can pay an extra dollar to have yours with pastrami, and it's well worth it. The sourness of the sauerkraut is an essential part of the classic Reuben and the Swiss cheese is irreplaceable, as it melts over the hot beef, mixing perfectly with the Russian dressing. All sandwiched in New York rye, a soft bread made with both rye flour and traditional strong white bread flour, giving a delicious subtle strength of flavour and texture. We mere mortals cannot hope to replicate this sandwich exactly – there are too many subtle variables and secrets – but below is my best guess.

A Reubenesque sandwich

good handful of sauerkraut

4 slices of Swiss cheese

300g (10½oz) thickly sliced, hot Pastrami this is a restrained guess – Katz's are immoderate, extravagant and borderline reckless in their portioning

2 slices of seedless New York rye bread

For the Russian dressing

1 tablespoon finely chopped onion

50ml (2fl oz) tomato ketchup

1 teaspoon Worcestershire sauce

1 teaspoon horseradish sauce

1 teaspoon hot sauce

Maldon sea salt flakes and freshly ground black pepper

In a small bowl, combine all the ingredients for the Russian dressing and correct the seasoning. Set aside.

Put the sauerkraut on a baking tray, top with the Swiss cheese slices and grill until the cheese has melted.

Pile the hot pastrami on a slice of New York rye.

Add the sauerkraut and cheese on top and smother the other slice of bread with a couple of spoonfuls of the dressing.

Close the sandwich and eat, with 2 hands and plenty of napkins.

One of our biggest sellers at Turner & George, these are intensely beefy and juicy. Don't skimp on the fat or breadcrumbs: fat adds juiciness and flavour and the breadcrumbs hold on to the meat juices while cooking and make for a juicier sausage. Sometimes 100 per cent beef can be a bad thing.

Steak sausages

500g (1lb 2oz) beef flank

500g (1lb 2oz) chuck steak

250g (9oz) beef fat

250g (9oz) bone marrow

125ml (4fl oz) Basic Beef Broth (see page 112)

250g (9oz) fresh breadcrumbs

30g (1oz) Maldon sea salt flakes

½ teaspoon freshly ground black pepper

You will also need

2m (6ft 6 inches) hog casing

a mincer with a sausage stuffer attachment

The meat should be kept as cold as possible, so work in a cool room and return the meat to the fridge when it is not needed.

Begin by roughly cutting the meat, fat and bone marrow so that is easy to feed through the mincer.

Soak the hog casing in cold water for about 1 hour to soften it, and loosen the salt in which it is packed. Place the wide end of the sausage stuffer up against the tap and run cold water through the inside of the casing to remove excess salt.

Mix the beef broth with the breadcrumbs to make a panade.

Fit a coarse disc into the mincer and mince the meat, fat and bone marrow into a large mixing bowl (or for very coarse sausages, chop by hand). Add the breadcrumb mixture, sprinkle over the salt and pepper and mix thoroughly. Cook a tester of the mixture in a hot frying pan to check the seasoning before making the sausages.

Cut the casing into 2 lengths and tie a small knot in the end of each. Fit the open end over the tip of the sausage stuffer and slide it on until the tip of the stuffer touches the knot, this stops excess air from getting into the casing. Fit the stuffer on to the meat grinder, or according to the directions that come with the stuffer, or hold the wide end of the stuffer against or over the opening by hand.

Fill the hopper with the sausage mixture. Turn the machine on and feed the sausage mix gradually into the hopper, for a manual machine; the sausage casing will fill and gradually inflate. Smooth out any bumps with your fingers, being careful not to push the stuffing out of the casing, and tie off the open end of the sausage tightly by making a knot in the end.

To form the links, hold the entire casing up by its middle and twist it to form the first link. Then twist at the required intervals, going in opposite directions for each sausage to prevent the links unravelling.

Hang for at least a few hours in the refrigerator to dry out before cooking.

To cook the sausages, use a heavy skillet or frying pan to diffuse the heat. Set over a low heat, and fry them low and slow for around 20 minutes. If they are colouring too fast, sprinkle them with a little water from time to time. If you are barbecuing, blanch them in boiling water for 10 minutes before cooking and cook over smouldering charcoal, low and slow. Make sure you cook them through – beef sausages should not be eaten pink. Serve with Mashed Potato and Onion Gravy (see pages 61, 111 and 115)

Sweetbreads come in two types: the throat, which is long in shape and used in stuffings and sausages as an ingredient, and the heart, which is round in shape and used as the principal ingredient in a dish. Sweetbreads should always be soaked for a few hours before cooking, to remove blood and freshen them up.

Sweetbread sausages

1 x 400g (14oz) veal sweetbread, from the throat, soaked, blanched, peeled and cut into 1cm (½ inch) cubes

ox bung casings

To poach & grill

25g (1oz) curing salt

1kg (2lb 4oz) veal belly, chopped

500g (1lb 2oz) pork fat, chopped

160ml (5½fl oz) iced water

75g (2¾oz) Confit Garlic (see page 162)

40g (1½oz) Onion Confit (see page 162)

To smoke & grill

2kg (4lb 8oz) mix of veal flank and veal shoulder, chopped

250g (9oz) pork back fat, chopped

250g (9oz) panade, made from equal quantities of milk and bread, soaked

50g (1¾oz) Maldon sea salt flakes

5g (⅛oz) ground mace

5g (⅛oz) ground coriander

5g (⅛oz) freshly ground white pepper

50g (1¾oz) garlic cloves, chopped

1 teaspoon thyme leaves

50g (1¾oz) dextrose

50g (1¾oz) Fermento (alternatively use buttermilk powder or dried yogurt powder) (see page 213)

250g (9oz) porcini or ceps, chopped and sautéed

To poach and grill: Add the curing salt to the veal belly and pork fat and toss together. Partially freeze this mixture, then mince on an 8mm (⅜ inch) die into a bowl set over ice.

Working in manageable batches and using the paddle attachment on a food processor, beat the mixture on medium speed for 10 seconds, before increasing the speed for roughly 1 minute while continuously streaming in the iced water. The mixture should be soft, tacky and firmly bound.

At this point cook a little bit of the mix to check for seasoning. If satisfied, fold in the sweetbreads, Confit Garlic and Onion Confit, being careful to make sure they are well incorporated but not over-mixed so they are broken down.

Stuff into large ox bung casings, or place on a sheet of ovenproof clingfilm, and roll it up and twist to form a cylinder around 15cm (6 inches) long. Poach in a pan of water at 70°C (160°C) for 1 hour, until an internal temperature of 60°C (140°F) is reached and the sausage is cooked through. Remove from the water and chill in iced water immediately.

When ready to use, cut into slices 3cm (1¼ inches) thick and fry until golden all over. Serve with a little jus or gravy.

To smoke and grill: Using a meat mincer, mince the veal flank, veal shoulder, pork back fat and panade through a 4mm (¼ inch) die and mix with the salt, then freeze for 1 hour. Mix in all the seasonings, garlic and thyme, dextrose and Fermento and mould into loose balls, then place in the freezer along with the clean mincer attachments until partially frozen.

Re-mince the partially frozen balls through the small die and reform the meat into small balls once more. Put back into the freezer along with a food processor blade attachment.

When partially frozen, place the balls in a food processor and whizz to a purée. Fold in the chopped sweetbreads and sautéed porcini.

Stuff into large ox bung casings, or place on a sheet of ovenproof clingfilm, and roll it up and twist to form a cylinder around 15cm (6 inches) long. Hot-smoke at 110°C (230°F) for 1 hour until an internal temperature of 60°C (140°F) is reached.

Leave to cool, then chill in the refrigerator. When ready to use, cut into slices 3cm (1¼ inches) thick and fry until golden all over. Serve with a little jus or gravy.

Confit garlic Makes 1 x 450ml (1lb) jar

2 garlic bulbs, cloves separated and peeled

olive oil

Place the garlic cloves in a small saucepan over a medium heat and pour over enough olive oil to cover them. As soon as the oil starts to simmer, reduce the heat to as low as it can go and poach for about 45 minutes, until the garlic is soft and tender. Transfer the garlic cloves to a sterilized (see opposite) jar and pour over the oil to cover.

Leave to cool, then seal the jar and keep in the fridge. It will keep unopened for several weeks, or you can decant into a freezable container and freeze it. Keep the garlic cloves covered in oil and always use a clean spoon to dip into the jar.

Onion confit Makes 40g (1½oz)

2 large Spanish onions, peeled and finely sliced

1 tablespoon vegetable oil

Maldon sea salt flakes, to taste

Heat the oil in a frying pan over a medium heat. When hot, add the onions to the pan and let them cook undisturbed for a few minutes. When the onions start to sweat and steam, toss and season with salt. Continue cooking for 20 minutes until the onions steadily colour and the liquid evaporates. Keep turning the whole pile of onions over on itself every few minutes to help distribute the caramelizing juice throughout.

After the onions have reduced in volume and are soft, reduce the heat to low and cook for 1 hour, stirring and turning the onions every 10 minutes to ensure they don't stick or burn at any point, until they develop a deep, caramelized savoury sweetness, and a soft texture.

Use immediately, or store in an airtight plastic container for up to 1 week in the refrigerator.

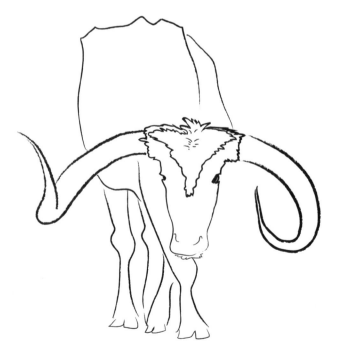

Preserved bone marrow

Makes as much as you need

Along with anchovies and Stilton cheese, I've a bit of a thing for bone marrow. And it occurred to me that it's an ideal ingredient for preserving. The amount of time it takes to sterilize or preserve depends on the size of the jar, and here I'm using 250ml (9fl oz) jars. Once cooked, it can be kept and used whenever a recipe calls for bone marrow.

bone marrow shafts, cut into 6cm (2½ inch) rounds (ask your butcher to cut them for you)

Basic Beef Rub (see page 40)

Soak the bone marrow shafts in iced water for 10 minutes, then refresh the water and soak for a further 10 minutes. The bone marrow should now pop out of the bones. Discard the bones and continue soaking the bone marrow for another 20 minutes to purge any blood.

To sterilize your jars, place them in boiling water or steam at 140°C (275°F), with an old tea towel under the jars to stop them rattling around and breaking.

Remove the clean bone marrow from the water and dry. Season heavily with plenty of Beef Rub and pack into heatproof glass jars, screwing on the lids reasonably tightly.

Put the jars back into the water or steamer for 30 minutes to cook and sterilize, then remove and allow to cool. The bone marrow can now be refrigerated for several weeks, or even months, until needed.

Pickled or brined ox tongue

Serves 12 as a starter

Ox tongues are often sold pickled or brined, but if you find yourself with a fresh tongue, this is how to do it yourself. Brining improves the flavour and texture of fresh tongue considerably.

3 litres (5¼ pints) water

300g (10½oz) Maldon sea salt flakes

100g (3½oz) light muscovado sugar

1 teaspoon black peppercorns

1 teaspoon juniper berries

2 cloves

1 fresh ox tongue

For simmering

1 faggot of herbs (thyme, bay and rosemary)

1 carrot, chopped

1 onion, peeled and chopped

1 celery stick, chopped

1 garlic bulb, halved horizontally

Bring 1 litre (1¾ pints) of the water to the boil with the salt, sugar and spices. Remove from the heat and allow to cool, then add the other 2 litres (3½ pints) of cold water.

Place the tongue in a large plastic container, then pour over the cool brine and weigh down the tongue in the liquid. Cover and refrigerate for 4–5 days.

Remove the tongue from the brine and soak in fresh water overnight in the refrigerator.

Place the salted tongue in a pot and add the simmering ingredients. Cover with cold water and bring to a simmer, then reduce the heat to very low and simmer for 4–5 hours. The tongue is ready when it is very soft.

Peel the tongue while still warm, and serve sliced, either warm or cold, with horseradish sauce and mustard.

Makes enough for a large crowd

Originating from the Valtellina Valley of northern Italy's Lombardy region in the Alps, bresaola is a cured and air-dried beef made from top inside round, a single muscle in the top of the leg and below the rump. Prague powder, though not absolutely essential, will make for a better result and is easily available online anywhere in the world.

Bresaola

1.5kg eye of round beef

50g Maldon sea salt flakes

50g caster sugar

5g Prague powder No. 2

5g juniper berries

5g black peppercorns

5g finely chopped rosemary leaves

5g finely chopped thyme leaves

piece of clean muslin (large enough to hold the beef), soaked in vinegar

Trim off all the surface fat and silverskin from the beef, but not the silverskin running through the centre of the muscle, or it will fall apart.

Grind the salt, sugar, Prague powder, spices and herbs to a powder, using a mortar and pestle.

Rub half the spice cure into the surface of the meat and seal it inside a freezer bag. Place the meat in the fridge and allow to cure for 1 week, turning daily.

After a week, take the meat out of the bag, dry it with kitchen paper, then rub it with the second half of the cure. Reseal and marinate for a second week, turning the meat daily.

Remove any remaining cure and pat dry with kitchen paper. Tie 2 pieces of string vertically around the meat, then tie a series of butcher's knots horizontally around and wrap in clean muslin.

Weigh the bresaola and make a note of its weight, then hang it at 15°C (60°F) and 60 per cent humidity (cool room temperature) for 1 month. The bresaola will be ready when it has lost 30 per cent of its weight.

Remove the bresaola from the muslin and rub down with clean muslin soaked in vinegar, then hang for a further 2 weeks without muslin.

Cut into paper-thin slices and serve either as it comes, or with extra virgin olive oil and lemon juice.

MOO

I recommend using metric measures for making this recipe as it is important to measure all the ingredients, especially the Prague powder, accurately.

Serves
6

A version of jerky originally made from game meats by the indigenous peoples of southern Africa, who preserved it by curing it with salt and hanging it up to dry. Biltong as it is today evolved from the dried meat carried by the wagon-travelling Voortrekkers, who needed stocks of durable food as they migrated north away from British rule. European settlers added spices in the early 17th century and later started using the same technique on their livestock.

Biltong

1kg (2lb 4oz) lean beef, such as rump or top round

30g (1oz) coriander seeds

30g (1oz) Maldon sea salt flakes

10g (¼oz) coarsely ground black pepper

Place the meat in the freezer for 1 hour so it's easier to slice thinly.

Toast the coriander seeds and crush lightly with a mortar and pestle together with the salt and pepper.

Slice the meat into strips 10cm (4 inches) long by 4cm (1½ inches) wide and 1cm (½ inch) thick, going against the grain, and dust liberally with the crushed seasoning. Place in a resealable plastic bag and refrigerate overnight.

Thread the beef strips on to wooden or metal skewers and hang them up to dry in a cool, dry, suitable spot where there is some movement of air and they are unlikely to be disturbed by flies. There is such a thing as a biltong dryer (see opposite), should a cool, breezy area be elusive!

Drying time is about 5 days, depending on the weather, and whether you prefer your biltong crisp or slightly moist. If the biltong is moist, store it in an airtight container in the fridge; if bone-dry it can be stored in a cool cupboard for up to 1 month.

It is worth noting that making this when the weather is dry with a degree of breeze will produce best results. Humid or damp conditions can produce mould.

Serves
8

I ate fresh beef jerky as a bar snack in a New York restaurant and was immediately smitten. Not quite as challenging to eat as commercially available jerky, this recipe makes a delightfully moreish beefy diversion.

Beef Jerky

1kg (2lb 4oz) top round
(from the rear leg)

For the marinade

50ml (2fl oz) sweet apple cider

50ml (2fl oz) cider vinegar

50ml (2fl oz) sriracha sauce

50ml (2fl oz) dark soy sauce

50ml (2fl oz) honey

50ml (2fl oz) sambal sauce

5 garlic cloves, crushed

freshly cracked black pepper

Place the meat in the freezer for 1 hour so it's easier to slice thinly.

Slice the meat into strips 10cm (4 inches) long by 4cm (1½ inches) wide and 1cm (½ inch) thick, going against the grain, and place in a resealable plastic bag.

Mix all the ingredients for the marinade and pour over the sliced meat, mixing everything around until all the strips are completely covered. Put the sealed bag into the fridge and leave overnight.

Remove the strips of meat from the marinade and place in single layers on 2 oven racks, letting the strips drip a little as you remove them from the marinade.

Place the racks high up in the oven and set the temperature to 75°C (170°F) or as low as your oven will go. Keep the oven door slightly open, so that the meat dries slowly without cooking.

Leave in the oven for about 2 hours, then flip the strips over and leave in there for another 2 hours or so. If you've used several racks, swap the positions around so the strips dry evenly. Total cooking time will depend a lot on the size and thickness of the strips. Your jerky will be done when it's dry enough to rip apart easily, but not so dry that it snaps if you bend it.

Leave the jerky out to cool for a couple of hours, then transfer to an airtight container, where it will keep unrefrigerated for a few weeks.

1kg (2lb 4oz) honeycomb tripe, cut into 10cm (4 inch) squares

500ml (18fl oz) Basic Beef Broth (see page 112)

2 carrots, chopped

1 onion, peeled and chopped

1 faggot of herbs (thyme, bay and rosemary)

1 spice bag (with plenty of cinnamon, star anise and white peppercorns)

Maldon sea salt and freshly ground black pepper

For a basic pickle brine

(Makes 500ml/18fl oz)

440ml (16fl oz) malt vinegar

50g (1¾oz) sugar

10g (¼oz) fine sea salt

1g (a large pinch) freshly ground white pepper

Pickled tripe

A Lancashire lass once told me the story of her grandmother feeding her family "dressed tripe" with salt, vinegar, white pepper and bread and butter when they were sick. (It didn't make them sick, you understand, it was what they called "invalid food" back then.) Made from the first three stomachs of a cow, there are a surprising number of dishes to be made from tripe all over the world. I imagine that like me you have managed to steer well clear of the stuff so far in your life, and I don't blame you. The thing is, some recipes are actually pretty good, and I think this is one of those.

Wrap the tripe in a clean tea towel or a cloth and gently beat it to discipline and tenderize it. Wash the tripe thoroughly, then place in a saucepan and cover with water. Bring to a simmer, cook for 5 minutes, then drain. Rinse with cold water, then put back into the pan and cover with the Beef Broth.

Add the remaining ingredients except those for the pickle brine. Cover the pan and simmer until the tripe is tender, around 1 hour.

Bring all the ingredients for the pickle brine to the boil and add to the braised tripe and broth, then remove from the heat and allow to cool.

Refrigerate overnight, and serve with bread and butter whenever feeling a little wan and in need of fortification. Lancashire grandmothers knew their stuff.

Slaughter

How an animal has been raised is obviously important, but the stress on it before slaughter, and then the stress that you put on the carcass as it's handled post-slaughter, are just as damaging – or as beneficial – to the flavour of meat. A farmer's hard work, good husbandry and passion can be undone with a poorly executed slaughter.

Minimizing the animal's stress

The well-being of the animal is paramount, but the reasons that a stress-free and humane slaughter is so important are actually two fold: not only do animals deserve to be killed in such a way that they feel no stress, but also the quality of the meat is affected by the stress that a badly run abattoir can produce in the animal. Go about slaughter in the wrong way and you can ruin a perfectly good body of beef, as adrenaline and other stress hormones cause muscles to tense up, making for tough meat. If you ever see a sheen on beef that is almost like an oil spill, along with patches of dark purple, you can be confident that the animal was stressed at the time of slaughter (and possibly beforehand) and that it will make for tough eating.

To keep stress levels at a minimum, cattle should travel as short a distance as possible and be allowed to rest overnight after the journey, to make sure that they are calm. Stress causes adrenaline to flood the muscles, which results in an unpleasant taste and texture in the meat.

Cattle are herded off the truck and through a race, or chute, to be weighed and then put into holding pens. These pens, holding 30–40 cattle each, separate the various grades, and even coat colour, of cattle that have to go through the slaughter facility. This makes it easier for the personnel in the slaughter plant to grade the various carcasses that are processed.

Most facilities employ in-house licensed veterinary surgeons, whose jobs involve witnessing the animals arriving and getting unloaded and checking that they are in good health. They also monitor how the animals are handled and whether they are properly stunned before slaughter. Cruelty and incompetence can all be reported, and ultimately the vet has the authority and power to shut down production. It's the vet's responsibility to manage meat inspections, health and hygiene and carry out ante-mortem (before death) inspection to detect any evidence of disease. If any such animal is found, a metal ear-tag is placed so as to give special post-mortem scrutiny, but if there is definite and conclusive evidence in the ante-mortem exam that the animal is not fit for human consumption, it is condemned and no post-mortem tests are necessary.

The cattle ready for slaughter are herded out of their holding pen down another race that leads into the plant. It's important that the cattle are kept in a calm state to avoid adversely affecting the quality of the meat. Cattle that are in a state of anxiety or panic will have darker-coloured meat than cattle that are calm and relatively relaxed. Reaching the kill floor, the cattle are herded into a movable cradle or box chute specially designed to block the animal's view of what's going on outside. The box is open above and the sides are high enough that the animal cannot see over them, even if it tries to raise its head. In addition, there is a solid-sided gate at the rear so that the cattle behind do not see what is going on in front of them. This is to help them remain calm and quiet. The animals move single-file into a curved race so that they have no awareness of what is in front.

Slaughtering stages

A two-stage process for the slaughter of animals is used in most countries. The first stage of the process, usually called stunning, renders the animal unconscious, but not dead; in the second stage, the animal is killed. This ensures that the animal is dispatched quickly and cleanly with the minimum of stress.

Stunning

Each animal is brought from the outdoor holding shed into the stunning pen individually. Once it is in the pen, the animal's head is swiftly secured and a captive bolt inserted into the brain, which renders the animal senseless. Then the animal is released from the restrainer and attached to a hook in the conveyor system that hoists it up. The stunned animal then travels to the proceeding areas to be bled out, skinned, gutted and halved.

Sticking, bleeding out & skinning

The point of a very sharp knife cuts into the animal's throat and through the dewlap, trachea, oesophagus and jugular vein immediately below the jawline to allow the blood to flow out. The cut can be made perpendicular or parallel to the neck, depending on the standards of the slaughter plant. Animals are bled out before being butchered, because it prevents blood from coagulating in the tissues and making the meat go rancid.

The hind shanks are skinned and removed at the hocks, by inserting beef hooks between the tibia and the tendon that runs from the tip of the hock, freeing the chain on one of the hind legs that had been used to hoist up the animal.

The hide is opened along the median line of the belly and is removed from the belly and sides. Down-pullers are used for removing the rest of the hide, including skinning the head.

Removal of the head, limbs, viscera or offal, spine & tail

The head is not severed from the carcass until the hide is completely removed. Until then, the legs, head, breast and aitch (rump) bones are split from the carcass by sawing. All internal organs are removed except the kidneys, and the offal is separated and taken away to other factories or butchers' shops.

The carcass is then split through the centre of the backbone and the tail is removed. The spinal cord is removed and discarded, and the split carcasses or halves are washed with cold water using a pressure-washer, then allowed to dry.

Chilling & distribution

The carcass is taken through a slow, gradual chilling process – it takes 24 hours to chill fully. Excessively rapid chilling early in the post-mortem can create something called cold shortening (conversion of glycogen to lactic acid) whereby the muscles contract to produce dry and tough meat.

Carcasses are then distributed to butchers and meat merchants where they are refrigerated for two to three weeks to allow the meat to age, before it is broken down into various cuts of beef.

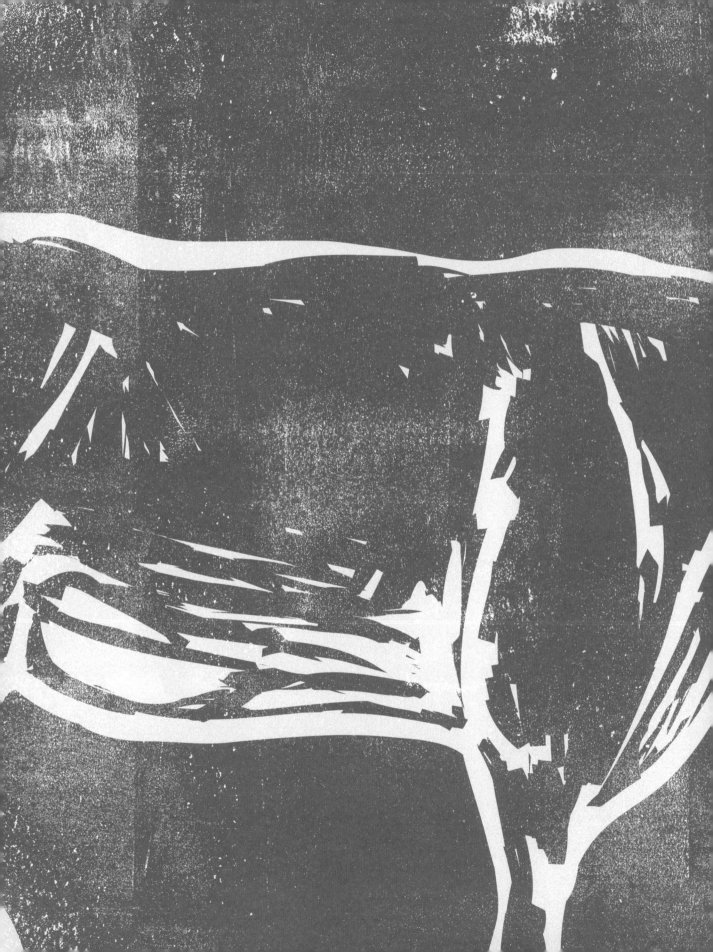

Fried 5

100g (3½oz) unsalted butter

4 slices of day-old bread

1kg (2lb 4oz) fillet steak,
cut into 4 equal pieces

4 x 50g (1¾oz) slices of foie gras

1 fresh black truffle, thinly sliced

200ml (7fl oz) Madeira Gravy
(see page 114)

Maldon sea salt flakes and
freshly ground black pepper

Tournedos Rossini

Tournedos Rossini is one of the most famous steak dishes, and was
created and named in honour of the Italian composer Gioachino Antonio
Rossini by the 19th-century chef Casimir Moissons, one of his close
friends. Rossini was a friend, critic and supporter of many of the greatest
chefs of his time, and was recognized as a truly knowledgeable gourmet
and an equally accomplished cook. Steak, foie gras, truffles and gravy
on toast. It was always going to work.

Heat half the butter in a skillet or frying pan over a medium heat and fry the bread slices
on both sides until golden. Arrange the fried bread on a serving platter and set aside.

Season the steaks, then heat the remaining butter in the skillet, still over a medium
heat, and cook them for about 3 minutes on each side, until medium-rare. Remove
from the pan, loosely cover with foil and allow to rest in a warm place for 10 minutes.

Clean the skillet and heat it again, this time over a high heat. Season the slices of foie
gras and sear for 1 minute on each side until deep golden brown.

Place a steak on each bread slice, arrange the foie gras on top and cover with the thinly
sliced truffle.

Heat the Madeira Gravy and pour over to serve.

2 onions, sliced

50g (1¾oz) beef dripping

200g (7oz) inside round (rump)

1–2 tablespoons plain flour

Maldon sea salt flakes and freshly ground black pepper

mashed potatoes, to serve (see pages 61 and 111)

Madeira Gravy, to serve (see page 114)

The Schatzkers' death-row chicken fried round of beef

"This is the height of simplicity. But damn it's good. You need a thinnish cutlet off a braising cut. The best is inside round (the equivalent British cut is rump) – the cut Germans use for *rouladen*. Basically, slice it about half an inch thick, then whack it down with a hammer or, my preference, the side of a cleaver. You don't want it scaloppini thin – not nearly. You just need to hurt it a bit, because that loosens up the fibers. Season with salt and pepper, then dredge it in flour. Then fry in a hot iron pan with plenty of fat. You want to get the outside browned before the inside overcooks. As far as fat goes, I'll leave that in your very capable hands. I guess you could use vegetable oil if that's all you have – I have, works fine – but I suspect lard is going to be better, or beef fat if you can get it. Serve it with mashed potatoes. And smother the fucker in fried onions. I can't stress how important it is to have loads and loads of them. Most people just don't make enough. I like to pre-fry the onions, then do the beef in that pan. This is similar to a chicken fried steak, but less seasoning, and a lesser cut. You could make a pan gravy, but I prefer without. Also, you need really good beef for this dish – using intensively-farmed meat will just leave you wondering why on earth I suggested this."
– Mark Schatzker

Fry the sliced onions in half the beef dripping until golden, then set aside. Do not wash the pan.

Slice the beef round about 1cm (½ inch) thick, then whack it down with the side of a cleaver. You just need to hurt it a bit, because that loosens up the fibres.

Season the beef with salt and pepper, then dredge in the flour.

Heat the remaining dripping until smoking and fry the floured meat until the outside is browned but the inside is still rare, flipping it over to colour both sides. Spread the fried onions over the top and flip again, pressing the onions down into the meat.

Remove from the pan and serve onion side up, with mashed potatoes and Madeira Gravy.

Serves 4

Lamesa, the county seat of Dawson County in Texas, claims to be the birthplace of country fried steak and hosts an annual celebration. Its origins are attributed to 19th-century German and Austrian immigrants who brought recipes for Wiener schnitzel to Texas from Europe. As always, use good-quality beef and do not be tempted to use any other cooking fat.

Country fried steak

4 fillet tails or "filet mignon", around 200g (7oz) each

100g (3½oz) beef dripping or bacon grease, for frying

hot pepper sauce, to serve

For the seasoning mixture

25g (1oz) Maldon sea salt flakes

5g (⅛oz) cayenne pepper

5g (⅛oz) garlic powder

5g (⅛oz) onion powder

5g (⅛oz) freshly ground black pepper

5g (⅛oz) paprika

For the seasoned flour

150g (5½oz) plain flour

50g (1¾oz) panko breadcrumbs, ground fine

20g (¾oz) rice flour

20g (¾oz) cornflour

First, prepare the seasoning mixture: combine all the ingredients in a mortar and pestle, and grind to a powder.

Flatten out the fillet tails with a mallet to make 1cm (½ inch) thick steaks and season them liberally, using just over half the seasoning mixture.

Mix all the ingredients for the seasoned flour together and combine with the remaining seasoning mixture. Place in a shallow tray.

Prepare a shallow bowl of cold water. Dip the steaks into the cold water, then coat well in the seasoned flour. Repeat this process once again.

Heat half the beef dripping or bacon grease in a cast-iron skillet or heavy-based frying pan over a medium-high heat. Shallow-fry the steaks, 2 at a time, until golden brown, then briefly drain on kitchen paper and serve hot, with hot pepper sauce.

This is really just a variation on bubble and squeak, but with the added oomph and spice of kimchi. It makes a great side for grilled steak, and is a perfect brunch dish in its own right. The trick is to take your time with long, slow, gentle frying and constant attention, tossing from time to time until it's crispy and golden all over.

Kimchi hash

50g (1¾oz) beef dripping

250g (9oz) baked potato
or leftover Roast Potatoes
(see page 327)

250g (9oz) Kimchi (see page 89)

50g (1¾oz) bone marrow, chopped

100g (3½oz) braised beef (leftover
Braised Short Ribs see page 265,
Daube de Boeuf see page 262
or Brasato al Barolo, see page 269),
chopped into bite-sized pieces

4 free-range eggs

Maldon sea salt flakes and
freshly ground black pepper

Preheat the oven to 180°C (350°F), Gas Mark 4.

Heat half the dripping in a skillet until hot, then add all the ingredients, except the eggs, and cook until crispy and golden, turning or tossing from time to time.

Season liberally and place in the preheated oven for 10 minutes.

While the hash is in the oven, fry the eggs in the other half of the dripping until just cooked but crispy on the outside edges.

Remove the hash from the oven and serve with fried eggs on top.

12 oysters

75g (2¾oz) mix of potato starch and plain flour seasoned with salt and pepper

2 free-range eggs, lightly beaten

100g (3½oz) fresh breadcrumbs

4 rose veal chops, 3–4cm (1¼–1½ inches) thick (300g/10½oz each)

oil, for frying

Maldon sea salt flakes and freshly ground black pepper

For the lemon parsley mayonnaise

1 unwaxed lemon

100ml (3½fl oz) good-quality mayonnaise

1 tablespoon chopped parsley

Veal chops with fried oysters & lemon parsley mayonnaise

Oysters have been eaten with meat in England for centuries, mostly because they were once so cheap and freely available that they made the meat go further in times of austerity. Times have changed, but this still works well because the flavour elements of fried crumbed protein combined with juicy grilled meat are really rather familiar, even if the exact delivery method is somewhat unorthodox.

To make the lemon parsley mayonnaise, first boil the unwaxed lemon whole for 20 minutes, then set aside and allow to cool.

Cut the lemon in half and scoop out the flesh, discarding the pith and rind. Discard the seeds and chop the flesh. Mix the mayonnaise with the chopped parsley and the hot lemon flesh and season to taste.

Open the oysters and remove the meat. Pat dry, then dip the oysters first into the seasoned flour, then into the beaten egg and finally into the breadcrumbs. Set aside.

Season the veal chops well, then sear in a little oil in a hot frying pan on both sides until well coloured but still pink. Set aside to rest.

Heat a deep-fat fryer to 200°C (400°F). Dip the oysters into the breadcrumbs for a final time, then deep-fry for a couple of minutes until golden brown. Drain on kitchen paper.

Serve the chops with a pile of fried oysters and plenty of lemon parsley mayonnaise.

Originally vegetarian and made with aubergine rather than meat, Parmigiana made its way over with Italian immigrants to America, where this variation appeared. Bloody delicious it is, too.

New York veal Parmigiana

3 tablespoons olive oil, plus extra for frying the escalopes

½ small onion, finely chopped

1 banana shallot, finely chopped

1 garlic clove, crushed

1 bay leaf

400g (14oz) can peeled chopped tomatoes

1 tablespoon chopped parsley

½ teaspoon dried oregano

½ teaspoon dried thyme

100g (3½oz) fresh breadcrumbs

50g (1¾oz) Parmesan cheese, finely grated

finely grated zest of 1 lemon

100g (3½oz) mix of potato flour and plain flour seasoned with salt and pepper

2 large free-range eggs, beaten

1kg (2lb 4oz) veal rump, cut into 4 and beaten to 2cm (¾ inch) thick

8 slices of Provolone cheese

Maldon sea salt flakes and freshly ground black pepper

To make the sauce, heat the olive oil in a large saucepan over a medium heat, then add the onion, shallot, garlic and bay leaf and cook until softened. Add the tomatoes and herbs and cook until thickened, about 20 minutes. Season to taste.

Preheat the oven to 180°C (350°F), Gas Mark 4.

To prepare the escalopes, mix the breadcrumbs in a bowl with the Parmesan and lemon zest. Lay out three plates in front of you. Put the seasoned flour on a plate, pour the eggs on to the next and put the breadcrumb mix on the third. Dip the escalopes, one at a time, into the flour, then into the egg and lastly into the breadcrumb mix, making sure to cover every part of the escalope.

Heat a large nonstick frying pan over a medium heat and add a good splash of olive oil. Add your escalopes in batches, adding a little extra oil if needed. Cook for a few minutes on each side, until lightly golden, and transfer to a plate lined with kitchen paper to drain.

Place the escalopes in a large shallow dish side by side and spoon a little of the tomato sauce over the top, followed by slices of Provolone cheese.

Bake in the preheated oven for 10 minutes, until golden and bubbling.

Serve with spaghetti or polenta, or as a sandwich in crusty bread.

Serves
4

Sichuan is a southwestern Chinese province and is also the name of its hot and spicy cuisine, which makes good and occasionally exuberant use of chilli. The Sichuan pepper itself is not hot or pungent but has a slight lemon flavour that produces a strange tingling, buzzing, numbing sensation, setting the stage for the chilli. It appears to act on several different kinds of nerve endings at once, inducing sensitivity to touch and cold and causing a kind of general pleasant neurological confusion.

Sichuan beef

2 tablespoons light soy sauce

2 tablespoons Shaoxing rice wine

6 tablespoons Oyster Sauce
(for homemade, see page 65)

2 teaspoons caster sugar

1 teaspoon freshly ground
Sichuan pepper

1 teaspoon cayenne pepper

4 tablespoons sunflower oil

800g (1lb 12oz) rump steak,
thinly sliced

200g (7oz) spring onions,
cut into 2cm (¾ inch) lengths

25g (1oz, or about 4) red chillies, seeds
left in and cut into 2cm (¾ inch)
lengths, or more if you like it hot

preserved plum, to garnish

steamed white rice, to serve

Combine the soy sauce, Shaoxing rice wine, oyster sauce, sugar, Sichuan pepper, cayenne and 2 tablespoons of the oil in a bowl. Add the beef, mix well, cover and leave to stand for 30 minutes.

Heat the remaining oil in a wok over a high heat. Drain the beef thoroughly, taking care to reserve the marinade. Add the drained beef to the wok and stir-fry for 3 minutes, until caramelized. Tip in the spring onions and chillies and stir-fry until just done and still crisp. Add the reserved marinade and continue to cook until heated through, about 30 seconds.

Serve with grated preserved plum sprinkled over the top and with steamed white rice.

Serves
4

Stir-frying is a Chinese cooking method in which ingredients are fried in a small amount of hot oil in a wok. In recent centuries, stir-frying has spread into the West with Chinese immigrants, and due to its simplicity it is a cooking method beloved by students and singletons alike. It's actually a great way to keep in maximum nutrients, as well as a lovely bit of crunch.

Stir-fried beef

100ml (3½fl oz) Basic Beef Broth
(see page 112)

10g (¼oz) dried orange zest, soaked
in hot water, pith removed, zest julienned

10cm (4 inches) fresh root ginger, peeled
and sliced thinly across the grain

50ml (2fl oz) light soy sauce

50ml (2fl oz) red wine vinegar

sesame oil, for frying

600g (1lb 5oz) rib-eye steak,
cut into thin strips

1–2 tablespoons cornflour seasoned
with salt and pepper

10 spring onions, cut into 2cm
(¾ inch) lengths

4 garlic cloves, finely sliced

½ bunch (about 15g/½oz)
of sweet basil, leaves picked

½ bunch (about 15g/½oz)
of coriander, leaves picked

Maldon sea salt flakes and freshly
ground black pepper

Bring the broth to a simmer with the orange zest, then add the ginger, soy sauce and vinegar and remove from the heat.

Heat a little oil in a wok until smoking, then toss the beef strips in the seasoned cornflour and quickly stir-fry over a high heat.

Add the spring onions, garlic and herbs, followed by the broth mixture, and remove from the heat.

Serve immediately, while the beef is just cooked and the vegetables are still crunchy. If you must have some carbs, steamed rice is the thing.

Serves
4
as a starter

Even an adventurous gourmet might draw the line at brains, but those who try speak highly of them. It's important that they are fresh, so either cook or freeze them on the day of purchase. Brains are rather rich, since they're loaded with cholesterol, and 500g (1lb 2oz) is more than enough for four people.

Fried calf's brains with fried potatoes & lemon

1 unwaxed lemon

20g (¾oz) Maldon sea salt flakes

1 calf's brain, about 500g (1lb 2oz)

½ carrot

½ onion, peeled

½ celery stick

1 tablespoon malt or cider vinegar

1 litre (1¾ pints) water

plain flour seasoned with salt and pepper

1 free-range egg, beaten

100g (3½oz) panko breadcrumbs

100g (3½oz) beef dripping

50g (1¾oz) butter

2 large potatoes, peeled and cut into fine matchsticks

a few rosemary sprigs, leaves picked

Maldon sea salt flakes and freshly ground black pepper

Lemon Parsley Mayonnaise, to serve (see page 181)

Zest the lemon into a mortar, then using a pestle, grind together with the sea salt and set aside.

Wash the brain thoroughly in cold water, then leave to soak in fresh cold water for 10 minutes. Drain, and carefully remove as much as possible of the surrounding membrane and blood vessels. Break into 4 pieces down the natural lines.

Put the vegetables, vinegar and 1 teaspoon salt into a saucepan with the water and bring to the boil. Drop in the brain chunks and, when the water has returned to a boil, cover the pan and adjust the heat to gently simmer for 5 minutes.

Drain, discard the vegetables and let the brain cool completely. When cool, refrigerate for about 10 minutes, or until very firm. Break each piece in half to form 8 smaller pieces. Dust with seasoned flour, then dip into beaten egg and then into the breadcrumbs.

Heat half the beef dripping, to a depth of about 1cm (½ inch), in a skillet over a high heat. When the dripping is hot, slip the breadcrumbed brain pieces into the pan. Fry until crisp and light golden brown, then add the butter, which will foam all over the brains. Remove them from the pan before the foaming butter starts to burn and transfer to kitchen paper to drain. Season with salt and pepper.

Clean out the skillet and heat the remaining dripping. Pat the potato matchsticks dry with kitchen paper, to remove any excess starch. Make sure you've got a slotted spoon and plenty more kitchen paper ready. Carefully fry the potatoes in batches for a couple of minutes until golden brown and crisp, adding the rosemary for the last 30 seconds. Using the slotted spoon, remove the potatoes and rosemary from the pan and drain on kitchen paper to soak up any excess dripping. Dust the potatoes with the lemon salt and serve on top of the fried brains with a squeeze of lemon juice and the Lemon Parsley Mayonnaise on the side.

These are much, much tastier than any chicken nugget could hope to be, and if served as a canapé before a special dinner, or as snack for a party, they will impress. They are molten hot once fried, so resist them for a few minutes before eating.

Fried beef nuggets with kimchi ketchup

1kg (2lb 4oz) Braised Short Ribs (see page 265), or cooked ox cheek or ox tail

½ bunch (about 15g/½oz) parsley

200g (7oz) Ogleshield cheese

100g (3½oz) plain flour seasoned with salt and pepper

3 free-range eggs

150g (5½oz) panko breadcrumbs

beef dripping or sunflower oil, for deep-frying

Maldon sea salt flakes and freshly ground black pepper

Kimchi Ketchup (see below) or Chipotle Ketchup (see page 41), to serve

Drain the braised beef and place the sauce in a pan. Shred the meat roughly into small pieces and add to the pan, then bring to the boil. Reduce to a medium heat and simmer until the sauce has all but reduced, but the meat is still moist. Chop the parsley and add to the pan, then taste, season and taste again until perfect.

Leave the meat to cool, then divide in half. Lay a large sheet of clingfilm on a work surface and spread half the beef out in a neat rectangle roughly 1cm (½ inch) thick. Cut the Ogleshield cheese into fat matchsticks or batons and lay half of them together in a line across the middle of the meat. Roll up the meat into a thick log, using the clingfilm to help you, so that the cheese is encased in the middle of the meat. Wrap tightly in more clingfilm and twist into a log shape. Repeat with the second half of the meat and cheese. Chill in the fridge for a good couple of hours, until firm. Remove the clingfilm and cut into 2cm (¾ inch) discs.

Dip each disc into seasoned flour, then egg, then breadcrumbs, then repeat each stage once more. Heat the dripping or oil to 180°C (350°F) in a deep-fat fryer, and fry the nuggets in batches until golden brown. Drain on kitchen paper for 2–3 minutes, which will allow them to cool a little. Serve with Kimchi Ketchup on the side.

Kimchi ketchup

100g (3½oz) garlic, sliced

100g (3½oz) fresh root ginger, peeled and sliced against the grain

100g (3½oz) *gochugaru* (Korean red pepper powder or flakes)

100g (3½oz) salted anchovy fillets

100g (3½oz) salted shrimp from a jar

100g (3½oz) sugar

100ml (3½oz) light soy sauce

200ml (7fl oz) water, or lactic pickle ferment juice if available

This sauce goes with Fried Beef Nuggets (above), but it can also be used in Kimchi Hollandaise (see page 37), a sauce I've always proudly taken credit for. Sadly mistakenly, as a bit of research shows Michael's Genuine Food and Drink in Miami to be its place of birth. Oh well, it's genius nonetheless.

Blend all the ingredients to a smooth ketchup.

If lactic pickle ferment juice is used it will of course continue fermenting, so avoid airtight bottles. This keeps in the fridge for up to a week.

Dude food at its best, or despicable worst, depending on your point of view. This is trashy as hell and as addictive as crack, I imagine.

Fried bacon cheese sliders

360g (12oz) minced beef (90 per cent chuck, 10 per cent bone marrow (see page 80)

70g (2½oz) Danish mozzarella or American burger cheese

2 x 350g (12oz) tubes of ready-to-make croissant dough (from the chiller section in most supermarkets)

12 rashers of smoked streaky bacon

plain flour, for dusting

beef dripping, for deep-frying

Maldon sea salt flakes and freshly ground black pepper

16 toothpicks

tomato ketchup and sliced Half Sours, to serve (see page 85)

Season the burger mince, then divide into small (about 30g/1oz, or 3cm/1¼ inch diameter) balls and flatten into ½–1cm/¼–½ inch thick patties. Cut the cheese into 1cm (½ inch) cubes and wrap each in burger mince to form a small meatball.

Unravel the croissant dough and, using a cookie cutter, cut out circles about 10cm (4 inches) in diameter. Place 1 meatball in the centre of each circle, wrap in the dough to completely enclose, then pinch the seams to seal.

Wrap each slider with a bacon rasher and gently secure with a toothpick. Place on a lightly floured tray, cover loosely with clingfilm and leave to rest for 1 hour at room temperature.

Heat the dripping in a deep-fat fryer to 170°C (325°F) and fry the sliders in batches for 4–5 minutes, or until the dough is golden brown on all sides. Allow the fat to come back up to temperature before frying subsequent batches.

Drain on kitchen paper, then remove the toothpicks and serve warm with ketchup and sliced Half Sours.

Serves
4
as a starter

Sweetbreads are glands situated in the neck or heart of a calf. Those from the "heart" are more spherical in shape, and are surrounded symmetrically by the cylindrical "throat" sweetbreads. They are neither sweet nor bread-like and are classified as offal. Here they are fried crisp and paired with some classic flavours that go well with veal and offal.

Fried veal sweetbreads with anchovy cream

500g (1lb 2oz) veal heart sweetbreads

1 thyme sprig

1 bay leaf

1 teaspoon black peppercorns

beef dripping, for deep-frying

1 lemon, sliced

100g (3½oz) plain flour seasoned with salt and pepper

To serve

2 tablespoons capers

2–3 tablespoons chopped flat leaf parsley leaves

Maldon sea salt flakes and freshly ground black pepper

malt vinegar

100ml (3½fl oz) Anchovy Cream (see page 141)

Soak the sweetbreads in cold water for 4 hours, then drain and rinse under more cold water.

Place the sweetbreads in a saucepan with the thyme, bay leaf and peppercorns. Cover with cold water, bring to the boil, then reduce to a simmer for 3 minutes. Drain in a colander and allow to cool slightly, then peel the outer membrane off the sweetbreads and slice them into quarters.

Heat some beef dripping to 180°C (350°F) in a deep-fat fryer.

Toss the sweetbread and lemon slices in the seasoned flour and shake off the excess. Cook in the hot beef dripping for 3 minutes, or until golden brown and crispy all over, then drain on a tray lined with kitchen paper to absorb the excess oil.

Fry the capers and parsley in the hot dripping until crispy and add to the paper-lined tray.

Season the sweetbreads with salt and malt vinegar, garnish with the fried lemon, capers and parsley, and serve with Anchovy Cream.

Hanging beef

Ageing, the process by which meat is hung after slaughter, allows some moisture to escape and to tenderize it. This is known as "hanging" or "dry-ageing". If beef is eaten fresh it is wet, can lack flavour and can be tough, but ageing it for even just a couple of weeks improves these elements. The technique has been practised for hundreds of years. After falling from favour in the 1960s, it underwent a surge of popularity in the 1990s and continues to be popular among connoisseurs of good beef today. One reason for its return to favour is that we are killing younger cattle, and the meat is more watery in younger animals.

The dry-ageing process

This process involves hanging beef in a controlled environment at 1–3°C (34–37°F); any warmer and the meat may spoil, any cooler and the water in the meat might freeze, stalling any ageing. Beef is hung on the quarter, the largest manageable size possible, where the weight of the quarter assists in the hanging process. Because the water needs to evaporate slowly, the room must be kept to a relative humidity of around 85 per cent, and to prevent bacteria developing on the meat, the room is kept well ventilated, often with fans. This process is monitored at regular intervals to ensure that it is working correctly.

As the water leaves the meat it concentrates the taste, making for a rich and savoury flavour. The meat also starts to break down. There are several theories about how this works (involving whether they are enzymatic or non-enzymatic) but the "calpain theory" of tenderization is recognized as the most probable. The job of calpains in living muscle is to break down proteins to be synthesized into newer proteins, and this process continues after slaughter but without the newer proteins being synthesized. The meat becomes tastier as those proteins are broken down into amino acids, including glutamic acid, which is related to umami. And so you get tender and tasty beef!

Beef's appearance also changes through the dry-ageing process. The meat will change colour from red to purple and will be much firmer than fresh meat.

The dry-ageing process takes at least two weeks. At this point, the meat will be noticeably tastier, but this length of time also results in a greater chance that the meat will spoil. Furthermore, dry-aged meat shrinks because much of the water has evaporated, and this loss of mass causes the meat to decrease by 10–15 per cent in weight. For these reasons, and because the process requires constant attention and a large room with specific environmental conditions, the price of hung meat is substantial. As a result, meat hanging has lost popularity in intensive meat production. Most butchers will only hang meat for 20–30 days, prioritizing profit over any intensifying of flavour.

Extreme ageing

A few butchers abroad are taking the dry-ageing process further. José Gordon of El Capricho in Spain, for example, ages meat for up to 200 days; the Peruvian butcher Renzo Garibaldi hangs it for up to 300 days; and the Northern Irish meat merchant Peter Hannan ages it for more than 400 days! This method of extreme ageing is practised with prime cuts more often than with full quarters. It's not for everyone – the meat picks up distinctly funky fermented flavours, and I find that it can mask the flavour of good beef when taken beyond a month or two. Similarly, in the wrong hands it could mask the flavour of inferior beef.

Wet-ageing in vacuum pack

In the 1960s a new process – wet-ageing in vacuum packs – led to the practice of meat hanging being almost stopped entirely. Wet-aged beef incurs considerably less moisture loss, which means in effect it can be up to 20 per cent cheaper than dry-aged. In the wet-ageing process, the meat is butchered then vacuum-sealed and left in the refrigerator to "age", when in fact it cannot change much if there's no contact with air and no moisture allowed to escape. It also doesn't benefit from the weight of the quarter pulling on muscle fibres. The process gives scope to advertise "aged beef" without technically lying, all the while keeping the weight of the product up and the margins high.

Storing uncut steak

Uncut primal muscle can be stored in a designated fridge for a week or so. The best way is to place them on a drip tray with plenty of room and air circulation around them. Do not store anything else at all in the fridge with your steak as it will influence or taint the flavour. In other words, you cannot age steak in a fridge that is used for other food.

6
Smoked

Serves
6

I first encountered smoked prime rib at Smitty's Market in Lockhart, Texas, on a research trip with the Pitt Cue team. As with brisket, you can use a rub, but salt and pepper gives a cleaner, purer flavour that I prefer.

Smoked prime rib

a 3-bone prime rib, chined but untrimmed, around 3kg (6lb 8oz) in weight

70g (2½oz) Maldon sea salt flakes

10g (¼oz) freshly ground black pepper

You will also need
a meat thermometer

To serve

Grilled Portobello Mushrooms (see page 22)

Smashed Grilled Beets (see page 200)

Kale Caesar Salad (see page 200)

Roast Potatoes (see page 327)

Preheat your smoker to 115°C (240°F).

Remove the beef from the fridge 1–2 hours before cooking and let it reach room temperature.

Season the meat heavily all over with the salt and pepper and colour on all sides over a charcoal grill. Place in the smoker with oak wood or chips.

Preheat a smoker according to the manufacturer's instructions.

Smoke at 115°C (240°F) for 2–3 hours, or until the internal temperature of the meat reaches 60°C (140°F) – the perfect temperature for prime rib.

As a guide, for medium-rare cook to 55–60°C (130–140°F); medium: 60–65°C (140–150°F), or medium-well done: 65–70°C (150–160°F).

Remove the rib from the smoker and rest in a warm place for at least 30 minutes (the ideal resting temperature is 58–60°C/136–140°F), then carve into single-bone portions, each for 2 to share.

Serve with Grilled Portobello Mushrooms, Smashed Grilled Beets, Kale Ceasar Salad and Roast Potatoes.

Smashed grilled beets Serves 4

As a fan of live fire cooking, I love these. Roots such as beetroot, sweet potatoes and potatoes take on a wonderful smoky flavour when baked in the dying embers of a barbecue. There's a trick to cooking in embers: too hot and the beets will burn irretrievably, not hot enough and they'll be part cooked. It takes practice and common sense.

4 medium red, orange or yellow beetroots, scrubbed, ends trimmed, and greens reserved

8 tablespoons extra virgin olive oil

5 tablespoons red wine vinegar

2 thyme sprigs, leaves picked

Maldon sea salt flakes and freshly ground black pepper

2–3 garlic cloves, finely sliced and fried until crisp, to garnish

Place the beetroots in the dying embers of a barbecue and leave to cook as the fire cools. After a few hours the beetroots should be cooked through. Peel them and press them with your hand to partially flatten them, while keeping them intact.

Season with salt and pepper and toss with half the olive oil. Charcoal-grill until slightly charred and crispy in places.

Whisk the remaining olive oil in a bowl with the vinegar to make a dressing. Trim and discard the thick stems from the beetroot greens and put the leaves into a medium bowl with the thyme leaves. Add some of the dressing, toss to combine, and season with salt and pepper.

Divide the beetroots between 4 plates and garnish with the salad and fried garlic chips.

Kale Caesar salad Serves 4

Many have tried and failed to improve on a good Caesar salad, and I'm reasonably sure it's not possible. However, this is my attempt to improve the vegetable of the moment – considered a superfood, kale has appeared on menus everywhere. While I'm not buying the superfood tag, I do think anything that encourages us to eat more green stuff is a good thing.

85g (3oz) mixed baby kale leaves

50g (1¾oz) leftover Trencher (see page 205), or similar loose-textured bread

10g (¼oz) finely grated Parmesan cheese

8 salted anchovy fillets, to garnish

Maldon sea salt flakes and freshly ground black pepper

For the Parmesan dressing

50g (1¾oz) finely grated Parmesan cheese

20ml (¾fl oz) Champagne vinegar (or use good-quality white wine or cider vinegar)

1 tablespoon lime juice

1 teaspoon Dijon mustard

½ teaspoon freshly ground black pepper

60ml (4 tablespoons) sunflower oil

20ml (¾fl oz) extra virgin olive oil

To make the dressing, blend the Parmesan, vinegar, lime juice, mustard, salt and pepper in a blender until smooth. With the machine running, gradually add both oils and blend until emulsified and well incorporated.

Wash and pick the baby kale, discarding the tough external leaves. Dry them really well.

Pull the bread into small, rough chunks, then bake at 180°C (350°F), Gas Mark 4 until golden, then season lightly.

Toss the whole baby kale leaves in the dressing and arrange on starter plates. Crunch the baked pulled bread over the dressed leaves, allowing small and medium pieces to fall over the salad. Grate the Parmesan over the top and garnish with the anchovies.

Serves 6-8

Kiełbasa is a smoked garlic sausage from Poland that's usually served with sauerkraut. The process of making kiełbasa is similar to that of hot dogs.

Kielbasa

500g (1lb 2oz) chuck steak, chopped

500g (1lb 2oz) pork back fat, chopped

5g (about ⅛oz) pink curing salt (93.75% salt, 6.25% nitrate), also called Prague powder No. 1

15g (½oz) Maldon sea salt flakes

10g (¼oz) caster sugar

3 garlic cloves, crushed

5g (⅛oz) English mustard powder

5g (about ⅛oz) freshly ground white pepper

30g (1oz) powdered milk

300g (10½oz) crushed ice

You will also need

2m (6ft 6 inches) hog casing

a mincer with a sausage stuffer attachment

a meat thermometer

sterilized needle

Cut the meat and fat into 3cm (1¼ inch) pieces and chill in the freezer for 1 hour or so, until partially frozen.

Soak the hog casing in cold water for about 1 hour to soften it, and loosen the salt in which it is packed. Place the wide end of the sausage stuffer up against the tap and run cold water through the inside of the casing to remove excess salt.

Combine the salts, sugar, garlic, mustard and pepper, then mix into the meat and fat with your hands. Return to the freezer for about 1 hour.

Fit a fine disk into the mincer and mince the meat into a large mixing bowl. Place the meat in a stand mixer, add the powdered milk and mix on a low speed for 3 minutes, to get the sausage mix to bind properly.

Stuff about 60cm (2ft) of sausage (see method on page 159), then pinch off the trailing end and pull off at least 15cm (6 inches) of casing from the stuffing tube.

Cut the casing with a knife and immediately pull out another 15cm (6 inches) or so of casing to form the loose end for the next long loop of sausage. This ensures that you will have enough casing to tie off the links. Leave the links untied for now.

Check each long link of kiełbasa for air pockets – you will probably have some. Using a sterilized needle, pierce the casing all around any air pockets. Gently compress the meat in the link from either end. Don't force it or the casing will burst. When you see no more air pockets, tie off the casings at either end and then tie into 15cm (6 inch) sausages. Hang them in a cool place overnight.

Next day, smoke the links for at least 4 hours, until an internal temperature of 70°C (160°F) is reached, then shock the links in iced water to cool quickly. Hang overnight to dry before eating. They will keep in the refrigerator for up to 2 weeks.

I recommend using metric measures for making this recipe, as it is important to measure all the ingredients, especially the Prague powder, accurately.

Serves
4

1 stick of fresh horseradish

500g (1lb 2oz) Maldon sea salt flakes

1kg (2lb 4oz) eye barrel of the rib-eye,
deckle removed, or fillet barrel
or popes eye)

Potato & Garlic Trencher, to serve
(see page 205)

You will also need

2 pieces of clean muslin or cotton
cloth (large enough to hold the meat),
dipped in cold water and wrung out

butcher's string

a meat thermometer

Dirty roasted steak

You don't need to use cloth for this recipe – the steak could be cooked
directly on the charcoal or wood – but this is a good gateway to that kind
of direct cooking, detailed in Jerked Steak & Cauliflower (see page 24).

Light a charcoal barbecue or grill, leaving the griddle bars off.

Grate the horseradish and mix with the salt. Arrange the muslin or cotton cloth on
a work surface and spread the salt mixture out on top so that it extends to 1cm (½ inch)
away from the edge.

Place the meat on top of the salt at the far end of the cloth. Roll the cloth and salt around
the meat – the idea is to make a compact roll. Secure the ends of the roll with butcher's
string, then tie in the middle, followed by another 2 ties between the middle and the ends
– you are aiming to form a tight cylindrical packet.

Lay the packet right on the coals, knot sides up. Grill for 9 minutes. Using tongs, turn
the package over and grill for another 9 minutes. The cloth should burn – it's meant to.

Using a meat thermometer and inserting it through the cloth and the salt into the centre
of the meat, check the temperature. When it's at 60°C (140°F), take it off the heat; it should
be cooked medium-rare.

Transfer the charred packet to a metal platter and allow to rest for at least 10 minutes.

Tap the packet hard with the back of a large, heavy chef's knife – the burnt shell should
crack and come off. Brush any excess salt off and transfer the meat to a clean platter.
Slice and serve on Potato & Garlic Trencher.

Potato & garlic trencher

Makes 4

Medieval in origin, trenchers were used before plates were commonplace, and if I get my way they will find favour again in grill restaurants.

For the sourdough

750ml (1¼ pints) water

200g (7oz) sourdough starter (either make your own, see below, or, better still, steal one with some maturity)

800g (1lb 12oz) strong white flour

200g (7oz) strong wholewheat flour

20g (¾oz) Maldon sea salt flakes

200g (7oz) beef dripping, with jelly if possible

For the trencher

1 garlic bulb, cloves peeled

2–3 tablespoons olive oil

10 fingerling or Anya potatoes

6 spring onions

50g (1¾oz) butter, melted

2 teaspoons fennel seeds

Maldon sea salt flakes and crushed black pepper

Garlic Butter, to serve (see page 113)

Reserve 50ml (2fl oz) of the water, and pour the rest into a large bowl along with the starter and both flours. Mix until a dough has formed. Place the dough in a large plastic container, cover loosely and leave to rest for 30 minutes – this allows the protein and starch in the dough to properly absorb the water.

Combine the salt and the remaining water together and mix into the dough with your fingers. Cover loosely and set aside to rise at room temperature for 3 hours, still in the plastic container. Every 30 minutes during the 3 hours, turn and fold the dough inside the plastic container, using wet hands.

Liberally grease the base and sides of four 20cm (8 inch) cast-iron skillets or ovenproof frying pans, or two 27 x 37cm (10¾ x 14½ inch) shallow roasting tins, with the beef dripping. Divide the dough into 4 equal pieces and press them down

into the skillets or roasting tins – the dough should be about 2cm (¾ inch) thick. Cover loosely with clingfilm and leave to do the final prove overnight in the fridge.

Preheat the oven to 220°C (425°F), Gas Mark 7 and remove the proved sourdough from the fridge.

Cook the peeled garlic cloves in the olive oil over a medium-low heat until just tender. Cook the potatoes until just tender in boiling salted water and drain. Slice the garlic cloves, potatoes and spring onions and press on to the surface of the bread.

Brush with melted butter, and sprinkle with fennel seeds, salt and crushed black pepper. Bake for 30–35 minutes, until golden brown, then leave to cool on a wire rack while you cook your meat.

When required, place the bread on a charcoal grill or in a hot oven to add a smoky flavour and heat through, then return to a cast-iron dish and dress with a spoonful of melted garlic butter and a spoonful of roast meat juices. Serve sliced grilled meats on top of the trencher to soak up more meat juices.

HOW TO MAKE A STARTER

Making a starter begins by making a culture – this happens when flour and water are combined and wild yeasts and bacteria present in the flour and the air begin to ferment. Once this happens you begin to feed this culture.

First put 200g (7oz) of rye flour into a jar, add an equal weight of tepid bottled water, mix well and cover with muslin. Put the jar somewhere warm and wait. Stir the mixture occasionally. After a few days you should start to see bubbles forming and the mixture beginning to rise or prove. This is your sign that wild yeasts have moved in. If nothing has happened after a week, throw it all out and try again.

After another day or so, once your starter is smelling sweet, bursting with bubbles and puffed up, it will be ready for feeding. Discard at least half of your original mixture before stirring in more flour and water. For a healthy starter, you need to at least double the quantity of culture with each feed, so this time add at least 100g (3½oz) flour and the same weight of water.

Once your starter has proved again, it's ready to use. Take as much as your recipe calls for, then give what's left another good feed and place it in the fridge, where your starter will continue to thrive but will need feeding less often, perhaps once a week.

Reduce your starter before every feed, either by baking with it or simply by throwing some away. This makes for a more vigorous culture, while also keeping the volume under control.

Serves
4

Another incredibly popular barbecue classic from Texas – this time the simplicity of salt and pepper is eschewed for a beef rub and a "slather" – a liquid glaze to brush over it.

Smoked short rib

50g (1¾oz) mustard

50ml (2fl oz) barbecue sauce

50ml (2fl oz) Madeira Gravy
(see page 114)

50g (1¾oz) beef dripping

1.5kg (3lb 5oz) short ribs, sawn in half widthways through the bone

50g (1¾oz) Basic Beef Rub
(see page 40)

You will also need

a meat thermometer

Mix the mustard, barbecue sauce, Madeira Gravy and beef dripping in a pan and bring to a simmer, then remove from the heat and allow to cool slightly. This is your "slather", or mop.

Brush the ribs with half this mixture and dust liberally with the rub, making sure every part is covered. Bang the ribs to remove the excess rub. The rub should seem quite wet now.

Preheat a smoker to 110°C (230°F) according to the manufacturer's instructions and add some lightly soaked oak wood. Place the ribs in the smoker for 8 hours, or until an internal temperature of around 90°C (195°F) is achieved. The inevitable stall will happen, but carry on smoking regardless.

Take the ribs out when they reach 90°C (195°F) – the temperature will continue to rise even after they have been removed from the smoker.

Cut between the ribs into 4 portions and brush with the remaining slather mixture. Place on a charcoal grill to colour the ribs, and serve with a salad of your choice.

Serves 4-6

Barbacoa originated in the Caribbean and is the root of the word "barbecue". It's usually made with a whole cow's head buried in a pit, but even I would struggle to find a whole head, so I've adapted it to suit modern tastes and availability of ingredients. If, however, you did find yourself with a whole head to cook, there are plenty of tasty bits to be rooted out with a bit of persistence. Barbacoa is now associated with Texas 'cue, hence the more Tex-Mex style of garnish.

Barbacoa

4 garlic cloves, finely chopped

2 tablespoons Maldon sea salt flakes

1 tablespoon coarsely ground black pepper

1 tablespoon ground cumin

a pinch of ground cloves

1 teaspoon dried oregano

1kg (2lb 4oz) ox cheek

200ml (7fl oz) Basic Beef Broth (see page 112)

100ml (3½fl oz) Chipotle Ketchup (see page 41)

100g (3½oz) beef dripping

juice of 1 lime

To serve

tortillas

Guacamole (see page 210)

Salsa Mexicana (see page 210)

You will also need

a meat thermometer

Mix the garlic, salt, spices and oregano together to make the rub. Coat the ox cheek with three-quarters of the rub, then cover and leave overnight in the fridge. Set the rest of the rub aside.

Preheat a barbecue or smoker according to the manufacturer's instructions. Smoke the ox cheeks at 110°C (230°F) for 4 hours, until an internal temperature of 90°C (194°F) is reached when the meat is tested with a meat thermometer or until tender and yielding to the touch.

Meanwhile prepare the sauce. In a saucepan bring the Basic Beef Broth, Chipotle Ketchup, beef dripping and lime juice to the boil, then simmer until reduced by half.

Shred the ox cheek just before serving and mix with the reduced sauce, then season with the extra rub and serve with warmed tortillas, Guacamole and Salsa Mexicana.

Guacamole Serves 4

This can be found in supermarket aisles the world over but they all contain preservatives by necessity, so making your own fresh guacamole is infinitely preferable.

1 large avocado

1 ripe tomato

½ red onion, peeled and finely chopped

juice of 1 lime

1 red chilli, deseeded and finely chopped

2 tablespoons chopped coriander

Maldon sea salt flakes

Peel and stone the avocado and chop the flesh into 1cm (½ inch) pieces.

Cut a cross on the underside of the tomato and cover it with boiling water. Leave for 30 seconds to loosen the skin, then peel, deseed and finely chop the flesh. Add to the avocado along with the chopped red onion, lime juice and chilli.

Add the chopped coriander and gently mix to combine. Season to taste and serve immediately.

Salsa Mexicana Serves 4

Freshly made Salsa Mexicana loaded with fresh chillies is ubiquitous in Mexico, and it's eaten for breakfast, lunch and dinner.

4 large ripe tomatoes

4 green chillies

½ red onion, peeled and finely chopped

1 garlic clove, crushed

2 tablespoons chopped coriander

juice of 1 lime

Maldon sea salt flakes

Cut a cross on the underside of the tomatoes, place in a bowl and cover with boiling water. Leave for 30 seconds to loosen the skin and then peel, deseed and finely chop the flesh.

Deseed and finely chop the chillies and mix with the tomatoes, red onion and garlic. Add the chopped coriander and the lime juice and gently mix together. Season to taste and serve immediately.

Serves
10

3–4kg (6½–9lb) brisket, packer or point end cut

70g (2½oz) Maldon sea salt flakes

10g (¼oz) freshly ground black pepper

1 litre (1¾ pints) water

100ml (3½fl oz) cider vinegar

50ml (2fl oz) light muscovado sugar

You will also need

a meat thermometer

Smoked brisket

In Texas, barbecue is about beef, and specifically brisket. Rich in connective tissue, it requires low-and-slow cooking to relax the muscle into melting tenderness – a pleasure that cannot be achieved quickly. In Texas they tend to season with just salt and pepper, which I approve of wholeheartedly, but you can use the Basic Beef Rub on page 40 if you prefer.

Preheat a smoker for indirect cooking at 115°C (240°F) according to the manufacturer's instructions.

Season the brisket heavily all over with the salt and pepper, and place fat side up in your smoker. Leave completely alone for 3 hours.

Combine the water, vinegar and sugar, stirring until the sugar dissolves.

After 3 hours, start periodically checking the colour of the brisket every 30 minutes or so. If it starts looking dry or going too dark, start spraying with a spritz of the vinegar mixture (this is called a gastrique in French cooking).

At 6 hours your brisket will hit "the stall", where it appears to stop cooking when the internal temperature reaches about 70°C (158°F) – this is when the moisture in the beef begins to evaporate, cooling the beef and therefore stalling its cooking progress. This is perfectly normal, so do not worry or do anything different.

Around 9 hours in, the beef should have reached 90°C (195°F). Give it a prod – it should have a wobble. When it reaches 90°C (195°F) the brisket should be removed from the smoker and wrapped in large sheets of greaseproof paper until needed.

The brisket contains 2 separate muscles: the "flat" and the "point". These muscles run in different directions, at a right angle from each other. They can simply be pulled away gently from each another by working your knife, or your fingers, between them. The fat will be so soft that it requires little effort, but be careful, it will be very hot. Now slice against the grain of both the flat and the point.

Smoked brisket is best served in white bread sandwiches with caramelized onions, Texas-style.

Frankfurters originated in Germany, where they were originally made with pork. Later, beef was added and eventually an all-beef version appeared in America. The term "dog" has been used for sausages since the 19th century, when the suspicion that sausage-makers used dog meat was common, and occasionally justified.

Franks or hot dogs

500g (1lb 2oz) aged beef flank

500g (1lb 2oz) aged beef shoulder

125g (4½oz) beef fat

125g (4½oz) bone marrow

15g (½oz) Maldon sea salt flakes

7g pink curing salt (93.75% salt 6.25% nitrate), also called Prague Powder No.1

250g (9oz) crushed ice

10g (1 rounded tablespoon) English mustard powder

2 teaspoons paprika

1 teaspoon ground coriander

1 teaspoon freshly ground white pepper

25g (1oz) dextrose

4 garlic cloves, finely chopped

40g (1½oz) Fermento, (used as a starter culture, it produces an immediate tangy flavour in semi-dry cured sausage – use dried yogurt powder or buttermilk powder if unavailable)

1 teaspoon finely chopped thyme leaves

You will also need

2m (6ft 6 inches) hog casings

a mincer with a sausage stuffer attachment

a meat thermometer

Chop all the meat, beef fat and bone marrow, then cover and place in the freezer for 1–2 hours until partially frozen.

Tip the meat into a food processor and blitz until finely chopped (you may need to do this in batches depending on the size of your processor bowl).

Add the salts and crushed ice, mix well, then freeze again for 1 hour.

Meanwhile, thoroughly wash and dry the food processor bowl and attachments. Soak the hog casings in cold water for about an hour to soften them, and loosen the salt in which they are packed. Place the wide end of the sausage stuffer up against the tap and run cold water through the inside of the casing to remove excess salt.

Mix the remaining ingredients with the meat and return to the freezer with the food processor bowl and blade. When the hot dog mixture has partially frozen, place it in the food processor and purée until it is as smooth as possible (again, you may need to do this in batches).

Cut the hog casing into 2 lengths and tie a small knot in the end of each. Fit the open end over the tip of the sausage stuffer and slide it on until the tip of the stuffer touches the knot – this stops excess air from getting into the casings. Fit the stuffer on to the meat grinder, or according to the manufacturer's instructions, or hold the wide end of the stuffer against or over the opening by hand.

Fill the hopper with the hot dog mixture. Turn the machine on and feed in the meat gradually – the sausage casing will fill and gradually inflate. Smooth out any bumps with your fingers, being careful not to push the stuffing out of the casing, and tie off the open end of the sausage tightly by making a knot in the end.

To form the links, hold the entire casing up by its middle and twist it to form the first 15cm (6 inch) link. Twist at the same intervals, going in opposite directions for each sausage to prevent the links unravelling.

To cook, preheat the smoker to 110°C (230°F) and cook the hot dogs for about 1 hour or until an internal temperature of 60°C (140°F) is reached. Chill in an ice bath and refrigerate until needed.

Butchery

More than two million years ago, early man hammered flint into the oldest-known cutting tools to carve up their kill. This early butchery is thought to have served as a major evolutionary force, as it slowly spread through Africa over the next 700 millennia. It is possible that these stone tools drove early human advancement, creating the conditions required for modern mankind to develop. Later, more sophisticated stone tools – hand-axes and cleavers – marked the next generation of tool technology, and mankind reached a level of communication that allowed these techniques to be taught and passed on. There is compelling evidence that the combined skills of butchery and fire-making were the driving factors for human evolution. To put it another way, we owe it all to the butchers and the cooks...

How beef is butchered

Animals are first broken down into larger sections called primal cuts, or "primals" (not the same as "prime cuts") and some of these can then be portioned into steaks. The carcass is split through the backbone into two sides, and each side is cut between the 12th and 13th ribs into the forequarter and hindquarter. From this point the quarters are usually hung for a minimum of two weeks before being broken down further in a variety of ways, depending on which style of butchery is favoured.

Chuck Taken from the shoulder, chuck contains a variety of muscles including the feather blade. It is sometimes sold as braising steak and is often minced to make burgers because of its almost perfect meat-to-fat ratio of 85:15. It is slightly less tough than the more common stewing steak and so can also be slow-roasted as a tied joint. The butler's steak (or flat iron steak) comes from the blade, and the seven-bone steak from the chuck eye, demonstrating the versatility of the shoulder. Chuck is one of the most economical cuts available. Its deep, rich flavour and toughness make it a prime candidate for marinating or using in braised dishes such as beef stew or pot roast.

Rib area This area of the cow yields ribs (as you might expect), as well as steak cuts. Larger cuts from this section, such as prime rib, are good for roasting, while short ribs (Jacob's ladder) taste their finest when braised. Well-marbled with a good amount of internal and external fat, this cut was usually boned and rolled as it makes the perfect roasting joint, until butchers realized that, if you removed the inner "eye" from its surrounding rib cap and bones, you could create a consistently flavoursome steak, now called the rib-eye. It is best hung for around five weeks, although it is often hung much longer. I prefer it cooked between medium and medium-rare, as this renders the fat a little and makes it more digestible. Prime rib is thicker and has a lower Maillard-to-meat ratio, so it tastes less intense and, because of the conductive effect of the bone, also cooks differently.

Loin area Sirloin sits next to the fillet, divided by the T-bone, and can be cooked on this bone, benefiting an occasionally tricky cut of meat. Steaks such as T-bone, porterhouse and entrecôte come from this area. Today, porterhouse is a premium steak cut, recognized as the first and sometimes second cut of the T-bone towards the thick end, purely to obtain the largest diameter of fillet on the steak. Historically in England, however, a porterhouse was a simple bone-in sirloin. Perplexing, I know – throughout the history of butchery this confusion was and still is commonplace. In the US this area is known as short loin.

Fillet Also coming from the loin area, fillet is one of the most popular but also most expensive cuts, because there is only 4–5kg (9–11lb) in each animal. It is the least used muscle and so is suitable for quick cooking on the grill or frying. It is best eaten medium-rare or raw in Steak Tartare (see page 138) or Carpaccio (see page 132). Chateaubriand, or rump fillet, comes from the thick end of the wedge-shaped fillet. Larger pieces are used for dishes such as Beef Wellington. In the US this cut is known as tenderloin, and is where the filet mignon is located, which is made from the very tip of the pointy end of the tenderloin.

Rump From the back end, or hindquarter, of the animal, rump is a cheaper prime cut than fillet or sirloin, as it's not quite as tender, although it has a better flavour than either sirloin or fillet. Despite its having a bit of chew, some steak aficionados will eat nothing else. Rump is less prone to becoming rancid when hung and it benefits from more ageing than other cuts, to soften the muscle fibres. It is best cooked medium-rare. In the US, rump is known as sirloin and is subdivided into top sirloin (the best quality) and bottom sirloin..

Silverside & topside Cut from the back of the thigh, silverside was traditionally salted and sold as a boiling joint or salt beef. This very lean piece of meat is now most often sold unsalted as a joint for roasting, although it will be tough if not pot-roasted low and slow to well done. Topside is a very lean round inner muscle of the leg and often has a layer of fat tied around it to baste it and help keep it moist while cooking. Much more suited to roasting than silverside, it should be cooked gently, at around 140°C (275°F). In the US, this area is known as round and is the choice for pot roast. Beef round is traditionally where we find cube steak, and cooks also use round to make burgers and jerky.

Oxtail Once discarded with bones and fat, oxtail is one of the most flavoursome and inexpensive cuts of beef. It is most often sold cut into individual vertebrae. Considered as offal, it will benefit from long and slow braising to release the excellent rich flavour, rewarding you with well-flavoured gravy and gelatinous meat.

Thick flank Also known as top rump, this cut comes from immediately above the hindquarter leg and is good for slow-roasting or braising. Leaner parts can be used for flash-frying or stir-frying, or in burger blends. When boned out, this cut will make a good salt beef. It is also great for quick fire dishes such as Fajitas (see page 33) and is popular in London Broils.

Leg or shin Often sold as braising steak, beef leg or beef shank, this is best suited to long, slow cooking in order to break down the connective tissues and dense fibres. Use it for stews and casseroles. It's extremely tough and full of connective tissue and so is mostly used for making stock, soups and stews.

Thin rib One of the denser forequarter cuts, thin rib is usually sold as minced (ground) beef.

Brisket From the lower chest area, brisket is suitable for slow-cooking or pot-roasting and is the go-to cut for an army of barbecue smokers. It is the cut that is traditionally cured and turned into pastrami, salt beef and corned beef, and it is also used for lean minced (ground) beef. Brisket is another tough cut commonly seen in pot roasts and on the barbecue. Slow-cooking methods are the way to go with brisket, because low and slow allows the meat to become extra tender.

Clod & sticking, or neck From the middle of the shoulder, this economical cut is rich and flavourful but less tender. Usually it is sold as stewing steak or used in burgers. It is also suitable for slow-cooking in braises.

Cheek or jowl This great cut is similar in flavour to oxtail. It is most often used in braises such as Daube de Boeuf (see page 262), but could also be smoked low and slow and then sliced by a skilled live fire cook. Tough and flavourful, it is well suited to heavy marinating and braising.

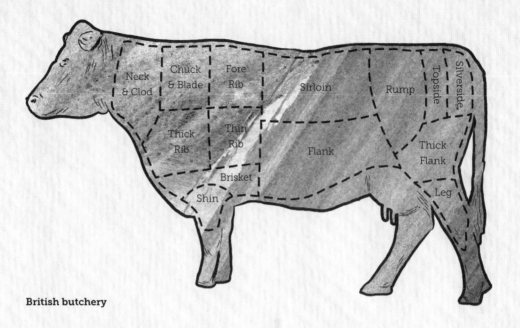

British butchery

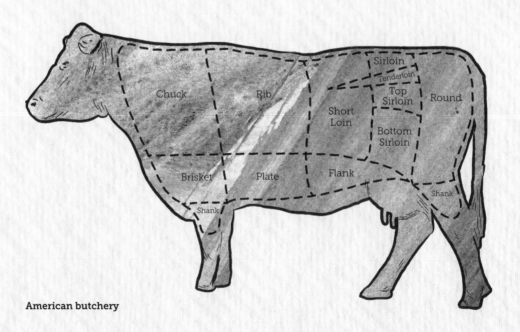

American butchery

How to cut steaks

If you've stored your steak as described on page 195, you will, of course, need to cut it into steaks. To do this, you will need a large, clean chopping board, a clean tea towel and a sharp, curved 25cm (10 inch) butcher's knife. You cannot cut steak well with a straight-bladed chef's knife, as the blade will not contact the chopping board at the proper angle. A butcher's knife needs to be very sharp – a sharp knife is less likely to cut you than a dull one, as you will not have to use undue force to cut with it. Butcher's knives are dangerous, and common sense is key. The knife, the meat and the chopping board should all be dry.

A common mistake is to put the meat on the block with the fat on top, thinking it looks "right side up", but that is incorrect. The fat is much harder and denser than the meat, so it needs to be on the bottom, with the softer meat exposed. If the fat is on the top, you need to exert more effort to get the knife through it, and the meat suffers (is compressed) underneath. When the meat is on the top, the knife glides into it with the hard fat supporting it, and you can then press the knife into the fat at the end of the cut, and get a clean edge against the board.

To begin cutting the steaks, place the knife at the top of the meat and lean over the top of it. You will see the meat curving away from the knife, and you'll also be at the perfect angle to check whether the cut is straight. Press the knife forward into the meat, trying not to saw. You may have to cut in a very slight fan pattern in order to make up for the natural shape of the meat.

Always clean as you go – both your board and your knife – and have a clean tray and butcher's paper or peach paper ready to receive the cut steaks as you work.

How to store cut steaks

Steak keeps best in whole pieces, but once cut it can be stored for a short time in trays at around 5°C (41°F). Individual steaks should be layered with butcher's paper or peach paper, with clingfilm over the top of the last paper. They can then be stored in the refrigerator. It's important to note that steak does not continue to "age" once butchered and portioned, and after a couple of days it will start to deteriorate.

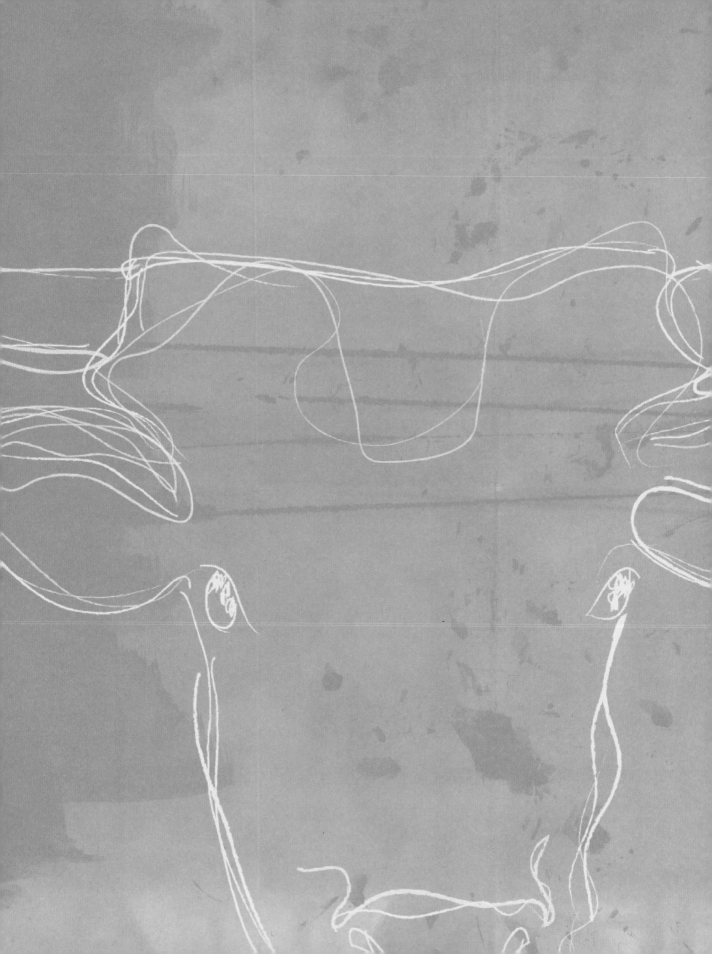

7 Braised

"Boiled beef and carrots,
Boiled beef and carrots,
That's the stuff for your 'Derby Kell',
Makes you fit and keeps you well.
Don't live like vegetarians
On food they give to parrots,
Blow out your kite, from Morn 'til night,
On boiled beef and carrots."

A comedic music hall song from the early 1900s extolling the virtues of this typically Cockney English dish.

Boiled beef & carrots

1kg (2lb 4oz) joint of silverside beef

1.5 litres (2¾ pints) Basic Beef Broth (see page 112)

2 carrots

1 leek, trimmed

1 onion, peeled

2–3 turnips, peeled

1 faggot of herbs (bay, thyme and rosemary)

1 spice bag (1 star anise, 1 teaspoon fennel seeds, 10 black peppercorns and 2 cloves)

1 x recipe Bone Marrow Dumplings (see page 222)

12 baby turnips, tops trimmed

12 baby carrots, tops trimmed

12 baby leeks, trimmed

Maldon sea salt flakes and freshly ground black pepper

Place the beef in a large pan and just cover with cold water. Bring it quickly to a simmer, then, using a ladle, skim off any scum that rises to the top. As you are doing this, you will also be removing some of the water. Pour in the beef broth and return it to a simmer.

Meanwhile, roughly chop the stock vegetables, then add them to the pan with the faggot of herbs and the spice bag and season lightly. Simmer the beef for about 2 hours, until the meat feels tender when pierced with a sharp knife. If the stock reduces too much, top it up with more water so the meat remains submerged.

When the beef is cooked, remove it from the pan and keep warm. Strain the cooking liquor into a clean pan and bring to a simmer. Add the dumplings, cover and simmer for 20 minutes, then uncover and cook for a final 10 minutes. Remove from the pan with a slotted spoon and keep warm. Add the baby vegetables and cook for about 3 minutes, until tender.

Slice the beef and season lightly. Serve in warmed bowls with the baby vegetables and dumplings. Strain the stock and pour over to serve.

Bone marrow dumplings

Makes 12

I use these in stews, where they suck up the stock or gravy to make intense gooey balls with a crunchy top. The addition of bone marrow (a superfood – no, really!) ramps up the beefiness of any dish.

250g (9oz) self-raising flour

75g (2¾oz) chilled butter

75g (2¾oz) chilled bone marrow

Maldon sea salt flakes and freshly ground black pepper

Place the flour in a mixing bowl. Using a coarse grater, grate the cold butter and bone marrow into the flour and season liberally. Using your fingers, gently rub the butter and bone marrow into the flour until it begins to resemble breadcrumbs. Add a little of the gravy from your stew (or Basic beef Broth, see page 112) to help bind it into a dough.

Divide the dough into 12 pieces and gently roll each one into a round dumpling.

Place the dumplings on top of your cooked stew, casserole or braise, and press them down lightly so that they're half submerged.

Cook in the oven or on the hob, over a medium heat with the lid on, for 20 minutes, then remove the lid and cook for a further 10 minutes.

Serves
4-6

Literally translated as "Beef Burgundy", bourguignon is a much-abused dish that is rather delightful if good-quality ingredients are used and shortcuts eschewed. Contrary to what many cooks might tell you, cheap wine is better drunk than cooked with, and this dish will succeed or fail upon the standard of wine used, though perhaps a Grand Cru isn't necessary.

Beef bourguignon

100g (3½oz) smoked bacon lardons, cut 1cm (½ inch) thick

1 rounded tablespoon plain flour

1kg (2lb 4oz) chuck steak, cut into 4cm (1½ inch) chunks

50g (1¾oz) beef dripping

20 button onions, peeled

20 button mushrooms

3 garlic cloves, crushed

1 faggot of herbs (bay, thyme and rosemary)

75cl bottle of good red Burgundy

250ml (9fl oz) Basic Beef Broth (see page 112)

Maldon sea salt flakes and freshly ground black pepper

Fry the bacon lardons until crispy in a heavy-based casserole over a medium-high heat, then remove to a plate, leaving behind the rendered bacon fat.

Mix the plain flour with plenty of salt and freshly ground black pepper. Toss the beef in the seasoned flour. Add half the dripping to the same casserole and, when melted, add half the flour-coated beef.

Colour the beef in the hot pan, browning the meat generously – this is crucial. Then, using a slotted spoon, remove the beef to the plate with the bacon. Add the remaining dripping and beef and brown as before, then transfer to the plate with the rest of the beef and bacon.

Add the onions to the pan and brown them lightly. Add the mushrooms, cook until golden, then remove both the onions and mushrooms to another plate.

Return the beef and bacon lardons to the casserole with the garlic, the faggot of herbs, the wine and the beef broth. Season, then cover and simmer gently over a low heat or in a low oven (preheated to 140°C/275°F/Gas Mark 1) for a good 1½ hours, until the meat is tender. This is not a recipe to hurry.

Add the onions and mushrooms to the pan and continue cooking for a further 30 minutes. Bourguignon improves if kept, so if you can make it the day before, all the better. Serve with noodles, mash or, even better, La Macaronade (see page 316).

A classic northern Italian stew closely related to the French Pot au Feu (see page 226). The resulting stock can be used to make soup or risotto. Mostarda di Cremona are mustard-spiced candied fruits available from Italian delis and even some supermarkets.

Bollito misto with salsa verde

1 whole calf's tongue

3 litres (5 pints) water

50ml (2fl oz) red wine vinegar

3 carrots, halved lengthways

2 celery sticks, halved

1 onion, peeled

4 cloves

1 faggot of herbs (thyme, rosemary and 2 bay leaves)

1 veal shank, about 2kg (4lb 8oz)

1 beef brisket, about 1.5kg (3lb 5oz)

2 beef cheeks

4 beef sausages

Mostarda di Cremona and freshly grated horseradish, to serve

For the salsa verde

a handful of parsley leaves

a handful of mint leaves

a few basil leaves

1 garlic clove

1 tablespoon capers

3 anchovy fillets

extra virgin olive oil

1 tablespoon red wine vinegar

1 tablespoon Dijon mustard

Maldon sea salt flakes and freshly ground black pepper

Blanch the tongue by covering it with boiling water and simmering for 30 minutes. Drain, cool, then peel off the outer skin and membrane.

Pour the water into a large casserole and add the vinegar, carrots and celery. Stick the onion with the cloves and add to the pan with the faggot of herbs and the veal shank. Place over a medium heat and bring to the boil, then reduce the heat and simmer for 30 minutes.

Add the brisket, beef cheeks, sausages and tongue and simmer for another hour. Remove each piece of meat and arrange on a platter.

To make the salsa verde, finely chop the herbs, garlic, capers and anchovies. Combine in a bowl and add enough extra virgin olive oil to loosen the mixture. Add the vinegar and mustard, and season with salt and freshly ground black pepper.

Thinly carve the meat and serve with Mostarda di Cremona, sea salt, the Salsa Verde and freshly grated horseradish.

1kg (2lb 4oz) beef brisket

1kg (2lb 4oz) beef shin

1kg (2lb 4oz) veal shank

500g (1lb 2oz) bone marrow shafts, cut into 8cm (3¼ inch) pieces (ask your butcher to do this)

2 onions, peeled and halved

2 large carrots, halved

1 faggot of herbs (bay leaves, thyme and parsley)

1 teaspoon Maldon sea salt flakes

a few black peppercorns

1 Morteau sausage

For the vegetables

6 carrots

6 medium-small parsnips, peeled

6 leeks

3 celery hearts

18 waxy potatoes, such as Charlotte, peeled

3 onions, peeled and halved

To serve

plenty of toasted sourdough

freshly grated nutmeg

pickled gherkins

Dijon mustard

Creamed Horseradish (see opposite)

Pot au feu

Traditionally, the broth is served first with a bit of nutmeg and the bone marrow, spread on toasted bread. Then the meat and the vegetables are served with coarse salt and strong Dijon mustard, horseradish sauce and pickled cornichons. This strikes me as an entirely civilized way to approach such a dish, and is why we owe so much to the French in terms of gastronomy: they just know how to eat. It is very hard to make this dish in domestic quantities, so I suggest making a large batch and working through it over a week. It keeps well in the fridge.

Place all the meats and the beef marrow bones in a large saucepan. Cover with cold water, then very slowly bring to a simmer and cook for 15 minutes, skimming all the time. Add the onions, carrots, the faggot of herbs, salt and peppercorns, return to a simmer, partly cover and cook gently for 2 hours.

Add the Morteau sausage and cook for a further hour, until everything is tender. Allow to cool and refrigerate overnight.

The next day, remove the fat from the top and discard the onions, carrots and faggot of herbs. Carefully strain off the broth through muslin into a large, clean pan, then place back over a medium heat and bring to a simmer.

Morteau sausage is a strong-flavoured French smoked sausage.

While the stock is reheating, prepare the vegetables to serve. Trim the carrots and parsnips, leaving them whole. Cut a thin slice from the base of the leeks and trim the tops, then remove the coarse outer leaves, wash thoroughly and split. Trim the celery hearts and cut into quarters through the root. Add all the vegetables to the pot and cook in the broth for 25 minutes, until tender.

Slice the brisket and sausage, pull the meat off the veal shank and beef shin and heat in the broth.

Serve the broth in bowls alongside a pile of toasted sourdough and the bone marrow for spreading. Arrange the meats and vegetables on a platter. Spoon over some broth to moisten, and serve with a grating of nutmeg, pickled gherkins, mustard, Creamed Horseradish and sea salt flakes.

This recipe depends entirely on the quality of the horseradish used. If you can find it growing wild – and it's not uncommon – then all the better. An obvious partner for roast beef hot or cold, it's also great with grilled steak, tongue or wherever a little fortitude is called for.

Creamed horseradish Makes 500ml (18fl oz)

125g (4½oz) fresh horseradish, wild for preference

1 teaspoon Maldon sea salt flakes

25g (1oz) caster sugar

125ml (4fl oz) organic cider vinegar, Braggs for preference

250g (9oz) crème fraîche

Grate the horseradish very finely indeed and mix with the salt, sugar and vinegar. Cover and allow to steep in the fridge for a few hours or overnight, the longer the better.

Remove from the fridge and squeeze out all the vinegar into a bowl, using a damp cloth such as a tea towel or double thickness muslin, taking care not to lose any – the more you can extract, the better the sauce. Once squeezed bone dry, you can discard the horseradish pulp.

Using a small food mixer, or by hand with a whisk, whip the crème fraîche with the infused vinegar until light and fluffy.

An American pot roast is a beauteous thing. A variation on the French dish *boeuf à la mode*, it is a great way to prepare a tougher cut of beef. The dish is prepared by first browning the beef in meat fat, and then half braising and half roasting in a liquid composed primarily of red wine, with garlic and root vegetables.

Pot roast

2kg (4lb 8oz) beef brisket

250ml (9fl oz) red wine

25g (1oz) beef dripping

3 large onions, peeled and sliced

6 garlic cloves, crushed

1 litre (1¾ pints) Basic Beef Broth (see page 112)

1 faggot of herbs (thyme, rosemary and bay leaf)

3 large carrots, cut into 4cm (1½ inch) chunks

1 tablespoon mustard (optional)

Maldon sea salt flakes and freshly ground black pepper

Onion Gravy (see page 115)

Mashed Potatoes (see pages 61 and 111), to serve

To prepare the brisket, using a sharp knife, score the fat in parallel lines, about 2cm (¾ inch) apart, and repeat in the opposite direction to make a criss-cross pattern. Season well, place in a bowl, then pour the wine over the top and let the meat sit at room temperature for 1 hour.

Preheat the oven to 150°C (300°F), Gas Mark 2.

Heat the beef dripping in a large casserole, then pat the brisket dry (reserving the wine) and brown it gently, fatty side down, over a medium-high heat. When the fat side is nicely browned, turn the brisket over and cook for a few more minutes to brown the other side.

Remove the brisket from the casserole and reserve. Add the sliced onions to the residue of rendered fat and sauté until they are lightly browned, then stir in the garlic and cook for a few more minutes.

Move the onions and garlic to the sides of the pot and nestle the brisket inside. Add the reserved wine, then the beef broth and the faggot of herbs. Season well, bring the broth to a simmer, then cover and place in the oven for 3 hours. Carefully turn the brisket halfway through, so that it cooks evenly.

After 3 hours, add the carrots and cook for another hour or until they are cooked through and the brisket is tender. Take the pot out of the oven, remove the brisket to a chopping board and cover it with foil. Take out and discard the herbs.

Skim the cooking liquor to remove all the fat and return to a gentle simmer, skimming constantly. Taste and correct the seasoning, adding the mustard, if using. Notice the lines of the muscle fibres of the roast: this is the "grain" of the meat. Slice across this grain in 1cm (½ inch) slices. Serve with the carrots, Onion Gravy and Mashed Potatoes.

Serves
4-6

A pared-down, luxury version of Pot au Feu (see page 226) with just one piece of meat, a fillet of beef, tied with a length of butcher's string long enough to grab, so that you can pull the beef from the broth and rightly call the dish "à la ficelle".

Fillet of beef "à la ficelle"

2 litres (3½ pints) Basic Beef Broth
(see page 112)

6 small potatoes, peeled and halved

6 small turnips, trimmed, peeled and halved

6 carrots, cut lengthways into 3

6 celery sticks, trimmed and cut into
5cm (2 inch) pieces

6 baby leeks, trimmed

6 shallots, peeled and halved

1kg (2lb 4oz) fillet steak barrel, tied at 5cm
(2 inch) intervals, with long strings attached

To serve

Pommery Meaux mustard

Creamed Horseradish (see page 227)

Maldon sea salt flakes and freshly
ground black pepper

Bring the beef broth to the boil in a pot large enough to fit the meat. Reduce the heat to a simmer and add the potatoes, turnips, carrots, and celery. After 8 minutes, add the leeks and shallots and cook for a further 8 minutes. When the vegetables are tender, lift them out of the broth and into a large bowl. Cover and set aside while you poach the beef.

Drop the beef into the simmering broth, tying the string loosely to the pot's handle, and poach for 10 minutes – it will be rare in the centre. Pull the beef from the pot using the string and transfer to a plate, then cover and leave to rest for 10 minutes.

Meanwhile, reheat the vegetables in the broth. Cut the beef into slices about 2cm (¾ inch) thick. For each portion, put 2 slices of beef in the centre of a shallow soup plate, surround it with some poached vegetables, and moisten with hot broth. Serve with Maldon sea salt flakes, a black pepper mill, Meaux mustard and Creamed Horseradish on the side, so you can season your own dish.

The best-known version of ossobuco hails from Milan, where it is served with saffron risotto, also made with bone marrow. Traditionally accompanied by gremolata – a chopped herb condiment classically made with lemon zest, garlic and parsley – here I've taken the small liberty of using orange instead. If you are Italian you've probably just thrown this book out of the window...

Ossobuco Milanese

1 small whole rose veal shank, around 2kg (4lb 8oz)

2–3 tablespoons plain flour seasoned with salt and pepper

75g (2¾oz) beef dripping

50g (1¾oz) bone marrow, chopped

1 onion, peeled and chopped

1 carrot, chopped

1 celery stick, chopped

1 garlic bulb, halved

pared zest and juice of 1 orange

4 sage leaves

300ml (½ pint) white wine

4 plum tomatoes, blanched, peeled and chopped, or 400g (14oz) can chopped tomatoes

300ml (½ pint) veal or chicken stock

Maldon sea salt and freshly ground black pepper

Risotto Milanese (see page 236), to serve

For the gremolata

finely grated zest and juice of 1 small orange

1 garlic clove, very finely chopped

½ bunch (about 15g/½ oz) of flat leaf parsley, finely chopped

Combine all the gremolata ingredients together and set aside.

Coat the veal shank in seasoned flour, then melt the beef dripping in a large heavy-based pan until hot and brown the veal shank well on all sides until golden and crusted. Set aside on a plate.

Reduce the heat and add the bone marrow to the pan. When melted, add the onion, carrot and celery, plus a sprinkle of salt, and cook until soft. Add the garlic halves, orange zest and sage and cook for a few minutes more.

Increase the heat and add the wine, chopped tomatoes and orange juice to the pan. Return the meat, standing it on top of the vegetables, and bubble until the wine has reduced by half. Pour in the stock and bring to a simmer.

Reduce the heat to its lowest, cover and simmer for 2 hours, carefully turning the meat over every 30 minutes or so, until it is tender enough to cut with a spoon. This can also be cooked in a 140°C (275°F), Gas Mark 1 oven. Serve with the gremolata and Risotto Milanese.

Risotto Milanese Serves 4

50g (1¾oz) butter

½ onion, finely chopped

1 litre (1¾ pints) Basic Beef Broth (see page 112)

pinch of saffron threads

350–400g (12–14oz) Carnaroli or Arborio rice

100ml (3½fl oz) white wine

50g (1¾oz) bone marrow, chopped

60g (2¼oz) Parmesan cheese, finely grated

50ml (2fl oz) double cream, lightly whipped

Maldon sea salt flakes

Melt half the butter in a large heavy-based saucepan and add the onion. Cook over a gentle heat until the onion is soft without taking on any colour.

Pour the broth into another saucepan and bring to the boil. Add the saffron, reduce the heat and keep it at a simmer.

Add the rice to the onion and stir until the rice looks glossy.

Pour the wine over the rice and onion and stir until it has almost completely been absorbed by the rice. Start adding the saffron broth a ladleful at a time, stirring constantly, only adding more once each ladle has been absorbed. It will take about 20 minutes to stir in all the liquid and for the risotto to cook – it should be soft and creamy but there should be a very slight bite in the centre of each grain.

Once all the broth has been absorbed, stir in the remaining butter, the bone marrow, Parmesan and lightly whipped cream and season to taste.

Although somewhat dated, *Le Repertoire de La Cuisine* (published in 1914) has proved invaluable over the years as a guide to a thousand flamboyant and occasionally extravagant dishes that can easily be updated or reinterpreted by a lively-minded cook. I've adapted this example of the gems that lie inside its pages – and note that there's not a tomato in sight.

French spaghetti bolognese

400g (14oz) fresh spaghetti

50g (1¾oz) unsalted butter

50ml (2fl oz) double cream

50g (1¾oz) Parmesan cheese, finely grated

1 onion, peeled and chopped

2–3 tablespoons olive oil

300ml (½ pint) Basic Beef Broth (see page 112)

1 small faggot of herbs (thyme, bay, rosemary)

400g (14oz) beef fillet, sliced 1cm (½ inch) thick

Maldon sea salt flakes and freshly ground black pepper

Cook the spaghetti in boiling salted water until al dente. Drain, taking care to keep a ladle of the cooking water, then tip the spaghetti back into the hot pan. Season, add the butter, cream and grated cheese and toss until the spaghetti is coated in a creamy sauce, adding the cooking water to loosen if necessary.

Fry the chopped onion in 1 tablespoon of the olive oil, then add the beef broth and the faggot of herbs. Bring to the boil and simmer until the broth has reduced by half.

Season the slices of beef fillet, then sear in the rest of the olive oil in a smoking-hot frying pan. Remove the pan from the heat and pour the hot sauce over the top to finish cooking, removing the faggot of herbs.

Pile the creamy spaghetti on to plates, place the fillet slices on top and serve with the beef sauce on the side.

Serves
4

Two things separate my spag bol from the thousands of versions out there. For one, I don't use spaghetti! Flat pasta is much better suited to meat sauces, so it's flat pasta that I use. Second, I toss my cooked pasta in a Parmesan and butter emulsion, creating a separate sauce around it, before topping it with the sauce. The result is the finest spag bol known to man, the kind that'll get you laid if you cook it for your date.

My spag bol

100g (3½oz) pancetta, chopped

1 large onion, peeled and chopped

1 carrot, chopped

1 celery stick, chopped

2 garlic cloves, crushed

500g (1lb 2oz) minced beef

250ml (9fl oz) red wine

400g (14oz) chopped ripe tomatoes (canned are fine)

1 bay leaf

500g (1lb 2oz) dried tagliatelle or pappardelle

100g (3½oz) Parmesan cheese, freshly grated

50g (1¾oz) grass-fed butter

Maldon sea salt flakes and freshly ground black pepper

4 basil sprigs, to garnish

Fry the pancetta over a medium heat until golden, using its own rendered fat. Add the onion, carrot and celery and fry until softened. Add the garlic and cook for a further minute, then increase the heat and add the minced beef. Fry the beef until browned, then pour in the wine, bring to the boil and cook until reduced by half. Reduce the heat under the pan, then stir in the tomatoes and bay leaf.

Season, then cover with a lid and simmer over a gentle heat for 2 hours, until the sauce is rich and thick, stirring occasionally.

Cook the pasta in plenty of boiling salted water, then partially drain, keeping at least a ladle of the cooking liquid. Toss the pasta with half the grated Parmesan, the butter and a little of the pasta cooking water, to form an emulsified sauce. Divide the pasta between plates and pour a ladle of sauce over the top (remove the bay leaf). Finish with a further scattering of cheese, a twist of black pepper and a basil sprig.

Serves
4

Today's beef stroganoff bears only a passing resemblance to the dish I enjoyed in Russia some years ago, not least because it seems to have developed a new spelling. My recipe is more akin to the original, a simpler affair served with fried potatoes, not rice. For those among you with working Russian, the original recipe is here:

Говядина по-строгоновски, съ горчицею. За два часа до приготовления взять кусокъ мягкой говядины, нарезать ее, сырую, маленькими квадратиками, посыпать солью и несколько перцомъ. Передъ обедомъ взять пол-осьмушки сливочнаго масла и ложку муки, размешать, поджарить слегка, развести двумя стаканами бульона, прокипятить, положить чайную ложку готовой сарептской горчицы, немного перцу, размешать, прокипятить, процедить. Передъ отпускомъ положить 2 столовые ложки самой свежей сметаны и ложку прожаренного уже томата. На сильномъ огне поджарить говядину с масломъ и лукомъ, положить ее въ соусъ, накрыть плотно крышкою, поставить на ¼ часа на край плиты, вскипятить, подавать.

Выдать: 3 фун. мягкой говядины, соли. 10-15 з. англ. перца, ¼ ф. масла. 1 ложку муки, 2 стол. ложки сметаны. Чайную ложку сарептской горчицы. 1 ложку томата.

Beef a la stroganov

600g (1lb 5oz) lean rump or sirloin steak, cut into 2cm (¾ inch) cubes

50g (1¾oz) plain flour seasoned with salt and pepper

50g (1¾oz) unsalted butter

100ml (3½fl oz) soured cream

50g (1¾oz) Dijon mustard

100ml (3½fl oz) Basic Beef Broth (see page 112)

Maldon sea salt flakes and freshly ground black pepper

fried straw potatoes or fries, to serve

Season the steak cubes with salt and pepper, then toss in the seasoned flour and shake off any excess.

Heat a nonstick pan over a medium high heat, add half the butter and fry the beef in batches, until browned.

Return all the beef to the pan and add the soured cream, mustard and beef broth. Cook until the sauce coats the meat, then correct the seasoning and serve with the fried potatoes, not rice.

Serves
4

2 litres (3½ pints) hot water

30g (1oz) packet of dried kombu seaweed

8 shiitake mushrooms, stems removed

½ Chinese cabbage, washed

1 carrot

100g (3½oz) enoki mushrooms, trimmed

500g (1lb 2oz) sirloin steak

350g (12oz) block of firm tofu

pon shabu sauce (a citrus soy, available from specialist shops or online)

4 portions of udon noodles, around 100g (3½oz) dry weight per person

Shabu-shabu

Based on the Chinese hotpot, shabu-shabu was first named in the restaurant Suehiro in Osaka, and is made by submerging thin slices of sirloin or rib-eye in a pot of boiling dashi broth made with kombu. Once the meat and vegetables have been eaten, the leftover broth from the pot is combined with noodles and the resulting soup is usually eaten last.

Pour the hot water into a large pot, then add the kombu and place over a low heat. Cut the shiitake mushrooms, Chinese cabbage and carrot into small thin slices and trim the enoki mushrooms. Cut the meat into small thin slices and the tofu into 2cm (¾ inch) cubes.

Before the pot of water comes to the boil, remove the kombu. Using chopsticks, dip the meat and vegetables into the hot stock to cook, then dip in pon shabu sauce and eat. Everyone eating should cook their own, so a tabletop burner or electric pan is useful here, to keep the broth at a bare simmer.

At the end of the meal, add the udon noodles to the remaining broth and allow to cook for a few minutes before finishing the meal by eating the noodles and broth.

Serves
4

There are two ways to make this Japanese hotpot-style dish – Eastern, and Western. Here in the Western, or Kansai, style, the meat is cooked first, then the sauces are added. The Eastern style is to add the sauces first.

Sukiyaki

500g (1lb 2oz) rump steak, thinly sliced into 4cm (1½ inch) squares

250g (9oz) packet of shirataki noodles, washed and drained, cut into 10cm (4 inch) lengths

8 shiitake mushrooms, stems removed

100g (3½oz) enoki mushrooms, trimmed

bunch of spring onions, cut into 4cm (1½ inch) lengths

½ Chinese cabbage, washed and cut into 4cm (1½ inch) wide pieces

150g (5½oz) piece of *yaki-dofu* (grilled tofu), cut into bite-sized pieces

100g (3½oz) *shungiku* (chrysanthemum greens), washed and cut into 4cm (1½ inch) lengths

1 tablespoon flavourless oil, such as vegetable oil

For the sukiyaki sauce

80ml (2½fl oz) soy sauce

30ml (1fl oz) sake

30g (1oz) sugar

150ml (¼ pint) water

For dipping

4 pasteurized free-range eggs, beaten

Arrange all the ingredients, except the oil, on a large plate and place the plate on the table. Mix the soy sauce, sake, sugar and water to make sukiyaki sauce. Set an electric pan or a skillet on the table.

Heat the oil in the pan and fry some beef slices, then pour the sukiyaki sauce into the pan. Add the other ingredients when the sauce starts to boil and simmer until everything has softened.

Pick pieces from the pan with chopsticks and dip in the raw egg before eating.

MOO

Yaki-dofu and *shungiku* can be bought in Asian food stores and markets or online.

Serves 4-6

50g (1¾oz) unsalted butter

1kg (2lb 4oz) chuck steak,
cut into 4cm (1½ inch) cubes

2 onions, sliced

3 garlic cloves, crushed

50g (1¾oz) Madras curry powder

600ml (1 pint) Basic Beef Broth
(see page 112)

50g (1¾oz) desiccated coconut

100g (3½oz) sultanas

2 ripe tomatoes, peeled,
deseeded and chopped

Maldon sea salt flakes and freshly
ground black pepper

To serve

Bombay duck (optional, see below)

apple chutney

finely chopped onion

finely chopped fresh mint
and coriander leaves

sliced bananas

coconut chips or flakes

poppadoms

steamed rice

British Army beef curry

We all love a curry; I have very fond memories of the cans of beef curry that used to be bartered and exchanged with vigour in the British Army. The dish most of us know is made from a commercially prepared mixture of spices dating back to the 18th century. Thought to have originally been prepared by Indian merchants for sale to members of the colonial British Army, no Indian chef worth his salt would entertain using such a curry powder. It is, however, still a delicious preparation.

Melt the butter in a large, sturdy pan over a medium heat. Season the beef and fry for a few minutes until browned all over, then add the onions and garlic and fry for 5 minutes, or until softened and golden brown. Stir in the curry powder and cook for 1 minute.

Add the broth, followed by the coconut and sultanas. Bring to a simmer, then cover and cook over a low heat, or in an oven preheated to 120°C (250°F), Gas Mark ½ for at least 1½ hours, or until the beef is tender.

Stir in the tomatoes and serve with grated Bombay duck (if using), apple chutney, chopped onion, mint and coriander, sliced bananas, grated coconut, poppadoms and rice.

MOO

Bombay duck is a dried fish
that is often grated over curry.
If you can't source it simply
leave it out.

Influenced by its neighbours India and China, a good Burmese beef curry is characterized by the inclusion of both pumpkin and potato and is flavoured with plenty of ginger. The Burmese eat with their right hand, forming the rice into a small ball with only the fingertips and mixing this with the curry before popping it into their mouths. If served with noodles, chopsticks should be used.

Burmese beef curry

1kg (2lb 4oz) chuck steak

2 large onions, peeled

small bunch (about 30g/1oz) of coriander, leaves picked

2.5cm (1 inch) piece of fresh root ginger, peeled and roughly chopped

2 large garlic cloves

2 red chillies, deseeded and roughly chopped

1 teaspoon ground cumin

1 teaspoon ground coriander

1 teaspoon ground turmeric

4 tablespoons sunflower oil

350g (12oz) Maris Piper potatoes, peeled and quartered

500ml (18fl oz) Basic Beef Broth (see page 112)

350g (12oz) pumpkin, peeled and cut into 3cm (1¼ inch) chunks

juice of ½ lime

Maldon sea salt flakes and freshly ground black pepper

cooked rice noodles, or rice, to serve

Trim any excess fat from the meat and cut into 3cm (1¼ inch) pieces.

Chop the onions, then put into a blender with the coriander leaves, ginger, garlic, chillies, cumin, coriander, turmeric and 1 tablespoon of oil and blend to a smooth paste.

Add the paste to the meat and mix well to thoroughly coat each piece, then cover and leave in the fridge to marinate for 2 hours.

Heat half the remaining oil (1½ tablespoons) in a wok or heavy-based frying pan. Add half the meat and, stirring frequently, fry until evenly browned. Remove from the pan and set aside, then add the remaining oil and meat to the pan and fry until brown. Remove the meat from the pan and set aside while you stir-fry the potatoes for another few minutes in the same pan. Set aside.

Return the meat to the pan, add the broth, stir well and bring to the boil. Reduce the heat, cover the pan and cook gently for 45 minutes. Add the potato and pumpkin and cook for a further 45 minutes, or until the meat and vegetables are tender. Taste, add a squeeze of lime juice and correct the seasoning. Serve with rice noodles or rice.

A caramelized curry dish from West Sumatra in Indonesia, reckoned to be one of the most delicious beef dishes on the planet by a CNN poll. Originally used as a method of preserving excess quantities of meat, this dish has spread throughout Asia due to the migrating culture of its originators, the Minangkabau.

Beef rendang

1kg (2lb 4oz) chuck steak

50g (1¾oz) beef dripping

2 cinnamon sticks

2 cloves

2 star anise

50g (1¾oz) desiccated coconut, toasted

500ml (18fl oz) coconut water (the kind sold fresh for drinking)

1 tablespoon tamarind paste

1 tablespoon fish sauce

1 tablespoon kecap manis or light soy sauce

2 kaffir lime leaves

250ml (9fl oz) Basic Beef Broth (see page 112)

juice of 1 lime

Maldon sea salt flakes and freshly ground black pepper

For the spice paste

100g (3½oz) shallots, peeled

1 garlic bulb, cloves peeled

50g (1¾oz) fresh root galangal, peeled

50g (1¾oz) fresh root ginger, peeled

3 red chillies

3 lemon grass stalks

50ml (2fl oz) water

For the coconut rice

300g (10½oz) basmati rice

700ml (1¼ pints) coconut water (the kind sold fresh for drinking)

First make the spice paste. Roughly chop the shallots, garlic, galangal, ginger, chillies and lemon grass, then place all the ingredients in a food processor and pulse, adding the water to make a fine paste. Set aside.

Cut the beef into 4cm (1½ inch) chunks. Heat a heavy-based pan over a medium heat and add half the dripping. Add the beef, in batches if necessary, and cook on all sides until browned, then remove from the pan and set aside. Add the remaining dripping and the spice paste and fry for 2 minutes, then add the cinnamon, cloves and star anise and cook for a further 2 minutes.

Return the browned beef to the pan, along with the toasted desiccated coconut. Stir well, then add the coconut water, tamarind paste, fish and soy sauces, lime leaves and beef broth and bring to the boil. Reduce the heat to a bare simmer, stirring regularly to make sure it doesn't stick. Cover with a lid and cook gently for 1½ hours, or until the meat is tender.

To make the coconut rice, place the rice and coconut water in a heavy-based pan over a medium heat and bring to the boil. Reduce the heat to a simmer, then cover and cook for 15 minutes. Remove from the heat and allow to stand for a few minutes before serving.

Meanwhile, remove the lid from the beef and cook for a further 15 minutes, until just thickened. Add the lime juice, season with salt and pepper and serve with the coconut rice.

Steamed meat puddings are traditional British comfort food at its best. Save this for when the evenings are closing in and there's a chill in the air. The first recipe for steak and kidney pudding appeared in a book by Mrs Beeton, though the dish is far older than the 19th century.

Beefsteak & kidney pudding

50g (1¾oz) beef dripping, plus extra if needed

1 onion, peeled and halved

1 carrot, halved

500g (1lb 2oz) chuck steak, cut into large chunks

1 whole rose veal kidney

20g (¾oz) plain flour seasoned with salt and pepper

1 leek, trimmed and halved

1 celery stick, trimmed and halved

200g (7oz) button mushrooms, sliced

500ml (18fl oz) Basic Beef Broth (see page 112)

small handful of curly parsley, chopped, plus extra to garnish

½ small bunch (about 15g/½oz) of thyme, leaves picked and chopped

Maldon sea salt flakes and freshly ground black pepper

steamed kale and potatoes, to serve

For the suet crust pastry

350g (12oz) plain flour, plus extra for dusting

175g (6oz) shredded suet

ice-cold water

Heat the beef dripping in a large pan and cook the onion and carrot until they are beginning to caramelize. Remove from the pan and place in a large casserole.

Toss the steak and kidney in the seasoned flour to coat. Add more fat to the pan if necessary, and brown the meat in batches, so it isn't overcrowded and doesn't stew in its own juices.

Place all the meat and vegetables in the casserole, cover with the beef broth, season and bring to a gentle simmer, skimming well. Half-cover the pan with a lid and continue cooking gently for 1 hour, until the meat is tender. Remove the meats and vegetables using a slotted spoon and allow to cool. Return the stock to the heat and bring to the boil. Reduce by half, then pass through a fine sieve and leave to cool.

Flake the steak with your fingers and chop the vegetables and kidney. Add the meat, chopped vegetables and chopped herbs to the cooled, reduced stock and reserve.

To make the suet pastry, tip the flour into a bowl and season with salt and pepper. Add the suet and mix to combine. Add ice-cold water, 1 tablespoon at a time, and mix in using a palette or round-bladed knife until the dough comes together. Gather into a ball using your hands, then flatten into a disc, cover with clingfilm and chill until ready to use.

On a lightly floured work surface, roll out two-thirds of the pastry and use it to line a 1.5–2 litre (2¾–3½ pint) pudding basin. Roll out the remaining one-third of the pastry to use as a lid.

Fill the pastry-lined basin with the meat mixture and seal the lid on top by moistening the edges with water. Trim off any excess pastry and cover the top securely with a cloth or foil.

Steam for 2 hours, then turn out carefully and serve with steamed kale and potatoes sprinkled with extra parsley.

The original *chile con carne* consisted of dried beef, suet, dried chilli peppers and salt, which were pounded together, formed into bricks and left to dry, to be boiled in pots while on the trail. Now the official dish of Texas, chilli is the subject of competitions, where contention is rife over the inclusion of beans, which are forbidden by most authorities on the subject. I include them, as I feel they add texture, but accept that to some this recipe is now null and void.

Chilli con carne

4 tablespoons beef dripping

4 onions, finely chopped

2 red peppers, finely chopped

5 dried habanero chillies, stalks removed, deseeded and crushed

2 garlic cloves, crushed

1 teaspoons ground coriander

2 teaspoons ground cumin

1 teaspoon ground cinnamon

1 teaspoon dried oregano

800g (1lb 12oz) minced chuck steak

200g (7oz) fresh beef suet

2 x 400g (14oz) cans of plum tomatoes

250ml (9fl oz) Basic Beef Broth (see page 112)

50g (1¾oz) dark chocolate (90% cocoa solids), grated

50ml (2fl oz) good wine vinegar

400g (14oz) can of beans (pinto is my choice)

For the cornbread

300g (10½oz) polenta

300g (10½oz) plain flour

100g (3½oz) light brown sugar

1 teaspoon baking powder

20g (¾oz) Maldon sea salt flakes

200g (7oz) free-range eggs (about 4 large)

480ml (17fl oz) milk

30g (1oz) unsalted butter, melted

beef dripping, for frying

To serve

4 small ripe avocados, mashed

400ml (14fl oz) soured cream

400g (14oz) Cheddar cheese, grated

4 spring onions, chopped

2 limes, cut into wedges

4 large, mild fresh red chillies, finely sliced

½ bunch (about 15g/½oz) of coriander, leaves ripped

Preheat the oven to 150°C (300°F), Gas Mark 2.

Heat the dripping in a very large lidded casserole and fry the onions, red peppers, chillies and garlic until they begin to soften. Add the spices and oregano and stir well, then add the minced beef and keep turning it to separate it as the meat browns.

Add the remaining ingredients, stir well, then cover and put into the oven to simmer gently for 2 hours, stirring from time to time.

If you have a double oven you can start the cornbread. Mix the dry ingredients together in a bowl and the whole eggs, milk and butter in another. Combine the 2 mixtures.

Preheat the oven to 180°C (350°F), Gas Mark 4. Heat a cast-iron skillet or oven-proof frying pan over a medium heat, then melt enough beef dripping to give a shallow depth – 2mm (1⁄16 inch) – and add the cornbread mixture. Let it sizzle and start to cook on the sides, then toss into the preheated oven for 20 minutes, or until a skewer comes out clean when inserted into the cornbread.

Reheat the chilli if necessary and serve the chilli with mashed ripe avocados, soured cream, grated Cheddar, finely chopped spring onions, lime wedges, chopped fresh chillies, plenty of fresh coriander and the cornbread on the side.

Serves
4-6

Gulyás is a meat soup seasoned with paprika and caraway and traditionally cooked in a bogrács, or iron kettle, over an open fire. It originated in the 9th century in Hungary, where it was eaten by shepherds who first cooked and flavoured the meat, then sun-dried it and packed it into bags produced from sheeps' stomachs. It then needed only water to rehydrate – the earliest example of a ready meal.

Gulyás (Hungarian goulash)

600g (1lb 5oz) chuck steak, cut into 3cm (1¼ inch) cubes

1 tablespoon sweet Hungarian paprika

2 tablespoons beef dripping

2 onions, peeled and chopped

2 garlic cloves, chopped

1 teaspoon ground caraway seed

1 bay leaf

1 litre (1¾ pints) Basic Beef Broth (see page 112)

2 carrots, chopped

1 parsnip, chopped

2 potatoes, peeled and diced

2 celery sticks, diced

2 tomatoes, peeled and chopped

2 green peppers, deseeded and chopped

Maldon sea salt flakes and freshly ground black pepper

For the csipetke (pinched) noodles

2 small free-range eggs

170g (6oz) plain flour

pinch of salt

1 teaspoon water

Season the beef with salt, pepper and the paprika. Heat the beef dripping in a large casserole and fry the beef until coloured all over. Add the chopped onions and fry until they get a nice golden brown colour. Add the garlic and the ground caraway seeds, stir well and cook for a further minute. Add the bay leaf, pour in the beef broth, bring to the boil and let it simmer, half-covered with a lid, over a low heat for 30 minutes.

Add the carrots, parsnip, potatoes and celery and season with salt and pepper. Continue cooking for another 30 minutes, then add the tomatoes and green peppers and let it cook over a low heat for a further 30 minutes.

Meanwhile make the csipetke noodles. Whisk the eggs, then add the flour, salt and water and knead to a stiff dough. Flatten the dough between your palms to about 1cm (½ inch) thick, pinch off small, bean-sized pieces, flatten them slightly between your fingers and add them to the boiling soup. Cook for 5 minutes, then serve.

Serves
6

A Peruvian beef hotpot that will delight and surprise. Cook this in summer and serve it with a South American salsa called Salsa Criolla – made with onions, coriander, pickled beetroot, boiled potatoes, avocado, chillies and tomatoes, to brighten the whole dish.

Sancochado

1kg (2lb 4oz) chuck steak

4 celery sticks, roughly chopped, leaves reserved

2 onions, halved

4 potatoes, peeled and halved

2 carrots, halved

500g (1lb 2oz) piece of cassava or yucca root, cut into 4cm (1½ inch) chunks

2 sweetcorn cobs, cut into 5cm (2 inch) chunks

2 small sweet potatoes, peeled and halved

1 small Savoy cabbage, cut into wedges

2 teaspoons picked oregano leaves

Maldon sea salt flakes and freshly ground black pepper

Salsa Criolla (see opposite), to serve

Put the beef into a large pan and cover well with cold water. Add the celery and onions, season with salt and pepper, then gently bring to a simmer, cover with a lid and cook for 1 hour.

Add the potatoes, carrots, cassava and corn and simmer for a further 20 minutes, until tender. Remove the veg from the pan with a slotted spoon and set aside.

Add the sweet potatoes to the pan and cook for 15 minutes, then add the cabbage and cook for a further 15 minutes. Transfer the meat to a board, sprinkle over the oregano and leave to rest for a few minutes. Return the cooked veg to the broth and bring back to the boil to warm through. Divide the veg between your bowls and top with the broth. Slice the beef and add to the bowls with the celery leaves. Serve with Salsa Criolla.

Salsa criolla

Serves 4–6

1 large avocado, peeled and stoned

1 whole pickled beetroot

1 waxy potato, peeled and boiled

1 ripe tomato, blanched, peeled and deseeded

½ red onion, peeled

juice of 1 lime

1 red chilli, deseeded and finely chopped

small handful of coriander, leaves picked and chopped

100ml (3½fl oz) olive oil

Maldon sea salt flakes

Chop the avocado, beetroot, potato, tomato and onion into 1cm (½ inch) cubes and put them into a bowl.

Gently mix in the lime juice, chilli, coriander and olive oil, and season to taste. Serve immediately.

The best way to describe this dish is that it's a sophisticated sweet-and-sour beef stew. Popular in 1970s bistros, it's been much adulterated – but my version is reasonably authentic, I believe.

Carbonnade à la Flamande

250g (9oz) large smoked bacon lardons

1kg (2lb 4oz) boneless shin of beef, cut into 4cm (1½ inch) cubes

1 rounded tablespoon plain flour, seasoned with salt and pepper

50g (1¾oz) beef dripping

6 onions, peeled and chopped

1 faggot of herbs (bay leaves and thyme)

½ teaspoon ground allspice

330ml (10½fl oz) dark Belgian beer

500ml (18fl oz) Basic Beef Broth (see page 112)

2 tablespoons dark brown muscovado sugar

2 tablespoons malt vinegar

200g (7oz) pain d'épice au miel (honey gingerbread, available online orin good bakeries), or pain de mie

3 tablespoons unsalted butter, at room temperature

3 tablespoons wholegrain mustard

50g (1¾oz) Gruyère cheese, grated

Maldon sea salt flakes and freshly ground black pepper

Fry the bacon lardons until crispy in a large, heavy-based casserole over a medium-high heat, then, using a slotted spoon, remove them to a plate leaving behind the rendered bacon fat.

Toss the beef in the seasoned flour. Heat half the beef dripping in the pan and add half the beef. Brown the meat generously – this is crucial – then remove to the plate with the bacon. Melt the remaining dripping and add the remaining beef, browning it in the same way. Remove from the pan with the slotted spoon.

Add the onions and brown them lightly in the fat. Return the beef and bacon lardons to the pan with the faggot of herbs, ground allspice, beer and beef broth. Season, then cover and simmer gently, either over a low flame on the hob or in a preheated oven at 140°C (275°F), Gas Mark 1, for at least 1½ hours, or until the meat is tender.

Skim off any excess fat that has risen to the surface, then remove the faggot of herbs, add the sugar and vinegar and adjust the seasoning.

This is not a recipe to hurry. Carbonnade improves if kept, so if you can make it the day before, all the better. Make it up to the point where the meat has been simmered for 1½ hours and before you top it with the sliced pain d'épice.

Slice the pain d'épice and mix together the butter and mustard. Spread the bread with the mustard butter and lay over the top of the carbonnade, slightly overlapping the slices. Sprinkle with the grated cheese and return to the oven for 30 minutes, until the top is golden and the carbonnade is bubbling. Serve with simple buttered boiled potatoes or French fries.

Serves 4

1kg (2lb 4oz) beef cheeks, trimmed of sinew

50g (1¾oz) plain flour seasoned with salt and pepper

50ml (2fl oz) beef dripping

1 litre (1¾ pints) full-bodied red wine

50g (1¾oz) butter

2 carrots, roughly chopped

1 onion, peeled and roughly chopped

2 garlic cloves

½ bunch (about 15g/½oz) of thyme

200g (7oz) bacon lardons

200g (7oz) button mushrooms

pared zest and juice of 1 small orange

1 litre (1¾ pints) Basic Beef Broth (see page 112)

Pig's Trotter Garnish (see page 264)

Maldon sea salt flakes and freshly ground black pepper

cooked carrots and Mashed Potatoes (see pages 61 and 111), to serve

Daube de boeuf

Daube de boeuf is a Provençal preparation usually served with its garnish of vegetables and bacon, but I've also seen it served with pig's trotters on top.

Preheat the oven to 110°C (225°F), Gas Mark ¼.

Season the beef with salt and pepper and dust with the seasoned flour. Heat 1 tablespoon of the dripping in a pan over a medium heat and gently sear the beef for 1 minute on each side, until golden. Remove the beef from the frying pan and set aside in a warm place. Add half a glass of the wine to the pan to deglaze, stir and set aside with the beef.

Set a pan over a medium heat and add ½ tablespoon of dripping and ½ tablespoon of butter. Once hot, add the carrots, onion, garlic and thyme and cook for 15–20 minutes.

Put the remaining butter and beef dripping into a separate pan and fry the bacon lardons and button mushrooms for 2 minutes. Add the lardons and mushrooms to the cooked vegetables, stir, then carefully drain any excess liquid from the pan.

Put the remaining red wine into a large saucepan, bring to the boil, then simmer until reduced to remove the alcohol. Put the reduced wine, beef, orange zest and juice and and beef broth into a braising pot and bring to a simmer. Cover with a lid and place in the oven for 2 hours, then add the vegetables and return to the oven for 30 minutes. Once ready, remove the meat and vegetables from the pot and carefully pass the sauce through a sieve into a saucepan. Simmer until reduced by half.

Cut the beef into 4 chunks, put back into the braising pot with the vegetables and the Pig's Trotter Garnish and pour over the sauce. Return to the oven for 10 minutes. Remove from the oven and allow to cool, then refrigerate until the next day to allow all the flavours to get to know each other.

Next day, reheat the daube for 30 minutes in the oven and serve with carrots and mash.

This dish is at its absolute best when made the day before and cooled, then reheated and eaten the next day.

Some years ago, in a very fine, old-school restaurant, I ate a dish of braised ox cheek, or *daube de joue de boeuf à l'ancienne*, as it was probably called. Sitting proudly atop three chunks of glistening cheek were three medallions of pig's trotter: genius. This is that garnish.

Pig's trotter garnish Serves 4

2 hind pig's trotters, deboned

100g (3½oz) onions, chopped, plus 1 small onion, finely chopped

100g (3½oz) carrots, chopped

150ml (5fl oz) pork broth

150ml (5fl oz) dry white wine

1 tablespoon white port

50g (1¾ oz) butter

250g (9oz) pork sausagemeat

Preheat the oven to 160°C (325°F), Gas Mark 3.

Begin by preparing the trotters. Put them into a large casserole dish with the onions and the carrots, broth, wine and white port. Cover with a lid and cook in the oven for 3 hours.

Meanwhile, put half the butter into a pan and heat until bubbling. Add the small, finely chopped onion and fry for 5 minutes, then allow to cool. When cool, combine with the sausagemeat.

Remove the trotters from the oven and allow to cool to room temperature.

Once the trotters are completely cool, drain them. Use the remaining butter to butter 2 large sheets of foil and lay a trotter on each piece of foil. Divide the stuffing mix between the trotters, then roll the trotters firmly around the filling to ensure there is no air trapped. Roll up the large sheets of foil to cover and tightly seal the trotters in a neat cyclindrical shape. Put into the fridge to firm up for at least 2 hours.

Remove the trotters from the fridge and, keeping them wrapped in the foil, place them in a steamer. Set over simmering water for 15 minutes, or until cooked through, then unwrap, slice into medallions and use to garnish the Daube de Boeuf (see page 262).

Serves
4-6

A simple base recipe upon which to build other dishes, short ribs were known as Jacob's Ladder in England and until recently were damned hard to find. Happily, most good butchers carry them now.

Braised short ribs

20g (¾oz) beef dripping

2kg (4lb 8oz) beef short ribs, cut into 4 x 500g (1lb 2oz) rib portions

1 onion, peeled and chopped

1 carrot, chopped

1 celery stick, chopped

2 garlic cloves, sliced

250ml (9fl oz) red wine

2 litres (3½ pints) Basic Beef Broth (see page 112)

Maldon sea salt flakes and freshly ground black pepper

Preheat the oven to 140°C (275°F), Gas Mark 1.

Heat the dripping in a heavy-based frying pan. Season the ribs and add to the pan. Brown all over, then transfer the ribs to a large casserole pan or a large, deep roasting tin. Add the vegetables and garlic to the frying pan, let them lightly brown, then add to the ribs.

Pour the red wine and broth over the ribs, bring to a simmer, skim off any froth that has risen to the surface and cover with a lid or foil.

Place in the oven for about 4 hours, or until tender. Turn the ribs halfway through cooking.

Remove from the oven and leave to cool for 30 minutes to allow any fat to rise to the surface. Skim the fat, then transfer the ribs to a dish or bowl and strain the cooking liquor through a sieve and into a clean saucepan. Discard the vegetables, then place the cooking liquor over a medium-high heat, bring to the boil and reduce by half, skimming off any fat as you go.

Pour the reduced sauce back over the short ribs. Allow to cool, then cover and refrigerate for use in other recipes in the book, such as pies and La Macaronade (see page 316). They can of course be served just as they are, with Mashed Potatoes (see pages 61 and 111).

Based on the French bistro classic *terrine de queue de boeuf*, this version makes use of lesser cuts from either end of the animal, which pleases me for some reason.

Cheek & tail terrine

For the terrine

1kg (2lb 4oz) oxtail, cut into pieces and trimmed of excess fat

800g (1lb 12oz) ox cheek, trimmed of sinew

50g (1¾oz) beef dripping

2 onions, peeled and roughly chopped

2 carrots, roughly chopped

4 garlic cloves, crushed

2 litres (3½ pints) Basic Beef Broth (see page 112)

1 faggot of herbs (bay leaves and thyme)

1 small bunch (about 30g/1oz) of parsley, leaves picked and chopped

3 tablespoons lemon juice

Maldon sea salt flakes and freshly ground black pepper

To serve

crusty bread

Green Sauce (see page 268) or Anchovy Cream (see page 141)

Preheat the oven to 150°C (300°F), Gas Mark 2.

Pat the oxtail pieces and ox cheeks dry, season with salt and pepper, then brown them in batches in the dripping over a medium-high heat, transferring them as they are browned to a casserole dish. Fry the onions, carrots and garlic until soft but not coloured, then add to the meat with the broth and the faggot of herbs and bring to the boil. Cover with a lid and braise in the preheated oven for 4 hours.

Using a slotted spoon, transfer the oxtail and cheeks to a bowl, reserving the liquid. Let them cool, then remove the meat, discarding any bones and fat. Strain the reserved cooking liquid through a sieve into a large bowl.

In another large bowl, stir together the picked meat with the parsley, lemon juice, plenty of salt and pepper, and 400–500ml (14–18fl oz) of the reserved broth until the mixture is combined well, using enough broth to hold the meat together. Reserve any remaining cooking liquid.

Rinse a terrine mould with cold water and pack the oxtail mixture into it, then carefully spoon over some of the reserved cooking liquid to just cover the mixture. Cover the terrine and chill overnight, or up to 2 days in advance.

Let the terrine stand at room temperature for 10 minutes. Run a thin knife around the edge to loosen it, then dip the terrine base into hot water for 20 seconds and place a chilled platter over the top. Invert the terrine with a sharp rap on to the platter and cut into 1cm (½ inch) thick slices with a very sharp, hot knife.

Serve with crusty bread and Green Sauce or Anchovy Cream.

Green sauce Makes 250ml (9fl oz)

Green sauce is found with variations throughout Europe, where it is often called salsa verde. Parsley is pretty ubiquitous, and basil or tarragon make appearances in Italy and France. My version goes particularly well with steak.

½ bunch (about 15g/½oz) of flat leaf parsley, leaves picked and chopped

½ bunch (about 15g/½oz) of mint, leaves picked and chopped

100ml (3½fl oz) light olive oil, plus extra if needed

2 garlic cloves

2 tablespoons salted capers, rinsed

5 anchovy fillets

2 tablespoons Dijon mustard

2 tablespoons red wine vinegar

freshly ground black pepper

Place the chopped herbs in a bowl and cover with the oil.

Peel the garlic and chop with the capers and anchovies. Add to the herbs and mix together.

Stir in the mustard and vinegar, season with black pepper and add more oil to loosen, if necessary.

Serves
4-6

Brasato al Barolo

1kg (2lb 4oz) piece of chuck roast – ask your butcher to tie it ready for roasting

1 faggot of herbs (thyme, bay and rosemary)

1 spice bag (1 star anise, 4 cloves)

75cl bottle of Barolo wine

3 tablespoons olive oil

3 carrots

2 onions

2 garlic cloves, crushed

50g (1¾oz) unsalted butter

Maldon sea salt flakes and freshly ground black pepper

finely grated Parmesan cheese, to serve

Place the meat in a dish with the faggot of herbs and the spice bag. Add the wine, then cover and leave to marinate overnight in the fridge, turning the meat after a few hours if it is not completely covered with the wine.

Preheat the oven to 150°C (300°F), Gas Mark 2.

Remove the meat from the marinade and dry thoroughly using kitchen paper. Heat the oil in a large frying pan over a medium heat, brown the meat on all sides, then remove from the pan.

Chop the carrots and onion into 3cm (1¼ inch) pieces. Add to the pan and fry for a few minutes, then add the garlic and fry for a further minute. Pour in all the marinade and season with salt and pepper. Using a slotted spoon, scoop the vegetables into an oval casserole large enough to hold the meat comfortably and add half the butter.

Place the meat on the bed of vegetables, then pour over the marinade and bring slowly to a simmer. Cover the pan with a tight-fitting lid and transfer to the oven. Cook for 3 hours, until tender, keeping an eye on the meat and turning it from time to time – it should cook at a steady simmer, so reduce the oven temperature to 140°C (275°F), Gas Mark 1 if it appears to be cooking too fast.

Transfer the meat to a chopping board, cover with foil and leave to rest for 10–15 minutes while you make the sauce. Pass the cooking liquid through a fine sieve into a clean pan, pressing the vegetables, faggot and spice bag to extract all the juices. Bring the sauce to a gentle boil, then slide the pan off the heat and whisk in the remaining butter.

Cut the meat into slices about 1cm (½ inch) thick, place in a serving dish, and pour over the sauce. Serve with plenty of grated Parmesan, and polenta or orzotto (see page 48) to soak up the juices.

It's said that India Pale Ales were brewed to withstand the rigours of being transported from England to India in the wooden-hulled ships of the time. This ox cheek curry makes fine use of IPA and shows off its character.

Ox cheek & IPA curry

1kg (2lb 4oz) ox cheeks

50g (1¾oz) beef dripping

500g (1lb 2oz) onions, peeled and thinly sliced

6 fat garlic cloves, finely grated

2 teaspoons whole fennel seeds

2 black cardamom pods, lightly smashed

1 star anise, freshly ground

1 teaspoon ground turmeric

½ teaspoon chilli powder

¼ teaspoon asafoetida

2 teaspoons Maldon sea salt flakes

850ml (1½ pints) IPA (beer)

200ml (7fl oz) Basic Beef Broth (see page 112)

30g (1oz) fresh root ginger, peeled and finely grated

2 tablespoons crème fraîche

1 red chilli, deseeded and finely chopped

a small handful (about 30g/1oz) of coriander leaves, finely chopped

rotis, to serve

Preheat the oven to 140°C (275°F), Gas Mark 1.

In a large casserole, brown the ox cheeks in half the dripping, then remove and set aside. In the same pot, sweat the onions in the remaining dripping until soft, then add the garlic. Stir, add the spices and salt and gently fry for 30 seconds.

Place the cheeks on top of the onions, then pour in the IPA and the broth and add the ginger. Stir, bring up to a bubble, pop the lid on, place in the oven and cook for 3 hours, until the meat is tender.

Remove the cheeks and put them on a warm plate. Cover and keep warm.

Pop the casserole back over a medium-high heat. Allow the sauce to bubble and reduce to "coating consistency", then pass through a fine sieve, add the crème fraîche and chopped chilli, and adjust the salt to taste.

Put the cheeks and their resting juices back into the pot, stir gently, bring back to bubbling heat, then serve immediately with coriander and rotis.

Serves
4

Paupiettes are an old Normandy dish made of meat, beaten thin, rolled around a stuffing, then fried or braised, or baked in wine or stock. They are popular in France, where they are sold ready-prepared in supermarkets and butchers.

Paupiettes of veal

16 smoked streaky bacon rashers

2 small onions, peeled and finely chopped

100g (3½oz) wild mushrooms, finely chopped

finely grated zest of 1 small lemon

10g (¼oz) fresh breadcrumbs

½ bunch (about 15g/½oz) of flat leaf parsley, finely chopped

1 tablespoon Dijon mustard

1 free-range egg, lightly beaten

600g (1lb 5oz) veal fillet

1 teaspoon thyme leaves

400ml (14fl oz) Basic Beef Broth (see page 112)

2 garlic cloves, crushed

100ml (3½fl oz) double cream

Maldon sea salt flakes and freshly ground black pepper

Finely chop half the bacon and fry over a medium heat with the onions and mushrooms for about 6 minutes or until nicely browned. Drain and set aside in a medium bowl, returning the bacon fat to the pan. Add the lemon zest, breadcrumbs, parsley, half the mustard and the beaten egg to the bowl, and season with salt and pepper. Mix to combine thoroughly, then set aside.

Cut the veal fillet into 8 even escalopes. Place each piece between 2 sheets of clingfilm and flatten, using a mallet or a rolling pin, then season each piece liberally with salt and black pepper and a few thyme leaves.

Spoon some of the reserved stuffing into the centre of each slice of veal, distributing evenly. Gather the edges up to create a round pouch, then wrap each pouch around its circumference with a bacon rasher and secure with butcher's string.

Heat the pan of reserved bacon fat over a medium-high heat and brown the veal paupiettes on all sides. Add just enough broth to cover and allow to simmer slowly for 10 minutes. Add the garlic, the cream and remaining mustard to the sauce, then bring to a simmer and serve with a potato dish such as a mash or gratin.

Serves 4

Veal consumption is contentious, as it is commonly produced unethically. I buy English rose veal that has been fed on its mother's milk. It grows more slowly, so it's over eight months old when it's slaughtered, and it's twice as expensive, but it's delicious and worth it. Old French dishes such as this blanquette de veau, stewed veal in a blanket of lemon-flavoured sauce served with rice, are seldom seen now. That's a shame: it's delicious.

Veal blanquette

1kg (2lb 4oz) breast of rose veal

2 litres (3½ pints) cold water

1 onion, peeled

2 cloves

2 carrots, halved

1 leek, white part only

faggot of herbs (flat leaf parsley, thyme, rosemary and bay leaf)

Maldon sea salt flakes and freshly ground white pepper

For the pilau rice

25g (1oz) unsalted butter

1 onion, peeled and finely chopped

1 garlic clove, finely chopped

300g (10½oz) basmati rice

500ml (18fl oz) veal cooking liquor (see recipe method)

For the onions & mushrooms

24 small button or pearl onions, peeled

24 (about 200g/7oz) small button mushrooms, trimmed

For the sauce

300ml (½ pint) double cream

3 free-range egg yolks

juice and finely grated zest of 1 unwaxed lemon

Cut the veal into 4cm (1½ inch) cubes and place in a large saucepan. Cover with the cold water and bring to a simmer for 30 minutes, skimming occasionally.

Stud the whole, peeled onion with the cloves and add to the pot with the carrots, leek, faggot of herbs and 1 teaspoon of salt and continue to simmer for 1 hour.

For the rice, heat the butter in a frying pan over a medium heat, then add the onion and garlic and fry for about 4 minutes, or until softened. Add the rice and stir well to coat. Pour in 500ml (18fl oz) of the veal cooking liquor, stir well and bring the mixture to a simmer. Cover the pan and cook over a low heat for 20 minutes, until the rice has absorbed the liquid and is tender. Taste and correct the seasoning, then keep warm.

When the veal pieces are tender, pass the remaining cooking liquor through a sieve into another pan containing the button onions. Reserve the veal in a warm place and discard the whole onion, carrots, leek and herbs. Simmer the button onions in the liquor for 10 minutes, then add the mushrooms and simmer for a further 10 minutes.

Strain the cooking liquid from the onions and mushrooms into a clean saucepan and add the onions and mushrooms to the veal. Over a medium heat reduce the cooking liquid by half, then stir in half the double cream and reduce by half again.

Meanwhile, in a bowl, mix together the egg yolks and remaining cream until well combined, and add a little lemon juice.

Remove the pan from the heat and stir in the egg yolk and cream mixture. Return to a low heat and stir continuously for 2 minutes, until the mixture is completely incorporated and the sauce has thickened slightly, to the consistency of a thin custard. Season with salt and pepper, then strain through a fine sieve and pour over the reserved veal, button onions and mushrooms. Serve with the pilau rice, lightly grating the lemon zest over the top.

An animal's extremities, such as tails and cheeks, are still relatively cheap and should not be thrown away. Another of those forgotten cuts, oxtail has its own unique flavour that reminds me of a childhood in my mother's kitchen. Yes, I know how that reads, but it does.

Oxtail stew

2kg (4lb 8oz) oxtail,
cut into large chunks

2 leeks

2 celery sticks

4 carrots

2 tablespoons plain flour

400g (14oz) can plum tomatoes

½ bottle (37.5cl) of red wine

1 faggot of herbs (thyme,
rosemary and bay leaves)

1 litre (1¾ pints) Basic Beef Broth
(see page 112)

Maldon sea salt flakes and freshly
ground black pepper

cooked, mashed carrots and parsnips,
and steamed greens, to serve

Place a large, deep roasting tray in the oven and preheat the oven to 200°C (400°F), Gas Mark 6. When the oven and the tray are hot, put the oxtail into the tray. Season, and roast in the hot oven for about 20 minutes, or until golden and caramelized.

Meanwhile, trim the leeks and celery and halve lengthways, then chop into rough chunks. Peel the carrots and chop into rough chunks. Add the vegetables to the oxtail and roast for another 10 minutes.

Take the roasting tray out of the oven and reduce the oven temperature to 150°C (300°F), Gas Mark 2.

Over a medium heat on the hob, add the flour to the roasting tray, stirring well to combine. Pour in the tomatoes and wine, add the herbs, season, then cover with the beef broth and stir well. Bring to a simmer, cover and return to the oven for around 4 hours, or until the meat falls away from the bone.

Remove the pan from the oven and leave to cool for about 10 minutes. Drain the oxtail and vegetables and pass the sauce through a fine sieve. Return the meat to the pan with the vegetables, discarding the faggot of herbs. Reheat, correct the seasoning and serve with mashed roots and steamed greens.

Serves
4

A traditional Yemeni dish made with oxtail – hence its name, *akwa*, meaning the thickest part of the tail. Long, low and slow cooking is important here. Serve with Zhoug, a kind of spicy Middle Eastern salsa verde.

Yemeni akwa

50g (1¾oz) beef dripping

1.5kg (3lb 5oz) oxtail, cut up on the bone

1.5 litres (2¾ pints) Basic Beef Broth (see page 112)

1 garlic bulb, cloves peeled

2 large waxy potatoes, peeled and chopped into 5cm (2 inch) chunks

2 large carrots, cut into 5cm (2 inch) chunks

1 onion, peeled and sliced into 5cm (2 inch) chunks

3 large celery sticks, trimmed and sliced into 5cm (2 inch) chunks

400g (14oz) can chopped tomatoes

1 spice bag (1 tablespoon each of coriander seed, cumin seed, cardamom pods and chopped turmeric root)

1 faggot of herbs (bay leaf, parsley and coriander)

1 lemon, cut into wedges

Maldon sea salt flakes and freshly ground black pepper

Zhoug, to serve (see below)

Preheat the oven to 150°C (300°F), Gas Mark 2.

Heat half the beef dripping in a large frying pan. Season the oxtail pieces and seal all over in the hot pan. Remove the meat, place in a large cast-iron, lidded pot, and add the beef broth. Bring to a gentle simmer, skimming any impurities off the surface.

Add the remaining dripping to the large frying pan, add the garlic, potatoes, carrots, onion and celery, and sauté gently until soft but not coloured.

Using a slotted spoon, transfer the vegetables to the oxtail, and add the chopped tomatoes, spice bag and faggot of herbs. Cover and place in the preheated oven for 2 hours, until the meat is falling off the bone and the vegetables are soft.

Lift out and discard the faggot of herbs and spice bag, correct the seasoning, and add a squeeze of lemon juice.

Serve with Zhoug and the remaining lemon wedges and sea salt flakes on the side.

Zhoug Makes 400g (14oz)

250g (9oz) green jalapeño chillies

½ bunch of coriander, chopped

½ bunch of flat leaf parsley, chopped

6 garlic cloves, peeled and roughly chopped

½ teaspoon ground cumin

100ml (3½fl oz) extra virgin olive oil

Maldon sea salt flakes and freshly ground black pepper

Trim, deseed and coarsely chop the chillies.

Blend the chillies, chopped herbs, garlic and cumin to a rough paste in a food processor, and season to taste with plenty of freshly ground salt and pepper. Add the oil and blend to combine. Pack into a glass jar, cover the top with olive oil, and store in the refrigerator for up to a month.

Poutine is a Canadian fast food dish first seen in 1950s rural Quebec. It is remarkably similar to the northern English dish of "Chips, Cheese and Gravy", eaten since 1901, and yet somehow that is considered to have "developed independently of poutine" as opposed to being the dish that inspired the Canadian classic. Whatever the origins, it's safe to say that the texture and squeak of the cheese curds is an improvement on finished cheese.

Poutine

75g (2½ oz) leftover braised beef with gravy (such as Braised Short Ribs or Daube de Boeuf (see pages 265 and 262)

200g (7oz) Beef Dripping Chips (see below)

75g (2¾oz) cheese curds

Maldon sea salt flakes and freshly ground black pepper

Bring the braised beef gravy, complete with bits of braised beef, to the boil.

Fry the chips until golden and drain on kitchen paper. Season lightly, then toss with the cheese curds.

Place the chips and cheese curds on a plate or in a bowl and pour the gravy over the top.

Cooking in rendered beef fat is something the English have done for centuries, and chippies up and down the country used to use beef dripping to cook both fish and chips – once tried there is no going back.

Beef dripping chips serves 4

1kg (2lb 4oz) chipping potatoes, peeled and hand-cut into chips

beef dripping, enough to fill your deep-fat fryer to the required level

malt vinegar

smoked Maldon sea salt flakes and freshly ground black pepper

Blanch the chips in a pan of salted boiling water for 10 minutes, or until just tender, then drain.

Heat the beef dripping in a deep-fat fryer to 130°C (265°F).

Fry the chips for 8–10 minutes, or until the oil stops bubbling, which means that the moisture has been removed. Remove the chips from the dripping and set aside to drain on kitchen paper.

Increase the temperature of the beef dripping to 190°C (375°F). Put the chips back into the dripping and fry for 4–5 minutes, or until crisp and golden brown. Remove them from the dripping, set aside to drain on kitchen paper and season to taste with smoked Maldon sea salt and ground black pepper.

Lightly spray with malt vinegar and serve.

Serves 8–10 as a starter or 4–5 as a main course

I grew up eating canned Heinz beef ravioli in tomato sauce, one of the great achievements of the 20th century (the ravioli, not my eating of). This is the dish that canned ravioli was trying to be.

Ravioli

For the pasta

600g (1lb 5oz) "00" flour

4 large free-range eggs, plus 6 free-range egg yolks

1 tablespoon olive oil

pinch of salt

1 free-range egg, beaten, for egg wash

For the filling

400g (14oz) Braised Short Ribs (see page 265)

50g (1¾oz) fresh white breadcrumbs

50g (1¾oz) Parmesan cheese, finely grated

1 free-range egg, lightly beaten

Maldon sea salt flakes and freshly ground black pepper

To serve

a good handful of finely grated Parmesan cheese

40g (1½oz) unsalted butter

First make your pasta. Place the flour in a food processor and slowly add the eggs and yolks, using the pulse button. Lastly add the olive oil and salt and remove from the processor. Knead for a few minutes, then wrap in clingfilm and place in the fridge for an hour to rest.

For the filling, separate the braised meat and sauce. Shred the meat finely and mix with the breadcrumbs, Parmesan, egg, and a few tablespoons of sauce. Taste for seasoning.

To make the ravioli, divide the pasta dough into 4 and, working in batches, use a pasta machine to roll it out thinly (I roll it through the penultimate setting on my machine). Spoon evenly-spaced teaspoons of the filling on the sheet of pasta and eggwash around the filling. Top with another pasta sheet and gently press around the mounds of filling to seal and expel any air. Use a pastry wheel or a cutter to cut out the little mounds to make 8cm (3¼ inch) squares. Make sure each raviolo is well-sealed by taking it in your hand and pressing all round the rim between your fingers, working your way round each one, otherwise they will split during cooking.

Lay the finished ravioli on a floured work surface or tray, and keep covered with a lightly dampened tea towel to prevent them drying out too much, then repeat with the remaining pasta dough and filling.

Cook the ravioli in a large pan of boiling salted water for about 4 minutes, until the pasta is tender. Partially drain the ravioli, reserving a small ladle of the cooking liquid. Toss with the butter to form an emulsified sauce. Serve with reheated braised beef sauce and extra Parmesan.

Serves
8

Pho originated in the early 20th century, south-east of Hanoi in the villages of Vân Cù and Dao Cù, Nam Định Province, northern Vietnam. It was originally sold at dawn and dusk by roaming street vendors, who shouldered mobile kitchens on carrying poles from which hung two wooden cabinets, one housing a cauldron over a wood fire, the other storing noodles, spices, cookware, and space to prepare the pho. With the 1954 partition of Vietnam, more than a million people fled from North to South Vietnam, taking pho with them. No longer confined to northern culinary traditions, variations in meat and broth appeared, and garnishes such as lime, beansprouts, coriander, Asian basil, hoisin and sriracha sauces became standard fare.

Vietnamese beef pho

500g (1lb 2oz) beef shin

500g (1lb 2oz) oxtail, cut into 2cm (¾ inch) thick slices

500g (1lb 2oz) chuck steak

500g (1lb 2oz) beef brisket

2 large onions, halved

8cm (3¼ inch) piece of fresh root ginger

2 whole star anise

1 cinnamon stick

1 teaspoon fennel seeds

3 cloves

1 teaspoon coriander seeds

75ml (2½fl oz) fish sauce

Maldon sea salt flakes

2 tablespoons yellow rock sugar

For the garnishes

6–8 servings of pho noodles

500g (1lb 2oz) fillet steak, sliced thinly against the grain

bunch each of coriander, Asian basil and mint

100g (3½oz) trimmed beansprouts

50g (1¾oz) sliced spring onions

2 thinly sliced Thai chillies, or 4 mild chillies

2 limes, each cut into 4 wedges

hoisin sauce

sriracha sauce

Blanch the beef shin, oxtail, chuck steak and brisket: place the meat in a large pot and cover with cold water, bring to the boil for 10 minutes, drain, then rinse thoroughly under cold water.

Charcoal-grill the onions and ginger, turning occasionally, until deeply blackened on all sides, about 10 minutes in total.

Put the blanched meats, burnt onions and ginger back into the pot, add the remaining ingredients, apart from the garnishes, and cover with cold water. Bring to a bare simmer and cook gently for 2 hours, skimming regularly. Remove the chuck steak and brisket and set aside to cool, then refrigerate.

Continue simmering the broth gently for 4 hours more, occasionally topping up with water if needed. Gently pass through muslin, taking care not to disturb any sediment.

Skim the broth and season to taste with extra fish sauce, salt and sugar. Pick the meat from the oxtail and beef shin, and slice the cold chuck steak and brisket.

Prepare the pho noodles according to the packet instructions.

To serve, place the rehydrated noodles in bowls, top with the reheated picked and sliced meat, and pour hot broth over the top. Discard the onion and ginger.

Serve hot, with sliced raw fillet steak, bunches of herbs, beansprouts, spring onions, chillies, lime wedges and the sauces in bowls on the side for people to help themselves.

Serves
8

Eastern European Jews served p'tcha with chopped eggs on the Sabbath in the 19th century, and Jewish immigrants in the United States continued to prepare the dish as an appetizer a hundred years later. In this age of ease and availability I doubt it is made very often, but it is a tasty use of an underused cut.

P'tcha or calves' foot jelly

2 calves' feet, cut into 3cm (1¼ inch) slices

2 large carrots, cut into 1cm (½ inch) chunks

1 large onion, peeled and cut into 1cm (½ inch) chunks

5 garlic cloves, crushed

3 hard-boiled free-range eggs, sliced

Maldon sea salt flakes and freshly ground black pepper

5 lemons, thinly sliced, to garnish

Blanch the calves' feet by covering in cold water and bringing to the boil, then drain and refresh in cold water. Cover with cold water again, bring to a gentle simmer and cook for 4 hours, skimming from time to time.

Add the carrots and onion, season well with salt and pepper and continue to cook on the lowest possible heat for a further 2 hours, until any adherent meat, cartilage, tendons and ligaments separate easily from the bones.

Pick out the bones and discard, then taste the broth and adjust the seasoning – be generous, as once set, the jelly will lose seasoning. Chop the meat, cartilage, softened tendons and ligaments into small pieces and mix with the garlic. Pass the broth through muslin and allow to cool a little. Pour 1cm (½ inch) of broth into a large flat-bottomed glass dish and refrigerate for 30 minutes, until set.

Place the sliced eggs neatly on top of the set jelly and evenly distribute the meat mixture on top. Over this pour the broth, including the onions and carrots, to a depth of about 4cm (1½ inches).

Place in the refrigerator until set. Any fat on the top of the mixture may be removed by skimming with the edge of a knife after the mixture sets firmly. Once set, the mixture can be cut into cubes and served cold as an appetizer, garnished with lemon slices, with any extra juice squeezed over the top.

2 tablespoons olive oil

1 oxtail, cut into thick slices

4 large carrots, chopped

4 large onions, peeled
and chopped

4 garlic cloves, chopped

1 spice bag (10 black
peppercorns, 1 star anise,
1 bay leaf, 1 sprig of thyme)

2 litres (3½ pints) Basic Beef
Broth (see page 112)

5 free-range egg whites

Maldon sea salt flakes and
freshly ground black pepper

black truffles or cooked
ox tongue, to garnish

Ox bone tea

A thermos of beef tea was traditionally the favoured way to fend off the
chill of winter matches for generations of British soccer enthusiasts, and
to this day, Bovril dissolved in hot water is sold in stadiums all over England.
Bovril beef tea was also the hot drink that Ernest Shackleton's team drank
when they were marooned on Elephant Island during the Endurance
expedition. I first came across it at Jonathon Jones's Anchor & Hope in
London some years ago and have been self-fortifying with it ever since.

Heat the olive oil in a large pot, then add the oxtail and brown it well all over. Add the
carrots, onions and garlic and cook until soft but not coloured. Add the spice bag
and the broth and bring to a soft boil, then half-cover the pan and cook for 4 hours
at a gentle simmer.

Remove from the heat and strain through a double thickness of muslin cloth.
Wash the muslin. Whisk the egg whites until foamy.

Return the tea to the pot and mix in the whisked egg whites. Return to a bare simmer,
without stirring, for 30 minutes.

Carefully make a hole in the centre of the egg white "cake" that has formed and ladle
the by now clear tea back through the washed muslin.

To serve, reheat, season to taste and garnish with freshly sliced truffles or a julienne
of cooked ox tongue.

Serves
8
as a starter

In today's sanitized market, beef heart is overlooked in favour of neatly packaged easy cooking cuts, and while your butcher may not carry hearts, he can usually get them with a little notice. As anyone who's tried it can attest, heart is a delicious offal cut, that just requires a little adventurous spirit.

Beef heart tea

1 beef heart

10g (¼oz) beef dripping

400g (14oz) chopped carrot

400g (14oz) chopped onion

4 garlic cloves

½ bottle (25cl) of Madeira

2 litres (3½ pints) Basic Beef Broth (see page 112)

1 small muslin spice bag, containing 10 black peppercorns and 1 star anise

1 faggot of herbs (thyme, bay and rosemary)

8 free-range egg whites

Preheat the oven to 160°C (325F), Gas Mark 3.

Clean the beef heart and cut it into 4 equal pieces. Mince or finely chop half the pieces of heart and reserve.

Melt the dripping in a casserole and cook the carrot, onion and garlic until softened. Add the Madeira and simmer until reduced by half, then add the beef broth, the spice bag and the faggot of herbs and bring to a simmer. Add the unchopped pieces of beef heart.

Cover with a lid and place in the oven for 4 hours, or until the meat is falling apart. Remove from the oven and drain off all the liquid into another pan, reserving the cooked pieces of beef heart.

Skim the broth well. Whisk the egg whites until foamy and mix with the raw minced heart, then add to the pan of broth. Place the casserole on the stove over a low heat and simmer without stirring for 20 minutes. A "cake" will form on the top of the broth: this is called the clarification.

Remove from the heat and gently strain through a double muslin cloth, a ladle at a time, taking care not to disturb the clarification.

Cut the cooked beef heart into 5mm (¼ inch) dice and place in 8 teacups. Season the beef heart tea to taste and pour it into clean teapots. Serve the teacups at the table, for people to add their own beef heart tea as a starter.

Alternatively the tea could be chilled to a jelly and served in the Victorian manner as an aspic – a much neglected preparation.

1 brined ox tongue, around 1kg (2lb 4oz) in weight

1 litre (1¾ pints) Basic Beef Broth (see page 112)

2 star anise

1 cinnamon stick

Little Gem hearts, to serve

Shaved Vegetable & Herb Slaw (see page 122), to serve

Braised ox tongue salad

I wasn't a fan of tongue until Mr Peng converted me with his version at Hunan in London's Pimlico. If you think you know and like Chinese food, I urge you to try his restaurant – I know of no better. This is my interpretation of his dish.

Soak the tongue in cold water overnight.

Next day, scrub the tongue thoroughly under cold running water until the surface is free of any blood, then soak again in cold, fresh water for another hour.

Preheat the oven to 120°C (250°F), Gas Mark ½.

Place the tongue in a large casserole, cover with cold water and bring to the boil. Drain, then refresh under cold running water. Return the tongue to the pan, add the beef broth and spices and bring to a very gentle simmer.

Cover the casserole and place in the preheated oven for 2½ hours, until the tongue is tender.

Remove the tongue from the liquor and allow to cool. Carefully peel – the outer skin should come away easily. Pass the braising liquor through a fine sieve back over the peeled tongue, then cover and refrigerate until needed.

To make the salad, remove the braised ox tongue from the liquor and slice thinly. Serve on a bed of shredded Little Gem hearts, and scatter the Shaved Vegetable & Herb Slaw over the top.

Serves
4-6

100g (3½oz) raisins

100ml (3½fl oz) Pedro Ximénez sherry

100ml (3½fl oz) Pedro Ximénez vinegar

1 small brined ox tongue, around 1kg (2lb 4oz) in weight, soaked in cold water overnight

2 litres (3½ pints) Basic Beef Broth (see page 112)

2 onions, peeled and sliced

2 carrots, sliced

2 celery sticks, sliced

2 garlic cloves, crushed

1 faggot of herbs (thyme, rosemary and bay leaf)

25g (1oz) unsalted butter

100g (3½oz) small whole blanched almonds

freshly ground black pepper, to taste

Mashed Potatoes with Extra Virgin Olive Oil, to serve (see page 61)

Ox tongue with raisins & almonds

Like other cuts of offal, tongue seems to be falling out of favour with the rise of intensive farming. As meat has become so cheap, we are valuing these cuts less. A shame, as tongue is considered a delicacy in many countries and is often the tastiest part of an animal.

Mix the raisins with the PX sherry and vinegar and set aside.

Scrub the tongue thoroughly under cold running water until the surface is free of any blood, then soak again for another hour.

Preheat the oven to 120°C (250°F), Gas Mark ½. Place the tongue in a large pan and cover with cold water. Bring to the boil, then drain and refresh under cold running water again. Return to the pan and pour over the beef broth, then add the vegetables, garlic and faggot of herbs, cover the pot and bring to a very gentle simmer. Place in the preheated oven for 2½ hours. The tongue is ready when it turns white and a knife easily pierces the thickest part. This takes around 15 minutes for every 100g (3½oz) of weight.

Remove the tongue and peel off the white layer as soon as the meat is cool enough to touch. While warm, this should come off easily after a few incisions with a sharp knife.

Melt the butter in a small frying pan, add the almonds and fry until golden brown. Add the raisins and 200ml (7fl oz) of the tongue cooking liquor and cook until reduced by half, then correct the seasoning.

Thinly slice the tongue and pour the raisin and almond sauce over the top. Serve with Mashed Potatoes with Extra Virgin Olive Oil.

Buying beef

Much of what we think we know about checking meat for quality is wrong. Some of it is based on what supermarkets have led us to believe good meat should look like, through years of marketing and advertising. Some is based on what the US Department of Agriculture (USDA) tells American citizens in an attempt to promote corn- and grain-fed beef, and the European public has subsequently picked up this information.

Take a good look at your beef. It should be dry, not wet, and should have a good layer of creamy yellow (not white) fat. The meat should be an appetizing deep red colour – muscle that has worked and is therefore tasty is darker than muscle that has not worked.

Marbling

Most experts will tell you that marbling is where the great steak flavour comes from. This idea originated with the USDA, which grades beef by the amount of white and creamy marbling on grain-fed beef. Marbling on grass-fed beef, however, is a pale yellow, if it's visible at all. Much of the marbling in grass-fed beef is intramuscular fat and is invisible to the naked eye; just because we can't see it doesn't make it any less tasty.

Smell

This is the most important characteristic for me. Your nose has evolved to divine information – if meat smells pleasant, it's good; unpleasant, it's bad. It really is that simple. Freshly cut steak should have a sweet, slightly meaty smell; meat cut too long ago will have an unpleasant, sour smell, as will anything wet-aged in a bag.

Touch

Good steak should not be wet or sticky to the touch, and it should feel firm rather than soft or mushy.

Colour

Grass-fed beef is a darker red colour than a well-marbled, grain-finished steak. When a freshly cut surface is exposed to oxygen, the myoglobin in the meat makes it turn a bright red hue, known as a "bloom". If the meat is not freshly cut, bright red indicates it has been kept in an oxygen-free environment such as a vacuum pack. Supermarkets vacuum-pack steaks to keep them fresh-looking, as steak will naturally oxidize and turn from bright red to brownish red as the day goes on. This doesn't make it bad – those steaks are just as good as the bright red ones – but it's harder to sell steaks at the end of the day if they've turned brownish red.

Labelling

Look carefully at the labels on supermarket meat. Only two of them really mean something: the Soil Association organic symbol and the RSPCA Freedom Food label. There are several others designed to fool people into thinking the meat is farmed well – ignore those.

What to look for

Great beef comes from animals that are grass-fed as nature intended, of a pure breed, free-range, at least two years old (preferably three), hormone-free, growth-promoter-free, and *happy*: they should have had a short journey to slaughter and have been killed quickly and humanely.

It is possible to buy meat online now, but do some research first, asking questions such as where and how the meat was farmed and how old it was at slaughter. Ask what breed it is – I wouldn't buy cross-breeds as they grow too quickly at the expense of flavour. Look out for "pure breeds" or "native breeds". Personal favourites are Dexter, Highland, Angus, Longhorn and Galloway.

If a company can answer these questions to your satisfaction, then place an order. Of course, the best way of all is to buy from a butcher. If he/she can answer those same questions, you have found someone with whom to build a relationship, to love and cherish. Be loyal and faithful to your butcher and they will reward you with untold meaty delights.

A question of priorities

Most of us could afford to spend a little more on our meat but buy less of it – when food is nutrient-dense, we don't require as much. We could buy meat, eggs and milk produced from animals that have lived their lives on pasture, rather than in cramped, dirty stalls or cages. We could refuse to participate in the brutality that is characteristic of factory farms. It costs more to raise

animals properly, the way we used to before farming became industrialized, so we should be willing to pay more to know that the animals we eat were treated well and with respect and to ensure they have been raised humanely.

If wealthy societies were willing to pay a little more for food, we could help ensure that farmers get paid what their produce is worth. We should also pay more for our food because good, tasty food takes time to grow and rear, and time costs money. Historically, people were happy to eat almost any cut from an animal, but these days we have eyes and stomachs mostly for the prime cuts, the easy bits, the luxury foods – fillets, loins, legs, roasts, chops – and we eschew bits that have built up a bit of muscle texture, connective tissue and, as a result, fat and flavour. These cuts are cheap *and* good value. They do take a little extra cooking skill, but it pays dividends in the end result. There is absolutely no doubt in my mind that slow-grown meat, though a little more expensive, tastes better than cheap, intensively farmed meat.

In a perfect world, we might buy organic where possible, not only for our own health but also to ensure that the land remains healthy for future generations. Pesticides are dangerous for everyone involved, not just us consumers, and they are damaging our soil, water and air. We should be willing to pay more for food that is safely and sustainably grown. Produce grown domestically often costs more than food shipped in from the other side of the world. Nevertheless, we should expect to pay extra for the food that didn't deplete the world's fossil fuels to get to us. This is just one small way we can help to reduce pollution.

It's actually more economical to invest in high-quality (whole, local, organic) food, because it results in improved health for us all. Less will need to be spent on drugs, dentistry, vitamin supplements and medical care. We can either pay the farmer or we can pay the hospital: we should choose to pay the farmer.

8
Baked

Serves
4

Probably nothing to do with the Duke of Wellington, as this is very much a 20th-century creation, this is a splendid thing to serve for Sunday lunch if you are feeling ambitious. Most recipes call for a layer of foie gras, which is authentic if a little grand – so it's optional here.

Beef Wellington

800g (1lb 12oz) fillet steak

1 tablespoon olive oil

250g (9oz) mixed wild mushrooms

50g (1¾oz) unsalted butter

1 large thyme sprig

100ml (3½fl oz) Madeira

250g (9oz) foie gras (optional)

8 slices of dry-cured ham

plain flour, for dusting

1 free-range egg, beaten

Maldon sea salt flakes and freshly ground black pepper

200ml (7fl oz) Madeira Gravy (see page 114), to serve

For the rough puff pastry

325g (11½oz) strong white flour

1 teaspoon fine sea salt

325g (11½oz) unsalted butter

150ml (¼ pint) cold water

First make the pastry. Sift the flour and salt into a bowl. Chop the butter, then add to the bowl and rub together to mix – there should still be small lumps of butter. Pour in the cold water and mix to form a firm dough – do not over-mix. Cover with clingfilm and refrigerate for 30 minutes to rest. Turn the pastry out on to a floured board and roll out into a square. There will be small streaks of butter running through the pastry – this is how it should be. Fold the right-hand third of the pastry halfway into the middle and repeat with the remaining left-hand side. Roll out again and repeat the folding process. Wrap the pastry in clingfilm and chill in the fridge for 30 minutes, or until needed.

Preheat your oven to 200°C (400°F), Gas Mark 6.

Season the meat and seal it on all sides in the olive oil in a smoking hot pan. Transfer it to the preheated oven and roast for 10 minutes. Remove from the oven, leave to cool, then chill in the fridge.

Meanwhile, finely chop the mushrooms. Heat the butter in a large pan and fry the mushrooms with the thyme sprig over a medium heat for about 10 minutes, stirring often, until you have a softened mixture. Season, pour over the Madeira and cook for a further 10 minutes, until all the liquid has been absorbed. The mixture should hold its shape when stirred. Remove the mushroom duxelle from the pan, discard the thyme and leave to cool.

Slice the foie gras, season, then pan-fry in a hot dry pan.

Overlap 2 pieces of clingfilm on a large chopping board.

Lay the ham on the clingfilm, slightly overlapping, in rows. Spread half the mushroom mix over the ham, then sit the sealed beef on it and spread the rest of the mushroom mix over the beef. Use the edges of the clingfilm to draw the ham around the fillet, then roll it into a sausage shape, twisting the ends of the clingfilm to tighten it as you go. Chill the rolled fillet in the refrigerator while you roll out the pastry.

On a lightly floured work surface, roll out one-third of the pastry to a strip about 3mm (⅛ inch) thick and 4cm (1½ inches) larger on all sides than the beef, ham and mushroom parcel. Place the pastry on a nonstick baking sheet or a baking tray covered with baking parchment. Roll out the remaining pastry to a rectangle about 3mm (⅛ inch) thick.

Carefully unwrap the fillet from the clingfilm and sit it in the centre of the smaller strip of pastry. Place the foie gras on top, then brush the edges of the pastry, and the top and sides of the wrapped fillet, with beaten egg. Using a rolling pin, carefully lift and drape the larger piece of pastry over the fillet, pressing well into the sides. Trim the edges to a rim about 4cm (1½ inches) wide and seal by pinching the pastry between your fingers or pressing together with a fork. Glaze with beaten egg and chill for at least 20 minutes.

Preheat the oven again to 200°C (400°F), Gas Mark 6. Brush the Wellington with a little more egg and cook for about 30 minutes, until golden and crisp. Allow to stand for 10–15 minutes, then serve cut in thick slices, with Madeira Gravy and sides of your choice.

A kind of pie was made by the Egyptians, the early Romans and the ancient Greeks, but the pastry was used for holding the filling, not for eating. By the time the pie arrived in medieval Europe the crust was edible and at some point it had become an integral part, eaten with the filling. There are two kinds of pie: a two-crust pie, and a top-crust pie, which is what we have here.

Steak & ale pie

about 50g (1¾oz) beef dripping

700g (1lb 9oz) chuck steak, cut into large chunks

20g (¾oz) plain flour seasoned with salt and pepper

200g (7oz) smoked bacon lardons

2 onions, peeled and chopped

2 large carrots, chopped

300ml (½ pint) bottle of dark ale

400ml (14fl oz) Basic Beef Broth (see page 112)

1 faggot of herbs (thyme, rosemary and bay leaf)

2 tablespoons brown sauce

1 bone marrow shaft, 7cm (2¾ inches) long

Maldon sea salt flakes and freshly ground black pepper

For the pastry

500g (1lb 2oz) self-raising flour, plus extra for dusting

1 teaspoon baking powder

½ teaspoon fine sea salt

100g (3½oz) unsalted butter, chilled and grated

100g (3½oz) bone marrow, chilled and grated

about 150ml (¼ pint) ice-cold milk, plus extra for glazing

Preheat the oven to 140°C (275°F), Gas Mark 1.

Heat the beef dripping in a large frying pan over a high heat. Toss the beef in the seasoned flour to coat and sear it in batches, taking care not to overcrowd the pan, until properly browned. Spoon the browned meat into an ovenproof casserole once done.

Reduce the heat slightly, add the lardons, onions and carrots to the frying pan and cook until the bacon fat begins to melt and the onions are golden brown on all sides. Then tip into the casserole.

Pour a little of the ale into the frying pan and bring to a simmer, scraping the base of the pan, then pour the whole lot into the casserole with the meat. Add the rest of the ale, the beef broth, faggot of herbs and brown sauce, then season and bring to a simmer. Cover, put into the oven for 2 hours, then uncover and cook, stirring occasionally, for a further hour, until the meat is tender.

Remove the casserole from the oven, correct the seasoning, remove the herbs and spoon it all into a pie dish. Leave to cool to room temperature.

Meanwhile, make the pastry. Mix the self-raising flour, baking powder and salt in a large bowl. Stir in the chilled, grated butter and bone marrow, then add enough iced milk to bring it together into a dough, using a palette knife to mix. Flatten into a disc, wrap in clingfilm and refrigerate for at least 1 hour.

Preheat the oven again, to 180°C (350°F), Gas Mark 4.

Lightly dust a work surface with flour and roll out the pastry to about 1cm (½ inch) thick. Place the bone marrow shaft in the centre of the pie, then place the pastry over the pie, pushing down around the edge to seal, and cutting a hole in the middle to allow the bone marrow shaft to protrude. Crimp the pastry edges between thumb and index finger. Brush with milk, then place on a baking tray and bake for about 45 minutes, until golden. Sprinkle with salt flakes before serving.

Lancashire is an English county of fine culinary traditions from Bury black pudding and black peas to Lancashire cheese and potted shrimp, its bounty is among the best in the country. Cowheel is a less well-known Lancashire delicacy but should most certainly not be forgotten; it's eaten cold in jelly with salt and vinegar, or used to add body to stews or pies as below. Desperate Dan was a fan, apparently...

Cowheel pie

1 cowheel, or cow hoof, split and cut into 4

1kg (2lb 4oz) boneless shin of beef, cut into 5cm (2 inch) pieces

50g (1¾oz) plain flour seasoned with salt and pepper

50g (1¾oz) beef dripping

1 litre (1¾ pints) Basic Beef Broth (see page 112)

2 large onions

2 large carrots

1 garlic clove

free-range egg and milk, for the egg wash

plain flour, for dusting

500g (1lb 2oz) shop-bought shortcrust pastry

Maldon sea salt flakes and freshly ground black pepper

Blanch the cowheel by covering it with cold water and bringing to the boil. Simmer for 30 seconds, then drain and refresh in cold water.

Preheat the oven to 150°C (300°F), Gas Mark 2.

Dust the diced beef shin with the seasoned flour and fry in batches in the beef dripping until well browned. Transfer to a casserole, then deglaze the pan with the beef broth and pour into the casserole. Add the cowheel, season, bring to a simmer, then cover and cook in the oven for 3 hours, until tender. Peel and chop the onions, carrots and garlic and add to the casserole, then return to the oven for a further hour.

Pass the contents of the casserole through a sieve into a clean pan, discarding the cowheel bones, which should have by now rendered the braise sticky and unctuous. Return the meat and vegetables to the sauce, place in a pie dish large enough to hold everything and leave to cool to room temperature.

Preheat the oven again to 180°C (350°F), Gas Mark 4.

Roll the shortcrust pastry out on a lightly floured work surface and cover the pie, sealing the edges with a little water. Brush with egg wash and bake the pie for about 30 minutes, until golden brown.

Makes
2

"Roast beef wrapped in a flat Yorkshire pudding, served with a dipping pot of gravy" is how this is described on the menu at Long Can Hall in Halifax, Yorkshire. It's a hybrid French dip-burrito-Yorkshire pudding and could easily be dismissed as a gimmick, were it not absolutely bloody delicious! There is a very fine line indeed between madness and genius...

Yorkshire pudding wrap

leftover roasting tray with drippings

Basic Beef Broth (see page 112)

Creamed Horseradish (see page 227) or mustard

2 large Yorkshire Puddings (see below)

leftover roast beef, shredded (see pages 326–9)

Take your leftover roasting tray and pour in the beef broth. Heat gently and stir and scrape to make a jus, then set aside to keep warm.

Spread horseradish or mustard on each Yorkshire pudding and pile the shredded roast beef at one end. Dress with a little of your prepared jus or gravy and roll into a burrito-like shape. Serve with more jus or gravy on the side, for dipping.

Despite half my family harking from North Yorkshire and growing up eating Yorkshire puddings every weekend, it took me years to master the perfect pudding. Originally they were cooked underneath roasting meats, to catch valuable meat drippings, and consequently they were much stodgier and heavier affairs. Now they are baked in an oven, the result is more crispy and voluminous, but I still like a soggy bottom soaked in drippings...

Yorkshire pudding

free-range eggs, Burford Browns for preference (allow 1 egg per person)

semi-skimmed milk

plain flour

beef dripping

Mix equal quantities BY VOLUME of eggs, milk and plain flour (2 eggs, for example, will make 2 large Yorkshire puddings). Store the batter overnight in the fridge.

Heat the beef dripping in Yorkshire pudding tins until smoking hot and pour in a ladle of Yorkshire pudding batter. If using a large baking tin to make a large Yorkshire pudding, fill to about 4cm (1½ inches) deep.

Bake in a hot oven at 200°C (400°F), Gas Mark 6 for about 20 minutes or until golden brown and risen, then turn over to colour the underneath.

Makes
4

I lived in St Mawes in Cornwall for a year and was rather partial to a Cornish pasty or two. The very best example I tasted was at The Gardens of Heligan and it contained a rogue ingredient – mustard. I've put it down as optional here, as it's not really traditional.

Cornish pasty

For the filling

450g (1lb) good-quality beef, such as skirt

450g (1lb) firm, waxy potatoes

250g (9oz) swede

200g (7oz) onions

1 tablespoon butter

1 tablespoon English mustard (optional)

Maldon sea salt flakes and freshly ground white pepper

For the pastry

120g (4¼oz) vegetable shortening or beef dripping

25g (1oz) cake margarine

500g (1lb 2oz) strong white bread flour, plus extra for dusting

5g (about 1 teaspoon) Maldon sea salt flakes

175ml (6fl oz) cold water

beaten free-range egg, for glazing

To make the pastry, use your fingers to rub the fat lightly into the flour until it resembles breadcrumbs. Transfer the mixture to the bowl of a stand mixer, add the salt and water and mix until the pastry comes together, moves away from the sides of the bowl and becomes elastic. This may take longer than normal pastry, but it gives it the strength that is needed to hold the filling and retain a good shape. Leave to rest for 3 hours in the refrigerator – this is a very important stage, as it is almost impossible to roll and shape the pastry when fresh.

Meanwhile, preheat the oven to 180°C (350°F), Gas Mark 4. Chop the beef and vegetables into 2cm (¾ inch) chunks.

Once the pastry is chilled, roll it out on a floured surface and cut out 4 circles measuring 18cm (7 inches) in diameter.

Layer one-quarter of the meat and vegetables on one side of each circle of pastry, adding plenty of seasoning. Mix the butter and mustard together and place on top. Bring the pastry over the filling and crimp the edges together. Crimping is the secret to a true Cornish pasty, but it really has to be taught – it's almost impossible to describe. Alternatively, just flatten like a turnover and mark with a fork. Glaze the pastry all over with beaten egg.

Place the pasties on a baking tray and bake for 1 hour, or until golden brown. Leave to cool for 30 minutes before eating.

Little pastry pockets called empanadas crop up all over Latin America, Spain and Portugal, and of course a version is found in our very own Cornwall, England. A Chilean pasty is made with beef, onion, hard-boiled egg, olives and raisins, and is called *pino* in Chile. While national pride dictates that the Cornish pasty be my favourite, I strongly urge you to try this. It is very, very good.

Empanada Chilena

235ml (8½fl oz) milk

300g (10½oz) beef dripping, melted

625g (1lb 6oz) plain flour,
plus extra for dusting

3 teaspoons Maldon sea salt flakes

3 large onions, peeled and chopped

3 garlic cloves, chopped

½ teaspoon hot paprika

½ teaspoon ground cumin

½ teaspoon ground cinnamon

400g (14oz) minced beef

100ml (3½fl oz) Basic Beef Broth
(see page 112)

150g (5½oz) raisins

150g (5½oz) black olives, chopped

4 hard-boiled free-range eggs, sliced

1 free-range egg yolk, beaten
with 2 tablespoons milk for the
egg wash

Maldon sea salt flakes and freshly
ground black pepper

Warm the milk and add 200g (7oz) of the melted beef dripping. Stir the flour and salt together in a large bowl, then pour the wet mixture into the dry and mix into a dough. Cover and leave to cool, then chill for 2 hours before using.

Heat the rest of the dripping in a large frying pan over a medium heat. Add the onions, garlic, paprika, cumin, cinnamon, salt and pepper, and cook for 8–10 minutes, until the onion is golden. Add the minced beef, stir and cook until completely browned. Drain the fat from the frying pan, add the beef broth and raisins and cook until almost dry.

Stir the olives and hard-boiled eggs into the mixture, then remove from the heat and set aside to cool.

Preheat the oven to 190°C (375°F), Gas Mark 5.

On a lightly floured board, roll the dough out to a thickness of about 3mm (⅛ inch). Using a cutter, stamp out 12cm (4½ inch) circles and drop equal portions of the filling into the centre of each. Fold each circle in half and press the edges together with a fork to seal. Brush the tops of the empanadas with the egg wash and arrange on baking paper-covered baking trays.

Bake for about 25 minutes, or until golden brown.

We all love cottage pie, and I sometimes use this as a pimped steak side instead of mash and gravy. In early cookery books, it was a means of using leftover meat of any kind, and the pie dish was lined with mashed potato as well as having a mashed potato crust on top. Here I've use braised short rib.

Hachis parmentier (Cottage pies)

1kg (2lb 4oz) large mashing potatoes

1kg (2lb 4oz) Braised Short Ribs recipe (see page 265)

4 tablespoons chopped flat leaf parsley

50g (¾oz) chopped bone marrow

1 tablespoon beef dripping, melted

250g (9oz) unsalted butter

250ml (9fl oz) double cream

6 free-range egg yolks

Maldon sea salt flakes and freshly ground black pepper

Place the potatoes on a baking tray and bake in a preheated oven at 180°C (350°F), Gas Mark 4 for 45 minutes, or until soft.

Remove the bones from the Braised Short Ribs, then shred all the meat and crush the vegetables. Put the meat and veg from the short ribs into a saucepan. Bring the braising liquor to the boil and pour it over the shredded meat and veg. Reduce by half until it is sticky and thick, then season to taste. Fold in the chopped parsley and bone marrow.

Remove the potatoes from the oven and allow to cool slightly, then scoop out the flesh, leaving a 5mm (¼ inch) layer of potato on the skin. Brush the skins with the beef dripping, season and return to the oven until crispy and golden.

In a separate pan, bring the butter and cream to a simmer. Pass the potato flesh through a mouli or ricer (or use a potato masher) and gradually combine with the butter and cream mix to make a warm mash. Remove from the heat and work in the egg yolks, mashing well. Season to taste, then spoon the finished mash into a piping bag and set aside.

Remove the potato skins from the oven and place on a cooling rack. Spoon the short rib mix into each skin until it is full, reserving some sauce, and pipe the mash on top.

Return to the oven for 10 minutes, or until golden and bubbling, then drizzle a little extra sauce over the top. Serve as a garnish to grilled steak or as a meal in itself.

8 sheets of fresh lasagne pasta sheets

600g (1lb 5oz) My Spag Bol sauce
(see page 238) or ragù

Parmesan cheese, finely grated

extra virgin olive oil

fresh herb leaves (parsley, oregano,
basil), to garnish

For the cheese sauce

125ml (4fl oz) milk

15g (½oz) unsalted butter

15g (½oz) plain flour

25g (1oz) Stilton cheese, grated

25g (1oz) Cheddar cheese, grated

25g (1oz) Ogleshield or other
washed rind cheese, grated

pinch of freshly grated nutmeg

Maldon sea salt flakes and freshly
ground white pepper

Open lasagne

Said to be one of the oldest pasta dishes, there is more than one way to
make lasagne. This is the individual plated version used in restaurants,
less like a cake or pie, and consequently much easier to present on a plate.

First make the cheese sauce. Pour the milk into a saucepan and bring to a foamy boil,
then reduce the heat to low and keep warm. In another saucepan, melt the butter over
a medium heat. Whisk in the flour and continue until a smooth, pale "roux" forms.

While whisking steadily, add the hot milk into the roux a spoonful at a time, whisking
all the time, and completely incorporate each spoonful before adding the next.

Once all the milk has been added, continue to whisk until the sauce thickens and bubbles
gently, about 2 minutes. Add the Stilton, Cheddar, Ogleshield, nutmeg, salt and pepper and
stir until completely melted.

Cook the pasta in boiling salted water until cooked through but very slightly al dente,
or firm to the touch.

Heat the sauce or ragù in a separate pan, and reheat the cheese sauce if necessary.

Spoon one-eighth of the sauce on to the centre of each warmed plate and top with
a sheet of cooked pasta. Repeat this, and finish with 50ml (2fl oz) or 2–3 tablespoons of
cheese sauce in the centre of the top sheet of pasta, taking care not to reach the edge.

Grate plenty of Parmesan over the top of each lasagne and place under a preheated grill to
melt the cheese and singe the pasta so that it starts to go golden and crisp, turning up at
the edges.

Dress with olive oil and scatter the herbs over the top.

This is a majestic dish for special occasions and events – the perfume emanating from the dish while you are turning it out will send you over the edge! Biryani is found from Iran to India and Pakistan in various guises. Not to be confused with a pilau, which is put together from raw and cooked, a biryani is always cooked before assembly and then baked to bring everything together.

Persian beef biryani

15g (½oz) finely chopped garlic cloves

15g (½oz) peeled and finely chopped fresh root ginger

15g (½oz) finely chopped green chillies

800g (1lb 12oz) chuck steak

400g (14oz) basmati rice

150g (5½oz) ghee or clarified butter

1 large onion, peeled and thinly sliced

2 green peppers, deseeded and thinly sliced

75g (2¾oz) dried apricots, chopped

50g (1¾oz) golden raisins

50g (1¾oz) flaked almonds

4 small cinnamon sticks

6 black cardamom pods

6 green cardamom pods

1 teaspoon whole black peppercorns, lightly crushed

½ teaspoon saffron threads

finely grated zest and juice of 1 small orange

2 carrots, grated

250ml (9fl oz) Basic Beef Broth (see page 112), heated

Maldon sea salt flakes and freshly ground black pepper

Crush the garlic, ginger and chillies to a smooth purée with a mortar and pestle.

Cut the beef into small strips, place in a shallow bowl and mix with the garlic, chilli and ginger paste. Cover and leave to marinate for 1 hour.

Preheat the oven to 170°C (340°F), Gas Mark 3½.

Cover the basmati rice with salted cold water and leave for 1 hour, then drain and rinse. Pour boiling water over the rice in a pan and simmer for 6 minutes, then drain.

Put a large frying pan over a medium-high heat and add 2 tablespoons of ghee.

Season the beef and sauté in batches, using fresh ghee each time. Remove the beef from the pan and set aside.

Add more ghee to the pan, then add the onion and peppers and fry for 10 minutes, stirring until the onion is caramelized and the peppers are soft. Remove from the pan and set aside.

Add another tablespoon of ghee and fry the fruits, almonds, spices and orange zest on a medium heat for 4–5 minutes, stirring, until the nuts are golden brown. Add the grated carrot, cook for 2 minutes, just to soften, then remove from the heat and add the orange juice.

Brush the inside of a 20cm (8 inch) ovenproof lidded casserole dish with ghee, then line the base and sides with greaseproof paper and brush this, too, with ghee.

Spread one-fifth of the par-cooked rice over the bottom of the casserole, followed by half the onion mix and half the beef. Season, then cover the beef with another layer of rice, followed by half the spiced carrot and fruit mix, then another layer of rice, spreading out each layer evenly.

Repeat the layers, finishing with rice. Pour over any juices and the hot beef broth, then cover with a clean tea towel and the lid. Bake for 45 minutes, until the rice is light, fluffy and crisp around the edges. Turn out on to a large platter, peel away the greaseproof paper and serve.

Serves
4

An authentic Macaronade is made from the juices of a meat stew such as the daube or *estouffade* of southern France. Once the noodles are cooked, they are moistened with the wine-rich broth, layered with freshly grated Parmesan cheese and browned in the oven. This is a version I've been serving for years as a side, or as a dish in its own right.

La Macaronade

250g (9oz) elbow (short) macaroni

250ml (9fl oz) Braised Short Ribs cooking liquid (see page 265)

100g (3½oz) Parmesan cheese, finely grated

50g (1¾oz) bone marrow, chopped

Maldon sea salt flakes and freshly ground black pepper

Preheat the oven to 150°C (300°F), Gas Mark 2.

Bring a pan of salted water to the boil and cook the macaroni for 10 minutes, or according to the packet instructions. Drain and reserve.

Mix the braised beef cooking liquid with half the cheese and the blanched hot macaroni and season to taste with salt and pepper. Add the bone marrow and mix to combine. Scoop into an ovenproof pot or baking dish and sprinkle the top with the remaining cheese, then bake for 10–15 minutes.

Finish under the grill, until the cheese is golden and bubbling, then allow to sit for a few minutes before serving.

Beef & the environment

Critics of the environmental impact of cattle farming assert that thousands of litres of water are required for every kilogram of beef reared. However, this claim is based on intensive farming practices connected with grain-fed beef. Grass-fed cattle are not voracious consumers of water, as they get most of their needs from grass, which can be as much as 75 per cent water. The most striking attribute of beef is that it can live on a simple diet of grass, which it forages for itself – and for protecting land, water, soil and climate, there is nothing better than dense grass.

Countering global movement

Grass-fed cattle could be the key to a promising strategy for countering global warming, through carbon capture (or sequestration) and the restoration of carbon to the soil. Up to 10 per cent of all human-caused carbon emissions in the last century are thought to have come from soil. This results from tillage, which releases carbon and strips the earth of protective vegetation, and from poor farming practices that fail to return nutrients and organic matter to the earth. Grazing pasture is ideal for carbon sequestration through photosynthesis and for holding it in stable forms in the soil; read on to find out how.

One of the worst greenhouse gases, methane, is produced by micro-organisms known as methanogens under anaerobic conditions (without oxygen), in animals and their manure. However, as beef manure is typically applied to the land while fresh, the anaerobic conditions necessary for methane production are impaired. The manure therefore accounts for only around 5 per cent of man-made emissions, and, in fact, pastured cattle have almost no carbon footprint.

Approaches as intuitive as good pasture management and as obscure as plentiful dung-beetle populations have been shown to reduce methane. Dung beetles encourage the growth of healthy grass through their burrowing in soil, which aerates it and allows rainwater and nutrients into the ground. The cattle manure provides nutrients to the dung beetles, which are in turn fed upon by birds and other creatures, and plants quickly utilize the readily available nitrogen in the urine. Most of the nutrients in the manure are a valuable source of fertilizer when applied to surrounding grassland, reducing the reliance on fertilizers and increasing the organic matter in soils.

What's more, grazing cattle stimulate vegetative growth through the "pruning" effect of their mouths, the trampling of their hoofs and the action of their digestive tracts, which promote seed germination and the recycling of nutrients. These beneficial disturbances, like those once created by wild grazing herds, help keep woody shrubs at bay and benefit grassland ecosystems, of which they are an integral part. They play an important role, with nutrients in manure and urine being dispersed as cattle move through the pasture seeking new areas to graze.

Research by the UK Soil Association shows that if cattle are raised principally on grass, and if good farming practices are followed, enough carbon could be sequestered to offset the methane emissions of all UK beef cattle, plus half the country's dairy herd.

Environmental gains

Grass is also one of the best ways to generate and safeguard soil and to protect water. Grass blades shield soil from erosive wind and water, while the roots form a mat that holds soil and water in place. According to soil experts, erosion from conventionally tilled fields can be between 10 and 100 times greater than from fields with native vegetation, such as that which is typically found on well-managed grazing lands. In fact, good pasturing technique can actually build soil.

As we consider the long-term prospects for feeding the rapidly expanding population of the human race, correctly raised, grass-fed cattle remain an essential element. Ruminants are the only livestock that can effectively convert hay – a byproduct of arable farming – into high-quality protein for human consumption. Raising beef cattle on grass is an environmental gain for the planet.

Roasted

9

My perfect roast

First you need to decide what cut you want. You can roast many parts of a cow. Classic roasting cuts, however, include silverside, topside, rump, sirloin, fillet or chateau and fore rib. All but the fore rib are usually sold boneless. If you're nervous about carving meat, the fore rib may not be tempting, but personally, I like to roast on the bone as I believe you end up with a more succulent piece of meat. If you must go boneless, I recommend rump, although it's not often sold as a roasting joint. For a smaller joint, you could do worse than rolled rib-eye, which is cut from the centre (or "eye") of the ribs.

Your beef should be dark in colour, indicating that it is well hung and mature. It should have a thick layer of yellow fat, which adds flavour and prevents it from drying out. Some visible marbling is good, but not excessive and certainly not thick clumps of fat. Remember, good marbling laid down slowly is often barely visible to the eye – but it's still there and will still moisten your roast.

Next you'll need to decide how much to buy. Don't worry about buying too much as everyone loves cold roast beef! As a guide, a 2kg (4½lb) bone-in or 1.4kg (3lb) boneless cut will feed six.

Temperatures & timings

Let the beef come to room temperature by removing it from the refrigerator at least an hour before cooking; this is called "tempering" in chef-speak. While your beef is tempering, you'll need to decide on the cooking temperature, which is obviously a personal preference and might even vary among members of the family. There are several opinions about the perfect temperature at which to cook roast beef, but in my experience starting the beef in a hot oven – 220°C (425°F), Gas Mark 7 – for the first 20 minutes, then reducing the temperature to 160°C (320°F), Gas Mark 2½ for the remaining cooking time will give you the best results. How long that remaining cooking time is depends on how you like to eat your roast beef.

- On the bone, medium-rare: 30 minutes per kg (14 minutes per lb) or until an internal temperature of 60°C (140°F) is reached.

- On the bone, medium: 35 minutes per kg (16 minutes per lb) or until an internal temperature of 65°C (150°F) is reached.

- On the bone, medium-well done: 40 minutes per kg (18 minutes per lb) or until an internal temperature of 70°C (160°F) is reached.

Resting

After roasting the beef, turn the oven off completely and allow the meat to start its resting period inside the oven, with its residual heat, for 20 minutes or so. The fibres in meat tighten up during cooking, and resting allows them to relax, releasing some of the meat juices, which results in a more tender piece of meat. Once it is removed from the oven, the meat then continues to rest. After 30 minutes' rest (in total), the joint is ready to carve, but you can leave it for up to an hour in a warm place – until its internal temperature is 55°C (130°F) – and its characteristics and indeed the flavour of the joint will improve over this time.

Carving

It's not over yet. Yes, I know the smell is killing you and, yes, you've probably sneaked a crispy bit while no one is looking – that's the cook's prerogative. If you've sourced a beautiful, properly hung piece of beef from a good herd, and have cooked and rested it carefully, it would be a terrible crime not to carve it properly.

First off, make sure your knives are sharp – the sharper the better. Always cut on a carving board. It's best not to use too much pressure when carving; let the knife do the work and use long, even strokes. You are looking for even, uniform slices that will look appetizing when neatly arranged on the plate. Too much pressure alters the shape of your roast and makes for uneven, misshapen slices, which get worse the further into the joint you carve. Keep an eye on the end of the knife, making sure it's in line with the handle, to avoid cutting wedges instead of slices. When carving a bone-in joint, take care not to scrape the bone, which would blunt your knife. Light use of a carving fork is sensible – not buried up to the hilt, but just holding the joint in place.

As to thickness, assuming you've chosen your meat wisely and cooked it judiciously, then the thickness of the slices is a matter of personal choice. I plump for thicker slices, confident in the knowledge that my roast is tender and juicy, as they will hold on to their heat much longer than thinner slices.

Rump makes a great flavoursome roast, but can sometimes be a little tough – cooking low and slow combats this and helps keep the meat fibres tender. It's important the meat is cut from a single muscle in the rump to avoid those meat fibres running in different directions when carving.

Slow-roast rump of beef

1kg (2lb 4oz) beef rump

beef dripping

Maldon sea salt flakes and freshly ground black pepper

You will also need

a meat thermometer

To serve

Yorkshire Pudding (see page 304)

Roast Potatoes (see opposite)

Mead-braised Carrots & Shallots (see opposite)

Mustard Greens (see page 328)

Madeira Gravy (see page 114)

Remove the beef from the fridge 1 hour before cooking. Preheat the oven to 75°C (170°F), Gas-as-low-as-it-will-go. Place a large griddle over a high heat and add some beef dripping. Once the griddle is smoking hot, season the meat with lots of salt and pepper, then sear the rump all over the surface.

Place it in a roasting tin and roast for 4 hours, removing it when the internal temperature of the meat reaches 57°C (135°F) for medium-rare and 60°C (140°F) for medium.

Leave to rest for at least 20 minutes while you make the Yorkshires, by which time the internal temperature will have risen by a couple of degrees. Serve with Yorkshire Pudding, Roast Potatoes, Mead-braised Carrots & Shallots, Mustard Greens and Madeira Gravy.

Roast potatoes Serves 4-6

I used to put bowls of these crispy, beefy golden roast potatoes on the bar of my pub the Albion every weekend, an East End London tradition. Leftover "roasties" make great hash and bubble and squeak, and are good smashed, then mixed with grated cheese, baked until gooey, and garnished with chopped spring onions.

1kg (2lb 4oz) roasting potatoes, peeled and cut into rough large chunks

200ml (7fl oz) beef dripping

1 garlic bulb, smashed

1 rosemary sprig

Maldon sea salt flakes

Boil the potatoes in heavily salted water until cooked through. Drain thoroughly, then toss the potatoes several times to roughen the edges. Allow to air-dry and cool, tossing again to roughen the edges still further.

Preheat the oven to 200°C (400°F), Gas Mark 6. Heat the beef dripping in roasting trays and add the garlic and potatoes. Roast in the oven for 30 minutes. Remove from the oven, season, add the rosemary, then toss the potatoes to mix thoroughly.

Return the potatoes to the oven for another 30 minutes, giving them the occasional toss.

When cooked through with a golden crust, remove from the oven and serve with your roast.

Mead-braised carrots & shallots Serves 4-6

250g (9oz) banana shallots

30ml (about 2 tablespoons) olive oil

100g (3½oz) smoked bacon lardons.

3 garlic cloves

3 thyme sprigs

250g (9oz) carrots

50ml (2fl oz) cider vinegar

250ml (9fl oz) medium/sweet mead

250ml (9fl oz) chicken stock

Maldon sea salt and freshly ground black pepper

Preheat the oven to 180°C (350°F), Gas Mark 4.

Peel the shallots and toss with the oil, a good teaspoon of salt, black pepper, the bacon lardons, garlic and thyme and place in a cast-iron casserole dish. Cook in the oven, stirring occasionally, for 45 minutes until the shallots are golden.

Add the carrots and deglaze the casserole (stir and scrape any sticky bits on the base of the casserole) with the vinegar followed by the mead.

Allow the vinegar and mead to reduce by one-third on the hob before adding the chicken stock and returning to the oven for a further 10 minutes. Season to taste before serving.

Mustard greens Serves 4

High in vitamins A and K, mustard greens (*Brassica juncea*) are more pungent than the closely related cabbage greens (*Brassica oleracea*), and are frequently mixed with these milder leaves in a dish of "mixed greens". Here I've gone the other way and intensified the heat of the leaves even further with a mustard dressing.

800g (1lb 12oz) mustard greens, washed

For the mustard dressing

50g (1¾oz) Dijon mustard

200ml (7fl oz) extra virgin olive oil

2 teaspoons red wine vinegar

Maldon sea salt flakes and freshly ground black pepper

Whisk all the dressing ingredients together.

Blanch the mustard greens briefly in boiling water, then refresh in cold water.

Reheat the greens in boiling salted water, then drain and toss with a generous amount of mustard dressing. Season to taste and serve.

Serves
4-6

1.5kg (3lb 5oz) aged rib of beef,
on the bone

beef dripping

Maldon sea salt flakes and freshly
ground black pepper

You will also need

a meat thermometer

Roast rib of beef

A roast rib of beef or a standing rib roast is the king of roasts – large
and impressive, it is helped by layers of tasty fat running through the
meat keeping it juicy and flavoursome. My favourite.

Preheat the oven to 220°C (425°F), Gas Mark 7.

Massage the whole joint with soft beef dripping and season lightly, all over, with salt
and pepper. Place on a roasting tray and put into the oven. Cook on this high heat
for about 20 minutes, until the meat is well browned and sizzling in the pan. Then
reduce the oven temperature to 160°C (325°F), Gas Mark 3 for a further 20 minutes,
or until the internal temperature of the meat reaches 57°C (135°F) for medium-rare
or 60°C (140°F) for medium (my preference for this cut).

Remove from the oven, place the joint on a warm serving plate or carving tray,
and leave to rest for no less than 30 minutes before carving and serving.

Serves 4-6

Chateaubriand comes from the end of the fillet and is also called rump fillet by some butchers. It is extremely tender, but lacks the flavour of rump or rib. It's also rather expensive, but if tender beef is what floats your boat then this is the cut for you.

Roast chateaubriand

1kg (2lb 4oz) Chateaubriand roast (the top, thick part of the tenderloin), trimmed of fat and silver skin, and tied at 1cm (½ inch) intervals with butcher's twine

20g (¾oz) beef dripping

20g (¾oz) unsalted butter

Maldon sea salt flakes and freshly ground black pepper

You will also need

a meat thermometer

To serve

Collard Greens & Gravy (see below)

Beef Dripping Chips (see page 280)

Preheat the oven to 200°C (400°F), Gas Mark 6.

Remove the beef from the fridge and let it sit at room temperature for 1 hour, then season liberally with salt and pepper.

Heat the dripping in a large ovenproof sauté pan over a high heat. Sear the meat until browned on all sides, about 8 minutes in total. Reduce the heat to low, and add the butter. Once the butter has melted, baste the meat with it, using a spoon. Put the pan into the oven for 5 minutes, then reduce the oven temperature to 160°C (325°F), Gas Mark 3 and cook until the internal temperature reaches 55°C (130°F) at the thickest part of the roast. Place the meat on a cutting board and let it rest for 30 minutes.

To serve, remove the twine from the meat, slice into 4 portions, and sprinkle with salt and pepper. Serve with Collard Greens & Gravy and Beef Dripping Chips.

Collard greens & gravy Serves 4

Trim 800g (1lb 12oz) of collard greens and wash them well. Blanch for 5 minutes in boiling seasoned water and drain well. Mix with ½ recipe of Braised Shallots & Garlic with Bone Marrow (see page 49), then correct the seasoning and serve with grilled steak or Roast Chateaubriand.

My instinct has always been to eschew any filler in a meat recipe in favour of MAXIMUM MEAT! However, I've come to understand that filler, in this case breadcrumbs, is integral for holding on to juices and flavour. Without it all the good stuff leaches out, leaving behind a dry meatball, and nobody likes a dry meatball. This mixture can also be formed into a meatloaf and baked as opposite.

Meatballs

100g (3½oz) white bread, cubed

100ml (3½fl oz) buttermilk

1 small onion, peeled and finely chopped

6 garlic cloves, crushed

100g (3½oz) Parmesan cheese, finely grated

½ bunch of flat leaf parsley, chopped

2 free-range eggs

100ml (3½fl oz) cold Basic Beef Broth (see page 112)

1 teaspoon ground fennel seeds

400g (14oz) minced beef (ideally short rib), 20% fat content

400g (14oz) minced veal shoulder

100g (3½oz) bone marrow, chopped

beef dripping, for frying

Maldon sea salt flakes and freshly ground black pepper

For the sauce

2 onions, peeled and chopped

2 shallots, peeled and chopped

1 garlic bulb, cloves chopped

100ml (3½fl oz) olive oil

2 x 400g (14oz) cans chopped tomatoes

1 faggot of herbs (thyme, oregano, bay leaf, rosemary)

Start with the sauce. Preheat the oven to 160°C (325°F), Gas Mark 3. In a deep casserole, fry the onions, shallots and garlic in the olive oil until translucent. Add the canned tomatoes and the faggot of herbs, bring to the boil, cover and place in the oven for 1 hour. Whiz with a stick blender, then pass through a fine sieve back into the pan and correct the seasoning.

Combine the bread with the buttermilk, tossing to coat. Let it stand until the bread is completely moist, about 10 minutes. Add the onion, garlic, half the grated Parmesan, the parsley, eggs, cold beef broth and fennel seeds. Season well, then add the minced meats and bone marrow and mix until thoroughly blended with the bread mixture.

Form the meat mixture into golfball-sized balls and fry in beef dripping until coloured all over. Add to the tomato sauce, cover and cook in the oven for 20 minutes.

Serve the meatballs with either pasta or polenta, spooning the sauce all over and grating the remaining Parmesan on top.

Rarely seen in restaurants, meatloaf is a proper "home-cooked" meal. My version makes use of the meatball recipe opposite, and is also not bad straight from the fridge, sliced and eaten cold in a sandwich.

Meatloaf

For the meatballs/meatloaf

1 x recipe Meatballs mixture, mixed, but not rolled into balls (see opposite)

For the glaze

ready-made barbecue sauce

Madeira Gravy (see page 114)

You will also need

a meat thermometer

Preheat the oven to 160°C (325°F) Gas Mark 3. Place the meatball mixture on a baking sheet and use your hands to gently form it into a rustic loaf shape, about 20cm (8 inches) long and 15cm (6 inches) wide. Place the meat mixture in a 450g (1lb) loaf tin lined with nonstick baking paper and use your hands to flatten the top.

Next make your glaze. In a small bowl add equal quantities of barbecue sauce and Madeira Gravy and stir to combine. Slather the glaze all over the meatloaf, then bake for about 1 hour, basting with the glaze halfway through, until the internal temperature registers 75°C (167°F). Allow to rest for 20 minutes before serving with extra Madeira Gravy.

A much-abused Italian-American classic sandwich which, when made using prime ingredients and with care and attention, can sing and be very special.

Meatball sandwich

4 large soft bread rolls

extra virgin olive oil

1 garlic clove

½ recipe of Meatballs (see page 332)

100g (3½oz) Parmesan cheese

200g (7oz) mozzarella cheese, cut into 8 slices

Preheat the oven to 180°C (350°F), Gas Mark 4.

Warm the rolls in the oven for 5–10 minutes, then cut them in half lengthways.

Drizzle the cut sides of each roll half with olive oil and rub with a cut clove of garlic until fragrant. Arrange the bottom roll halves on a baking sheet, cut sides up, and spoon a generous layer of the meatball tomato sauce on to each.

Slice each meatball in half and arrange on top of the tomato sauce, overlapping as necessary for even coverage. Spoon more tomato sauce on top of the meatball halves and grate the Parmesan all over.

Lay slices of mozzarella on top of the meatballs. Transfer the baking sheet to the oven and bake for about 4 minutes, until the cheese is fully melted. Warm the top roll halves in the oven for the last minute of cooking. Close the sandwiches and serve immediately.

Makes
1

Two LA restaurants claim to be the originators of the French dip sandwich, Philippe The Original and Cole's Pacific Electric Buffet. In the name of research I visited both, and they are very similar: the roll is dipped in the hot beef juices before assembly and is served "wet" or "double-dipped" and *au jus*, with more jus and mustard on the side. Both restaurants were established in 1908. However, Cole's claims to have originated the sandwich shortly after the restaurant opened in 1908, while Philippe's claims that owner Philippe Mathieu invented it in 1918. Whatever the truth is, a French Dip is a mighty sandwich indeed. My interpretation includes cheese and onion, which can be left out if you favour authenticity.

French dip

200ml (7fl oz) Basic Beef Broth (see page 112)

roast beef juices and drippings from the roast beef

15–20cm (6–8 inch) small soft French stick

1 tablespoon American mustard, French's for preference

2–3 tablespoons Onion Confit (see page 162), optional

200g (7oz) rare Roast Rib of Beef (see page 329), very thinly sliced

50g (1¾oz) sliced Cheddar or, if you can find it, Ogleshield cheese

To make your jus: deglaze the beef roasting dish with beef broth, then pour in any roasting juices and dripping. Reduce to your taste (but authentic *au jus* is quite thin).

Slice the bread in half and toast the cut sides. Spread mustard on the bottom half of the bread and dip the top side of the bread in the prepared jus or gravy.

Pile the onions, if using, on to the bottom half of the bread, then the warm, sliced roast rib on top. Scatter over the cheese and place under a preheated grill until it melts.

Place the lid on top and serve with more jus on the side for dipping.

Serves
6 as a starter
or 4 as a main
course

Loosely based on the Italian *vitello tonnato*, this is great on a Victorian-style cold cuts board. Known as lunch or deli meats, cold cuts are reappearing on restaurant menus – and that can only be a good thing.

Roast veal with boiled eggs & anchovy cream

800g (1lb 12oz) rose veal rump

2 tablespoons olive oil

4 free-range eggs, Burford Browns for preference

200ml (7fl oz) Anchovy Cream (see page 141)

Maldon sea salt flakes and freshly ground black pepper

To garnish

salted anchovy fillets

deep-fried parsley

thyme sprigs

Preheat the oven to 160°C (325°F), Gas Mark 3.

Lightly season the veal rump, then heat the olive oil in a frying pan over a high heat. Add the veal and seal on all sides until golden brown all over. Place in the oven and roast for 30 minutes, then turn the oven off and leave the meat inside to cool.

Cook the eggs in boiling water for 4 minutes and remove from the heat, leaving them to cool in their water.

When everything is at room temperature, remove the veal rump from the oven and set aside. Peel the eggs and slice. Rinse the salt from the anchovies and pat dry on kitchen paper.

Thinly slice the roast veal on to a platter and dress with the Anchovy Cream and slices of boiled egg. Garnish with anchovy fillets, deep-fried parsley and thyme sprigs. A suitable side might be potato salad.

Serves
4

4 x 250g (9oz) untrimmed tomahawk rose veal chops (see below)

100g (3½oz) white bread, chopped

200ml (7fl oz) milk

1 free-range egg

2 tablespoons beef dripping

100g (3½oz) caul fat, soaked and washed in cold water

250g (9oz) unsalted butter

Maldon sea salt flakes and freshly ground black pepper

To serve

cooked spinach

toast

Braised Shallots & Garlic with Bone Marrow (see page 49)

lemon wedges

Veal chop Pojarski

An authentic Veal Pojarski is really a giant meatball reformed around its bone, created by Pojarsky for Czar Nicholas I of Russia. My conscience won't allow me to chop the loin off the meat, so this is my version.

Preheat the oven to 180°C (350°F), Gas Mark 4.

Trim the meat off the long bones, keeping the eyes of the chops attached to the bone – you could ask your butcher to do this for you, and he/she might even mince it for you! If not, chop all the trimmed meat very finely (you could also use a food processor).

Soak the bread in the milk and mix with the chopped veal. Add the egg and season aggressively with salt and pepper.

Heat a spoonful of beef dripping in a frying pan, then season the trimmed chops, add to the hot pan and colour all over but without cooking through. Remove from the pan and allow to cool. Top one side of each chop with a ball of the chopped veal mixture and mould it over the top.

Spread out your washed caul fat and wrap each veal chop in a parcel-like fashion, leaving the bone totally exposed.

Heat a large cocotte dish or ovenproof sauté pan with the remaining spoonful of dripping and fry the wrapped chops until coloured all over. Add the butter and allow to foam, then spoon this foaming butter all over the chops and place in the preheated oven for 20 minutes.

Remove from the oven and allow to rest for 20 minutes, then serve with cooked spinach on toast, Braised Shallots & Garlic with Bone Marrow and lemon wedges.

MOO

Tomahawk chops are also known as bone-in rib-eye steaks with the bones left long.

A version of this was on the menu at Le Gavroche way back in the late Eighties, and it's one of my favourite offal dishes even now. The Roux version, *rognon de veau aux trois moutardes*, was made with the addition of tarragon mustard.

Roast veal kidney with mustard

100g (3½oz) unsalted butter

1 whole veal kidney, about 400g (14oz) in weight, in its caul fat

1 banana shallot, finely chopped

100ml (3½fl oz) dry white wine

100ml (3½fl oz) double cream

1 tablespoon Dijon mustard

1 tablespoon grain mustard

1 teaspoon thyme leaves

Maldon sea salt flakes and freshly ground black pepper

fresh egg noodles, pasta or toast, to serve

Preheat the oven to 220°C (425°F), Gas Mark 7.

Heat a heavy-based cast-iron pan and add half the butter. Season the whole kidney liberally, add to the pan and colour all over, then place in the preheated oven for 5 minutes. Turn the kidney over, spooning the foaming butter over the top, and roast for a further 5 minutes, until the outside of the kidney is golden and crispy. Remove from the oven and place on a warm plate to rest.

Pour off the excess fat from the pan and add the shallot. Sauté until translucent, then add the white wine, let it reduce by two-thirds, and add the cream. Bring to a simmer, then add the mustards, the remaining butter and the thyme. Correct the seasoning and remove from the heat.

Slice the kidney and serve with fresh egg noodles or pasta or toast and the mustard sauce. Or I really love this on toast!

Health & beef

It's safe to say that red meat has been persistently vilified for many of the ills of Western society, with meat consumption increasingly blamed for everything from cancer to heart disease. The press fills its front pages with fear-fuelled headlines about red meat, but the claims are ill-founded and misleading.

The flaw in these scare stories is that they don't differentiate between intensively farmed and extensively farmed beef. When compared with beef that is intensively farmed, well-reared, high welfare beef routinely has less total fat, more omega-3 fatty acids, more conjugated linoleic acid and more antioxidant vitamins. (These are all good things.)

One of the reasons for this difference is that in order to achieve large increases in production, modern farming uses aggressive, intensive farming techniques, with feeds that are rich in omega-6 fats, as opposed to grass, which is naturally higher in omega-3 fatty acids and vitamins. Consequently, the nutrient content in much of our beef is reduced.

Vitamins

Consumption of high-quality beef can contribute significantly to overall vitamin intake. It contains a vitamin D metabolite which is assimilated much more quickly and easily than other dietary forms of vitamin D. It also has significant levels of B vitamins, including thiamine, riboflavin, pantothenic acid, folate, niacin, vitamin B6 and vitamin B12, all vital to proper functioning of nearly every system in your body. B12 deficiency can play a role in everything from ageing, neurological disorders and mental illness to cancer, cardiovascular disease and infertility.

Minerals

Beef contains haem (or heme) iron, a form that is absorbed and utilized much more efficiently than the non-haem iron found in plant foods. Furthermore, even small amounts of meat can aid in the absorption of non-haem iron. This is particularly important for women in pregnancy, as iron is crucial for the growth of the developing foetal brain.

Beef is also an important source of the essential mineral zinc.

As with vitamin D and iron, the zinc present in beef is highly bioavailable – even a small amount of beef in the diet can increase zinc utilization from all sources. Zinc is crucial to many physiological functions, and people eating meat-free diets are at greater risk of zinc deficiency. In addition, beef contains significant levels of other vital minerals such as magnesium, copper, cobalt, phosphorus, chromium, nickel and selenium.

Fatty acids

Where grass-fed beef really shines is in its fatty acid profile. The ratio of saturated to monounsaturated to polyunsaturated fat in beef is similar regardless of the animal's diet – so, irrespective of whether your beef is grain-fed or grass-fed, you'll be getting about 40–50 per cent saturated fat, about 40–50 per cent monounsaturated fat and somewhere near 10 per cent polyunsaturated fat.

However, the diet of the cow does significantly influence the types of each fat present. Within the broad categories of saturated, monounsaturated and polyunsaturated, there are several individual fatty acids with different chemical compositions, each of which has a unique effect on your body. The two fatty acids you are probably most familiar with are omega-3 and omega-6, both of which are polyunsaturated. Recent research indicates that although beef contains consistent levels of omega-6 regardless of diet, significantly higher levels of omega-3 are found in grass-fed beef. Depending on the breed of cow, grass-fed beef contains between two and five times more omega-3 than grain-fed beef does.

Omega-3 fats are essential for normal growth in humans, and they may play an important role in the prevention and treatment of coronary heart disease, obesity, hypertension, arthritis, autoimmune disorders and cancer. These fats cannot be made in the body and so must come from our diet. We need sufficient amounts of both omega-6 and omega-3 fats, but they must be balanced for normal development. If the ratio of omega-6 fats to omega-3 fats in our diet exceeds 4:1, we may be more prone to health problems. This is especially significant because intensively farmed beef can have ratios that exceed 20:1, whereas extensively farmed beef is down to around 3:1.

There are three main types of saturated fat found in red meat: stearic acid, palmitic acid and myristic acid. Grass-fed beef consistently contains a higher proportion of stearic acid, which does not raise blood cholesterol levels. This higher proportion of stearic acid means, of course, that grass-fed beef contains lower proportions of palmitic and myristic acid, which can raise cholesterol.

Conjugated linoleic acid (CLA) is a type of polyunsaturated fat that appears to be a potent antioxidant, and research indicates that it might be protective against heart disease, diabetes and cancer. Beef is one of the best dietary sources of CLA, and grass-fed beef contains an average of two to three times more CLA than grain-fed beef. This is because grain-based diets reduce the pH (alkalinity) of the digestive system in ruminant animals, which inhibits the growth of the bacterium that produces CLA.

Other antioxidants

Grass-fed meat also contains other antioxidants in greater proportions than grain-fed beef does. Carotenoids, such as beta-carotene, are precursors to vitamin A that are found as pigments in plants. Grain-fed beef does not contain appreciable levels of carotenoids, for the simple reason that grains don't contain them. However, cattle that eat carotenoid-rich grass and forage are incorporating significant amounts of these compounds into their tissues. The carotenoids make the fat from grass-fed beef more

yellow than the fat from grain-fed beef, so fat colour can be a good indicator of how nutrient-rich your meat is.

Grass-fed beef also contains significantly more of the antioxidants vitamin E, glutathione, superoxide dismutase and catalase than grain-fed beef. These antioxidants play an important role in protecting our cells from oxidation, especially delicate fats in the cell membrane such as omega-3 and omega-6. Antioxidants such as vitamin E and beta-carotene also work together synergistically to protect the meat itself from damage during the journey from butcher to plate. These antioxidants are especially important if you choose to fry or grill your meat, because those high-heat cooking methods can be more damaging to meat than wet, low-heat methods such as stewing or braising.

Testosterone

There is strong evidence that extensively farmed beef can be part of a healthy and balanced diet, and if that isn't enough, Timothy Ferriss asserts in his book *The 4-Hour Body* that eating grass-fed steak can increase testosterone significantly. Why might that be of interest, you ask. Men whose testosterone levels are slightly above average are less likely to have high blood pressure, to experience a heart attack, to be obese and to rate their own health as only fair or poor. And according to Ferriss, they are also more likely to have an active sex life. But, men don't have the monopoly on testosterone – although women produce and require less of this hormone, it's still an important part of their health, helping with the same things.

You are what you eat

When it comes to red meat, quality makes a big difference. While not everyone can afford grass-fed meat, it is more nutrient-dense than grain-fed meat is, so even though it is more expensive, you're getting more nutrition gram for gram. The saying "you are what you eat" applies to cows as well as to humans. There are significant differences in the nutrient quality of beef depending on how the animal was fed, which is why extensively farmed grass-fed beef is a better choice than intensively farmed grain-fed beef. In fact, I consider extensively farmed grass-fed red meat to be one of the healthiest foods you can eat.

Index

Glossary

Acknowledgements

The author would like to thank:
Karen McBride for reading everything and acting as my filter.
Matt Brown, Emily Kidd and Annie Rigg for their talent and help in testing and cooking.
Mark Schatzker, Jessica Wragg, Phillip Warren, Peter Hannan and James George for being my sounding boards on some of the essays.
The guys at Turner & George for their good-humoured supply of all the beef, and pandering to my weird and peculiar demands.

David Ezrine at Alfresco Concepts for loaning me the Big Green Egg used in many of the recipes and photography.
Paul Winch-Furness for being a general photog-deity and fearless shirt wearing.
Stephanie Jackson, Caroline Brown, Sybella Stephens and Juliette Norsworthy at Octopus Publishing for their continued patience and indulgence.

To Basil
Always remember -
never forget
Sincerely
yours

Shmuel Lowensohn
24/10/90

With very best wishes
Bertha Leverton

I CAME ALONE
The Stories of the Kindertransports

DOVER COURT RECEPTION CAMP
Reprinted by kind permission of the Hulton-Deutsch Collection.

I CAME ALONE
The Stories of the Kindertransports

Joint Editors

Bertha Leverton and Shmuel Lowensohn

Forewords by

The Chief Rabbi
The Right Hon. The Lord Jakobovits

and

The Most Reverend
The Right Hon. The Lord Archbishop of Canterbury

The Book Guild Ltd
Sussex, England

The Book Guild Ltd.
25 High Street,
Lewes, Sussex.
First published 1990
© Bertha Leverton and Shmuel Lowensohn 1990
Set in Baskerville
Typesetting by Kudos Graphics,
Slinfold, West Sussex.
Printed in Great Britain by
Antony Rowe Ltd.,
Chippenham, Wiltshire.

British Library Cataloguing in Publication Data
I Came Alone: The Stories of the Kindertransports
I. Leverton, Bertha II. Lowensohn, Shmuel
325.210922

ISBN 0 86332 566 1

ISRAEL AND THE WORLD SHALL REMEMBER
THIRTY THOUSAND JEWS
EXTERMINATED IN THE CONCENTRATION CAMP
OF BERGEN—BELSEN
AT THE HANDS OF THE MURDEROUS NAZIS

EARTH CONCEAL NOT THE BLOOD
SHED ON THEE!

FIRST ANNIVERSARY OF LIBERATION
15th APRIL 1946
(14th NISSAN 5706)

CENTRAL JEWISH COMMITTEE
BRITISH ZONE

This book is dedicated to the memory of all the parents who made the supreme sacrifice of sending their children away never to see them again. It was not in vain; we have started a new generation again and enhanced the re-birth of the Jewish people.

FOREWORD

BY THE CHIEF RABBI, THE RT HON THE LORD JAKOBOVITS

While I myself was mercifully sent by my late parents from Germany to find refuge in Britain at the end of 1936, and was not therefore with the Kindertransport three years later as the cloud of war and wholesale destruction of Jews by the million was about to burst over Europe, I was close enough to the events to feel profoundly involved in the current commemoration of those infinitely dark days.

If there were any, even remote, silver linings on the cloud of disaster which overwhelmed Europe and its wealth of Jewish life and culture, it consisted in the wonderful rescue efforts by people with exceptional hearts, culminating in the Kindertransport, many of whose members were or became very close to me at the time and for many years thereafter.

Equally heartening is the wonderful rise to success, in some cases to great communal or national eminence, of many who arrived here torn from their families, interrupted in their education, and placed in an environment originally utterly alien to them. The magnificent men and women who organised the Kindertransport and then adopted these children as wards of the community will earn their and our everlasting gratitude for a humanitarian act of nobility and foresight with few parallels in modern history.

I therefore most sincerely pay tribute to Mrs Bertha Leverton for her loving and painstaking work in assembling so much valuable material on one of the truly heartening episodes in modern Jewish history. May the examples of selflessness the editors record be an inspiration to future generations.

FOREWORD

BY THE MOST REVEREND, THE RT HON THE LORD
ARCHBISHOP OF CANTERBURY

1939 was a bleak year for Europe. There are not many
good stories to tell about international cooperation then.
There is, though, one major exception – the story of
Kindertransport. This book lets the Jewish children who
found a new home in Britain that year tell the tale of
their exodus, as they now recall it fifty years on.

It is heartening to remember that, in those dark days
of division in Europe, the Christian churches cooperated
with Jewish groups in giving these young Jewish
children new homes and fresh hope. Lives were saved as
a result of Kindertransport. Let us continue to cherish
and extend that spirit of affection and cooperation
today.

Dear Friends and Readers

This book is a collective effort by the children who came to England fifty years ago, from 2 December 1938 to 1 September 1939, unaccompanied by parents, to find refuge from Nazi persecution. Our only crime was to be Jewish, or even half or quarter Jewish. After the infamous Kristallnacht on 9 November 1938, Jewish places of worship in Germany and Austria were set alight, Jewish properties smashed and many Jews arrested and killed. It was then the world began to realize the horror to come.

Britain offered entry visas to ten thousand children from three months to seventeen years. This was an act of mercy, not equalled anywhere else in the world. It was also in part to make up for their refusal to open the doors of Palestine, which could have saved a large number of European Jewry.

To process those children, a great deal of work was done by many people of many denominations. Committees were formed to establish hostels and find homes. Vast sums of money were collected as £50 per child was required, so as not to be a burden on the state, and of course the children had to be maintained after their arrival. About half of the number were housed in hostels, the other half in private homes, Jewish and non-Jewish. In this book it is not possible to mention and give credit to all the various bodies and individuals who took part in our rescue.

Let me state here that I am not a historian and I would not have been able to enumerate everyone who did such wonderful work on our behalf, but in some of the stories you will find mention of those who helped. All of our contributors were willing to state their names and particulars, thus proving the authenticity of their stories. Most of the children lost their parents in the Holocaust and thus became part of history. If some of the stories seem repetitive, please realize that our experiences were often identical; for instance the journey, described so many times by so many of us, was a trauma, as was the realization of having become orphans when the rest of the world celebrated victory.

These stories came into my possession in the following way. One day, in June 1988, I realised that it was forty nine years ago that I had come to this country, and looked in vain for any sign of a commemoration to be held for our forthcoming fiftieth jubilee year. Also, looking at my grandchildren, one of whom was exactly the same age as I on leaving Germany, made me think and realize what our parents and relatives must have felt to let their children go. I then started to organize a fifty year jubilee reunion, and it soon became apparent that the local reunion I had envisaged was far too narrow in concept. News travelled fast, and shortly I had a world-wide two-day reunion on my hands. This proved to be a wonderful success, reuniting former friends and resulting in off-shoot smaller reunions being held all over the world. A Souvenir Brochure was produced, compiled and edited by Shmuel Lowensohn, listing names, former names and addresses both of participants and non-participants, thus enabling people to get in touch with one another. Several miracles happened whereby relatives who had not known of each other's existence for fifty years were reunited through the reunion. I will only highlight two.

Grace Stocken had heard me speak on Woman's Hour and realized that she may be one of the Kinder. She had arrived with her twin sister on her third birthday, adopted by a Baptist minister and never been told of her heritage, only that they came from an orphanage abroad. She asked my help in tracing her origin and had just found her real mother's name (Bechhofer) and that she came from Munich. I broadcast that name on the Israel Radio with the result that she now has several cousins and an aunt in America and has reverted to her given name of Susie. She has found her real identity after fifty years and has written a book about her life. The BBC made a documentary of her story. Her twin sister died some years ago.

Gwen Richards had also heard my talk. She was seven and her sister nine when they arrived on the last transport before the war from Poland. She too had become a Christian and been adopted. She sent me copies of her mother's letters which those young children had kept for fifty years. All their family had perished in the Holocaust. Some weeks later I was asked by a Professor from Jerusalem if he could distribute some research material at our reunion. He enclosed a note from his wife for our search column. She said that she was a concentration camp survivor and remembered two cousins two years older than herself, (she was only six years old when taken to the camp) who came on the Kindertransport. Their name was Fraidenreich. I made the connection immediately, for that was the name on Gwen's mother's letters. I will never forget being present at the cousins' meeting.

Those of you fortunate to be surrounded by loving families, will find it hard to realise what it means to grow up without a single relative in the world.

I also received a great deal of archive material from the Kinder which has been made into a large pictorial exhibition. The consultant photographer for this exhibition was Stephanie Colasanti. The research was, and is still being conducted, by Paula Hill. To both of them I extend my sincere thanks. The exhibition is available for travel.

I also wish to express my thanks to Jesse Zierler who is responsible for the artwork and captions for the exhibition and who designed the cover and other items for the brochure and the jacket of this book.

The amount of work in connection with this book was tremendous and proved to be beyond me. My good friend Shmuel Lowensohn compiled and edited our now famous Fiftieth Anniversary Souvenir Brochure, and in desperation I turned to him for help. As always Shmuel rose to the occasion and gave a fantastic amount of time, energy and expertise. He is joint editor of this book.

October 1989   Bertha Leverton

Günther Abrahamson

(Berlin), Ottawa, Canada

My father, a lawyer, killed himself when the Nazis came to power. A secret that was kept from me at the time. I was twelve when I left Germany in 1939, less than two months before war broke out. My sister, who was five years older, had left a year earlier for Palestine. Her departure was accelerated by a Gestapo officer's suggestion to her that she might enjoy 'planting flowers at Oranienburg', a nearby concentration camp. At sixteen, my sister was asserting her independence. Already a committed Zionist, she had attended *Hachshara,* a farm training school programme which prepared young people for emigration and work on the land in Palestine. As the younger child, I was the more attached and displayed greater affection. I discovered later that my mother found the thought of sending me away heart-rending. But in the months that followed she prepared me for emigration as an experience to enjoy. Two options were discussed. Palestine or England; I didn't know on what basis the decision was eventually made.

I was put on the train with a suitcase, and ten Reichsmarks in my pocket. I exchanged them in England for a shilling which I soon converted into my new discovery – Mars bars. The journey to England was unremarkable. We boarded the ferry to England at Hook of Holland and arrived at Harwich the following morning where a bus took us to a reception camp; Barham House, Claydon, near Ipswich.

We assembled for registration. I remember the incredulity of the woman who took down my particulars when I insisted that I wanted to be a carpenter when I grew up. We were then assigned to one of the houses. Each one was named after a prominent British politician. Mine was 'Baldwin House'. Our housemaster, Max Haybrook, who spoke and understood some German, took a personal interest in us, and provided an introduction to English manners and customs.

Haybrook assigned Hans Silberstein, who had arrived before me and was six months older, to be my mentor. Hans had the privilege of looking after the camp's poultry and he allowed me to assist him. I enjoyed Barham House. It was mid-summer and it seemed like a long vacation. Haybrook made us write letters home. After war was declared we were allowed to write twenty-five words monthly on forms provided by the International Red Cross, and received replies of similar length. In 1942 my brief letters to my mother were returned as undeliverable. I learned after the war that she had been deported to the extermination camp at Riga.

A Rabbi conducted classes for boys preparing for their *Bar Mitzva.* I was cheeky, he slapped me, and I left his class never to return. So, I never had a *Bar Mitzva.*

I do not recall anybody telling me what plans, if any, there were for my future. Boys were constantly leaving the camp to join relatives or families who had agreed to accept refugees, or to stay in foster-homes. Hans and I were to go to Scotland. Hans left before me for a visit en route with an aunt in London. Before I got away the camp was struck by successive outbreaks of measles and the camp was quarantined for three weeks each time. It was October before I left for Scotland.

I was going to Selkirk in the Scottish Borders. The train ride took twelve hours and involved changing trains twice. I was ill with motion-sickness when I got off to wait for another train at a small station in Northumberland. A dear old granny who seemed to run the station took charge, held my head and made me drink very sweet tea. Neither of us understood what the other said but she knew a sick child when she saw one and I will never forget her kindness. A few hours later I arrived in Selkirk.

At the railway station I was met by a tall man with a white mustache and patrician bearing who was somehow connected with the Priory, a children's home in a Victorian mansion, to which I had been sent. He was also the father of the matron who was in charge of the Priory.

He warned me that if I behaved myself all would be well. I did not have the vocabulary to enquire about my fate if I did not behave myself, but had a foreboding that I was not going to like the Priory.

Once again Hans Silberstein was put in charge of me. He was thirteen. According to Hans, I had a choice of going to the public school for vocational subjects, or the high school for academic subjects. Hans recommended the latter and I followed his advice. An interview with the headmaster quickly established my lack of English. I was put in the most junior form.

As I was the only boy there was considerable incentive to learn English. The girls were always prepared to do my homework. At the Priory nobody cared if I studied or did well at school. Motivated and mature individuals like Hans did well and walked away with the school prizes. The headmaster told me years later that his teachers often wished that they had more refugees in their classes. Despite our strange clothes and accents we were readily accepted by the Scots children and were often invited into their homes.

The people of Selkirk showed us much kindness and we established friendships that have endured for over fifty years. I was unhappy at the Priory. The food was poor and, as growing children, we were almost always hungry. Discipline was in the hands of some older boys and I resented the bullying. I complained to Haybrook at Barham House and asked whether I could return. He must have made enquiries but I didn't find out till all the refugees were assembled in the Matron's private sitting room, a part of the house that was usually out of bounds. There the Matron tall and resplendent in a matron's uniform, complete with a white, starched veil, and in the presence of her father down from Edinburgh, announced that one of us had not only written to complain about the Priory, but worse, had breached a rule which required us to pass all our letters, unsealed, to her for posting. A requirement which, she alleged, had been imposed by the police. Since all the persons in positions of authority were looking at me, I readily admitted the transgression. There was no direct punishment but henceforth I was expected to buy my own stamps. We received no pocket-money.

On Sundays, regardless of our religious persuasion, we were marched twice a day to the local Church of Scotland. While this was compulsory, I do not believe that there was any intent to convert us. Those who protested were told that it would do them no harm. I became a regular visitor at the manse where I took English lessons from the minister's sister and enjoyed regular high tea prepared by his mother. No attempts were made to influence me in my religious beliefs or lack of them. The minister bought me a bicycle and I sometimes accompanied him on his rounds in the country. On one occasion we visited a farm family with whom I subsequently spent every weekend and every school holiday. They treated me as one of the family and, at fifteen, I was happy to leave school and the Priory to work on their farm where I stayed till 1946. They still regard me as a member of the family and I visit with them whenever I am in Scotland.

After the war I received a bursary from the Secretary of State for Scotland to study at the College of Agriculture and the University of Edinburgh. Following graduation, and a brief visit to Israel, I left Britain to work my way around the world. I did not get beyond Canada. On my way to the Pacific coast, a forester whom I met suggested that to leave Canada without having seen the Arctic was not to have seen Canada at all. A job with a mining company took me to Yellowknife in the Northwest Territories.

I lived in a cabin by a beach on the edge of Great Slave Lake. I acquired a canoe and a sailboat and spent weeks on the water exploring virtually uninhabited lakes and rivers. A boyhood dream come true.

I later moved north of the Arctic Circle to take a job with the Canadian Government managing its herd of 8,000 reindeer which foraged on a twelve million acre reserve on the edge of the Arctic Ocean. Headquarters were at Reindeer Station, on the banks of the Mackenzie River. A village of about 100 souls, most of whom were Eskimos and all of whom were connected with the reindeer project. I met my wife there, a dentist and a recent immigrant from Berlin. I was one of her first patients. My wife loved Reindeer Station and grieved when a promotion had me posted to Ottawa.

In this brief account I have mentioned by name two people whose faces leapt into my memory as I was thinking about events of fifty years ago. There are, of course, many others to whom I shall always be grateful. One of these is Netta Pringle who was an assistant at the Priory for a brief period before she joined the army. She took a personal interest in the refugees and provided the link that kept a number of us in touch over the decades. Her house in Edinburgh continues to be my second home.

*   *   *

Lorraine Allard

(Sulzbacher, Fürth), London, UK

I was born in Fürth, Bavaria, on 8 December 1924 as Lorse Sulzbacher. My mother was from Würzburg and my father was born in Fürth, as was his father before him. My father inherited the family business, which collapsed as did all Jewish businesses.

I left Germany on 18 April 1939 – number 4435 – with a Kindertransport. I had my accordion with me and had to play it at the border to prove that it was not just a valuable object being taken out of Germany for gain. I was so scared that I played very badly.

When we arrived at Liverpool Street station, I was one of the last children to be collected by my guardians, because their train from Lincoln had been delayed. It was my home for the next four years. My guardians saved my life, but they were very different to my parents in every way. They were not at all affectionate to me or to each other. The reason for my acceptance in their home was most unusual. Their only son, aged seventeen, had a non–Jewish girlfriend and I – just fourteen years old – was supposed to break up this alliance! As it turned out she converted to Judaism and they lived happily ever after. He became my big brother and we had a very good relationship.

I had no further schooling in Lincoln, but eventually won a scholarship to the Lincoln School of Art. What I learned there helped me in later life. During all my time in Lincoln I worked in my guardians' dress shops and was also responsible for the cleaning of the house we lived in. In addition, with my very poor English, I took to knocking on the doors of big houses to try and find a home and guarantor for my parents and others. I actually succeeded in getting jobs for my parents as gardener and housekeeper, and also for a friend and two cousins. Unfortunately only my friend, Stefan Wiesengrund, made it before the war started.

I shed many tears in Lincoln, mainly because I was homesick and felt utter emotional loneliness and hopelessness when the war started.

In June 1943 I left Lincoln and joined the ATS.

*   *   *

Gabrielle Allen

(Wulff/Hamburg), Toronto, Canada

Music turned out to be the reason I was able to leave Hamburg on 10 May 1939. I was met by my teacher and my sponsor David MacCallum and his wife Dorothy the next day, on 11 May, in London. I was sixteen.

Mr MacCallum was then the Concert Master of the Royal Philharmonic Orchestra. I would be useful helping with the two boys, with the household and as a sort of apprentice accompanist to his forthcoming solo performances. It was a brilliant spring and summer that year, both weather-wise and for the Royal Philharmonic, to say nothing of the many musical events I was able to attend. After one recording session, Sir Thomas Beecham shook my hand. Imagine! Not that I had played any part in that session – he merely wished this particular refugee well. Just before the war broke out, Sir Thomas went to the United States leaving the orchestra temporarily disbanded; the MacCallums went to Scotland and my own education changed direction for a while too.

The mass evacuation of children from the large cities, particularly London and Liverpool, produced another type of small displaced person. Many had to be looked after in a home with a matron in charge. The Committee sent me to one in Poole, Dorset to become a 'nurse in training'. It seemed to work out well for my fellow refugee Erika, originally from Frankfurt on the Oder, but not so well for me. However Mrs Franklin-Cohen of the Bournemouth Committee found me an ideal spot there. Mr and Mrs Apsey and Miss M Apsey needed a *Haustochter* but I was also to receive further musical training, for Miss Apsey was a music teacher who volunteered to prepare me for the English Conservatory examination standards. Music is a universal language – but is it? It was easy for us young refugees to learn to speak and write fluently in English but it takes time to learn musical theory and its terminology in a new language. Nonetheless I had an ideal time there until Dunkirk.

Next stop for some of us was the hostel in Reading, a curious time for us what with the Battle of Britain and the scare of invasion.

Let me finish by referring to our particular guardian angel on the Reading Committee; Professor, later Dame, Edith Morley. Through training she actively helped so many of us to achieve our first measure of independence.

*　　*　　*

Gerta Ambrozek

(Jassem/Vienna), New York, USA

The train left Vienna in the early evening. My father placed my small suitcase onto the overhead rack and had to leave the train. We children crowded around the window to receive last minute instructions. Despite the quietly shed tears, the desperate hopelessness of the people left behind was not really grasped by us. The youngest of the children was three years old, and the oldest fourteen. Many children were bewildered as they did not understand why they were leaving their homes and their parents, while to others it appeared as though this was an outing to a far and romantic land. We all had curious, if somewhat stereotyped pictures of England in our minds. We imagined that all English people walked about dressed like Sherlock Holmes or like the prim English girls seen in old copies of *The Tatler*. It wasn't quite clear to us why our parents, standing in small groups on the platform, were quietly sobbing.

Two months earlier my sister Lily had put an advertisement in the London *Times* and had left for England with another girl. She got a job as a chambermaid and her friend as a cook. Neither of them had even boiled an egg or made a bed. Their only preparation for their new life had been a few intensive lessons in English. Lily had found my sponsors through another advertisement in *The Times*, an elderly couple whose grown-up children were no longer living at home.

Six years went by before I saw my parents again. I left as a child and when I next saw them I was a married woman.

*   *   *

Shulamit Amir

(Englander/Prague), Jerusalem, Israel

I arrived in London on 13 May 1939. The transports were organised by the Quakers who obtained the required permission from the SS. I do not know what the criteria for inclusion were, but my father, who happened to be in London on a business trip at the time of the Nazi takeover, managed to secure a British guarantor for me, and this enabled my mother to arrange my trip.

The scene at the railway station before our departure will remain in my memory for ever. Most of the children were crying at the prospect of being parted from their parents, and the parents were trying to put on a brave face.

My mother assured me that our parting would only be temporary and that she would follow me 'very soon' to London. I tried very hard to believe her. Most of the parents were fated, like my mother, never to see their children again. It must have taken superhuman courage to save them by sending them away in the knowledge that it was for ever.

Our group consisted of over 120 children. I was just twelve and among the oldest. I was entrusted with two toddlers of less than two years old for whom I cared and was totally responsible throughout the journey which lasted three days. I used the overhead luggage racks to bed them down, whilst we older children sat up all night and tried to keep warm. Finally our train arrived at the Hook of Holland and we crossed to England by boat.

I was among the lucky few who had a parent waiting for them. My father collected me and we spent the next eight years together in London. He died in 1971 and I went on *Aliya* to Israel in 1947.

*   *   *

Mary Arnold

(Griminger/Vienna), London, UK

I was born 24 January 1934 and five years old when I came to England. Praterstrasse No 1 was where we lived in Vienna. The street leads down to the famous old fair, with the giant wheel and the roundabouts, and where the band used to play. We lived in one of those old houses with a passage way that led into a wide open cobbled courtyard. The flats were arranged around the courtyard. When you went through the archway, to the left, three flights up was our home. We lived in one room. You opened the front door and there was a little passage with a toilet in it, and then our room had another door to open; there was my parents' double bed, my cot, a table near the window with some chairs and a stove.

My father always used to sit me on his knee, teaching me songs, and bouncing me up and down. He was a lovely father. Well, this day was no different to any other. My father was teaching me a song which I have never forgotten. He made me sing it over and over again. It went like this:

Fur fur gesunterheit, Gott soll dich beglicken,
Sollst du nicht fergessen a Briefele tzu schicken.

It was a nice easy tune and meant: 'Travel travel, in the best of health, God shall guide you, but you shouldn't forget to send a letter!' He also taught me to speak a little Polish; I spoke German and, of course, Yiddish, which we spoke at home.

My mother had told me we were going to Poland for a holiday to see an

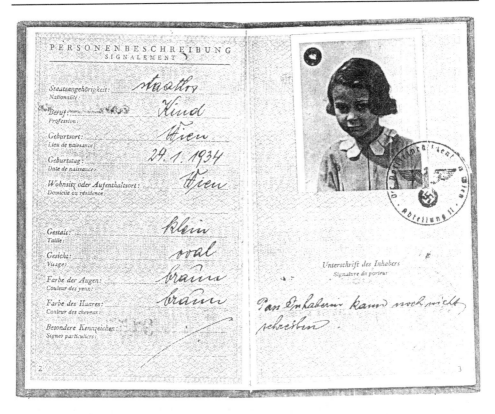

aunty there, and I was looking forward to it. I knew what *Tak* and *Nei* was
('Yes' and 'No') in Polish. My father told me that if ever I would hear 'Yes'
and 'No' that would mean I was in England. I didn't know why he said that.

The next morning was the same as usual. My mother dressed me and there
was a knock on the door. It was my aunty who was coming with us. Mother
put my coat on. I said goodbye to my father who was standing by the stove.
He seemed to be standing there for such a long time stirring the tea. I said
goodbye again and he didn't answer or turn round. I was standing close
behind him for a kiss and he turned round, tears running down his cheeks.
He kissed me and couldn't speak. I gave him a big kiss; poor Papa, I didn't
know why he was sad. It wasn't like him. Anyway, we went, my mother,
aunty and me. When we arrived at the station it was full of people, you could
hardly move. My aunty was now holding my hand. I didn't know where my
mother was; she had let go of my hand and seemed to have got lost. My aunt
pushed her way through the crowd. She put me on the train. My aunt had
now left, I was alone. Where was my mother? The train was packed with
other children. I went into the corridor to look out of the window. I could
hardly see, but pulled myself up by the rail across the window. I couldn't see
my mother anywhere. I started to cry; the train started to move. I was

sobbing till I went to sleep. When we were woken up, it was dark and we went on a boat. We washed and went to sleep. When we woke and got dressed I didn't know that I had been across water. We got off the boat and a lady met me who spoke German. I asked this lady if she was taking me home, and I thought we were going back to Vienna. The lady said we were going home and I was going to see my mother. I stopped crying. We got off the train and walked to a big house. A woman opened the door and we went in. We had some tea. I wouldn't let go of this pretty lady's hand. I was frightened she would run away from me, but she promised she wouldn't leave me and took me into the garden to ride on the swing. So I swung for a while, then decided to go back into the house. She had gone; nobody seemed to be around. The front door was slightly ajar, so I ran out into the street. I wanted to get back to the station, get onto the train and back to Vienna. I knew I was in England, as I heard people saying 'Yes' and 'No'. I ran down the street, when this other woman caught me. She took me back to the house. She was a nice woman and spoke to me in German. There was a knock on the door, and there stood a small woman with short dark hair, holding a little girl's hand, who was just a little taller than I was. She asked me to go home with her and her daughter. We walked for a little while and got to her house. It wasn't as large as the other lady's house. I couldn't understand anything they said as they couldn't speak German. This woman's name was Margery Coles. Sonia, her daughter, and myself slept in the same room. In the morning the first thing I looked for were my new boots, which my mother had bought for me. They weren't there. I looked everywhere; I couldn't find them. I asked Mrs Coles where she had put my boots, and she said I couldn't have them. I never saw them again.

I met Mr Coles (his first name was Tom) the next day. He was a very nice man. He sat me on his knee and tried to understand what I was saying. He had a German/English dictionary in his hand. He tried to speak to me.

The following day we went into the garden to play. There was a red three-wheeled bicycle. I ran to it and started to ride it. Sonia told me to get off. I didn't want to, so she went inside the house to tell her mother, who then pulled me off the bicycle. One day Sonia asked me to go out and play with her. I didn't want to, so her mother said I had to do as Sonia said as I came to be her playmate. I was learning English quickly, as I used to copy everything Sonia said. When she said 'Goodbye Mummy' I said the same, so I was calling them Mummy and Daddy. What an insult to the precious names!

We came in from playing; it was rather cold, and we were both hungry. Tea was laid and we sat down to eat. I had two pieces of bread. I was just going to take another piece when Mrs Coles took it away from me and said I was only allowed to have two pieces of bread for my tea, and one in the morning for my breakfast. It wasn't fair, as Sonia could have as much as she wanted. I was very hungry. I started to creep downstairs at night and when everyone was alseep, steal some bread and butter and marmalade; they never missed it!

We started going to school. Mrs Coles took us. I was put at the back of the class as I couldn't speak English very well, and the teacher gave me cards with drawings on and names at the bottom of the card. Nobody took much notice of me. One day after school, a boy started shouting and pointing his finger at me shouting 'German Jew'. I didn't know what he meant. I didn't know what a German Jew was.

A man used to come to Mrs Coles' house. He spoke German – a very nice man. I now think he must have come from the Jewish Board of Refugees. I didn't know then. Mrs Coles said I had a letter from my mother, and she got this man over to translate it. She seemed to hear a lot from my mother but she didn't bother to get the other letters translated. On my marriage my husband came with me to Mrs Coles' house and said he would go to the police if she would not return the letters she still had from my mother. She was taken by surprise and handed over what was left of them.

She was horrible. One day after school, Sonia and I were going out to play. Mrs Coles stopped me and said that I hadn't come over only to play with Sonia and I was sent to do the housework. She was contradicting herself. She told me to go into the kitchen and peel potatoes. The water was very cold, and I ran some warm water. She told me off, as I had to use cold water. My fingers felt numb. She then showed me how to lay the table. After tea, I had to wash up. Sonia didn't do any of this. One day Sonia asked me out to play. I said I couldn't go as her mother had told me I was to do the housework. She tried to push me, and we were at the top of the stairs. I pushed her so hard that she fell down. Mrs Coles hit me, and said I had to do what Sonia told me, and also do the housework. She then gave me a duster and showed me how to dust everything. When I had finished she went round with her finger and found some dust, and told me to do it all over again.

Every time I did something Sonia didn't like, she would hit me. I was frightened of her now. I was small, and Sonia was growing faster than I was. One day Mr Coles told his wife that she was treating me very badly and to try and be nicer to me. She told him to be quiet. He was a weak man. He wasn't in the army. At weekends Mrs Coles made me take tea up to her and Mr Coles. I was nervous I wouldn't wake up early enough to make the tea. One day the man came who spoke German, and wanted to see me. Mrs Coles told me to go upstairs and not make a sound. She went to the door, and I heard her tell him that I was out playing with Sonia. Little did he know that I was working in the house. He came often, but I was never allowed to see him. One day, Mrs Coles said she had a letter from my mother, and she read it to me. She said: 'Your mother writes that she hopes you are being a good girl and working hard, as that is what she wants you to do, and do as Sonia tells you.' She made it up, as she couldn't read German anyway. I couldn't read very well, or write, I didn't want to learn; it wasn't important. I was worried what was happening to my parents. I used to cry myself to sleep, hoping it was all a bad dream and that I would wake up to find my mother lying next to me. I prayed to God all the time. I saw the letters from my mother piling up in Mrs. Coles' bedroom; she never told me she had heard. If only I could have read them!

The bombs were dropping down badly. Mrs Coles told me I was going to a family in Bath. There I stayed with a Mr and Mrs Bartlett. Lovely people. They had a daughter my age. The husband was a policeman. I went to school there and was very happy. One day they told me that Mr Coles was coming to collect me and take me back to London. I said I didn't want to go. The morning Mr Coles arrived, I was crying as I didn't want to leave. Mrs Bartlett and her daughter were crying too, and asked Mr Coles to let me stay with them, but he said I had to go back with him.

I wasn't happy to be back with the Coles family. I had to do all the work again. I asked Mrs Coles to be kind to me and love me. She cuddled me for a few minutes and I thought she would be nicer to me, but she wasn't for long. Why didn't she love me? Why was she so unkind to me?

I started to wet the bed and Mrs Coles used to wake me up when she was going to bed, take me to the toilet, and I would then go to sleep.

Mrs Coles got pregnant and I was sent to a hostel in Hemel Hempstead. I hated the hostel. I begged to be put somewhere else. I was there for about six months. I went back to Mrs Coles, but was then sent to Tunbridge Wells, the Beacon Hostel. As soon as I got there I felt at home. There were all German and Austrian girls there, all Jewish. I didn't know I was Jewish, I just felt I belonged for the first time. There were about thirty-five girls there and I was put in a dormitory of eight. A lot of girls spoke with accents. The older ones even spoke German. I had forgotten all my German. As I was leaving Mrs Coles to go to Tunbridge Wells I was taking my money box, but she took it away and said it was for her baby and I couldn't take it. Although the money that was in it was given to me by the Coles' relatives and visitors, she said it was hers, as she had kept me for years and nobody gave her any money for me. I loved my money box and a few presents I had, but I couldn't take anything with me.

The Beacon hostel was a lovely big house. The grounds were twenty-two acres and three lakes. At the end of the garden was the cook's cottage, Mrs Heywood. A lovely warm English lady, who loved all the girls.

The years rolled by and I came to London (hostel) and met Eddie Arnold, famous comedian/impressionist, who broke all records at the London Palladium in the 1950s. Sadly he became ill with a tumour on the brain and died in 1962, leaving me with a daughter aged seven years.

*   *   *

Harry Arvay

(Vienna), Givatayim, Israel

I arrived in Harwich on 29 April 1939. I was thirteen years old and in charge of about a dozen much younger children who came from Austria. We travelled by train, without food and water, via Germany, picking up more and more children along our route, ending up in Holland.

There many of the youngsters remained, only later to fall into German hands. We were luckier and, after a most unpleasant episode on a Dutch cargo ship whose captain threatened to take us back to Germany if more cash was not handed over for our fare, we arrived safely in our new homeland – Britain.

Editors' note: Harry Arvay is a well known author, having written fourteen fiction books and recently two further books of his unusually interesting memoirs.

*   *   *

Joachim Auerbach

(Berlin), Birmingham, UK

I came to England in July 1939 with the Refugee Children's Movement and went straight away to Bunce Court School, run by Miss Essinger. My parents did not succeed in getting out of Germany and were killed in Auschwitz.

*   *   *

Anneliese Barth

(Baumann/Leipzig), Rugby, UK

My maternal grandfather left England well over a hundred years ago and settled in Chemnitz, now East Germany. He had married a lady from Danzig who did not like England. In due course, they had four children, my mother being the third. In her teens she was escorted by her elder brothers to Gillingham, Kent, to stay with her aunt and uncle for about a year. She loved her cousins there, but never saw them again. However my grandfather and his brothers corresponded

continued on page 24

BEAVER LODGE · RICHMOND GREEN

SURREY TW9 1NQ   01-940 7234

Sir Richard Attenborough, C.B.E. · Lady Attenborough, J.P. · Claude Fielding

12th June
1989

Sidney Samuelson, Esq.,

my dear Sydney,

        You asked me to let you have some gen about my two
adopted sisters. My father chaired a committee when Principal
of Leicester University College devoted to bringing Jewish
refugees out of Hitler's Germany. In a large number of cases
it merely meant housing them for a relatively brief period of
time while they obtained visas to go to relatives in either
the United States or Canada (this applied particularly to children).

        On the particular occasion, my Mama - known as Mary, my
father being known as the Governor - went to London to collect two
girls whose father was one of the medical officers for Berlin.
They arrived back home, Irene aged 12 and Helga 9, the former with a
dreadful nervous mannerism and the latter almost covered in sores.

        As far as my two brothers and I were concerned, they were
just two further lost children who seemed to inhabit our house every
few weeks. However, the difference was that during their time with
us, war was declared. One day on our return from school, David,
John and I were asked to go and see the Governor in his study.
Mary was also there. They both explained to us that the two girls
who were at present staying in the house were by virtue of the
threatened war totally stranded. They had little news of their
father, their mother and elder sister were in concentration camps
(perhaps I should add that by some miracle their elder sister
survived, but they never saw their mother or father again). Equally
there was now no possibility of a visa to go to America and so Mary
and the Governor had decided that with our agreement the two girls

/Cont

Registered in London: Number 489773

Sidney Samuelson, Esq.   12th June 1989

should remain with us for as long as the war lasted and until they
could rejoin their family. My parents were adamant that there was
only one condition under which this was possible and it was that
they should to all intents and purposes adopt the two girls. It
would mean, they explained, that we would no longer be a family of
five but a family of seven, and that the family would only engage
in any form of activity - holidays, outings, supply of clothes etc -
that we could afford as a family of seven. The girls would be
treated in exactly the same way and that my parents would love them
as they loved their three sons. In other words, they were to become
our "sisters" on a totally equal standing with the three of us, the
only difference being that whereas we referred to Mary and the
Governor as Mother and Father, the girls would call them Aunt and
Uncle, naturally in the expectation that they would eventually be
reunited with their own parents.

        The decision, the Governor said, is up to you boys. If
they are to live with us, your Mother and I are convinced that this
is the only proper way in which we should anticipate the future.
Naturally the three of us agreed at once and I am sure David and John
would agree that it was one of the best decisions we have ever made.

        We became devoted to Irene and Helga and have remained so
for the last 50 years. They both live in the United States now,
both were married (although sadly Irene's husband Sam Goldschmit
has died), but Helga remains married to Herman Waldman and they have
two daughters.

        So my dear Sydney that is how David and John and I came
to acquire two sisters.

Richard Attenborough

Letter from Sir Richard Attenborough, CBE, reference Irene Goldschmit and Helga Waldman (from Berlin), USA

Reprinted by kind permission of Sidney Samuelson and Sir Richard Attenborough.

regularly so that all news reached them across the Channel.

As the troubles in Germany increased, one of the Kent cousins, now married to a doctor in South Wales, invited my sister and me to stay with them but this invitation was refused by the consul in Dresden. This was in June 1938.

My 'aunt' in Wales then approached her MP, Mr William Mainwaring, who supplied her with entry permits for my sister and me.

Meanwhile, the Kristallnacht took place and my sister and I were hidden in the home of non-Jewish friends. Our school was closed and my parents started to prepare for our departure.

As my parents, and especially my mother, were active in the *Bnai Brith*, we were offered places in the first Kindertransport, provided we were ready in twenty-four hours!

At that moment my parents' courage failed them and they pleaded for more time. I think the following transports were made up of very sad cases, in desperate need of help, and we were no longer eligible.

Around Christmas time, our permits arrived and we were attached to a transport early in February 1939.

We were full of hope and expectation, having read a lot about life in England and being fairly fluent in the language.

In Amsterdam we were met by an aunt and uncle who had lived there a number of years. Then on to Hoek van Holland where another aunt, more recently arrived in England, met us. That same day we were put on a train to Cardiff to be met by our adoptive parents. Our own parents finally obtained entry permits and planned to arrive in England on 5 September. War started on 3 September. We never saw them again.

So we grew up in the Rhondda Valley, away from bombs and other refugees. We both graduated from Cardiff University. I worked for a few years, first in Exeter which boasted two Jewish families, and then in Coventry with a more sizeable community. Here I met my husband, a GP in Rugby, and have lived here ever since.

*　*　*

Edith Basch

(Schwarz/Graz), Los Angeles, USA

After the 'Kristallnacht' with all its well-known horrors, my mother managed to get a permit to go to England as a 'parlour maid'. I had been on the list for the Kindertransport right from its inception but I was somehow never included. We lived in Graz. When my mother went to the British Consulate in Vienna in order to pick up her visa, she told them that she had a fourteen year old daughter and asked what could she do with her. Their reply was that she could take me with her, but would have to find a place in England for me. An aunt of mine, already in England, also working as a maid, found a 'place'.

And so we went! The border crossing into Belgium was the usual nightmare of harrassment, being stripped and searched even in the most private parts of our anatomy – so much so that we missed the train to Ostend and the channel crossing to Dover. With the help of the Refugee Committee in Brussels we spent the night there and the next day arrived at Dover. We had our freedom but my father was still in Austria.

The place that was found for me did not materialize unfortunately.

It was Friday afternoon at the beginning of February 1939, a cold, foggy and drizzly day as we made our way to Bloomsbury House. There was a big sign on the door which said they would not open up again until Monday morning – so we stood outside talking German of course, and discussing our dilemma. Suddenly a kind and charming lady, whom I will never forget, came by and asked us in German what our problem was. When we told her, it seemed as if magic had happened. She opened up the office, made a cup of tea and informed my mother that she would send me to Broadreed Camp in Selsey-on-Sea where some of the children from the Kindertransport were. She seemed like a good fairy and made things happen so fast, it was unbelievable. She phoned the administrator of the camp, took us by taxi to the railway station, talked some people into looking after me, and said that someone would meet me, even though I would be arriving at eleven o'clock at night! She then took my mother to a hotel, paid the bill for her overnight stay, arranged for a taxi to take her to her destination the next day and made arrangements for her to find out that I arrived safely.

I enjoyed being with my contemporaries. Shortly after my arrival, we were transferred to Tunbridge Wells, Kent, where we stayed in a girls' hostel. In April I was informed that I was going to be sent to the Heaton Secondary School for Girls in Newcastle-on-Tyne. The headmistress, Miss Cooper, met me and took me to the home of a family whose daughter attended the same school. They were kind and wonderful and made me feel most welcome, but of course I was terribly homesick for my parents. The school guaranteed to take care of me until I was eighteen. I learned to speak English very quickly and I loved the school. Meanwhile my father luckily managed to get into the Kitchener Camp in Sandwich, England, and although we were all over the place, we were safe thanks to the efforts of a country second to none – this small island which saved more lives than anyone else had even attempted to.

The war started and the school was evacuated to Kendal in the Lake District – a peaceful haven. My parents eventually joined me there and life became somewhat normal again. I matriculated, went to business school and started work. After the war I joined the Civil Censorship Division of the U.S. Army as an 'Allied Civilian' and worked as an interpreter in Offenbach, Germany. There I met my husband, who was also a refugee from Berlin, and anxiously awaiting his quota number for the United States. This happened in January 1947 – we got married in February and left for the United States in June 1947.

* * *

Alfred Batzdorff

(Breslau), Santa Rosa, California, USA

Those Channel ships have a tough time ploughing their way across the water from the Continent to the British Isles during the rough winter months. Together with a dozen Jewish children I was on one of them during the night of 1 to 2 December 1938, breathing free as we were approaching a haven of safety, yet deeply concerned for our dear ones.

There were buses waiting for us when we disembarked at Harwich. A short ride brought us to a camp, the Dovercourt Bay Holiday Lido. I spent a couple of weeks there. We were housed in small cabins and well fed in a large army-style mess hall. Somehow we could keep busy just maintaining the place and ourselves and entertaining the younger children. Some programmes were organized to fill the afternoons with cultural and English language classes; we saw movies, and on one occasion Sir Samuel Hoare came to speak to us. Time and again cars would drive up; people would alight and proceed to the administration office. There they would dig through the ever-growing file of life histories of the camp's young residents and select a number of children to be interviewed. We would then be looked at, talked to, evaluated, and either eliminated or accepted. This meant that a family agreed to take one or two children into their home. It now seems so obvious how generous these good people were. Is it not a tremendous obligation, a huge sacrifice financially and otherwise, to accept a strange foreign child, to make a home for him, to give him love and affection, to care for him as for one's own child?

Some people were financially able and eager to help those refugee children at the Lido. In a number of cases, some of these people would organize a hostel under a competent leader. They would then adopt a group of children of similar background and age and care for them under one roof. One of these hostels was organized by the hastily formed Swanage (Dorset) Refugee Committee, and I was fortunate enough to have been amongst those selected to benefit from their generosity.

Shortly after New Year's Day we all moved into our new hostel. Kingscastle was a beautiful place. A large one-family house, temporarily vacant, located high up on the cliffs with a magnificent view of Swanage Bay, the Channel and the Isle of Wight. Mr and Mrs Ellington, an American couple, looked after us, and they were soon joined by Mr Phil Carter, a schoolteacher and scoutmaster. They procured books and games for us, taught us English, songs and games. But in spite of all their endeavours they could not keep us sufficiently occupied. Man's greatest demoralizing agent, idleness, made itself felt in the house. Again we had to go to the people of Swanage for help. Again they found the answer. We were given a chance to work. Some of us worked in garages, others in stores, one fellow was a page in a law office, another a barber's helper. Our life became fuller as we worked, met more people, made new friends, and had a little spending money to buy a few things or go to the pictures.

A few months later, the Swanage hostel was to be closed. A new site had been selected in Bournemouth. Yet before we could move to the new hostel, there was another period of homelessness. Kingscastle had been closed, and Bournemouth was not yet ready.

This time it was our friend Roger Browne who offered a group of us asylum. Mr Browne was a rich bachelor, who occupied a splendid house high up on a cliff overlooking the Channel. His mansion had many rooms, and his heart was full of charity. During the summer months he would invite groups of underprivileged city children to share his luxurious dwelling place. He would feed them well and buy them fine clothes. Now he extended comparable benefits to us. But soon this vacation came to an end. The hostel was ready and we moved to Bournemouth.

At first our new hostel was much like the one in Swanage, but the larger town gave us better employment possibilities. Now we could seek jobs where we could learn a trade and build up earning potential for ourselves. I started work at the Durley Dean Hotel as a dish washer and decided to make the hotel business my temporary career. During the evening hours I was able to attend classes at the Bournemouth Municipal College to further my education, which was slated to go into the field of engineering but was so prematurely interrupted by the happenings during those eventful years.

The reason why I was working in the hotel business was twofold. Firstly, this was the only line of work where a foreigner did not require a work permit; secondly, I worked my way up. I earned my money, and I enjoyed my work, although I realized that my life's ambition was not satisfied in this endeavour. I had always been interested in physics, and especially in mechanics, and had always been good at handicrafts and in the use of tools. I realized that I should change my career to engineering or an allied profession or trade. Thus, when I found an advertisement in the *Daily Telegraph*, where a surgical instrument maker and inventor was looking for an apprentice, I wrote a letter to the gentleman offering the position, telling him in detail about my background and the necessity for me – should I become eligible for the position – to procure a work permit.

Soon after, I received a letter from Mr Davis in Cardiff, inviting me to come there for an interview. I was forced to reply that I had neither the money for the trip to Wales nor could I afford to lose a couple of days' pay at my present job. In answer, I received a prepaid bus ticket and the assurance that a hotel room had been reserved for me and paid for. This new example of English generosity moved me much. I went to Cardiff the following week, only to find that Mr Davis had been called out of town. Mrs Davis, however, received me well. She invited me for lunch at her house, and we had a fine talk and got well acquainted.

After my return home, I received a communication from Mr Davis that on the judgement of his wife he would be happy to have me join his company. He was willing to give me spending money of fifteen shillings a week while I learned. There was a splendid opportunity for me. A man who put a lot of trust in me though he had never met me. And yet I felt forced to tell him that I could not accept his offer. The remuneration he offered would not suffice to pay for my upkeep. But Mr Davis would not take no for an answer. He talked the case over with his wife and wrote that they had decided to room and board me at their house free of charge in addition to the fifteen shilling payment. This was the greatest generosity I ever saw an employer extend to one of his men.

Together with Mr Davis I applied for a work permit. It took many months of tiresome waiting. In the meantime an opportunity opened up for me to go to the United States. As my endeavours to procure working papers seemed so hopeless, I notified Mr Davis that I felt compelled to give up the idea of building up my career in England.

Late in May 1940, heading for a new but uncertain haven, I looked back from the boat to the English shoreline. I felt a deep emotion, full of gratitude and respect to a great and splendid country, to an unselfish and charitable people, to a group of friends whom I considered the Lifeguards of Democracy.

*   *   *

Rosalind Baum

(Berlinger/Schweinfurt), Michigan, USA

Where to begin? I was born in Schweinfurt and my maiden name was Rosi Berlinger. My father, who had such a powerful influence on my life, was the Cantor as well as the Art and Music teacher at the Lyceum. In 1937 he opened the *Gemeinde* School in Schweinfurt, a one room school house where he taught grades one to twelve. On 10 November this schoolhouse, as well as the rest of the *Gemeinde* house with my mother and I in it, was set on fire. We managed to get out and I am still here to write this story. My father was taken to Dachau in November 1938 and released around the end of 1938. When he came back both my parents realized that everyone had to leave Germany as quickly as possible. How it came about that I was on a children's transport I don't know. I still have some letters sent to my foster parents. My parents filled out a form asking for an orthodox placement and I was very lucky. Mr and Mrs Broder were my foster parents and I still correspond with Mrs Broder and visit with her and her sons every time I go to England. They were very kind to me until I left in 1944 to live at the Willesden Lane Hostel.

I met my husband, Heini, through a room-mate at the hostel who was a friend of his sister's. We arrived separately in the US and lived in New York with relatives. Heini, also a Kindertransport child, and I have now been happily married for forty years. We were unable to find jobs in New York so after we got married we moved to Detroit. We started our life in Michigan with ninety-five dollars in debts, two cups for milk and two plates and two soup bowls for meat. The first place we lived in was a rented furnished room where I did all my washing up in the bathroom and all my cooking on a two burner plate.

We were very blessed in that God has constantly helped us and guided us as we moved upward from a furnished room, to a four room flat and a single house and from one neighbourhood to another. We have three children all of whom attended a *yeshiva* day school as we involved ourselves in the orthodox community of Detroit. Our oldest son is an attorney, our daughter an executive secretary at *Agudas Israel* in New York and our youngest son is a doctor. In addition, we have over a dozen grandchildren.

A word or two about my husband. His father was first *Chazan* (Cantor) in the main orthodox Synagogue in Cologne. When he was deported to Poland in October 1938, Heini's mother undertook the responsibility of sending the two children to England. Heini, now Henry, together with his sister Margot and other children, were transported from Cologne through the special efforts of the principal, Dr Joseph Klibansky, who in the end was unable to save himself and his family.

Henry was sent to a hostel in Brighton where he lived together with twenty six other boys from Germany and Austria.

Henry attended the Brighton Senior Boys School. He stayed there for a year and a half until the age of fourteen. In the meantime he learned how to iron shirts and press trousers as part of his duties in the hostel. When he left school he was apprenticed to a furrier, a trade he learned and which kept him employed later on in London and, after we were married, in America.

At the age of twenty-eight, Henry decided to enrol at Wayne State University where he received all his degrees, the last – his Ph.D. – in 1975. He worked for the Detroit Board of Education as a teacher counsellor and for the last eleven years as a principal of Detroit's largest high school with over three thousand students.

This year Henry retired from the Detroit school system but still continues his affiliation with Jewish education. He is active in many Jewish organizations and seems to be busier than ever before.

We have a lot for which to be thankful. Henry and I came from orthodox homes and were forced into situations which completely removed us from such observances. We consider ourselves fortunate that, with the help of many people, we were able to return to that which was rooted in us by our parents. We have found great happiness and satisfaction in seeing our parents' examples mirrored in all our children and grandchildren.

*   *   *

Gideon Behrendt

(Berlin), Natanya, Israel

Another bleak November morning in Berlin. The fog and the cold drizzle got to my skin by the time I reached my school in *Rykestrasse*. School and Synagogue formed one complex unit and the school yard was between the two buildings. I could smell burnt wood and furniture. There had been a fire during the night but I could not detect any sign of a fire brigade having been there. A policeman stood near the burnt entrance of the Synagogue. He looked bored. We entered school as usual but talked to each other in whispers. We did not realize that we had witnessed history in the making the morning after the Kristallnacht.

In retrospect it seems as though I dreamed this period. I just accepted being different from my classmates. I had to run and escape the mob of boys who found it fun to wait for me on my way home to pounce on me like a pack of dogs on a rabbit. I didn't keep count of the torn trousers and shirts, the black eyes, the bruises, bloody knees, elbows, the tears and my father's reproaches. 'A Jewish boy doesn't brawl in the streets, just run away', he said. In a short time I became a good runner. By 1936 – I was eleven years old – I even became fairly good at boxing and wrestling. That year I had to leave my German school for the Jewish school in *Rykestrasse*.

Jews were not to mingle with Aryans. I still see the signs in shop windows saying '*Juden verboten*', '*Juden unerwünscht*', the writing on the wall, '*Juden raus*', '*Judas verrecke*', drawings everywhere, the yellow benches in public parks marked '*Nur für Juden*'.

On 13 June 1938 at exactly 5.50 am – it was already light – someone knocked on our door. I opened it. Two tall men stood in the doorway and asked quite politely for my father.

'Just a few routine questions to be answered at the local police station. He'll be home in a matter of minutes', they said.

The two were Gestapo. I went to school and didn't even notice that three of my classmates did not come to school that morning. Only the next day did I hear that their fathers too were visited by the Gestapo. Four weeks passed without a word or sign from my father until the day a printed post card arrived from Buchenwald saying 'I am well, please send some money'. Since my mother had died years before, this is how I became *de facto* an orphan and was accepted into a Jewish orphanage.

On 1 December 1938 some of Berlin's Jewish orphans were sent to England with a Kindertransport. There were no heart-rending scenes since none of us left much behind. Those who stayed behind envied us. My brother Heinz wished me farewell as the train left the station and I awoke from my childhood nightmare.

Some of us were given a home with English families; others like myself left

Dovercourt for hostels in different parts of Britain. About fifty of us went to Leeds which became our home town, to the hostel in Stainbeck Lane which became just 'home'.

We were lucky and had the local refugee committee to support us and take care of our daily needs. Members of the refugee committee, mostly in the clothing industry, donated our clothing. One fine day we found ourselves all wearing the same type and colour of suits, the same hats, shirts and ties etc. We must have been quite conspicuous seen together in our refugee hostel uniform.

There was good old Mr Bently and two young teachers teaching us English. The grand old man tried his utmost to turn us into perfect English gentlemen overnight. We learned English manners, customs, community singing and history.

Mr Model, himself a refugee from Hamburg, acted as our housemaster but really he was more of a father, friend, educator and choirmaster all in one. We all loved Model deeply. He made us forget the wounds and scars of 'over there' and enabled us to settle down to some sort of normal life.

I have to mention those close friends who were like brothers to me when I had no family. There were four of us inhabiting a room in a small cottage: David Goldberg, Simon Issman, Walter Kohn and me. We studied and worked together, and also went out together. There were our first dances at the Judean Club and our first meetings with the fairer sex and of course the sharing of our innocent experiences. I'll always cherish the happy hours spent at the teenage parties on Sunday nights where all four of us were invited. Like the Musketeers, one wouldn't go without the others. On my first date, I took a lovely girl to the pictures to see *Gunga Din*. However, I had only one shilling so I bought two front row seats, the very cheapest, and told my date that I was short sighted.

All too soon the war started. Priorities changed and instead of learning how to be gentlemen we went to work in the factories. Model, our father figure, was taken away from us and replaced by Mr Meier and, shortly after, by Mr S and his wife who made the once so happy hostel in Stainbeck Lane into a place that can best be compared to the orphanage described by Dickens in Oliver Twist.

By 1940 or 1941 most of us were fifteen and sixteen years of age and started to go out into the wide world. Each one went his own way. When the war ended we had something in common again, the building up of homes, the warm family homes we had yearned for and never had.

The four musketeers took different routes. David Goldberg settled in Edinburgh and, together with his lovely wife Ray, raised a wonderful family. Simon Issman went and made his home in New York and worked hard to establish himself. He will tell his two children and his grandchildren all about his personal nightmare and his happy childhood in Leeds. What has become of you, Walter Kohn? We have not heard of you for nearly fifty years. But we have not forgotten you and wish you the very best. Myself? After serving in the army, I decided that once the war was over I would not be a refugee any more and that what I needed most was a homeland. So I got myself a homeland, Israel.

*　　*　　*

Stella Bell

(Salomon/Luzendorf-bei-Wien), Melbourne, Australia

We lived in Luzendorf-bei-Wien, a small place just outside Vienna. Everyone knew we were Jewish and many acted Nazi fashion. I was glad to leave, not knowing that I would not return and never again see my parents.

A cousin, Julius Stener, came to England in 1938, and canvassed families to shelter refugee children. I knew in advance therefore that I would live with Ettie and Harry Grosberg and their thirteen year old daughter Stella in Stoke-on-Trent.

There followed a difficult adjustment period for all of us. I know the family tried to make me feel welcome, but in spite of all the warmth and generosity around me, I somehow could not respond. I felt very lonely and different and withdrew, hardly talking, and doing very little. Stella with her cheerfulness helped me a lot and so did going to school. I was permitted just to sit and listen. Often the headmistress, Miss Bennett, would allow me to spend time in her room where she talked and encouraged me and said healing things like 'We'll show that Hitler he can't do things like that!' I'll never forget Miss Bennett.

I arrived in England in January 1939, aged twelve. In 1941 the family moved to Canada for two years to escape the hardships of the war. During that time I lived with Mrs Grosberg's parents and sisters in Southport. I was a fairly well-adjusted teenager, working as a stenographer enjoying life and definitely feeling as English as everybody else. Eventually I married Mrs Grosberg's youngest brother. We live in Melbourne, Australia, now, but are in close touch with the family we share in common and which I hold in great affection.

*　　*　　*

George Bendori

(Rechelmann/Stettin), Rishon Le Zion, Israel

Separation: Our parents knew they would never see us again. We, the children, understood only that we would not see our families for a long time. We will never forget the heartbreak, the clinging together for the last time.

Freedom: Who can ever forget the feeling of having escaped it all even though we were only eleven years of age.

Crossing the German-Dutch border the train could not move quickly enough for us as we feared a last-minute hitch. The final inspection of documents, the ruthless way of going through our meagre possessions carried out by stern SS men whose menacing looks left no doubt in our minds as to what they would have liked to do to us.

And then the kind smiling Dutch ticket collectors who came into the compartment to ensure that nothing untoward would happen to us from then on. It was all behind us, we were free. Only our unfortunate parents were left behind to face it all. Because of their foresight we were saved.

A feeling, impossible to put into words. Impossible for someone to grasp who has not experienced it.

And then to Dovercourt. Bitterly cold in the winter of 1938-39 but still heavenly. The dedicated and kind staff who looked after us and did their utmost to make us forget what our little minds had absorbed.

We had funny moments too at Dovercourt. Inspected by prospective foster parents we felt like we were in a zoo. On Saturday and Sunday you had to be spick and span. It was a game and we quickly got used to it.

Let us give a moment's thought to those who made it possible. The aftermath of the Crystal Night of 9 November 1938 brought about another of Britain's finest hours. The British have always championed the cause of the oppressed, and Britain was one of the very few democracies at that time to open its gates to us – absorbing more children than many other countries combined. It is something in which Britain can take pride.

There are too many names to mention, all those gallant and righteous people who combined together to spur the government into action. Let it suffice to say 'We are forever grateful.'

Let us never forget those numerous noble people who were not Jewish, but who felt a deep shame at the inhumanity exploding in Europe. They opened their arms to many of us, took us into their homes, provided for and kept us – giving us their very best.

In conclusion, let it be said

'Britain, without you we would not be here today, thanks.'

* * *

Professor Tom Bermann

(Hronov, Czechoslovakia), Kibbutz Amiad, Israel

A letter from his mother to Mrs Miller who gave him a home in Scotland.

Hronov, 14 June 1939

Dear Mrs Miller,

Your letter of 11 June which we fervently expected has moved us to tears and we thank Heaven that has led our only child into the house of so generous and good people. Though we have not known more than your name until now (as well as you of us) upon reading your kind letter we can now form an idea of you and I need not assure you of our happiness to know that our child is in such good hands.

We thank you with all our hearts for your great love and care you surround our child with and we only wish that Tommy in his childish ignorance may not presume upon your kindness by his naughtiness. Though Tommy is kind-hearted, yet he is a very lively and obstinate boy. I beg you very much to have not only love and goodness for him, but strictness as well, as he must not be allowed all. We are persuaded that the child feels like at home and that his new 'Auntie' and 'Uncle' will soon take him to their hearts.

We are extremely longing for the child, the house is as quiet as the grave and we are very lonely. But if we bring the great sacrifice of parting with the child to save him perhaps from great suffering and know that he is so well kept safe, we master our pain and trust in God who onward may not leave us.

As I have already written to you I am sorry to say that Tommy is a very weak eater and there are few things that seem enticing to him. As you are so extremely good as to be inclined to prepare his favourite dishes, I shall gladly tell you what Tommy likes to eat. He is mostly fond of soups and I gave him them first after meat and vegetable dishes. He does not even dislike vegetable dishes, but least he likes the meat and fish he refused at all. As to the farinaceous food he ate little as well, but he mostly liked a chocolate tart without cream. He is very fond of fruit, especially bananas. His favourite soups are: vermicelli, mushroom, potato, vegetable, lentil, cumin with vermicelli. Vegetable: spinach, carrots, potatoes, cabbage, cauliflower. I prepare that vegetable as follows: I boil it in salted water till it is soft, then I mingle it with lightly roasted flour. He eats all sorts of meat, poultry as well, but only cut to very small pieces. But please, don't worry about his eating, but the child wants particularly little and with a good or bad grace we have not been able to force him to eat more. God may give that he keeps well, it is more than a sacrifice of you if you wish to do for him all in any way and we do not even know how to thank you. Tommy was born on 25 February 1934, he is no more than five years and six months, but he is rather wide-awake for his age, he knows to tell already the time, he can count till one hundert and knows already many letters, he even writes them. I suppose that going to school will surely be a good thing for him and that he will already be able to do so. We beg you to kiss and bless him instead of us. I leave it to your consideration to give our picture into the child's room. I think he would be pleased with it.

Now I wish to tell you something about us for we may well imagine that even you would like to know whose child you have in your house. My husband is forty-one, a commercial and technical manager of a big factory for textiles and hosiery the owner of which stays in London and to whom you may apply for information. The present owner's father and my husband's father were cousins. My husband has worked himself up to his present position, at the age of twenty-two he became a confidential clerk and since the time he has finished the school for textiles he has been engaged in one and the same firm, Edmund Pick, mechanical weaving and knitting factory of Velké Poříčí, which is ten minutes distant from Hronov. At present my husband cannot leave the factory. Yet we do not know how long still, whether six months or only three months. My husband is not only a good and fully reliable man in any line, but a well-known expert in his branch. Alas! We do not know in which way he will be able to make use of his qualifications. We possess an affidavit to USA, Colorado where our relations live. They are Dr Waldapfel, laryngologist, and his wife. Though we have registered in March we were told at the American consulate that it may take years till we may get the possibility of emigrating the quota being overcharged. Therefore we should like to go to England if it were possible, of course it is very difficult to get a permit there. A cousin of ours in London who is herself an Austrian emigrant writes to us that I should be able to receive a permit only if I took the position in a domesticity which I should gladly take as I can lead the most pretentious domesticity, perfectly cook and bake. But it is much more difficult for my husband as I cannot leave him here until he would get a permit. There may be found a way out by time, we pray to God every day that he may help us. I myself am thirty-three, I have secretarial training, but I was very much engaged in the domesticity and now I have attended many special courses as cold meat, English cookery and I have learned how to make Carlsbad wafers. Next time I shall send you a sample as Tommy likes them as well. My father is a physician and because of his age of seventy, he is living now retired with my mother in Brno. My father's father has been a territorial and chief Rabbi and lecturer of oriental languages at the University of Cernauti and my mother's father has been a cantor. My only sister has married a lawyer and has no children.

On the day of Tommy's leave I have some photographs taken and I send you some pictures as well as some pictures of our house and I beg you to show them to Tommy for, as I suppose he will enjoy them. Please, let me know whether he cries sometimes and about that whether he annoys you and refuses to obey as I know well that the child has bad points which will be polished by time.

Dear Mrs Miller, you make us happy by your detailed writing about our child and I can assure you that we remember you with great thankfulness as well as full of affliction that our child is so far from us, but we are filled with happiness that he had the chance of coming just to you.

We thank you still many thousand times and remain, dear Mrs Miller,

faithfully yours

Charles and Lenka Bermann

*   *   *

Guy Bishop

(Brüg/Gera), Newtown, USA

I arrived with a Kindertransport in July 1939 under my original name of Günter Brüg, born in Gera/Thüringen on 9 April 1926. The Kindertransport left from Leipzig and we arrived at Harwich.

I was without a sponsor and was sent to the refugee camp at Barham House, Claydon near Ipswich, Suffolk. I eventually found a sponsor and in January 1940 started at the Hammersmith School of Arts and Crafts, then evacuated to Bath, Somerset and lived as an evacuee with a family until mid-1941, when the school became residential in Trowbridge, Wilts. While I had no direct contact with my sponsor who, however, took care of my financial needs, I became a member of the Bishop family who took me in as an evacuee in Bath and this relationship has continued to this day.

For my protection, I assumed the name of Guy Bishop when I went on active service and my name was changed by deed poll. I became a naturalized British subject while in the army.

I volunteered as soon as I reached the age of seventeen and a half and enlisted on 20 April 1944. After basic training with the Highland Light Infantry in Glasgow and the Royal Fusiliers in Essex, I embarked for active service in the European theatre of war in December 1944. I was assigned to the 7th Battalion of the Black Watch (RHR) and joined its Intelligence section with which I served until February 1946. I was then transferred to the Intelligence Corps, where I was rapidly promoted and reached the rank of Warrant Officer II in December 1946. I was demobilised in November 1947.

I have lived in the United States since December 1952 and am now a United States citizen. I am married but have no children.

*   *   *

Tom Bermann grew up in the Miller's house from 1939 to 1952. They had no children of their own. Mrs Miller is still alive, but Tom's parents perished in Europe. Below is his entry certificate into England. He now lives in Israel.

5986

This document of identity is issued with the approval of His Majesty's Government in the United Kingdom to young persons to be admitted to the United Kingdom for educational purposes under the care of the Inter-Aid Committee for children.

THIS DOCUMENT REQUIRES NO VISA.

PERSONAL PARTICULARS.

Name BERMANN   THOMAS

Sex MALE   Date of Birth 25.2.34.

Place KÖNIGGRÄTZ

Full Names and Address of Parents

BERMANN   KARL & LENKA

U. NACHODA

KRONOV/MMET

BRITISH COMMITTEE FOR CHILDREN IN PRAGUE.

An original lino cut by Mr Bishop.

*   *   *

Lotti Blumenthal

(Gruber/Hamburg), San Diego, USA

'My dear parents,' I wrote on 16 December 1938, from Dovercourt, 'do not worry about me. I am fine. I arrived safely but it is terribly cold in England and although I have plenty of warm clothes these do not seem to be sufficient.'

I was thirteen years old at the time and completely unaware of what lay in store for the Jews of Europe.

There did not seem to be a language barrier with the warm and friendly people who took care of us and I think that most of us learned to speak English quickly. Every day people arrived at the camp to take children into their homes or whole groups were sent to various places. Some gentlemen from an organisation named Grand Order Sons of Jacob spoke to a group of children and invited them to come to their convalescent home in Sussex, not very far from London. I decided to go there and although I was completely unaware of what lay ahead I soon realized that I had made the right decision. On 1 January 1939, along with twenty or thirty other girls, I arrived at Wyberlye, a beautiful estate in the little town of Burgess Hill. Wyberlye was run by a strict matron who ruled with an iron hand. Some time later our number increased so that we were now about fifty girls ranging in ages from six to sixteen. The younger ones attended school and then had their assigned chores while the older ones worked in the home.

I recall that most of the girls got along well with each other although their backgrounds were so dissimilar. We taught each other various skills, shared treasured books which we had brought with us and talked about our families. We all shared one common wish, to be reunited with our families as quickly as possible.

We settled into a routine and more or less accepted the fact that we were separated from our families. We attended school every day, walking two by two through the little town. We had become accustomed to the school and did our homework diligently. We looked forward eagerly to the moment each day when Matron handed out mail and spent many hours writing to our families. When the war broke out, since Wyberlye was located near the coast and the air raids were increasing daily, the home closed in 1940 and all the girls were relocated to other homes and youth hostels in London. I am sure that many of my old Wyberlye friends lost their loved ones and had to start a whole new life without their families.

I was lucky. My parents had arrived in London just prior to the outbreak of World War Two. We survived the difficult war years and emigrated to the United States in 1947.

*   *   *

Alice Boddy

(Grünwald/Vienna), California, USA

The day I had been hoping and praying for for so long had finally come. What a relief to know that I was scheduled to leave the city of my birth, Vienna. For over a year my family and I had suffered during the Nazi occupation, trying everything to get out. Though we had registered with practically every consulate and various foreign transports, my mother and I had not made much progress other than getting my brother out.

Following the Kristallnacht pogrom of 10 November 1938 I registered for the Kindertransport being arranged by Gertrud Wijsmuller-Meijer and jumped for joy when, early in the spring of 1939, I was notified by the *Israelitische Kultusgemeinde* that I would be included in their Kindertransport in April leaving Vienna for London.

Just as I was saying a tearful goodbye to my mother, uncle and aunts and starting to climb the first step to our train, a young woman rushed up to me and handed me her little girl. Chokingly she said, 'Please look after my child. She is so young and still so helpless. At least you are one of the older children and I trust you'. Funny how this total stranger somehow sensed that I had always loved children. I was delighted and took the child in my arms and got into a compartment.

The train started to pull out of the station and we pressed our faces against the closed windows waving goodbye as tears stained our faces. The mother of my little charge fainted and I'll never forget the sight of her lying on the ground of the platform as we left the station behind for ever. The little girl in my arms soon developed a high fever and I had to turn her over to our escorts.

It was a slow journey and I finally fell asleep in the corner of our compartment. Suddenly I heard a commotion and saw a man in a grey uniform standing by the door. I was sleepy and hungry but I had heard voices and jumped up. 'What did you say?' I asked the man. 'Dutch Red Cross' he replied, smiling. I couldn't believe my ears. I charged towards him and fell around his neck. He dropped the juice and coffee he was carrying. I'll never forget that moment. Suddenly all the pent-up emotion escaped, some kids started praying while others screamed for sheer joy when they heard the words 'Welcome to Holland'.

I remember very clearly the handsome young man sent by Great Britain to escort us across the Channel. Once there, we were assembled in a big hall with children on one side and 'parents' on the other. As each name was called out we were to come up and meet the people to whom we had been assigned.

I was very lucky and my English family were both good to me and good for me. Mother and father were educators, their three sons were a barrister, solicitor and medical student. They still consider me to be their little sister and only last week they wrote 'We always, all of us, think of you with much love and feel lucky that you were the child who came to us'. Most of the kids, as I found out, did not fare as well. Many complained of being hungry and I brought them 'home' to my house. In September war broke out and I moved again – this time with my 'family'. We left London for Wolverhampton on September 1st just before the great London Exodus started.

*   *   *

Ingeborg Bower

(Morser/Berlin), Sheffield, UK

THE LESSON OF THE KINDERTRANSPORT

When Nazi said
　　'Du bist ein Unmensch'
When stranger said
　　'You will be my servant'
When Synagogue said
　　'You are an inconvenience'
When child in school of 1941 said
　　'Go home, German pig'
　　　　　I felt a no-one

But it was not to me, individually;
It was from the circumstance of prejudice,
It was from the System
That the words were spoken.
　　　　　Yet I felt a no-one

When *Mutti* said
　　'Go, and go on living'
When headmaster said
　　'Come, learn and be a teacher'
When husband said
　　'You are my beloved'
When children said
　　'You are our best Mummy'
When friend said
　　'With guts you have done it'
　　　　　I felt a some-one

Now it was to me, the individual;
To my own personhood
That the words were spoken.
　　　　　And I felt a some-one

No-one, some-one
It is our humanity that says it
Each to another.

*　　*　　*

Edith Bown

(Jacobowitz/Berlin), Maidstone, UK

When I came to this country fifty years ago, I was too old to go to school, but not too old to learn. After the first few weeks in a refugee hostel in Belfast, Northern Ireland, all the children were sent into the country, to a *Hachshara* farm in Millisle, County Down. This had been intended for *chalutzim* who were being prepared to go to Palestine, but the Jewish Refugee Committee felt that there was enough room for the children for whom they were responsible.

Our dining-room was an old stable, where the rain trickled in gently. The sleeping accommodation consisted of two large tents, into which camp-beds were put side by side. The following night we moved into a cowshed which had been whitewashed. The days were rather pleasant, that July before the war. If we had not been waiting for news of our loved ones, it could have been fun. On 3rd September, I remember standing at the bottom of the farmhouse steps listening to the news. Who can sleep when one is homesick, hates the country of one's birth and almost mourns for loved ones!

I worked on the farm for some time. I was fifteen years then. For a time I went back to Belfast and worked in the factory of my guardian, Mr Hurwitz. I sewed on buttons all day and lived again in the refugee hostel. Some time later I became the nanny to the only Jewish grocer in Belfast. I pushed the baby through the back streets of Belfast and read Dickens and Thackeray while she slept. For this I was given five shillings a week, from which I had to give two shillings and sixpence to the hostel. In the end I went back to the farm, as my employer told me that she was only 'keeping' me out of pity.

I must mention that I came to Northern Ireland with my ten-year-old brother, after our parents had been arrested in May 1939. He had been on the farm the whole time, and at school in Millisle village. The community there gave a kind of family environment, especially after war broke out and we were all classed as enemy aliens. Two weeks before I was eighteen years old, I started my nursing training at Ards District Hospital, Newtownards. It had not been easy to persuade the committee to let me go. 'You will cease to be a Jew and become converted', said Rabbi Schachter. I told him that after all that had happened to me, I would not forget so quickly.

My early nursing training was full of pitfalls, but I qualified in 1945.

I left Ireland in 1946 and went to Liverpool to train for tropical diseases, prior to what I hoped would be my *Aliya* to Israel. While there I met the son of Ben Gurion and saw him married to an English girl. I left nursing for a time and stayed with some good non-Jewish friends. From there I went on to study midwifery.

Shortly after that I met my husband. We married on the understanding that we could divorce if it did not work. This year we celebrate our fortieth anniversary. My only son Stefan (after Stefan Zweig), was born in 1950. He married in 1980 and we now have a grandson, Nicholas William, born on the 101st birthdate of my late father, who died in Dachau. My mother died in Auschwitz. During the years of my marrige I studied and became a health visitor, in which field I worked in Kent for over twenty years and only stopped when I was discovered to have leukemia. It has been a very good life so far. My only regret is that my parents were not alive to enjoy it with us.

* * *

Lotte Bray

(Löwenstein/Halle), Chippenham, UK

On a cold January day in 1939 my parents saw me on to the *ss Deutschland* at Bremerhaven – en route to England. I did not travel as a member of a children's transport although there were many children travelling together on that trip and we banded together. I was to be met at Victoria station by my future foster mother. We didn't know each other.

To me, at just seventeen years old, it was a great adventure. For years, I had pressed my parents to emigrate or at least let me go to a kibbutz in Palestine, as it was then, but my father would not hear of it.

'*Du bist ja nur ein Kind*', he would say – how could I possibly know what to do for the best? Germany saw me off in typical fashion, a thorough search by a woman who stole my watch and a small signet ring; I hoped it would bring her bad luck.

The journey was uneventful and as we landed at Southampton we saw our first British bobby and – wonder of wonders – he smiled at us. I think it was then I made up my mind that I would never leave England if it was at all possible – a country where a policeman actually smiled must be a good place to settle. The boat train soon landed us at Victoria station and there I was on my own. I walked along the platform and wondered how on earth I would find the lady who was supposed to meet me. Just outside the gate a lady with a photograph in her hand waved to me. She had recognised me and gave me a big hug – welcome Lotte. We caught another train and got to my new home very late at night and so began my absorption into an English family. There were two children younger than myself, mother, father and two grand-mothers who shared a bungalow at the bottom of the garden. It was not an easy time, my English was poor and no one spoke German. This turned out to be an asset because it forced me to learn fast. That kindly English Protestant family closed around me and made me one of their own. I had found a new home. My own parents went to Shanghai soon after I left but I stayed with my foster parents until I was able to join the ATS in 1941. They were – and still are – a wonderful family. As for me, I married a British soldier and settled down here after the war. I have never once regretted it.

*   *   *

Professor Leslie Brent

B.Sc., Ph.D., F.Inst.Biol., Hon.M.R.C.P.

(Lothar Baruch/Köslin), London, UK

I arrived in Dovercourt Camp on 2 December 1938, together with many other children who had travelled from Berlin to the Hook of Holland. I was thirteen years old. Fate had decreed that my best friend Fred Gerstel be sent only as far as Holland; I never saw him again. At the time of our selection by the director and staff of the Jewish Orphanage in Pankow for the first Kindertransport both of us must have been seen by others as among the lucky ones. For Fred it turned out not to be so.

In Dovercourt Camp I spent a good many hours playing table tennis. One of the boys with whom I played from time to time (Gabi Adler) was a few years older and he was a helper in the camp. He told me about his school in Kent (Bunce Court) – a German-Jewish co-educational boarding school that had been transplanted from Southern Germany as early as 1933 by a farsighted headmistress (Anna Essinger). She intended to take a number of children from the camp and he would mention my name to her. Gabi must have been as good as his word, for one day I ran through a doorway and collided with a stout lady, who peered down at me shortsightedly and asked me who I was. On hearing my name she asked me whether I would like to go to her school in Kent; I said 'yes, please' and thus began a very important chapter in my life.

My first impression of Kent, with its narrow lanes and hedgerows buried in snow, and of the imposing country house that was to become my home, was magical. The school itself was extremely well ordered without seeming to be authoritarian, and the staff – many but not all German Jews – were utterly devoted to the children even though some of them had to carry great personal burdens of their own, having left their families and friends behind. I was made to feel welcome and cherished and I soon came to appreciate the high quality of the lessons, which were given in small classes of about a dozen. I made the most of the opportunity to engage in sports, particularly in hockey, at which I later excelled. I fell in love for the first time – alas, a case of love unrequited; and I took part in extramural activities such as the performance of part of *The Magic Flute*, in which my friend Ernst Weinberg and I were among the Moorish attendants, covered with a mixture of butter and cocoa.

One of the rules, enforced with only limited success despite the vigilance of the headmistress, was that all children had to rest on their beds after lunch.

We were then summoned by a bell to read the list allocating various practical duties we were expected to perform daily. By choice I spent my time mainly in the kitchen, wood workshop and garden, thus learning skills that have stood me in good stead later in life.

Excellent as the school was academically (the lack of science teaching other than biology was its most serious shortcoming), its most important feature was the informal and friendly relationship between teachers and pupils. I was very fortunate in that several teachers became lifelong friends. The school, which was evacuated to Shropshire in 1941, literally became my home and I returned to it whenever I had a holiday or an army leave until its demise in the early fities, its task more or less completed. This made it possible for me to cement friendships and to forge new ones.

Having taken my School Certificate with Matriculation I left school at the age of sixteen. Anna Essinger was at that time in touch with the Midlands Secretary of the Jewish Refugees Committee, Ruth Simmons, and after discussing it with her I accepted a job as laboratory technician in the Chemistry Department of Birmingham Central Technical College. There I was exposed to chemistry for the first time and I continued my education with evening and weekend classes in physics, chemistry, botany and zoology. I earned the princely wage of £56 per annum and more or less got by on it, with a little occasional assistance from Ruth Simmons and the kindness and generosity of Mr and Mrs Widdowson, in whose house I shared a room with another boy from Bunce Court and to whom I paid ten shillings a week for board and lodging! Financial exigency encouraged me to ride into the city by bicycle, a form of transportation for which I have retained a liking all my life. Cycling fifty-odd miles on the occasional Friday evening, after work, in order to spend a weekend in my old school (by then evacuated to Shropshire) was one of the pleasures and challenges of life.

I was to have taken the Intermediate examination in the summer of 1944. In the event I decided to join the Army late in 1943 and so as not to waste my studies I took the examinations six months early. Although it didn't seem to matter any more I passed all subjects except physics. I had already spent a year with the Home Guard, the war was going badly, and Birmingham was being bombed (I had joined the firewatching rota at the College, a rather eerie experience made bearable only by my colleague Dennis Wood playing Walton marches and Chopin preludes on the piano in the deserted building). I had received the last of my parents' Red Cross messages, which had sounded cryptic and ominous: '*wir verreisen*' In an earlier message my father had written, of course in German: ' . . . we feel sure that all will go well with you for you are, after all, *ein Sonntagskind* (Sunday's child). As soon as 'enemy aliens' were allowed to join the Army I volunteered.

Although I was quite well prepared for the Army in several ways – I was used to institutional life and had undergone training with the Home Guard – the first five weeks spent in Maryhill ('Merry Hell') Barracks in Glasgow came as something of a shock and an eye opener. I was exposed for the first time to language in which four letter words abounded and, what with my foreign name, my 'superior' education and the fact that whenever we 'fell out for a smoke', as the hourly ten minute break was called, I pulled out my pocket edition of *War and Peace*, I must have appeared to the other recruits as something of an oddball. Fortunately my ability to cope well with the physical demands of the tough training and the fact that I proved to be a first-class shot earned me their respect. Had that not been the case I might well have been given a rough ride. When interviewed about my future in the Army I expressed an interest in joining the Medical Corps. (My father had been a stretcher bearer, in the German Army of course, in the First World War.) However, it was suggested that I should opt for training to become an officer, and after some months with the Royal Warwickshire Regiment I was sent to a camp in Kent, where we were subjected to intensive training and selection prior to being sent to an officers' training camp in Lancashire.

This is not intended to be a biography and I will conclude by summarising the rest of my life. I was released from the Army in the autumn of 1947 with the rank of Acting Captain and, thanks to a Ministry of Education grant, I proceeded to Birmingham University to study Zoology. Soon after the end of the war in Europe I spent a hectic and traumatic week on compassionate leave in war-ravaged Berlin, attempting to trace my parents and sister and other relatives, only to be told eventually that they had been 'sent East by transport' in 1943. The real and awful significance of this only fully sank in when, shortly afterwards, I saw a film about the liberation of Belsen concentration camp.

I had four very busy years studying Zoology. I played hockey for the University, British Universities and Staffordshire and I became involved in the affairs of the Students' Union, of which I became President in my final year. Fate once again intervened. First, the woman who was to become my wife (Joanne Manley) was elected to be my Vice-President; and second, my intention of becoming a school master was fatally undermined by an invitation from the head of the Zoology Department, Professor P. B. Medawar, who was later to receive the Nobel Prize in Medicine and to be knighted, to become his Ph.D student. Thus began forty years of academic life and research in immunology, which are about to end in retirement.

Although, like others, I have had to work through some emotional problems over the years – connected with my early history, the loss of my family and the fact that I had been rather good at sweeping the more troublesome thoughts under the carpet – I have had a remarkably happy life in Britain. I feel thoroughly adjusted to my adopted country and part of it.

I was helped greatly in facing the past by recent participation in the BBC film *No Time to Say Goodbye* and by being interviewed in depth by one of the researchers of Barry Turner's book on the Kindertransports. This encouraged me to take the plunge and visit the town in which I was born and in which I spent the first eleven years of my life – Köslin, now in Poland. I went there accompanied by Joanne and my son Simon, whose support I valued enormously. Even so it proved to be a cathartic visit. The Kindertransports Reunion organised by Bertha Leverton was another important milestone in this respect. Although it is probably impossible to come fully to terms with the death of my family, I feel that I can now acknowledge it, ponder on it and go through the kind of mourning that was lacking earlier. How indeed does one mourn the death of one's loved ones when there is no grave, and whilst their death remained an uncertainty? I derive great satisfaction from the progress through life of our three children: Simon, Susanna and Jennifer, all following careers of their choosing and engaged in work they love – forestry, circus aerialism and acting. Not unnaturally I harbour some regrets about my life but this is hardly the place to enlarge on that.

I have encountered very little antisemitism in Britain at a personal level, though I was enraged when I came across a soapbox fascist in a London street in 1952. Earlier, when my foreign background was more obvious, I came across antisemitism only once, at the Technical College in Birmingham. On reflection I am not sure whether the lecturer's antipathy to me was because of my German origin or my Jewishness. What unpleasantness he generated was more than outweighed by the great kindness extended to me by other members of staff, who went out of their way to be helpful. I have never particularly flaunted my origins (except in the BBC film!), nor have I attempted to hide them. It is a fact, perhaps sad, that I grew away from Judaism after my arrival in England – first because religion (as opposed to religious knowledge) was not encouraged by the agnostic headmistress of Bunce Court school, and later because I developed a rationalist view of life that left no room for religion. I have always instinctively shied away from the nationalist fervour of Zionism but was glad when the State of Israel was established.

Ein Sonntagskind? Well, maybe.

Professor Brent is Professor of Immunology at St. Mary's Medical School, London.

*   *   *

J. L. Brent

(Bernstein/ Berlin), Australia

Eight months after war was declared I alighted from the bus I had boarded at Morden Underground station early in the evening. It was five minutes' walk to the refugee boys' hostel that was my home just off High Street.

As I made my way briskly around the corner into a side street, my heart was light and my spirits were high. Perhaps paradoxically so, for I had just visited my mother who had a room in north-west London, an hour's journey away. I had been there to say farewell. I was to report to Sutton police station on Friday morning, together with the other Sutton hostel boys who were sixteen or over. I was to be interned. Internment was to most people a calamity. To me, a boy of seventeen, it was a welcome change from the dreary routine of rising at half past five, slipping into moist clothes, downing my cup of coffee and, still half asleep, joining the crowds of workmen converging on the inner London suburbs by tube, trolley bus, bike and train. This was followed by nine-and-a-half hours of clock-watching from quarter to eight to six o'clock. I had a job as an instrument maker trainee in Lambeth. With its pie shops, its iron picket fences, its urchins playing in the gutter beside the crumbling pavements, it was not a world in which I felt at home.

Internment was not going to be all that long. The police sergeant who had called at the hostel some days previously to alert us, had made it known that it wasn't likely to take more than four weeks and he had suggested we take our tennis racquets. No, it wouldn't take long. And wasn't I in an 'essential industry'? A skilled worker?

These were my thoughts as I strolled down the tree-lined street. Soon I focussed on the party to be held the following night, Thursday. We had been asked to report to the police station on the following Friday morning. So we had written to the Marys and Margarets and Mollys and pooled our savings to buy chocolates, biscuits, cakes and two bottles of the cheapest wine we could find. And for days we had lived for and planned for THE PARTY. For we were sixteen and seventeen and, in 1940, dancing was thrilling and girls were still mysterious and unexplored.

As I entered the hostel through the open front door, I noticed the gloom on everyone's face. There was an oppressive silence in the air. 'What was the matter?' I asked. 'Well', they said, 'there was a change of plan'. A bobby had called that day to advise that four of our boys were to report for internment a day early, on Thursday. The other four were to go to the police station the following day. We would all join up at the same place, wherever that would be.

This threw a spanner into our plans for our break-up party. Not that anyone cared whether one was interned a day earlier or later. That didn't really matter. But nobody wanted to miss out on the Thursday night party into which had gone so much planning, care and thought.

We decided to draw lots and eight screwed-up pieces of paper went into a hat, four of them with pencilled crosses to indicate that the unlucky recipient was to report on Thursday morning. So we dipped into it for the sake of a song, for the sake of a few new dance steps, and hopefully, for the sake of a kiss in the dark. On Friday or Saturday we would all be together again.

What we did not know was that it was a dip into the future, into fate. The four of us who drew the crosses were shipped to Australia. The four who drew the blanks had their party, together with the under-sixteens. When they reported to the police in the morning, they were asked to return the following day. When they did so they were told that the Black Maria was full and could not take any more. During the following weekend, the indiscriminate internment policy came to a halt.

After the war, I tried to contact two of the boys with whom I had been particularly friendly. Both had joined the army. One could not be traced. The other was reported killed in action in 1944. To this day, nearly half a century later, I have been unable to establish what happened to the other boys.

* * *

Ruth Brunell

(Lewin/Berlin), Illinois, USA

Just after Kristallnacht, 9 November 1938, our cleaning lady told my mother that one of her other families was sending their two girls to England to school. My mother immediately contacted that family and with their help got in touch with the right people in England and eventually I received an affidavit from the headmistress of Fonnereau House School in Ipswich.

My parents took me to the station in Berlin. Little did I know that this would be the very last time that I ever saw them. But what fourteen year old child would think she would never see her parents again?

At the school there were two other refugee girls, also from Berlin. We didn't get along at first but this changed during the next few months.

When I was about fifteen years old, I asked my headmistress if I could learn shorthand and typing at a school across from ours. She was reluctant at first but I persuaded her and went there twice a week, doing rather well, and it has earned me a good living ever since.

Then the war broke out and no more mail from home, other than Red Cross messages or letters via Portugal. I was so homesick and still hoped that my parents and I would be reunited.

A year later, 12 September 1940, children were evacuated from Ipswich to the Midlands for safety and my friend Lilly and I decided to stick together. We asked the billeting officer to keep us together. The following day, he took us to the house of Mr and Mrs Potter where Lilly and I then resided for six years. I worked in Leicester at various jobs. Mr and Mrs Potter treated us like their own children, included us in all functions and took us every Friday to the Odeon, where Mr Potter was a manager, and we saw many good movies.

I remember many of the people whom I met, who treated me with much kindness, generosity and friendship, and most of them remained friends and I have seen them again over the past years. But my six years in Leicester were not always easy; I had many ups and downs before I departed for the United States.

The war years were difficult but I will never forget how wonderful people were to me, a little girl without parents, without money, trying to make my life as easy as it could be under the circumstances. To all those, I am deeply indebted for life.

Now, I have been in the United States for just over forty years, got married, have three children and four wonderful grandchildren. Again, life has not always been easy . . . but that is life.

*   *   *

Renate Buchthal
(Vienna)

I joined the Children's Transport in Vienna one evening in June 1939. I was ten, Vera, my little sister, nearly six. My clearest memory is of the sea of parents' faces at the station; most of them would never see their children again. We were two of the lucky ones, our father was already in London, our mother was to join him later, she came over on the last ship before war was declared.

The train ride seemed to go on for ever. It was dark when we embarked in Holland and I was disappointed that we could not see the sea properly. I had never seen the sea and had looked forward to this. At Harwich it was grey and damp. In the big hall at Liverpool Street station we were found by our new foster parents who recognised us from the photographs they had been sent of us. Our father was with them which was a great relief.

'Auntie' and 'Uncle', our foster parents, did not have the easiest time with me. I was homesick, fiercely loyal to my parents and determined to do things their way, not the English way. I had no wish to become a nice little English girl which was Auntie's ambition for me. At the time my attitude seemed to me entirely reasonable; in retrospect I must have been a trying child. My little sister more than made up for it and was soon as devoted to Auntie and Uncle as they were to her. They had no children of their own and Vera became theirs, she never really bonded to our parents again when years later she came to live with them once more.

My parents worked as domestic servants for a local dentist and we saw them most weekends. These meetings were painful for everybody. It was hard for our parents to see us as someone else's children and I found each parting agonising, expressing this by more sullen and resentful behaviour to my long suffering foster parents. Later our parents moved further away and we visited them only for school holidays, an arrangement kinder to everyone.

I was able to live with my parents again after less than a year with Auntie and Uncle. I knew they loved my sister best and I felt quite guilty when I came upon Auntie crying bitterly about my planned departure – they cared for me more than I had thought and considerably more than I deserved.

Auntie died some years ago, Uncle lives near my sister. Our own parents are both dead now and he is the only 'parent' we have left. We love and value him greatly.

There is still the guilt – that I was saved when so many children were not.

*   *   *

Gertrude Burns

(Hatschek), London, UK

This is not the story of a sad refugee, but is a sort of adventure. All I can clearly remember is arriving at the West-Bahnhof in Vienna one evening in June 1939 with my very tearful parents, and a small suitcase. I was to join a Kindertransport train via Holland to Harwich. Being nearly sixteen years old I was 'in charge' of some younger children during the journey.

When we arrived there was a call over the tannoy system:

'Would Gertrude Hatschek please come to the Purser's office at once.'

I had visions of white slavers, Gestapo, etc and went with much trepidation. Mr Stuart had come to collect me, a youngish blond, Scottish giant, completely unknown to me, who greeted me very warmly and told me he was taking me to meet his wife and then on to a school.

Fortunately I spoke fluent English at that time, my mother having decided many years earlier, that – if all the other girls were to have 'Mademoiselles' – her daughter would have a 'Miss'. I have blessed her snobbism ever since, it enabled me to go straight into an English school, take up lessons more or less where I had left off and take my School Certificate with flying colours.

I enjoyed my life at school on the whole, but the change from being an only child, with my own room and lots of privacy, to sharing a dormitory with five others and every minute of the day fully accounted for, was quite a wrench. The girls were very friendly, as were the staff. My headmistress, J. Vernon-Harcourt, was of the old school, made me read to her every night from the *Financial Times* to improve my accent, made me sit next to one of the staff at every mealtime, to be trained in making polite conversation during meals.

We had set times for letter writing, everything was censored by matron and she greatly disapproved of my writing to boys or men, those being uncles, cousins and school colleagues already in England. But I did get permission in the end to keep up my correspondence. I was the only foreign

– and Jewish – girl in the school and thus decided to join in Church parade on Sunday, rather than let the Committee send me religious material from London. Thus, when I finally left school and did come to London in the summer of 1940, it was my first meeting with the Refugee Committee. I was accommodated in Mrs Glücksmann's hostel at 27 Belsize Park and attended the Barrett Street Trade School to learn dressmaking and tailoring.

* * *

Kenneth Carey

(Heilbrunn/Goslar), Southampton, UK

I was born on 17 December 1921 as Kurt Heinz Heilbrunn, in the ancient city of Goslar in the Harz Mountains in what was then the province of Hannover in Central Germany.

All members of my family were Jews by religion, although they were not orthodox and did not actively practise their faith except on the major holidays. I have no recollection of feeling different from other children until the persecutions began with the arrival of the Nazis.

My father had a particular affection for the Harz mountains where he liked to spend what little free time he allowed himself. I did not realize it at the time, but he must have found these outings extremely strenuous. During the First World War he had, like so many German Jews of his generation, volunteered for front-line service and had received a severe abdominal wound. The hole was so deep that, even though it had scarred over, I was able to put my fist into it. This injury was to plague him for the rest of his life.

In common with the 100,000 Jews of Germany who had served their country, he foolishly assumed himself and his family to be immune from the extremes of Nazi persecution.

I enjoyed my early years at school. The teaching in the junior school was progressive and included frequent class nature study outings which I liked.

All this changed as the power of the Nazi party grew, although early on I had felt somewhat protected from the gravest excesses because of my father's standing in the town and particularly because of his army service. In a military town such things were still important and my father still counted among his good acquaintances and customers a number of the garrison officers.

By this time I was at the local *Realgymnasium*, the same school which my father and his brother had attended as boys. Most of the teachers were of my father's generation and had also served in the army. They behaved in a neutral manner towards me and I was conscious that some tried to protect me from physical and verbal attacks by the most rabidly anti-semitic pupils. But among the teachers there was one, the History master, who took every opportunity to humiliate me and later, actively to persecute me. I recall being called out in front of the class. (I had long been made to sit by myself so that I should not 'contaminate' the Aryans.) He then shouted at me and ordered me to leave the room. As the only Jewish child in the school I had to endure the full measure of his venom.

Persecution was becoming commonplace. During one of Hitler's visits to Goslar in either 1935 or 1936 I was made to stand in the entrance to our shop whilst a Gestapo agent held a gun to my back remarking that if anything happened to the high-ranking Nazis in the motor cavalcade my fate would be sealed.

In 1935 my father was denounced for having insulted Julius Streicher, the *Gauleiter* of Franconia and editor of the notorious anti-semitic tabloid *Der Stürmer.* He appeared before a local court, was convicted and initially sentenced to four months' imprisonment, commuted to a fine of one thousand marks. The court considered that clemency was appropriate because of his service at the Front and his war wound. (The fine was the equivalent of a shop assistant's annual wage.) Failure to pay would incur a day's imprisonment for every ten marks outstanding. None of this seemed to break his spirit.

Because of the gravity of the situation at the *Realgymnasium,* my father decided, as an interim measure, to transfer me to a Jewish boarding school. This school, with a full Jewish staff, was still allowed to operate at Caputh near Potsdam. It catered for both boys and girls and lessons were conducted in small groups. For the few months there I felt free and happy and in a caring atmosphere, conducive to learning. Sadly, it was soon clear that my father could no longer afford the school fees, and in the autumn of the same year he arranged for me to enter a Jewish firm of outfitters belonging to a business contact, and still functioning in Magdeburg.

Shortly after my arrival I was woken early one morning by two plain clothes officers who took me to Magdeburg jail. I occupied a cell of my own and remember nothing more than that I was suddenly told to get out. (This must have been several days later.) My aged boss was released at the same time and we were given to understand that we were lucky: he was too old, and I, at not yet seventeen, was too young to be sent to a concentration camp. The other Jews rounded up at the same time were not as fortunate.

The morning of my arrest in Magdeburg was, as I was later to realize, the infamous 'Kristallnacht', the night of 9-10 November 1938, when the Nazi machine went on the rampage.

On my release from prison, I vaguely remember making my way by rail to Goslar. As I neared our shop I saw a lot of people staring at what to me looked like a pile of rubble. The shop was empty, deserted and all the windows were without glass.

I became even more frightened than I had been. I do not know what prompted me to do so, but I left the scene and walked quickly to the house of a Jewish friend. I found my mother with other terrified and confused women. We were all distressed and in a state of shock and it took some time for me to discover what had happened.

Mother had been alone with her father in the flat above the shop. For some years he had been living with us. He was elderly and had become increasingly frail.

My father had gone on business to Berlin. During the night a mob of Stormtroopers had broken into the shop and had begun to ransack the place and loot its contents. On hearing the sounds of this orgy of destruction, my mother had managed to phone Berlin and warn my father. Apparently such was the noise as the Stormtroopers smashed their way into the flat that he could hear it clearly over the telephone.

In spite of his age, grandfather was pushed down the steep stairs and then dragged off to prison. Mother had to watch all this. I do not know how she eventually escaped to her friends.

I returned later that week to the shop and flat. All the merchandise had been removed along with much of our personal property including most of mother's jewellery.

On his return to Goslar, my father had also been taken to prison, but was soon released probably because of his war wound. Grandfather, too, was eventually released, bowed and bruised, but not broken.

At the end of November, a lady called on my parents and suggested that no time was to be lost in attempting to get me out of Germany. I was told that she belonged to the Society of Friends, the Quakers, who were working in England to remove threatened Jewish children from Germany. As I was nearly seventeen it was felt that I had to leave without delay. Of course my parents consented immediately.

I joined the children's transport on 5 January and can still feel the oppressive silence in the compartment of the train until we were in Holland and had left Germany behind us.

On arrival in England, we were all taken to a vacant holiday camp in Dovercourt. It was used as temporary accommodation for refugee children. From there I was lucky enough to be put in a refugee hostel under the care of the Oxford Refugee Committee and allowed to go to Southfield Grammar School in Oxford, where the little English I had learned in Germany had to be turned into acceptable speech.

At seventeen a young man is very impressionable and with events and changes crowding in on me, I was certainly no exception. We were received with kindness and consideration and, although conditions were far from luxurious, the sense of being free was overwhelming. We were restricted in our movements in the transit camp and later because lack of English reduced the opportunities of exploring and making contact with people. But we were free! Everyone was helpful and did his best to make us feel at home as quickly as possible. I could not remember feeling homesick, but I did have one main thought in mind: how to get my mother, father and grandfather out of Germany. My parents had managed to send my bicycle to Oxford and I was still in correspondence with them, although I felt that I had to be very careful what I wrote. Just before the outbreak of war I asked the warden of the hostel to be allowed to cycle to London. I cycled through the night and arrived at the headquarters of the Board of Deputies of British Jews early in the morning to seek advice on whom I might consult with a view to bringing my family to England. In retrospect I realize how naive it was to expect anyone to respond to a penniless young man with the urgency I demanded. I continued to talk to as many people as I thought could help my parents, but then the war came and time had run out. The last contact I had with them was through one or two Red Cross postcards. Then there was silence.

I heard nothing more of them until after the cessation of hostilities in Europe when, with the help of the Army, I discovered that they had all been killed in concentration camps.

As for myself, I spent a happy time at the Grammar School in Oxford, where I became proficient in English and where I was increasingly able to grasp the immense benefits which were mine, just by being in England.

After Dunkirk our movements were restricted and most of us were interned. My own internment lasted only a short time. I volunteered to join the British Army. At the time only the Pioneer Corps was open to us. On 23 October 1940 I enlisted at Liverpool. I was then not yet nineteen years old. I volunteered my way out of the Pioneer Corps and joined the Royal Artillery in October 1943, having earlier that year been given permission to change my name. Those of us who intended to go on active service abroad had been advised to do so. Henceforth I became Kenneth Richard Carey. The name was really picked out of the air.

After training as an Anti-Tank Gunner I was posted overseas and saw active service in Italy.

I was demobilized from the Army in October 1947 holding the rank of War Substantive Sergeant.

After demobilisation I became a teacher and until my retirement served as head of the Geography department in a Southampton comprehensive school.

I am married, have a daughter from a previous marriage and two grandsons.

In 1977 I had a chance encounter with a Mr Cramer, who as a boy had been our neighbour in the *Werenberg Strasse*. He was moved as a result of this meeting to make it his continuing task to discover the fate of the few Jewish families living in Goslar before the war. He has recently published his major work of documenting their martyrdom. It was not until after 1985 that I finally learned the full details of the fate of my parents.

Anita Chard

(Graetzer/Olomvoc), Sydney, Australia

My name was Anita Graetzer and I was just eight years old. I was one of the lucky ones because I was with my older sister Eva who was thirteen. It was a very frightening experience, suddenly being sent away and travelling on many trains a long way.

Our first view of London was this large station waiting-room where we waited so long to be collected. Nearly all the children had gone when at last our distant relative came to pick us up. We went to his elderly mother's place and were allowed to sleep for what seemed like ten minutes and were then taken to be fitted for our new school uniforms. The best part of this was travelling on a red double decker bus right on the front seat upstairs; an experience which I had never had and it was very exciting.

Late that night, our relative took us by car to Macauley House College in Cuckfield, Sussex. All I wanted to do was sleep after this long journey. When we arrived I had the worst fright I could ever remember. There were the headmaster and his wife all in black. She was in a long black dress and there was this huge open fireplace. I was so afraid and imagined that any minute I would be thrown into the roaring fire and burnt alive. Also all the canes lining the walls were not a pleasant sight, although I am not sure that I knew what they were at that point.

We were taken into a dormitory and although we were really tired and it was well after midnight we had to have a bath in two inches of water and then to unpack our suitcases. The matron then sent us into a dormitory full of girls to go to bed in the dark. How was I to know where to get into bed? The sheets and blankets were tucked in all around. By this time I was really crying but was told to be quiet and not wake the others, although I didn't understand a word of English. This was my first day in England – not a very happy one. Child psychology and understanding of young children who had been suddenly parted from their parents was unheard of here it seemed.

*   *   *

Paul Cohn

(Hamburg), London, UK

I grew up in Hamburg as an only child. My father was an accountant; and both my parents' families had lived in Hamburg for generations. For this reason my parents did not really contemplate emigration until it was too late.

After the Kristallnacht my father was taken to Sachsenhausen concentration camp, and was only released (in view of his First War record) after several months of effort by my mother. We now made serious attempts to emigrate, but the only place willing to take refugees was Shanghai, and there was a long queue. Late in 1938 Holland agreed to take unaccompanied children, so my mother registered me. A little later England made a similar offer, and my parents promptly changed my registration, reasoning that England would be safer than Holland. Refugee Committees in England were trying to find families willing to guarantee refugee children. The Müller-Hartmanns, relations of ours who had emigrated to London, were able to find a farmer willing to guarantee two boys through the Dorking Refugee Committee. The idea was for these boys to be trained on his poultry farm and then to go to one of the Dominions, where they would be able to find work. My cousin Peter, who came to England early in 1939, was taken on by the farmer and I was to join him there.

Our transport was to leave on 21 May 1939. My parents made light of the parting, saying that they would follow soon, but they must have known that they would probably not see me again. In fact, they were taken to Riga concentration camp in 1941. They never returned.

We travelled by train to Hook of Holland and then by boat to Harwich. At the quayside we were transferred to a train. The train brought us to Liverpool Street station, where relatives and friends were waiting. Here I saw Mrs Müller-Hartmann, whom I remembered well from Hamburg. She had come to meet me and take me on the tube (Underground) to Victoria and put me on the train to Dorking. I was met by a lady from the Refugee Committee who drove me to my destination, the farm in Newdigate. Here was my first chance to practise my English; after six years' study at school I was pleased to find that I could keep up a conversation without too much difficulty.

The farm was eleven acres of land just outside Newdigate, where Mr Panning and his wife kept about five thousand chickens. They found that the work was a bit too much to do unaided, and this is where my cousin and I came in. When I arrived, Peter had been there about four weeks and things had not gone too well; perhaps Mr Panning's expectations had been too high, possibly Peter, who was a year older than I, had found the life too constricting, and so it had been decided to transfer Peter to another farm once I had settled in. I had been brought up very much as a town child and did not look forward to such tasks like killing and plucking chickens but seeing the farmer first do it made it look so easy that I soon tried it myself. There were many other jobs to be done: mainly feeding, watering and 'mucking-out'. I picked up these tasks quickly and then settled down to a somewhat dull routine, working some seventy-plus hours a week, with half a day off each week and every other Sunday afternoon. For this I had my board and lodging plus 2s. 6d. (12½p.) per week pocket money, but this gradually increased. On my half day I would take the bus to Dorking and there go to the cinema. For 6d. (2½p.) I would have six hours of viewing, seeing each film twice, to improve my English.

The Duke of Newcastle had large estates near Dorking and had offered to accept refugees to help out; after a few weeks Peter left to work on one of the Duke's farms. As September approached and war clouds gathered, some Londoners began to look for accommodation in the country. On our farm we had a little hut, literally a single room, used for sorting eggs. This hut was now let to a couple from London.

On 3 September, as Mr Chamberlain made his memorable broadcast, Mr Panning and I were digging a shelter in the yard behind the farm house. When we had a hole big enough we made steps into it, reinforced by wood and covered the whole with corrugated iron and earth. We never actually used the shelter, which was just as well, since it soon filled with water.

In other ways the war brought variety to farm life. We acquired two cows, as well as a number of sheep. I soon learnt to milk the cows and this more than anything gave me the feeling of being a real countryman.

The sheep needed very little care. They had to be shorn from time to time, but mostly they were self-sufficient and except in the winter, spent the nights out of doors.

An important daily task was 'locking-up', that is shutting all the poultry houses at night, after making sure none of the inhabitants were left out. This was to guard against foxes.

At the outbreak of war I was still fifteen and when I reached sixteen in January 1940 I became a 'friendly alien' but in June, after the fall of France, lots of refugees were interned and I awaited my fate with some anxiety. When I had to renew my alien's registration book at the Dorking Police Station, I took the opportunity to ask the desk sergeant when I would be interned. He leaned across the desk, glowered at me and growled:

'You don't *want* to be interned, do you?'

I never raised the topic again and in fact was not interned.

During the Battle of Britain we saw many planes overhead, both friendly and enemy, and occasional dog-fights. At the time of the invasion scare in 1940, the farmer started putting padlocks on the poultry houses, 'because of the soldiers'.

'Why do you expect German soldiers?' I asked somewhat apprehensively.

'Oh no,' he laughed, 'we're having some Allied soldiers quartered in the village'.

They turned out to be Scots Canadians, who soon came to visit us on the farm, and played their bagpipes for us. During the day they sometimes came for shooting practice; I noticed that as I walked past (close to their line of fire) they stopped, and I then realized that they were not just firing blanks. Their favourite target practice was the overhead telephone wire; they brought it down once, but soon afterwards were transferred.

As the war went on, animal feedings stuffs became more and more difficult to get. The cows and sheep were no problem, but we had to cut down on the number of chickens, and eventually, late in 1941, the farmer decided to give up his farm. By now I was able to get permission to work and I was to be sent to a Government Training Centre to be trained as a fitter. This was a welcome change and I looked forward to a job more in line with my interests, after two and a half years of farming., Nevertheless, it was a somewhat melancholy feeling to walk around the farm on the day of the auction and to see everything disappearing under the hammer.

* * *

Elfriede Colman

(Janda/Vienna), London, UK

June 1939. I was five and so excited: I was going alone by train to visit Aunt Rella in Hamburg. My parents saw me on to the train in Vienna and my only concern was making sure that a packet of sponge fingers was in my rucksack. I slept on the floor of the train. Then there was shiny white paint and wooden planks (a ship, of course), and then a large shed where I had to identify some luggage. I can only recall my rucksack, but since that was probably with me already, maybe it was a suitcase which I still have. Then on to the offices of the Catholic Committee for Refugees from Germany. My 'aunt' arrived and took me to a house in Hendon which she shared with another teacher. I was put into a pretty dress and was dismayed when I discovered it was a nightdress and I had to go to bed. At no stage do I recall being sad or frightened or bewildered. My Jewish mother had become a Catholic before I was born and it had been decided that I should go to Catholics in England. I was the adored child of father (seventy-two) and mother (forty-six) and I had a huge repertoire of songs and nursery rhymes. There were several half brothers and a half sister from my father's first marriage.

My 'aunt' was kind and loving and I soon became attached to her. This caused resentment in the other teacher who was a religious maniac and a bully. It was only in my teens that it was pointed out that she was a lesbian. There followed thirteen years of tension/fear/repression/rows between the two women, and religious brainwashing. Certainly no room for personal or emotional development; fun and spontaneity were dirty words. I came from a musical background – my father was a *Kapellmeister* – so piano and violin lessons were arranged. I was made to excel, won competitions, but never derived any pleasure from this activity. When I was nine the nice 'aunt' got the other woman to agree to 'lay off' me and foster her own child. So a poor little five year old girl was procured from a Catholic orphanage. Of course I was bullied as before but the new child was beaten as well. We were both too cowed to complain to anyone.

In 1940 a Red Cross letter came telling me of my father's death. After the war a letter came from my half sister, forty years my senior, sending photos, details of my family about which I had known nothing, and the news that my mother had been denounced by someone wanting her flat. When she knew that she would be taken away my mother had given my half sister my address in England. Two of my mother's sisters had been taken also. As returning to Vienna was impossible for me, my nice 'aunt' formally adopted me in 1949 when I was fifteen. She is now eighty-five and very frail and I am totally responsible for her, and having no one else to care for her she recently came to live with me.

My first school was a convent run by German nuns. As they were pro Nazi I was an embarrassment and they excused my presence by saying there must have been something wrong with my family if I had to be sent away. After eight years at another convent, I went to a technical college for my final matriculation year and heaven – there were boys and no religion! Our menage was exclusively female, the only male being the occasional visit from a priest. Although it had been decided that I should attend a music college, it was considered wise to take a secretarial course first. As soon as the course finished I found a job and left to live in a hostel.

I married at twenty, a lovely man who was forbearing and patient, and who was a loving father to our two children. My deficient childhood made me incapable of giving the unstinting love they all deserved, and it wasn't until in my late thirties that an extended period of psychotherapy turned me into a reasonably adequate human being. By that time the marriage was at an end; my husband deserved much better.

In 1983 I returned to Vienna for the first time, primarily to visit an old aunt who had spent the war years in Shanghai with her husband and daughter, but also to try and establish some national affinity since I had never had any religious or national identity. Whilst there, I tried to obtain copies of marriage and death certificates. The attitude of Catholic clergy was strange and unhelpful, people in municipal offices just wanted to be rid of me but finally someone took an interest and I achieved some success. In the same building that houses my aunt's old peoples' home (well guarded by a soldier with machine gun/electric door/passport control) are the offices of the *Israelitische Kultusgemeinde*, who most efficiently produced documentary proof of my mother's demise via 'Theresienstadt, Auschwitz and camp unknown'. I returned to England feeling truly British. I had not known about reparations until the 1980s so with my documentary proof and the kind help of Neville Sandelson, MP and the Austrian Consul in London the Austrian Government were hugely generous – £581.96! Apparently this was the 'going rate' for my mother's incarceration from 1942 to 1945!

I'm lucky to be alive, have two smashing children who are settled with their own partners, some good friends, gregarious Sunday walks with the Jewish Senior Ramblers and my first *real* identity. I AM ONE OF THE KINDER.

* * *

Hans Danziger

(Berlin), London, UK

My sister Marion Goldwater and I came to England aged five and eight respectively in March 1939 from Berlin. We lived in Putney learning English and attending school for one or two months. It was quite a culture shock. In August we all went on holiday to a Sainsbury home in Bexhill and on our return my sister and I were evacuated to J B Sainsbury's hunting lodge in Leighton Buzzard. We were looked after by the groom and his wife for about a year after which we went to her daughter in Harpenden for four years. We were happy and she gave us a stable home. Her husband was in the army. Mr Sainsbury sometimes came to see us. My sister and I attended the local school. I joined the Scouts and attended the Methodist Sunday School which was run by a marvellous lady who never let us forget that we were Jewish. At the age of thirteen it was decided that we should both go to the St Albans *Cheder* run by a Mr Wolfson who taught me *Bar Mitzvah* which was celebrated by Rabbi M Landy. Members of the community put us up and gave a party. I had made some friends as I was by then attending St Albans County School for Boys.

It was then felt that I should be in a Jewish environment and I went to live with a German Jewish family. The husband had been invalided out of the Pioneer Corps and could help to support me and the son of a friend, Willy Naymann, who came from a Leeds hostel to be as a brother to me. My sister went to Stoatley Rough, a boarding school in Haslemere. During the war we received messages from my parents in Germany who used a false name. They miraculously survived in Berlin due to the help of Christian friends and others who deliberately turned a blind eye. They obtained false papers. After a spell in a Kibbutz set up in Fulda, they came to England paid for by the refugee committee and Mr Sainsbury who always invited us to tea to hear of our progress. We all lived together for a short while after which they went to live with the Hahn-Warburgs, whose house they tended, and who gave them a quiet and peaceful time and a place for us all to meet at weekends. I was now an apprentice, training as a designer, and my sister was at Hendon Tech taking her NNEB. My parents, after ten years of working for other people, decided that they could afford to retire if they returned to Fulda.

I was married to a Viennese girl whom I met at the *Achdut* Club organised by the Refugee Committee, but she died in 1976. I have a married daughter who teaches music and another who, after taking an English degree and working as a social worker, is now working for a degree in that field. I have remarried, have a delightful nine year old daughter, a joy to us all. My wife, who is English, disproves the notion that one must have the same background to be happy.

*   *   *

Clare David

(Dresden), Southport, UK

I lived in Dresden, and was part of a large and happy family. Father, mother, three sisters and a brother. In 1935 a Jewish school was opened because of the anti-semitism in German schools. We children had our own social activities and only mixed with Jewish people, and were quite happy and contented in spite of the anti-semitism until that eventful day when our little world suddenly collapsed around us. Our school was closed down, never to be re-opened.

That night all Jewish shop windows were smashed and many of our friends disappeared, having been either deported or arrested. A few evenings later, while my father was out, there was a ring at the door. My mother answered it and there stood two tall men in Nazi uniform. I was close behind my mother and was quite frightened, but she, who was only small, never turned a hair and asked them to come in. They said they had orders to search for weapons, and they went right through the house. Fortunately they did not break anything and went away without doing any damage. I like to think that it was my mother's courage which made them behave and I admired her so much that evening.

I was chosen as one of the children to join a Kindertransport to England. Two of my school friends were going too. It was all arranged so quickly. We hardly realized what was happening and suddenly I was spending my last night at home. How sad my parents must have felt, knowing that they might never see their children again.

After my arrival in England, I spent some weeks at the reception camp in Dovercourt. I was sad to be parted from my two school friends. They were sent south and I was taken to two old ladies in Wallasey near Liverpool. They were very kind to me. I started going to school and began to learn English. I settled down to my new way of life, but I missed my home and family very much and waited anxiously for news of them. We corresponded regularly until war broke out. After that I heard nothing more of them.

Ellen Davies

(Wertheim/Hoof bei Kasstle), Swansea, Wales, UK

I was born in 1929 in Hoof bei Kasstle in Germany. My maternal grandparents emigrated to Argentina in 1935/6, while my paternal grandparents left for America about the same time. I arrived in Swansea, South Wales on 30 June 1939.

My father escaped from a concentration camp and arrived in England in August 1939 and was sent to Australia in 1940. My mother, four brothers and two sisters, (one born in August 1939), were left behind. News received from the Red Cross in 1942 reported that mother and all the children were sent to the gas chambers in 1941. At twelve years old I would not believe this document – did not want to believe it. Subsequently all documentation was destroyed, when the house in Swansea received a direct hit.

An early marriage to an orthodox Jew produced two delightful children, now forty and thirty-four, and now two grandchildren. This marriage failed. My second husband is an understanding man, though not Jewish. I spent a great deal of time trying to trace siblings, but to no avail. Years went by; heartaches never diminished. At all times, my wish and dream has always been 'Next Year in Jerusalem'. Five years ago, on the spur of the moment, I decided I would go to Israel. It took just four days to arrange and one nervous middle-aged lady was going through the El Al security not believing that this was happening. I spent five days touring and then decided to return to Jerusalem and *Yad Yashem*. No words can describe the agony, hell, but at last, I was able to mourn my dead. I had been trying, but my stubborn disbelief had become so ingrained that it was almost a complete amnesia, with just stray memories filtering through.

I spent nearly an hour going through files with the help of a most understanding man. It seemed as if the name Wertheim did not exist. I left *Yad Yashem* with names and addresses of tracing agencies in Germany. On my return home, I wrote to two and waited and waited. During this wait I had a letter from someone in charge of records at *Yad Yashem* who had checked even further. There was a lady, who fifteen years ago, had been trying to trace her family named Katz; and her married name was, would you believe, Wertheim, address New York. Next a letter arrived from one of the agencies; it could have been a copy of the Red Cross letter received in 1942, only more detailed. I thought I knew what grief was . . . That letter shattered me.

My husband suggested that I wrote to New York to check out that Wertheim. To my amazement and delight, the husband was my late father's second or third cousin. Again on impulse I went to New York, how could I not?

I arrived at Kennedy Airport and got a taxi to the address. As you can imagine, there was joy and tears all round with everyone talking at the same time. The telephone rang all the time for me from family I didn't even know. It was enough that they had grown up with my father. The telephone rang again for me. The voice at the other end kept saying through tears 'You're Julius' daughter' over and over again. Then she kept insisting that as she was my only second cousin, I had to come to California to her. Having scraped just enough money to get to New York, this was out of the question. She was insistent. Her husband eventually came to the telephone giving me a dozen numbers to copy and insisting I took a flight to Los Angeles using these numbers which were his American Express card. After being in New York for a week, I flew to LA and an unimaginable welcome.

During the first evening, Toni, my cousin, asked me 'Have you ever been in touch with your Uncle David?' My mouth dropped. 'Who's my Uncle David?' The information then given was that he was my father's eldest brother who lived in Miami and Erika also lived there. This name I knew. She was my father's youngest sister just two years older than me. Toni picked up the phone and dialled Miami. Poor Uncle David, he's eighty-four. I thought he would have a heart attack. Again the question, 'When are you coming?' Sorry, I had to return in a week and in no way could I get to Miami. Perhaps next year, please God.

I had a wonderful week, my cousin could not stop talking and would burst into German periodically. As I had not spoken German for fifty years I could not answer her, but to my amazement I did understand.

Time flew. During that year I corresponded with my aunt Erika and she asked in one letter if I knew that I had cousins in Cincinnati who had come from the Argentine. Of course the answer was no, so she gave me the address and I wrote. By now it was February 1988 – the first trip was 1987 – and I made arrangements to spend *Pesach* in Miami and then a few weeks in LA.

Within ten days of my letter to Cincinnati, the telephone rang one Sunday and a voice said 'This is Sal from Cincinnati'. I was so shocked all I could say was, 'I just wrote to you'.

'Yes,' he replied, 'that is why I am phoning you. We are having our Silver Wedding on 16 March and I have sent you plane tickets to Miami because we so want you to be with us'. In Cincinnati I met three distant cousins, two second cousins and the rest were cousins of cousins both maternal and paternal, as one of my mother's sisters married one of my father's brothers. How close can you get?

Letters now come and go like confetti, only filled with love and affection. After fifty years I have at last found my family. My husband, children and grandchildren mean the world to me, but my new-found family have given my life a new dimension and so very much missed love now found. At last part of my dream has come true.

*   *   *

Lenore Davies

(Ritter/Vienna), Guildford, Surrey, UK

I wonder if you can imagine what it is like to realize at age thirteen that because there has been a change in government you no longer have a place in society? You are a non-person. Overnight the girl who has shared your desk at school will no longer talk to you, the neighbours whom you have known all your life, with whom you have been away on holiday, shun you.

One thing is certain – you grow up overnight.

I had been very fortunate to be selected as one of thirty children, all labelled, and I can still hear the voice at the barrier which looked at my label and said 'There she is' and with that I was handed to a lady who was waiting. We knew absolutely nothing about each other.

Next morning like a well-brought up little girl I took my bed to pieces, stripped the sheet, placed the pillows on the window sill, upended the mattress – and suddenly my hostess stood in the door, threw her hands up in horror and said: 'Shocking, what will the neighbours say!'

That was the first of many innocent misunderstandings to come; my table manners were different, not wrong; my phraseology was poor, not impolite; my English general knowledge was limited, not stupid. Yes, I did have too many clothes, but that was the only thing I could bring with me and mother did not want anybody else to have the additional expense of clothing me.

After three weeks my hostess phoned the Society of Friends, under whose auspices I had come, and said that she could not put up with me any longer – and so suddenly I was out on my ear ... that same day my parents were leaving Vienna for an uncertain destination. We spoke to each other on the telephone and it took many more years before I could face trunks calls again. Next morning my hostess took me to Bloomsbury House, kissed me fondly on the cheek and left me half way up an imposing staircase.

I was sent to a hostel for adults which was about to open in South London and I was their first resident apart from a refugee couple who had been engaged as caretakers. I went to school, I joined the Girl Guides and made many new friends.

When war broke out, I was evacuated with my school. This time I was the more experienced – I had seen it all before, not knowing where I would be the following night or who would be with me. My best friend Audrey and I arranged to be together and now I was able to support her when she felt homesick. Suddenly I was no longer different, everybody else needed to be looked after also. Audrey and I were billeted with a charming family in a large house. They were understanding, helpful and everything one would wish; life became more settled, my English improved by leaps and bounds. Meanwhile my parents had been allowed to settle in Venezuela, but alas, there was no chance of joining them until after the war.

On my sixteenth birthday I became an 'enemy alien' overnight. Later I was a 'friendly alien' again and the restrictions were more lenient.

I passed my exams, but as there was no money to go to university and as I was not eligible for any grants and I had not won a scholarship, it was obvious to me that there was only one thing to do. I would join the Forces. You would not believe how many people, who should have known better, were only too willing to tell me that I would not be accepted. With the optimism of youth I persisted and was rewarded.

I joined the WAAF in September 1943 at a time when 'friendly aliens' were allowed to be in trades other than orderlies or cooks, and I became an Instrument Repairer. Actually I passed the aptitude test to be a wireless mechanic. This was a highly skilled category subject to the official secrets act ... However, the WAAF were very discreet and put me through a special medical which discovered that my eyes crossed in the wrong place and therefore I was unacceptable as a wireless mechanic. I was happy to work with aeroplanes in any capacity. At the end of the war in Europe I transferred to the Education Department and in 1947 I was demobbed. By now I had not seen my parents for eight and a half years and was anxious to do so before I began my studies at university. Passport difficulties were immense and it was touch and go whether I would manage to get to Venezuela and back before term started. Only after I returned and had started to read for my degree in Physics was I allowed to swear allegiance to the King and gain British nationality.

After graduating I took a post with a British oil company in Trinidad as a research physicist. I wanted to be at least on the same side of the Atlantic as my parents. There were still those who knew better and chided me for deserting the country which had sheltered me ...

I met and married my husband in Trinidad.

We returned to England permanently in 1957 and shortly after that I became a grammar school physics mistress. When in 1964 one of my pupils gained a Physics Exhibition to Cambridge, I felt that after twenty-five years I had arrived.

*   *   *

Louis De Groot

(Arnhem), California, USA

I grew up in Arnhem, the Netherlands, where my parents were active with the Jewish refugee committee. Among my memories is the arrival at our home of two young sisters from Vienna who were on their way to England

and who needed overnight lodging before they could continue their journey.

They arrived on a wintry Saturday afternoon in December. Their belongings consisted of the clothes they were wearing and little else. My parents took them to our store to purchase some clothing which led to the revelation that their parents also owned a store in Vienna.

The younger girl who I guess was about my age, eight or nine years old, was terribly upset about being uprooted. I remember that my father presented her with a doll hoping that it would make her feel a little more at ease with her new situation.

My memories of the older sister are limited to her efforts of comforting and reassuring the younger one. This may very well be because the older girl was closer in age to my sister.

While many refugees from Germany and Austria passed through my parental home on their way to the Hook of Holland during those years the two Viennese sisters have always remained vividly in my memory. One of these girls' names was Hannelore.

*   *   *

Ruth Doniger

(Traum/Vienna), Moshav Habonim, Israel

My brother and I, Ruth and Alfred Traum, thirteen and ten respectively, left Vienna and our family on 20 June 1939 and arrived in England on 22 June. We were going to an English Christian family in London. The family Griggs had contacted us through Bloomsbury House and offered to take us and promised my parents to take care of us. I feel that if some data is now being compiled that I must take the opportunity to tell someone about this ordinary working class family with two younger children of their own, who just felt that they had to help us. At the outbreak of war we were all evacuated with our different schools and being the eldest and first to finish school, I was the first to return to London. Mrs Griggs had in the meantime passed away, and as the three children finished school they all returned to London, where we lived together until the father died and the house was sold. My brother and I moved into a Jewish environment in Manchester. We had had no contact with any Jewish people in London at all.

I was married in 1947 to a Manchester man and we all, my husband, two sons and brother came on *Aliya* in 1956. My brother married an American girl and lives in the States. My younger son was killed in the *Yom Kippur* war and my husband passed away about a year later. My other son is married with two children and we all live at Moshav Habonim.

To this day we have remained in close contact with the daughter of the Griggs family, who has even been to visit us a couple of times in Israel.

*　　*　　*

Dorothea Douglas

(Koniec/Bratislava), Fife, Scotland, UK

This is an account of an event, just after the war, while I was serving in the ATS in Germany.

A notice came round from Company Office, offering compassionate leave to those of us who originated from central Europe and would like, for whatever reason, to visit it again.

When my Unit first arrived in Germany, I wrote a letter to our former address in Bratislava, although I knew that my parents were no longer there. I had had a message previously from the British Red Cross stating that our parents had been sent to Poland in June 1942. I was hoping that somebody would see my letter and reply. I did in fact receive a letter from a former neighbour, confirming what the Red Cross message had already told me.

In the summer of 1946 I returned to Bratislava. I had made no arrangements for my stay, but simply took a taxi to the address of our former home. When I got there, I found the place totally empty. The only sign that anyone had lived there was the marks on the wall where pictures had hung, and behind the kitchen door, strangely, pencil marks made by our mother charting our rate of growth over the years and the initials D and H. A Mrs Cupakova, a former neighbour, appeared on the scene and greeted me and invited me to stay in her flat. She and her husband lived in a new block of flats, next door to our former home. They were at that time still very short of food, but they were very kind and freely shared what they had with me. Mrs Cupakova came with me to various places in the town, where my parents had stayed. In one place I was handed a bulging box tied up with string. It contained 103 letters written by my brother Herbert and myself. Our parents had tried, by every means possible, to supply addresses in neutral countries to which letters could be sent, and which amazingly found their way to Bratislava. The date of the last letter which my parents received was July 1941 and the last letter we received from home was dated November 1941.

At another house, the lady handed me a wedding ring. She told me that the day the Germans came for my mother (I do not know what happened to my father) she pulled her wedding ring off and threw it behind her. The lady of the house noticed it and put her foot on it and later put it safely away. It was placed on my finger at our wedding in Edinburgh on 27 May 1950. I had left Prague on 27 May 1939.

Olga Drucker

(Lenk/Stuttgart), Merrick, NY, USA

Everything changed last night. When Mama tucked me into my bed, I was still a fairy-princess. But this morning it's all different. Now I'm just an ordinary ten-year old girl, going on eleven, and pretty scared.

I heard footsteps stomping up our stairs in the night, and strange, gruff voices. Some doors banged. I think I heard Mama crying softly. That frightened me more than anything else. I stuffed my handkerchief into my mouth and lay very quietly, hardly breathing. What were those men doing in our house? It got even more scary after they left. My door opened. I heard Mama tiptoe in. I felt her cool hand on my head. But I feigned sleep. She left, leaving my door open a little so I could see the light from the hall.

Next morning. 'Where's Papa?' I say first thing. Mama's eyes are red, she looks terrible.

'He . . . he's had to go away for a while.' It doesn't sound right. I don't think she's telling the truth.

'When will he be back?' I know I shouldn't talk with my mouth full, but she doesn't seem to notice it. She shrugs and hides her face in her coffee cup. Now I know something is wrong.

'What shall I wear to school, Mama? I'll be late if I don't . . .'

'You can't go to school today.' Am I hearing her right?

'Why not?'

'Because . . . you just can't.'

'But Fräulein Böhme . . . ' I love my teacher.

'Soon you'll go to a new school, Olga. In a few days.'

'What's wrong with the old one?' But Mama isn't listening to me any more. She has picked up the telephone and is yelling something into it. I think it has to do with Papa.

I try to read. Papa is an important children's book publisher in Stuttgart. I always feel very lucky to have such a Papa. But I can't keep my mind on it today.

One week later. Mama is forever on the phone. A word keeps coming up: DACHAU. It's where Papa is. It sounds like a dreadful place. Mama cries a lot, though she tries to hide it from me.

Two weeks. I've started Jewish school. It's nearly *Chanukah,* they tell us. Mama and I find the *Chanukia.* We're going to celebrate the Festival of Lights and Freedom for the first time in my life. I brought home a sheet with music and Hebrew words from school, so we can sing tonight. I wish Papa were here. We were told that the night they came for Papa, they came for thousands of other Papas too. Jewish store windows were smashed downtown, the Synagogue was burned down. Someone called it Kristall-nacht. Papa is still not back.

Six weeks. My birthday, 28 December. Papa is back! But he's changed. He's so thin, and his hair is white, and he doesn't joke with me any more. Frieda, my nanny since I can remember, had to leave us because she let her boyfriend come to our house in his Nazi uniform. Everything is so scary!

January. A man comes to our house to teach me English. I am to go to England for a while. He is bony and has greasy hair. I hate him. I've learned to say: 'The dog is under the table.'

February. At school they talked about Haman. This evening when Mama helps me get ready for bed, I say:

'I think Haman was as bad as Hitler.'

Mama turns pale and tells me not to say such things. 'The walls have ears,' she says. I look, but I can't see any.

A few days later. I have a temperature, my head hurts and I threw up my breakfast. Mama calls the doctor. He says it's the measles. And it's only three weeks till I'm supposed to leave for England! Our seamstress has been sewing my clothes. I like the school uniforms. Mrs Lieberman, the lady I'm to stay with, sent us a drawing of one. I think I look quite good in it, except my legs are too skinny. Mama has been packing all my stuff in crates and boxes, while an SS man watches her. He asks about my cello.

'What's that?'

'Oh,' Mama answers, 'It's just an old thing.' He loses interest. She's even packed my favourite doll, Peter. But I don't think I'll have much use for him in England.

We got a letter from the Liebermans in Norwich, England, yesterday. There was a coloured picture of the family in it. Their daughter is about my age. The pastel colours make them look weird, and their lips are too red. I ask Mama what if they don't like me.

'Of course they'll like you.' But I doubt I'm going to like them.

3 March. Today is the day! Cousin Hildegard is coming too. Mama comes with us as far as Wiesbaden, where Omama lives. I kiss Papa goodbye. Also Herr and Frau Gumbel, our next-door neighbours.

'It's only for a few weeks, Kaetzle. Six at most,' Papa promises.

Omama meets us in Wiesbaden. Mama gets off the train. My nose is flat against the dirty windowpane, until I can't see them any more. The train fills up with children. My eyes are wet, and I have to go to the bathroom. When I come out, some children are laughing and pointing at me. My blue wool-knit dress is tucked into my matching underpants. I am furious! I sit stiffly next to Hildegard, who is three years older than I, and rub my wet eyes. I have no idea that six weeks will stretch into six years.

*   *   *

Olga Drucker

(Lenk/Stuttgart), Merrick, NY, USA

by Mrs Marianne Woolley aged 85, Essex, UK (Foster Mother)

In the early summer of 1943 – the twins were five or six months old, and it must have been a Sunday, for my husband was with me, and, as headmaster of the local grammar school he was free only on a Sunday. We wheeled the two babies in the big double pram and stopped half way down Hatton Road to greet Mrs Callis, who came out to admire our two boys.

'Come here, Olga!' she called over her shoulder. 'Here's something you'd like to see.'

A shy little girl with enormous plaintive eyes came out of the house. Sixteen? Seventeen? It was hard to tell.

Mrs Callis introduced us and explained Olga's presence.

We began to talk.

Olga was going to Cambridge in August, for a holiday.

So were we!

Olga was going to Adams Road. She had a cousin who lived at No 9.

I began to laugh. 'My sister lives at No 9, and we are going to her for our holiday!'

And that's how it all started.

While staying at the other address Olga developed measles. My sister is a doctor. Of course Olga came to No 9. She was a darling – the babies loved her – everyone loved her. Nothing was too much trouble.

'Olga' I said, treacherous in my selfishness, 'you have got to come to us!' And a few weeks later Olga did come, and immediately (as far as I was concerned) became my eldest daughter.

I am, evidently, a Victorian mother. I think my eldest daughter worked very hard, helping with the children and the housework. It was a large house, and the eldest of the six children was only eight or nine.

And there were always other families living with us, and air force men from all over the world having a few days leave with us.

I can never remember that she ever protested or complained.

In some ways it seemed we lived together for years. In fact, it was only nine months; and one of the greyest days of my life was when I took my little Olga to Swansea in the autumn of 1944, to board the boat that was to take her to America and her parents.

*   *   *

Olga Drucker

(Lenk/Stuttgart), Merrick, NY, USA

by Jane Rowland (Foster Sister)

I was twenty-two when I met Olga properly. The last time she had seen me was when I was four and she fourteen or so, in 1944. I don't remember her from those days but my parents and Emily (our family 'help') talked about Olga regularly and so we children grew up, as it were, with Olga. She had gone to America towards the end of the war to be with her parents, whom she hadn't seen since she had boarded the boat which brought her and many other apprehensive and frightened Jewish children to England. She and my mother corresponded nearly every year and in 1962 I had the opportunity of going to Long Island, about sixty miles from where Olga and her family lived, to be an 'au pair'. Of course, I got in touch with Olga to let her know I was coming and travelled to meet her at her home, some two or three weeks after I had arrived in America. Her first words, as she gazed up at me (I was large and tall, she petite) were

'You've changed hardly at all!'

She, her husband and three children became wonderful friends to me, especially after a very serious car accident I had four months after my arrival in the States. Olga and Rolf, her husband, came to see me in hospital nearly every day and would ring my mother in England to let her and my family know how I was faring; they then had me to stay with them while I recuperated and, after two weeks, paid my fare home! That was the beginning of a marvellous 'love' affair between the Drucker and Woolley families. At least six or seven of my parents' family, children and friends have been to stay with the Druckers. In 1978 my husband, two sons and myself stayed with Olga and Rolf and used their house as a base from which we travelled to Washington, Boston, and New Jersey. In 1988 the Rowland family travelled to the West Coast of America, and our two sons stayed with their eldest daughter Jane, who was called after me, in her lovely apartment in Studio City, Los Angeles. The following Christmas saw all but one of the Drucker family at my mother's home, where we were too, and over the past fifteen years various Druckers have stayed with us in London.

*   *   *

Fred Dunston

(Deutsch/Vienna), London, UK

After the premises of the *Youth Aliyah* School in Vienna had been destroyed during the night of 10 November 1938, some of the staff helped out with the office work in the *Palestine Amt* until other suitable premises could be found to continue the work of the school. *Palestine Amt* was the roof organisation for all the various Zionist movement committees and fund raising organisations and there was obviously a lot of work to be done – lots of lists and card indexes of children of various age groups had been started but could not be completed because the people who worked on them had left everything behind from one day to the next when their chance to emigrate had arrived. Often they could not pass on or explain the work they were doing to their successor.

One morning early in December, whilst I was working on these records, an urgent message arrived from the *Israelitische Kultusgemeinde*. The Home Office in London had agreed to admit a number of unaccompanied Jewish children up to the age of seventeen. If the formalities were settled, the first transport of about three hundred children would leave for England within a week. The *Kultusgemeinde* were willing to let us have one hundred places as long as the documentation was completed and handed into their office on the following afternoon. If we could not meet the deadline they would fill the places from their own lists. As they had received the information much earlier than we, they were already better prepared to cope with the situation. We were, however, quite determined to take full advantage of this opportunity to send so many children to safety but how could this be done?

We thought that we could extract enough names and addresses of suitable children from our existing records within a few hours. Naturally we would have to get at least two hundred names or more to make sure to get one hundred accepted and to be prepared for future occasions. The task was to get them with a parent and birth certificate etc to our office as quickly as possible, so that they could be interviewed and, if we thought them eligible, to prepare the paper work, and to get them ready to travel at very short notice. We also had to arrange for a photographer and a doctor to be on hand. I enlisted the help of my former Scout troop. It worked so well that a big queue formed outside the office within an hour. A team of interviewers started work at once to carry on non-stop until late in the evening when the last of the children were attended to.

I was one of the interviewers, a strange, moving and exhausting experience. Anxious parents were begging and pleading, often crying, trying to make sure that their child would be on the list for the first transport. They thought the decision depended on us but this was not the case. We only did the paper work. We could only promise these poor tortured people that we would do our best, and even if their child would not be on the first transport others would follow in weekly intervals. Many parents talked to us as if the life of their children depended on us. It was a difficult situation and we had to convince them that there was no favouritism. Life plays strange tricks.

The door opened yet again and I found myself confronted by a teacher who had tried not very successfully to teach me religion in the grammar school. He had come to bring his son. A few years ago he was my teacher sitting at his desk. I was the pupil sitting at the bench. Now I was sitting behind the desk and he was an applicant imploring my favours. He had recognised me and thought that by humiliating himself (I had difficulty in preventing him from kneeling down) he could persuade me to do more for his son that I would do in my normal course of duty. It was sad and pathetic. He said that he had always been good to me, which was true, so he thought it was now up to me to be good to him. It was an unforgettable moment. I completed my part of the formalities but I never found out whether or not his boy got on a children's transport.

It was almost midnight when we had a sufficient number of files ready, but another task was still ahead of us. A complete typed list of all the names and addresses and birth certificates and birth places with seven copies was asked for. So two typists were required to type simultaneously to the dictation of a third person. Most people had gone home by now completely exhausted and apart from one of the office staff who was a very fast and competent typist, I was the only one who could type, so we just had to get on with it. I managed to match the speed of the other typist and it was extraordinary how we found the ability to do what the occasion demanded. The job was completed when the other workers started arriving in the morning.

The transports went off pretty regularly from then on – week by week up to the end of July 1939 when the outbreak of war brought them to an end altogether. Over nine thousand children came to England on these transports and found safety and a new life in this country. I am glad that I and some of my friends had the opportunity to help make it all possible and these exciting days will always stay alive in my memory.

*   *   *

Fred Durst

(Munich), London, UK

In September 1938 at approximately three o'clock in the morning at our flat in Munich, I was woken by the proverbial knock on the door made by rifle butts. There stood thugs in brown shirts demanding that my father, sixteen year old sister and I (fourteen) pack a few things and go with them to Stadelheim Prison, just outside Munich. They said we would be deported from Germany and sent to Poland.

After three days in prison we were taken to the railway station under armed guard. The train headed east towards Poland. After about forty-eight hours it stopped near the border and we were told that we would be returning to Munich. I found out later that the Poles had started to retaliate and expelled German citizens.

Meanwhile in England the Inter-Aid committee was formed and the children's transports started.

My father was told that Munich was allocated ten to twelve places, and he said he would be happy if my sister and I could go to England.

We met the other children on 3 January 1939 at the railway station. After brief goodbyes most of us never saw our parents again.

When we crossed the German border into Holland and saw the last Swastika flags and the first Dutch flags, it was an indescribable feeling, even for a fourteen year old boy. At that time Germany was allowing all Jews to leave, but very few countries opened their frontiers. Had the State of Israel already existed, all the Jews of Europe could have been saved.

We arrived at Harwich all wearing labels, and were housed in a Warners' summer holiday camp. There was enough room for eight hundred children.

After three months the camp closed and those children who had not been selected to live with private families (mostly boys – girls were often found homes, perhaps because they could be domestically useful) were sent to hostels all over England.

At the beginning of April 1939 with a group of forty boys I was sent to a hostel in North Kensington. We were well looked after, and went to the local Jewish council school. I quite enjoyed school, getting used to the prefect system and playing cricket, and also feeling slightly odd because none of our crowd could afford uniforms.

After some months my form master spoke German quite fluently. I also received a postcard from Victoria station informing me of the arrival of my bicycle.

As soon as the war started the school was evacuated to a small village in Wiltshire. I stayed with a very kind family in a tiny cottage with outside toilets, and a tin bath. I learned to look after an allotment and feed chickens, and also joined the Boys Scouts. It was a very happy time.

When I reached sixteen I had to return to the hostel in London. In due course I was apprenticed to a firm of diamond mounters near Hatton Garden.

A boy in those days was the lowest form of existence. During my first year I had to sweep up, make sandpaper buffs, polish my master's shoes and do errands. These included taking gold to the assay office and going to the bullion dealers. There was no danger to carrying any amount of precious metals or diamonds, other than being hit by bombs or later, flying bombs or rockets.

At the hostel I had also met my friend John Najmann again. He was subsequently apprenticed at the same firm and much later became my business partner.

As my shoes and other clothing were wearing out and I was growing out of them, I decided to sell my bicycle. I advertised it in a local newsagents and received a crisp white £5 note for it. I had to show such wealth to all the boys at the hostel. With it I managed to buy a completely new set of clothes and shoes in Portobello Road market.

This was the beginning of a new life. I wished only that the children's transport could have taken out many more children. I have been grateful ever since, and spend considerable time on social matters to try and repay my debt to society.

Fred Durst went on, with John Najmann, to found Fred Manshaw Ltd. He is a Past President of the British Jewellery and Giftware Federation and served as chairman of the British Jewellers' Association twice. He is a member of the British Hallmarking Council, a Liveryman of the Worshipful Company of Goldsmiths, and chairman of an old people's home.

Reprinted by kind permission from the *British Jeweller,* June 1989.

* * *

John Edelnand

(Halberstadt), Luton, UK

Little did I guess what was in store for me in a new land when I waved goodbye to my parents and twelve year old sister, never to see them again on the day I fled Germany, just one week befor war broke out in 1939.

There were about two hundred children in our party and we stayed just outside Ashford, in a field in the middle of nowhere where we found two enormous marquees furnished with bunk beds, camp beds, trestle tables and benches. We were told that this was only temporary accommodation and that very soon we would be leaving to move into a castle. A real castle, I thought, it cannot be true.

One September, nearly forty-six years to the day after I first set foot in Wales, I went off to Abergele with a desire to relive those happy days and to find out as much as possible about the life of the refugees at Gwrych Castle. I drove from my home in Luton, Bedfordshire, and when I first saw the sign post to Abergele I must confess my heart missed a beat or two. As I came closer to Abergele, the peace and tranquility as the September sun penetrated the mist gently covering the luscious green meadows, rekindled my thoughts and experiences of those happy days. I was eager to learn as much as I could, particularly what the natives thought about those strangers at the castle, shy and reserved, their heads invariably covered with small round skull caps and speaking in a foreign tongue, not realising that these foreigners were soon to be classified as 'enemy aliens'.

I re-visited all the places I once knew. My first call was at the sheep and cattle auction market, just off Market Street. There had been very little change there; new faces, of course, and more sophisticated transport vehicles perhaps, but the atmosphere which fascinated me as a fourteen year old boy and the Welsh language, which intrigued me even more, remained. I walked along Market Street and stopped outside *Siop Bach*. Mr and Mrs Jones used to be in that shop. Mr Jones had a glass eye and he frequently presented me with a bar of chocolate without payment as he was aware that we did not receive any money for our work nor from the Gwrych Castle management. Before I explain this further I must tell you that our stay in the United Kingdom was purely to prepare and train us for life in Palestine as it then was. Entry into Palestine was limited because of prevailing political circumstances at the time – our stay in Abergele was to be a stopover only. The camp at the Castle was run like a kibbutz, there are many now in Israel. We were fed, clothed and looked after well– share and share alike was our motto. Everything was evenly distributed and even visits to the local cinema were taken in rotation. Mr Parry, who was in charge of the cinema, allowed me entry on my own twice a week free of charge. In return I had to rewind the films in the projection room ready for the next performance. I enjoyed this job very much indeed as it was certainly very different from the daily chores like tree felling, gardening and working on the farm.

I returned to the car park and drove towards the Castle. I stared past the lodge. The road to the Castle was no longer there, it was completely overgrown and impassable.

Tan-y-Gopa Road has a particular significance for me as it was here that I met my first local gentleman. I later learned that his name was Wil Davies, always dressed in wellington boots and always chewing tobacco. I was walking down Tan-y-Gopa Road towards Abergele on the very first morning after my arrival in 1939 when Wil Davies came striding towards me. I must practice my English, I muttered to myself having learned the language for a short period in the private Jewish school in Germany.

'*Goot mornink*' I said in a very crude German accent. He looked at me and, after a pause said,

'*Bore da, boi bach. Sut 'dachi beddiw?*' to my utter amazement. I did not realize at the time that Wales existed with its own language and culture. Wil Davies taught me quite a bit of Welsh, including most swear words, and he took the greatest delight in listening to me when I tried to repeat them. He also taught me to say

Llanfairpwllgwyngllgogerychwyrndrobwllllantysiliogogogoch

which I am able to pronounce to this day. I called at Mr Edwin Roberts' farm and there he was, a spritely seventy-five year old, keeping himself busy by helping his son who now runs the farm. When I introduced myself he could not recall me working at the farm, but he did remember the refugees who worked there. I enquired about Wil Davies but learned that he had since died at the ripe old age of ninety-one years.

I later visited Mrs Jessie Edwards, widow of Dick Edwards who used to supply us with bread and whose bakery was in Llanddulas at the time. He delivered to the Castle daily in a rather tatty old van which would never pass its MOT today. Mrs Edwards reminded me of the times when I managed to hide in the back of the van when Dick called at the Castle and was in a hurry to get home for his tea. When we arrived at his house in Llwyn Morfa, where Mrs Edwards still lives today, I suddenly appeared as if from nowhere and Mrs Edwards had no alternative but to ask me to join them for tea. I suspect that Dick Edwards knew of my presence in his van all the time. Kind, generous Dick Edwards. For over two hours I talked with this dear charming old lady and we were later joined by her son Ken who has continued in his father's footsteps in a newly built bakery in Old Colwyn.

Now the moment of visiting the Castle and its grounds had come. My eyes first focussed on the Castle itself. From a distance very little had changed but as I approached the now derelict and neglected building, which was a home and refuge for three hundred young Jewish children, it was a sorry sight to behold. I cannot describe how shattered I felt. But the people of Abergele, those I have met again and those whose acquaintance I have made for the first time in the shops and restaurants and the Rotary club endorsed once again the friendly and considerate people they still are. I shall certainly never forget that they took us into their midst, made us feel at home and tolerated us despite our peculiar backgrounds. There was indeed a welcome in the hillside.

*   *   *

Ilse Eden

California, USA

I came to England in March 1939 at the age of ten on a children's transport as one of twelve children sponsored by a Jewish paediatrician, Dr Bernard Schlesinger and his wife Winifred, who had five children of their own. The twelve of us with staff lived together in a hostel and went to the local school until war broke out and we eventually all landed in boarding schools. The Schlesingers have stayed in touch with eleven of us until their deaths and we have had several reunions. I now live in the United States and am working as a social worker. I am married and have two children. My mother escaped, my father did not.

* * *

Lee Edwards

(Carlebach/Frankfurt), California, USA

THE NECKLACE

It has nine pearls and twenty-six little diamonds. I know, because I just looked at it again. I can't say I look at it very often – maybe once or twice a year, and I NEVER WEAR IT, but just looking at it brings back all the memories; some sad, some bitter-sweet; some joyful.

I am sixty-five years old and the necklace and I go back fifty years. I remember the dark gray railway station in Frankfurt-on-Main. It's March 1939 and a whole group of children are huddled together under the watchful eyes of the Nazi police. The children are wearing numbered labels around their necks – no names, just numbers – and their mothers and fathers are bidding them a tearful goodbye. We are off to England, without our parents, to a strange land, strange people who offered to take us into their homes; thus saving our very lives. But we don't realize this on this gray March morning, we are leaving our loved ones behind; we don't know it, but most of us will never see our parents again. My mother is wiping her eyes with a little dainty handkerchief, and I help her smooth the wool blanket on top of the suitcase after the police have searched it and allowed it to be closed.

When we reach England after the crossing from Hoeck van Holland to Harwich, the British customs open the suitcase; I lift the blanket, and there, in the crumpled little handkerchief my mother used to wipe her eyes, is The Necklace, and a few other trinkets she wanted me to have. The customs and the children – we all huddled around staring at this necklace. If the Nazi police had found it, God only knows what they would have done to all of us.

My home was to be with a young Jewish family in Coventry. They were newly married, had no money, but wanted to save a Jewish child from certain death. Sometimes, when the bombs fell on Coventry, and we were all busy carrying water buckets to douse the flames, I took out my necklace and looked at the little diamonds dancing in the lamplight.

The war was over and I joined an American Civil Censorship group in Germany. I was stationed in Esslingen, near Stuttgart and met a handsome young man – a refugee like myself – who had served six years in the British Army – and had joined the same Censorship Division. On our wedding day, 1 March 1947 in Frankfurt – in the same Registry office where I had been registered at birth – I was thinking of my necklace. My mother had died in Auschwitz, my father had committed suicide; they would have loved me to wear it on my wedding day; but it was in a bank safe in England.

Back in England, we apply to go to Canada and we sail on the old *Empress of Canada* in November 1948. I was so sea-sick I was sure I was going to die – and then who would wear my necklace?

Four years in Vancouver; we both work hard, but we haven't got a lot to show for it, and no grand occasions worthy of wearing my necklace.

10 March 1952 – everything happens in March – we didn't have an affidavit, but we had saved up three thousand dollars and the American Consul in Vancouver must have thought we were responsible people; – he gave us an immigration visa, and we are off to the Promised Land – Southern California.

Is it possible we have lived and worked in Los Angeles and its suburbs from 1952 to 1980 – twenty-eight years, and I have never worn my necklace? There were festive occasions, but I always judged it to be too ornate and not suitable for the inexpensive clothes I wore.

In 1980 we retired and moved to our 'Leisure Village' retirement community, about fifty miles from Los Angeles – and my necklace is sitting in the bank safe. Will I never wear it?

Now we have come full cycle since the start of this little story. It's March 1989 and we plan to join a reunion of many 'children' now all in their fifties and sixties – who had come to England with a Children's transport in 1939. The reunion will be in Harrow in June.

From there we will go back to Frankfurt to help my only brother celebrate his seventy-fifth birthday. He survived many years in a concentration camp. But I won't be wearing my necklace; it will have been left behind in its safe deposit box.

My mother achieved her wish on that gray March morning at the Frankfurt railway station in 1939: I could not treasure her; I never saw her again, but I treasure her necklace for ever.

*　　*　　*

Albert Edwards

(Eisner/Vienna), Manchester, UK

THE DAY I WAS MORE POPULAR THAN FIELD MARSHAL MONTGOMERY

When I reached military age I fought my way into the British Army, not the usual Pioneer Corps background, but straight into the Royal North Lancashire Infantry Regiment.

Eventually I landed in Normandy on D+6 and joined 2nd Army HQ, Intelligence Section. The war went on, we broke out of Normandy and eventually reached and liberated Belgium.

Our HQ set up a few miles from Brussels and I managed to get a day off duty to go to Brussels on the day after its liberation. These were the days when people danced in the main squares and stopped us soldiers in the street for our autographs.

I walked into a shop near Gare du Nord to buy something. A middle-aged woman before me spoke French so badly that I suspected her to be 'one of us' and I waited outside the shop to talk to her.

She turned out to be a Jewish woman from Vienna and she and her husband had been hiding in her flat for about two years with her Gentile neighbours buying food for them.

Naturally, they were delighted to meet a British Corporal who was in fact a fellow Viennese, but after half an hour they explained that there was a Cottage Hospital full of Jews, mainly from Germany and Austria, who were just saved from being deported to the Extermination Camps, and would I go with them to visit them.

Remember, they had only been liberated the day before.

What an experience. I had to go from bed to bed and have a little chat with them and their delight to speak to a British Corporal who was really one of them and could speak their language is really beyond description. It was impossible to take short cuts, I just had to walk from bed to bed and talk to each patient individually.

Our postal address ended with 'BLA'. This stood for British Liberation Army.

On that day, more than any other day, I felt that this is indeed what we were.

then Cpl Albert Edwards,
14436727,
General Staff Intelligence,
2nd Army HQ,
British Liberation Army.

*   *   *

Joseph Eisinger

(Vienna), New York, USA.

(Department of Physiology and Biophysics, Mount Sinai School of Medicine, New York.)

I was almost fourteen when Hitler invaded Austria in 1938 and the first few months of the occupation were disruptive but hardly traumatic for me. Conversations among the adults were dominated by rumours about emigration opportunities and by learning new and useful trades, which were said to hold the key to emigration. I enrolled first in a course to become an electrician and then, making what at the time seemed like a very practical choice, I apprenticed myself to a blacksmith.

Eventually my name appeared on a list of children selected for a Kindertransport to England. There was feverish activity in our home, my suitcase was packed, my father spoke a blessing over me, and then it was time to assemble at the railway station. The rules for the ensuing farewell and departure were carefully orchestrated by the authorities: there was to be no display of emotion or grief by parents or children and as the train pulled out of the station, amid the derisive laughter of the Nazis observing the scene, we all sang '*Muss I denn, muss I denn zum Städtle hinaus . . .* '

Soon we found ourselves sitting in a large hall at Victoria station in London. As each child's British sponsor signed the necessary papers and deposited the required bond, our ranks thinned. I was then given the distressing news that nobody had come forward to sponsor me and that I would therefore be returned to Germany. At about the same time a young man sidled up to me (he turned out to be the son of my sister's host and sponsor) and after telling me who he was, told me (in English!) that upon his signal, he would grab my suitcase and we would together make a dash for the side door. This opened onto a narrow lane where his father pulled up in a car. We jumped in and took off into the London traffic.

After being shunted among kindly friends and relatives, themselves refugees from Vienna, a refugee committee, somewhat put out by my unorthodox entry into Britain, sent me to an agricultural school in Haslemere, Surrey. There I was put to work peeling large quantities of potatoes and excavating a swimming pool with pick and shovel. I believe my training at the school was intended to prepare me for a career in agriculture, for after a few weeks I was dispatched to Bishop Monkton, a small village in Yorkshire, where I worked as a farm hand.

After a year on the farm my sister wrote to tell me of a position as a dish washer in a hotel in Brighton, with the opportunity of apprenticing to a chef. I gave a month's notice and travelled south.

The Park Royal Hotel provided me with a bunk in a windowless boiler room, a dubious improvement on my unheated, but windowed room on the farm. My primary duty was to provide spotless crockery and cutlery for the few hundred guests, four times a day.

In the summer of 1940, after the fall of France and soon after I had turned sixteen, two policemen appeared at the hotel and politely asked me to accompany them. I collected my coat and toothbrush, pleased to have an excuse to abandon my pantry, and we drove to the police station. Thus began an odyssey of eighteen months' internment, which eventually landed me in the New World, ever further from my roots. My arrest was the result of the British government's decision to intern all 'enemy aliens'.

The overwhelming majority of the internees were Jewish or political refugees and while internment embittered many of them by adding insult to injury, it was akin to liberation for me. The loss of freedom, the primitive living conditions and the sparse diet seemed unimportant compared to the companionship with young men of my own age which I had gained.

During our internment on the Isle of Man volunteers were called for to relocate to Canada. I was one of them, and we eventually sailed on the former passenger liner *Sobieski* There were about fifteen hundred of us in cramped and dirty conditions. We travelled in a large convoy guarded by corvettes and destroyers, until the *Sobieski* lost one of her propellers and we found ourselves abandoned by the convoy, alone in the U-boat infested Atlantic. As it turned out, despite our slow speed we finally reached St Johns, Newfoundland without being attacked. Eventually we landed in Quebec where we were searched once again, this time by Canadian soldiers who confiscated what money, watches and fountain pens remained in our possession. Our contingent which consisted predominantly of Jewish refugees, was then marched through heavily-armed lines of soldiers first to a train and then through the streets of Trois Rivieres into a converted sport stadium, which already housed captured German submarine crews! They were amazed at our arrival and 'war' soon broke out in the camp. The Canadians quickly erected an additional barbed wire fence to separate Nazis from anti-Nazis.

The story of our life in the Canadian internment camps and the internees' struggle to be recognized and released as ardent enemies of Hitler, has been admirably told in Eric Koch's *Deemed Suspect* (Methuen). Our weapons in this struggle for refugee status were work strikes, hunger strikes and appeals to the world beyond the wire. The Canadian camp commander, for his part, countered by endless roll calls and round-ups of work parties and would revoke various privileges, the most dreaded one being the removal of a tube from the only radio in the camp and therefore our only source of news and music. Our confrontations punctuated an otherwise peaceful existence, and we never lost sight of our good fortune of being prisoners of ill-informed but benign Canadians instead of the Nazis.

We worked as lumberjacks in the cold, snowy woods of New Brunswick. For me lumbering was an invigorating and satisfying experience after the months of detention in crowded camps. (I now own a small tree farm in New Jersey and still wield a double-edged axe with much pleasure!) We were also put to work making camouflage nets for artillery. Our pay was twenty-five cents per day.

On three of our six work days, internees who had registered as students of the camp school were given the afternoon off for study and to prepare for the McGill University matriculation exam, which was required to be written within the city limits of Montreal. This gave rise to one of the strangest interludes of my internment, for an enterprising refugee committee persuaded our Camp Commander to transfer us for one week to an Italian POW camp which happened to be located in a seventeenth century fort on St Helena Island, in the St Lawrence River – in Montreal. The fort had ten foot thick walls and a tiny courtyard where the Italians had learned to play soccer brilliantly. We played them after we had completed our exams and they defeated us soundly.

In time I was released as a student under the sponsorship of Dr Bruno Mendel and his family in Toronto, themselves immigrant German Jews and strangers to me until then. The Mendels had selected me and my close friend, Walter Kohn, who had been a student of the *Akademische Gymnasium* in Vienna with me, because they were music lovers and had heard that in the camp Walter and I played recorder duets together. Following our release from internment, Walter and I lived with the family and I attended the University of Toronto for one year.

In the summer of 1943 it became possible for non-citizens to serve in the Canadian armed services and I volunteered for service first in the RCAF and then in the Canadian Army.

I resumed my studies in physics and astronomy after my discharge, and was drawn towards academic research.

My parents had escaped from Vienna during the war on a ship which took them on a long and dangerous journey down the Danube, through the Black Sea to Crete, which they reached a week before the German paratroopers. Escaping again, their ship ran out of fuel and after being towed into Haifa, the British put them and their party on a boat bound for Madagascar. When the ship sank after being sabotaged by the Jewish underground, they were rescued, interned and finally released in Palestine. In 1947, lacking the means for commercial travel, I signed on as a seaman on the freighter *Oceanside*, due to sail from Montreal to the Mediterranean with a bunkering stop in Haifa. After two weeks in Bizerte, Tunisia we docked in Limassol, Cyprus. There the captain kindly gave me leave to take a passenger steamer sailing to Beirut and Haifa, where I was finally re-united with my parents. After touring around the still British, and already strife-torn Palestine, I rejoined the *Oceanside* when she came to bunker in Haifa and returned to Canada.

By now a measure of normality had returned to the world. I had become a Canadian citizen. In time I was drawn to the United States by my scientific activities, which are as peripatetic as the wanderings of my youth, and include research in physics, biology, medicine and history. The good fortune, to which I owe my survival of the Holocaust has not abandoned me and I have a loving and like-minded family, to whom this autobiographical fragment is dedicated with deep affection.

*   *   *

Philip Engelberg
(Chemnitz), London, UK

Some fifty years ago, a frightened little boy left Chemnitz, Germany. The Holocaust was in the making, only I did not know, nor did my fellow Jews, what was in store for us. As I stand today on a cold, dilapidated platform in East Berlin, with my daughter Jackie, waiting for the train to take me back to Chemnitz, I watch the people and listen to their conversation, complaining about the cold. In 1938, I too, stood with many thousands, in the bitter cold, at a Berlin railway station, to be taken in goods trucks – destination – a concentration camp. Obviously, my mind started wandering back and I felt very emotional and churned up inside.

Here we were, on 20 November 1988, just looking out of the window, travelling from Schöneweide to Chemnitz, now known as Karl Marx Stadt.

A very interesting couple joined us in our compartment and we got talking to them. The man spoke very good English and we got to know a lot about their lives in East Germany and their ambitions and aspirations. Like people all over the world, all they wanted was to work and be happy. Judging from the two hours we spent talking, I could not see any difference between them and the youth of any other country. In fact, I arranged to meet them again the following evening, so that I could discuss with them the horror of the past and assess their reactions. Of course, they knew about the Holocaust and felt that this period was a black mark in the history of the German people.

We set out early the next morning, 21 November. We were elated to see huge posters outside a museum which was showing the history of the Jews of Chemnitz from 1750 to present day – including the Holocaust. It emphasised the benefits that Chemnitz had gained through its Jewish citizens, over the centuries, in every field – commercially, culturally, medically, etc.

Because of the exhibition, we were privileged to meet the President of the Association of Jewish Communities in the GDR, Sigmund Rotstein who, in fact, survived Theresienstadt. We learned that only twelve Jewish families had returned there, out of approximately 50,000 Jews who had originally lived in Chemnitz in 1933!

If I could measure the depth of my emotions then, surely 22 November must rate amongst the most memorable days of my life! It was the day I went to visit the actual street in which I spent my childhood. Would the sight of it convey anything to me? Would I, at last, grasp and understand the invisible force that urged me, for so long, to return? It certainly was not curiosity – it was the return of a survivor who, through providence, had returned to the roots of his youth.

As I stood with my daughter in front of the house I had lived in, the span of time did not seem to matter to me any more. Suddenly, many incidents came back to me. The wall down the road, covered in big red letters 'Death to the Jews' and 'Jews back to Jerusalem'; the friend across the street with whom I did my homework, and who was suddenly not allowed to associate with me. Above all, the vivid memory of my parents. It drained me emotionally! There was my mother's anxious look when I played football across the street; my father's return from business and I, standing at the corner, waiting for him, his hug, and my excitement telling him about the day's events at school.

I have no regrets about coming back, because – for a short time – I was able to re-live my past in its authentic surroundings. As I stood deep in thought, I suddenly felt very lonely, almost as if I, alone, had reached the peak of the mountain, friends and relatives encouraging me to go on, while they perished on the way.

Back in London, I had time to reflect and think. What is the difference between East and West Germany's ideology on the issue of the Holocaust? The curriculum in West Germany's schools, until recently, hardly touched on the rise of Hitler or the period 1933–45 at all. It is true that compensation has been paid to those who managed to escape. However, I am not sure what the West German government is trying to achieve. A more positive policy, teaching the coming generations about racial tolerance would, in the long run, one hopes, avoid tragedies.

In contrast, East Germany has taught, and is teaching, its new generations the evil of fascism. They are taught about the Holocaust in great detail.

As a survivor and proud Jew, I cannot and will not blame the new German generation for the sins of their fathers. However, there should be no let-up in pursuing the monsters who, either directly or indirectly, were responsible for those hideous crimes. I, for one, cannot 'forgive and forget' those involved in any way.

My journey through life has been full of ups and downs. The jackboots of the SS kicking me all over the place, the weeks of humiliation and denegration in a concentration camp, the unsuccessful attempt to escape from Germany; all that for a boy of fifteen years of age.

I have now come to terms with my past. Because of my experiences, my values – I feel – have always been in their proper perspective. Looking back, I am now aware that I was closer to death than I had realized. The day will come when the voices of survivors will no longer be heard. It is important, therefore, for those who have witnessed the horrors of the Holocaust, to convey this message to historians and future generations.

Miriam Eris

(Keller/Leipzig), Safed, Israel

The events of the morning of 28 October 1938 changed my life – and the lives of my family – for all time.

The night before, an uncle in Berlin called our home in Leipzig to warn my father of what the Germans called an 'action' – which meant a raid, arrest and worse. My father did not believe that any such 'action' would materialize.

But, on the very next morning, when he heard two men at the front door of our apartment asking for him, he scrambled out of a window, got into his car and drove around town until evening, unaware of what had happened in his absence. When he returned, he was appalled to discover that his wife had been arrested, along with his three children. I was then fourteen years old, my sister was twelve and my brother eight.

All four of us were taken into custody and deported to a 'No Man's Land' between Germany and Poland. The Germans had decided to deport people of Polish origin, (my parents came to Germany in their teens and were married there; my sister, brother and I were all born in Germany). But Poland did not want us. We spent the night in the woods and fields. SS troops, armed with rifles, had warned us that we would be shot if we tried to re-enter Germany.

Finally, the Poles relented and we were permitted to enter the village of Sbazsyn. We were exhausted, frightened and hungry. From the nearby town of Katowice, Jews came with hot food. In a short time, all sorts of committees were formed. We were advised that we were free to go to other parts of the country.

My mother decided that we would go to Cracow, a large city. There, she was given a room for herself and for my younger sister and brother. I was boarded with a Polish Jewish doctor's family. Meanwhile, the 'action' had been halted, my father had returned to our old flat, and my parents managed to communicate with each other by telephone. They decided to attempt to have me smuggled back into Germany so that I might be able to leave from there for the United States on a student's visa, which was valid only from my land of birth – Germany.

My father travelled to Beuten on the German border and made contact with a local smuggler to bring me back to Germany. My mother brought me to Katowice and we met the smuggler there. This was 3 January 1939 – my fifteenth birthday. My mother had great misgivings about this adventure. She was then thirty-nine years old – and it was the last day I saw her, my sister and my brother.

After an horrific journey the smuggler brought me to a flat where my father awaited me. He put through a telephone call immediately to my mother in

Katowice and advised her, in guarded tones, that the 'mission' had been successful. My father and I then took a train to Leipzig to make immediate preparations for my departure. I hoped to be able to travel to the US.

Some months later, in May, I was in Berlin for the weekend when two German officials arrived at our flat in Leipzig to check the list of the items I would take with me to the US. They were not happy with the list, as prepared, and asked my father to come with them to see a higher official. This particular official was not available and my father was jailed with a number of drunks being kept overnight. On Monday, I returned to our flat in Leipzig and found that it had been officially sealed.

My father was kept in prison for 'investigation' while a legal case was being prepared against him. We had known of people kept in custody for years. My father was now very anxious to find a lawyer, but not (because of the racial prejudice) a Jewish one. We found a German lawyer willing to take the case – if the Polish Consulate would write a letter asking him to represent my father as a Pole and not as a Jew. However, the Consulate would not issue such a document.

I was forced to handle the contact work with the police and legal authorities. They were trying desperately to find some irregularity in my father's business, foreign currency (strictly forbidden) or any detail which would help in building up their case against my father. On their visits to our flat, they helped themselves to whatever caught their fancy. A typewriter and a silver tea set, bought as gifts for (we hoped) our relatives in California, were stolen by them.

I visited my father every Tuesday, bringing him clean clothes and newspapers, and we planned strategy. The Holland-America Line vessel, on which I was supposed to sail for the US, had already left. My father instructed me to go to the Jewish Community Offices to have my name included for a transport of children to England. By this time, an official order had been issued, decreeing that all Jews had to leave Leipzig by 4 July 1939. Soon thereafter, I was advised that I was booked on a transport leaving before that date. I consulted with my father, who told me that I must go – even if that left him with no contact outside the prison. This wrenching decision proved unnecessary as the court informed me that I could not leave: I was required to be present at my father's trial scheduled for 26 August.

My father was convinced that, if only he could get a trial, he would be freed. In this respect, he was correct. When sentence was pronounced, the time he had spent in custody plus a monetary fine, corrected the wrong he had supposedly committed.

My father sent me to Berlin in order to obtain a transit visa to any country in the world on the strength of the valid American visa I held. When I arrived, my aunt informed me that she had heard of a children's transport leaving that very night for England. After considerable difficulty, we managed to contact my father by telephone and he gave his permission for me to leave on that transport.

He had considerable difficulty in making his way to Berlin, but arrived thirty minutes before our departure, bringing me a suitcase full of clothes. He did his best in those few moments to give me some guidance on how to conduct myself among strangers in a foreign land. We said goodbye. I never saw my father again.

The children's transport travelled overnight to Cologne. We crossed the German border at Kleve and were driven by bus across Holland to the Hook of Holland. We arrived at Harwich, England, on Friday morning, 1 September 1939.

The first thing we learned was that Germany had invaded Poland.

*   *   *

Marion Feigl

(Feiglova/Prague), New York, USA

'The Germans are here'. The words were spoken by my mother as she stood at the foot of my bed. I jumped up in a panic. But my mother appeared to be calm. She wasn't really but she knew that she had to appear so. It was 15 March 1939 and my father had left a few days earlier for Paris on his way to the USA. My mother had urged him to go for months but he was reluctant to leave, unable to imagine that anyone could seriously want to harm us. Now she and I and our household helper were alone in our apartment.

One night my mother received a telephone call from her sister Hanni. There were some people here arranging for children's transports to England. The next morning my mother put my name down for the trip. She herself had a visitor's visa for the USA, but I had nothing and that is why she had stayed behind with me.

When she explained to me that I would be going to England with a group of other children I didn't want to hear about it. I was nine years old and had never been anywhere without my parents. But my mother said that it had to be. It would be nice to live with my aunt Trude and my cousin Achim in London, she said.

Once my place on the transport was assured my mother prepared for her own trip to the USA, via Berlin, where she wanted to say goodbye to her mother and brother. She later told me that she was so terrified about going to the German authorities for her exit visa that she had to drink several glasses of wine to work up the nerve to go in. Fortunately it was granted. After my mother left I stayed with my aunt Hanni who carefully packed a knapsack for my trip. In her orderly way she labelled the packages 'lunch for today', 'breakfast for tomorrow'. She and my cousin Evi saw me off at the railway station where I joined the Kindertransport. That was the last time I saw them.

It was warm in my bunk in the boat coming to England, but I must have fallen asleep because I remember waking in the dark to the unfamiliar sensation of slowly rising and falling.

Then we were at the railway station in London and there were my aunt and cousin. I didn't know then just how lucky I was. The transport had saved both my mother and me.

* * *

Charles Feld

(Vienna), Easton, Conn, USA

WRITTEN IN 1951 AT THE AGE OF FOURTEEN YEARS

At the age of five, when my father died, I was sent by my mother to an orphanage in Baden-bei-Wien, a small town near Vienna. My younger brother, Moshe, followed me a few years later to this dismal institution. The horrible years we spent there have no bearing on this story other than to connect the place with the events of March 1938, which happened in Austria.

On 12 March 1938, the German army marched into Austria to complete the *Anschluss*. I recall being bunched around the radio with the other orphan boys and listening to conflicting stories. Chancellor Schuschnigg was assuring everyone that Austria would be free forever, when a report came in announcing that the German army had invaded Austria. We were shocked when we looked out the window and noticed a number of flags with swastikas flying from several houses.

We were still in a state of shock as our director called us into our chapel where, in our time honoured tradition, we began to recite psalms. We prayed and knew that it was all in God's hand. Within a few days Stormtroopers appeared, arrested our director and his staff, took over the orphanage and put us children out on the street. I managed to get to Vienna, where I put my brother in a State orphanage, where he was temporarily safe, while I went to a relative to live.

With many others I was arrested on Kristallnacht on 10 November 1938. I was taken to a school in the Karl Meisel Strasse. All the windows had been painted black and hundreds of us were herded into the gymnasium. The Nazis kept themselves amused by torturing the old people, making them exercise on the gym equipment until they dropped. Periodically a bunch of brownshirted hoodlums would run amuck and beat everyone with rifle butts and sticks.

Since there was only one bathroom for the hundreds of people there, the

Gestapo permitted us to have a continuous line to go to the bathroom. I stepped out of line to see how much longer I would have to wait. I was struck immediately and was told to get back into line. I leaned over to see what was happening at the end of another line. I noticed an SS man with a clipboard calling off names. I realized instantly that the Gestapo was separating people to be shipped to a concentration camp. Resigned to my fate I stepped up and gave the SS man my name.

'Feld . . . Feld . . ., I have no Feld on this list . . . *Raus* (out)'. I stood there dumbfounded not knowing what to do. I think that I admired the German bureaucratic mind and started inching toward the nearest door. Once I reached the door I just started running and running and running . . .

I went to the American consulate until I was finally able to register for the 'quota' system for the United States. After 'escaping' from the camp in Vienna, I was able to secure permission from a friendly Christian lady to sleep in her hallway.

I went every day to visit the *Kultusgemeinde* in Vienna to see if there was any possibility of leaving the country, knowing full well that if arrested again I certainly would be deported to a camp in Germany or Poland. Totally by accident, I met a fellow named Shapsi who was with me at the orphanage home. I don't remember his last name but when we struck up a conversation he told me that he was involved in the transport of children that was leaving for London. I told him of my arrest and my fears, and pleaded with him to be one of the children to leave, since I had no one who could help me. After a time he agreed to put me on the list of children. I then told him that I could not possibly leave without my nine year old brother for whom at the age of fourteen I was responsible. He finally agreed and so both my brother Moshe and I came to London with the Kindertransport.

I think all of us got who got out alive have a story of miracles and such incidents to tell, but the 'why me?' syndrome still haunts me.

*   *   *

Rev. John Fieldsend

(Feige/Troppau), St Albans, UK

The memory of saying goodbye to my parents on Wigstadtl station in Czech Sudetenland in the spring of 1939 is still clear in my mind, though little did I then realise that I would not see them again. I am one of the children brought over by Nicholas Winton, the wonderful man who saved six hundred Czech children though unlike most of the others in his transports, I came through Germany, spending some weeks in a boarding school in Hanover, finally arriving with others on the 3 July transport. On arrival in England I was fostered by a Christian family with whom I spent three years before being sent by the Jewish Refugee Committee to a boarding school in Surrey. I still returned to my foster parents during holidays. I was thus exposed to both faiths in my mid teens. Whilst being prepared for my *Bar Mitzvah* at school, I made a clear decision instead to ask for Baptism, which took place subsequent to an appointment made for me to discuss the matter with a Rabbi.

At the completion of my secondary education I went to university, graduated in electrical engineering, served in the Royal Air Force, spent some time in the electronics industry, and then, following what I experienced as a clear calling from God, trained for the Christian ministry, being ordained in 1961, just a few weeks after my marriage to Elizabeth.

In the early 1970s deep and wholly unexpected stirrings came into my life. Through a series of events, which would take too long to enter into here, my by now all but lost Jewish identity began to break through into my life. Without, I hope, sounding arrogant, I felt I could understand how Moses felt when he realised that he wasn't an Egyptian! Shortly after these experiences, and in the most amazing chain of circumstances, I was reunited with an uncle and a cousin whom I had last seen in Germany in about 1936, and another cousin who had survived Belsen. Next, one of the now well known *That's Life* programmes, which again took me totally by surprise anchored my roots yet more firmly in my Jewish identity. In all these events I have had to re-examine many of my presuppositions, and re-orientate many of my priorities. Much that I had valued had to be re-assessed, and some things have had to change. But in and through all these events I have honestly and plainly to say that the reality of my fundamental conviction that Yeshua is the Messiah has been deepened and, not by my choice but by his calling, I identify myself as a Messianic Jew, and to him I testify with joy and gratitude for all that he has done in and with my life.

*   *   *

Dorothy Fleming and her sister

(Oppenheimer/Vienna), Sheffield, UK

Part of a letter from the guardians to their parents:

London, 14 January 1939

Dear Friends,
In the meantime you will have also received the second telegram that both your children have landed happily in Leeds. Mrs Ross writes to me today:

'Dora and Lieserl arrived radiantly happy. The Halls are already thrilled with them, they are delightful children. We are all convinced that they will be very happy in the Hall home' – so, there's nothing better one could hear, is there?

On Wednesday afternoon Mrs Ross telephoned me from Leeds and told me that the children would be arriving on Thursday at three o'clock and would I then send them straight on to Leeds. I didn't want to agree to that; I was worried that the children would be too tired to travel onward unaccompanied. Thus Mrs Ross promised me to come herself to fetch the children. We agreed on a sign of recognition and everything else. Then I rang Olga and Bruno and also managed to reach Paly.

On Thursday at three o'clock we were all at the station with thumping hearts. Punctually the train drew in and it was very moving how all the small and big children streamed out; there were surely none on that platform who didn't have tears in their eyes. I quickly found both of ours, waiting very nicely, hand in hand.

We were all so happy that the children belonged to us for a while and not yet to the Halls. Dorli naturally comported herself wonderfully but the little one was still very tired. Olga requested that both of them should come to her; we stowed them into a taxi and at home they were quickly refreshed and the little one was immediately put to bed where she soon dropped off to sleep peacefully. At this time, as always, your 'big' daughter showed such touching selflessness and such motherliness to the little one, one could only be amazed. When Lieserl was already in bed, Dorli was still in her coat and could not be moved to think of herself. I have never seen such a thing in a ten year old. Everyone was full of praise for her. Both of them then slept well all night, had a good bath the next morning to be rid of travel grime and when my husband and I collected them at eleven o'clock both were cheerful and lively.

I put them on a train to Leeds. Then I saw a Salvation Army officer getting in; a respectable looking man with glasses who was stowing away his luggage opposite the children. I asked if he was also travelling to Leeds and whether I might put the little ones in his care. At first he was somewhat surprised but then he smiled kindly and agreed.

So, my dear Mrs Oppenheimer, such children can really be sent into the outside world with confidence. They will do one credit everywhere. I can't get over your Dorli and I am telling everyone about it. This ten year old behaved like someone aged at least fifteen, so wise and straightforward and responsible and still absolutely undemanding and childlike. I wanted to explain English money to her, but she already knew all that by heart. And her little notebook with all the addresses and telephone numbers . . . and how she always had everything necessary for the little one ready with a few quick and confident moves – it is hard to believe. She's the best possible nurse one could find for the little one; always loving and caring and sometimes also a bit forceful. That really is tremendous.

The beautiful little one was naturally a singular delight for everyone. We could already have 'lost' her a few times at the station; there were immediate admirers all around. She was the most delightful child of the whole transport group. Even the taxi driver took her quite gently in his arms as she was so tired and all the porters and station officials smiled and were clearly touched. At the departure for Leeds, as she stood at the barrier still with the big number on her chest, the ticket collector punched her ticket, looked at her, said: 'Come along, seventy three!' at which she then proudly marched through.

Both your children are very affectionate but not at all emotional and that will be of great help to them when they have to get used to everything being new.

They rode off with rosy cheeks and shining eyes and seemed quite pleased to be rid of us. It was, after all, a splendid adventure!

My dear Hanna, you speak specifically of the possibility of your entering into domestic service and ask for my opinion. But this is all now resolved due to the fact that Mr L has invited *both* of you here. This is really a great stroke of luck and I have high hopes that everything will be settled soon because he is outside London.

Now, dear friends, I think this has been a long letter and hopefully you are a bit cheered now and hold your head high and trust to good fortune. I am pretty firmly convinced that all that remains will now go very quickly.

Many warmest greetings, to all the grandparents and to you both from both of us.

Your,
A. and H.

How many pairs of pants was the little one really wearing? It was very sensible to do it like that. There was a little dumpling ambling along the station platform, and afterwards, when all the layers were shed, there was a very graceful and slim little girl.

*　　*　　*

Edith Forrester

(Welkemeyer/Nordhausen), Fife, Scotland, UK

Annaliese and I were walking through the town of Nordhausen on what must have been a shopping expedition. I adored our maid who always took time to explain everything I wanted to know. Suddenly there was the sound of breaking glass and Annaliese seized me urgently by the hand pulling me away from the gathering crowds.

'Why have they broken that shop window?' I wanted to know, but this time dear, gentle Annaliese wasted no time to explain. We reached home in record time and I was quite breathless. It was November 1938 and the whole incident left me, a seven year old child, quite bewildered.

Similar incidents were to take place over the next few weeks and months, this time affecting close friends in our neighbourhood and then relatives living in the same town. Houses were ransacked, furniture smashed and hurled out of windows. Nightly raids were made by SS men on Jewish homes. Then I began to know fear for the first time in my life. Why, oh why, were such awful things happening in our town?

Then the night came when it was our turn to have our house searched. The Jewish men from the two other flats were taken away, as was my father. He was, however, released many hours later and I was so happy to see him again. He had undoubtedly been warned what could happen to us all, but being a Gentile, he was allowed home. How upset I was when the two SS soldiers forced my dying grandmother out of bed! To this day I am thankful that she died in March 1939 and was spared the fate of her beloved only daughter Erna and that of her sister, brother-in-law and other relatives.

Everything was happening much too fast for a seven year old. Suddenly I was taken to shop for every conceivable item under the sun, from underwear to coats, dresses and even two suitcases. We were going on a journey, perhaps we were about to embark on a wonderful holiday.

I think I began to have a sense of foreboding the day my mother accompanied me to school. Although I had begun to dislike the name calling that was going on, I did like going to school and I had a great affection for my teacher, Herr Krieghof. Looking back he reminded me of Schubert with his rosy cheeks, twinkling eyes and spectacles. When I left him that day the tears were running down his cheeks. How strange to see him cry, but why?

All the time the preparations were going on, I failed to notice how silent and glum everybody had become. I assumed, of course, that I would be going on this journey with my parents. Little did I know that my mother would be taking me as far as Hanover and then we would be parting for ever.

We waved goodbye to my father in such a way that I felt sure he would be joining us shortly. After all he was a busy man and could not always join us, but we were a family and we did everything together. My mother tried to explain, but with the trusting nature of a much loved only child, I felt secure and did not grasp the awfulness of the situation, until I found myself alone on a train which was bursting at the seams with what seemed to me to be hundreds of children. What was even worse, I could not get near a window to see my beloved mother. Suddenly I heard my cry of '*Mutti! Mutti!*' and somebody lifted me up and I was able to catch a last glimpse of her face, her lovely, sad eyes frantically searching for me. To my dying day I shall never forget the expression on her face. I was no longer a bewildered child, but a very frightened one. Where was I going and what was going to happen to me?

We seemed to travel by train, by boat and bus for a lifetime. Eventually we arrived in London and were taken to a huge hall where we were given food. My journey was not over yet, for I soon found myself on yet another bus and another train until I arrived in a quiet little town in the Borders of Scotland, called Selkirk. Why Scotland? To this day I do not know the answer to that question. I had no relatives anywhere in Britain because the surviving members of our family had managed to escape to America and South Africa.

On Friday 17 March 1939, a photograph of our group appeared in a local paper. A Scottish couple saw this picture, saw me in the front row holding the hand of a little boy, and decided they would like to take me into their home. They came to the home and it was love at first sight. We were unable to communicate, they speaking no German and I speaking no English. After many formalities, I was the first child in the group, perhaps because I was the youngest, to find a new home.

My beloved foster parents have both died, but to me they made life worthwhile again. I shall thank God to my dying day that he dealt so kindly with me by bringing me to a loving home, by selecting me to live. They not only gave me a home and love, but a wonderful education so that I have had the privilege as a teacher of influencing thousands of young lives.

*   *   *

Ya'acov Friedler

(Oberhausen), Haifa, Israel

We didn't know that we were making some sort of history, the last Kindertransport out of burning Europe, as we instinctively lay supine on the deck of the old Dutch freighter, ss *Bodegraven,* pulling out of the port of Ymuiden, near Amsterdam on the evening of 14 May 1940.

We were concerned about the two German planes which, after dropping their bombs, swooped in low over us and started to machinegun the ship. No one was hurt. The bullets struck just too high, on the bridge and ventilation funnels. After a minute or two I turned round to look. I could see the pilots and the crackling fire from their guns. For a moment or two the sailors, who had been issued rifles, were taking ineffective pot-shots at the planes. Then the captain ordered them to cease fire. Over his bridge radio he heard that Holland had just surrendered and he was keeping to the rules. The Germans kept on firing, but finally they too gave up and flew away. Next morning the captain posted notices that Berlin radio had announced the sinking of the 'important' steamer *Bodegraven.* We knew better, fortunately.

'We' were the eighty children from Germany and Austria who had been living in the *Burgerweeshuijs*, the almost five hundred year old city orphanage in the very centre of Amsterdam. One of its wings had been cleared of the Christian wards and allotted to the Jewish refugee children. Just a month before the German invasion, we had been placed in a nearby primary school as we had been considered to have learned enough Dutch to go to a regular school.

When the Germans launched their invasion on 10 May, we were no longer allowed out. Queen Wilhelmina, caught up in the general fifth column scare, ordered all foreigners off the streets. Occasionally we saw a German plane fly over our home, usually pursued by an orange-marked Dutch fighter. It was on the third day of our strange curfew that talk about fleeing to England started. We thought that it was impossible for any ship to get to Britain. It simply wouldn't get through the airtight barrier of mines, submarines, patrol boats and shore defences. Nevertheless, when next morning we were told to get ready to move at a moment's notice, we complied. We managed to get together our most prized possessions before a couple of buses pulled up outside the ancient portals of our home and took us through a series of roadblocks to Ymuiden. Truus Wijsmuller-Meijer, the courageous Dutch woman, who had already saved so many children from Germany, had not let the actual outbreak of war stop her. She remembered the *Burgerweeshuijs* and got together the buses and the permits to see us through.

The guns were already audible as we left town and the sky was filled with puffs of smoke and with what we took to be German paratroopers descending on one side of the city as we moved out of the other.

At Ymuiden we were quickly embarked, together with several dozens of Dutch Jews whom Wijsmuller-Meijer had picked up. As the journey was to take only a few hours we were told to settle on the deck of the old freighter. After the German attack, the captain ordered the holds to be opened and for everybody to go below. We were scared of the steep descent on the plank ladders, and the sailors, Indonesians from the Dutch East Indies, took us in their arms and slid down with us. In the holds we bedded down on the board floors and sooner or later fell asleep.

Next morning and four mornings more we were still at sea. Unknown to us the British had refused to let us land at Harwich and the *Bodegraven* made her way up the east coast. The first day the sailors shared their meagre portions of rice with us, afterwards we had only the stone-hard ships' biscuits, which had to be sucked and chewed, bite by bite, before they went down.

Finally we landed at Liverpool to a hero's welcome. For the first time the Liverpudlians were actually seeing real life refugees from the Nazi dreadnought that was sweeping across Europe. The police had to clear a path for us through the cheering crowds, and we felt very important. We were put up in a Sailors' Home near the port and in order to allow us to stretch our legs the police would occasionally cordon off a stretch of the street outside to let us promenade, goggled at and cheered by the populace.

After three days, we children were taken to nearby Wigan, the butt of so many jokes, ('Wigan Pier' is the one that springs to mind first) where we were put up in a Scout Hall. Soon the women of Wigan came to claim us for teas and suppers and pony riding and every other treat they could press on us. Rarely have so many done so much for so few, a description that Mr Winston Churchill later changed into so memorable a phrase.

After a few weeks, having been taught some basic English, we were moved again, to a house in Salford, Manchester. There, between the barrage balloons and the sirens and the Ack Ack fire we were sent to school. It was not unlike being tossed into the water to learn to swim. We were spending more time in the makeshift shelters than in the classrooms. There, standing up, to die with our boots on if need be, we sang along with our Liverpudlian classmates: '*Roll out the Barrel*', '*Run Hitler*' and '*The Siegfried Line*'. We didn't understand everything, but who in those hectic days did?

Through the Red Cross my older sister, who had come to England before the war, like many others on a maid's visa, found us, myself and my younger brother. She had been interned on the Isle of Man as an 'Enemy Alien' like every other refugee we knew, and arranged for us to join her. We spent a happy year in the Breakwater Hotel at Port Erin, the 'women's camp' housed in the deserted hotels of Port Erin and neighbouring Port St Mary. After a year, our sister was brought before a tribunal again and as automatically as she had been designated 'Enemy' in the spy-scare days of 1940, she was now declared 'Friendly' and we were sent back to the mainland, for her to join the war effort and us to go to school. I attended the Jewish Free School, evacuated to Ely, where I became proficient enough to be awarded a scholarship to a Public School in the 1942 examinations.

So I found myself on the railway station of Frome, Somerset, a forlorn little boy with a poor little suitcase. The billeting officer of the Coopers Company School, a retired sergeant major, who had come back to replace younger men and taught gymnastics, had little trouble in identifying me. He took me to the home of the town chemist, Mr Maggs and his wife Lilian, their son Vivian, a little younger than me and another refugee evacuee, Karl Oberweger from Austria. The Maggses taught me to be English and to behave like a gentleman. In the year I spent with them I think they had some success. Then, joined by my brother whom the headmaster agreed to accept without a scholarship because he had found me so 'pleasant and intelligent a lad', as he wrote to the Jewish Refugees Committee, we moved to a working-class couple. Vic and Dorothy Crook lived in an old cottage, with gas light in the living-room, candles in the bedroom and a Saturday night bath in a tin tub in the kitchen. They dismissed the Maggses as 'tuppeny ha'penny aristocrats' but wanted to know every detail of their behaviour and table manners. Unwittingly I played a little part in bridging the English social gap. Then the Rabbis discovered us, had us transferred to a kosher boarding house in Stamford Hill and enrolled us in the Brewers Company school in Islington. Then we were evacuated once more, when the V1 buzzbombs started, to the Jewish Secondary School in Shefford, where we stayed until the end of the war. I took the Matriculation exams of London University just after hosilities ceased. After three years, my younger brother and I went to Israel.

Space prevents me from recording much more, not least an eightieth birthday exchange of letters with the Queen Mother about what she did for our family personally after the war.

* * *

Ester Friedman

(Müller/Vienna), Norwich, UK

THE TAPESTRY

The Tapestry? What has a tapestry got to do with the death of my father, mother, sister, uncles, aunts, cousins and six million Jews? If you bear with me I will tell you its story and now, on the fiftieth anniversary of the Kristall Night, is the time to remember. What happened on the Kristallnacht, you all know – but the story of the tapestry started seventy years ago, when my mother started embroidering it before her marriage to my father.

My mother loved sewing, so she became a dressmaker. Here in England you would call her a 'Court Dressmaker' as she made dresses for *Bundeskanzler* Schuschnigg's sisters. We lived in Vienna. My mother was born in Vienna; my father in Czechoslovakia. His mother and father walked to Vienna with four children after a pogrom. But that is another story.

It was hard to make a living in Vienna in the days of my childhood. I can see in front of my eyes the mesh of my cot rail, the chink of light under the door and hear the sound of cutting, cutting, cutting, till deep into the night. Thinking back, I seem to have been a strange child, worrying about my mother working so hard. She had little time to relax, but sometimes, and that very seldom, she would take out the tapestry and sit and embroider it. And I would sit on a little wooden stool at her feet, so happy oh, so happy, to have my mother to myself and to know that she was relaxed and content. I would sort out the colours and tidily roll up the silks. What precious moments – what happy memories!

The day came for me to leave – I did not see my mother shed a tear. She must have, but in my presence she showed nothing but calm. I loved both my parents, but my mother I loved to distraction – if she had shown any emotion, the seriousness of the situation would have been brought home to me, but as it was, I took it as an adventure. The first time in my life to travel on my own! My sister was sixteen and a half, and was called back while already at the station, several months after I had left Austria. We were six hundred children, four hundred to go to England and two hundred to Holland. Most of those who went to Holland perished.

This transport left Vienna on 12 December 1938 and I was fourteen years old. The organisation dealing with refugees found a place for fifty of us in a *Bnei Brith* convalescent home in Sussex. We had it so good, but I could not rest from trying to get my family over to England as well. The sense of adventure had turned into a pain of longing to have my family with me. Within the next year I received only two letters from them – 'We are well, hope you are happy'. Someone had the bright idea to write to namesakes found in the telephone book: 'We may be related, please help my family'! My name was Müller, a very German name and there were four Müllers in the phone book. Three of them answered and one was prepared to help my sister. She was then seventeen years old. Had the war started two days later, she would have been safely in England.

Life continued for me. I must have been fifteen when one day, feeling very much alone, sitting in the dormitory, I ached with longing for my loved ones. In the distance I heard the voices of the other girls but in my heart was only one voice, one ache. I took a piece of paper and out poured the pain, tears ran down my face onto the paper. I found it the other day, while packing to leave. A smudged scrap of cheap paper. I sat and read and remembered the day I wrote to ease the pain as I am remembering now:

I had a home once and knew laughter and joy,
I was a child once, playing with dolls and with toy,
I had a mother, so gentle and good
Loving me, as only a mother could.
A father, strict and stern,
Always teaching – there was so much to learn.
He taught me to work hard and be honest in my life.
He told me that happiness cannot be bought with worldly goods.
With love and contentment it must be fed
And that often a hard crust covers a heart longing for understanding.
He taught me this and many a thing
And now that I am older I know
That he not only spoke, but that all his life he kept to this code.
Such good people – they died with six million others – WHY?

This piece of paper is forty-nine years old. I gave it to my daughter who, I know, will treasure it.

Time passed, the war continued. I had a few letters from my parents through the Red Cross until 1942 and then SILENCE. We children, like so many others, had no idea what was going on in Germany, Poland, Czechoslovakia and we did not know about concentration camps. All this was brought home to us after the war. Survivors looked for their families or what might be left of them. The then Home Secretary, Mr Chuter Ede, helped me personally to look for my family by contacting the authorities and governments involved, but to no avail. I contacted a firm of private investigators, sent them photos and particulars and they put up posters in public places with pictures of my parents and sister, their old address, and, as by then I was training to be a nurse, my hospital address.

One day I was studying in my room in the nurses' home when there was a knock at the door. A stranger stood in the doorway and he told me the following:-

He saw one of my notices and as his intention was to come to England, he went to my old address. Someone who knew nothing of my parents, opened the door. Unable to get information from her, he tried the neighbour below our flat. Frau Silber was an old lady as long as I can remember and whenever we children were too boisterous my mother used to say: 'Pst, Frau Silber will come up.' Strangely, she never came up or complained, but it always worked and we stopped jumping on the wooden floor. This Mrs Silber, not being Jewish, was still alive and she told my visitor the following:

My mother lost most of her clients as they were not allowed to give Jews work. In 1940 my family was forced to give up three rooms of our flat to another family and had to move – the three of them – into the fitting room. A tiny room with the window facing the wall opposite. How long were they there? How did they live? My mother's permit to work was withdrawn. It was then that my mother found time to work on the tapestry. This tapestry, when finished, my mother gave to Mrs Silber for safekeeping.

One day the SS came – heavy boots on the stairs, truncheons splintering the door, truncheons wrecking and breaking the furniture, breaking all that was breakable. Strong, rough hands grabbing my beloved mother, father, sister – dragging them downstairs into the lorries already full with other helpless men, women and children. That ended Frau Silber's story – she did not know any more.

She kept the tapestry throughout the war.

And so, he, a stranger, came to me.

What is there of greater value to me than this heirloom worked in times of happiness with love and in utter despair.

The only thing that escaped destruction – the only thing left of them except their ashes in a mass grave in Auschwitz. Please God, let them rest in peace.

*　　*　　*

Gerald Friedman

(Berlin) New York, USA

As a sixteen year old student in a Jewish school in Berlin, I received a visa for entering England to visit a British family for the summer 1938 vacation. This family was that of my father's cousin.

Luckily I had an unexpired German passport at this critical time. It had been issued in 1937. By mistake it was made out for five and a half years. Passports for Jews at that time were valid for only one year, whereas non-Jews received theirs for five years. Theoretically my passport should have been returned to the Nazi authorities in 1938 at the end of its one year validation.

On 28/29 June 1938 I was in a train at the German border in possession of a five year passport and mistaken for a non-Jew or so-called Aryan. The SS man at the border confirmed this mistaken identity by demanding my military papers. However before demanding them he had stared at me for several minutes, while examining the passports of others. Apparently I must have aroused his suspicion. As Jews were not conscripted to the German army I knew nothing about military papers, but luckily had seen a notice in Berlin demanding that those born in 1919 and 1920 should register as conscripts. Since I was born in 1921 I said coolly:

'Ich bin Jahrgang 1921'

meaning I was born in 1921 and have to wait one more year for military papers, too naive to know that if my religion be revealed he would have taken me off the train to face an uncertain fate. Apparently the SS man was satisfied and the train left for Holland.

The first night after my arrival in London I spent in the home of my father's cousin, Leo Goldstein. Next morning he brought me to the Jewish Aid Committee who placed me at Townley Castle School in Swiss Cottage, London where I lived till November 1938. Thereafter Woburn House sent me to a farmer in Barley, near Royston, in Hertfordshire, where I remained for six months.

My mentor in Barley was Dr R. N. Salaman, FRS through whose effort and that of my mother's cousin Erich Gumpert in London I brought my brother Horst Joachim (now Kenneth Freeman) and my sister Traute (now Traute Eckersdorff) to England through a Kindertransport. My brother arrived in January 1939. He found a job in the East End of London with a candy manufacturer called Clarnico. One of Clarnico's managers sponsored our parents' transit visa to England as part of their passage to Shanghai (China) and/or the United States. My father Martin arrived in June 1939 and my mother Frieda (nee Cohn) with her sister in August 1939, just a few days before the outbreak of World War II.

*   *   *

Walter F. Friedman

(Vienna), Vermont, USA

It was ten minutes before midnight of 11 December 1937, ten minutes before my fifteenth birthday, when my father briefly came out of a coma and then died. Almost to a minute, a year later I left Vienna for England, where I arrived the next day on my sixteenth birthday, 12 December 1938.

In this one year, and the year after in England, I not only grew up rapidly, but was party to one of the most eventful times of our history, a period which fortunately left a very positive imprint on my future life.

I was born into an upper middle class Jewish family in Vienna, brought up as a spoiled brat with many privileges. My mother came from a well-known old-line Jewish family and was highly concerned that I should continue in the tradition of the famous Rabbis of this family.

It was three months after my father died that Hitler came to power in Austria. Our lives, as well as everyone else's who was Jewish, changed drastically. Almost a week after the *Anschluss,* my sister was taken as a hostage by the Gestapo to blackmail my mother and force her to bring our foreign accounts into the German Reich. I was transferred to a Jewish school where I fortunately finished fifth *Gymnasium* grade.

About that time, Adolph Eichmann was transferred to Vienna in charge of the Gestapo's Jewish affairs. He and three of his deputies needed a place to live. They surveyed desirable apartment buildings in various sections of Vienna. They decided on four flats in a building which was owned by my family including, through inheritance, by myself. My uncle Hugo was the executor of my father's estate and managed this building. He thus came into almost daily contact with Eichmann in redecorating and making ready these apartments. Eichmann, for example, had to have all of the toilets replaced because the previous tenants were Jewish and he would not sit on a toilet on which a Jew had sat.

I, like most other Jews, was looking for a means to learn a trade or at least to get started with something that could become useful, in emigration. Through a friend of my father's, I obtained a job as an apprentice in a repair garage. I had always been mechanically inclined and enjoyed working with my hands. I liked to build things, watch construction and at an early age I played with mechanical toys. This job seemed right for me.

It was a few days after the Kristallnacht that my uncle, Hugo, was in Eichmann's office on some matter, that had to be settled in his flat. At that time, Eichmann asked him,

'Don't you have daughters?'

Uncle Hugo said,

'Yes, I do. I have three daughters.'

'How old are they?' he asked. Uncle Hugo replied: 'They are fifteen, seventeen and twenty-one.' Eichmann said at that point: 'The British and the Dutch are arranging for some children's transports to their respective countries. I think I can get your two daughters, the fifteen and seventeen year olds, on the first transport.' Whereupon my uncle asked, 'Do you think you might also get my nephew, Walter, on this transport?' He said he would try.

It was a few days later that I was notified to leave on 11 December on a train to England.

On the train, I sat in a compartment with two brothers whom I befriended and stayed in touch with all through our lives. Unfortunately, the older brother, Otto, committed suicide in Chicago about ten years ago. Henry, the other brother, was kind enough to take one of my two watches. We were afraid that they would be confiscated if they inspected us at the border.

Unfortunately, 1938 had one of the coldest winters in the history of England. The camp we arrived at was beautiful and had all the sport and entertainment facilities for a good time in warm weather. But we froze, huddled around the single fireplace in a common hall where this was the only source of heat. Fortunately, through the immense efforts of the Refugee Committee of Bloomsbury House, new quarters for us were soon found. We were split up into groups, assigned to boarding schools, where the students went home during the Christmas recess, and boarded there.

We stayed until about the second or third of January and then we were transferred to some First World War barracks in Essex near Colchester.

As a whole, we seemed to have a very good time being with other youngsters and being for the first time away from home for a long period of time. Some of us went to foster parents, others went to jobs. While we waited, there were some kind people in the area who visited us at weekends and even took some of us out to their homes and other places to entertain us and to make us feel at home in England. I met a wonderful family, and we became great friends for a number of years. Unfortunately, I lost contact, but re-established it again about ten to twelve years ago on one of my trips to London. I invited the wife (the husband had since died), who had helped refugees and soldiers to make them more comfortable during this critical time, to come to the United States about ten years ago. She enjoyed the trip to Florida, where we have our winter home, immensely.

Finally, the news came of my assignment to a trainee job in London with a lorry repair facility of the Shell-Mex Company. Apparently, my brief background as an apprentice in automotive repairs had paid off. I was further assigned to live in an orphanage in South London. I was unhappy to leave my newly-found friends, but the anticipation of a new future in London with a purposeful job was overriding all my anxieties.

At the orphanage, I really didn't make any friends, because we were all tired when we got home. We ate together and then most of us went straight to bed. Our things were kept in lockers in the basement where there were also the common washrooms, with one shower, for the thirty boys. It was perhaps after one week when one morning I went to the locker to get my shaving things, and discovered that there was a big hole in my toilet bag. The mice had been busy. I decided that this home was really not for me and I was determined to leave it as soon as possible.

I had a sympathetic aunt in London who came there a few weeks after me. She said she would help me and put an advert in *The Times* for a boarding house, with food and board. The cost was to be one pound. At that time, I earned one guinea, which was twenty-one shillings. My aunt promised me another five shillings as pocket money. This was not very much, but would certainly help me with incidentals after my living expenses were taken care of. The advert produced results. I moved to a boarding house in Kensington.

About that time, in order to save money, I purchased a used bike for five shillings. This became my transportation for quite a while. I always enjoyed riding a bike and it gave me a great deal of independence. I particularly enjoyed riding behind double-decker buses where the vacuum behind the bus actually pulled the bike along. In those days, I think without a bike, I would not have been able to see as much of London and not been able to get together with some of my friends whom I had met in the various places where I had stayed, prior to coming to London.

However, my mother, who corresponded with both of my aunts who were by then in London, felt that this lifestyle was not the right thing for a nice sixteen year old Jewish boy. Unknown to me, they made inquiries for a place for me to stay. They heard about the former owner of the *Drei Husaren*, a five star Viennese restaurant, who had bought a house in Chelsea and who took in boarders to help support himself. Arrangements were made for me to move there in a small, but comfortable room on the top floor and to eat with them their excellent Viennese meals, including wonderful pastries. The Dieners (that was their name) had a daughter, about three years older than I, with whom I got along very well. In a short while, she taught me dancing in a small den. Ever since then, I dance in circles, because that's how I had to dance because of the limitations of the room. As a whole, my stay was a happy one and I got excellent food and good company.

About the time that I moved to this boarding house, I joined a Boy Scout troop in Kensington. I had been a very devout Scout in Vienna, having been a member of a group of almost exclusive Jewish Scouts. The troop that I joined was located in a church, the Scoutmaster was a London Bobby, an extremely nice person in his middle thirties. We met once a week. The members of this troop were really very nice and fully accepted me as an outsider. We had many outings and camps in outlying areas of London. My English was broadened with additional slang words and the Cockney dialect. On the whole I enjoyed my affiliation with this troop and it added to my perspective on the English people.

I also enrolled in the Bayswater Polytechnic where I started an evening course in Mechanical Engineering. This involved two evenings per week. The course was quite simple for me; there were a few language problems, but I had no difficulties in keeping up and getting far better grades than I had ever achieved in mathematics and related subjects in Vienna.

This relatively peaceful life came to an abrupt end during the Battle of Britain, when all 'enemy aliens' were being interned. Not even the influence of the London Bobby, my scoutmaster, could keep me from having to go into an internment camp.

I was released from camp after four transfers after three months, because I got an affidavit from the owner of the boarding house that I had lived with an English family and I was under seventeen years old. From then on, I stayed in a couple of hostels until my sister and I moved together into our own flat. During this period, we had a very active social life with Austrian youth, and in spite of the Blitz, immensely enjoyed London life including the theatre and the many parks, and of course the many friends that I had made during my first year in London, during internment, and after. I left with my sister with great apprehension for New York, to where our mother had emigrated two years earlier.

My four and a half years in England will always be remembered, in spite of the many hardships, as a very happy period where I learned a great deal, not only about English customs, but how to become self-sufficient and to appreciate the full value of education, proper work habits and solid friendships.

After a stint in the US Navy, I completed my studies in engineering. For the last twenty years, I headed a management counselling practice. I am now retired, living in Vermont and Florida.

*   *   *

Kurt Fuchel

(Fuchsl/Vienna), Rocky Point, NY, USA

In 1938 life in Vienna fell apart. The Nazis occupied Austria, a rape with the victim enjoying every minute of it. A law was promulagated which effectively allowed anyone in good standing with the Nazis to simply expropriate an apartment occupied by Jews. Thus on the infamous *Kristallnacht* we were evicted with only a few hours' notice. As recounted by my mother, a Frau Janaba had seen a photo of our apartment in the shop of an interior decorator. She visited us and asked if the apartment was for sale, but was told that it was not. A few days later my father received a summons to go to the headquarters of the Nazi Party. My mother, knowing his pride and short temper, wouldn't let him go and went in his place. She was told that we had to leave our home and everything in it by nine that night, as Frau Janaba was taking it over. My mother protested that she had a sick child at home who was already asleep, so the officer agreed to let us stay until six next morning. Frau Janaba asked: 'What if they take some of *my* things?', to which the officer replied: 'They wouldn't dare.'

Next morning, Frau Janaba showed up; my father told her that she was stealing what he and my mother had worked for. She said: 'Stop talking like that, or I'll have you sent to a concentration camp.' At that moment I, aged seven, burst into the room and told Frau Janaba: 'You are a bad woman. You came here before and lied to us.' Janaba was so disconcerted to be confronted by a child that she screamed: 'Get the boy out of here!'
A kind friend took us in, and we lived all three packed into one small, dingy room until we could leave.

I used to go to school by tramway: my mother would put me on at one stop, and a school aid would await me at a stop further down the line. One day people told my mother that I was a very talkative little boy, and that I had told everyone in the tram just what that bad man Hitler had done to my father and what exactly I thought of him. After that, I did not travel alone.

My parents took up an offer to have me sent to England and live there with a family until they could establish themselves elsewhere. After some correspondence, the Cohen family in Norwich was selected for me, and one day in February 1939 a piece of cardboard with a number was fixed around my neck and I was put on a train bound for England.

The train from Vienna took its frightened flock of children, instant refugees, to Antwerp and from there a ship carried us to Harwich on the east coast of England. Next morning the Cohens picked me up and drove me to Norwich. I remember walking into the house: a little boy dressed in his Austrian finery: short pants, jacket, long wool stockings held up by a suspender belt, and high-rising boots, the effect somewhat marred by the grubbiness accumulated during three days of travel. Ahead of me were the stairs going up to the second floor. Near the top sat John, a little boy of five, shyly looking at this new brother. I was stripped, scrubbed from head to toe, my clothes burnt, new ones provided, and then the family gathered around the table for a magnificent chicken dinner. A smile returned to my face: here was a language I could understand.

Learning English was next on the agenda. For this purpose an elderly German who lived down the block was hired. He wore thick glasses, had a brusque manner and I was terrified of him. Perhaps spurred on by my distaste for the man I learned English in record time. Six weeks later I wrote to my parents in English: 'I no longer speak German,' and from that day on I never have.

One of the more vivid memories of that period was an invention known as the Morrison shelter. This replaced the dining room table; it was about the size of a double bed, the top was a quarter of an inch thick steel plate, the legs heavy steel angle irons, the bottom was made of steel strips supported by springs, and removable wire netting sides completed the arrangement. The idea was that if the house collapsed during an air raid, the occupants of the shelter would be safe. My adoptive brother, John, and I slept in this contraption for quite a while during the worst of the bombings. When the sirens sounded, the rest of the family would crawl in with us. Sleeping in the shelter was really quite fun. One could make believe that one was a caged lion or some other animal, snarling through the heavy wire mesh sides.

One of the first things to be sacrificed in the war was the lawn behind the house. It was spaded over, and assorted vegetables planted on half of it; the rest was fenced in and a shed built for chickens which were expected to supplement our ration of one egg a week per person. On special holidays or other occasions the decision was made to eat one of our chickens. This was always a traumatic event; after all we were on a first name basis with them. My sadness did not diminish my appetite.

*   *   *

Walter Fulop

(Vienna), Broxbourne, Herts., UK

I switched on the radio to listen to the latest news. At 7.30 the Chancellor came on announcing the German ultimatum forcing his resignation in favour of a German appointee. His speech ended with an emotional 'God save Austria.'

I felt that the world around me had collapsed and burst into tears. From the street you could hear the marching of the formerly illegal Nazi sympathisers shouting their slogans with frenzied chorus precision. I tried quickly to recover my poise in case any of my family returned. It would not do for a fifteen year old boy, approaching adulthood, to be found crying.

November came and with it Kristallnacht and we had hurriedly and secretly to leave our home and hide nearby in an empty flat in the building containing our workshop which the concierge kindly offered us. He surely saved us in diverting marauding bands of Nazis looking for Jews. In addition, the woman owning the local grocer's shop supplied us with food as it was impossible to go out without running enormous risks of being apprehended. My aunt and uncle joined us in hiding as the outlying district where they lived made them too vulnerable.

Things grew more threatening and sinister and with emigration from

Austria growing increasingly more difficult it seemed to us that the world had slammed its doors in our faces.

Luckily I heard from a friend of mine about children's transports being organised to England. As my older sister had already emigrated there as a domestic servant, this seemed a good escape route. I managed to get myself on the list.

Early in January 1939 I left Vienna by train for London after a tearful separation from my parents, wondering whether I would ever see them again.

At midnight, bleary eyed, we boarded the boat at the Hook of Holland destined for Harwich where we arrived early on a freezing January morning. Off to London and Woburn House where I met Captain Davidson who provided avuncular advice and assurances.

Being beyond school age, I was given an errand boy's job at a gentlemen's outfitters in Kentish Town. On the first morning, when I reported for work, dressed in continental fashion in plus fours, I dutifully clicked my heels and bowed my head and offered my hand to be shaken. The boss looked quizzically at me, examined me from head to toe and then burst out 'You haven't come here to play golf.' A second-hand suit was quickly organised.

I looked younger than my age and all the men in the shop took a fatherly interest in my welfare making sure, among other things, that I was properly introduced to the more salty regions of the English language.

Came March 1939 and the swallowing of Czechoslovakia into the Reich. We felt war would not be far off, so my sister and I redoubled our efforts to enable our parents to join us. Their only hope of entering the UK was to seek domestic service, so we went to see an endless number of potential employers until we finally secured them a post. Whereas we could well imagine our mother successfully operating in the kitchen, the idea of my stepfather as a butler passed the realm of imagination. I had never seen him even boil an egg let alone polish shoes. They managed to arrive a few days before the outbreak of war.

War broke out and with the fall of France I found myself interned at the ripe old age of seventeen, obviously potentially more dangerous than my stepfather who, at the appropriate tribunal hearing, was assigned a more harmless category and escaped internment for a few more months. This further unsettling experience made a deep impression – as indeed it must have done on thousands of others – on this rather impressionable young man.

One frightening event engraved itself upon my memory. After Kempton Park Race Course we were transported to a disused mill (Warth Mills) somewhere in Lancashire. Hundreds of internees with no toilet facilities quickly remedied by holes dug into the ground, greenish stagnant pools of water next to our palliasses, looking out over broken glass roofs and windows. The internees were seething as they collected in one of the vast empty derelict factory halls and shouts of revolt were reverberating. The guards around the barbed wire perimeter got jumpy and an officer could be heard shouting commands to the guards, possibly fix bayonets although I am not sure. I really had no stomach to join such a revolt against armed guards and looked round in fear for support as it looked far too dangerous to try to detach oneself from such mass hysteria. In a corner away from the screaming internees I saw a group of youngsters equally frightened as myself gathered around a middle-aged man offering them support and I eagerly joined them. Just as it seemed that the situation would boil over, in stormed a big burly man with a powerful rasping voice, positioned himself on top of some boxes and harangued the crowd in German not to be so foolish as to lose their heads. I listened open-mouthed as he swung the mood of the crowd and calmed them. It was a close thing.

This DIY orator became the leader of the camp and negotiated with the military camp commander. This incident became the subject of questions in Parliament and an inquiry was set up. As a result a General inspecting Warth Mills – obviously a former cavalry officer as he wore breeches – was overheard to say that he would not put his horses into this camp.

We were subsequently transferred to Onchan on the Isle of Man. There, a much more relaxed regime prevailed. In the empty holiday boarding houses an almost bourgeois lifestyle developed.

At one stage the camp half emptied with some of the internees being transferred overseas and a batch of new arrivals was expected. I had a premonition that this would include my stepfather though I had no news from home for some time. Knowing his love of comforts I prepared a bed and room for us as best I could. Sure enough, he did arrive. In the gathering dusk I dragged him inside and installed him in our house. With camp life highly developed by then he adapted well to it for there were already coffee houses serving tea, coffee, and cream cakes – though heaven knows how these were obtained – with cards and chess being played all day. Barbed wire apart, my stepfather seemed to relish such coffee house life.

Among the internees – business men apart – were a lot of scientists and artists so that lectures and concerts were organised. Norbert Brainin of the subsequent Amadeus Quartet often played the violin for us and in the evenings I attended lectures given by an earnest young man on Nietzsche's 'Thus spake Zarathustra'. Sport and particularly football also figured large and I thoroughly enjoyed participating. Just the small matter of the company of girls was missing.

In mid-1944, with the Russian Army storming into Rumania, disaster struck all my relatives as a result of the Eichmann action, which with close co-operation of the Hungarian security forces led to their deportation to Auschwitz where most of them perished.

News of this reached us shortly after the end of the war and it was shattering.

Of course the events of the thirties and forties had a profound influence on my outlook on life. My belief in the civilizing influence and supremacy of European culture, and the ability of its monotheistic Judean-Christian religion to act as a spiritual bulwark and restraining hand on barbaric high (state) organised excesses on a massive scale, lay in utter ruins, never to recover again. The role of fanatic fundamentalism both in the political and religious domain had, and still has, a fatal corrosive dehumanising effect, as we regretfully observe still to this day.

In an interview with Terry Coleman of *The Guardian*, the incumbent Chief Rabbi conceded that as far as the Holocaust was concerned there is a problem as yet unresolved. Where was God then? Good point that, and full marks for courage and honesty.

*   *   *

Margaret Furst

(Romberg/Astheim), Dallas, USA

I was born in a very small town, Astheim, Germany between Darmstadt and Mainz on 30 May 1929.

My parents had married in July 1927. My father was a banker by profession, but when he married my mother he moved into my grandfather's house and helped with the business, which was a general merchandise grain store for the area. My brother arrived 17 July 1930.

My grandfather died three months before I was born and the burden of the business fell upon my parents and grandmother. As far back as I can remember we were a happy family. We lived quite well, not ostentatiously, but comfortably.

My father died in March 1934 at the age of forty-four from a severe heart attack. Hitler was already in power. Mama had a very hard time getting over my father's death and coping with the business. Anti-semitism was rearing its ugly head. There were only two Jewish families in our town and as time went on matters got worse. I started school in 1935, but at the beginning of 1936 Mama decided to sell the business and move. We moved to Eschwege on the Werra not far from Kassel, where my aunt Paula lived with her family. My brother and I both entered the Jewish school where we were taught by the Cantor of the Synagogue and one Jewish secular teacher. We lived in an apartment owned by Jews, and had to move twice in three years. There were non-Jews all around us and we were hardly able to walk in the streets. Food was difficult to come by. After Kristallnacht and the burning of the Synagogues we were in dire straits. My brother and I had a visa to go to

Sweden in May 1939. The day before we were due to leave, our mother received her affidavit from England to go as a domestic servant in a distant relative's home, together with our permit to go on the Kindertransport. We left on 21 May 1939. As children, we looked forward to the adventure. Mama probably felt a lot different, leaving her mother and all our other relatives behind, but for the sake of her children she had to be brave.

I cannot recall the train ride until the train finally rolled across the Dutch border and we were free!

I stayed in an orphanage in the suburbs of London for four weeks. I remember very clearly my feeling of loneliness and homesickness. I couldn't speak English and although I was treated very kindly I was very unhappy. We had never been separated before.

Bert was eventually placed with a Gentile family in Coventry where he was reasonably happy. The Shepherds tried very hard to make him feel comfortable. 'Mom' was a bus conductor and 'Pop' was a postal worker. They had two children, a boy and a girl, older than Bert. Bert had piano lessons every week with their hard earned money.

I was placed with the Simons family in Coventry. Mrs Simons was very kind to me and tried to make me feel at home. I went to school and was lucky enough to have a Jewish teacher, Mrs Jacobs, who sensed my plight and helped me a great deal. The headmistress' name was Miss Smith and I had a hard time getting it straight. Most of the time I said 'Miss Miss' to the delight of the other children.

After school, when I came home, I had to clean the house and I worked to the best of my ability (which wasn't very good). More often than not I burned the stuff or ruined it in some fashion. At ten years old I wasn't too adept in the kitchen.

When I had been with the Simons two months, the war broke out and my personal life went from bad to worse. Mr Simons' wife worked very hard and he did nothing. The son John teased me incessantly and always had me in tears. John was four years older than I. The daughter Esther was two years younger. Esther shared a bed with me, which she wet every night.

My writing paper and stamps began to disappear and I had no money with which to purchase more, therefore I couldn't write to my mother to let her know how I felt.

My brother lived just a few streets away, but I never had enough time to see him, except when we went to *Cheder* once a week. That too came to an end when the bombing started.

Coventry seemed to be a favourite target of the Nazis. As matters became worse the Simons fled to the country. Mrs Simons knew some people through her dress shop business. They offered to take all of us in – five people, and so we moved to Edgehills near Banbury, a tiny hamlet. It was idyllic – the nearest place to heaven that I had ever seen, but it was because of 'us Germans that they had to leave their home.' We stayed in Edgehills two weeks and then moved to Kineton at the bottom of the hill. Mrs Simons went to Coventry to her shop twice a week and came home in the evening. Whenever I was alone in the house with Mr Simons he would chase me all around the table and assault me. I took as much abuse as I could stand and finally had enough guts to let my mother know what was going on.

With the help of Bloomsbury House I went to a Home Training School at Westmill near Buntingford which had been evacuated from London. The teachers were like mothers to us. There were thirty-six girls, three of whom were Jewish. We lived on an estate which belonged to a colonel fighting in North Africa and was used by the school for the duration of the war. Each of us had chores to attend to every day, and we also had to take care of the animals. I was assigned to Alma the goat. I had to clean Alma's stall out and feed her. Alma smelled like all goats, but I didn't care. I was happy. It was here that I met my dear friend Rita Hauser whom I met again at the Kindertransport reunion in Harrow. I had thought she was in Israel. The grounds were beautiful. We had fresh vegetables and fruit, a flower garden, a pond with tadpoles, we even had a hockey field, and daffodils as far as the eye could see in the spring. It was here that I learned to cook. I have loved it ever since.

At holiday times I went home to visit my mother in London, who in the meantime had rented an apartment with three other friends and was working making raincoats in a factory. My brother came from Hertford where he had been placed with a very warm and loving family so that he could attend the Battersea Grammar School, which was also evacuated from London.

Despite the bombings we were happy together and looked forward to the precious days. I started to appreciate Shakespeare. I went to see Laurence Olivier at the Old Vic. I attended my first opera at Covent Garden. My cultural life began to awaken because our mother encouraged us despite having very little money. I had to leave Westmill at age fifteen, since that was as far as the school was equipped to teach. That was June 1944 and the war in Europe was in full swing.

I went to work for a dentist in Barnet. After nine months we received our affidavits to go to the USA.

We left from Greenock on the hospital ship *Aquitania* and arrived in New York on 12 April, one day before Roosevelt died. Our relatives met us in New York. We have had a good and fruitful life ever since.

I thank Britain for saving us, but I think the world could have done more for humanity as it stood by and watched.

*   *   *

Laura Gabriel

(Eichengrün, Gelsenkirchen), New Jersey, USA

I remember my parents and grandparents seeing us off at the railroad station – my parents reassuring us that we would soon be reunited, and my grandmother crying; she and my grandfather died at Theresienstadt – it was the last time we would see them.

The memories of the train-ride and the Channel crossing are dim to me now, but I do recall the feeling of being assembled with all the other children in a large hall, where our foster-parents were waiting for us. When my name was called, I was greeted with a warm hug by a lady in a fur coat and her husband – Esther and Jack Benabo from North Finchley. My brother went to an acquaintance of theirs – so we were able to be in touch.

I was taken home to North Finchley to meet my new brothers and sisters: John sixteen, Peggy who was just my age, Ted six and Ann five. So these wonderful generous people had decided to take a refugee child in addition to their own four. Peggy, shortly after her twelfth birthday, was dressed in a pink evening gown, topped by the school blazer and school hat, on her way to a school dance. I was very impressed indeed. Thanks to my parents' foresight, I had been given private English lessons, so was able to converse, though not exactly fluently, with my new family. The day after my arrival, Peggy and I went to the pictures, something we had no longer been permitted to do in Germany. I still remember it: *That Certain Age* with Robert Stack and Deanna Durbin singing *My Own*. To me, it was the best film I ever saw because I was free to go in and enjoy it, without fear. There are so many memories of those first days and all those that followed during the two-year sojourn in England.

What makes my experience with my new family even more outstanding is that once I explained to my foster parents my parents' dilemma of waiting for their American Quota numbers to come up, they obtained for them a permit to come to England during the waiting period. Mr Benabo even gave my dad a job in his business. So, three weeks before the war began, my parents arrived in England thanks to my foster parents' generosity. My brother joined them in London but I continued living with my English family – going to school with Peggy – until we left for the United States in October 1940. I spent weekends with my parents – weekdays with my other family.

Through all these years we've kept in touch. Mr and Mrs. Benabo passed away in the early 1980s. But they visited us in the United States in the 1950s and my husband and I helped them and the family celebrate their fiftieth and sixtieth wedding anniversaries. Peggy – now Margaret Hallet – and her husband Tony is still like my sister today – we have visited each other across the Atlantic a number of times and are in constant touch. John, while in the Services, visited us during the war; I am also in touch with the other children.

An interesting aside: only Mr Benabo was Jewish in the family!

Thanks to pure chance – my life was permanently enriched by these wonderful people – and my parents' lives were saved.

*   *   *

Herbert Gale

(Groschler, Jever), London, UK

I came from a little garden town in Friesland, Northern Germany called Jever, near Oldenburg.

In December 1938, the Rabbi from Oldenburg told my parents of a children's transport which was leaving for England in nine days' time – collecting point Hamburg. I was fifteen, my brother twelve at the time. Our parents decided that we should leave. We said our sad goodbyes, promising to write often, not knowing what the future would bring. I was very bewildered and could not fully understand what was going on.

The next morning, after a rough crossing, we docked at Harwich and from there were taken to Dovercourt Holiday Camp. We stayed in Dovercourt for a week or so and were invited by local families for tea. After a few days we were asked to choose whether we would like to go to a hostel in Belfast, Leeds or London. I chose Leeds. I remember that, although my young brother was with me, I felt very lonely and homesick, but everybody had problems and personal miseries. One boy was always wetting the bed and there were lots of arguments and fights.

As time went on we were given lessons and Hebrew services. We were invited sometimes to the members of the Jewish committee's homes and went to Jewish clubs. We were given sixpence per week spending money. After six months, the boys who were old enough were sent out to work. I was sent to an upholstery firm, where I had to sew one side of a cushion in readiness for it to be stuffed for a three piece suite. I was given fare money and a packed lunch. After a while I changed my job and became an assistant to a barber and hairdresser.

My younger brother was due to have his *Bar Mitzvah*. A small service was held for him at the hostel. My cousin remembers going to this and has since told me how pathetic it all was, in his ill-fitting suit! But they all did the best they could!

I had only heard from my parents a couple of times and a parcel with a suit arrived, then no more news.

I asked one of our Jewish customers, who had a large factory, to give me a job rebuilding old sewing machines and he did! I was taught the work. A few of my workmates were very kind, but some were anti-semitic. A favourite past-time of theirs was to fill my pocket with grease and to thread a 6"x½" bolt through the buttonholes of my coat, put a nut on the end and damaging the thread of the bolt making it impossible for me to remove it without putting it in a vice and hacksawing it.

At the digs where I was living, the landlord was a decorator, and I helped him at week-ends to earn a bit more money. I changed my job again and became a sewing machine mechanic with a large menswear factory. I worked with nice people and really learned the trade. I ended up in charge of the repairs for all of the machines, but I was restless and seeked adventure, being the age that I was. I heard that the Jewish Brigade was being formed, and I volunteered. My workmates and boss were sorry to see me go, but I felt that I had to. I sold all my clothes and went to London to collect my uniform. Later on I went into the British Army and became an interpreter. I thought that somehow I could get back into Germany to look for my parents. This I did, and discovered that they had died in Auschwitz concentration camp.

We have since returned to Jever, as guests of a charming young history teacher, who was writing a book about the history of the Jews of Jever, together with a group of his students who were determined to make amends. A block of flats now stands where my father's house once stood. We were treated with kindness, generosity, and respect from the moment we arrived, but felt uneasy as we remembered the animosity that once prevailed. I felt alien in the town in which I was born; felt the guilt of the old residents as they clammed up in conversation. But we could not ignore the eagerness and enthusiasm of the young students anxious to please us, and their zest for knowledge as they tried to understand why there appeared to be a gap in the history of their country, as they questioned their parents. In their search for the truth they were beginning to unravel the misdeeds of their forefathers and we admired their determination to work for a better future.

*   *   *

Ingrid Gassman

(Hamburg), Kidlington, Oxon, UK

I came to England in December 1938, aged nine and a half, and was at Dovercourt for about one month. The thought of the journey was exciting until I was separated from my two brothers at the Hook of Holland. I did not find them again for what seemed like months, but it could only have been about two weeks. On 3 January we were moved to a farm in Pluckley, Kent, and soon after I was sent to a Christian family with three sons of similar ages to mine.

Like most Kinder, I passed through my own traumas and was a very difficult adolescent. My foster parents had the patience of Job. They always reminded me of my family and insisted that I wrote to my brothers and sister. The whole family accepted me as one of their own (and still do). I learned a great deal of English in the middle of the night, when I would awaken the household by having a nightmare – a legacy from three months in hospital in Hamburg in 1938.

My confusion was threefold. Firstly, for years I could not be sure if I was German or English, Jew or Gentile. I used to say that I got sore from sitting on the fence. In recent years, however, I have resolved these problems and at last come to terms with myself. Secondly, I had a thirst for education. In my foster home higher education was not a priority, although they were prepared to pay for it. However, when in my thirties, I attained a Teaching Certificate, and later a degree. The third cause of conflict stemmed from my own family. My mother survived the war, but was a jealous and unpredictable person. I was constantly hoping to get a little of her approval, but never did.

Without the placid security of my foster parents' home, I doubt whether I would ever have reached my goal of becoming a well-balanced person.

* * *

Gabrielle Gatzert

(Moos, Ulm), Reston, Va., USA

What really saved my life was that my father and my sixteen-year old brother had been in the concentration camp after Kristallnacht. This made my mother realize that I had to leave Germany as soon as possible. But where to go and how, was the big question. I remember sitting in our living room in Ulm with my mother, when she suddenly remembered she had a very close friend, who was the sister of Anna Essinger, the principal of the New Herrlingen school that immigrated to England from Germany. My mother wrote to her and arranged for me to be accepted in the school. The only way I could leave Germany was with a children's transport and we applied immediately. Since my mother was not well I bought all the clothes for England myself and sewed name tags on everything. Every day I watched the mail, waiting for the letter that would enable me to leave Germany. On top of that, in January 1939, I broke my leg at several places and luckily I did not get the notice until 13 June, when I was able to leave.

I met a lot of other children who were leaving Germany from Bremen on the *Europa*. The picture I will never forget as long as I live and which upset me most at the time, was a beautiful little girl, her head full of curls, and her mother kissing her goodbye. I do not know what happened to this little girl and whether she ever was reunited with her family.

I was terribly sick during the boat trip and could not get out of my cabin. In addition someone got scarlet fever. What did this mean? I could not go to New Herrlingen as I might be contagious. For hours we sat in Victoria station until it was finally decided that we would be sent to a hospital in London for complete isolation. After about three weeks in the hospital, I finally arrived at the New Herrlingen school in Kent. When war broke out, the school was evacuated to Shropshire to be away from the coast. The thing that made an everlasting impression on me was that, when we stopped in the middle of a town with our bus, the people heard that we were refugees and made a collection and gave us the money. I was overwhelmed by their kindness.

I found the time at school difficult because I did not know whether my parents were alive. They had initially gone to Luxemburg, finally ending up in the USA.

After finishing my schooling in Shropshire, a wonderful English lady helped me to go to Birmingham where I learned shorthand and typing in order to be self-supporting. I also met some distant relatives there who were like second parents. I still am in touch with them – both are very old.

In Birmingham I lived at first in an all girls' hostel with Sophie Friedländer and Hilde Jarecki being in charge. It was one big family there. When that closed I moved to another hostel for boys and girls. I remember one of the wardens being blind and it was hard for him to control all of us. After that I rented a room with a girl friend where I had a landlady who was quite a character. Every day she wore a red robe and tied a stocking around her waist as a belt. Her brother came home drunk every night, but she cooked very good meals and gave us part of her rations. I had a job doing war work. I was financially independent, earning thirty-five shillings, out of which I paid twenty-five shillings in rent. After the war I was reunited with my parents in June 1946 in Rochester, New York. It was a very hard adjustment as we had been separated for seven years and they were struggling for their existence and extremely poor.

My experiences in England taught me to become a stronger person as I was alone from the age of thirteen to twenty. This helped me later on in life. When I lost my husband after thirty-two years, I felt I was able to fight and make it alone again and I DID! I have a wonderful daughter and son-in-law, love it in Virginia and make the most of life.

I appreciate the opportunity to put some of my history on record.

* * *

Eva Gladdish

(Berger, Vienna), High Wycombe, UK

I come from Vienna. One day I saw people I knew by sight scrubbing the pavement, supervised by a uniformed man with an armband. I heard a woman screaming, terrified one night; there was a bonfire of books in a road near us. I had to go to a different school. I overheard how a professor friend of ours with a weak heart had been made to climb the horizontal bars in a gymnasium; when he collapsed, water had been thrown over him until eventually he died. And there was the day I was coming home, when someone grabbed me shouting 'Look out'. A bang followed and the Synagogue I was about to pass collapsed.

Our world had radically divided into 'them and us'; and the heartache of 'Mischlings', those of mixed marriages. At the time I could not understand it, nor that our lives would change for ever.

About November I was told that I would soon be going to Sweden or England and naturally assumed it would be with my parents. There was a new coat and hat, even a muff to match. I had my picture taken in a new dress, disappointed that only a little of it showed; I didn't know about passport pictures. My half sister visited us from Czechoslovakia.

Then one day friends called in to say goodbye; that evening we went off to the station carrying a small case. It was cold, dark and wet. The platform was crowded with other families – and then all the children were put on the train. So that was why my parents had been so sad for weeks past; they were staying behind and I was going alone with a lot of children I didn't know.

They were ordered to stand way back from the train; all we could do was look at them – the train was delayed! After seemingly forever they were allowed on to the train again. Everyone wanted a last kiss, to hold hands. The little girl by me couldn't reach, so I tried to help her. 'Take care of Dorli' said one of our mothers.

Eventually there was the excitement of crossing the border at Aachen; finally the train stopped at the Hook of Holland and we were told to get off.

Onto the ship we went and were allocated places. It wasn't long before the motion of the ship sent us off to sleep.

We were just in time to join the last children down the gangplank. Someone put a name and number label round our necks as we did.

After arriving in England we got on the last coach; we turned off into a gate – the Holiday Camp, Harwich. Next we were allocated to huts along muddy roadways. Three beds had small cases on them, so I put mine on the fourth. It was very cold in the hut. Outside a group of older children were passing, so I followed them and found myself in a very big hall; children everywhere and lots of noise. Food was being served so I went and waited my turn to eat. Bedtime came and I got lost; one road of huts looked much like another in the dark. I thought of a warm bed and sleep. It wasn't warm, but I slept just the same.

The second day started like the first, except another stove had appeared and things seemed to be more organized generally. Intermittently some people walked round and a child here and there was called away. A silver-haired lady accompanied by a man stopped at our group, walked on. Then one of us was called and presently I was too. Mrs Duncan questioned me in English, the man interpreted and she noted down my answers. I was sent back to my group – what was this all about? Soon a helper told me to get my things. Returning I found a little group gathered round Mrs Duncan, and we all went off.

Next thing we were on a train, excited, warm, sharing round our remaining titbits. Suddenly it happened again; the train stopped and we were told to get off; hurry up, shut cases, put on coats and away down the platform to sit down at some tables. Our interpreter brought tea and food – and horrors – I missed my muff with my three treasures in it: Mother's silver coin bracelet from Father's POW days in Russia; grandmother's gold pocket-watch, and the new little pen and pencil set in a case for which I had saved for ages. Must have left it in the train; so Mrs Duncan went off to find them. Her sad face told me the answer when she returned; but the loss had been reported and they were sure to be found. I was inconsolable. I felt I had lost the last tangible bits of my parents.

We boarded the next train. Darkness descended long before we reached Bath. There we were taken to a hall where some people sat waiting. We were to be distributed among them.

My turn came and I was introduced to Mrs White, who started chatting as we left; I smiled and felt foolish . . . and yes, a bit frightened. We got on a crowded tram and were offered tiny spaces facing each other on the benches at the back. The people around and Mrs White started chatting, looking at me. How I wished I could understand, explain why I looked such a mess – and above all I wished I were back with my parents, in my warm home, among people not speaking a foreign language. Those thoughts were to haunt me for a long time to come.

There followed my first introduction to cold English bedrooms with washbasins and jugs of cold water. And to English mustard – too much and I burnt my mouth; my hosts and their two adult children thought it was funny, but how to explain? What a joy to meet up with the rest of our little group next day and chat a short time while pictures were taken.

To my surprise Christmas Eve brought no festivities, but next morning I was given a dog pyjama-case. I had always wanted a dog, so this was the next best thing. We all went out to tea and party games! I tried to follow the instructions for running round chairs to music, hunting a thimble and join in the laughter.

A few days later Mrs Duncan arrived. I was to move again – too old to be adopted by the Whites, not old enough to be an 'au pair'. Please leave your dog behind for the next child, have a little pincushion dolly instead. So off I went without my dog for comfort.

We ended up at one of those tall Bath houses with only one or two rooms per storey and were greeted by two, what seemed to me, very old ladies. My room was at the very top of the house, freezing cold. They lived mainly on the first floor, their deaf and dumb sister on the ground floor. I spent hours in my room writing to my parents and couldn't understand why I had not had the letter they had promised. I knitted what was to be my school scarf on the first floor, did jigsaws and learned sign language with their sister and got warm running up and down stairs. Navy clothes and black shoes were bought – and I was taken to a pantomime. Funny child, not laughing and shouting like the others! Early in January, after a long car journey, I found myself in a convent.

I was told that my beloved mother had died in Vienna. Some months later my father fled to Yugoslavia.

Altogether I spent three years at the Convent boarding school, with lessons, crocodile walks, games. There were much loved music lessons, helping with the tiny tots, Saturday night dancing to the gramophone – and long holidays with no home to go to, except occasionally a schoolfriend's. But probably by its very nature the school routine kept me on a reasonably even keel and did its best to turn me into a young English lady.

On my sixteenth birthday my headmistress took me to the police station to be issued with an Alien's Pass; and the constable said: 'No, I couldn't spend a few days away at my friend's house fifteen miles away'. After all I might be a spy!

* * *

Walter Glückman

(Berlin), Elstree, Herts., UK

EALING HOSTEL 50 YEARS LATER. A SUCCESS STORY

'Opened June 1939 and fully subsidized by the Ealing Jewish Community for approximately twenty Kindertransport boys aged fifteen to sixteen years. Its purpose to give them a home, teach them English and a trade or craft so that within three years they should become totally independent. Closed in 1942, its aim having been fully achieved.'

This would be a very brief description, but could never convey the friendship and feeling that gradually grew among its inmates due to a large extent by the leadership, guidance and warmth shown by its Matron, the late Miss Irma Rose. Here were twenty boys thrown together from different parts of Germany and Austria, most of them never to see their parents and family again. Circumstances could certainly not have been more difficult. War broke out with all its traumas, half the boys, plus the hostel's cook and her husband, being interned; one boy losing his life when the ship taking him to internment was torpedoed. Then there was the black-out, rationing and 'English' food that could never be quite like home. A shilling pocket money had to last the week; our wages having to be submitted.

I well remember one of the highlights, being a special treat of coffee and cake after dinner every Friday night. When the hostel closed in 1942 and the boys now being spread out in various digs, Miss Rose extended to us an open invitation to her little flat for coffee and cake and a chat every Friday night, thus helping us all not to lose contact.

Some of the boys subsequently volunteered to join the Armed Forces and at the end of the war about half emigrated. However the foresight and inspiration of the weekly get-together eventually almost created a new 'family'. After we married and established our own homes we started to take turns for what ultimately became a regular monthly meeting. We shared most of our *Simchas* and our children regarded Miss Rose and her sister as second grandparents; the ladies never missing their birthdays with a little gift.

On the occasion of the fiftieth anniversary we felt that we wanted to thank the Ealing community by suggesting our attendance from far and wide at a *Shabbat* Service and special *Kiddush,* at which we intended to make a donation in memory of 1939-42. Unfortunately this idea was not accepted, probably due to the old generation no longer being around. Instead we joined in with the Harrow reunion and the gift went to the Great Ormond Street Children's Hospital appeal. At this wonderful function we actually rediscovered the whereabouts of two ex-hostel boys, one of whom had come all the way from the USA.

I called this a success story. Out of terrible circumstances something good and positive has come. Although mostly retired, the ex-Ealing hostel boys still hold their monthly meetings and we will continue to do so as long as we can.

*   *   *

Lisa Golabek Roberts

(Jura, Vienna), Los Angeles, USA

I left Vienna with a children's transport in 1938, aged fourteen, for London, where I stayed with relatives and looked after babies. When the Blitz got too much for the family, they left and arranged for me to work in the country, about 220 miles from London. There I was employed as a kitchen maid, later on as a parlour and lady's maid. This was in a beautiful castle. The owner was a former captain in the British army. He was about sixty years old. His wife was a young woman of about twenty-five. There was a butler, a cook, two other maids and myself. I stayed there for a few months and, although the lady of the house was very kind to me, I was very lonely. So one day I took my bicycle and ran away.

Abandoning the bike, I took the train from Brighton to London. I begged the Jewish Family Service to help me learn a profession. They put me into a hostel and I went to work in a factory. My type of work was millinery, dressmaking, shorthand and typing.

My lucky day came when the matron of the hostel made me enter a piano competition so that I could win a four year scholarship to the Royal Academy of Music. I had studied piano for quite a few years as a little girl in Vienna, and had been fortunate to be able to continue practising in the hostel. I entered this audition with some of the repertoire which I had learned in Vienna and was delighted when I won first prize. This enabled me to study for some years with one of the most prestigious Professors, Mabel Floyd, of the Royal Academy of Music.

I met my husband in Paris whilst on a benefit recital for Israel. He had fought many years in the underground in Paris and received the 'Croix de Guerre' from General Charles de Gaulle. We left immediately for Los Angeles, California. We have two daughters, Mona and Renee, who are now famous pianists in the United States. I lost my husband Michel in 1977. In 1981 I married Bill Roberts, a famous orchestra leader in the USA.

* * *

Marion Goldwater

(Danziger, Berlin), London, UK

My brother Hans and I came to England, unaccompanied, with a Kindertransport from Berlin on 1 March 1939. We came under the guarantorship of Lord Alan Sainsbury together with twenty-five other children. He paid for our education and well-being until we were both eighteen years old.

* * *

Joseph Goldsmith

(Goldschmidt, Munich), Newcastle-upon-Tyne, UK

My story really begins with my sister Sofie who came to England from Munich in 1933 at age thirteen. My parents had been advised by the headmaster of her school that nothing more could be done to further her education as she was very gifted. Fortunately, they were able to find a sponsor for her where her being Jewish would not prevent her full potential being developed. It is therefore primarily because of her that the rest of the Goldschmidt family eventually came to England. Sofie was by then able to find sponsors or guarantors for us.

After leaving school in July 1938 I was working at a *Lehrgartnerei* in Munich until 9 November 1938, when it was closed down by the Nazis. On 16 March 1939 I left Munich, having obtained a permit to come to England as an agricultural student. I met my guarantor in London. From there I was sent to Chichester in Sussex, where I worked on a farm, then on to Wallingford doing the same type of work.

My parents came separately, my father in June and my mother together with my younger sister Berta aged two in late August 1939.

I was interned in Huyton, Liverpool, and then on the Isle of Man for three months. From there I was sent to Canada – sailing one day after the *Arandorra Star* was sunk. My mother, who knew that I was destined for Canada, made enquiries as to losses, and saw a list with the near enough same name – G. GOLDSCHMIDT, and thought that it was me. She had a nervous breakdown and because of this, my father, who was at that time also interned, was released on compassionate grounds.

I spent thirteen months in Canada doing all kinds of work. On my return I was sent back to the Isle of Man for another three months. After that I was released and spent the rest of the war working on a farm in Guildford.

Eventually, at the end of hostilities, I got a job in a bakery, worked at different companies in London, finally at the Dorchester Hotel.

I met my wife in 1952 and we married in 1954. Our first son Michael was born in 1957. We moved to Newcastle in 1960 where our second son Alan was born. Michael works for British Rail, and Alan is in the Civil Service. I have been retired just over two years, and am now enjoying a more restful life.

*   *   *

Marga Goren-Gothelf
(Brandenburg), Rishon LeZion, Israel

I was one of fifty-six children, aged thirteen to fifteen, who were given permission to enter England from Zbaszyn. We had been deported from Germany to Zbaszyn on 28 October 1938 because our parents were Polish passport holders. The Polish Government had announced that it would not renew these passports if the holders had been living outside Poland for more than five years. The Germans decided to deport all Jewish Polish subjects. This deportation was the cause of CRYSTAL NIGHT, as Hershel Grynspan's parents were amongst the deportees from Hanover who had been shot at near the Polish borders.

Our group left Zbaszyn on 15 January 1939 for Gdynia, where we boarded the Polish ship *Warszawa* for London. Both the Baltic and the North Sea were very rough. When the German officials boarded the ship at the entrance to the Kiel Canal we were scared as we thought this was the end. I was thirteen years old at the time and the whole situation was very frightening. We arrived at the London Docks on 15 February 1939.

There was a reception committee waiting for us and, after we were given our first meal on British soil, they decided what our fate would be. There was Rabbi Schneider from the Gateshead *Yeshiva* looking for suitable candidates. There were families looking for a foster-child, there were relatives who came for their kin, and there was Rabbi Louis Yitzchak Rabinovitz of Walm Lane Synagogue in Cricklewood, London. The Walm Lane community had at that time opened two hostels for two classes of the Yavne School from Cologne and since we were the right age, Rabbi Rabinovitz took us with him. The boys were taken to the hostel in Minster Road. The girls' hostel wasn't ready yet and so we were sent to stay with families. I stayed with the Lipmans at Sidmouth Road. I didn't know a word of English and they didn't speak any German. That made communicating very difficult. They had two children who were studying Hebrew and it was from their Hebrew textbooks that I learnt my first English words. After about two weeks the hostel at 243 Willesden Lane, Willesden Green, London was ready to welcome us and at the beginning of March we moved in. It was a spacious house with a back garden and lawn where we spent time at sports and games. We took turns in cleaning, working in the garden and helping in the kitchen. The hostel was run by the matron, Mrs Cohen from Berlin, and a cook, Mrs Glazer, from Prague.

Our days were well planned, we got up early, tidied and cleaned our rooms, prayed together, had breakfast and went to school (Chamberlayne Wood Road School). The walk took us about twenty-five minutes. We returned to the hostel for lunch and went back to finish our studies. The teachers at the school couldn't be bothered with those of us who didn't speak

English, there was no special programme for us. They used to tell us to write letters home or bring some handicrafts.

Friday nights and Saturday mornings we went to the Synagogue in Walm Lane and there we used to meet the boys from the boys' hostel. Sunday mornings we attended lessons at the *Talmud Torah* at the Synagogue and sometimes in the afternoons a few of the committee ladies would come in their cars and take some of us sightseeing in London.

Our life went on in this way till the middle of August 1939 when we were invited by *Habonim* to take part in their big summer camp in Bedfordshire. We spent a very enjoyable fortnight there. As soon as we returned to London we were evacuated like all the other London school-children. We, the girls, were evacuated to Northampton and were billeted in pairs with Gentile families. The boys were sent to Bedford. A small group of us (boys and girls) went from there to a *Youth Aliya Hachshara* at the David Eder Farm at Harrietsham, Maidstone in Kent in spring 1940.

I can't really finish this account without stressing the great part Rabbi Louis Yitzchak Rabinovitz played in our lives at that crucial period. He not only provided for us (he himself used to bring and carry crates of fruit and vegetables to our hostel early in the morning) but he was aware of and concerned about the problems we faced being separated at such a young age from our families. He talked to us individually when he saw the need and corresponded with our families whenever necessary. He conducted one of our *Seder*-nights and often spent a Friday night or *Shabbat* lunch with us. All that at a time when he was very busy trying to find more sponsors to save more children from Germany and had of course a family of his own.

I stayed in England until May 1946. The last six months or so I spent working with children who had survived the concentration camps and were given a fresh start in England. I was with them for a few months at Wintershill Hall near Southampton and later transferred with a group who had suffered from TB, to Cardross in Scotland.

*   *   *

Susanne Graham

(Burghardt, Hamburg), Welwyn Garden City, UK

I was ten and my brother eight at the beginning of 1939. I cannot recall how Hans and I got onto *Le Normandie*, but I do remember lying in the cabin feeling ill. Later I was told that that feeling was sea-sickness.

In the evening a large group of us gathered on deck and sang German, Hebrew and Yiddish songs. I knew many songs and put my heart into this group singing. An adult passed, I felt his eyes, expressing sadness, compassion. I told Hans to be brave and not to cry. It was I who felt the need to be brave! Neither of us did cry.

Next morning someone sought me out. I was made to sit on a chair on deck in the middle of a group of strangers. A Rabbi tried to speak to me in Yiddish, which I did not understand. Nor did I speak French. My mother had given a French steward a diamond ring and my name. She would have been willing for the steward to pocket the ring, rather than the Nazis appropriate it. Thus I arrived in England with one case, one Deutschmark and a diamond ring.

A French boy, some years older than me, and I played deck quoits. We shared a good game and I long cherished the feeling that human beings could understand one another, even without a common language.

On arrival we stayed overnight in a Southampton convent. Next day we waited in a sombre hall to be collected. Hans and I waited longest. Later we travelled across London by taxi with Miss Modell who was collecting us for our sponsors. She seemed very kind and gave me two very large coins to keep – two pennies. We were set down in Lewisham some way from yet another transit point. My one permitted case was heavily packed, so that I could just lift it, but not carry it. Miss Modell took my brother's hand and his case and went ahead. I struggled on behind and soon felt unable to go on. I put the case down and tried to push it along the pavement, without success. My heart sank, I despaired – I wished I'd never come. That feeling of despair is still vividly recalled.

We were finally deposited at a small boarding school in Birchington and were happy there. The couple in charge had sons of their own.

We were moved to a new small boarding school. Oh so different! There were fourteen children and fourteen dogs. The dogs had preferential treatment. We were allowed one bath a fortnight. The five elderly spinster sisters did not seem to like children. They had adopted Stephen – an orphan. Stephen was sixteen and spent much of his day peeling potatoes and doing other menial jobs. Twice he attempted to run away to sea and was brought back.

Mother had managed to come to England and was working in a hospital in Lincolnshire. I wrote asking whether we could be near her. I said that I was not happy and mentioned that we were having to pray for our 'daily severely rationed bread'! Before we left, I was taken into the huge, dark and unused dining room, and told how ungrateful I was, that Hans and I had been accepted for less than the normal fees and that I would regret what I had done, and would never again receive a good education. Luckily it turned out otherwise.

For a very short while the three of us were together in the same small town of Grantham. Hans and I stayed with Mr and Mrs Marsden and their two daughters. Then war was declared. Mr Marsden was moved by his firm and

Mother was forced to leave her work in the maternity unit. Mother went to work on the land. Hans went to live with a vicar twenty-five miles away. I stayed on in Grantham.

So, aged eleven, I was the only refugee in the town. Only with hindsight can I acknowledge the loneliness and the isolation experienced in the war years. Some people were kind and thoughtful, others were not. After several foster home moves, I settled happily with Auntie Win and Uncle Ernest Jealous and at sixteen, at last, I was allowed to be just me.

I was in the long busy school cloakroom when a girl announced loudly and venomously that I was a Nazi and a Jew. Quietly I continued to dry my hands on the roller towel – shattered. Another time classmates and I were playing Monopoly, sitting on the floor around the board. One of the girls spat on my money. The others followed suit. Once more I sat very still hurting inside. Years later one of them, Frances, told me how much she regretted that incident.

To be alone and to be an 'enemy alien' was hard. For instance one day a school prefect hissed in my ear,

'You know you are not wanted here.'

Money was naturally very short. This was felt as a challenge rather than hardship. I picked potatoes and peas, and did cleaning jobs. Also rosehips, gathered for their Vitamin C, brought in twopence per pound. I saved hard and bought a Raleigh cycle. It was wonderful to have a good bike and I frequently went on long country rides.

At school, the morning after the VE Day celebrations in the town, two of our young teachers were twittering about an overwhelmingly handsome Air Force officer. That officer had walked me home and kissed me good night. I am not beautiful but on VE day was presumably endowed with a special radiance.

Hostilities were over.

*   *   *

Bea Green, J.P., M.A.

(Siegel, Munich), London, UK

One minute to midnight – the train for Frankfurt hisses its imminent departure from the Munich Hauptbahnhof. It is 27 June 1939.

I am fourteen years old and I am wearing a suit, a raincoat, a hat on the back of my head and gloves. I feel quite grown up and excited. I have already made friends with two girls in my compartment, one older than I and one little orphan, a pretty girl. There is some shouting and waving and slowly the

train moves forward. I see my mother stepping behind my father so I shouldn't see her cry. I see the gesture and suddenly feel hollow in my stomach. But I cannot cry or I won't cry, I don't remember. My uncle takes a photograph, and we are off. Goodbye Munich. Goodbye parents. Goodbye to that mixture of security of a warm Jewish home and to events since 1933, when my father was beaten up by Nazi thugs and led around Munich with a placard round his neck; of Walchensee where we had a little house and the notice at its entrance that said '*Juden sind hier unerwünscht*'.

We spend what is left of the night in a big hall in Frankfurt where a lot more children join us and then we're off to the Hoek van Holland. We come to the border of Holland and before leaving Germany we have to show our passports with the letter 'J' stamped on the front page in red. Also I have been given an additional name, I am now Maria Beate *Sarah* Siegel. I rather like it. I think it's nice that all the other girls are also called Sarah. The border guards look at our passports. I am a bit nervous because my mother has hidden a couple of extra ten mark notes wrapped up in one of my sandwiches. It's all right. The border guard is not interested in my sandwiches. More puffing and hissing of the engine and we are in Holland.

It's night time when we get to the ship. We sleep in bunks and arrive in Harwich at dawn. A little girl cries and keeps repeating '*Mutti, Mutti*'. I put my arm round her and tell her she'll see her soon.

We are shepherded into a large, dark hall where we sit on wooden benches. I am separated from my Munich companions by now. I am not homesick, I am not unhappy. I feel I am in a grey vacuum. 'S' is far down the alphabet. Most kids seem to have been called for. Then I hear my name. I am being collected by a lady in a lilac-coloured suit. She has a very soft voice and asks me how I am or how I do; I don't quite understand. We find my luggage and are driven in a very large car with a chauffeur to a very large flat in Portland Place. A room and a lovely bed await me. Miss Williams turns down the covers and I go to sleep.

Miss Williams is the daughter of my guardian, Mrs Williams of Brasted Hall, near Sevenoaks, Kent. We drive down in the same big car the next day. Mrs Williams gives me a little kiss on the cheek. She is small but determined. Margot comes into the drawing room. She's been looking forward to having someone to speak German to. Then I meet Miss Currie-Smith, Mrs Williams' lady companion. She cannot figure where to put Margot and me socially. She is a bit put out. Margot and I share a bedroom and are given the billiard room for our sitting room. The house is big and there are a lot of servants. I like the house.

I am supposed to settle in for a day or two but I want to go to school. I haven't been since Kristallnacht. So I am allowed to go next day. I am wearing my dirndl and am stared at. The headmistress balks at my name: Beate. Did I have another? I suggest the other two but she decides on 'Bay-ar-tar'.

Margot has been with Mrs Williams for two weeks. A few days after my arrival, I ask her how long it has taken her to get over being homesick. She says she hasn't yet. My heart sinks.

Can it really be fifty years ago? My home is here now; I even feel English, Anglaise, Inglesa, when I'm abroad. I've been back to Munich and I cannot honestly say that I feel German. And yet ... there is that little trace of homesickness and I don't know what for.

*   *   *

Olga Grilli

(Gabanyiova, Prague), Poughkeepsie, NY, USA

It was 31 July 1939, 11.30 at night. We were at the railroad station in Prague and the children were assembled in groups, all with rucksacks on their back, each with a number tied on a string dangling from the neck. The last goodbyes were said and we were put on the train. Slowly it pulled out of Prague – I was looking out of the window and could see the platform full of parents wiping their eyes, waving their last goodbyes to us until we moved out of sight.

Next day we reached England. I was met by my sponsor and was soon on my way to the Manchester area where I was to spend the next two years.

A new life lay in store for all of us – I did not know then that I would never see my parents again and that one of the darkest periods in the history of the world and the Jews was just beginning.

* * *

Gusta Gross

(Moszkowicz, Danzig), Tel Aviv, Israel

I came to England through Bloomsbury House from Danzig in May 1939 with a children's transport. I was fifteen years old at the time. Another girl and myself went to York. I stayed with a very nice family, Mr and Mrs. Watsham. They were Gentiles and very kind. As I came from a religious Jewish family I wanted to stay with Jews, so after a while I was sent to Harrogate to a Jewish girls' hostel. I didn't like it very much, so the family in York took me back. When Mr Watsham went to the Army I had to leave them and I wandered from family to family. I learned English in a night school and as I learned it rather quickly and knew German and Polish, I got a job in London with the Polish Government in exile at the end of 1942. I earned well so I could keep myself and stayed in a boarding house. I married in 1945, had a son in 1946 and in 1948 came to Israel. My maiden name was Moszkowicz.

My younger brother, Pesach, arrived in York with the last transport during the last week of August 1939. He stayed for a short time with a Jewish family in York, then was sent to a boys' hostel in Leeds. At the age of seventeen and a half he joined the British Army, became an officer and after his release in 1947 came to Israel. He also lives in Tel Aviv, is a lawyer and has a family.

* * *

Gerta Grün

(Weiniger, Vienna), New York, USA

My name is Gerta Weiniger Grün. I came to England from Vienna, in December 1938 with one of the children's transports. Since I was one of the older ones, I was asked to take care of some of the younger children, who were terribly homesick. This was at Dovercourt.

I am sure that whoever was in charge of the arrangements, meant very well, but they forgot to give us stationery and, more importantly, a stamp to write a letter home. Knowing how much my parents were worried about their only daughter, I did the next best thing and worked for a stamp. I went into the kitchen and found a kind dishwasher who gave me a stamp in return for an hour's work helping him stacking dishes. When my parents, Hans and Grete Weiniger, received this letter, most joyously, they immediately took it to the Vienna *Kultusgemeinde*, to share this 'treasure' with the other parents who were still waiting for a sign that their children had arrived safely in England.

I finally got to my destination, a Quaker Children's House in the East End of London and met some very kind and generous people. I am still in correspondence with one lady who was the secretary at the time. Her name is Jean Anderson and she now lives in Glasgow, Scotland. She was one of those who really went out of her way to make us refugees feel at home. She tried to teach me English and, having never done this before, she thought that Shakespeare would be a good book to start, until I pointed out to her that we should perhaps try the *Daily News* instead.

After about three months, and with the help of my little charges (three to five year olds) who took me around the room, pointing to objects and saying 'This is a chair' and 'This is a table', etc., I managed to make myself understood; so much so that I was soon accepted at the Montessori International Training Course, given by Madam Montessori herself. She spoke in Italian, her nephew translated paragraph by paragraph into English. I finally passed the exam and received my certificate to teach children up to the age of twelve years by the Montessori method.

In the meantime, my parents were lucky to escape from Vienna on one of the last planes, before war broke out on 3 September 1939. They entered domestic service near Manchester.

Soon afterwards I was evacuated from London, as the Blitz had just started, to live with a Jewish family, Mr and Mrs Harry Towb, in Newcastle on Tyne, to take care of their two lovely little girls, Elizabeth and Ursula, three and five years old.

I left England for America during August 1940; settling finally in New York City. My younger brother, Harry, had come to America, with another children's transport and I wanted to be with him. I became a Kindergarten teacher; then married William Grün (another Viennese) in New York, where we have been living ever since. I continued to go to school at night, working during the day, and finally got my Master's degree in Public Health at Columbia University in 1981 and am now a Consultant in Geriatrics.

*   *   *

Bernard Grünberg

(Lingen, Ems), Derby, UK

I was born on 22 March 1923 in Lingen, Ems, Germany. The last nine months I spent at the *Umschichtungstelle* in Berlin. From here I came with the Kindertransport to England on 14 December 1938. After landing at Harwich we went to a holiday camp at Lowestoft. After a short stay there, a group of about twenty children was moved to the Salvation Army Hostel for Seamen at Harwich. The persons running the hostel gave us, as I recall it, a splendid time. I will always remember, everyone tried so hard to ease our ordeal and make us feel more at home. As it was now getting nearer the outbreak of World War II, we were sent to Turners Court near Wallingford in Berkshire. Here were about fifty boys brought together with the object of getting agricultural training, prior to working on farms in Britain. Turners Court turned out to be an approved school and I personally felt like one of the inmates, and so at the beginning was very depressed. My late father was a cattle dealer, and I had learned to milk cows at home. I therefore asked if I could work in the dairy as part of my training and so be able to prove my ability to hold a job on a farm. Luck was on my side. I proved to the instructor, that I was a first-class milker, and so succeeded in being sent to a farm just before the outbreak of war. From then on I stood on my own two feet and finally settled in the Derby area for the past thirty years.

Another boy who came to England in January 1939 with a children's transport, came to the same farm as I, and after the outbreak of war we both volunteered for the British Army. He was a year older than I, and was accepted, I was not. I never saw him again as he eventually became a Commando and was killed in action on a pre-invasion raid into France. He was born in Erfurt and was in Berlin during my stay there. I very much regret that I cannot recall his name.

* * *

Ilse Haas

(Philippsohn, Leipzig), Torquay, UK

Before I left Germany in June 1939 my father took me to see his seventy-nine year old mother in Sachsenhagen near Hanover. My ancestors had lived there since the seventeenth century. I had spent many happy holidays in Sachsenhagen. My grandmother was living in very reduced circumstances with her eldest son, who had been blinded in the First World War, and his wife. Their twelve year old daughter was away at a Jewish boarding school.

While my parents had been very factual about my departure, bidding farewell to my relations was very emotional. I talked through the night with my beloved aunt about their prospects and my escape into the unknown.

Earlier that day I had said goodbye to my mother and brother in Leipzig. Until I had my own children I never knew how my poor mother must have felt. At fifteen my main pre-occupation was not to burst into tears.

The next day my father took me to Hanover to a Kindertransport; we met up with his only sister on the way. Quite by chance my father spotted some cousins on the station platform, whose only daughter Friedel, aged about five, was going to England all alone on the same transport.

Friedel and I took an instant liking to each other. We spent the entire journey together but thereafter I have never been able to make contact with her again. Now I have even forgotten her surname.

My guardians, an English curate and his wife, met me in London. Out of the goodness of their hearts they had decided to sponsor a strange German Jewish child and I was the lucky one. They drove me to their cottage in Sussex where they lived with their young family. I am still in touch with them. They have been the only 'grandparents' my children have known, their children are my children's aunts and uncles and their grandchildren their cousins. They were extremely kind to me. All the same in those early days in my new environment I was very lonely and more homesick than I realized. I only lived for the letters from my parents and friends.

When I heard war had broken out I cried and cried and cried as I knew exactly what fate awaited the Jews left behind in Germany. No close relations of mine had managed to emigrate. Of course nobody believed me and thought that I was a bit hysterical.

For a while I received letters from my parents via their cousins in Luxemburg. However, my English family did not like this because it was of course highly illegal. They had moved to Weymouth by this time and I was able to go to school there. But I had to leave the coastal area because I became classified as an 'enemy alien'. I had a tribunal eventually and was allowed to remain free.

Not until 1942 did I really settle. Then I started to train as a nurse at Guys Hospital. Guys at that time was the only London teaching hospital which accepted foreigners in their School of Nursing, thanks to their enlightened liberal matron.

A student nurse's life was hard. We had to work very long hours and adhere to a very strict regime at all times. I earned only thirty shillings (£1.50) per month! I made many friends and though life had its ups and downs, I enjoyed the work and felt fulfilled. At the beginning of 1943 the Red Cross messages to which I had become accustomed, from my parents roughly once a month ceased to arrive and I was devastated.

Luckily there were several other refugee girls at Guys and we consoled each other as best we could, really knowing the bitter truth.

On VJ day I met my future husband, then a medical student, who had come to England with his parents from Czechoslovakia. He joined the army in 1948 and on the strength of that we got married in a Synagogue on 18 May 1948. My guardians gave me a wonderful wedding. Shortly after that my husband was sent abroad. While he was abroad I finished my midwifery training and then returned to Guys as a staff nurse on the children's ward at the princely salary of £140 per annum.

In 1948 I was struck down with severe paralytic poliomyelitis from which I never fully recovered. Some hard years followed. My son was born in 1958 followed by a daughter in 1960. Soon after that my husband became a consultant paediatrician in Torquay and Exeter and we moved to glorious Devon. There I had two more daughters, one sadly a spina bifida baby who only lived for six weeks. The other three are now grown up, all educated to degree level.

Besides bringing up the family and running the house from a wheelchair, I worked for many years at the Citizens' Advice Bureau and I have been involved with various committees and charitable appeals.

We have travelled quite extensively but have always been glad to return to our lovely home in England, the country of our adoption that has been very good to us.

*　　*　　*

Inge Hack

(Wertheimer, Nuremberg), Kent, UK

WRITTEN AFTER ONLY ONE YEAR IN ENGLAND, AGED THIRTEEN YEARS

It was a very sad *Chanuka*. My father had been taken away, Mummy was sad and I was waiting for my transport to England. One day we received the notice that I was to go at 1.00 am. in the morning. My family, consisting of my mother, an aunt who lived with us, and our loyal and loving maid came to the station with me. We said a very fond goodbye, not knowing then that it was the last time we would ever see each other. The snow was lying deep when we left the station at Nuremberg and travelled into the night. Arriving in Frankfurt at 5.00 am., more girls joined us. Castles, towers and ruins came into view until we finally reached Cologne. Yet more children joined us and we sped to the German-Dutch border. The Dutch were so friendly. We were greeted everywhere and waved at all the people we saw in the countryside.

We marvelled at the many windmills. I was twelve years old at the time and
many were even younger.

When we went ashore in England, an omnibus was waiting for us. This
was the first bus I had ever seen which had an upstairs. Of course we all
trooped upstairs. Soon we arrived at our camp which was called Dovercourt.
The camp had shower rooms, a concert room, a tennis court as well as table
tennis. We spent a lovely time there. We went to the cinema and sometimes
we had entertainment in the Palm Room. The Lord and Lady Mayor were
our guests.

One Sunday I received a message to go to London where I was to meet my
new foster family. With several other children who had been contacted by
their new families I packed my bag, said goodbye to those left behind, to
make the journey to London.

*   *   *

David Hackel

(Karlsruhe), Bath, Avon, UK

Pakefield Hall 'holiday' camp.

Two young men in their twenties were in charge of us, refugees like the rest
of us, but with a modicum of English. They had already taught us songs the
Nazis had banned. The morning after our arrival we were treated to a pep
talk, in German naturally.

'Boys you know, of course, how important it is to be on our best behaviour
at all times, but particularly now that we are in a small town where we are
conspicuous as strangers. We must make a good impression, we must not be
sloppy and make the place look untidy. When going out we shall all go
together. In order not to lose sight of you in an untidy straggly line we shall
march in columns of three. Of course, I shall not bellow commands but
quietly say one, two, three and off we march.'

We were not exactly delighted about this decision but we saw the point – it
would be tidier.

And so we marched through the narrow streets of Harwich, through the
park to the sea front, along the promenade of Dovercourt singing the songs
the Nazis had banned. But not for long. On the second day, word came from
the Town Hall to stop it – the townspeople did not like German songs being
sung in the streets of England, no matter what their subject matter. Naturally
we stopped singing, and marching, forthwith.

There is a happy ending to this story. We were not in the dog house for
long. A week or so later the Mayor of Harwich paid us an official visit and

bid us welcome. What none of us realized at the time was that this incident was the beginning of our '*Entdeutschung*'.

*   *   *

Melissa Hacker
(Vienna), New York, USA

The synopsis of a film
My Knees Were Jumping
55 min. 16mm colour

> '*When they brought my father home from jail I listened from the next room as the secret policeman called to ask if he should take my father back. I knew if they took him I wouldn't see him again. And I fainted. I remember feeling that my knees were jumping out of my skin. That's when my parents knew that I wouldn't make it and that they had to send me away.*'

This film tells the story of the childhood of my mother, Ruth Morley (neé Birnholz). Now a successful costume designer, in the late 1930s she was an assimilated upper middle class Viennese Jewish child. Her parents, like so many others, could not believe that what was happening in Germany would ever happen in Austria. They stayed in Vienna until after the night of rioting and murder of Jews known as Kristallnacht and then put their young daughter, who had never so much as crossed a street alone, on a train carrying refugee children to London. She waved goodbye, excited at the prospect of this great adventure, only to realize hours later that she was truly alone, going to a strange country. And that she might never see her parents again.

This experience affects Ruth strongly to this day and her trauma has been passed on to the second generation, my sister and myself. These scars run deeply through our lives, as they do in the lives of all children whose parents have survived unfathomable horrors. Many Americans are the children of parents who have lived through events which we can barely comprehend. From survivors of the Holocaust to survivors of the atrocities of the Khmer Rouge, parents are struggling to lead normal lives and raise children in this new country.

Yet we children have blood ties to the old. We speak English, we go to American schools, we were born here. But under the surface there is much pain and alienation. We have been marked by events we did not experience, but the repercussions of which permeate our lives. As a child I grew up hearing bits of stories of life in Vienna and of the horrifying changes after the *Anschluss*. Stories of male children carrying guns on city streets and pointing them at the Jewish school children (my mother among them); forced to ride in the front section of the streetcars. Of my grandfather's house being broken into, my grandfather being randomly arrested and just as randomly let go.

I grew up with a mother who was afraid. Afraid of crowds, of people in uniform, of young men. This was unspoken, but almost from the time I could walk I carried with me a second sense. A second set of eyes and ears constantly on the alert for potential threats to my mother's tenuous sense of security. I always felt that I had to protect my mother. From what – I was never quite sure, but I knew that the world was very dangerous and fragile. Leaving her out of my sight for too long could spell disaster. But all of this was unspoken, implicit, until now. We, the second generation, children of Holocaust survivors, are only just beginning to tell our stories.

This film (which is available from me in New York, (212) 255-5081) is both an exorcism of this heritage and an important addition to the culture of remembrance; an examination of the shadows still cast by one of the key historical events of the twentieth century. The current rise in anti-semitism, as evidenced most pertinently in Austria makes this work now more topical then ever.

* * *

Rose Harburger

(Mainzer, Frankfurt), Arizona, USA

Over-protected and raised with a great deal of love, my greatest difficulty came at the age of eleven – when I was thrust into a totally different kind of environment. On 12 June 1939, assembled with hundreds of other children – sponsored by the Kindertransport – I clung to my mother for the last time. Moments later, grief-stricken and shattered, I was on a train headed for the English Channel.

I kept thinking about my mother and sister, wondering if I would ever see them again. I didn't!

Later that morning we were gathered in one of London's immense stations. As 'Big Ben' struck three o'clock, I was the only one left in this colossal structure. Its startling noises and echoing sounds only added to my state of anxiety. Salty tears flowed freely – the taste filtering through my lips and into my mouth. A young woman with short wispy blond hair and a warm smile came towads me. She put me on a train bound for Leeds. Explaining my presence to others in the compartment, she gave me a brief hug and disappeared. Motionless I sat next to the window while the English countryside whizzed by – feeling the tears welling up again, hot and burning. Though I didn't know any English, I knew they were talking about me. Nodding heads and sympathetic eyes focused in my direction, as comments about the 'little Jewish refugee' were being bantered about.

When I finally arrived I searched the strange faces of passers-by. Suddenly, a short, pudgy woman in her thirties emerged out of nowhere. In broken German she asked my name. Ignoring my wretchedness she steered me out of the station and onto a streetcar. In silence we rode for about twenty minutes. When we came to the end of the line, a handsome man of medium build with black wavy hair was waiting. He smiled as he lifted me off the trolley. She introduced him as her husband. He worked in a nearby factory. Instantly I perceived him as a sweet gentle man and throughout my seven years with the family my perceptions were confirmed time and time again. He took my suitcase and we started to walk. Exhausted from lack of sleep and food I dragged behind. Endless cobblestone streets lay beneath rows and rows of small terraced houses – all identical – facing one another. As I climbed up the steep concrete steps, the door to my guardians' home opened and my new life began.

Everything was in complete contrast to the way I was brought up. The wife was a spiteful domineering woman, ruling the tiny slovenly-kept house like a commanding general. Luckily, their five-year old son – a lovable tyke – was usually on my side. It was not easy! My struggle to survive those early years – emotionally more than anything else – seemed doubtful at times. But I came through – most probably because of my age! I feel I'm a better person for it – taking nothing for granted.

*　　*　　*

Arnold and Annie Harris

AS TOLD BY THEIR SON ANSEL HARRIS, LONDON

I thumbed through the souvenir brochure for the reunion in June 1989 and immediately saw the names: John (Manfred) Silberman, Alfred Jeckel and Kurt Marx. They were all 'our' Bedford boys.

My late father Arnold Harris' diary for 17 October 1939 reads as follows: 'Moved into 2 Sidney Road, Bedford'. And four days later: 'We held the first *Shabbat* Service here. There were present thirty-six hostel boys and six other refugee girls. The service was followed by *Kiddush*'.

To begin to understand what that could have meant to those forty-two young people, I must offer you a brief background.

Who were these 'hostel boys'? Boys who had been uprooted from their orthodox middle class homes, mainly in Cologne, and brought to England in Kindertransports early in 1939. Some were less than ten years old, none older than fifteen. Others had arrived as late as August 1939. They came under the auspices of the Weekly Appeal Fund of the Dollis Hill and Cricklewood Refugee Committee. Its inspiration and driving force was my Rebbe and a close friend of my parents, the late Louis Rabinowitz. My parents were active members of that Committee.

The children, evacuated to Bedford, had as a result been uprooted a second time within a year. But this time they had been transported to an even more complex almost incomprehensible foreign environment: enemy aliens, billeted in largely working class homes, not yet speaking the language and to a town whose only Jewish resident was Colonel Waley Cohen. They were totally lost and bewildered.

And so, when in the first days of the war Captain Louis Rabinowitz, now a chaplain, called my parents and asked if they could go up to Bedford to see how the children were faring, they could only agree. *Rosh Hashanah* that year fell on 14 September. By that date my father was in Bedford, and had organised Services. My parents had decided that they had a duty and responsibility to try to provide in small measure for what these children had lost and so desperately needed. And so they moved to Bedford. The diary a few months later records that one Friday evening nine boys stayed for dinner. 23 February 1940: 'It entailed much work for Annie. She however said: "It was worthwhile. But for the Grace of God my own boy might have been one of those lads".'

Our home was open house to these children. Occasionally if a child was in particular need he or she would actually live with us. Gisela Jeckel I recall was one. Our home ultimately became 'The Centre', the Bedford Jewish Youth Centre and the centre for the growing community of Jewish evacuees, and Jewish servicemen and women.

Apart from running the family home (actually it often took second place), teaching in the Hebrew classes they established, visiting outlying communities where some children were housed, my mother acted as foster mother to the children who of course continued to live in their billets. She also counselled the foster mothers who almost without exception showed remarkable love and care for these 'German children'. She established such a reputation that as the diary recalls: 'The billeting master at Owen's School, having difficulty in finding accommodation for his boys reported, "At many houses where I call to try and place my boys the answer very often is that if they are Mrs Harris' boys, we'll have them".'

My father tended the boys' *Bar Mitzvah* preparation. He fought to secure jobs for the older boys. He managed to get John Silberman his first job, as a transport clerk. He managed to get two of the boys free places at Bedford

Modern School. The headmaster saw it as the school's contribution to the welfare of the refugee children. Rolf Weinberg went on to read English at Trinity College, Cambridge. Walter Hausmann was sadly killed in a flying accident. He helped others like Shmuel Königshoffer to *Hachshara* and ultimately *Aliyah*.

I am frequently reminded of the inestimable role my parents played in the lives of these bereft boys and girls. On my father's seventieth birthday (1964) they presented them with a specially bound and inscribed copy of Karen Gerson's book ' *They Came as Children*', which contains a tribute to him. And amongst the many JNF Tree Certificates on the occasion of their Golden Wedding in August 1970 is one from the Tomaschoff brothers in Israel.

Louis Rabinowitz wrote in his obituary to Arnold Harris: 'Our Rabbis taught that he who saves one soul is regarded as though he had saved a whole world – what then shall I say of one to whom it was given to save some hundreds? Arnold and Annie Harris were in the forefront of this work of mercy in every way . . . no children had greater love and devotion showered upon them by their natural parents than these children had by their foster parents Arnold and Annie Harris'.

* * *

Harry Harrison

(Nadel, Berlin), UK

AS TOLD BY LESLIE BRENT

Harry Harrison has died at the age of seventy-nine. One might ask why this particular event should be noticed, for in many ways there was nothing especially remarkable about him. Yet on two occasions in his life, this gentle and unassuming man had behaved with notable spirit and bravery.

Born Heinz Nadel in Berlin to Jewish parents, he became a teacher and pedagogue, with a talent for middle-distance running. Eventually he became a housefather and teacher in the Jewish orphanage in Berlin-Pankow, and it was there, in the summer of 1938, that he displayed high courage.

Several months before the infamous *Kristallnacht*, the orphanage was stormed by an organised mob, and the ground floor, including the school's Synagogue, ransacked. The children had fled in terror to distant parts of the building and attempts to contact the police were mysteriously unsuccessful. As the mob surged up the rather grand staircase Harry went to meet them – alone, but carrying a small boy in his arms.

The mob stopped in their tracks, and in the surprised pause, Harry was able to remind them quietly that they had invaded an orphanage. He asked them not to frighten the children any further and to be so kind as to leave, and, unbelievably, they did.

Just before the war Harry managed to escape, with his brother, to England. He joined the Pioneer Corps, transferring later to the Intelligence Corps when that became possible for 'enemy aliens'. His unit entered Belsen concentration camp on 15 April 1945.

He was later highly praised by his commanding officer for the way he had helped to restore some semblance of order, establishing a school for the surviving children, compèring the first stage show produced and performed by camp survivors, and helping with the evacuation of some five hundred sick people to Sweden.

After the war, he worked for a few years with Freud's architect son and he was latterly employed as interpreter, translator, and finally assistant to the managing director of a machine tool firm. Thereafter, with his books and love of opera and informed interest in athletics, he lived quietly with the companion of more than thirty years, Edward Harrison, whose family had befriended him when he settled in this country and whose surname he had taken.

No wonder that Harry, whose own parents had died in the Holocaust, later suffered from the most appalling nightmares. Even some of his closest friends knew little about his conduct before and during the war. I knew because I was one of the boys in that orphanage.

Reprinted by kind permission from *The Guardian,* 20 November 1989.

*   *   *

Harry Heber

(Vienna), London, UK

My sister Ruth and I arrived at Harwich with the Kindertransport on 18 December 1938, one month before my eighth birthday.

Before embarking on our journey into the unknown, my parents had stressed that brother and sister must look out for one another and not allow ourselves to be parted; so when someone came up to Ruth to tell her that she was being taken to a new home, she spoke up and insisted that her little brother Heinzi must come too!

We were taken by motor car, driven by a kindly-looking gentleman, Mr Ogden, and subsequently my sister was accommodated with him and his young family. I was, however, dropped off some miles away with an elderly farmer and his wife in an old country cottage that had still not been introduced to electricity.

To say the least, the experience for a little boy was traumatic. Having been used to an ordered home life, I had been parted from my parents about a week earlier and now even my older sister had been taken away. My surroundings were strange and bleak with only the snow-covered country-side around as far as the eye could see. My hosts spoke no German, so I was unable to talk to them and communicate my feelings of despondency and isolation. The only thing I could do was what all children resort to when they are unhappy – I cried and cried. I wept and sobbed throughout the Christmas period before my new foster parents were able to alert the local Refugee Committee of my plight. I was then collected with my few belongings and after being allowed to see my sister and assured that all would be well, I was taken to a small boarding school in the village of Goudhurst in Kent. I remember when I first entered the common room where about twenty children were playing or reading, everyone stopped what they were doing to look at this tear-stained young stranger who had been placed in their midst. Without taking their eyes off me their conversation stopped and then became animated, but of course I could not undertstand what they were saying. They were pointing their fingers at the strange sight in front of them. He was obviously a boy, but he was dressed like a girl! Yes, I did look different from the other children – I was wearing long stockings held up by suspenders under my short trousers! In Austria at the time, because of the severe winters, it was customary, not only for girls, but also for boys to wear long stockings to protect them from the cold, but in England, where conditions were more spartan, little boys were expected to brave the elements. Within the next few days I became suitably attired as an English schoolboy and my knees continued to be exposed until I acquired my first pair of long trousers on the occasion of my *Bar Mitzvah* some five years later.

I quickly settled into my new surroundings in the company of other children, with the result that nine months later when I was happily reunited with my parents who had arrived in England only three days before the outbreak of war, I could only speak English and had forgotten my mother tongue.

*   *   *

Bernhard Heikel

(Berlin), Cheshire, UK

My story is a simple one. I am not Jewish, but was counted as a 'Mischling' (mixed blood), being three-eighths Jewish on my mother's side. As I was only thirteen years old, and my parents were divorced, I went where my mother went; hence I joined the Kindertransport.

I left my home city of Berlin on 5 June 1939 as one of a large party of children from Friedrichstrasse station, where I was seen off by my grandmother. That was a sad moment – I thought I would never see her again, and I loved her with all my boyish heart. I never did see her again.

After arriving in England we got into a London train. There we were split up into groups. My group, about eight or ten of us, were taken to Kings Cross and put aboard a train going North.

In Doncaster I was told to get out on my own and ask for a train to take me to Goole, in Yorkshire, where my prospective foster parents lived. This was the most worrying part of my journey; how would I be able to ask for my train in my very poor English? Somehow I did it and arrived shortly afterwards in Goole. What next?

A very large and energetic lady descended upon me on the station platform and began mopping my sweaty brow with her handkerchief soaked in eau-de-cologne. As a boy I was not too keen on this, but I was probably not too clean after my long journey.

I was taken home by Mrs Frankland, my new foster mother, and there met a tall and lanky gentleman, Mr Frankland. A very kindly and understanding man, headmaster of a local primary school, he understood and truly cared about children.

Thus began my new life in England on 6 June 1939.

Now, fifty years later, what are my main impressions? A sense of overwhelming gratitude to the Society of Friends, the Quakers, who organized the Kindertransport. The very real love and generosity which I received from Mr and Mrs Frankland, who could not have treated me better if I had been their natural son. The attitude of the people of England in general, who were willing to accept and keep us unknown children of oppression in a foreign country.

*   *   *

Ruth Heinemann

(Simon, Choppenburg), Dundee, Ill., USA

In December 1938, my sister, Hilde Simon (Gernsheimer) and myself, Ruth Simon Heinemann, emigrated to England from Hamburg, Germany.

Our mother, Selma Simon, was alerted to the fact that there would be a children's transport departing in early December through our Oldenburg Jewish Congregation. Our Rabbi's wife was handling the immigration details in conjunction with HIAS, as our Rabbi had been taken into custody, along with all the other men in our community, on the day of Kristallnight.

Only two children from each family were allowed to participate in this transport. A decision had to be made as to which of her four daughters my mother would send. She chose Hilde and myself, her two middle children. My eldest sister, Edith, and my youngest sister, Ilse, would remain at home with my mother.

Upon our arrival in England we were informed of an opportunity to stay in Harrogate, Yorkshire, in the Jewish Convalescent Home for Children. Hilde and I accepted this generous offer along with twenty-five other girls.

We were well cared for and remained in the charge of the most philanthropic men and women of Leeds and Harrogate for six years before emigrating to the United States.

Hilde and I have both raised lovely families since meeting our husbands and marrying here in America.

My husband, Fred, and I returned to Harrogate in 1985. We made contact with a Mr Carl Rosen (who has since passed away). Mr Rosen was the secretary of the Jewish Congregation of Harrogate, whose members cared for us during the war.

We wanted to dedicate a memorial of appreciation to the gallant and generous members of the congregation to show our gratitude. We placed a plaque in the Harrogate Synagogue to those men and women of valour. The remaining funds were used to purchase an Ark Curtain and *Bima* Cover embroidered in Israel.

The gifts arrived in time to be used at a wedding in the Shul, the first wedding performed there in a long time.

* * *

Michael Hellman

(Vienna), London, UK

Railway station Westbahnhof, Vienna; a December night in 1938. A crowd of children, bound for England, are taking leave of their parents. I was one of those children, aged fifteen, saying goodbye to my mother. My father had died in 1931.

Our transport came under the auspices of the late Rabbi Schonfeld. We were put up in two hostels: the girls in Stamford Hill and the boys around the corner, in Amhurst Park. A teacher came to our hostel and gave us English lessons and also taught us some English songs. I had already acquired some basic English from a textbook. We were taken on a sight-seeing tour of London and treated to a cinema visit.

After about three weeks in the North London hostel some of the boys, including myself, were sent to Manchester and accommodated in the Cassel-Fox hostel. It was the beginning of a new life, in a new and strange environment. Adjustment to this new life was no doubt easier for us youngsters than for older refugees, but it was by no means painless.

In August 1939 the Jewish Lads' Brigade invited us refugee boys to participate in their summer camp near Llandudno in North Wales. We were issued with JLB uniforms – and did a fair amount of square-bashing; a mild foretaste of the military life for those of us who were later to join the British Army. It was quite an enjoyable experience and a welcome break from work in a factory, which I had been doing since March, when I had also moved from the hostel into lodgings.

A very few weeks after returning from the JLB camp World War II broke out. For us refugees, the start of the war brought us the status of 'enemy aliens' and examination before aliens' tribunals. Above all, it was a time of increasing anxiety about the fate of those we left behind.

*   *   *

Paula Hill, M.A.

(Moise, Braunschweig), London, UK

As the train sped away that fateful morning in January 1939, I stood at the window for a last look at the world I was leaving behind. I watched the receding figure of my widowed mother, holding my little brother's hand rapidly fade from sight. This scene, so often to disturb my adult life, was not unique to me. Prisoners of fate, my companions and I travelled in silence, each consumed with our own thoughts. Somewhere in another part of this train, was my thirteen year old brother, but where? We already knew that any act of brutality was possible. The appearance of a group of uniformed compassionless zombies, in the corridor of the train, evoked terror in my heart.

Happily journey's end came without incident. Harwich dull and grey but peaceful – just the crashing of the foaming winter waves against the sea wall, seemed like the Garden of Eden to me. No noise of marching jackboots, no hysterical shriekings. My brother found me and we embraced. Safe at last or so we thought!

A new kind of terror greeted us at Dovercourt – the selections, which sealed our fate as to where and with whom we would go.

Dainty, blond, blue-eyed and almost ten years old, I was made to stand in line and invariably picked. I suppose I should have been flattered but I was not. For the homes and hosts selected for me were not Jewish and I, as an orthodox Jewish child, deeply resented that. My reasons were totally rational. Were not the Nazis Christians? To a child not yet accustomed to deep intellectual thought, one kind of Christian was like another. I was simply afraid and resorted to hiding behind the camp huts, so that I could not be found for the dreaded selections. But I was not always in luck! My brother, deeply religious and fearing for my Jewish soul, thanked the kind ladies who wanted me to be their own, but insisted 'My sister must stay among Jews.' This did not pacify the beautiful childless fur-coated elegant lady, who with tears in her eyes pleaded with my brother 'I will arrange kosher food for your sister.' 'That is not enough,' said my brother, 'she must continue her Jewish education.' Not daunted, the lovely lady replied: 'I will arrange for that too.' To no avail – my brother stood his ground.

The 'they' who now had control over our lives, took my brother to task.

'How dare you behave like that. You are lucky to be here and we no longer have Jewish homes willing to take refugee children. We will have to send you back to Germany,' they threatened. Stoically, my brother replied: 'Then that is what you must do.'

But then a miracle occurred. Two ladies appeared who said they were here to select children for Jewish families in Birmingham, and would we like to go. Would we indeed! My brother and I rushed to our huts, packed our meagre belongings and once more found ourselves on a train.

My brother, his courage still far from daunted, set out on his next mission. He informed the ladies while still on the train that he intended to save his mother and brother, and could they please help. They smiled at this remarkable child and promised to see what they could do.

But first we must settle ourselves. I was placed with a Jewish couple of advancing years, who were neither prepared nor equipped for the traumatized child who had entered their lives.

My brother fared far better. He joined a widow and her two children whose Jewish culture was near to our own.

Soon, my brother started asking around for anyone who might need the services of a domestic (the only way my mother could get out) and after several months succeeded in his quest.

My mother had a visa but obstacles were placed in her way by the Refugee Committee refusing to guarantee a place for my little brother. The reason given was that they had already sent two of her children to England, whereas from some families they had not yet taken one.

War was imminent and my mother pleaded her case. At last the Committee relented and she saw her youngest child off at the station where seven months earlier, she had taken leave of her two older children. In August 1939 she succeeded in coming to England and we set up home together.

My remarkable older brother, forced into the adult world long before his time, and to whom childhood was denied, emigrated to Israel together with his family nine years ago. Soon after his arrival he suffered a severe stroke from which he has only partially recovered. My mother lived to see all but one of her grandchildren. And the decimated family is now being rebuilt.

* * *

Peter Hirsch

(Berlin), Denville, NJ, USA

It must have been a bad time for a seven-year old to leave his mother (Hilde F Hirsch, née van Gelder), because I can remember almost nothing of the trip. I don't know the name of the town from which the boat left, nor at which it arrived, nor how I got to the departure point from Berlin. I cannot remember actually leaving my mother, although I have spent considerable effort, some of it on a psychiatrist's couch, to recapture what must have been a painful experience.

There was a boy on the transport whose name was Reinhold, and another named Eisenberg. Reinhold was my friend. Eisenberg's name sticks in memory because an 'Iron Mountain' seemed a strange concept. I have no memory of any of the Kindertransport children being with me in any of my schools.

My memory, unsupported by any scrap of a document, says I left Germany on 21 June 1939, and arrived in England on 22. I went first to a boarding school in Sevenoaks, Kent, but very soon thereafter to the Manor House School at Bromley Green, near Ashford, Kent, where I spent the next three years. I remember being homesick the first three nights, and having some trouble with English, but the sadness soon faded and the language came quickly. Seven years later I knew no German, except the numbers, '*Ja*', '*Nein*', and the meaning of '*Zwiebel*'.

All those seven years, with the exception of the last three months, were spent in boarding schools. The closest I had to a family life was with a Mrs Franklin ('The Honourable' (?) Mrs Franklin) of 50 Porchester Terrace, London. She was the sister of a Mrs Montague, who was evidently very active in the refugee problem. Mrs Franklin invited me to visit Porchester Terrace periodically. Mr Franklin taught me manners and gave me two weeks' holiday in County Donegal, Ireland, with a number of other children. I don't know whether she had children of her own, but if so, and if any of them (or any following generation) read this, please know that there is a man in Denville, NJ, USA who owes you a rather large debt of kindness and would be delighted to repay it.

My parents survived. My father (Ernst L Hirsch MD) had left Berlin before me, a last minute berth on one of the Exodus ships to Palestine with room for a physician, but not his family. There he enlisted in the British Army Medical Corps, followed the troops up Italy, then to Germany where he found my mother again in 1945. She had lived illegally in Berlin until the end. After the war they set up house again in Berlin and brought me home in December 1946. We left Germany (again) as 'Displaced Persons' for the USA in 1949. My mother died in 1951 – far too young – she was denied the reward of her courage and strength in the war years. My father married again, passed the medical boards in his fifties, and practised medicine in Queens, NY until he was seventy-eight. He died in 1986, at age ninety-one.

Of my years in England, there is not much more to say. I was not consciously unhappy, but the lack of family life has left scars. A number of people did their best for me, notably Mrs Franklin and Miss Garrard, whom her staff and pupils knew as 'Gerry'. I have no complaint. On the contrary, I owe the organisers of the Kindertransport my life and health. On balance, they were good years.

* * *

Herbert Holden

(Holzinger, Pilsen) Cambridge, UK

I thought that leaving Czechoslovakia late in July 1939 was a great adventure. Although I was sorry to leave my parents and younger sister behind, I knew that it was only a matter of time before we would get together again, as we had planned to meet up in America soon afterwards.

Whilst I was very excited, my sister who was three years younger than I (I was thirteen at the time) was upset by the parting and spent the whole of the journey in tears.

My confidence weakened when we arrived at Liverpool Street station and were taken to a hall to wait for someone to take us to our new temporary families. Finally a gentleman arrived, puffing and panting. He had been delayed because he was still trying to find us a home. Fortunately some acquaintances of his who had guaranteed to take a Jewish refugee boy from the next transport, which sadly never materialised, said they would look after us whilst more permanent accommodation could be found. Eventually my sister was taken in by relatives of theirs and I moved to a hostel in Birmingham.

Our first day in Birmingham was hell. It suddenly hit me that we were in a foreign country without knowing the language, with no relatives or friends. I was trying desperately hard to be as brave as a thirteen year old boy was expected to be, and I spent most of that day in and out of the toilet so that no one would see the tears which were running down my cheeks.

As time went on one became acclimatised to the surroundings. I enjoyed going to school although it was difficult for me to understand why 'yes' should be pronounced 'yessa' until someone explained that this was the respectful way to reply to one's teacher and that the spelling was 'yes sir'.

We went to church regularly (the family were Christadelphian) and I looked forward to this as someone would invariably give me sixpence or even a shilling. Once, in fact I was given half a crown – I couldn't wait to meet that particular lady again. Most of this money was spent either on fish and chips, which I loved, or on a halfpenny's worth of broken biscuits from Marks and Spencer.

When I moved to Rugby I changed school and was very proud when I won the English prize (from thirty-nine English pupils). Unfortunately during that period grammar schools were still fee-paying, so I had to leave at the age of fourteen to find a job.

During this period I managed to locate a sort of relative. He certainly wasn't a close relative, in fact not really a relation at all, although I managed to track down the family connection. He was responsible for bringing over thirty of his own family to this country from Germany. I heard that he had just become a grandfather so I wrote to congratulate him and, at the same time, asked him whether he would buy me an overcoat. Such *chutzpa*, I couldn't do it today! We met and he offered me a job at his factory in London and I also got my overcoat. He organised my digs and arranged with my landlady to pay her twenty-five shillings per week – all my wages. After one week I had to ask for a rise which enabled me to clean my teeth with a toothbrush and toothpaste, as well as being able to go to the cinema.

Excitement when at the end of the war I obtained a list of concentration camp survivors with the names of my parents and sister on it, only to be shattered by the news that this information was incorect and out of date! Whilst most of my family perished, I was fortunate in so far that my grandmother, aunt and cousin survived Terezin. Another aunt survived forced labour in Estonia.

Life progressed satisfactorily from there on. I married, have three kids and only recently retired, but I am still working in a different capacity. Although I don't come from a particularly religious background, I got involved in our local Synagogue and suddenly had the urge to have *Bar Mitzvah,* having missed out in 1939. So at the age of fifty, with our Rabbi's agreement, I made up for the lost opportunity.

Much to our delight the party was arranged on the day of the Entebbe rescue, so our celebration was doubly enjoyable. Not only was it a memorable day but it helped to collect a considerable sum for medical supplies to Israel in lieu of presents.

Quite recently I discovered that I am one of Nicholas Winton's boys and needless to say I owe him a tremendous debt of gratitude. After all, it is really as a result of his action that I am alive today.

Editors' Note:

Nicholas Winton M.B.E., together with two friends, went to Czechoslovakia in 1939 and rescued about six hundred children. He was a special guest at our Reunion in June 1989. He loves to hear from 'his children'. Address on request from The Editors.

Gretel Howard

(Simon, Bodenfelde), Oxford, UK

I was born in a small place called Bodenfelde. It was a very friendly place and because my parents owned the only big store, we were involved with all that went on in the village. My brother and I had a very happy childhood and lots of friends.

I was eleven at the time and had just won a place to go to high school in nearby Uslar, a train journey of only thirty minutes. Although I was never actually abused by my school mates on the train, I felt most uncomfortable and more often than not ended up sitting in a compartment on my own. After a while the children at the school became very unpleasant. They would call me names, refuse to sit by me in class and actually hit me during breaks for no apparent reason, and my parents were asked to remove me for my own safety.

So back I went to the local school, amongst my friends, as I thought, only to find that they weren't friends any more. Apart from the jeers at having to leave the high school, the former pattern of abuse repeated itself, only worse.

We were not allowed to go swimming (we might dirty the water), go to the cinema or into a restaurant or cafe. Everywhere notices appeared saying 'Jews forbidden'.

My father's shop was out of bounds, and the few kind and loyal people would come round the back after dark to buy a few things, just to show that they were not Nazis. Had they been caught, they would have been severely punished. During the day a Nazi would actually stand guard outside the shop to make sure no one could enter.

In 1936 my brother, at the age of sixteen, managed to flee to Holland and my parents decided that I too must leave home, but where could I go? In the end, they sent me to a Jewish orphanage in a place called Padderborn and there I stayed until I was fourteen. I never saw my home again because my parents were forced into selling it, well below its value, to the biggest local Nazi, and then had to leave themselves.

They moved to a big town called Bochum in Westphalia, where they took over the management of a big Jewish hotel. I joined them there and we all loved the life. But that too was very short-lived. On 9 November 1938, like the Synagogues everywhere, it was burned down. It was a miracle that no lives were lost and this was entirely due to a complete stranger who came rushing in at nine o'clock at night, in a terrible state, shouting for everyone to leave, as the Nazis were on their way to burn it down. Terrified, we fled to the top of the house and barricaded ourselves in one of the bedrooms. The beasts had got in and we could hear them smashing up furniture, crockery and anything they could find, on their way to search for us.

After a while - it seemed like hours - all was silent. Looking out of the window, the crowds were still there, so what could have happened? We took down the barricade and gingerly opened the door and knew at once what had happened. We smelt smoke and heard the crackling of the smashed furniture as it burned. We made for the stairs, but the smoke was so thick that we were driven back. As we were on the third floor, it had obviously been going for some time, hence the silence both inside and outside the house. We went back into the front bedroom, knotted together some sheets, opened the window and prepared to let ourselves down, but the crowd outside shouted 'There they are' and a row of Nazis stood below us holding up their axes and shouting 'Go back Jews.' The message was clear. We were meant to burn with the place. Horrified, we had no option but to crouch in a corner and await our fate. How long we sat there I do not know, but suddenly there was a banging and shouting on the door, and an order to move the wardrobe and let whoever was outside in. Powerless to move and absolutely terrified, we did nothing. The door was finally broken down and there stood an enormous SS man. In a gentle voice he said 'I won't hurt you, I've come to help you.' Of course we didn't believe him and did not move. He just stood there and waited. After a while, the smell of the fire penetrated into the bedroom and we realised that time would be up shortly anyway. Either we would suffocate or die at the hands of the Nazis, so we really had nothing to lose. We all linked hands and stumbled after him down the stairs and into the yard outside.

So, once again, we walked the streets looking over our shoulders all the time and waiting to be grabbed. We called at various Jewish friends' houses and found panic and destruction everywhere. Some had left everything and fled, no one knew where, others tried to cope as best they could. We finally came to a house where there was very little damage, because the house and shop had recently been sold to a non-Jew and our friends were just waiting for a visa to go to America. They very kindly offered us shelter.

Next morning there was a commotion of a different kind. An open lorry screeched to a halt and we could see men and boys we knew sitting miserably in it. Some officers came to collect my father and the man and son of the house for questioning at the police station, we were told. But none of us believed it and they never came back. In due course we learned they had all been taken to a concentration camp.

One morning some strange ladies came to see my mother. It seemed that because of what had happened, England had offered to take in a number of children, leaving the choice to the Welfare Committee. Because we were homeless I rated as one of the first to be chosen.

After a broadcast about us, people from all over England had offered hospitality to a child. Others came personally to make their choice. The young ones went quickly, us older ones, people were not so keen to have. I was sent to a family in Wallasey, near Liverpool, supposedly as a companion for their twelve-year old daughter, but what they really wanted me for was cheap domestic labour. Not surprisingly I wasn't very happy there. My dearest wish was to go to boarding school but, of course, that needed money. I couldn't even go to ordinary school, because at the time school-leaving age was fourteen.

We had no idea where my father was or even if he was dead or alive. Nor he, of course, knew what happened to us, so you can imagine his state when he was released from concentration camp, and found my mother eventually only to learn that his child had been sent to England, which, at that time, must have seemed unattainable to him. Not surprisingly he had a complete nervous breakdown.

One could only get out of Germany on a domestic permit, and my parents were lucky to get a job in Oxford. So a few days before war broke out, my parents left Germany, stopping en route in Holland to persuade my brother to come with them to England. He was now twenty, had not seen his parents for four years and was happy with the family who had adopted him. He did, however, promise to come for a visit that Christmas, but by then it was too late and war had broken out.

After the war we learned that he and the kind family who had hidden him for three years during the occupation, had been shot two weeks before the liberation, when somebody gave them away to the Germans. I don't think that my father ever recovered properly and he died a few years later. My mother lived until eighty-five and died in Oxford in 1983.

*   *   *

Renate Inow

(Elberfeld), London, UK

We were lucky in our family to have a very rich great-uncle in England, the brother of my grandmother. He had come to England at the beginning of the century, at a very early age, in order to miss conscription into the German army. He soon went to South Africa digging for gold.

Because of him, some members of my family managed to get out of Germany. Unfortunately, not my parents.

As small children in Germany, we had of course heard of Uncle Rudolph and Auntie Vi, but we were far more interested in their car, a Rolls Royce.

The farewell from my parents was as sad as with most children, and even thinking of it today, is still very painful. There are some memories of the journey to England, but it is only since comparatively recently, that a smile comes to my face when I think of my reception at Liverpool Street station. I was busy talking to one of the other children next to me when I suddenly noticed a very good-looking elderly lady leaning over me, with a photo of my brother in her hand, asking whether I was Renate. I could not believe that this very good-looking lady could possibly be Auntie Vi. And, although she said 'Yes' when I asked her if she was Auntie Vi, I still wanted to be quite quite sure, and the only way I could think of at the time was to ask 'Rolls Royce?' She not only answered 'Yes' but pointed to the white-gloved driver who was standing behind her. And so, with a deep great sadness in my heart, I was taken to my aunt, my mother's sister, and her three boys, who had also recently arrived here, kneeling on the back seat of a Rolls Royce looking out of the window.

* * *

Betty Israel

(Scheiner, Leipzig), London, UK

My brother and I, aged thirteen and fourteen respectively, left Leipzig with the children's transport on or about 18 April 1939.

Recalling that day my most vivid memory was parting from my mother, who fortunately later followed to England. Arriving at the Leipzig Hauptbahnhof and passing the barrier to the platform we saw large numbers of the dreaded Gestapo and SS, the latter in their black jackboots, lining the full length of the platform. The silence was eerie and we found ourselves conversing in whispers.

I saw a very young child being passed to a helper through the open window of a carriage by its mother. The thoughts and feelings of that poor mother handing over that tiny tot to a complete stranger still haunt me today.

The absence of any visible emotion or tears was chilling and I still 'feel' that horrible silence after fifty years. How well-drilled were the children of the Nazi era. Fear prevented them from expressing their emotions.

* * *

Rosa Jacobs

(Granek, Breslau), London, England

I arrived at Harwich on 15 December 1938 along with my sister. I was fifteen years of age and my sister a year older. My family name was Granek and our home was in Breslau.

We were taken to Dovercourt Bay Holiday Camp in Essex where we stayed until early February.

My first surprise was when I went to have breakfast and saw what was offered to eat, porridge, eggs, kippers, toast and marmalade. My first thought was that we were having an early lunch.

My impression of the tea served with milk was also confusing and I thought it tasted horrible. However I got used to it and now, funnily enough, it is my favourite drink and I would miss it very much.

The local Boy Scouts came to entertain us and the managers of the local cinemas allowed us free entrance, provided we had labels or tickets to identify where we were staying. In general the local people were very kind to us.

On Sundays families who were interested in adopting or fostering us would come to look and decide whether we were suitable for them.

We used to go into a special room where they would take a look at us more personally. I remember wondering whether my nose was straight enough or if there was anything else physically they would not like. My particular problem was that at fifteen I was among the older children who prospective parents thought might be a greater responsibility.

Eventually I went to a family as a foster child. I stayed there for thirteen years until I got married. I worked very hard in this home because I came under the child scheme and had to agree that I would not take other employment.

* * *

Ruth Jacobs

(Heber, Vienna), London, UK

I arrived in England on 18 December 1938 with the Kindertransport from Vienna. I was ten years old and my brother, who came with me, was seven. We had both been born in Innsbruck, a town with a small Jewish community of about a hundred families. We had been forced from our home in Innsbruck and taken under guard to Vienna.

After a few days at Dovercourt a member of the Refugee Committee took me, my brother and several other children to Heathfield, Sussex. This was Mr Ogden who took me into his own home with his wife and three small children. My brother was sent to an elderly couple where he was most unhappy, so after a few weeks he was sent to a boarding school in Kent. He settled down there and stayed for several years.

Mr and Mrs. Ogden were very kind to me. They also sent for my parents to come to England as domestics to work for them. My parents arrived just three days before war broke out. I am extremely grateful to Mr and Mrs Ogden who saved my parents from certain death.

A place was offered at the Stroud High School for girls for a refugee. I was lucky enough to be chosen and once again I had the greatest of good fortune to be sent to Mr and Mrs White who treated me as a daughter. I spent very happy years with them finishing my education. Our ties are as strong as ever. We are constantly in touch and I regard them as family. I came to London where my parents had managed to establish a home; my brother was already living there and so finally we became a united family once more.

*　　*　　*

Irene Jacoby

(Danzig), Norfolk, UK

My brother and I arrived in London and were immediately put on a train to Derby where we were met by our guardians. It was some considerable time since we had eaten and so we looked forward to some food on the train. We were placed side by side in a carriage and of course were now on our own. I was not yet nine and my brother was just twelve.

After some considerable time we were brought some sandwiches and milk. I was absolutely delighted as I was by now very very hungry. My brother looked at the sandwiches – they were ham. I think I would have gone on eating them quite happily as it was food but my brother refused to allow me to eat, and we spent the rest of the journey to Derby looking at sandwiches that we could not eat. At the time I remember crying, but now I can look back with some amusement.

*　　*　　*

Sessi Jakobovits

(Dzialowski, Leipzig), Montreal, Canada

My two brothers, aged fifteen and thirteen, and myself aged eleven left Leipzig on 29 November for the meeting place in Berlin of children chosen from several cities.

Over the years I have repeatedly looked at my own children and grandchildren as they reached the age of eleven, and asked myself 'Could I send this child into the unknown, even to save its life?'

As instructed by our beloved mother, we were all at the window when the train pulled out of the Berlin station next morning, and soon passed over the anticipated bridge where she stood below, as promised, to get one more glimpse of her treasured offsprings and to wave just one more brave and smiling farewell – a scene I will remember for ever!

In order to pass the time, and having no better partners, my brothers taught me the rudiments of playing chess, and from then on, in every conceivable way, took over the responsibilities of both father and mother to me, which they have kept up until this very day. We travelled with a cousin three years my senior.

How great was our relief on crossing safely into Holland! As the train again gathered speed, two young ladies walked the length of the train, opening each compartment doors. Imagine our joy when they opened our door and enquired: 'Are there any Dzialowski children in here?' They were my father's Dutch cousins, who joined the train on entering Holland, providing sandwiches and fruit for all the children on board, sponsored by the Rotterdam and Amsterdam Jewish communities.

By afternoon we had been billeted in the huts of a lovely summer holiday resort called Dovercourt Bay.

Though it was still a great adventure, as a group of some sixty-five orthodox youngsters amongst over 250 in all, we now faced our first challenge of adult life. The primary purpose had been to save our lives, and it now fell on the shoulders of fourteen and fifteen year olds to save our traditions. A few boys emerged as our leaders. They organized prayer meetings and general duties. Soon it was Friday night, and we grouped ourselves in one corner and sang *Zemirot*, the traditional Sabbath melodies as we had been taught at home.

Several Jewish delegations came to visit. Our attempts at keeping our strong traditions were now recognized, and we were supplied with prayer books and even a small *Torah* for Services. Amongst the visitors were some wonderful people from Leeds, led by the late Mr Mark Labowitch. The Leeds delegation decided to act, and act they did. Leeds Jewry has always been very traditional at home and positive in its identification with Jewish causes. Many had themselves fled Europe at the turn of the century and from Czarist Russia and Poland thereafter. A lot had done very well (eg. Sir Montague Burton, the Ziff/Lewis families) and they now responded wholeheartedly.

In Harrogate was a convalescent home for Jewish children. Kosher, and staffed with a Matron, it was presently empty. What better use to make of it, than to house those thirty-five or so observant girls from Dovercourt. We had been in this resort just one week when our opportunity knocked. For me however, it was an unhappy moment. I had said farewell to my beloved parents, and was now expected to leave my brothers as well. But the latter took charge and urged me strongly to go. 'You will be with your cousin Esther, who has promised to look after you. Go, it will be for the best!' Sadly, my hut-companion from Dovercourt and I packed our few belongings, when suddenly the door burst open and her brother and mine rushed in. 'Imagine, we are going too,' they shouted excitedly. The Leeds committee had decided that they did not wish to separate siblings. The brothers of any girls going to the hostel would be taken into private families in Leeds, until a boys' hostel could be opened there shortly. Leeds was, after all, only a short distance from Harrogate. I was overjoyed!

I remember well Matron's kindly face and disposition. But honestly, I think she did not know what had hit her when we descended upon her. Here she was, in charge of a boisterous group of healthy young girls, with unbounding energy. How to keep them out of mischief? We were supplied with games and mountains of wool and knitting needles. The older girls taught the younger ones to knit. How handy this was just two years later, as I was able to do my bit for the war effort by knitting gloves, socks and scarves for English soldiers. We were so happy to be able to go to the Synagogue again on *Shabbat* morning. In the afternoon several ladies invited us and introduced us to High Tea.

Our brothers meanwhile were taken into private families in Leeds. All were housed, but mine. No-one had offered to take two boys. The last call was made to a unique couple – Jimmy and Fanny Lewis. 'Fanny, we have two brothers here and though we know you offered your home for only one boy, how about taking two?' Mrs Lewis did not hesitate for a single second. 'Of course I'll find room for two.' And she found room to sleep, and room in her heart. Three weeks later she was called again. 'Fanny, your boys have a third brother. The Nazis incarcerated him on Kristallnacht, though he was only seventeen. He was released by virtue of entrance papers to London University, but this was only a fake procedure to help to get him released and out of the country. He has now arrived in England – how about it?' And Mrs. Lewis again replied: 'I found room for two, we'll push the beds together and have room for three.' (When we left for England we did not know if our brother was alive at all. A fourth, the eldest, stayed with our parents, and spent the war years in hiding in Holland and miraculously survived.)

When my brothers joined the Lewis household it did not take them long to get to know each other, especially as the Lewis' also had a son of thirteen. Their daughter was at boarding school. Of course they talked about their eleven year old only sister and that first Sunday afternoon Mr Lewis piled everyone into his car and came to visit me in Harrogate. On sight, Mrs Lewis threw her arms around me in a warm, motherly hug and pressed a half-crown into my hand. Somewhat bewildered by this total stranger's kindness, I looked at my first English money, not comprehending its value. All I sensed was that here was a tiny lady, barely five feet, with an outsized heart, and unlimited generosity.

True to their intentions, some six weeks later, the Leeds committee opened a boys' hostel. My three brothers moved into the hostel and I came to live in the Lewis' home and in their hearts.

* * *

Inge Joseph

(Pollak, Vienna), Sheffield, UK

Extracts from her diary, written at age twelve

30 June 1939

I am twelve year old Inge Pollak and you are my darling diary to whom I'll tell everything and you'll of course keep it all to yourself.

I'm in England! In Falmouth, Cornwall, to be precise, at the house of Mr and Mrs Robins. The house is large and very nice and the journey was quite good, but something travelled with me, something I didn't want and which here too is my constant companion. It is homesickness. Not a pleasant feeling. We have a private tutor. She teaches us English amongst other things. She told Mr Robins that I don't work hard enough. I do try, but everything is so strange here. It seems to me that I've been torn out of my own warm nest, and it hurts terribly. But nobody must know this, only you and I.

I'm tortured by homesickness. If only I could be back in Vienna, going for walks on Sunday mornings with my parents. Dreams! Childish, wishful dreams. Everything is destroyed. But I must keep telling myself that everything will be alright in the end.

2 July 1939

The 'Miss' still thinks I'm lazy. I don't like Mrs Robins, but Mr Robins is nice. I feel a bit guilty and ungrateful. After all, the Robins's have done a wonderful deed, taking in two strange children.

Homesickness is terrible. Last night in bed I remembered how I used to pray and long, in my bed at night in Vienna, for my visa to come to England. Now I'm lying here in bed and pray and long to be back in Vienna. To think I may be here for months, years! I feel I shall die of misery. But then I fetch you out, darling diary, and tell you everything. If Mummy had the slightest suspicion, how upset and unhappy she'd be! She must never, never know! It hurts me to lie to her in my letters, but one mustn't only think of oneself, must one? Nobody must know how unhappy I'm here, only you.

Daddy wrote from Paris to say if anything is wrong we can write to him or to Uncle Hans. Shall I? Better not.

8 July 1939
Mr Robins has written to Mummy saying I should try and learn English soon.
I'm so happy he didn't say anything worse about me!

Mrs Robins was in a very bad mood yesterday. She keeps correcting my
English in front of other people. There will never be any room for her in my
heart. Only hope sustains me, hope that I shall soon be united with my
family.

25 August 1939
Mrs R again told us off for not doing our room properly.

'We give you a home,' she shouted, 'but you must keep it tidy.'
I think it's Alice, one of the maids, who tells tales about us. Mary is much
nicer.

I can be justly proud of what I've experienced at only twelve years old, I
think, and all the other Jewish children, too. I'm sure we've all become more
mature, sensible and clever. Unfortunately also sadder. Sometimes, when I
chat and laugh at mealtimes, I suddenly stop and ask myself: What reason
have you to laugh? Your situation is much too terrible for you to laugh. So
STOP!

Just imagine, Lieselotte has become homesick! She says she has had
enough of living in strangers' houses, riding in their cars and taking their
charity. The further the good old days slip back into the past, the more vivid
their memory becomes.

Yesterday, in a shop, the shop assistant asked me how I was getting on with
my English. Before I could reply, Mrs Robins said: 'She's a bit lazy.' This
really hurt me, because it was unfair. Everyone else says how well I speak
English now. She's so unjust. I hate her.

I'm still in love with Mr Robins – but not all the time.

2 September 1939
Germany and Poland are at war. It can't be long now till England and France
join in. I'm sure you're thinking, how can I write that down so calmly? Well, I'm
not calm. I'm in a terrible state. But my imagination fails me for once. What will
war be like? If there is really a war, will I ever see my parents again?

3 September 1939
Heaven help us! My eyes are full of tears and my heart is pounding. It is
WAR! It has come at last, the spectre of horrors I feared so long. Mummy,
Daddy, shall I see you again, and when? Now all hope has gone.

6 September 1939
First days of war. No sign of it here yet, except that we get no letters from
home. I don't know what has happened to my parents in Vienna and Paris.

14 September 1939
Lieselotte started at the High School today. She passed her Entrance Exam in
the summer. My turn next, but I'm sure I'll fail.

Ihr wart doch beide so jung noch und zart
Und als wir alleine nach Hause gingen
Da meinte ich das Hertz müsste im Leib mir zerspringen.
Gar oft hab ich geweint, das glaubet mir
Und trotzdem bin ich froh Ihr seid nicht hier.
Die fremden Menschen, die sich Euer angenommen
Die werden sicher einst in den Himmel kommen.
Ich segne sie mit jedem Atemzug
Und wie Ihr sie auch liebt, es ist doch nicht genug!

Es ist so trüb geworden um mich her
Gott nahm mir alles, mir blieb nichts mehr,
Den goldnen Vater, die Heimat! Nicht ein Winkel blieb,
Nichts, nichts, das mir wert und lieb!
Wie Vieh gezeichnet geh'n wir durch die Gassen
Nur unsern Namen hat man uns noch gelassen.
Oft auch Nummern um den Hals, das macht mir alles nicht aus,
Wenn unser Papsch nur noch lebte, wär ich auch hier zu haus!
Im Leben war ich noch nie so allein
Oft wünschte ich mir beim goldenen Papsch zu sein!

So viele sind gedrängt in einem Raum
Und wenn nebenan einer stirbt, man fühlt es kaum.
Leib liegt an Leib, man sieht des andern Leid
Und fühlt voll Schmerzen die eigne Einsamkeit.
  Kinder, seid Ihr gesund und brav?
Jetzt küsst Euch wohl niemand mehr in den Schlaf.
Manchmal des Nachts, da will es scheinen mir
Ich fühle Euch, Ihr lieget beide neben mir!
Denk nun, wenn wir uns einmal wiederseh'n
Wir werden einander nicht mehr versteh'n.
Ihr habt Euer Deutsch verlernt im jetzigen Leben
Und ich kann halt nur wenig Englisch reden.
Wird das nicht komisch sein, ach wär's nur schon so weit
Mich dünkt's es dauert noch eine Ewigkeit.

Ich lieg jetzt im Krankenhaus,
Tante Ernest macht meine Freude aus,
Sie füttert mich für Euch mit Liebe gesund
Und wenn sie kommt ist im Tage die schönste Stund
Meine Gedanken fliegen zu Euch beiden
Und bin doch froh Ihr seid nicht hier und will lieber um Euch leiden.
Ich trage es gerne, ist es auch hart,
Euch beiden blieb ja doch viel Hässliches erspart.

Das Leben hat mir halt alles Schöne genommen
Gott allein weiss, warum um alles Glück ich gekommen.
Doch litt ich gerne noch tausendfach Qualen,
Wüsst ich nur, ich könnt Euer Glück damit bezahlen.

Nun ist es spät, ich will schlafen gehen
Könnt' ich Euch beide nur einen Augenblick sehen!
So aber kann ich nichts als Briefe Euch schreiben,
Die voller Sehnsucht sind und doch liegen bleiben.

Geschrieben im November 1943 im Spital, Theresienstadt.

My darling girls,

It was almost five years ago that you journeyed into the world all alone. I still see you there in Vienna in the train compartment turning your little heads with eyes begging to let you stay with me. It seemed hard that we had let you go. You were both so young and vulnerable and as we went home alone it seemed as if my heart would break. Believe me, many times the tears rolled down my cheek. Nevertheless, I am glad that you are not here. The strangers who have taken care of you will surely go to heaven. I bless them with every breath. However much you may love them – it is not enough!

It has got so dark around me. God took everything, there was nothing left to me, he took your golden father, my country, not a corner was left, nothing that I appreciated and loved. We are walking the streets marked like cattle, they have left us nothing except our names. Often they also put numbers round our necks; all this would matter little to me, if only our Papa were still alive I would be at home even here. Never in my life have I been so alone. I often wished I were with golden Papa!

So many people are forced together in one room and when someone dies next to one, one hardly notices. Body close to body, one feels the pain of the others as well as one's own pain and one's loneliness.

Children, are you in good health and are you well behaved? I don't suppose that anyone kisses you goodnight. Sometimes at night I imagine I feel you both, that you are lying next to me. Just think, if ever we meet again we won't understand each other any more. You have forgotten your German in this life and I know only a very little English. Won't this be funny? Oh, would that the time had come! It seems to me it is taking an eternity!

I am now in hospital. Auntie Ernest is the source of my pleasure. She feeds me with love so that I might get better for your sakes and when she comes this is the most beautiful hour of the day. Our thoughts fly to you both; nevertheless I am glad that you are not here and I would rather suffer (than have you here). However hard it is, I suffer it gladly knowing that so much ugliness has been spared you. Life has taken everything from me; God alone knows why I have lost all my happiness. Yet, I would willingly suffer a thousand tortures if only I knew that this would pay for *your* happiness.

It is late now and I am going to sleep; if only I could see you just for a tiny moment. But, as it is, I can only write letters full of longing and which nevertheless stay unposted.

Written in the hospital, Theresienstadt, November 1943 and dedicated to my two beloved children with faithful love.

Your old mummy.

*   *   *

Kurt Landes

(Vienna), Jerusalem, Israel

I was eleven years old and we started at the railway station in Vienna, late 1938.

Fritzi, my sister, cried very much when we said good-bye to our dear parents. I had been away before from home, to summer camps, the Alps and even Yugoslavia, and took this to be just another good-bye. My sister, who is a bit older, must have realized that this was going to be something quite different.

The memories were of the train journey and stopping at night across the border in Belgium, and where we were served a bitter tasting coffee which I did not like but was told to drink it 'because we were in Belgium'.

Arriving at the Dovercourt holiday camp and being allocated a chalet was the first rest we had, although the place was for summer vacations and there was no heating. We wore all our clothes.

Christmas came and some kind ladies put up a huge tree in the dining hall for those who wanted to celebrate, and I remember a fight between the kids for or against celebrating. I, being a natural coward, stayed out of the fighting and concentrated on the extra refreshment provided for the occasion.

Shortly after, a group of girls were sent to 'Harritch', and I was sent along with my sister who insisted on looking after me.

'Harritch' was another happy holiday camp. This time with wooden chalets, and I remember sleeping under a pile of blankets, and clothes, with hot water bottles.

People began to arrive and to look us over as suitable candidates for, either to give their affection to, or 'doing their duty', or simply slavery (as happened to my sister).

I finished off with a kind, religious and childless couple in Birmingham, who saw me through the war years, the bombings and evacuation. I have remained in contact with my foster parents to this day.

Then there was the Aldridge hostel, then Wheelys Road hostel, and into the world of studies, work, marriage, fatherhood and conformity.

I sometimes wonder how I would have faced up to the challenge of deciding whether to send my children off to a foreign land, or even becoming foster parents to children with a strange language and strange clothes.

The sadness that my parents could never join us and had to die, together with most of our families, had not diminished over the years, and I turned towards the religious side of Jewishness together with the need and duty to live in our Jewish country.

My children shout at each other in Hebrew and take it for granted that they belong somewhere, and could fight for their rights as equal human beings here in our own land.

*   *   *

Gerd Lederman

(Berlin), Kathmandu, Nepal

'A short account of my life since I went to Nepal?' Actually I have just finished writing an account of my life with nature, solitary, on a 7,000ft mountain, for relatives and friends, some of whom are interested in more detail, but that certainly is not 'short'.

Looking back to 1939, this is probably the least dramatic or eventful chapter of my life. It is more of a philosophic culmination of many world wide experiences of fifty years, a distillation of various ways of life and trying to come to terms with my understanding of material and spiritual values – that elusive quest for the ultimate in happiness and contributing in the best possible way towards the well-being of others and the environment. Quite a mouthful! In other words it would be easier to write about my war years in Scotland, cycling to Israel to be part of the new State, serving in the IDF, again cycling across Europe and North America, on the way working in Hammerfest, Nordkop, Helsinki, looking after reindeer and walking across Lapland in the process, engineering in Canada and in the Arctic at 55° below zero, with snow shoes and husky sleds. Getting married in Mexico (to another Berlin Kind) and helping to run a Health Ranch. Driving a jeep down the unmade Pan American Highway through Central America to Panama followed by three months backpacking with a five year old son from

Colombia to Rio de Janeiro, including a month marooned in the Amazonian jungle. Finally fifteen years on a two hundred acre farm in Queensland, Australia, running an independent school and Buddhist meditation courses.

Also two years Colombo Plan Foreign Aid in Central Pakistan followed by an eighteen months Landrover journey from London to Singapore (my first visit to Nepal in 1963) including Iran, Pakistan, nine months in India, Malaya, Thailand, Cambodia, Vietnam before returning to Australia. And during the last ten years working for the Shah in Teheran until Khomeni arrived! Six years rehabilitation of British 'boat people' then tracing Tibetan refugee families in Shasa after a three week trans-Siberian train journey from London to Hong Kong through Mongolia, the Gobi Desert, China ... and since then in Asia, choosing Nepal as my final destination – meanwhile!! – after a year of Sanskrit

Gerd Lederman on a week's hike crossing 10,000 foot ranges in the mountains near his land, Nepal 1989.

at the University – using solar energy to cook my food and heat water and a hydraulic turbine to provide light for my twelve foot by twelve foot rock and mud house.

So now you probably see what I mean about Nepal. It is a beautiful, very peaceful place with friendly, helpful people, where my idea of a simple, very basic life close to nature is possible.

My former wife is now a Buddhist nun with her own monastery in Sri Lanka!

At the reunion it was of course interesting to meet former Glasgow hostel boys after forty years (having spent ten years together) and to exchange experiences, but very little common ground ... well, that's another story.

Shalom and *Namaste* (my soul touches your soul).

*   *   *

This document of identity is issued with the approval of His Majesty's Government in the United Kingdom to young persons to be admitted to the United Kingdom for educational purposes under the care of the Inter-Aid Committee for children.

THIS DOCUMENT REQUIRES NO VISA.

PERSONAL PARTICULARS.

Name ENGELHARD   Berta

Sex Female   Date of Birth 23.10.23

Place MUNICH

Full Names and Address of Parents

ENGELHARD   Moses + Rosa

9 Mariahilfstr.

MUNICH

Bertha Leverton
(Engelhard, Munich), London, UK

Looking back over the years, one normally recalls not the ordinary things that happened in one's life, but the happy or sad events. They may recede into the background but are never forgotten.

The memory of five years I spent with my foster family can never be erased. On the bonus side they also kept my younger brother Theo, aged twelve, and my sister Inge, aged nine. I was just fifteen on my arrival in England.

The treatment of me by 'Aunty Vera' I can now put down to her resentment of my good health, she being a semi-invalid. But her torment of us and me in particular was nothing compared to 'Uncle' Billy's 'friendliness' which I successfully managed to avoid for five years.

The first year was more endurable. We lived in Coventry, having been sponsored by Coventry Cathedral, but knew nothing about any Jewish refugee committee. However, Theo was *Bar Mitzvah* in the little *Shool* in Barras Lane and we were invited to the Rabbi's house for the *Seder* nights. But returning home with a packet of *Matzot* made the yearning for a real Jewish homelife even harder to bear. On the rare occasions that we were allowed to go to the Sabbath Service (a two mile walk), not one of the small congregation seemed to notice the three forlorn children who so much wanted to be part of Jewish life. One day, Theo came home crying and limping from school. He had fallen into a bomb crater. For several days he was made to go to school and told not to be a cry baby. I too was told not to be silly when I suggested he should see a doctor. In the end his foot swelled up so much that he had to be seen by a doctor and it was found he had walked with a broken ankle for days.

Many times Inge's little arms were full of bruises from being pinched by aunty for some trivial naughtiness. When we were banished to the kitchen to have our meals, we did not mind in the least.

After the blitz on Coventry, we were evacuated with the family to a small town in Yorkshire. Now we were really cut off from any Jewish contact; but there must have been a Committee who knew about us, for I remember that twice a year a young Rabbi, whose job it was to visit children in non-Jewish homes, came to see us. There was no point in complaining to him about our treatment. It was our word against theirs, and by that time we were so cowed, we just accepted our fate.

I was sent to work in a nearby cotton mill, doing the housework at night and weekends, and Theo worked in a factory from age fourteen. Inge went to school and won a scholarship. I liked to work because it took me away from 'home' and the girls there were kind and accepted me. We were on piece work and within a short time I earned top rates. But of course Theo and I had to hand over our pay packets intact, getting half a crown back from each pound earned – one eighth! But that was in theory only. For after a day or so even that small sum was 'borrowed' back, never to be returned.

There were times when we rebelled and did unheard of things like asking for our sweet coupons. Then aunty would fall into a 'faint', accusing us of impairing her health and being ungrateful. Uncle and aunty liked playing Monopoly, but it wasn't much fun just played by two, so we were usually invited to play with them. We soon found that if we won, they did not like it and tormented us afterwards. So we developed a skilful strategy of losing. This made them happy and earned us treats like tea and biscuits, or some sweets.

I recall one wonderful week in January. Aunty and uncle went to visit her mother in Coventry and we were given permission to open our wage packets and take out our allowance and a little extra for food. It was my twenty-first and Inge's fourteenth birthday during that week. We went to Oldham, the nearest town, lunched in a cafe on eggs, beans and chips, saw the sights and then went to the swimming baths where I taught Inge to swim and then had our photographs taken. The happiness and freedom of that birthday will remain for ever in my memory. But even more happiness was in store for us.

Our parents had managed to escape in 1940 and, after five years journeying, ended up in Portugal. It was still war time. A law had been passed in parliament permitting close relatives from neutral countries to travel to England, providing they had children under fifteen there. Inge qualified on that score. Aunty's mother had bought another house in Coventry (she ran boarding houses) on hearing about our parents coming. It

was intended to install them as housekeepers there so that they could earn
their keep. However, when they arrived and saw the state we were in (I had
no shoes, only wooden clogs for working in the cotton mill where they were
the usual footwear), there was a terrible rumpus. We children had decided
not to say anything bad about Aunty and Uncle, but during the night Mutti
had wormed the whole story out of me. Inge had lost all and Theo most of his
German. Parents are not deceived and I shall never know how, but Papa, via
the village telephone, and not speaking any English, managed to contact the
nearest Refugee Committee (Manchester) and within two hours they arrived
by car and we were taken away. My parents insisted that I was bought a pair
of shoes on the way. This was a few days after my twenty-first birthday.
When I recently bought my records from the CBF I found we had been
labelled troublemakers for complaining to our parents.

A new, happy era started. We settled in Birmingham. I married and raised
a family and have two daughters and nine wonderful grandchildren in
England and Israel. I am no stranger to tragedy either, having lost a
wonderful son, Danny, at the age of twenty-one. Also Theo died forty-three
years old. But I console myself with the knowledge that I can visit their and
my parents' grave, a comfort which, unfortunately, is denied to so many of
my generation of Kinder.

*Our parents on their arrival
in England, January 1944.*

PARLIAMENTARY COMMITTEE ON REFUGEES

CHAIRMAN:
MAJOR VICTOR CAZALET, M.P.
VICE-CHAIRMEN:
LORD MARLEY
H. GRAHAM WHITE, M.P.
HON. SECRETARY:
MISS ELEANOR RATHBONE, M.P.

SECRETARY:
MISS VERA CRAIG

7, COWLEY STREET, S.W.1.
TELEPHONE ABBEY 2249

ABBey 3131.

From: 5, Tufton Court,
Westminster, S.W.1.

28th June, 1943.

Dear Miss Engelhard,

In reply to your letter of June 1st, I think from the
facts as you tell them to me that you now have a chance,
which did not exist until recently, of getting permission
for your parents to come to this country.

In the Debate of May 19th, Mr. Peake, the Under-Secretary
for the Home Office, announced three new categories of aliens
who, subject to security conditions, would be considered
eligible for admission and one of these was:

"Parents of children under sixteen who are already
here and who came here unaccompanied".

I gather that you have a brother and a sister both under
sixteen and that they did arrive here "unaccompanied" at least
by any adult member of the family.

As you say the matter is already in the hands of the Home
Office and the Polish Consulate, I do not think that anything
would be gained by my making representations. But I enclose
an additional copy of this letter which you could send, if you
liked, to the Polish Consulate so as to draw attention to the
fact I have indicated. I should be interested to know what
answer you get from the Home Office.

Whatever happens as to this, I think you are to be
congratulated on the fact that your parents are in Lisbon
where from all that we hear they are in no great danger. But
I can understand your and their wish to be re-united. Hoping
you will succeed in this,

Yours sincerely,

Eleanor F. Rathbone

Miss Bertha Engelhard,
c/o Sharpe,
Rosehill,   Delph,
Near Oldham,   Lancs.

Letter from Miss Eleanor Rathbone M.P. to Bertha Engelhard, now Leverton

INSTRUCTIONS FROM COLONEL LEVEY.
FOR ALL HOSTEL MASTERS.

--   9th July, 1941

I have received information that there is considerable
slackness with regard to the boys getting out of bed
sharp at 6. o'clock in the morning. I have information
that within the last 48 hours several boys have remained
in bed until as late as 6.15. a.m.

No boy will be allowed to remain in bed on any day in the
week, which includes Sundays; one minute after 6.0. o'clock.

I shall hold the master of each Hostel responsible for
this instruction being most strictly carried out.

The leader of each room will be held responsible to the
Hostelmaster for every boy being out of bed at one minute
after 6.0.

The next report I receive of boys being allowed to remain
in bed after 6.0. will mean that the boy will forfeit
his Foster Parents money for 3 months and I shall appoint
as quickly as possible a fresh Hostelmaster.

BY ORDER:

(Lieut.Col.J.H.Levey)

INSTRUCTIONS FROM COLONEL LEVEY
FOR ALL HOSTEL MASTERS.
9 July 1941

Dov Levy

(Vienna), Ashkelon, Israel

We were a family of five when Hitler occupied Austria. I was fifteen years old, my two sisters were thirteen and twelve. When my parents realized the danger we were in, they tried to get us children out of the country. There was some talk about sending fifty boys to a *Yeshiva* in England, but the committee which dealt with the matter seemed to take their time and nothing ever came of it. Then, on 10 November 1938, my father was arrested. A few weeks later he was released and given two weeks to leave the country.

It was only then that we first heard of the children's transport to England which Dr Schonfeld was organizing. He cut red tape and didn't rest days and nights until he succeeded in obtaining permits for five hundred children. Our parents registered us at once and we left Vienna on 12 December 1938. Four days later, during *Chanukkah* week, we arrived in England. Among the other children in the transport were the girl who eventually became my wife, her sister, and my little cousin. Had it not been for this wonderful man, Rabbi Dr Schonfeld, what would have become of those five hundred children?

Since the Avigdor High School was then closed for *Chanukkah,* we were placed temporarily at the school until arrangements could be made to move us elsewhere. The youngest children were taken to Rabbi Dr Schonfeld's private residence, where he and other volunteers looked after them. The refugee committees, which were supposed to be helping the refugees, refused to help us, claiming that Dr Schonfeld, who had brought us over, should look after us himself. To this day, I can't understand why this man who saved our lives should have been refused cooperation from the 'Establishment'.

In the meantime several Synagogue committees were formed; they put up some hostels to look after us. I was placed at first into a hostel at 65 Lordship Road. Later on I was assigned to a hostel at 44 Rectory Road until we were evacuated with the Jewish Secondary School at the outbreak of the war. My two sisters and my future wife and her sister were placed into a well-run hostel, financed by a joint committee of the Grove Lane and Egerton Road Synagogues. My little five-year-old cousin was adopted by a family. But after a few months that family sent her back to Rabbi Schonfeld.

When we were evacuated to Shefford with the Jewish Secondary School, our hostel in Rectory Road was abandoned and all our belongings which we had managed to bring from home were stolen or destroyed. Rabbi Schonfeld took us back and arranged to get us clothing, pocket money and other needs.

When I started work as an apprentice after leaving the Jewish Secondary School in Shefford and I didn't earn enough to pay for lodgings, Rabbi Schonfeld supported me until I earned enough to pay my own way. When I returned to London toward the end of the war and started to work as a carpenter, he helped me again by employing me as a teacher at a small

Talmud Torah at his premises at 86 Amhurst Park. When I left for Israel in 1951 he tried to encourage me to enter the teaching profession because I had made a success of my work at the *Talmud Torah.* Eventually I took his advice and to this day have never regretted it.

He even visited us a few years ago when we were on vacation in Jerusalem and when my wife mentioned to him what he had done for us, that he had actually saved our lives, he didn't want to hear about it. 'Forget what has been,' he said. But we have not forgotten. The six children whom he took out of the Nazi hell have now produced a total of forty children and grandchildren. We hope there will be many more to come. We will always remember this wonderful man, who sacrificed much to save thousands of children, to give them new homes and to make them an asset to *Am Yisrael.*

*   *   *

Kate Lewin

(Berlin), Paris, France

I left Berlin in April 1939 with a Kindertransport and was adopted by a family in Bristol. When war broke out, the husband was called up, and they were unable to keep me any longer. The school which I had been attending as a day student kindly took me in as a boarder for one term. In the meantime my parents had been able to leave Berlin also; but of course they were not allowed to work in England. We were waiting for our visas to the USA to come through, so they stayed with friends in London, where they were unable to have me. After one term, the school refused to keep me any longer. In the meantime bombings had begun in Bristol and we students (I was thirteen at the time) spent nights in the school's air raid shelter. The parents of one of the other students kindly offered to take me in.

At that point my father was interned on the Isle of Man. My mother was afraid to be alone, and asked me to come and join her. So I left Bristol for London. Almost as soon as I got there, the bombings began there too. I did not attend school for six months and used to take out books from the local library during all-clears. We spent our nights in the shelter on Hampstead Heath. Finally our visa for the US came through and my father was released from internment. We left for New York in November 1940, from Liverpool, in a convoy where we had nightly training in what to do should we be attacked.

I stayed in New York throughout 1947, finishing high school and going to college there. I then came to France, intending to stay for a year and have, with some intervals, been living here ever since.

Martin Lewis

(Lewin, Berlin), California, USA

I was born in January 1922 in Tempelburg, Pommern, Germany. After graduating under most difficult circumstances from *Mittelschule*, April 1938, I moved to Berlin to attend Ortschool.

On Kristallnacht I was arrested, sixteen years old, and spent two months in Sachsenhausen concentration camp. I was released through Bloomsbury House's help, and arrived in England, Dovercourt Camp on 7 February with a Kindertransport from Berlin.

I never saw my family again. I eventually was sent to a Children's hostel at 243 Willesden Lane London. In June 1940 I was interned on the Isle of Man.

In December 1940 I volunteered to join the Pioneer Corps. In 1942 I volunteered to join the 21st Independent Parachute Company, 1st Airborne Division.

I served in North Africa, was wounded in Italy, recovered and fought in the Battle of Arnhem, and later invaded Norway and participated in the surrender of all German forces in Norway which signalled the end of the war. I was released in 1946 after serving six years.

I married Irene Ohnstein in 1947, also arrived from Berlin via a children's transport. In 1948 we left for New York and after four months we arrived in Los Angeles, California. We had three children, lost one son, and four years ago I lost my lovely wife. I am still very active in my business.

*   *   *

The following article is reprinted by kind permission from the *Hampstead and Highgate Express*, 25 October 1946

A twenty-four year-old Jewish refugee who was dragged from his home in Pomerania eight years ago by the Gestapo and thrown into a concentration camp, has now, after many thrilling experiences, settled down in Hilltop Road, West Hampstead, and is seeking British nationality.

He is Mr Martin David Lewis. Born at Tempelburg in 1922, he said goodbye to his parents when he was fourteen and went to Berlin to study at an engineering college. Things went well for two years, and then his father died. Martin returned home for his father's funeral.

On the day he arrived at Tempelburg, Himmler launched his Jewish 'purge' to revenge the death of a prominent Nazi murdered by a young Jew. After he had been only three hours at his father's bedside with his mother, a number of Gestapo thugs smashed their way into the house and dragged young Lewis out. He never saw his mother again.

In an interview with an '*Express*' reporter this week, he described his adventures over the next eight years.

'I was taken, together with many other young Jews, to a concentration camp at Sachsenhausen, accused of murdering the prominent Nazi. All of us, of course, were innocent.'

The conditions in the camp were dreadful and they received rough treatment from the guards.

'It was plain that the Nazis were preparing for the extermination of the Jews on a large scale,' he said.

He spent six weeks in the camp and was eventually released by order of the International Child Welfare Organisation and brought to this country. He was lodged at a hostel for Jewish refugees in Willesden where he studied the English language. At the outbreak of war he was interned with enemy aliens in the Isle of Man, but in 1940, when he was eighteen, he volunteered for service with the British Army. His application was granted and he joined the Pioneer Corps. Later he volunteered for the paratroopers and by 1942 was wearing the familiar red beret.

His officers recognised Lewis as a keen soldier and he quickly gained promotion. As staff-sergeant he served in Italy and took part in the famous Taranto operation. He was later wounded and sent to Tunisia. His really great day came when he took part in the Arnhem campaign.

'As one of the marker force I was almost the first to land.'

Lewis remarked that the fight got hotter every hour, and after a day or two the German artillery was murderous. 'I got away, I suppose I was one of the lucky ones,' he said.

Last month he was one of the party who revisited Arnhem to pay homage to their comrades who fell in the battle.

With no relations in this country, Mr Lewis's application to become a British subject has been sponsored by his commanding officer. He hopes to start work in a leather factory very shortly.

*   *   *

Nina Lieberman, Ph.D.

(Margules, Salzburg), Woodstock, USA

KINDERTRANSPORT REUNION: REMINISCENCES AND REFLECTIONS

20 June 1989, 9 am. – Northern Line of the London Underground. I spotted them on the train and turning to my husband, I said: 'I think they're also going to the Reunion.' Middle-aged, somewhat self-conscious in their Sunday finery on a weekday, they seemed to be a mirror-image of ourselves. And yes, they did get off at Harrow-on-the-Hill, then disappeared briefly, only to rejoin a crowd of us later on the shuttle bus to the Leisure Centre in Harrow, the meeting place of the Fiftieth Reunion of those brought over mainly from Germany and Austria under the humanitarian action by the British Government, which gave 10,000 unaccompanied children refuge from Nazi persecution.

The bus trip was a foretaste of things to come. Men and women introduced themselves to one another. Across the aisle from us, sat a retired engineer from California, originally from Hamburg, and in front of him a woman whose face looked strangely familiar to me. An exchange of words, a recognition. As a young girl she had lived in a hostel in Cambridge. At that

time, I was working in the regional office of the refugee Children's
Movement which had under its care some eight hundred refugee boys and
girls who, like other children from London, had been evacuated to the
countryside to escape the bombing of that city. Previously, her cousin had
made contact with me in the United States, and we had an emotional 'mini-
reunion' in Cold Spring on the Hudson, a place midway between where he
and I lived.

Once arrived at the Harrow Leisure Centre, another cousin, now an
elegantly coiffured grandmother, introduced herself to me. Of course, I
remembered Paula. We hugged and kissed, the spouses shook hands.

It was now eleven o'clock. The doors of the hall would not open for
another half an hour. London was experiencing a heat-wave, with temperatures in the middle eighties. We had met my sister on the bus and the three of
us were now moving in and out of a constantly shifting mass of people who
not only sought the shade but one another. The badges told of place of origin
and current place of residence. We did not expect to meet anyone from
Salzburg, our own home-town, but there were hundreds of people from
Vienna with whom we shared memories. Once inside the hall, this was borne
out by tables marked 'Vienna', which filled almost a quarter of the space.
What had started on the bus as excited chatter now rose to a crescendo of
voices, a pouring out of stories to one another. People were milling about;
they sat down first in one spot; then found some long-lost friend from the
1940s and moved to another table. Soon towns of origin and towns of
residence became intermingled. The air became heavy from the outside heat
and charged with the emotions of the close to 1,000 people crowded into the
hall.

I, too, decided to make the rounds of the tables, joined by my sister. As we
skirted the tables for Berlin, Hamburg, Karlsruhe, Leipzig, we finally arrived
at some smaller tables, one of which was set up for invited notables. And lo
and behold, there sat Ms Joan Stiebel, one of the movers and shakers at
Bloomsbury House who not only knew us, but had known most of the
members of the Cambridge Refugee Committee, with whom I had worked
from 1940 to 1946. Looking back, we could have had a good laugh about the
fights carried on by one of the members, the wife of a Cambridge don, whose
speciality was finding intellectually gifted children and getting them into
prestigious public schools, sometimes over the protests of headquarters at
Bloomsbury House. Many a legal scholar, physicist, or mathematician owes
his or her career to the bulldog determination of this tiny woman, Greta
Burkill. Non-Jewish herself, as were all the other members of the Committee,
she readily sought my father's advice on the children's religious education.
He was a Rabbi, strictly traditional, who, because of his own exposure to
secular education, could appreciate and convey to others the possibility of
combining Judaism with science, law, and needless to say, the humanities.
My sister and I had been fortunate enough to be reunited with my parents

and living in Cambridge and we, too, benefited from my father's attitude of how to maintain a Jewish identity in a mainly Gentile environment.

Voices from the podium cut through our conversation and the flood of memories. It was now close to 12.30 and the official programme, starting with a Memorial Service, was about to begin. Three Rabbis and a Cantor, all original 'Kinder', led those assembled in the chanting of Psalms in Hebrew and English, the recitation of '*El Male Rachamim*', followed by *Kaddish*, not only for those of the Kinder who lost their lives fighting with the Allied Forces or in the Israel War of Independence, but also those who died of natural causes. And, of course, in everybody's mind were the parents, grandparents, aunts, uncles, cousins who died of unnatural causes, at the hands of the Nazis and their collaborators.

The Opening Ceremony, with the official greetings from the representatives of the British Government and the Anglo-Jewish Community struck a different note. Socio-historical in nature, they presented the factors leading up to the admission of 10,000 Kinder in 1938/39 and surveyed the contributions made by these orphans to the communities and countries which adopted them and whose loyal citizens they are today. The Minister of State for Home Affairs, Mr Timothy Renton, MP, quoted Emma Lazarus' lines, incised on the Statue of Liberty. I looked around me: the once wretched refuse were now well-dressed, comfortable-looking men and women, seemingly sure of themselves and of their place in the world. And yet, is all well that ends well? Perhaps a glimpse of the underlying pain was revealed in a question asked later by one of the Kinder:

'I often wonder, when I think of the million and a half children who perished in Hitler's concentration camps, why I was spared? What was so special about me that I survived?'

As we look inward, all of us who survived have to answer that question for ourselves at one point or another. Do we have a special responsibility to those who died? Is it incumbent upon us to compensate for their unlived lives? Am I writing these lines today for Anne Frank, whose talents were so brutally cut short?

There are no easy answers. Each one of us carries the guilt of the survivor as a permanent burden, but also as an ever-present challenge; to make a mark with the life that was given to us twice.

*   *   *

Nina Lieberman

(Margules, Salzburg), Woodstock, USA.

GRETA BURKILL – A GREAT HUMANITARIAN REMEMBERED

To have known Greta Burkill was a privilege. To have worked with her was an experience never to be forgotten. I was fortunate to have known and worked with this very special woman.

In 1940 I was appointed to work in the regional office of the Refugee Children's Movement in Cambridge. Hundreds of children had been evacuated to the countryside, among them the children who had been brought over under the aegis of the Movement just before the war. Since the Movement was in *loco parentis,* they needed to be visited, supervised and cared for. Among the chaos and dislocation of the war, this was a stupendous task. Barely acclimatised to their new surroundings in the cities where most of them had been placed with their guarantors, they were once more uprooted.

Greta Burkill, then a member of the Cambridge Committee looking after these children, proved a power of strength not only to her co-workers but also to the children whom she truly befriended. She was especially interested in those boys and girls who were intellectually gifted and managed to place a good number of them in public schools and later on, at universities. Many a physicist, mathematician or legal scholar owes his or her career opportunities to the tenacity of Greta Burkill. Indeed, when thwarted by bureaucrats, she could be like a tigress fighting for her cubs.

I learned many things from Greta Burkill, not the least of them never to give up on your original goal. I achieved my own educational fulfilment in the United States, where I obtained my doctorate in educational psychology. On my visits back to Cambridge, she was always most gracious to me and my husband, who also came to admire her greatly. Truly, she continues to live on in the lives she influenced.

*   *   *

Manfred Lindenbaum

(Unna), USA

For me this year has been a year of remembrance. This is the fiftieth anniversary of the beginning of World War II and even though I was only a child, I have vivid memories of the months which preceded the outbreak of war. The war against the Jews started earlier. I remember in my first years of school the constant propaganda against Jews and other foreigners by teachers in the classroom – with Jewish children present. At first we were outcasts – and then we were beaten.

In the autumn of 1938 shortly after the High Holidays, the Nazis announced that all Jews with Polish passports would be returned to Poland. This included my parents even though they were already second generation immigrants. We were required to report to the police station, we were allowed ten marks in German currency and a suitcase; everything else was confiscated. We were taken to the railway station in Dortmund, and forced to board a train. Our family included my mother and father, my older sister, younger brother and my grandfather who was blind. It was a Friday evening. None of us had ever travelled on *Shabbat*.

I remember getting on the train, but very little of the journey. Perhaps we survive the trials of childhood by knowing when to sleep. This scene took place at all major rail centres of Germany. Some twenty-five thousand people were transported to the border town of Zbaszyn. Many were chased across the no man's land separating Germany and Poland by the German SS. Men, women and children, without regard to age or health were forced to run at gun point. I was eight years old – but I remember!

We lived in Zbaszyn under primitive circumstances for about ten months. We slept on straw in a partially completed factory building as many as fifty people to a single room. Food and some clothing was provided by Jewish communities in Poland. But war was imminent. News of the Kristallnacht atrocities in Germany came to us and I remember being told that our Synagogue in Unna had been destroyed.

Jewish communities throughout the world heard of these outrages and appealed to their governments to intervene. The Jewish congregations of the United Kingdom appealed to the British Government to admit Jewish children whose lives were in danger throughout Europe. It was agreed that up to 10,000 children would be admitted on condition that a bond be posted for each child and that a guarantor would be identified so that the new immigrants would not become a burden. Committees were formed to organize this effort. Speed was essential.

The danger of a German invasion of Poland at any time was obvious among the thousands of refugees in Zbaszyn. We heard of the efforts in Great Britain to bring in Jewish children. Many parents registered their children with the Kindertransport Committees. But some did not. Not all could accept the grim necessity of relinquishing their children for a safer haven.

My parents decided during the summer of 1939 that we would all travel East to Grodno, away from the German border. I remember all of us again going to a railway station. We were waiting on the platform for the train to Grodno; suddenly a man ran onto the platform. He was out of breath; he asked everyone to listen. He was a Kindertransport representative. He had a list of names of children who should not get on the train, their papers for travel to England had arrived.

My parents had but a few moments to decide to leave their children. My sister Ruth was thirteen, my brother Manfred was seven and I was nine. We watched the train pull out of the station. My brother and I arrived in London on 29 August 1939; three days before the invasion of Poland. My sister was to have been on the next ship . . .

My brother and I lived in England through the war in relative safety and at least our physical needs were met.

Much has already been written and recorded. We must remember and remind those who might forget, and we must teach those who are not aware and we must confront those who chose not to be reminded. It is only by our remembrance that we can invoke the will of God that this shall not happen again.

This Rosh Hashanah – fifty years later – we must ask two questions.

'Can there be another Holocaust?' Sadly we must conclude that 'Yes, it can happen again.' The second question is: 'Is a recurrence of the Holocaust inevitable?' And to this question we must hope and pray that our vigilance, and our remembrance can prevent a repetition, so that we can affirm:

'No, it is not inevitable. No! it must not be.'

*   *   *

Professor Siegfried Lindenbaum

(Unna), Lawrence, Kansas, USA

My brother and I were among a number of children who came from Zbaszyn, Poland, where we lived under temporary, primitive conditions after having been deported from Germany during the autumn of 1938 – shortly before Kristallnacht. We were separated from our parents in the summer of 1939 and sent to England on the ship *Warszawa* We arrived in London on 29 August 1939 – probably the last refugee boat before the war. I was nine years old and my brother Manfred was not quite eight. Eventually we were taken to a Jewish Boys' home in Ely, Cambridgeshire, which was the community to which the Jews' Free School was evacuated. There were approximately fifty boys, nearly all refugees. The home was under the direction of Rabbi A. Kon. After the war, the home continued for some time in London at 167 Amhurst Road, London E8. I am not sure what happened to the home after my brother and I left in 1946 to join relatives in the United States.

Just a brief note about myself – I am a professor of Pharmaceutical Chemistry at the University of Kansas. My wife Loraine is American born and an elementary school teacher. We have three children Jeff, aged twenty-nine, a physician in New York, a daughter Ann, aged twenty-seven, an attorney in Los Angeles and a daughter, Beth, age nineteen, a student at the University of Wisconsin.

*   *   *

Irene Liron
(Borchardt), Israel

At the beginning of May 1939 I arrived with a Kindertransport in London. There I met my new foster parents. Of course I knew no English, so communication was almost impossible, but I meekly followed them to their car, and then began our long drive to the little village in Sussex where they lived. They were very good to me in every aspect. The father of the family was a gentleman farmer, nearly the whole village belonged to him, and from a materialistic point of view, I was very well off.

Evidently I was a bit of a tomboy, and after a few days of settling down in my new home, started climbing trees. My foster mother wrote of this to my parents, and straight away I got an urgent letter from my mother. 'You mustn't climb trees,' she wrote, 'You must not add worries to your new family. You must not be wild. You must be obedient. You must be quiet. You must be grateful that they took you. You must be very good. You must do all you are asked, and even read their wishes from their lips before they are said.'

Actually all her letters were somewhat similar. Always reminding me to be good and grateful, and always complaining that I wrote so little in my letters to them. But looking back now, I don't see how a ten year old child could be expected to write long letters every week, but I do understand my mother's worries about my possible bad behaviour (and the possibility of being sent back). I should hate to be in her situation where she had to send her youngest daughter to unknown people in a foreign country.

Meanwhile a single lady was found who was willing to take in my thirteen and a half year old sister. She was supposed to come in August, and my adoptive family was going to take me to London to meet her on her arrival, but then this woman decided to take a holiday first, and the date was changed till the middle of September. She never made it, of course, because the war started, so my complete family perished in Hitler's death camps. As far as I know I have no living relatives at all in the world.

In September I started school. I was sent with my adopted brothers to boarding school in Devon, and till this day I am grateful for the good education which I received there. Then, because of the bombing, we attended the village school for about two months.

This school consisted of one large room with two teachers. I don't know if I learned anything during this period, but I tried very much to 'belong' and not be different from the other children. I wasn't very successful in that, as I was considered a German (they didn't know what Jewish was) and as England was at war with Germany, it made things even more difficult for me. But what was most difficult for me at this school was the weekly visit to the village church for prayers. My parents were traditional but not religious Jews, but all the same I felt that by going to church I was sinning. I pretended to pray, with the rest, listened to the vicar's sermon, but it was a terrible ordeal for me. Of course I know that if I had said one sentence, that I was Jewish and didn't want to go to church, nobody could have made me – which just goes to show how foolish children are, because their one desire is not to be different.

Luckily the next term we returned to boarding school, where we had no religious instruction at all. But then somehow the Jewish refugee committee got hold of me. Hearing that I got no religious instruction, they decided that I must take a correspondence course in Bible lessons. I was sent a Bible and weekly lessons to my school. The lessons themselves were simple, but what disturbed me was that on the envelope was clearly printed 'Bible lessons' and I was afraid that the other children would laugh at me if they knew about this. So on the day of the expected envelope I would rush to where the post was delivered, to get hold of this discriminating evidence before anyone else managed to see it. Evidently nobody ever did, because it was never mentioned.

So much for childhood memories. After finishing school, I went to work as an assistant in a home for children who had been brought to England from the concentration camps, and it was here that I met other Jews for the first time since arriving in England. Ernest Bevin, who was then Minister of Foreign Affairs and a great anti-Semite and anti-Zionist, turned me into both Jew and Zionist, and in October 1948 I emigrated to Israel, where I served in the army, married, gave birth to three children, and am now the proud grandmother of seven (with another two on the way).

*   *   *

Shmuel Lowensohn

(Vienna), Radlett, Herts, UK

Reprinted from *Link*, the Magazine of the Borehamwood Elstree and Radlett Jewish Community, September 1989

Amongst all the accounts of the abominable horrors of the Nazi era there is at least one story that warms the heart. The British Government agreed to allow an unspecified number of unaccompanied children up to seventeen years old from Germany, Austria and Czechoslovakia to come to this country as 'transmigrants', provided they would not be a financial burden on the state. A refugee organization based in Britain (now the CBF World Jewish Relief) was set up to bring Jewish children out of the Nazi hell to freedom. Just under 10,000 children were saved through the efforts of Jews and many Gentiles as well. To achieve this marvellous aim called for much organization, but two problems had to be overcome; firstly a great deal of money was needed, and secondly the committees had to try and arrange to provide for their foster children for an unknown period.

Many of these children are today approaching retirement. A good proportion of the Kindertransport children have had notable careers and have become well-known personalities. In our community we have such a man; he has given his working (and now retired) life to Jewish institutions, such as The Federation of Zionist Youth, the Jewish National Fund and the Joint Israel Appeal, holding the highest office in each. We interviewed this remarkable man – Shmuel Lowensohn – for LINK and this is his story:

'My parents, my sister and I lived in a flat in Vienna in the 1930s but life became almost impossible when the Nazis came to power with the *Anschluss* in March 1938. My father's business was taken away from him and he had to resort to menial jobs to keep us going. Our situation worsened rapidly and almost all aspects of civilized life were denied to us. A Nazi official took a great liking to our flat and he took it from us. We were thrown out on to the street but managed to find shelter with friends. Jews were harrassed on the streets; my sister and I were picked up and held for several days. My sister was forced to scrub pavements and I was expelled from school (Gymnasium) at the age of thirteen.

We then got to hear of a scheme set up in Britain to save Jewish children by getting them out of Nazi countries. Although I was very young I did voluntary work at the *Israelitische Kultusgemeinde* (Jewish Community) offices in Vienna, and my father insisted that I include my name on one of the lists of children to be saved. He knew full well that, if I were to leave, we would be unlikely to see each other ever again. The day came when my parents took me to the railway station. I need not, nor can I, describe our feelings as the train pulled out of the station.

ISRAEL. KULTUSGEMEINDE WIEN

Wien, am ....Oct.29th,1946.... 194....
I., Schottenring 25

     Mr.S.Loewensohn,
     12, Stirling Road,
     <u>Edgbaston, Birmingham,16,</u>
          England.

Dear Sir:-

         Referring to your esteemed letter of the Aug.11th,
last, we have to inform you to our greatest regret that nothing
is known to us about the fate of all the persons, who have
been deported to·Izbica in 1942. For your guidance we beg
to mention that about 5.ooo Jews from Vienna have been evacuated to this place but, as far as we know, nobody has returned from there.
         We regret very much not to be in a position to give
you any definite information regarding this case and remain,
dear Sir,

                             Yours very truly

ISRAEL. KULTUSGEMEINDE WIEN
Z.3/E

Wien, am Dez.15th   6
I, Schottenring 25   194....

     Mr.S.Loewensohn,
     12 Stirling Road
     Edgbaston
     Birmingham 16,

           ————————————

Dear Sir,
                  Referring to your esteemed letter of
the April 24th, last we have to inform you to our greatest
regret that   Vienna
        Loewensohn Isser, last address/2.Ferdinandsstr.31/25
        Loewensohn Mina   "   "   "

have been evacuated to IZBICA on 15/5/1942, not ret'd.

We are Sir,   Yours very truly

I now admire their herosim, and they were not even allowed to come near to the train to say goodbye but were held back by the Nazi police behind a barrier. I never saw my parents again – they died in a Nazi gas oven. None of the thousands of children who were brought out to life and freedom, can ever forget the selfless gesture of their beloved parents. Most fortunately, my sister managed to get to Palestine in June 1939 and after the war we were able to meet again. She lived in Palestine, later Israel, until her untimely death two years ago.

As for me, all I had with me on the train and boat to Britain to begin my new life was a pack of food, a tiny case of belongings and a number on a string round my neck. Two days later we landed at Dovercourt on the Essex coast. Every day we stood in line to be inspected and selected by the host families, a scene repeated at several other locations. I and other boys of fourteen years were not chosen and were sent to Barham House, a special school near Ipswich.

I was able to correspond with my parents via the Red Cross, but as the months went by this became increasingly difficult and there were long periods when I heard nothing from Vienna. The last communication I had was in 1942. I do not know exactly what happened to my dear parents – where they were taken to and what miseries they had to endure in their last days and this alone gives me much grief. I ascertained after the war that they were taken to Izbica concentration camp where they perished.

Some of the 'unadopted' children were not cared for by Jews and I was sent to live in a hostel in Birmingham, which was set up and financed by Christadelphians. When I reached the age of sixteen, I was interned as an 'enemy alien'. We were shunted around the country and finally finished up in the Isle of Man. There it was that I began to arrange classes in Ivrit and Jewish Studies. I was fortunate to be released after a comparatively short time and reclassified as a 'Friendly Alien of Enemy Origin'! I returned to the hostel in Birmingham and managed to scratch a living working in a munitions factory and later in the fish market and a paper factory, finally becoming articled to a well-known firm of Chartered Accountants. I also studied as an external student at Birmingham University and became more and more deeply involved with Jewish Zionist organizations. I was chairman of the Birmingham Zionist Youth Council and on the executive of the Federation of Zionist Youth.

Shortly after the end of the war, I was fortunate to be selected to study Youth Leadership and Methodology at the 'Institute for Youth Leaders from Abroad' in Jerusalem and in November 1947 I went to Palestine where I met my sister, for the first time since 1938. I was privileged to play a part in the Israel War of Independence. When I returned from Israel, my involvement with Jewish Zionist organizations became my career – with the Federation of Zionist Youth, the Jewish National Fund and finally with the Joint Israel Appeal, and in all organizations I was privileged to hold positions of responsibility for very long periods.

My wife and I produced three daughters, one of them now lives in Israel, and we have two grandsons. Recently my wife and I moved to Radlett in my 'retirement'. In my working life I have had the opportunity to meet and get to know many of the luminaries of the Jewish (and also not-so-Jewish) world – but that is quite another story! One of my more pleasant duties was to visit Israel very often on behalf of the various organizations, especially Joint Israel Appeal Missions.'

This is only a brief outline of Shmuel's moving story. In his 'retirement' Shmuel still works for the Jewish Community. He helped to form and is the first chairman of the Borehamwood, Elstree and Radlett JACS (Jewish Association of Cultural Societies) and also helped with the recent Reunion of Kindertransports by collating and producing a most interesting and lovely Souvenir Brochure.

One may say that Shmuel has left his mark on every aspect of Jewish life here and abroad (his wife calls him the Jewish 'Mr Chips'). He is a warm-hearted and most respected gentleman. We are honoured to have him in our Community.

Shmuel Lowensohn interviewed by Bernard Gerstein

*   *   *

Shmuel Lowensohn

(Vienna), Radlett, Herts, UK

SHMUEL'S FORTY YEARS FOR ISRAEL

Reprinted from the Joint Israel Appeal of Great Britain and Ireland *Reporter*

The Joint Israel Appeal's Director of Wills, Bequests and Missions, Shmuel Lowensohn, is retiring after forty memorable years of service to Israel and the Jewish people. As we celebrate forty years of Israel's growth and independence, it is most significant to note the forty years of commitment in the career of Shmuel Lowensohn.

A special memory he holds of his childhood in Vienna was that when his parents wanted to talk privately, without the children knowing what was being said, they spoke in Polish. When Shmuel and his father spoke of things which they didn't want his mother and sister to hear, they spoke in Ivrit. Yet, when he and his sister shared secrets, they spoke in the small amount of

English they knew. All the family spoke German of course, as well as Yiddish.

As a young man, Shmuel held a variety of jobs, while attending Birmingham University as an external student. They ranged from working in the Birmingham Wholesale Fish Market to being articled to a firm of accountants. At that time one had to pay the employer during one's apprenticeship, thus Shmuel was forced to leave his job because he just couldn't afford it!

After the war, Shmuel became a naturalized British citizen. In 1947, he was accepted as a student representing the Federation of Zionist Youth to the Youth Leadership Institute in Jerusalem. On 5 November 1947 he landed in Palestine with a student visa. This was the first time he had seen his sister since the war.

In Israel, Shmuel studied and worked. He was in Jerusalem when the War of Independence came and he stayed to fight with the *Haganah*. During the siege of Jerusalem, he was on duty at night in a trench, opposite the Egyptian lines. He felt as if he were 'being eaten alive by mosquitoes.' He started slapping at them with his rifle butt. The gun went off. Immediately a hail of bullets shot forth from the Egyptians. Nobody was hurt, but he never heard the end of it.

Returning to England in 1949, he worked as National Secretary and *Shaliach* to the Federation of Zionist Youth. In 1950, he became Director of the Youth and Education Department of the Jewish National Fund. One of his major responsibilities there was the publication of children's books, the most famous of which was an Annual called *Moledet*, which means 'Homeland'. These books were translated and sold all over the world.

Other publications he co-edited were the *Aleph Bet Book Series*, which serve to teach children the *Aleph Bet*. These books included the *Aleph Bet Festivals*, the *Aleph Bet Animal Series*, and the *Aleph Bet Nature Series* and others.

Shmuel progressed within the Jewish National Fund and became the assistant director in charge of Young Jewish National Fund, Jewish National Fund Fellowships, and Development. It was here he became closely associated with Trevor Chinn, (now Sir Trevor), who was the chairman of Young Jewish National Fund at that time. It was Trevor who asked Shmuel to join the Joint Palestine Appeal and take over Young Leadership. At the Jewish National Fund, Shmuel had organized Young Missions to Israel, and did the same for the Joint Palestine Appeal upon joining the organization. These fact-finding tours were a huge success, as they allowed members of the British Jewish community to witness at first-hand how their contributions were being used to help Israel and her people. Because of this success, Shmuel started Missions for senior members of what had become by then the Joint Israel Appeal (JIA).

The first impetus for Missions came immediately after the Six Day War, when Shmuel organized fifteen Missions. It was an exhausting, but greatly gratifying experience.

In 1975, Shmuel Lowensohn completed twenty-five years of service to both the Jewish National Fund and the Joint Israel Appeal. Greatly esteemed by his colleagues, he was honoured by receiving a gold watch from the late Michael Sacher, then chairman of the Joint Israel Appeal. Shmuel still wears that watch to this day.

Although he has organized Missions throughout his working life, that was only a part of the many roles he has played. He oversaw the Projects Department and became campaign coordinator from 1983 to 1985. This proved to be an extremely stressful job and, owing to a minor heart attack he had experienced years earlier, he was advised to relinquish that part of his job, as it was detrimental to his health.

In 1985, Shmuel formed a new department for the Joint Israel Appeal, that of Wills and Bequests. This department has grown substantially, as people realize that they can continue to show their love of Israel after they have passed on, by including a bequest in their Will.

Shmuel will actually only be partially retiring. Being the vital person he is, he will continue to act as a consultant for the Joint Israel Appeal, primarily for the Wills and Bequests Department, but acting wherever he's needed. Having forty years' experience with travel, he also now serves as an adviser for a travel agency.

Away from work, he is an avid philatelist, and regarded as an Israeli stamp expert. He runs the Israel Stamp Collectors Club, and plays a reasonably good game of bridge.

The great support of his family, which includes two married daughters in England and one in Israel, have seen him through many incredible years. Shmuel admits to owing a great deal of his success to his wife, Deborah, herself an active social worker. He says, 'Without the support of my wife, I could never have done my job.'

So, after forty years the question is asked, why did Shmuel Lowensohn decide to devote his life to Israel and the Jewish people? Practically all his family were annihilated in the Nazi ovens, and in his own words:

'I was determined to do whatever I could, to ensure that what happened to my parents would never happen to my children.'

He took to heart the saying, 'Whatever WE don't do, will not be done.'

* * *

Rudy Lowenstein

(Düsseldorf), Winnipeg, Canada

As parents and children entered the Düsseldorf railway station that afternoon, 7 February 1939, I remember a German man passing us saying 'This is the exodus of the children of Israel.'
Would it had been a complete one like that of our ancestors from Egypt!

The Jewish community of Düsseldorf was fortunate to have a nursing sister, *Gemeinde Schwester*, known to everybody as Schwester Ella (Elfriede Bial) employed by the community. She accompanied us on the German portion of the train trip to the Dutch border at Emmerich.

I still sense the feeling of relief and muted joy after we entered Holland, when we immediately received gifts of sweets from Dutch Committees on the train, who obviously knew of this coach full of Jewish children passing through. In one of the Dutch cities, where the train stopped, the father of one of the boys who had escaped to Holland was at the station to see his son for a few minutes as he passed through. I hope they had a happy reunion later that year in England or after the war. The next morning we set foot on British soil and freedom.

A few weeks ago I spoke to a friend who was one of the boys on that Kindertransport, and one of the first things he said to me was: 'Remember *Schwester* Ella?' Unfortunately she was not able to make her own trip to freedom, and on this occasion tribute should be paid to her and to the Jewish Community offices on the local levels, but especially to the leaders of the Jewish Central body in Berlin for their great efforts. The movement for the care of children from Germany in London and the help and consent of the British authorities made possible our rescue at that turning point of our lives. It stands out as a shining example of humanity at this tragic period of Jewish history.

*   *   *

Larry Mandon, M.A.

(Gassmann, Hamburg), Doncaster, UK

My brother, sister and I arrived in England on 3 December 1938 from Hamburg. Later there was to be considerable publicity in a variety of newspapers and magazines about us being adopted by a syndicate in Kent.

My name was Hans-Eugen Gassmann and the family had been established in Hamburg since 1910. I was born in 1927. My father had sportswear shops and he was also very much interested in politics. He died in 1933.

I have lived in England since 1938 although I have travelled extensively throughout the world. I am married and we have one son, Paul, who is a Dental Surgeon. I lecture for the Health Authority.

As a psycho-therapist I have spoken to many people who experienced being refugees who had many complex personal problems.

I think it is interesting how many unresolved problems still very much plague so many people after all these years. It is often the case that people during their working lives had little time to think about the atrocities, and now in later life it is becoming a very real problem for them to put all the pieces together.

I am regularly consulted by a wide range of people who find it still very hard to come to terms with what was done to them and their families between 1933 and 1945 by the Nazis, and some of the deep-seated pain is still very evident. I am always very willing to spend time with these people, some of whom are the children or grandchildren of those who suffered at the hands of the Nazis. No one finds it easy to accept the horror of it all.

* * *

Peter Mansbacher

(Lübeck), Olympia Fields, USA

On 25 August 1922 I was born as Fritz Ludwig Mansbacher in the town of Lübeck, Germany. As an only child, I was constantly surrounded by the love of my parents, Martin and Julia. I grew up like any other boy at that time in Germany. I believed myself to be a human being first, then a German citizen and then a member of the Jewish religion, in that sequence.

Never in my wildest dreams had I imagined that I was neither human nor German nor a citizen of the town of Lübeck. This thought hit me quite suddenly and was unexpected.

Suddenly, many neighbours and friends no longer knew us and avoided us. Many of my schoolmates called me a 'Dirty Jew'. On the morning of 10 November 1938 two SS men arrived at five o'clock in the morning to arrest my father.

I was excited about the prospect of going to England, never giving a thought to the seriousness of the moment of parting from my parents, my home, my world. This was to be the last day on which I would see my parents!

We were happy to be in England. We were also tired, hungry and cold by the time we arrived at the Lowestoft Pakefield Holiday Camp on the east coast.

During *Chanukah* arrangements had been made in the dining hall for a celebration. A *Chanukia* was set up on the stage and the visiting Rabbi gave the blessings.

Soon we were moved to the St Felix School in Southwold, a girls' college, temporarily vacated for the Christmas holidays. After Lowestoft this school seemed like paradise. There were beds with white sheets and blankets and the washroom boasted hot water! The food was cooked and served by cooks and teachers who had volunteered to stay on over the Christmas holidays.

Everyone was so nice and friendly to us. The teachers taught us English, English history, English table manners and traditional British dances. We savoured our stay at the school and we all pitched in helping with cleaning, dining room and dishwashing tasks.

Alas, everything comes to an end and we soon had to leave the school at the end of the Christmas holidays. We left a 'thank you' note over our beds for the girls, who had so kindly left us a greeting as we arrived.

Miss Southern and Mr Turner of the St Felix School were still with us and taught us English daily. The heated dining hall served as our school rooms and assembly hall for get-togethers and group singing.

Finally we were moved to the Dovercourt Holiday Camp nearby. Entertainers came to make life pleasant for us and families arrived to look us over in order to choose those children they were willing to take into their homes.

Slowly children from our camp were taken in by foster parents. Others left as they received their visas for other countries. Some left to stay with relatives. Fifty of us boys volunteered for work at the Lord Kitchener Camp, abandoned since World War I, which needed restoration. It was hoped that, upon completion, this camp would serve as home for 3,000 men from concentration camps.

* * *

Sonja Marco

(Jura, Vienna), Los Angeles, USA

Departing from Vienna in 1939, when I was twelve years old, was a sudden step in leaving my childhood behind. I had the terrible feeling of never seeing my parents again; a fact that unfortunately materialized.

I was welcomed at Liverpool Street station by my sister and an uncle. My sister had preceded me by several months to England.

I lived with my cousins Rose and Sid and their young son, Martin. My education was continued at Mount Pleasant Lane Elementary School, in

Clapton, London. It was with this school that I was evacuated to Bishops Stortford just prior to the outbreak of World War II.

Upon reaching the age of fourteen, it was decided that it was time for me to seek employment. Next came·three of the most memorable years of my life living at a hostel at 243 Willesden Lane, London. The matron in charge, Mrs Cohn, was a kind and able lady who herself had to leave Germany under duress. We were approximately thirty-five young adults, boys and girls, thrown together during the Blitz. I remember my life there fondly. Time was not without stress but the cameraderie, the support, we gave each other, was a great help to us young people. Friendships were made that have endured to this very day.

I attended night-school to further my education. Work was in a small clothing factory; I learned a trade. It was there that I met my dear husband, Sol, who was born in London. We were married in June 1947. In due course we opened our own business. Our son, Alan, was born in 1950, and our daughter, Denise, in 1953.

In spite of being well settled and having many dear friends, we decided, in 1959, to join my two sisters in Los Angeles, California. From the very first day we loved California with its sunshine and way of life and we still do. We were in business for many years and are now semi-retired. We have two darling grand daughters, courtesy of our daughter; our son is still looking!

I am fortunate in having as my very close friends, some of those people from the hostel, who are living here in Los Angeles.

*   *   *

Chava Markowitz

(Bachrach, Essen), Tel Aviv, Israel

I was an only child, twelve years old. A cousin of mine living in Manchester knew a young Christian lady who was willing to take a refugee child for a few months. So Miss Kathleen Morley, aged twenty-eight, a nursery school teacher, became my guarantor.

I left my home town, Essen, on 21 June 1939 on a Kindertransport. I remember being very excited, my first journey abroad, but also sad and insecure, feeling that I might not see my parents again. With me was another girl from Essen – Edith Ogutsch – who now lives in the USA.

I was told that Miss Morley's father would come to collect me as he and his wife lived in Purley, near London. I was introduced to Mr Morley and he took me with him. He spoke no German and my spoken English was limited, although I understood most of what was said to me. Miss Morley was still working at the nursery school in Nelson, Lancs., so, for the first month I stayed with her parents in Purley.

The first week I was very homesick and cried myself to sleep every night, but then I began to feel more secure.

I would like to describe the Morley family. Dr Morley, at that time already a pensioner, had been a school inspector for mathematics and had written several books. He had received an OBE but hardly ever used his title of Dr. Mrs Morley was a housewife. One of their sons, John, was a doctor and lived with his family in Yeovil. The other, Arthur, was a parson in Buckinghamshire. Kathleen was the daughter I came to. The elderly Morleys took me to visit their sons and I came to know typical English Christian families who put themselves out to make me feel as comfortable and happy as possible.

I also spoke to my parents on the phone three times before war broke out, each time getting very excited and sad.

Miss Morley, to whom I feel I owe my life, because I don't think that my parents would have found another family before the outbreak of the war, took me to Nelson, Lancs., and we got to know each other. What an enormous task for a young single lady to take on, to look after a twelve year old girl! Nelson, at that time, was a poor and depressed area.

We lived in rented rooms and I went to an elementary school. There, I was the only Jewish refugee child in the whole school and I had a lot of explaining to do as to why I was there. I enjoyed my two years at school and the teachers and children were all very helpful. I am still in contact with two former classmates.

At the outbreak of the war the contact with my parents was cut and I was very worried about them. Miss Morley agreed that I should stay with her as long as it was necessary, and on the whole we got on very well. As I was still a child going into adolescence I was not always easy to deal with. I left school, and Kathleen, when I was fourteen. I felt that I was a burden to her, and through relatives a place was found for me at a little Jewish boarding school, which had been evacuated to Somerset. I had to help looking after the younger children, and in return received my board and lodgings and some tuition. I was not happy there and after a year and a half returned to Kathleen who had moved to Durham, working as the headmistress of a nursery school. We found lodgings with the Ramsey family. Canon Ramsey, besides serving in the Cathedral, was also a lecturer of Theology at Durham University. We lived right in the Cathedral Close, and again I soaked up a different type of English atmosphere. For one year I attended Durham girls grammar school, which I enjoyed very much as I liked learning. This was facilitated with the help of the Ramseys, who also did everything to make me feel at home and comfortable.

As we were living right near the Cathedral, I used to attend the Sunday services. No one told me to go to the services. On the contrary, Canon Ramsey came to speak to me and Kathleen. He suggested that I should not attend the services because I was Jewish. As I was at an impressionable age, he did not want me to be influenced by the Christian religion and rites. I valued this thought highly and stopped attending the services.

Dr Michael Ramsey became the Archbishop of Canterbury and when he and his wife came to Israel for one day in April 1966, I met them and spent some time with them in Jerusalem.

In the summer of 1944 I left Durham. Rumours of the Holocaust had reached England and I felt that, as a Jew, I wanted to settle in a home and country of my own. Therefore I went to a *Habonim Hachshara* and in 1946 came on *Aliya,* after spending four months in a Cyprus detention camp.

I am still in contact with Miss Morley, now Mrs Hersom, to this day. I visit her and her family whenever I am in England. She married in 1947 and has one son of her own, but also adopted three other children. She and her husband have the true spirit of helping people. It has been an honour to know them. I can never thank her enough for what she did for me!

My parents did not manage to leave Germany before the war broke out. They were deported to Poland and perished in the Holocaust.

*   *   *

Marion Marston

(Dreyer, Halle), London, UK

In our home town of Halle, now in East Germany, my parents had been making what proved to be unsuccessful preparations to emigrate to Israel. At thirteen, like others, I was banned from my original school and then from the Catholic school to which my parents transferred me hoping to continue my education. At night, in secret, and at great personal risk, loyal Catholic school friends visited me at home to relay the events of the day. After Kristallnacht my parents decided that I should join a children's transport sponsored by *Bnei Brith.* A family friend already in London vetted the Jewish family who were to be my guardians, through Woburn House.

Two weeks after my arrival in London, I attended the local Technical College in Wandsworth, where everyone was very kind and friendly. Before long I became very conscious that I was not being treated as one of the family. Having strong Jewish and Zionist roots, I soon found the way from Wandsworth to Brondesbury for the weekly *Habonim* meeting. Uppermost in my mind throughout was the thought of my parents still in Germany, though eventually my father managed to get to the Kitchener transit camp in Deal, Kent, on a temporary visa. In desperation I began knocking on strangers' doors in Wandsworth appealing for help to get my mother out.

Help came from a Quaker family who obtained a domestic work permit for her.

September arrived and I was evacuated with my school to Reading and with a school friend was billeted with a young English couple with a baby son. It was my first *Yom Kippur* in England and I was excused school to go to Synagogue. That very morning a letter arrived from my guardians saying, to my utter disbelief and dismay, that, due to the present circumstances (the war situation) they felt unable to be responsible for me and were forwarding my belongings. I was shattered and didn't know what to do. Instead of going to Synagogue I went to see my headmistress. She consoled and assured me that though my guardians had abandoned me and ceased paying my school fees, I would be able to continue at the school. I should not have been so surprised at my guardians' behaviour. They were a wealthy Jewish family, but I remember the time when they went on a shopping trip in Oxford Street. I sat waiting for them in the car. They came out loaded with parcels for themselves, never thinking of getting anything for me, then thirteen years old.

The non-Jewish family with whom I was billeted told me I would always have a home with them. As it happened we were moved on again and after more moves I qualified as a Nursery Nurse after three years' study and training at Dauntsey Park, a Wiltshire stately home, where a nursery for evacuated slum children was sponsored by the Americans.

*   *   *

Alice Masters

(Eberstark, Trstena, Czechoslovakia), Maryland, USA

THE THREE EBERSTARK GIRLS

Near the foothills of the Tatra Mountains in Czechoslovakia, lived Salamon and Sidonia (Sidi) Eberstark, in the village of Trstena, Orava, Slovakia. They had three daughters. There was a small, but thriving Jewish community in Trstena, with its own Synagogue.

The little girls grew up in an idyllic, almost rustic fashion. Their favourite playground was the Haleckova Woods, with its wild flowers, berries and mushrooms, and they had the shallow river, Orava, to swim in and skate on. In the winter, they sledded, skated and skied whenever possible. To get to the nearest high school (*Gymnasium*) meant a two-hour journey to Dolny Kubin by train. Getting up before dawn, Salamon Eberstark would lead the way to the railway station with a lantern.

Salamon Eberstark was a building contractor, specializing in roofing and metal works. He had a Tatra automobile and a new house which he had just finished building for the young family. He was a respected and well-liked member of the community. One day, when lightning had struck the cross on top of the steeple of the village church, he was the only man who dared to climb up to that dizzy height. The whole village had turned out to watch, and they cheered when he fixed the damage. But soon after occupation they rounded him up with all the Jewish men in the village. The Eberstarks were worried about the family's future. A letter came from Sidi's younger brother Heino, who lived in London, urging them to send their children to England with the Kindertransport which was being organized there. They agonized over what to do, but Heino's writing had sounded so insistent that his warning could not be ignored. He was much more aware of what was going on in the world than the Eberstarks in their small mountain village. Salamon Eberstark began to guide Jews in flight from the Nazis over the mountains to the 'safety' of Poland. At long last the emigration paperwork was done – and Heino came through with his part. He had arranged for the girls to leave on what turned out to be the last Kindertransport.

Salamon and Sidi felt that they could not leave Czechoslovakia themselves, because they did not want to abandon three of their elderly parents who lived in the village and could not come along. Besides, visas were almost impossible to obtain. But the Kindertransport would at least get the children out. Josi was fifteen, Alice fourteen and Elli ten. The parents asked Josi to be a mother to the other two – and she assumed that role.

The morning of their departure came, and the girls remember that it was the only time they had heard their father cry, not in front of them, but sobbing in the next room. It was 28 June 1939. The family travelled by train to Bratislava, where the children said goodbye to their parents. Three times the mother took the youngest from the train – she felt Elli was too young to go out into a strange world. Three times she put her back, fighting her emotions.

After arriving in London, the Ebertark girls were taken to Burgess Hill, Sussex, to a refugee children's home – an old red brick mansion called 'Wyberley' – for their guardians could not take them in. There were fifty other children there from Germany and Austria.

The three children often felt that the parents must have suffered, wondering whether they had done the right thing in sending them away. They were the only ones in the village to do so and they were often asked 'How could you have done such a thing?'
They must have had painful moments of soul–searching, especially when they heard the Nazi propaganda, that England was being heavily bombed. But when the parents were sent in cattle-cars to the gas chambers of Auschwitz, they must have felt some comfort that their tremendous sacrifice had not been in vain.

The Eberstark girls never saw their parents again, nor their three grandparents, nor aunts, uncles, cousins and schoolfriends – all of them, no matter how old or how young, were murdered by the Nazis.

We should like to voice our gratitude to Mr Nicholas Winton, who helped to save our lives, without a doubt, though we did not know that at the time, nor indeed until just recently.
We should also like to thank the guardians that were found for us, the late Dame Myra Hess for Josi and Elli, and Ms Fanny Bendit, now ninety-two, for Alice.

*   *   *

Ruth Michaelis

(Berlin), London, UK

Fifty years ago I came to England as a four year old child, one of many children to escape Hitler's Final Solution. There seems to be something significant about this 50th anniversary. Perhaps it is only now that we can look properly at what happened then without shying away from the thoughts and feelings involved, feelings that were too frightening or unacceptable to be allowed at the time. I remember feeling terrible because I didn't feel grateful for being rescued by all those good people who planned to get me out Germany and then looked after me until I had grown up. Angry, hateful feelings were out of the question, protest was unthinkable. I remember trying to pretend gratitude that I patently did not feel. I punished myself mercilessly by thinking I ought to have perished instead of some other child who would have made much better use of the chance to survive than I did. It was only years later that I learnt about what is technically called 'survivor guilt'. I had just felt it during my childhood. And I realise now, only fairly recently, that with all this I made things far harder for myself than they need have been.

Last spring my husband and I took up the Bürgermeister's invitation to all former refugees from Berlin to spend a week there. I knew very well that I was going to search for memories I had lost. And, sure enough, at the Bahnhof Zoo I remembered the start of our journey to England. We had arrived there in a car and I threw a tantrum because I didn't want to go on the train to England. I wanted to go and visit my favourite monkeys in the zoo where my Tante Ella used to take me. I am pretty sure it was the last tantrum I threw as I think perhaps I connected being abandoned in a foreign country with punishment for being so naughty.

Try as I might, I could not get in touch with any other memories in Berlin but I was unusually anxious whenever I heard any noise that I could not immediately identify. In the Weisensee cemetery in East Berlin we found my grandmother's grave. It was an icy cold day and there were many frightening noises. Most horrific was a leaking tap in the cemetery spurting water rhythmically. Until I saw what it was, the sound conjured up the marching of jack-booted stormtroopers.

I remember the journey to England in considerable detail. It seemed endless. I was amazed that the world was so big that you could go on and on without coming to the end. The boat was huge and I couldn't understand how anything that big could possibly float and not sink. I was put to bed in a bunk when the boat left the docks. I don't remember the sea trip or docking in England, but I remember being very very sick in my bunk.

Without my brother, three years older than me, I cannot imagine surviving those first weeks in England. Indeed, I have always been grateful that we were allowed to be together, or at least in touch with each other, the whole time in England. It was my brother who explained to me all the things that were frightening and bewildering. I think some of his explanations were quite wide of the mark, but they always satisfied me. I think it was just as important for him to have to keep going in order to look after me. I am pretty sure our parents' last instructions to him would have been to look after his little sister. And he did.

We were forbidden to speak German. I learnt English very quickly. I remember not getting food at the table unless I asked for it in perfect English. Many nights I went to bed hungry. Only Martin knew how hungry I was and he crept downstairs and raided the larder in the dead of night to feed me. And how dead the nights were. For a city child the night in the countryside is terrifyingly black. I had to sleep in a room all alone and I remember lying in the black nothingness and wondering in terror whether anything still existed and whether I was still alive.

I was far too frightened to get out of bed to go to the toilet in the dark so I dreamt that I had gone. I can still remember the dream, feeling the cold floor under my feet and the cold ring of the seat as I sat down on the toilet and then the horror of the warm wetness and discovering that I had been in my bed all the time. I was beaten with a leather belt by the Rector's wife for the bed-wetting. I tried so hard but I just had that awful dream again and again. I remember sleeping on my stomach because my back was too sore from all the beatings. And then the relief when I went to a Quaker boarding school at the age of six and the matron told me to stop worrying. She said nearly all the children wet their beds and that they had rubber covered mattresses, so that it wouldn't matter.

*   *   *

With Max Schwarz, on arrival in England.

Paul and Eva Minikes in the Children's Home, 1940.

Eva Minikes

(Leipzig), Kfar Shmaryahu, Israel

We lived in Leipzig, Germany. A few months after Kristallnacht I sent my only child – just fifteen months old and still in nappies – to freedom in England.

The children's transport was arranged by Mr Harry Jacobs, director of the Times Furnishing Company in London. On hearing of the danger we were in, this benefactor took ten toddlers up to the age of five and sent them to a children's home in London. He guaranteed their upbringing, including education, up to the age of eighteen years. When war broke out, he transferred the ten children to his summer home in Surrey and converted one wing of his beautiful home into a nursery. He engaged a cook, two nurses and a maid.

When Mr Jacobs was called up for military service, he had to close up his home, so he moved the children to a children's home in Hemel Hempstead where the same conditions prevailed under his supervision.

When I came to England, just three days before the war, I worked in several households until Mr Jacobs accepted me to serve at the Home in Surrey. His only condition was that I did not disclose that I was the mother of one of the children, in order to avoid making the other children sad.

I saw with my own eyes what this benefactor – this wonderful man – did for these toddlers. He deserves to be praised and honoured.

I am now eighty-five years old and look back on the disaster that befell us (my late husband was in Buchenwald). I am sure that without the help of Mr Jacobs my little son and I would have perished like millions of our fellow Jews.

My son is now fifty-one years old – a lawyer, married to a *Sabra*, and has three lovely children.

Emmy Mogilensky
(Hubert, Cronheim), Baltimore, USA

Emmy Mogilensky was born in Cronheim, Bavaria and was sent out of Germany on a children's transport to England in 1939. She served in the British Army during part of the war, after which she obtained a Teacher's Certificate from the University of London. Mrs Mogilensky came to the United States in 1950 and obtained a Bachelor's Degree from the State University of New York. She worked for SUNY Central Administration for almost twenty years as a Computer Programmer, Systems Analyst and Associate for Institutional Research. During, and since that time, she spoke and continues to speak in high schools, colleges and to Jewish and non-Jewish audiences on the Holocaust, and has written several published articles on the subject.

She served on the Advisory Committee to the New York State Department of Education for the creation of a Holocaust Studies curriculum, the product of which is now in every high school throughout New York State. She also serves on State Senator Manfred Ohrenstein's Advisory Committee for the Permanent Holocaust Exhibit and Research Centre in the New York State Education Department Museum in Albany. She is now a Director of that Exhibit and Research Centre. Last year New York State Governor Mario Quomo appointed her to the New York Holocaust Memorial Commission.

Emmy attended the 1981 World Gathering of Jewish Holocaust Survivors in Jerusalem. An Albany television station made a one-hour documentary called 'EMMY – A JOURNEY FROM THE PAST', which records her experiences during, and reactions to, the Gathering. This film was underwritten in part by the Jewish Federation of Albany, and won the Bronze medal at the 1982 International Film and Television Festival.

Emmy is now retired and spends part of her time speaking and writing, and as a volunteer for the American Gathering and Federation of Jewish Holocaust Survivors; she is a member of its National Executive Committee. She is also the Programme Coordinator of the Jewish Historical Society of Maryland on a part-time basis. Emmy has three children and six grandchildren and moved to Baltimore in 1987 to be near them.

A WAY TO LIVE – A WAY TO DIE
by Emmy Mogilensky

'Whoever lives through a trial or takes part in an event that weighs on man's destiny or frees him, is duty-bound to transmit what he has seen, felt or feared.' – Elie Wiesel.

You are fourteen years old. Your parents put you on a train with five hundred other children. No adults. The train is to leave at midnight (is there a harder time to say goodbye?) and they hug and bless you. You own a suitcase with a few clothes and a paper bag with two sandwiches and an apple. The whistle blows and you know you will never see them again. And you know they know it, too.

A way to live – a way to die.

No tears. You are way beyond tears. You are aware of the other children in your compartment, frozen with nameless terrors. Suddenly the compartment door is pulled open. A laundry basket is pushed in. The door closes. The train gathers speed. What is in the basket? Naked terror fills the train car. Why is everyone staring at you? With a shock you know you are the oldest. You must go and open the basket.

A way to live – a way to die.

How fertile is the imagination of a fourteen year old? You think of every bizarre horror the basket might contain, while you walk the length of the corridor to where it stands. You fumble with the clasp, raise the wicker lid – and stare at two peacefully sleeping infants. Twins!

Slowly some of the other children come to look and stare, too. How do we care for them? Are they listed to be on the train? Surely not. What will happen at the border? To them? To you?

A way to live – a way to die.

Reason returns gradually. Almost reluctantly. There are several ten or eleven year olds – they can help with the babies. Everyone over six must help the smaller ones. You find there is a toilet. There is water. Good. The children are starting to talk to each other, to comfort those who whimper, to dry the tears of those who weep soundlessly. The ice is breaking. And then you notice him. In a corner, unmoving, stiff, staring into space. How old is he? Seven? Eight? You talk to him, you ask him his name, you touch his hair, you smile at him. Did you know you could still smile? No response, nothing. You touch his hand. Ice. Would he like to look at the babies? Silence. What to do?

A way to live – a way to die.

You say the *Shema* together and are settled down to sleep. You wake with a start – the babies are crying! They must need feeding, changing. How? What? You pick one up and you see the bottles. Two bottles of milk, two clean nappies. You feed one baby, someone else feeds the other. They each drink almost half the bottle of milk. How many more feedings will there be? Who is good at changing nappies? Consultations, even giggles. You change one. Girls; two beautiful, sweet little girls. The train is to cross all of Germany to the Dutch border. Hours and hours. You fill both bottles with water to make the remaining milk go further.

A way to live – a way to die.

The boy has not moved. Nothing you do, nothing anyone does, reaches him. He does not eat; he does not cry. He does not go to the toilet. He just stares. You wash the nappies in cold water and dry them over the seats. You collect large handkerchiefs from the boys as additional nappies. How long will the water on the train last? There is no milk left now, only water. And the babies are uncomfortable. They cry and cry and you can do nothing. And your children are hungry, too. When did they all become your children? The little food they brought has long since gone. There is nothing, nothing.

A way to live – a way to die.

A sign! 'Three kilometers to the border.' The babies!! We put them in the basket and close the lid. They sleep only fitfully now, they are bloated with water and starving. The train stops. A German guard jumps into the compartment. You freeze. 'Whose basket is this?' he demands. 'It is mine' you say. 'You are not allowed to bring more than one suitcase. Open the basket!' Silence. Is anyone breathing? You cannot move. You just look at the guard. He is quite young. 'Are you deaf?' he shouts and aims his rifle at the basket. A thin wail. He looks at the basket, he looks at you. He reaches for the clasp on the lid.

They are both crying. One always wakes the other, the basket is so small. The guard stares. He looks at his list and you know they are not there. He reaches for the basket. Your babies – your beautiful babies! If he – . He closes the lid, turns and walks out without another word. Does this mean they are safe or is the whole train doomed? Five hundred children?

A way to live – a way to die.

You pick them both up and hold them, tight, tight. You look at the boy in the corner. He has not moved in forty-six hours. How much longer? What will happen now? The train slows, stops, moves, stops again. The engine is uncoupled. What does it mean: Another engine. Moving again, slowly, painfully slowly. The sign! German border. Entering Holland. Is the train safe? Are your babies safe?

A way to live – a way to die.

The train stops again. The door bursts open and a whole group of Dutch women enter with baskets, distributing thick slices of bread and butter, cheese and milk. They hold the babies, feed them, coo to them. They hug the children and the children hug them back. How is it that there is no need to speak the same language? These are poor women, you can see that. Are they depriving their own families to feed you? Their families – your family! The first time you have let yourself think of them.

A way to live – a way to die!

She sits with him in the corner. She talks quietly and she hugs him and hugs him. She sits him on her ample lap. She feeds him milk – and he drinks! She takes his hand and walks with him to the bathroom. The other women leave. Marvellous, wonderful, loving Dutch women! The train moves again, on its way to the coast, for the boat that will take you to England. But she stays with him, talking, hugging, feeding, loving. Does she not have a family waiting for her? And how will she get back to them? How did she know what to do for him? You look at the babies, sleeping soundly. All the children, fed and dozing. An enormous weight has been lifted from your shoulders and suddenly the tears come, cleansing, relieving, oddly comforting.

A way to live – a way to die.

Jewish Agency people are everywhere. Welcoming, understanding, kind. You are safe. Your children are safe. But the babies – they are a problem – they were not expected – no arrangements have been made – an orphanage, temporarily of course – No!! Did you scream like that? If Jewish families in England will take five hundred children into their homes, will they not take two more? They are yours and you will not leave them in Holland. All right, all right. We will telegraph – see what can be done – make arrangements with the British authorities. You do not let the basket out of your sight. Imagine, your babies – a problem!

A way to live – a way to die.

So long ago. So many things happened – good, bad. What brought it all back to vividly – The plane–loads of Vietnamese children? You remember that not a single German Jewish child was permitted into the US. And the children from Vietnam were not marked for extinction.
– The persecution of your brothers in Russia, Syria? – *Yom Hashoa?* You attended the commemoration at the Jewish Community Centre and you felt like a stranger. Girls and boys in blue jeans, singing, giggling. Whom do they remember? What do they remember? Your parents' faces on the train platform at midnight – that is your memory. The special leave from the British Army after the end of the war to look for them. The trail with its inevitable ending – that is your memory.

A way to live – a way to die.

*   *   *

Ilse Morgenstern

(Meyer, Essen), UK

WRITTEN BY EVA BUICK (Morgenstern), UK

Ilse arrived in Britain with the last Kindertransport. Both parents were left behind in Essen, Germany.

Coming from the security of a well-situated family, as the only child, Ilse was plunged into the extremely hard conditions of a farm-hand at the age of fourteen. She survived and hardened thanks to a strong will, a love of animals and a marked sense of responsibility towards the elderly couple she served. They exploited her, of course – but Ilse felt that this was better than life under Nazi rule. A relative living in Britain managed to get her away from the farm into a school, where she matriculated and then was trained as a physiotherapist. During the war she served in the ATS.

After the war she went for a time to Canada, to see a bit of the world and, presumably, to test herself.

Back in England, she studied at the university – Biology and Psychology. She married Franz Stephan Morgenstern, then a medical student, in Oxford. In the course of the years they accumulated a family of ten besides their own son – adopted children of various races. They now have three 'grandchildren', and all their children have found their place in life.

* * *

Gerda Moses

(Platz, Vienna), Dallas, Texas, USA

BY HER SON DAVID GERSHATER

Gerda was born in 1925. Her parents were Max and Helen Platz. The Platzes were naturalized Austrians, originally from Poland. They were middle class, not particularly religious, and had three children: Joseph, Marlene (also saved by the transport), and Gerda.

Though she rarely speaks of her life before the war, I have learned from her and her nanny that she lived in Vienna, near the giant ferris wheel. She enjoyed trips to the Austrian countryside. She had a few piano and French lessons. For several years before the war she was pelted with stones by children calling out 'Jüdin'.

When the Nazis took over, Max and Helen were taken out on daily marches through the streets of Vienna. Other torments included irregular apartment ransackings – called 'Weapon Searches' and the destroying of the local Synagogue. When I was a child I found a single square of leaded glass tucked near the bottom of a drawer. The glass was from her Synagogue, burned down by the Nazis on Kristallnacht, and she had risked her life to keep it.

The oldest child, Joseph Platz, was fifteen when the family found a soldier willing to smuggle him out of the country in return for jewellery. He was under fire during part of his escape to Belgium. He left Europe via a boat heading for Palestine – where he settled and joined the British army. Marlene Platz was thirteen years old when her name came up on the Kindertransport list. Marlene went about London putting Gerda's name on lists and begging people to help her little sister get out of Vienna.

Max Platz did not return from what started as a daily march. A few months later Gerda was sent to London on a Kindertransport. Working days as a seamstress in a London garment factory and nights as a movie-house usherette, Gerda supported herself while living in London.

As it turned out, the parents were still alive several years after her escape. Helen and Max went first to Dachau and then other concentration camps. They had vague hopes of escaping to America, but President Roosevelt had stopped immigration. The facts of their being put to death were recorded by the Nazis. There was also a farewell letter Helen Platz had given to a Polish farmer in 1944. She had to work as a labourer before being gassed.

In 1942 Gerda gave up her jobs and joined the Royal Air Force, where she served first in the motor pool and then in nursing. In 1947 she left the WAAFs. After her release she emigrated to Israel and joined the Israeli Army. For two years Gerda and her brother, Joseph, were in the same country. Marlene remained in London a few more years. She had married and had a child. In the early 1950s, after divorcing her husband, Marlene and her son moved to Israel.

In Tel Aviv, soon after Israel's independence, Gerda met an American, Eddie Gershater. Like Gerda, he had fought both in Europe and Israel. He had been an air force tail-gunner, the lone survivor of a combat plane that crashed in the Netherlands, and a prisoner of war. Six weeks after meeting, Gerda and Eddie were married; they left Israel and travelled to Europe.

Eddie was working for H.I.A.S. in Germany. They had their first two children in Nuremberg and Munich.

When the H.I.A.S. job ended, the Gershaters emigrated to America, had a third child, and settled in Dallas, Texas. With the aid of a spunky British friend, Margaret Ford (whose parents had died in the Blitz), Gerda obtained work as a sales clerk. The customers liked Gerda, and she looked great in the clothes the store carried.

Gerda and Eddie were divorced in 1969. Three years later Gerda married Leo Moses, who, like her father, was in the textile business. Leo, a Lithuanian, had survived a concentration camp.

Gerda continued working, taking longer vacations so that she and Leo could travel. They often went to England and Israel, where they visited family and friends. Gerda retired last year.

Liesl Munden

(Heilbronner, Düsseldorf), Sussex, UK

TO MY PARENTS

You gave me life
And nurtured it with love;
You taught me right from wrong
Trust in the One above.

For fifteen years I stayed
Within the family fold
Then sent away from you
To England I was told.

You gave me life anew
With greater pangs of pain
Since you were well aware
We'd never meet again.

You made a choice
So many years ago
Such selfless love
When you did need me so.

And in a way
My need was much the same
Though never given voice
Adds sadness to my shame.

Could I have known
Or felt what you went through
I should have tried to be
Much more in debt to you.

For I am here
And lived a life so free,
Which you twice over gave
So generously to me.

On 24 August 1939, I left my home, my parents and all my other relatives and many friends. I was fifteen years old.

* * *

Henry Myers
Salford, UK

My three sisters and I arrived at Harwich in January 1939 and from there we were taken to a camp at Dovercourt where we stayed for a few days. We were interviewed by two women from Middlesborough. One of them was a Mrs Goldberg. It appears they were looking especially for girls. The hostel was at 5 The Avenue and the person in charge was a Professor Mahler. The Minister to the Middlesborough Hebrew congregation at that time was a Rev Wohl. During the three years we were there we were photographed many times, and articles about us were published in the local press.

* * *

John Najmann
(Breslau), London, UK

The night our sorrow began . . .

On 9 November 1938 my childhood ended and my world fell apart. It was the week of my fourteenth birthday in the city of Breslau, Germany (now Wrozlaw in Poland) where my family lived and I was born.

Although Germany's war against the Jews had started five-and-a-half years earlier I suppose I had a reasonably happy childhood. I went to a Jewish school and lived in an intensely religious Jewish atmosphere.

I was only vaguely aware of what my parents must have suffered during those years although I well remember the problems caused by the tightening of the anti-Jewish laws: the closing of the kosher butcher shops, the doubling up in classrooms when Jewish children were forced to leave non-Jewish schools, not being allowed into cinemas, the swimming bath, skating ring or my usual playground and park.

Fathers of school friends were taken in the middle of the night to the 'brown house' beaten up and found in the gutter in the morning. Our family doctor committed suicide.

But worst of all was the waiting for month after month for our turn to receive a certificate to emigrate to Palestine.

It never came but I remember the queueing outside consulates from morning to night and sometimes through the night because rumours went around that Cuba or Peru or Bolivia would hand out a limited number of visas. I remember well my father coming home one day asking me for my school atlas. He had heard that San Domingo was issuing visas. He wanted to know where it was.

After the war I found my father's prayer book and in it were steamship tickets he had bought for the whole family to sail to San Domingo.

With my childish perception I must have thought that this was the norm, the natural order of things – until 9 November, the Kristallnacht. That night marked the start of the physical destruction of the German Jews and eventually, as everyone now knows, the deaths of millions more throughout Europe.

That morning I left for school as usual. As I walked out of our building I saw my form teacher rushing along with his hat pulled down and his collar up. I spoke to him; he whispered to me to go away, to leave him alone.

'There will be no school today,' he said.

I continued past the small department store; all its windows were smashed and German stormtroopers in uniform were throwing clothing and household goods from the upper floors onto the street. Police holding hands formed a cordon to stop the crowd being hit by the flying objects. When the store had been emptied of stock the police stepped back and the spectators took armfuls from the huge pile lying there.

I walked on and passed the prayer rooms where my family worshipped on the ground floor of a block of flats. The scrolls of the *Torah* had been taken out, dumped on the pavement and were burning there. That scene haunted me for most of my life, until I had a *Torah* written and presented it to a Synagogue.

When I got home my mother, two younger brothers and sister were there. My mother and I wept. It was the first time I saw my mother weep.

My father had gone into hiding. For three days and nights he hid amongst the trees and shrubs on a local heath. He had arranged that I would bring some food when it was dark, to be left near a wastepaper basket where he would pick it up – for Jews were being arrested everywhere on sight and sent to concentration camps.

After that he hid with several other men in the flat of a widowed lady teacher of mine. On Sabbath morning we held a Service there. It happened to be the first anniversary of my *Bar Mitzvah*. I read the weekly portion of the *Torah* but not from a proper scroll for there was none and I read it in a low voice so neighbours would not hear.

During that night in Breslau, about ten Jews were beaten to death and about twenty-five committed suicide. All Synagogues were burned.

On 12 December I had the good fortune to be told that I had been included in the children's transport to England, and left for England on 15 December. My second brother aged nine also came on the children's transport in April 1939. In June my mother took my small brother and sister twins, aged three and a half, to the railway station just as another transport was leaving. She pushed them into the melee among the other children and walked away. They too came to England.

Meanwhile, my father had smuggled himself on foot into Belgium on New Year's night 1939 and from there to France. My mother after sending off the twins went to Poland from where she hoped to join my father in Paris where they would wait for that elusive certificate to Palestine. It never came.

When war broke out they were trapped. My father who had offered himself as a volunteer for the French army was arrested by the French on 23 June 1942 and was handed over to the Germans for transportation to Auschwitz extermination camp on 27 July 1942 where he was killed.

My mother was arrested by the Germans in 1939 and spent the war in ghettos, concentration camps and the Auschwitz death camp. She survived the infamous death march from Auschwitz to Saxony in December 1944.

I found myself at the end of the war with the Allied Control Commission in Germany where eventually I discovered my mother in a displaced persons' camp. She was a broken woman. She came to England where she died a few years later as a direct result of her suffering.

I married a girl who had escaped two weeks before the war from Vienna and I found happiness with her and our family of three children.

As the years go by and some of the details become blurred, the enormity, the obscenity of Kristallnacht becomes more incomprehensible to me. The pain and the sorrow does not lessen.

How do I tell our children that their grandparents and family did not die because of some spontaneous riot or some drunken mob got out of control, but that they died because an entire people were handed over by a legitimate Government to officers of state organized by the authorities and trained to hunt and kill with the single purpose that every Jew, whether man, woman or child, should be exterminated in slaughter houses constructed especially for human beings.

What began fifty years ago no Jew can ever forget.

Reprinted by kind permission from the *Evening Standard*, 7 November 1988

* * *

Ursula Nelson Schlochauer

(Kantorowicz, Berlin), New York, USA

My name was Ursel Kantorowicz, born in Berlin in 1921. I came with a children's transport to London on 18 April 1939. I was seventeen and a half years old.

We were conducted to a youth hostel to stay one night before going on to Glasgow the next morning.

At the station in Glasgow my foster parents awaited me – a tall grey haired lady and a somewhat smaller husband at her side with a big car and driver. It was most impressive.

It was a bonus to arrive on a Friday night. The family was religious, but not orthodox – they went to the Synagogue each Saturday morning. On Friday night, the family gathered and the table was beautifully set with flowers and the best silver. There were two daughters and husbands that first night. There were also three grandchildren whom I got to know on the following day. The oldest little granddaughter came for lunch each Saturday. She was a sweet little girl of seven, and had a baby brother, who came later on to collect her with his nurse. It was a more affluent life than the one I had been used to. It was all so different from home in Berlin. My mother was a divorced working woman who supported herself and me. She was very independent, interested in music, art and politics.

Back to my life in Glasgow – it was a relatively nice one, I was supposed to be the daughter of the house but never really felt at home, the atmosphere was so very different and I was homesick.

I did get news of my parents via friends in Holland and in this I was luckier than most refugees, since my parents finally managed to leave Germany in May of 1940 and reached the USA.

I was eighteen in July 1939 and thought that it was time for me to learn something with which I could earn my living later on – but my foster father, though he was kind, did not want to pay for an education. I could stay with them for as long as I liked, he said, but no money for an education was forthcoming. In that case I thought it best to leave. Luckily for me, my stepfather's sister, my aunt, lived in London and she took me in.

I parted from my foster parents with thanks to them for their help to get me out of Germany – they had saved my life after all and I stayed in touch with them for a few years after I left them.

Now my life as a refugee began, since I was living among my own kind – it was not like living in England really – it was a little oasis of life among family. My aunt took a kindly interest in me and got in touch with Bloomsbury House on my behalf. I was granted the sum of 10s. 6d. (52½ pence) per week for my keep, since I lived with relatives and not on my own. I also took a sewing course which I enjoyed, not because I liked sewing, but because I met others – my sewing did not improve much, however.

The bombing started and we were evacuated to Reading where there was a girls' hostel which was willing to take my cousin and myself. We were about twenty girls – all in similar circumstances far from home and on our own. We were very fortunate in that the Committee in Reading had been founded by a retired professor of German from Reading University, who was not only very capable in helping to solve problems, but who was familiar with our language and background and believed in education. This was, of course, hard to come by without any funds. I was granted a course in stenography and typing for which they paid while I lived at the hostel.

The hostel was sparsely furnished, but the matron in charge was a Viennese lady and she was a good cook and made the most of the rations. I made a number of friends at the hostel who have remained lifelong friends – I suppose adversity brings one closer.

After I had completed my typing course I was fortunate enough to find employment with the Society of Authors who had been evacuated to Mortimer about half an hour away from Reading.

I had married in the meantime, an English soldier, and was receiving my allowance – which I tried to save for later on – and my mother would occasionally send some money from the States and clothes which were very welcome, so I looked perhaps a bit more stylish than I would otherwise have done. The theatre became my over-riding joy and as I earned more and was able to go to London more often I saw most of the then current and famous performers in the West End.

When the war ended and the fate of the Jews who had remained in Germany became known, many of my friends knew that they would never see their parents and relatives again and there was a good deal of emotional re-adjustment. Most of them had married by that time and were beginning to build new lives – but the wounds never healed.

In 1947 I went to the United States with my husband. I did not really want to leave, though life was by no means easy. I had many friends by that time and basically liked England and its ways, the humour, the traditions and the stoicism displayed during the war. I would find life very different in the US and it took years until I settled down.

I started work with Doubleday and Company, a name familiar to me through my work at the Society of Authors and we rented an apartment in the Inwood section of Manhattan. I was happy to have my own home, though it was only an apartment in a walk-up, but I had my own front door which I could shut against the world. Work at Doubleday was quite different than it had been at the Society – I found that my colleagues were nice, but out for their own advantages. In England one was asked for tea, here one invited onself. The work was not too hard, though I had to get used to the American ways and different usage of the language.

I have lived in the States for over forty years now and one should assume that I have settled down. I have been married three times, though I do not have any children. I don't know what would have happened had I stayed in England – I do know though that my years there have made me into an Anglophile for ever.

* * *

Rabbi Professor Dr Ya'acov Newman

(Neumann), Jerusalem, Israel

Jeremiah, on beholding the tragedy of the Jewish people of his generation, proclaimed: 'He hath made me dwell in darkness as those who have been long dead' (Lam 3, 6).

When we come to contemplate the catastrophe that visited the Jewish people, which is today known as the Holocaust, we are left in utter darkness. Logic and understanding fail, and a dark gloomy cloud envelopes us. The story of the Holocaust will never be told to the end. And as the endless reportage unfolds, we search constantly for understanding, perception, meaning, which elude us. Yet it continues to occupy our mental resources and as we hover on the peripheries of this all-shattering event we entreat Heavenly resources for a glimmer of hope, of light, of comfort.

One of those borders of this gruesome episode is the series of events which the group of Kindertransport lived and experienced, and which we are recording here. The existing literature on the subject of the *Sho'ah* by now fills libraries, yet the tale is far from having been explored to the full. And now the time has come to give due mention to the stories of the 'Kinder', in as much as it is possible to deal with personal histories of such profound and traumatic nature.

I may humbly claim to having been witness to the affliction of some thousand young souls who wrestled with circumstances that defied human understanding. I listened to episodes, circumstances and events that shook me to the deepest corner of my conscious existence. My eyes beheld the agony that was mirrored in the forlorn looks of young tormented souls crying for help, for explanations, for sympathy. I struggled to find the right word, the correct response. And at times there was little else I could do or say beyond a deep sigh, a choking sound that escaped from my own helplessness.

For all those whose anguish I was unable to lessen, and those who turned to me for assistance which I was unable to render, my heart bled and pained all the more, because I proved to be so utterly lacking in remedies of a material or spiritual nature at a time when it was most needed. At the time I was myself an apprentice at learning to live with the news that reached us in all its unbelievable horror. The days were nightmarish, the nights sleepless for fear of dreams.

The Beginnings

The peace within the parental home became disturbed and profoundly upset even before the outbreak of the war. The war-cry of the soul-less enemy was heard loud and clear by every Jew, and more specifically the Jewish parent who trembled in contemplation of future events. The polluted air of Jewish existence in Europe contained the menace of stark mad days to come, though no one would have assumed the immensity of the gigantic wave of destruction that was to engulf millions. No child could have escaped the underlying disquiet that prevailed in the shadowy corners of the home. Of course parents did all they could to spare the child worry, but we all know how susceptible children are even at a very tender age to the slightest wave of unrest in the hearts of mother and father.

It was in that atmosphere that the child was taken out of the arms of a parent, sometimes crying and sometimes play-acting smiling cheer, promising good times ahead. The child was taken to the place of assembly, to a train or boat to be wafted helplessly into the unknown.

The effects of such an experience would be more than sufficient to fill a book of tragedy of Homeric proportions. Yet this was the experience of the fortunate children, who managed to escape the brutal hands of the savage enemy. The traumatic fate of these children who did find refuge and voyaged into an obscure future, suddenly thrown into a world where they were not understood when they tried to express an urgent request, a desperate need, cannot be fully described. Can a person overcome such an experience without remaining scarred by it? There is probably no definitive answer to this, but by and large the children who went through this tunnel of darkness emerged whole, strong and courageous human beings. Was it perhaps the Jewish genius for survival, for wrestling with the angel and prevailing though limping somewhat thereafter, that brought them through to face life and conquer?

Some of the Problems Encountered

My first encounters with refugee children date back to late 1942, and lasted to the end of 1945. I did however gain glimpses into the earlier phase of their lives from a number of out-pourings, from casual or more seriously couched references indicative of earlier confrontations. By the time I came in contact with them, new problems and concerns had superseded their past struggles. Yet the grooves of sorrow were still discernible, though pushed into the background. With the exception of a few isolated cases, contact with parents had by then been broken. The deepfelt concern about this was buried temporarily to allow more pressing problems to come to the fore. These mostly concerned unhappiness with the circumstances or surroundings of their lives.

About these problems I learned indirectly since my area of concern was essentially related to matters of faith and religious belief. At the same time in human matters it is never possible to separate one aspect from the whole of personal involvement.

This might be the appropriate place to recall one incident that stands out with particular poignancy in my memory.

I shall call her Naomi. She asked to see me and I proceeded to the boarding school where she was housed. The school had a religious character and the matron and head teacher were dressed like nuns.

They questioned what brought me there to see Naomi. I realized that I had to weigh my words carefully and said that it was my task to visit refugee children and that I was working under the auspices of a joint committee on which the Home Office was also represented. 'Could I see the girl in their presence,' they asked. I answered:

'No. I would prefer to see her privately.'

In silence the two exchanged looks. I was told again that they would prefer to be present. To this I retorted that if they barred me from interviewing Naomi privately I would leave. The matron then said: 'We will allow you to see her by yourself, but please do not keep her too long.' My answer was clear and sharp:

'I shall keep her as long as it will take for her to tell me her story.'

Naomi appeared. She was a girl of about fourteen. After entering the room she watched to see that the door behind the nuns was closed properly before bursting forth: 'Rabbi, please take me out of here.' She wanted to walk outside with me. As soon as we were away from the school she repeated her first request. I explained to her that in order to effect a transfer it would be necessary for her to give me details of what was troubling her. Tears gathered in her eyes and made a slow stream down her face. Once again she said: 'Just take me out.'

I explained to her that unless I could place before my committee some serious reasons for her request it would not be possible for drastic action to result quickly. The best I could do would be to refer her case to a welfare counsellor.

We walked on slowly as she guided me to the nearest bus stop. She calmed down, but she still would not give me any more information about the reason for her distress. She sat with me until the bus arrived and again I saw in her eyes that disturbed look as she burst out with one last parting plea: 'Please, take me out of here quickly!'

All I could do was report the case as it had happened. The picture of that lonesome troubled girl never left me and now, more than forty-five years later, I still recall it vividly.

The Religious Realm

A question that seemed to trouble the minds of several young people was the finding of a connection between their fate and being Jewish. Though I recognised such queries as the very essence of my task in helping my charges, it was the most difficult to handle. The demand was always for a rational elucidation. But is there any logic to be applied in explaining the fate and destiny of the Jewish people? After trying several times to use the argument of religious belief, I learned that young people with troubled spirits cannot be pacified by reference to a blind and unquestioning faith.

The questioner was always quick to forge further with the deeper probing of the mind. Doesn't faith mean belief in G-d, and how am I to understand that the Almighty, Who is described as the Absolute Good and the Absolute Just, is letting people suffer without their having sinned? What have we Jews done to deserve it? Are we really as evil as the world would have us believe?

When I was confronted with such probings, I reverted to a private silent prayer of my own to be granted the inspiration to lighten the mind of the young person facing me, who deserved a consoling explanation.

It was much easier to find an answer and give religious guidance in everyday life in regard to observing the minutiae of religious law. The prevailing war conditions allowed for leniency wherever possible for the maintenance of good health.

Perhaps another incident may serve as a telling example.

Solly visited Manchester and called on me. He was a young lad, thirteen or fourteen years of age, lean and of a rather nervous demeanour.

He came from Germany, where he had left parents and siblings behind. He now had a few questions to ask. Would I be willing to help him? 'Of course,' I answered.

'Are you a proper Rabbi?'

I looked at him, somewhat astounded.

'Go ahead with your questions,' I said. 'We will discuss my qualifications later.'

'Well, you see,' he stammered, 'I would like to know what the position of the soul is according to Jewish teaching.'

'If your question is whether we believe in the eternal quality of the soul, the answer is very definitely yes!'

'Well, that is the first part of my question.'

'Well, then, carry on,' I encouraged him.

With a deep breath he continued:

'I hear that all the Jewish people left in Germany are being killed. I think if my parents were dead by now, their souls would have contacted me. Isn't that so? Can I assume that they are still alive?'

The tortured state of his spirit was of course evident. I explained that there is no room for doubt about the eternal quality of the soul. But the nature of the soul-life in the Hereafter is hidden from man. Cautiously I carried on: 'There is however evidence of some souls having contacted the living, but then there is also evidence that a living person may reach out to one near to him. This realm of study is called parapsychology. We know little about the workings of the occult. At this stage you can do no better than hope.'

My young visitor rose from his seat and asked outright: 'Do you hope that the Jewish people left there will be saved? I cannot believe. Does that make me bad in your eyes?' He then offered: 'I think you are a real Rabbi.' He moved to the door, opened it, looked back and said: 'Thank you. You helped me.' He left.

I remained bewildered. So young, and so troubled. So adult-like, and so afraid. Our discussion took but a few minutes, but for a day or so my paperwork lay unattended.

It was natural that most of the cases brought specially to my care had to do with spiritual problems and fears. It was then that I became convinced that a Rabbi in a modern world cannot discharge his tasks adequately without having some scholastic training in the fields of psychology and sociology.

The difficulties which arose for the Kinder *vis-à-vis* superiors were in most cases due to the prevailing attitude to aliens in England. There is a natural tendency for any person to become integrated and accept the local customs and behaviour. But little allowance was made to the young newcomer, who was not always able to acclimatize quickly to the new environment. The adult in charge was eager to see the children adapt quickly, and if this was not the case there was often little understanding, sympathy or tolerance. This not only made the life of the young person harder than it should have been, but in fact handicapped complete integration later.

I remember on one occasion the headmistress of a very big school, when complaining about a young refugee, saying: 'We are at war with the people in the country from which this boy comes, yet he is making no effort to integrate.'

I found it practically impossible in such a case to achieve better relations between the parties concerned.

On the other hand I found a much greater understanding for the child's religious upbringing, though many of the instructors had never encountered a Jewish person before.

Worry about Parents left behind

The case of little Miriam illustrated well the hidden ongoing anxiety about the fate of parents and siblings left behind. When I met Miriam, a girl of twelve, she was of very serious disposition. In fact that was the first complaint against her from her class teacher. The latter stated that Miriam hardly ever participated in extra-mural activities. She never smiled and seemed to go her own way all the time.

My contact with Miriam, by contrast, was a very close one. She always showed attachment and pleasure in being able to talk about her past life, though she did not share her deeper concerns with me. One day she asked me whether I would be able to take money from her and deposit it in a safe place in her name. I told her that this was something I could not do. I asked her where she got money, and she answered curtly: 'From friends.' She added in an undertone: 'I would be grateful to you if you could let me have a bit of money from time to time.' On the one hand she seemed to have money to deposit, yet at the same time she asked me for support. I naturally tried to obtain more information from her, without success.

On another occasion, when she repeated her request for money, I said to her firmly that I wanted to know why she was saving money and asking for more. To this she replied:

'After this war comes to an end I would like to be in a position to help my parents. They will be without means and there will be no one else but me to come to their rescue.'

A while later I received an urgent call from the school. By then various complaints had been lodged against Miriam and she faced the possibility of being expelled. Yet she would not reveal her concerns and her plans in regard to her family. I went to the school and extracted a promise from her that she would not continue with her private campaign. When I explained the matter to the teachers, they began to treat her with much more sympathy.

A Variety of Causes

The multitude of problems encountered by my 'Kinder' can hardly be enumerated. Even if the nature of the problems was similar, the details varied considerably. Taking all the differing problems as a whole, the young people displayed tremendous resources of character, principles and spiritual strength. I think of them as the heroes within the context of the Holocaust. Most of them grew out of their initial predicament and became upright, fine and solid citizens of the country which adopted them. Their courage in prevailing over mighty odds should be written with bold letters in the golden history of the Jewish people.

* * *

Eddie Nussbaum, B.Sc.

(Hamburg), Los Angeles, USA

At a time when we remember with sorrow the lack of help by the then Roosevelt administration in the USA, it is worth recalling the heroic efforts made by British people of good will to save these Jewish children. Helped by newspaper accounts of the 9/10 November Nazi horrors, these activists were able to get their pleas across to the Chamberlain government. Of great assistance were such progressive Members of Parliament as Josiah Wedgwood, Philip Noel-Baker and Eleanor Rathbone. The result was the creation of an unusual special visa category, allowing unaccompanied children from Germany, Austria and Czechoslovakia to enter Britain. Arrangements had to be made for them to stay with British families or in one of the many youth hostels set up by the Refugee Children's Committee, with financial aid by the Central British Fund.

The entire Kindertransport action must go down in history as a 'True Good Deed' by a country far less powerful than the United States and facing difficult economic circumstances. The action allowed these children to escape the Holocaust. Now that the word 'Transport' has such a deathly meaning, it is worth recalling the positive connotation of those cross-Channel 'Kindertransporte'!

The logistics of the entire campaign was staggering: British families had to be found to become sponsors, hostels had to be set up and staffed, funds had to be raised and liaison established with the Jewish communities in the various European cities.

My own case: I was an only child, attending the Jewish Secondary School in Hamburg. I was lucky to be a 'guaranteed' case, going to a sponsor family living in London who were friends of my family. Each transport of some 150 children was accompanied by a prominent person, such as Dr Spier and Dr Jonas, respective headmasters of the Boys' and Girls' Jewish Secondary Schools in Hamburg. These adults were given 'leave of absence' by the Nazis but had to return to Germany after tasting freedom briefly in England.

From the train window at Hamburg Hauptbahnhof I saw my parents on the platform, for the last time ever. I was just sixteen. But to return to the less subjective matters of general organization of the transports. There was, of course, the problem of language, only partially alleviated because many British Jews were able to communicate with their charges in Yiddish. Then there was the problem of matching the host families' religious observance to that of the children. In this regard mention must be made of Dr Solomon Schonfeld, the young, dynamic London-born Rabbi who formed a virtual one-man organization for the rescue of orthodox Jewish children. His close connections with the Home Office produced an abundance of visas, and he personally went to Vienna and other cities to bring hundreds of children to the UK. It is also worth mentioning that Lord Jakobovits, the present Chief Rabbi of Great Britain, was one of the children Dr Schonfeld brought out of Germany.

And thus began life in a strange but free country for thousands of children now officially classified as 'Refugees from Nazi Oppression'. Unfortunately, those of German citizenship became Enemy Aliens when war broke out in September. For those over sixteen, this led to the internment episode in May 1940. I personally got the full treatment, courtesy of HM Government!

On 10 July about 2,500 internees embarked on the infamous troopship *Dunera.* We were supposed to be sailing to Canada but were switched to Australia at the last moment on orders from Whitehall. Two days after leaving Liverpool we were attacked by a German U-boat, but thanks to good zig-zag manoeuvres by the captain the torpedo fired at the ship brushed off the side without exploding.

After disembarking in Sydney in September we were moved to a camp at Hay, New South Wales, and later to a camp in a milder climate at Tatura, Victoria. In camp the children were able to maintain some form of educational activity, including study for their 'matric' certificates (equals High School Diplomas in the USA). My release came through early, and I was returned to Britain as a free man on another troopship, the 'Stirling Castle', in November 1941.

The rest of my own Kindertransport story is relatively unexciting. War-time life in London, war work in an engineering factory, Air Raid patrol duty at night, and part-time college leading to a London University B.Sc. Engineering degree. Finally, in 1948 came my grant of British citizenship. This effectively ended my coming under the auspices of the Committee located at famous Bloomsbury House in London's West End.

So mine was a positive, pro-British experience, except perhaps for the internment interlude. Even that can be understood, if not excused, by the Fifth Column hysteria in the spring of 1940. The then Home Secretary, Sir John Anderson, admitted afterwards that 'regrettable and deplorable mistakes' had occurred. To quote Major Cazalet, MP speaking in the House of Commons on 22 August 1940: 'No ordinary excuse, such as that there is a war on and that officials are overworked, is sufficient to explain what happened. Frankly, I shall not feel happy, either as an Englishman or a supporter of this Government, until this bespattered page of our history has been cleaned up and rewritten.'

In my case, winning a post-graduate Fellowship brought me to the United States in 1949. On returning to the UK I was not happy with the policies of the newly elected Labour Government, and, with my new bride, I decided to settle in New York. We now have two married children and three grandchildren.

Reprinted by kind permission from the *Hampstead and Highgate Express*.

*   *   *

Sonja Pach

(Skapa, Berlin), Jerusalem, Israel

My parents had been born in Poland and emigrated to Berlin in the early 1920s. They had four children: three girls and one boy. Mutti turned to her three brothers in London for help, and a reply soon came. They were very sorry that they could not help us, but they would forward the matter to a committee in Coventry. Would we send photographs and doctor's certificates of the children as soon as possible? Some family would certainly be willing to take a child. I, the second oldest, happened to be chosen. I was fourteen years old at the time. Little did I know then that these documents were the vital factors in deciding who would be chosen to live and who to die.

The desperation that had prompted my parents to send me away alone, not knowing when and if they would ever see me again, must have been heartbreaking. Papa, with tears streaming down his face, put both his hands on my head. He wanted to part from me with the traditional Jewish blessing of the Priests. (Both my parents were *Cohanim.*) Those short verses of spiritual blessing were the last I ever heard Papa's voice speak.

A refugee committee was on hand to welcome us in London, and also my new foster parents, Mr and Mrs Lee of Coventry. My meagre knowledge of school English did help me to answer a few questions. The Lees were good Protestants and made my fortnight's stay with them as comfortable as possible. They respected my Jewish religious background and made very clear to me that I would not be given any meat, let alone bacon.

Despite the beautiful room I was given, I was very homesick. Every letter I received from home caused me very deep depression. I would have given anything to be able to go home again. I would sit near the fireplace and cry for hours. This must have been very disturbing to that elderly couple. The Rabbi of Coventry was summoned for advice and as a result, our relations in London were made to take me.

My uncle, his wife and their three children, two boys aged sixteen and twelve and one daughter, nine years old. I could have fitted in if they had wanted me, but I soon realised that they had really been made to take me. My aunt raised hell: 'If I have to take a child then the other brother also has to take one,' was her slogan. That saved the life of my oldest sister. She came out with one of the last Kindertransports, just before the war started.

For four long years, throughout the Blitz in London, I used to write twenty-five words home to my parents through the Red Cross. My letters were always answered, and they are in my possession until this very day. The morning I joined the ATS (19 February 1943), I received my last letter from home. My next twenty-five words were never answered, and I understood that something had happened.

Years later I realized what a lucky step I had taken by joining the ATS. By sheer luck, I was called to report to an officer. Out of the blue he decided that I was an artist. I assured him that I had had no training in that field, but he was determined to try me out. So I became a graphic artist, working in the education and entertainment department for the duration of the war.

For the first time since I had parted from my parents, I did not have to worry about clothing, while in the British army, the uniform put an end to that. I received the medical and especially dental treatment that I needed so urgently. To crown it all, on a long week-end leave in Birmingham, where I had arranged to meet my old schoolfriend Anni who was also serving in the ATS at the Jewish Forces Club, I met a very handsome young religious Jewish Dutch soldier by the name of Abraham. I soon learned from him how he had escaped from Holland via France, Gibraltar, Iran and Algeria to England. After meeting Abraham a few times, I realized how close I felt toward this new friend, not knowing that Abraham felt the same. He was determined to marry me, on one condition: that I agree to live with him in Palestine. That was always his ideal and he could not give it up for anything in this world. The decision I had to make engrossed me day and night. If only I had parents to ask for advice. Could I speak to my aunt and uncle about this? In the end I found the courage to inform them by letter of my next visit to them and of a surprise.

In the evening I wrote the following in my diary: 'Uncle and aunty did not mind at all. "Once you are twenty one, you'll do as you please", they remarked.' They were free of their heavy refugee burden.

My sister was not at all happy that I was going to leave her. But Abraham was determined to marry me and live in the Promised Land in spite of any pressure to the contrary. He was not taking any chances of losing me. For months I struggled, torn between two worlds. I informed my relatives of my decision to marry Abraham. At that stage, Mutti's oldest brother, with whom my sister lived, felt some responsibility toward me. 'I will give you £20 as a wedding gift,' he offered generously. He made a deal with me: '£10 I'll give you now, and if you are a good girl I'll give you the other £10 later.' Perhaps I was not a good girl. I never received the second £10.

My aunt and uncle, Mutti's second brother, who had taken me into their house from the kind Coventry guarantors, also felt responsibility.

'Do you want a tea dance wedding party, or do you prefer the money instead?' I was asked. Abraham soon found out in Holland that there was no family of his left after the Holocaust whom he could invite to our wedding. We both preferred the money. We received £50.

Since I was under twenty-one years of age, the marriage had to be approved by a judge, according to English law. The day came when we had to appear in court. I was given the Bible to take the oath. The judge looked up from his desk after having read the application, removed his spectacles and asked: 'Do you want to marry this man?' 'Yes, sir, I do', was my confident answer. He went on, 'And where are you ging to live?' 'It may take some time travelling, but our aim is to live in Palestine.'

Now it was Abraham's turn. He also had to take the oath. The same question. 'Do you want to marry this woman?'

'Yes, sir', replied Abraham, very sure of himself. 'What are you going to do in Palestine? How will you support your future wife?'

'I am going to be a farmer just like my ancestors before me', he said, pointing to the Bible. With a knock of the hammer on his desk, the judge approved and signed. A farmer, I thought, not daring to interrupt. Good heavens, I have never been near a farm, let alone milked a cow or held a live chicken; what am I undertaking?

Now we could make arrangements for the wedding. Abraham had to go back to Holland to be demobilized. We had very little money to spend on luxuries. Fortunately it was fashionable to get married in uniform. A lady in the London Jewish community took pride in lending out her wedding dress to brides. Luckily, the dress fitted me.

The Sabbath before the wedding we went to the Synagogue. Prayers had always given me confidence and strength during the worst times. I started to read the portion of the week. Genesis, Chapter XII-XVII, history of the Patriarchs: 'Now the Lord said unto Abram: Go forth from your native land and from your father's house to a land that I will show you; and I will make of you a great nation and I will bless you, and make your name great; And you shall be a blessing: And Abram took Sarah his wife. . .' Those were our names too. We had made the same decision. Suddenly I felt so strong and confident. I knew now our course of action was right. The answer had come from Heaven.

It was a very crisp autumn morning that day, 14 October 1945, in London. The sun broke through later, and by the time our wedding ceremony had taken place, it had become summer.

The Rabbi's sermon, friendly, firm and warm, made a great impression on me:

'You two young people are starting a new life and are at the beginning of a new road. The portion of this week in our holy Bible begins: "Go from your country, your home and go to the land that I will show you." The way which you two have chosen is one of idealism. You are going to a country whose problems and difficulties you don't know. But don't be intimidated by these thoughts because you are taking the path you feel you should and which you consider your duty. You, my dear Abraham, have chosen to follow the way which our forefather Abraham was told to take by the Almighty. He took his wife Sarah with him to be of help to him. You too are taking your Sarah with you. She too will be a help to you to overcome problems and advise you when necessary. We know that our forefather Abraham had complete confidence in the Holy One, praised be He. We can imagine a man, well-established in his father's house, going away to an unknown country, leaving so much behind, but trusting in G-d who had told him to go, and who had promised that country to him and to his descendants. Our history teaches us how the promise to Abraham was kept and the country became the Promised Land, the land where the Jewish kings established themselves and built their homeland. But the time will come, with G-d's help, when we will return to that country and rebuild it. People will come from all corners of the earth and be reunited in the Promised Land of the Jewish people. You have lost your beloved ones in the Holocaust. You have helped to overcome the enemy. You have found each other while doing your duty in this country of your adoption. You have decided to. live for each other and make up as much as possible for the great loss you have suffered.'

In the evening, Abraham's friends, Hilde and Isi Engleman, made us an unforgettable party and presented us with silver candlesticks which we both cherish until this very day. It was in the Engleman's home that Abraham had found a house which he could call his home, where he was accepted as warmly as if he were a member of their family. Whenever I look at our wedding photos, the sensation of great happiness returns to my heart, in spite of the problems and difficulties we had to face during forty-four years of married life.

*   *   *

Vera Penney

(Apter, Warnsdorf), Chesham, Bucks., UK

I was born in Warnsdorf, Czechoslovakia, on 27 April 1929. My parents had moved there from Vienna in the early 1920s. I have a sister, Hella, who is four and a half years older than I. Warnsdorf is in what is known as the Sudetenland – formerly part of Germany prior to the formation of Czechoslovakia. In the detached house where we lived, we had the upper apartment, whilst in the lower apartment, my Uncle Samuel and Aunt Pepi lived with their three children, Sonja the eldest, who was seven years older than I, Friedle, her brother, and Edith the youngest girl who was one week older than I.

I have in my possession, a number of letters from my parents which were written over a period of two years. During my first three months in England I received one letter a week, but after that they asked me to send my letters to someone in Switzerland, and I only received a few more, very intermittently, till the last one in April 1941 just prior to my twelfth birthday.

Through my young years, I remember being very confused about to which country and people my loyalties belonged. On the radio news we kept hearing about the Jews in Palestine fighting English soldiers, and there I was, having been taken in and cared for by kind English people. What was I supposed to do or feel? I remember running out of the room one day when the news was on, with my head in my hands, not knowing what to do or think. I loved my parents and wanted them desperately, but felt I could not talk about it and no one asked me to anyway. In my young mind, I suppose I felt let down and rejected. My parents had written of their hopes that we would be reunited. The political implications were obviously not real to me then. I was not in touch with any Jewish people whatsoever, apart from an occasional letter from an uncle in Palestine to whom I felt, quite wrongly I realize now, I could not write as by then I could only speak and write in English.

*   *   *

Arno A. Penzias, B.S., M.A., Ph.D.
(Munich), New Jersey, USA

I was born in Munich, Germany, in 1933. I spent the first six years of my life comfortably, as an adored child in a closely-knit middle-class family. Even when my family was rounded up for deportation to Poland, it didn't occur to me that anything could happen to us. All I remember is a long train trip and scrambling up and down three tiers of narrow beds attached to the walls of a very large room. After some days of back and forth we were returned to Munich. All the grown-ups were happy and relieved, but I began to realize that there were bad things that my parents couldn't completely control, something to do with being Jewish. I learned that everything would be fine if we could only get to 'America'.

One night, shortly after my sixth birthday, my parents put their two boys on a train for England. They told me to be sure and take care of my younger brother. I remember telling him:

Jetzt sind wir allein,

as the train pulled out.

My mother received her exit permit a few weeks before the war broke out and joined us in England. My father had arrived in England almost as soon as the two of us, but we didn't see him because he was interned.

We sailed for America toward the end of December 1939 on the Cunard liner *Georgic* using tickets that my father had foresightedly bought in Germany a year and a half earlier.

We arrived in New York in January 1940. My brother and I started school and my parents looked for work. Soon we became 'supers' (superintendents of an apartment building). Our basement apartment was rent free and it meant that our family would have a much-needed second income without my mother having to leave us alone at home. As we got older and things got better, we left our 'super' job and my mother got a sewing job in a coat factory; my father's increasing wood-working skills helped him land a job in the carpentry shop of the Metropolitan Museum of Art.

It was taken for granted that I would go to college, studying science, presumably chemistry, the only science we knew much about. College meant City College of New York, a municipally supported institution then beginning its second century of moving the children of New York's immigrant poor into the American middle class. I discovered physics in my freshman year and switched my 'major' from chemical engineering. Graduation, marriage and two years in the US Army Signal Corps, saw me applying to Columbia University in 1956.

My army experience helped me get a research assistantship in the Columbia Radiation Laboratory, then heavily involved in microwave physics. After a painful, but largely successful struggle with courses and qualifying exams, I began my thesis work. I was given the task of building a maser amplifier in a radio-astronomy experiment of my choosing.

In 1961, with my thesis complete, I went in search of a temporary job at Bell Laboratories, Holmdel, New Jersey. Their unique facilities made it an ideal place to finish the observations I had begun during my thesis work. 'Why not take a permanent job? You can always quit,' was the advice of Rudi Kompfner, then Director of the Radio Research Laboratory. I took his advice, and have remained here ever since.

From the first, I made it my business to engage in the communications work at Bell Labs in addition to my astronomical research. It seemed only reasonable to contribute to the pool of technology from which I was drawing. Similarly, Bell Labs has always been a contributor to, as well as a user of, the store of basic knowledge, as evidenced by their hiring of a radio astronomer in the first place.

As time went on, the applied portion of my efforts included administrative responsibilities. In 1972 I became the Head of the Radio Physics Research Department upon the retirement of A. B. Crawford, the brilliant engineer who built the horn antenna Wilson and I used in our work. In 1976, I became the Director of the Radio Research Laboratory, an organization of some sixty people engaged in a wide variety of research activities principally related to the understanding of radio and its communication applications.

I have also been a visiting member of the Astrophysical Sciences Department at Princeton University since 1972. My occasional lecturing and research supervision have been more than amply repaid by stimulating professional and personal relationships with faculty members and students.

Finally, most important of all is the love and support of my family, my wife Anne and our three children, David, Mindy and Laurie.

B.S., City College of New York, 1954
M.A., Columbia University, 1958
Ph.D., Columbia University, 1962

Docteur Honoris Causa, Paris Observatory, 1976

Henry Draper Medal, National Academy of Sciences, 1977
Herschel Medal, Royal Astronomical Society, 1977

Joint Nobel Prize Winner for Physics, 1978, for 'Discovery of Cosmic Microwave Background Radiation'

Member, National Academy of Sciences
Fellow, American Academy of Arts and Sciences
Fellow, American Physical Society
Member, American Astronomical Society
Member, International Astronomical Union
Member, International Union of Radio Science

*   *   *

Rabbi Professor Dr Jakob J. Petuchowski

(Berlin), Cincinnati, USA

BRITISH MUSEUM, BLOOM'S, AND CHARLIE CHAPLIN

What do the British Museum, Bloom's Kosher Restaurant, and Charlie Chaplin have in common? Only that they were all crowded into the space of but a few hours within a forty-eight hour period which changed – and saved – my life. A document in my possession, entitled Aliens Order 1920 – Certificate of Registration issued in East Lothian, Scotland, on 30 July 1941, my sixteenth birthday, testifies to the fact that I arrived in the United Kingdom on 22 May 1939 and notes my 'Profession or Occupation' as that of an 'Agricultural Trainee'. There is a photograph attached to that document, which indeed shows me in the overalls of an agricultural trainee. It also pictures me with a face far from happy. Perhaps, by nature and by nurture, I was not cut out to be an agricultural trainee. In fact, when I ultimately left the farm school in Scotland, in order to pursue my rabbinic studies, someone remarked: 'The farmers will always say that you are a good Rabbi, and the Rabbis will say that you are a good farmer'. Perhaps they do. At any rate, being an 'agricultural trainee' helped to save me from internment on my sixteenth birthday.

But it is the 22 May 1939, the day of my arrival in the United Kingdom, which really leads me to the topic of the British Museum, Bloom's and Charlie Chaplin. That day was also the birthday of my dear mother, her first birthday since I was born, which I did not spend with her. Nor would I ever spend another of her birthdays together with her. The day before, on 21 May

1939, we had said a tearful farewell on the platform of a Berlin railway station. It was the very last time that I ever saw her. She became part of the 'Six Million'. That, of course, nobody could foresee at the time – not even as late as May 1939. There was hope for a reunion in England – soon. Still, it was bad enough for a *Muttersöhnchen* like me to be torn away from his familiar surroundings and from being spoiled by his loving mother. The train trip to the Dutch border was uneventful.

We boarded a ferry to take us to Harwich, England. It was an overnight crossing and the next morning, on deck, I, for the first time in my life, took a cup of tea with milk. It was not bad at all. However, for some mysterious reason, it is only in Britain that, to this day, I am able to drink tea with milk. I just cannot manage to do it in any other place – America, Israel, Germany, France, Spain, or Mexico. Tea with milk must go with the British venue.

Upon arrival in Harwich, we were shepherded into a train, which would take us to London. When we arrived, there were members of the Refugee Committee welcoming us, and coaches waiting to take us to our next stop.

What does one do with dozens of German-Jewish refugee children who had left Germany more than twenty-four hours ago, and who had now arrived tired, unwashed and hungry in the capital of the British Empire? The answer seemed to be quite obvious to the kindhearted members of our reception committee, if not, perhaps, to the refugee children themselves. The buses deposited us at the British Museum, where we were given a tour of its treasures! Frankly, I no longer remember just what we saw in the British Museum on 22 May 1939. I am not even sure that I managed to keep my eyes open all the time. At any rate, the British Museum was my first exposure to cultural life in Great Britain. In retrospect it even makes sense that culture should have been given precedence over food, although at the time we children might have felt differently about that.

At long last, however, we reboarded the coaches, and were taken to Bloom's Kosher Restaurant for our first real meal since leaving Germany. I no longer recall what we ate. What mattered then was the fact that we were being fed; and we were grateful.

London, however, was not the ultimate destination of some of us on that Kindertransport. We were headed for the Whittingehame Farm School in Scotland. Yet the night train to Edinburgh would not leave until much later. To while away the time, we were taken to a cinema, and there we saw Charlie Chaplin in *The Great Dictator.* One year's English in a Berlin Jewish school may not have prepared me sufficiently to get every nuance of the dialogue, although Chaplin's acting made up for what I may have missed linguistically. At any rate, it was enough, some thirty hours out of Nazi Germany, to see the Führer being made fun of, and to be able to laugh at Nazism with impunity and without any danger whatsoever. Now we knew for sure that we had arrived in a land of freedom, and we breathed more freely.

During the train ride to Edinburgh through the night not many of us were able to sleep. All the new impressions, gathered during the last few hours, not to mention the delicious kosher sausages, still had to be digested; and the uncertainties of the future, too, kept us awake. We duly arrived in Scotland on 23 May 1939. That happened to be *Erev Shavuot* that year; and at the Whittingehame Farm School, where we finally arrived, the traditional custom was observed – by those who wanted to observe it – of staying awake the whole night in order to study the first pericope of every *Torah* portion in the Pentateuch, as well as other biblical and rabbinic texts. Not yet having completed the year in which my *Bar Mitzvah* had been celebrated, I was obviously eager to participate as a Jewish adult in that all–night study session. We had not even quite covered the second of the Five Books of Moses when sleep finally overtook me.

I have visited the British Museum since then. I also did some research in its library in 1978. I have had some delicious meals at Bloom's too, and I have had the opportunity of seeing *The Great Dictator* once or twice more in later years. But none of the repeat performances were as significant in my life as had been the juxtaposition of the three initial experiences on that 22 May 1939. Then they symbolized freedom. Today the memory of them still fills me with feelings of gratitude towards those who saved my life.

Editors' Note:
Jakob J. Petuchowski is the Sol and Arlene Bronstein Professor of Judaeo-Christian Studies, and the Research Professor of Jewish Theology and Liturgy at the Hebrew Union College – Jewish Institute of Religion in Cincinnati, Ohio, USA. He has written or edited thirty-two books, and published more than six hundred articles in English, Hebrew and German. For the last thirty-two years he has been serving as part-time Rabbi of Temple *B'nai Israel,* Laredo, Texas, in his 'spare time'.

*   *   *

Ronald Preston

(Polak, Vienna), Greenford, Middlesex, UK

BEI UNS IM PRIORY PLACE, SHEFFIELD

Most of us boys enjoyed life at the hostel very much and we had three very nice German Jewish refugee ladies looking after us. There was Miss Mayer, who was in charge of everyone, Miss Dukat and Miss Hanff who assisted her.

The boys went to a local school and three of us, including myself, played in the school football team. We were very proud and felt that it was quite an achievement to have three of us refugees playing for the school.

The year was 1941 and although we had many air raid warnings, the German planes usually passed over in the distance and we often heard some anti-aircraft guns firing away, but the All Clear was soon sounded.

The cellar in our hostel had been reinforced as was the practice in those days. On one occasion we realized that things were different and the gunfire was getting louder all the time. It soon became obvious that this time Sheffield was the target of the German bombers and the noise of the gunfire and the bombs falling became worse and worse. We all kept calm or at least tried to do so in the circumstances, and were singing songs to drown the noise outside. Then suddenly there was a terrific crash and bang, the lights went out and we were sitting there in total darkness.

It seemed like a very long night and in the early hours we heard voices coming down to us. It was the Air Raid Wardens who managed to clear some of the rubble away to get to us in the cellar.

'You have been hit,' one of them said. 'Are you all right?'

'Yes,' we answered.

'Half the hostel has been torn away and a lot of the building has collapsed,' said one of the wardens. 'We will get you out and take you to a rest centre at a local church.'

They got us out and we stumbled over broken bricks and all sorts of debris and there was dust and smoke everywhere.

They were very nice to us at the church hall and gave us hot tea and blankets and told us not to worry, everything will turn out all right.

We stayed at the church hall a few days after which time the Jewish community had arranged to put us up at the Synagogue in Wilson Road. There was a large hall and we slept on comfortable mattresses all laid out next to one another.

We made good use of the table tennis table and the congregation made good use of us boys, as they were always short of people to make up a *Minyan*, so one of them always came rushing into the hall shouting 'I want two boys.' Needless to say, to us table tennis was a greater priority than a *Minyan*, so we always made ourselves rather scarce when the man came rushing in.

It was at about this time that the question of my *Bar Mitzvah* came up and it was decided that a certain Mr Gittleson would be my teacher. I won't pretend that I was a good pupil, because frankly Hebrew was never a good subject of mine, and how I got through it all I will never know, but I did. In fact in the end, three of us boys had *Bar Mitzvah* together and it all ended well.

Our stay at Wilson Road Synagogue was no long term solution and after some months it was decided by the powers that be that another hostel must be found for us. In a way we were sorry to hear this, as by then we had got quite used to our new surroundings and we even got used to making up the *Minyanim*, but obviously this could not go on, so eventually another hostel, also in Sheffield, was found for us and another chapter in our lives started.

The new hostel was in Glossop Road and was run by a very nice non-Jewish married couple and who deserve a lot of credit for putting up with the antics of us boys, most of whom were by now working mostly in factories on war-work.

In retrospect, Priory Place hostel will always be somehow special to me.

* * *

Rena Prozzer
(Margulies), London, UK

The earliest memories of most children consist, I suppose, of family outings, holidays, playing with grandparents. Mine are different – mine are of lying in bed on a Friday night, listening to perhaps fifty female voices singing downstairs, or of going round with my mother in the morning as she woke up lazy young girls by pulling the bedclothes off their feet (I thought this very cruel!).

I was born in the middle of the war. My parents, Dora and Siegmund Margulies – later known as 'Matron' and 'Mr M' – were refugees from Vienna in 1938, and, having been in England for a year, they were asked by the Jewish Refugee Committee to run a hostel for orthodox girls. This was my world until I was about seven years old, when the hostel closed. By then, of course, I had realized that other children had one mother, one father and perhaps one or two brothers or sisters, whereas I had to share my parents with about fifty other girls who, I thought, were adults, although some of them were only about thirteen years old when I was a baby.

I had my favourites among these girls. Some played with me, or told me stories – these I loved. Others made a fuss of me and picked me up, and these I did not like, but they couldn't understand why.

I remember my father, the only man in this female world, dressing cut knees and lancing boils. He was very happy being father to all the girls, and they loved him! I also remember the huge kitchen table covered with chickens, being drawn (to my disgust!) in preparation for the *Seder*. Oh, the smell!

There are many more memories, and with hindsight I know that the prevailing atmosphere was a happy one. But one incident was symptomatic of the situation and how it affected me. My mother explained to me that a new batch of girls was arriving, from Hungary I believe, and they didn't know any English and she would be teaching them – I was not to interrupt the lessons. I was annoyed: they were taking my mother away from me. I now realize that this must have been a group liberated from the camps, and everyone was treading very carefully with them. But I didn't know anything of this at the time, and I did resent the intrusion.

As a child, one takes everything for granted, and my parents, who later often spoke happily of 'hostel times', and who kept in touch with many of the girls after the hostel closed, were modest people who did not boast about their achievements. But the glowing tributes I received when first my father, and later my mother, passed away, testify to the fact that they really were like parents to these girls, and tried to give them as normal a home life as possible. To me, it was far from normal, but I now know that the experience of being a 'hostel baby' enriched my life, and it can be no coincidence that I am now a social worker!

*　　*　　*

Rabbi John Rayner

(Rahmer, Berlin), London, UK

A few weeks ago I found a note from my secretary which, from a cursory glance, seemed to say: 'Ring so-and-so at the BBC about kidney transplants'. As I have recently become involved in a medical ethics group, the message seemed only slightly odd. But when I rang the BBC and spoke to the producer in question, she told me that the programme she was making was not about kidney transplants but about Kindertransports.

How did it all come about? So as not to go too far back, let us start with Kristallnacht, the Night of the Broken Glass, 9/10 November 1938. That increased the urgency for Jews from Germany, Austria and Czechoslovakia, all under Nazi rule, to get out, and therefore also the pressure on the governments of other countries to take them in.

In the House of Commons the 'Jewish refugee problem' was debated on 21 November 1938 and on the same day the British Government announced that it was ready to admit an unspecified number, later set at 10,000, of Jewish children up to the age of seventeen from German-occupied lands.

The decision galvanized into action a whole conglomeration of Jewish, Christian and national organizations, as well as many private citizens. Among Christians, the Quakers especially played a noble role.

The first Kindertransport arrived on 2 December 1938. One of the last, which included me, arrived on 11 August 1939.

It was on a dull and drizzly afternoon that I found myself on the platform of a Berlin railway station, saying good-bye to my parents. How they must have felt is, given the circumstances, obvious; but on my part, the anxiety as to whether I would ever see them again soon became commingled with a sense of adventure.

There were about four hundred of us, mostly younger than myself, and a youth leader who tried to keep up our spirits by going from coach to coach, making us sing songs. We disembarked at Harwich and were taken out into some fields. The sun was shining, the air clean, the grass greener than any I had ever seen, and if ever freedom was a tangible thing, it was so that morning in Harwich.

At Liverpool Street station I was the last one to be collected. A strange lady came for me and put me on a train to Newcastle-upon-Tyne.

During school holidays, I lived with a Christian family. Red Cross messages, limited to twenty-five words, were exchanged with parents until no more messages came from them.

We also tried to keep in touch with our benefactors who helped to bring us over. There was, for instance, a lady called Mrs Atkinson who had played a part in making the arrangements for me. I never met her, but corresponded with her for a number of years, and it was only relatively recently that I had my first opportunity to visit her home in Dorset, which turned out to be a lonely farm in the middle of nowhere. She had died some years before, but her bachelor son was still living there, and showed us into a drawing-room full of armchairs occupied by dogs! During the war, he told us, the same room had been crowded with Jewish children from Germany!

I mention these details to convey something of the spirit of active concern and compassion which animated many people in this country in our time of need. Not all, of course. There was insensitivity, too, and many criticisms have been justly levelled against British policy during the Nazi years, which could no doubt have saved many more refugees if the will had been there. But those of us who found hospitality in this country will always feel a deep sense of gratitude on that account which no such qualifications can diminish.

* * *

Mitzi Raynor

(Schreier, Vienna), Ilford, Essex, UK

My sister and I said good-bye to our parents, uncle and aunt on the platform of the Westbahnhof, Vienna, not knowing when we would see them again, but not imagining that this would be the last time we would see them alive.

The eldest brother of my mother, who had emigrated to England before the First World War was our guarantor. He always wrote that he was poor, but I did not expect such bad living conditions. I shall never forget the disappointment of seeing my uncle's home in Hanbury Street, Spitalsfield, London. My sister and I slept on a sofabed in the kitchen.

My uncle could not afford to keep us, so Bloomsbury House, seeing our living conditions, found a hostel in Kensington for my sister, and I looked for a job. The only work I was allowed to do was trainee dressmaking. I managed to find a job in a small establishment, earning 12s. 6d. weekly, minus stamps. I had to give ten shillings a week to my aunt for my keep. I was quick and was put on the machine sewing sleeves and other small parts. Only speed mattered, and I did not mind the job. There was another girl from Vienna working with me and we became friends. I remember going to Hyde Park with Helen and spending our meagre pocket money on sweets and having to walk back all the way to the East End.

When I went to see my sister in Kensington, I realized that there was a nicer part of London, so different from the dreary East End. However, my sister did not stay there long. One day I was informed that she had been sent to Tunbridge Wells. As I could not afford the fare to go and see her at the time, I was devastated.

I found a domestic position for my mother, but there were so many obstacles from the *Kultusgemeinde* in Vienna, that war broke out before she could leave. My uncle, who was a sick man, died in January 1940, before the Blitz, and my aunt and I were bombed out and moved to Stoke Newington. I spent the war years in London and really admired the spirit of the English people during those hazardous times.

I managed to get an office job at John Lewis, where I worked happily till I was called up for war work. Somehow those six years passed and peace came at last. The worst part was the rude awakening; that most of us were orphans and our parents and other relatives and friends had met such a tragic end.

However, life goes on and when you are young you realize that you must make a life for yourself, and eventually I married and settled down. I have two daughters and four grandchildren and my sister has two sons. We shall never forget what happened to us, but we count our blessings and hope that our offspring will live in peace.

*   *   *

Gila Raz

(Silberberg, Wadersloh), Kibbutz Ma'ayan Baruch, Israel

My name was Frederika Silberberg, born 30 July 1931, in the small village of Wadersloh, Westfalia. I believe that only six Jewish families lived there. My parents were Martha (née Bonwitt) and Ludwig Silberberg. I had one older brother, Julius, born in 1927. No one survived the Holocaust.

After Kristallnacht my parents moved to Hanover. From there I was sent to a Jewish boarding school in Arlem to join my brother who had been sent there previously. During that period my parents were in contact with a Jewish family, Leah and Jacob Clark of Sunderland, who agreed to accept me into their family as their daughter. From the date of my arrival in England in June 1939, I lived with the Clarks for nine years.

In 1949 I finally made *Aliyah* and became a member of a small northern kibbutz in the Upper Galilee, Kibbutz Ma'ayan Baruch. Since settling on the kibbutz I have married, had four children and two grandchildren. Professionally I am now a social worker specializing in Geriatrics.

*   *   *

Karola Regent

(Hannele Zürndorfer, Düsseldorf), Scotland, UK

At last everything was ready and we had received notification that our transport train was leaving Düsseldorf station on 3 May 1939. I think it was one of the last Children's transports that stopped to pick up in Düsseldorf.

The night before we left my father wrote a final poem into our autograph albums and my mother also wrote some loving lines. I was to read these again and again during the years that followed.

Before we left the house that morning, my father and my mother laid their hands on our heads and blessed us, as they always did on Friday evenings, for the last time.

It was a very long train. I don't know how many children it was carrying, but it had come a long way, picking up children at different towns. I think that Düsseldorf was the last pick-up point. It all passed like a dream. I do remember when the unbelievable moment of separation actually came. We were all busy with the preoccupations of finding the right coach and compartment, of stowing the luggage. Then the last clinging embrace: my face against the familiar tweed of my father's coat and the comforting feel of my mother's fur collar.

Then we were on the train. We didn't cry then. We all knew we mustn't. Not Mummy either. She was so brave. I think Lotte and I waved goodbye happily, still hearing their last firm assurances: 'We are coming soon . . . in a few weeks . . . '

Then, as I saw their lonely figures receding as the train drew out, looking so forsaken, I cried, but not for long. There were so many new faces to take in, so much to think about, and then there was Lotte, weeping away beside me. 'Look after Lotte!' were their last instructions and I promised myself that I would. It was the least I could do, now that we were on our own.

What I didn't know at the time, but learnt only after the war, was that my father, anxious to see that we got safely across the border, had jumped on to the train at the very end, where it curved around a corner and we could not see from where we were, and had travelled on it all the way to the Dutch border. My father left the train as unobtrusively as he had got on, and watched it snake its way across the frontier into Holland and safety; a train full of children, full of hope, leaving behind the broken hearts of mothers and fathers, empty homes and a future of 'night and fog'.

We travelled by night-boat from the Hook of Holland to Harwich and from there by train to Liverpool Street station where we were to be checked and claimed by our sponsors and relatives.

I faintly remember meeting my dear friend, Inge Lewin, at Rotterdam. Her father had emigrated to Cuba, and the rest of her family had left Düsseldorf just one month before us and were now waiting in Holland for permission to join him. My father had written to them, and now they came to see us as we passed through. But the whole journey had a somnambulistic quality – train, boat, train, interspersed with endless standing in long, labelled lines. I suppose that with all the excitement and emotional strain of farewells, frontier hold-ups and apprehensions, we were tired out.

The first clear picture that emerges is of our arrival at Liverpool Street station, a vast glass dome swirling with steam, and of filing through a door into a great hall with windows high up in the walls and a grey light filtering through them. As we entered, our names were checked off a list and were each given a packet of sandwiches, some chocolate and an orange. It's funny how children always remember food. Certainly this orange, round and brightly glowing in the grey surroundings, suddenly cheered me and brought back a sort of excitement and anticipation.

I suppose we were hungry by then, but I don't remember actually eating the orange. Perhaps I was still clutching it when we arrived at my aunt's flat.

It seemed hours and hours that we sat in that grey hall on wooden benches. I have an impression of a gallery where relatives and sponsors sat waiting for their charges. I think we must have been dealt with alphabetically, for we two Zürndorfers heard name after name being called and saw nearly all the children who had travelled with us leave.

But where were Tante Rosel and Inge? I could not see them in the gallery. What if they had not come? Would we be sent back, or would we have to stay in this depressing hall? Lotte began to fidget and weep. Then, when there were only a few unclaimed children scattered about the hall, our names were called: 'Hannele and Lotte Zürndorfer!'

We stood up and a lady led us to a desk where our labels were taken off our necks, and we were handed over to our official English sponsor, Mrs Ettinghausen, a kind, smiling lady. And there stood Tante Rosel, small and

continued on page 253

B'nai   **B'rith**

B'nai B'rith Care Committee for Refugee Children

150, SOUTHAMPTON ROW, W.C.1.
Telephone : Terminus 2261

OE/LA   16th February, 1939.

Leo Anker, Esq.,

Maida Vale,
W. 9.

Dear Sir,

    Thanking you for your very kind offer to take
into your home a refugee child, we would like to
inform you that Else and Heinz, Karplus, Berlin,
are arriving in this country on one of the next
transports.

    Would you please be good enough to state
whether 48 hours notice will be sufficient for you.

                    Yours faithfully,

                    p.p. Mrs. O. Epstein.

                    Lori Adam.

You can help to make a Refugee child happy.   Will you ?

anxious, and Inge. We were no longer baggages, numbers, labels, but children with a loving aunt who hugged and hugged us and took us away from that stuffy hall as soon as formalities had been completed and the luggage collected. I looked back and the boy who had sat next to us on the bench was still there, looking so lost and lonely. I wondered what was going to happen to him.

We went by taxi and I kept thinking to myself, 'This is England!' We drove through crowded streets full of shops and people bustling about. All the notices were in English, and all these people were talking English. It really was exciting! Then the taxi stopped in front of a large, cream-coloured house fronted by a porch with flaking pillars. And out of the window at the very top of the house looked Uncle Ala, waving and pulling funny faces. When we had climbed the three flights of stone stairs, Ala tried hard to make us laugh, but he looked older and sadder than I remembered him and I felt a bit like crying. We were made so welcome and cousin Egon hopped excitedly from foot to foot and immediately started teaching us English, 'Good afternoon girls,' he said. It was comforting to be with relatives. A telegram was dispatched to Mummy and Daddy.

An excerpt from ' *The Ninth of November*' by Hannele Zürndorfer

* * *

Vera Reichman

(Aziza, Beuthen), Montreal, Canada

I have now been living in the same house for the past twenty-three years. Each time I think about it I am astonished and marvel at the stability I have finally attained. It was not always so.

I was born in 1931 in Beuthen, Upper Silesia. My immediate family consisted of my parents, an older and a younger brother and myself.

One day, suddenly, we were at the station; my parents, my two brothers and I. When my turn came my parents gave me a hug and a gentle push and reminded me to obey the people in charge. That was the last I saw of them. It was May 1939.

On arrival in England, I vaguely recall standing in a room full of people. My name was called and when I came forward, someone handed me over to a lady who led me away. It was a traumatic moment. Until then I had been together with other children in the same situation as myself, who spoke the same language. Now I was cut off from everything familiar and my parents were far away. I felt a lump in my throat but I was ashamed to cry. This was something I was to experience time and again whenever I moved and found myself in unfamiliar surroundings, even as an adult with children of my own.

The first family to give me shelter in England was far more affluent than mine and the size of their house amazed me. The head of the household was a doctor. There was one child, a boy, two years older than me. I think my foster parents must have been rather active socially for they were often out and I was, for the most part, taken care of by their live-in maid.

When war broke out my foster parents, possibly tired of the responsibility (I was not an easy child), had me transferred to a refugee school in Folkestone, Kent.

The school was headed by an exceptionally kind and intelligent woman. She was an experienced teacher and principal, having had her own very successful school in Berlin. Unfortunately the town of Folkestone was on the South East coast of England over which German bombers passed on their way to London and other cities. In June 1940 our school had to close and we, as well as many other Folkestone children, were evacuated. Our destination was South Wales, and my group ended up in the small village of Caerwent, Monmouthshire.

We were temporarily billeted with an elderly couple until, after several days, I was taken to a family in Tintern who had offered to look after me. I was surprised to find that the father was Jewish, although his wife and daughter, a girl of my age, were both practising Catholics.

I lived quite contentedly with them from July 1940 until January 1942 when the *Bnai Brith* committee responsible for refugee children arranged for me to be moved to a more Jewish environment in the city of Newport, some forty miles from Tintern. My new home – a hostel for twelve girls from the ages of ten (myself) to sixteen, was not a very happy experience. The hostel was run by a matron and cook, two singularly unpleasant women. Food was insufficient and the discipline rough. To our relief, in November 1942 the place was closed and the girls dispersed to different homes and hostels. Two of the younger girls and myself were sent temporarily to a hostel in London.

I had been there for about three weeks when the family, hearing that I was in London, came to take me back to Tintern until a new home could be found for me in a safer area. I was more than happy to go back, for I had come to regard that family almost as my own. In January 1943 a place became available in a hostel for evacuees in Surrey. For the umpteenth time I packed my little black suitcase and left for a new home.

I arrived at the Rowledge hostel late one January afternoon. A young woman took me upstairs to a bedroom with four bunk-beds and two dressers. I was shown the bed I was to occupy and the drawer where I could keep my clothes and then I was left alone. The by now familiar lump rose in my throat as I surveyed the unfamiliar surroundings. A little later the young woman returned and took me to the dining room where I was introduced to everyone and given a seat at one of the four tables. So began two and a half of the happiest years I spent in England.

The hostel was run by a dedicated staff of young people – all under thirty – headed by a Rabbi and his wife, members of the Jewish orthodox youth movement *Bnei Akiva* and remained enthusiastically Zionist. It was, therefore, natural for me at the age of eighteen to decide to go on the movement's *Hachshara* programme as a preparation for eventual settlement on a kibbutz in Israel. In September 1949 I joined the *Bachad* Farm at Thaxted where I stayed for one year, going on to work in other areas of the organization for another year.

So much for preparation! I never did get to Israel. Chance intervened. I met and married a young teacher from Morocco and lived there for six years until the political situation brought us with our two young children, first to the US and then, shortly after, to Montreal, Canada where, twenty-two years ago, our youngest child was born.

I am profoundly grateful to all the selfless people who took me in at various times, or invited me to their homes and made me feel wanted. To the staff of the Rowledge hostel I owe an extra measure of gratitude for their patience and devotion; their high standard of care and their efforts to instil in us the moral and ethical values appropriate to our ages and an appreciation of our Jewish culture and religious heritage which gave me firm roots in a turbulent post-war world.

But my deepest love and gratitude go to my parents whose courage and foresight saved our lives. Their sacrifice is vindicated by the survival of their children, grandchildren and great-grandchildren, helping to ensure the future of the Jewish people.

*   *   *

Professor Nicolas Daniel Reis

(Königsberger, Berlin), Haifa, Israel

RECOLLECTIONS OF CHILDHOOD 1938-1939

One morning I left the house as usual to catch the bus to school. My brother was not with me. Some of the shop windows were smashed and the pavement was littered with glass. People were standing about confused. Then I saw some fires: smoke seemed to be billowing out of a Synagogue. At the Kaiserdamm the school gates were closed. A small group of pupils stood about waiting not knowing what to do. Ginger was there. He told us they had been wakened in the middle of the night by Nazis; then they smashed into his father's fur shop and stole all the furs.

We decided to go home. When I arrived at our house, my mother told me that I need not go to school any more. Soon after, Mother told us we would be leaving for England. Mother and the grandparents took my brother and myself to the station. The platform was crowded. Suddenly it dawned on me that mother was not coming with us. I made myself stiff as a board and lay down on the platform screaming. Nobody could pacify me or persuade me to get on the train. Only when my brother said: 'You sissy, I knew you'd make a fuss!' did I overcome my hysteria. We waved goodbye.

In Hamburg we boarded the *United States*, an enormous luxury liner. Everything was exciting: the cabin, the meals, the activities. There was a party: we sang Hebrew songs in high spirits. On the second day we docked in Southampton. I had a cardboard identification card with a piece of string round my neck: it said 'Klaus Wolfgang Königsberger', a number and the name of our guarantor.

A train took us to Victoria station. Uncle Karl, whom I had never seen before, was there. After some formalities he took us to our first foster parents: the Kohns at Ashbourne Avenue, London NW11. It was a Friday. The next day we wandered along the Finchley Road: the most amazing sight was huge mountains of butter in the windows of Sainsbury's.

On Monday we went to the Hampstead Garden Suburb Elementary School. We knew no English. But my brother Max was top in everything at the end of the first term. He was also the marbles king and the cigarette card banker. We would get beatings regularly and we were always ready with thin exercise books stuffed in between our underpants and our trousers.

The nights were cold and damp and we would sleep fully dressed. We worked for the United Dairies milkman on Saturdays – ten pence a week plus a bottle of Jersey full cream milk. It was by now summer 1939. I had forgotten Berlin and had almost suppressed the memory of my mother.

I was fully immersed in my new life without parents and my main preoccupation was the new game of cricket which I was trying to master. When I was told at the beginning of August that mother would be arriving in a few days at Croydon airport – I was glad but not terribly overjoyed. I had no appreciation of the gravity of the situation or of the mortal danger facing all Jews. When mother arrived she asked to see her sons: she was told they had gone into town! We were making one of our visits to an Oxford Street amusement arcade: Max, my brother, was a wizard at winning from the machines.

Mother began her studies as a student mid-wife at Queen Charlotte's Hospital. She was allowed to meet her sons once a fortnight on a Sunday. We would wait for her on the Marylebone Road. Shortly after my ninth birthday the sirens went off. We were walking past Hendon airport at that very moment on the way to lunch with Uncle Karl and Auntie Grete. They were glued to the radio: England had declared war on Germany. So ended our first six months in England. We were to grow to love England and all she stood for, although we later followed our destiny in Israel; our first love from the days of our schooling at the *Theodor Herzl Schule* in Berlin.

9775

This document of identity is issued with the approval of His Majesty's Government in the United Kingdom to young persons to be admitted to the United Kingdom for educational purposes under the care of the Inter-Aid Committee for children.

THIS DOCUMENT REQUIRES NO VISA.

PERSONAL PARTICULARS.

Name FRAJDENREICH   HEDWIG

Sex FEMALE   Date of Birth 16-11-31

Place DANZIG

Full Names and Address of Parents

FRAJDENREICH Schejwa & Dydia
25, Brzezinska
LODZ

Gwen Richards

(Frajdenreich, Lodz, Poland), Devon, UK

When Paula, nine and I, Hedwig, seven, left Lodz, our parents, brothers and sisters came to the station to wave goodbye. They said that we would all meet up in London, then make our home in Israel. We were heading for a camp called Otwock, until the ship came. I remember we had long hair, which we had to have shaved off. The ship came to take us to England. We stayed with a Jewish family in London and went to Highgate school. When the war came in September, we were evacuated to Devon to a Christian family.

I remember living in Danzig, where the streets were cobbled. I remember going to the Synagogue every Friday night and coming home eating *gefilte fish* with carrots. My father was a tailor. I remember my father asking me to get him some cotton and when I returned with it there were Germans hitting him with a long iron bar. We last had a letter from Poland in 1942. We have tried many places to trace any of our large family, but without success.

In 1949 this family adopted us, saying we had no one left. We then had to become Christian and at the age of twenty I married a Christian man, but deep down in my heart I am still a Polish Jewess.

*   *   *

Thea Richardson

(Wessely, Vienna), Stanmore, Middlesex, UK

My name was Thea Wessely before I was married, and I am from Vienna. How I came to England at the age of fifteen shows what an important part fate plays in our lives.

I was learning English at my school in Vienna, when two girls from the Hastings High School for Girls came to visit the school. It must have been some time in 1937. I, together with two other children, wanted to improve our English and we approached the girls from England and asked them if they could give us the names of pen-friends. They gave us the name of the headmistress and told us to write to her. I wrote a letter which was read out at assembly and three girls agreed to write to us. The other two Viennese girls were not Jewish and the fact that I was Jewish was not mentioned. I exchanged about half a dozen letters with my pen-friend and then Hitler marched into Austria and my whole world collapsed.

We lost our home and my father lost his job and I had to leave school. My parents and I did not know anybody abroad, so one day I had the bright idea of writing to my pen-friend about our plight. She, her parents and the whole Hastings school were amazed and horrified to hear what went on; they had no Jewish connections and were not aware of the situation. My pen-friend wrote to me by return of mail that I should come and live with her and go to school with her, and they would try to find somebody to send permits for my parents. Sadly, although some of the teachers of the High School agreed to take my parents, this took too long, and my parents did not survive, but my life was saved. I am still in constant touch with my 'pen-friend'.

*   *   *

Eric Richmond

(Reichmann, Vienna), London, UK

My name was Erich Reichman from Vienna. On 10 December 1938 my parents took me to the Westbahnhof for my journey to Holland and England. I was fourteen years of age and this was the first children's transport from Vienna with boys and girls of a similar age.

I remember one of the girls in my compartment. She was called Erika Furke and her father was a Rabbi in the Tempelgasse Synagogue where I had my *Bar Mitzvah.* The atmosphere on the train was strange, some of the children cried, others – not quite grasping the fact that they might never again see their loved ones – just played around or sang.

We spent two days on our journey and arrived on 12 December in Harwich, to be accommodated in a Warner Holiday Camp in Parkfield right by the sea. The wooden huts held just two children each and it was very cold and wet. During the night we were all flooded and had to be moved to Lowestoft to sleep on the ballroom floor of one of the hotels.

The next destination was a holiday camp – and a very large one it was – in Dovercourt. We were all divided into groups and I remember my housemaster was a man called Haybrook. Every Sunday visitors arrived to see us and some children were adopted that way.

Eventually we were moved to Ipswich to a most depressing old building and then some of us were moved to London to various hostels. I finished up with my old school friend Henry Roberts (formerly Hans Robitschek) in the St Marks Road hostel, London W10. We were first sent to a local Jewish school and then found jobs. The letters I received weekly from my mother up to the beginning of the war were heart-rending. I cried myself to sleep nightly and I am sure she did as well. I was an only child.

Ironically we were classed as 'enemy aliens' at the age of sixteen, and had to report to Notting Hill Gate police station. Some of our boys were sent to internment camps in Canada. I must have presented a sorry sight, for the interviewing officer gave me a sweet and sent me back to the hostel.

* * *

Ilse Richtman

(Schächter, Vienna), East St Kilda, Australia

In April 1939 I left Vienna with a Kindertransport for England. I was eleven years old at the time and was accompanied by my brother who was five years older. As for most other Jewish families, the year previous to this had been very traumatic and I was a very frightened, sad little girl when I said goodbye to my parents at the Wiener Westbahnhof. Boys and girls were separated on the train and so I was not with my brother but with a school friend whose name was Gertie Bernstein with whom unfortunately I have lost contact. I will never forget the kindness shown to us by Dutch women who boarded the train in Holland and gave us refreshments. It was such a contrast to what we had been through.

On arrival in London we were 'sorted out' at Liverpool Street station and, accompanied by a Committee lady, I was taken on a trolley bus to the Cazenove Road Girls' hostel where the door was opened by Mrs D Margulies, the Matron, who had been my Hebrew teacher in Vienna. Being very shy and timid at the time, my pleasure at seeing a familiar face cannot be put into words. On 2 September 1939, we were evacuated with the school to Bishop's Stortford and I stayed there until 1942 when I returned to the hostel, where I stayed until I came to Australia in 1947. Unknown to me, my brother was interned in 1940 and sent to Australia on the infamous *Dunera*

Times in England were very hard but I will never forget the friendships I made during that time and the many instances of kindness shown to me during my eight years' stay in England.

*   *   *

Edith Riemer

(Lefor, Ludwigshafen), Cherry Valley, USA

In early June 1939, six months after leaving Ludwigshafen/Rhein on a Kindertransport, I settled in at the Lexington Gardens hostel in London. I had just fled from the family, who was supposed to take care of me; the head of the household had been severely injured in a car accident and was prone to bizarre and frightening behaviour that could occur without prior warning. True, his wife and servant had given me instructions on how to protect myself, to always lock myself into my bedroom, but his last outburst hit far too close to home. After staying with friends for the first few days, the Refugee Committee suggested the hostel.

It was a large house on a quiet residential street, not far from the Earls Court Underground. The population was in a constant state of flux, depending on how many children had found foster homes and how many were stranded – at least temporarily – after their transports arrived. We were never more than perhaps twenty to twenty-five, but there was a big age variable. I will never forget one toddler, who was crying inconsolably for his mother, taking only short naps, refusing to eat, holding on tightly to his bottle. We all took turns holding and cuddling him, trying to catch his interest, all to no avail – with one notable exception. A refugee family of four was renting a flat next to our bedroom; generally they kept to themselves, but when the constant crying got on their nerves, the father came to lend a hand; it was the only time the child merely sobbed. All of us were happy when foster parents were found for him.

Birthdays at home had always been very special occasions; there were presents of course and, when I was little, parties, but it was more than that – it was a day of doing special things together with my parents and friends, an intensification of the bonds that held us. I wondered how I would cope with my coming birthday without their support. That day breakfast was served as usual, then we played ball in the park, but after lunch a group of children wished me a 'Happy Birthday' and presented me with enough money to buy a movie ticket – an unbelievable treat. I was surprised and moved; they had saved and sacrificed their precious weekly allowance (I think it was a shilling), barely enough to pay for the postage needed to write home. Of all the birthday presents I ever got it was by far the most memorable one.

War clouds were gathering. On 25 August 1939 we were transferred to Rusthall Beacon, Tunbridge Wells, considered to be a safer location than London. When we arrived we could hardly believe our eyes – we were in a country estate.

Starting in April 1941 I worked briefly (cut short by illness) at the Rothsay Gardens, Bedford, hostel which was also run by the Jewish Refugee Committee. It was more of a Children's Home than a hostel since it provided long-term care for new-borns to school-age youngsters, whose parents could not care for them. A few single mothers worked in the Home, either in the kitchen or in housekeeping. Their, visiting hours were restricted, not only to prevent interference with their own work schedules, but also to reduce stress for the child-care staff and their own children, deeming their unexpected appearances disruptive and upsetting. Oh, how attitudes in child-rearing have changed – thank Heavens. I can still hear the crying of the little ones sitting on their 'potties', tied by cloth restraints to the bars of a large playpen. Only one little girl, with large dark eyes, stared quietly at the others; her name was Marion Levy. Her mother was in the Forces. Most children lacked the personal attention needed for normal physical and emotional growth. I was already sharing most of my free time with Marion; it was the first time she was taken to a store and just before I left, I had her photograph taken professionally. I often wondered what became of her.

We worked long hours, not only looking after the children themselves, but we were also responsible for the laundry (I can still remember having to boil the nappies), sterilization of bottles, making up formulas, straining food and cleaning the nursery. Yet I loved the work with the children and was sad when I had to leave.

The Belsize Park hostel in London was, once again, a totally different entity. Run by Bloomsbury House it provided board and loading for a great many girls past the mandatory school age. Some were apprenticed to learn a trade, others had jobs, but their earnings could not support them outside a subsidized, sheltered environment. Although financially expedient there was a more compelling reason for them to choose the hostel; with several girls sharing a room, friendships flourished, an easy cameraderie developed, it gave them a sense of belonging. In essence the hostel acted as a surrogate family. There was also the added security of having a nurse present and a six-bed sick-room available.

The director, Mrs Glücksmann, together with her staff, was also running a British restaurant on the same premises. The cooks and bakers worked magic, conjuring up delicious menus despite food rationing. Though it was meant particularly to provide war workers with nutritious food at reasonable prices, most of our clientele were Jewish refugees living in the neighbourhood. The hostel girls had their own dining-room, but the food was the same. Eventually I moved out of the hostel proper to another house, also owned by Bloomsbury House, just minutes away, where I shared a room with just one other girl. Most of the other tenants were also young Jewish refugees. Choosing a less structured environment was the last step towards total independence.

*　　*　　*

Helga Roboz

(Liebenau/Leigh, Berlin), Vancouver, Canada

There is very little I remember of that day, 4 May 1939, when my brother and I left Berlin with the Kindertransport. I do not even recall the name of the station from which our train departed. I do remember that we stopped again at another station in Berlin and that my parents, wanting to catch another glimpse of us, had rushed to this stop to say good-bye once again. They both died in the Holocaust.

My brother, twelve years old, and I, fifteen years old, were separated and sat in different compartments. The only other memory I have of that day is that I started to cry at some point and a girl, very nicely, asked me to pull myself together; that I was a bad example for the small children, and that we were all, so to speak, in the same boat. She was absolutely right, of course.

*　　*　　*

Brigitte Rohaczeck

(Neumann, Prague), Schwaig, West Germany

Prague – July or August 1939 . . . SS men in uniforms were standing around with guns in attention watching our every movement. I was frightened. We kissed our Pappa for the last time and we were told to join the other children on the special train to go all the way to the Netherlands via Germany. In Amsterdam we would board a ship for England.

Liesl, my sister, was eleven; I was nine years old. Both Liesl and I carried school satchels on our backs with all our little treasures inside; a few photographs, a new fountain pen, a four-colour pencil, and a book.

Mamma was born in Aussig/Elbe; Pappa was born in Litau/Mähren, but his family moved to Schönpriesen near Aussig when he was a child. Liesl and I were born in Aussig. While my mother came from a Jewish background, my father's family was Austrian. While my father's relatives survived the war by leaving the country in time or by incredible chance (my father was imprisoned in the concentration camp Oranienburg/Sachsenhausen for political reasons), my mother's family was less fortunate. That's why I would like to mention them here. They have perished, but they will always be a part of me as long as I live.

In the autumn of 1938 Hitler occupied the whole of the Sudetenland. All my parents' friends joined the NSDAP (the National Democratic Party). My father was asked to become a member as well. He refused. His comment was: 'I am a social democrat and that is what I am going to stay!' As a result of this he immediately lost his job. He was not even allowed to treat private patients.

When we arrived in England, we were very nervous. Onkel Helmi was somebody we knew from tales but whom we had never met in our lives. And now we were going to live with him and his family. Our cousins Edith and Melitta were complete strangers to us. There was the problem for Pappa who had no idea of the size of the station we would arrive at. So he decided to make sure that Onkel Helmi would recognize us by our clothes and by our hats. We wore light-blue knitted dresses and had red *Tirolerhüte* with long feathers on our heads. We must have been a strange sight for our fellow travellers. We loved Onkel Helmi the moment we saw him, he was so very much like Pappa. We had our difficulties with Tante Trude. She was not the least bit like our gentle warmhearted Mamma. But I don't want to be unfair to her. It was a difficult situation with little money.

It was there at the station that we met Miss Jones, our future schoolmistress, for the very first time. She had come to the station with some of her pupils from the village school of Sellatyn to welcome us. They gave us a big box of toffees. After this nice welcome we were taken to the hostel in Sellatyn, near Oswestry in Shropshire. It was a small village at that time with a big church, a vicarage, a village school and a schoolhouse where Miss Jones lived with her sister. There was a small village shop and a tiny post-office, and a pub. This pub was very interesting. It was exactly on the Welsh border. It had a signboard that said 'Last Inn Out' when you came from the English side and 'First Inn In' when you approached it from Wales.

Miss Jones was a very nice person who not only taught us English in a very short time but made school a pleasure. But I owe her another thing which became very precious for me. I told you already that I took a book on the journey and left all my toys behind. It was Miss Jones who bought me a doll. Thank you so much . . .

The people in Sellatyn were very pleasant. We used to go to church on

Sundays and we were very often invited for tea by the farmers in the hills, by the vicar and, of course, by Miss Jones. The pupils of the girls' high school in Oswestry used to arrange lovely Christmas parties for all the refugee children. I want to express my thanks to all the kind people who helped to save our lives and who made us so welcome.

Many thanks to Miss Hilda Francis. I spent many happy and unforgettable days with her and her old father at Craigside, Pant, near Oswestry. She was a real lady with a kind heart who helped to save many lives. She tried helping Mamma to come to England but it was not possible any more.

Thanks to Mrs Williams in Oswestry. She moved to London later and died there in 1946 . . .

Thanks to Miss Rogers, the warden of the hostel in Coboyn for taking us to the cinema and for spoiling us with chocolates . . .

to Miss Roberts who helped us with our English like Miss Jones . . .

to the group of very cheerful English friends who used to visit us on Tuesday evenings. We had so much fun with them . . .

to all of them THANKS THANKS THANKS . . .

We left Sellatyn in 1942 to go to the Czech school which had been founded for the children who would return to Czechoslovakia after the war. Onkel Helmi and his family moved first to Nottingham and later to London. I returned to Czechoslovakia after the war in 1947, while Liesl stayed in England. Later I regretted my decision, but I felt I had to join Pappa.

What had happened back home in the meantime?

Pappa was arrested in March 1940, put on trial as a traitor to Hitler's Germany and sentenced to prison. Later he was sent to a concentration camp where he stayed till he was liberated by the Russians. Before that the whole camp was set marching on the so-called 'death march'. After the liberation he was not allowed to return to Czechoslovakia, the Red Army needed doctors. In September he managed to escape from them and it took another month before he was back, safe and alive.

Mamma was arrested in 1944 and deported to Theresienstadt (Terezin) and from there to Auschwitz in January 1945.

My grandfather, my aunts, my uncles, and my cousin Lotte were all deported to Theresienstadt and from there to Treblinka, Auschwitz, and Warsaw in January 1942.

Liesl and I would have surely shared their sad fate if we had not had the chance to go to England. I would like to express my thanks to this generous country that gave us shelter in that dark period of European history.

I have written this in 1989 in Schwaig, near Nuremberg, a town that acquired a sad reputation during Hitler's power; the racial laws were passed there in 1935 and Hitler built himself a kind of colosseum to demonstrate his power and to parade his troops. It is a town where the vast majority of the population suffered from acute loss of memory after the war and where most do not wish to discuss such matters.

Mordechai Ron

(Fröhlich, Breslau), Kibbutz Neot Mordechai, Israel

It seems like yesterday, and yet, fifty years have gone by. It was a dismal cold February morning in 1939, that we met and parted on Anhalter Bahnhof in Berlin. We met almost one hundred youngsters from all over Germany between the ages of twelve to sixteen, and we parted from our parents and dear ones, many never to meet again. We were surrounded by German police and I still have the teutonic barking in my ears as we were herded into special carriages reserved for us Jewish brats. Our parents were not allowed onto the platform for fear of creating scenes and thus shielding the good Germans from witnessing the disgusting spectacle of tears of good-bye.

A tragic-comic incident occurred as the train finally pulled out of the station. The compartments were locked and we crowded into the corridor. Just as the conductor opened the locked doors, a local train pulled abreast of us and some of us espied our parents waving to us. We rushed into the opened compartments in order to occupy seats and to return to the corridor windows. As it happened, one girl, in a hurry to rush back, hung her rucksack mistakenly on the handle of the emergency brake and the train screeched to a halt. Commotion broke out when it was discovered that the Jews had sabotaged the *Reichsbahn* and we saw ourselves returned and tried. It took the transport leader sweat, persuasion and courage to calm the infuriated train personnel and after fines were deposited we were allowed to proceed.

Crossing into Holland was a rare experience and at the first stop we were greeted by some kind-hearted ladies from the local Jewish community who showered us with sandwiches and sweets.

On a foggy dark and cold morning we stepped on to English soil. We were benumbed, tired and hungry. Some of the younger ones cried for their mummies as the reaction of parting from home set in. We soon were dispersed to private homes, some to hostels and I was sent to one of the Warners Holiday Camps in Dovercourt, and eventually joined a *Youth Aliyah* group which was formed there and which was destined to be established in Scotland on the estate of the late Lord Balfour.

On our way there I recall another episode. We were about twenty boys, the vanguard of the future *Youth Aliya* group to be set up. We were supposed to catch the night train but arrived somewhat early in London. Our group leader decided to show us some of the sights of London which included refreshments at the then famous Lyons Corner House. A table was reserved for us and on entering, the orchestra, probably advised of our arrival in advance, played some continental tunes including some Viennese waltzes, and naturally we were very much impressed.

At a table nearby sat several gentlemen. One of them rose and approached our table and introduced himself as a member of the Labour Party and handed some banknotes to our group leader with the best wishes of his colleagues, to be used for our enjoyment in London. It later transpired that he was Clement Attlee, leader of his party and later to become Prime Minister.

England was for me more than a haven. I learned to love the country and her people and their way of life and I soon realized that here was the cradle of democracy. I met kindness, understanding and compassion and to this day I admire the way the people conducted themselves during the bitter days of total war. I founded a family there but, having remained true to the ideals of my youth, I eventually left and came to Israel and helped to establish a *kibbutz,* but to the end of my days I shall always cherish the memory of those years I spent in Great Britain. Yes, it seems like yesterday, and yet fifty years have gone by.

*   *   *

Lillyan Rosenberg

(Cohn, Halberstadt), New York, USA

I was born Lilly Cohn, daughter of Ernst and Margarete Cohn, in Halberstadt, Germany on 30 January 1928.

On Kristallnacht I was ten years old and I remember my father being picked up by the SS and taken to the concentration camp at Buchenwald. My brother was in hiding, he was fifteen. After five weeks my father returned home, thin and head shaven.

In March of 1939 the news arrived that guardians had been found for me in England, Mr and Mrs Herbert Allen of Rochdale, Lancashire. An aunt, who had emigrated to England, visited the Allens and assured my parents that they would take very good care of me.

I was taken to the train to meet the Kindertransport. The photos taken at the station were the last of our family, my brother Werner, my parents and me. I never saw my parents again.

I was too young to understand the political implications, but I knew they were horrendous. Before my departure my mother explained 'the facts of life' to me, although I was too young to comprehend at age ten. She also tried to make me feel that I was a lucky girl to be able to go and live with the Allens.

The Allens owned a large bus company. Mrs Allen was a kindly lady. Mr Allen was a very aristocratic gentleman, and their son Hubert was about thirty years old. I was told he was my new brother. The early days were frustrating. I tried to teach the Allens German but to no avail. Mr Allen was ill in bed and had great patience teaching me English by pointing to objects and pictures.

Within a few weeks I was enrolled at the Convent High School. The nuns at the convent were of German origin and this was most helpful. I was soon able to participate in classes with the exception of the religious class.

A few months later war broke out and ended direct letters out of England. At the convent I met a priest and it is my recollection that he sat in a large room with stained glass windows and we were reading the *Chumash* together, translating from Hebrew into English, from where I had left off at the Jewish school in Halberstadt.

My brother Werner arrived in England one day before the war began and at fifteen he had to fend for himself. The Allens did not wish us to have contact since they wanted me to forget my past. They were now 'Mam' and 'Pop' and wanted to adopt me. My aunt and brother strongly objected as we had hopes of being reunited with our parents after the war.

Letters, via the Red Cross or friends in Switzerland, arrived sporadically. We were told (there was a limit of twenty-five words) that my grandmother had been deported to a camp. We learned that my parents were among those sent to Auschwitz. I still have all the letters my parents sent. It is too painful to read them but I keep them as they are all I have left.

The years that followed were shared with other girls at the Beacon hostel in Tunbridge Wells, Kent. There we tried to make the best of our life and were like a family. Many of us are still in touch, in England and the United States.

In Tunbridge Wells, I took an exam for a special school in Tonbridge. Although I passed the exam, I was informed that as an 'enemy alien' I could not be accepted. At fifteen I was however accepted at the School of Arts and Crafts in Tunbridge Wells and studied art and dress designing. This was paid for by the 'Committee', and led to an apprenticeship at Jacqmar in London where I lived throughout the rest of the war with Mr and Mrs Hayward, who were most influential in my future life. I continued to study music and art at night.

In 1946, my brother insisted that we go to the United States. I would never have left England. We received a visa from an uncle and I soon followed my brother to New York. My brother and I rented a room in New York and I was able to obtain a very good job, sketching and dress designing, and another new life began.

I met my husband Jerry Rosenberg while visiting an uncle in New York. We were engaged and married in 1948. We were blessed with two sons; Steven, born in 1950 and Ralph, born in 1952. Jerry was in the airline catering business. We travelled through most major countries of the world and our sons had excellent experiences.

Steven married Susan Soto. Before their marriage, Susan converted to Judaism. I gave her the *Magen David* I wore when I left my parents. My guardians had not allowed me to wear it because of its association with my past. This completed the cycle back to Judaism. Steven is a dermatologist in Palm Beach, Florida, and he and Susan have a two year old daughter, Miranda.

Ralph is an internist. He married Hilda Slivka who is a paediatrician in
Hartford, Connecticut. They have two children, Jake, four and Julia one.
Julia is named after both Jerry's and my mother.

I am working as a tour manager in New York City, dealing with tourists
from all over the world and am putting all my acquired knowledge,
particularly of German/English, to the best possible advantage.

Somehow life seems brighter.

*   *   *

Ilse Rosenduft

(Durst, Munich), London, UK

I was born in Munich and my parents were Pauline Durst (nee Reinach) and
Bernhard (Chaim Baruch). Two years later my brother Fred (Manfred)
arrived. We both attended the *Hohenzollern* School and later the Jewish school.
Fred spent a short while in the *Real Gymnasium.* As I was good at needlework,
my teacher recommended me to the firm of Rothenberg where I learnt
dressmaking for eight months. Apart from the loss of our dear mother on 5
April 1935 life was fairly peaceful.

At the time of the *Polen Aktion* on 28 October 1938 our family was arrested
and sent to Poland. On the way we spent a night in Adelheim prison. I
remember *Challot* being brought there by the Jewish community as it was a
Friday night. Luckily we got to the border too late and so we returned home,
paying for the return journey ourselves. A week later, on 9 November 1938,
the Kristallnacht pogrom made many Jews realize that it was time to leave
Germany.

9,354 children found a home in Britain as a result of arriving on
Kindertransports under the auspices of Bloomsbury House. With the help of
Munich's *Kultusgemeinde,* with £1 each in our pockets, my father took us to the
station. I was sixteen and my brother fourteen years old and at the time it
seemed like an adventure. I have only a vague recollection of saying goodbye
to our father, not realizing that we would never see each other again. Of
course we hoped to be reunited in America but he emigrated to Shanghai
and we received a Red Cross letter stating that he had died a natural death in
1943.

We left for Holland where we had a really wonderful reception. I still
remember the beautiful white bread, just like cake. At night we embarked at
the Hook of Holland, arriving at Harwich in the morning. My friend Bertie
Engelhard (Leverton) shared a cabin with me.

We were taken to Dovercourt where it was bitterly cold. Sometimes we slept three in a bed to keep warm in the small wooden chalets. At the camp we tasted our first porridge and other strange food like kippers, toast and also tea with milk. Everybody was full of gratitude for being safe.

We learnt songs like 'Underneath the Spreading Chestnut Tree' and 'Daisy, Daisy'. At first I did not realize why some orderlies called me 'Scotty'. However after a time it dawned on me that it was because of the checked dress I wore. Marks and Spencer sent a huge supply of clothing and I enjoyed helping in the store.

After a few months all the girls were sent to Selsey. From there, an English Jewish couple picked me out and brought me to London. There were two sons besides Uncle and Aunty. For doing all the housework and helping in two shops I received six pence pocket money a week until I helped the Taylors, and then I earned seven shillings and sixpence a week. Often I was told that, if it were not for them, my foster parents, Hitler would have had me and that the only good German was a dead German, even though I came from Germany. I was also told that I was very lucky to be here – which of course was true. Nevertheless they were very pleased to steal from me all the material goods which my father sent and which he intended me to have. This included some valuable crystal he managed to send me.

At the beginning of the war Fred was evacuated to Holt in Wiltshire. I stayed for two years with the family in London, and then went to the Klarfeld Hostel in Oxford Gardens, London W10 where I made many long-lasting friends. I found a job as a dressmaker in Bond Street which was what I had always wanted to do. However, as I wanted to help the war effort, I spent sixteen weeks at a Government Training Centre. Afterwards I worked at an X-ray factory in Finchley, where I met Gus, my husband. Three girls and myself left the hostel and moved to a private address in Shepherds Bush. I believe Gus and I were the first children from a Kindertransport under the auspices of Bloomsbury House to get married in 1943. As we were both under age we had to get the court's permission. Ladies from Bloomsbury House were so excited about our wedding that they sent us a huge parcel containing two beautiful hand crocheted blankets which we still treasure today.

After living in furnished accommodation in Hampstead we found an unfurnished flat in W10 and moved in together with Fred and John Najmann, Fred's business partner.

It was a joyful occasion when, in 1947, our daughter Esther Pauline arrived. She is now married and has two lovely daughters. Now we are happy to have a new family, after losing so many relations.

After the war we were naturalized, but because of my accent people still ask where I come from. I tell them that I was a Polish refugee from Nazi oppression. We feel that it is our duty to tell the next generation about the Holocaust. We had misgivings about accepting restitution from Germany for loss of schooling and a deprived childhood. We thank God that we managed to escape and find peace and contentment in England. We are survivors and we will always be grateful to England for admitting us. However it is a great shame that not many more people were saved.

*   *   *

Herbert Rosinger, B.Sc., F.R.S.C.

(Vienna), Kent, UK

My name is Herbert Paul Rosinger, born 25 April 1924 in Vienna, Austria. I left Vienna at midnight on 10 December 1938 and landed in England with a large refugee children's transport at Harwich on 12 December 1938. After spending some time in Dovercourt and Westcliff-on-Sea, I came to the Refugee hostel in Manningham, Bradford, in March 1939.

At the outset of the war, I was interned, together with many other Jewish refugees, on the Isle of Man. I joined the British Army in 1942 when I was eighteen years old, having served the previous two years with the Home Guard in Bradford. As we were all considered enemy aliens in those early days of the war I, together with many others, could only join the Pioneer Corps. I then volunteered at the first opportunity for service in a fighting unit, and ended up in the Reconnaissance Corps as a dispatch-rider.

My unit landed on the beach in Normandy a few days after D-Day in June 1944, and went through France, Belgium and Holland until we reached a small village half-way between Nijmegen and Arnhem, called Elst. Whilst sleeping one night in a small farm cottage near Elst, a direct hit buried me under the ruins of the farm house. I spent several months in army hospitals in Belgium and finally at a convalescing depot near Ostend. I ended up the last two years of my army service in the Intelligence Corps, serving all over West Germany, until I was demobbed in April 1947.

During my hostel days in Bradford I was trained to be a chef in catering, but I was always very interested in the science subjects, and up to the time of joining the army had studied Physics, Chemistry and Maths at the Bradford Technical College. After my demob I lived for a while with my elder brother Heinz and carried on working as a chef in a hotel and restaurant in Morecambe until 1948, when I decided to go into scientific research.

I got myself a job as an analyst in the research department of a firm called Lansil, and started my part-time studies again in the science subjects from 1948 until 1956 when I qualified. For the first four years I studied at the Lancaster Technical College, then the next two years at Liverpool and the last two years at the Medway Technical College at Chatham, Kent. I obtained a B.Sc. in Physics at Liverpool, and became a Fellow of the Royal

Institute of Chemistry. In 1952 I joined Shell Research Ltd., at their research establishment at Ellesmere Port where I stayed until 1955, when the company asked me to move to their newly opened Agricultural Research Centre at Woodstock. I worked for Shell as a Senior Scientist for thirty-two years, mainly on the development of new agricultural chemicals, until my retirement at the age of sixty in April 1984.

I had met my wife in 1945 and we were married on Boxing Day 1947 in Lancaster. I have two children, a daughter called Monica born in 1953 and a son Christopher born in 1957. My daughter has two boys, John eight years old and Stephen five. My son Christopher is a Ph.D in Botany and does research at Saffron Walden near Cambridge, and his wife is a teacher.

My parents had six children; my mother, father and youngest sister were killed in the extermination camps. My only brother Heinz lives in South East London, and of my two older remaining sisters, one lives in Australia and the other in California, USA. The other sister died a few years ago of cancer in Brisbane, Australia.

I will be sixty-five years old next April, and since my retirement have kept myself very busy with a wide range of interests.

*   *   *

Eli Rosner

(Berlin), NY, USA

My name is Eli Rosner. I was born in Berlin, Germany in 1927, and I didn't feel too much of the Hitler era that started in 1933. My recollections as a child include having been beaten going to and from school and, of course, the marching bands and the flags which were all over Germany. I remember that when a German flag passed, everybody had to salute and say 'Heil Hitler', but Jews were not allowed to say 'Heil Hitler'. If you did say it, you were beaten. If you didn't say it, they knew you were a Jew and you were beaten anyway. Some of my family left for Israel and my parents waited for a visa to America, which came through in 1940 when it was just too late.

I remember 28 October 1938, when the Germans came. We had a grocery store. My father used to go to the market every day at 3am and he came back at about 5.30 to 6am and went straight to the store, even though we lived right next to it. This morning, for some reason or other, he came straight to the house from the market and the Gestapo were waiting for him and took him away. They came into our store and broke everything open and threw everything out into the street. They came to the apartment because one of the leaders was the son of the landlord of the house, and they started smashing up our furniture until the landlord came down and said 'Haven't you done enough already?' and chased them out. In the end he was pretty nice, but they were all afraid because the children were turning against the parents. They were asked to inform: they were regarded as heroes if they told what happened in the home, what the parents talked about and, of course, they wanted to be big shots. It was unbelievable that people with whom you were born and raised could change and act like animals.

That was the day they deported all Polish citizens, pushed them over the border into Poland and put troops to guard them so that they should not be able to get back ... So a camp was born in Zbaszyn, right on the border of Germany and Poland. Thousands of Polish Jews were kept there. My mother decided that there was just no way we could stay there and wait.

Plans were made for us to leave. The only way out at that time was to go to Holland and children only were taken. Adults were not taken without papers, and Germany did not issue them. So my mother decided that she would save the children, meaning my sister – eight years old, my brother – three years old, and me – eleven at the time, and there was a cousin also with us and she was around thirteen. In December 1938 my mother went with us by train to the Dutch border and there she left us and we crossed the border ourselves. The Jewish Refugee Committee was waiting at the Dutch station as it was a daily occurrence that children were sent over the border. We were put into a little camp with about fifty other children on a temporary basis. The Dutch people were lovely, and were very good to us.

We stayed in Holland until April 1939 when my brother and I were sent to England. My sister jumped on the moving train because she was being separated, and they had to drag her off by force. She was hysterical but we had nothing to say in the matter. We thought it was a catastrophe. The two boys in England, my sister in Holland, my mother in Germany, my father in Poland – we were spread all over Europe. After some time my mother managed to smuggle herself into Belgium, and my sister also got to Belgium, so my mother and sister were together. Then my father asked for permission to go back to Germany for a week or two to collect some money, and after a while the Germans granted it to him, figuring that after he collected his money they would take it from him and send him back. But my father went straight to Cologne and hired someone to smuggle him into Belgium. The first time, in spring 1939, the smuggler abandoned him in the snow. The second time he hired a smuggler they couldn't get through, as there were too many German patrols, and they had to turn back. The third time they managed to get through, and so my parents and my sister were reunited in Belgium.

My parents hid in Brussels and were moving back and forth from one apartment to another every few months. It was a room, a basement, a garage; whatever they could find and wherever they felt they could trust someone by bribing him with a piece of silverware, a damask tablecloth, etc. There was a teacher living in the same building who taught my sister French. After a while my sister put on a necklace with a cross when she went shopping; carrots, beets, these kind of things at the market (not at the stores, people might know her). They made beet soup. My father started fasting every Monday and Thursday so that my sister should have more food. There were daily and weekly occurrences and if you got through the day it was a miracle. There were times when they didn't leave the house for three or four months at a time. At two o'clock in the morning they would open the window, when everybody was sleeping, to get a little fresh air.

When I got to England in April 1939, my brother and I were put in a camp with about two hundred boys, most of them from Vienna. My brother was the youngest there and everybody made a big fuss of him. The Jewish Committee told me that they had a flight for me if I wanted to go to America with a visa, but there was only one space left. I didn't want to go without my brother. They then said that they would arrange for a family to adopt him. I didn't want this because if he was adopted by a family at three years old he would never know his real family. So we stayed in the camp for about a year. About an hour's ride away there was a camp for small children, and I arranged for my brother to go there. His camp was kosher, run by Jews, but the nearest *Shul* was thirty-five miles away. Maybe once in three or four months they travelled there and had two hours of learning. There were no Services.

I had an uncle in the British army who landed in Normandy. When Brussels was liberated, he had got a special pass and went there and found my parents. He found them in a shocking condition. My uncle got undressed, took off his underclothes and socks and left them for my father along with a bar of soap that he had.

As soon as he came back to England I packed my things and managed to get a visa to Belgium and joined my family again.

* * *

Fred Rosner M.D., F.A.C.P.

(Berlin), New York, USA

Director, Department of Medicine, Queens Hospital Centre, Affiliation of the Long Island Jewish Medical Centre, and Professor of Medicine, Health Sciences Centre, State University of New York at Stony Brook.

WHY I RETURNED TO BERLIN FIFTY YEARS
AFTER KRISTALLNACHT

Extracts from his address to the First International Jewish Congress on Medicine and *Halacha,* Berlin, Germany, 16-20 November 1988:

In November 1988, memorial events took place throughout the world to commemorate the infamous 9-10 November 1938 Kristallnacht, the first all-out assault by the Nazis upon the survival of the Jewish people.

Why did I return to Berlin exactly fifty years after Kristallnacht which my family and I lived through? Why, many years ago, did I swear never again to set foot on German soil, never to purchase German products, never to ride in a German car, never to read a German book, never to listen to German music, never to enjoy anything German? Why have I steadfastly refused an offer by the Berlin municipality for an all-expenses-paid seven-day excursion to Berlin – an offer extended to all Berlin natives who were forced to flee their birthplace from the Nazis? Why did my revulsion for the German language compel me to lecture in Berlin in English even though I speak German fluently? Why did I accept the invitation of the organizers of the First International Jewish Congress on Medicine and *Halacha* (Jewish Law) to participate in that Congress in Berlin? What rational thinking or divine inspiration or guidance motivated me to return to Berlin in November 1988, exactly fifty years after I fled that city?

I was born in Berlin on 3 October 1935 into a very large family, my father being one of ten siblings and my mother one of six siblings. On 28 October 1938, my father and my paternal grandfather were deported to a concentration camp in Poland called Zbancion (Neu Benshen) from which my grandfather never returned. Less than two weeks later, on the night of 9 November 1938, the Nazis unleashed gangs of storm troopers to carry out widespread attacks on Jews, Jewish-owned property and Synagogues throughout Germany and Austria. At least 30,000 Jews were arrested and sent to concentration camps at Sachsenhausen, Buchenwald and Dachau. Hundreds of Synagogues were set on fire or completely demolished and thousands of shops and homes were destroyed, looted, set on fire or otherwise desecrated. Among them were my family's house and store. Our belongings were thrown out onto the street, our piano was smashed, our cabinets broken and our store produce ruined. There was no place to hide.

The Nazis called it Kristallnacht – night of shattered glass – an almost poetic appellation for that night of arson, terror and murder. But another horror of that awful night was what happened around the world. Nothing! No one cared. No country in the world was willing to accept even a fraction of the several hundred thousand German Jews. Even my adopted country, the United States of America, closed its doors and the Jewish people were shut out in their greatest hour of need.

My maternal grandfather witnessed the burning and total destruction of the Synagogue across the street from his apartment. He saw the *Torah* scrolls, Bibles, prayer books and other sacred objects thrown onto the street, doused with gasoline and set on fire. He collapsed in a state of shock, lapsed into a coma, never regained consciousness and died several months later. He lies buried in what is today East Berlin.

Less than a month after Kristallnacht, on 8 December 1938, my brother, sister and I were taken by train to the German-Dutch border where we miraculously were able to cross into Holland. My mother had to relinquish all rights to her children and signed us over into the custody of the Jewish Refugee Committee. She was accused by some members of the family of being a 'raven mother' for abandoning her children. Other members of the family comforted her saying 'At least you saved the children.' Two hundred children and no adults were on that train.

On 18 April 1939, my brother and I were shipped to England with the Kindertransport where we spent the entire war in relative safety. My sister remained in Holland, but was later smuggled into Belgium by a Christian family who pretended that she was their daughter. Here she joined my mother, who had also smuggled herself into Belgium. In the Spring of 1939, having bribed his way out of the Polish concentration camp, my father returned to Berlin, traced my mother and sister to Belgium and joined them there. My parents and sister were hidden in Belgium by several Christian families, moving from hideout to hideout every few months, to remain ahead of the Nazis who were constantly searching for Jews. Most of my parents' numerous brothers and sisters and their children as well as my two grandmothers were apprehended in Antwerp, Belgium and deported to the concentration camps in Theresienstadt and Auschwitz from which they never returned. Several hundred members of my extended family were murdered in Auschwitz. Only a handful survived to be liberated by Allied forces. To this day they have concentration camp numbers tattooed on their forearms and horrible memories indelibly and forever emblazoned in their hearts and minds.

One uncle and aunt were able to reach England posing as a butler and a maid on 2 September 1939, one day before the war broke out. One cousin escaped to the United States via Marseilles, France on a forged visa. Other members of the family who made it to France on their way to Marseilles were cut off by advancing German forces and were compelled to return to Belgium where they were apprehended and deported to Auschwitz.

My parents and sister were liberated by American forces in the summer of 1944 in Brussels, Belgium. My brother and I had lost contact with them for some time and were unaware of their exact whereabouts. A British soldier who landed in Normandy, France with the Allied forces in 1944 took temporary leave from his army unit to go to Belgium to search for them. He located them in Brussels and shortly thereafter, my brother and I were reunited with them.

On 1 July 1949, we arrived in New York and were greeted by the Statue of Liberty. We adopted the United States of America as our homeland, became citizens, have lived there happily ever since.

With this background, I again pose the question: why did I return to Berlin exactly fifty years after the infamous Kristallnacht? Why did I accept an invitation to participate in the First International Congress on Medicine and Jewish Law? Why did I return to the city in which I was born but from which I was forced to flee at the tender age of three years?

In the United States, I was privileged to pursue a career in academic medicine. As a physician, I regard with abhorrence the participation of Nazi physicians in the killing of millions of Jews and others. The heinous acts of medical experimentation and torture chronicled at the Nuremberg trials had a chilling effect on the world at large and the medical profession in particular. In his recent book, ' *The Nazi Doctors*', Robert Lifton recounts in great detail the medical horrors at Auschwitz and the involvement of German physicians in the torture and killing of thousands of innocent human beings. The Nazis began with a programme of sterilization and euthanasia under which German physicians actually carried out the murder of countless children and adults considered 'unworthy of life', because they were physically or mentally ill, or socially undesirable, such as Jews. At Auschwitz doctors performed the selections, both on the ramp among arriving transports of prisoners, and later in the camps and on the medical blocks.

In Auschwitz, doctors supervised the killing in the gas chambers and decided when the victims were dead. Doctors ordered and supervised, and at times carried out, direct killing of debilitated patients on the medical blocks. At the same time, they kept up a pretence of medical legitimacy, signing false death certificates listing spurious illnesses. Doctors consulted actively on how best to keep selections running smoothly; on how many people to permit to remain alive to fill the slave labour requirements of the I.G. Farben enterprise at Auschwitz; and on how to burn the enormous number of bodies that strained the facilities of the crematoria.

Then there was a radical escalation in the technology of mass murder at Auschwitz where Jews, Gypsies, and others were subjected to sterilization by injection, radiation, or surgery, to the injection of vaccines made from dental infections, and to massive bleedings for blood-group experiments. Then there was the use of human tissue for culture media and the making of lampshades and tobacco pouches, brainwashing with chemicals, deliberate infection with typhus, and the application of toxic substances to various parts of the body. There were vivisections and mass killings by phenol injections, gassing, shooting, and other cruel and inhumane methods. How many of my relatives were used to make lampshades or bars of soap? My twin cousins who survived Auschwitz were designated by the infamous arch-evil Doctor Joseph Mengele, known as the 'angel of death', for human experimentation. He had a passionate fascination with twins whose lives had existential value. Twins were given desirable jobs and were not to be harmed because they were needed for Mengele's experiments and were kept alive for his anthropological research. About fifteen percent of the twins were killed, some as a consequence of the experiments performed on them.

These experiments and killings were only a small part of the role Nazi doctors played in Hitler's Final Solution. In fact, doctors supervised the entire killing process at Auschwitz from beginning to end. How were physicians, sworn by oath and conviction to ease suffering, transformed from healers to systematic killers?

When I received the invitation to participate in the International Jewish Congress on Medicine and Jewish Law in Berlin, I did not know how to respond. My sister said: 'Absolutely not! Under no circumstances should you go back to Berlin, ever.' My brother said:

'You're not going as a tourist. You are going to strengthen the Jewish community there, so go.' When I consulted my father, he did not say yes or no but only responded: 'If you go, visit your grandfather's grave in East Berlin.'

I returned to Berlin for two reasons: one had a rational, personal, intellectual and perhaps emotional basis. On pure rational grounds, I went to Berlin to visit and pray at my grandfather's grave. It is the only grave whose location is known of all the members of my family who perished in the Holocaust. To me that grave symbolizes my grandmothers, uncles, aunts and countless cousins who perished in Auschwitz and who have no known graves. To me that grave also symbolizes the six million Jews and four million others who perished at the hands of the Nazis and who have no graves to visit and no tombstones at which to pray. At my grandfather's grave, I came face to face with my past.

The second reason I returned to Berlin was to give strength and encouragement to the small Jewish community of Berlin, a mere shadow of its previous glory of the 1920s and 1930s.

The light of Judaism shines for ever. Its brightness may at times be dimmed as it was fifty years ago, but the flickering flame is never extinguished. The Third Reich has come and gone and the miracle of our generation is that the Jewish people are still here as they have been for thousands of years. The Nazis were unsuccessful in their attempt to blot out the light of the Jews.

*   *   *

Marietta Ryba

(Pollak, Prague), Tulsa, USA

It is now fifty years since my family's eviction from our lovely home in a small town in Moravia. My father was manager of a chocolate factory there and the house we lived in was part of the benefits of his position. My memories of that time and the years that followed have been carefully stored and hidden in the darkest crevices of my mind. Yet for the sake of my dearest parents, the preservation of their memory, I find myself compelled to dig up that past and put it on paper. Our children have asked me repeatedly to do so . . .

The events that lead to that dreadful morning in March 1939 should have prepared me for the events that followed. At the age of thirteen I had heard and read many reports of the persecution of Jews in Germany, had listened to Hitler's insane speeches on the radio, followed the news of Austria's take over and Chancellor Schuschnig's collaboration. My own cousins, Peter seventeen and Liesl my age, were threatened, forced to clean toilets in their school until desperate measures were taken to get them out of the country.

How well I remembered our almost monthly trips to Vienna, five and a half hours by car from our village. Our grandparents and father's two married sisters with children lived in that city and we would arrive laden with chocolate and Bata shoes. The custom officials on the Czech-Austrian border knew us and accepted gifts of chocolate or slivovitz. Besides the kindly teasing of our grandfather whom I remember as an invalid in a wheel chair, I looked forward to my visit to the Prater with its huge ferris wheel, chamber of horrors and other exciting attractions.

Father and mother believed fighting would take place as soon as the Germans approached our borders, that England and France would surely come to our assistance and so plans were made for us children to be moved further inland. All this is history now, our poor small country was sacrificed and my family evicted from the home I knew for thirteen years.

I was sent to England with a children's refugee transport in June 1939. My father became acquainted with Mr Cadbury during one of his business trips abroad and it was my understanding that Daddy turned to this kind gentleman for help. My father broke the news of my imminent departure as gently as possible.

I did not want to leave my parents, my sister and beloved dog Billy. How well I remember the walks we took with Daddy when he told me about the English countryside with tall hedges separating fields and winding country roads. The pretty English gardens, which were the pride of the English people. The strong belief in fair play and decency by the people of that island. He was trying to correct my loss of faith in England caused by the recent turn of events that left the citizens of our country in a state of shock and disbelief.

Finally came the day of departure and reluctant farewells to my friends. We were all assembled at Wilson railroad station in Prague and shortly after arrival there, various German officials and soldiers parted the children from their parents, promising the parents they would later see their children again. My mind is vague on the rest of that day and my next recollection is of my father climbing the side of the railway carriage so he could kiss me goodbye through the window. My mother and sister stood on the platform with the other parents desperately waving and blowing kisses, shouting farewells that we could not hear.

There were several inspections by German custom officials during our journey out of Czechoslovakia and through Germany. The smaller children were crying and we older ones comforted them and sang songs.

We boarded a British vessel to make the Channel crossing, greatly relieved to hear English instead of the feared and despised German language. We could not understand what the sailors were saying to us but felt from their good-natured laughter and body language they were being kind. I tasted my first 'cuppa char' strong, sweet and somehow comforting.

The English train was impressive to all of us with the upholstered seats and mirrors above the seats. My next recollection is of being on another train from London to Birmingham with two other Czech girls.

Mr and Mrs Jones and their oldest son Brian were waiting for me on the platform, we shook hands formally, walked to their car and drove to their home.

So many new impressions, different customs, smells, yet through it all the similarity of a normal family. Phil, the nine year old son came home from some school outing and eyed me suspiciously all during our first meal together as if wondering how his life would be affected by my presence. I met the youngest member the next morning when the little blond curly-headed boy surprised me in the bathroom, and told me his name was Colin. It was this wee cherub who became my constant companion and fellow student. We were both learning English. He never laughed at my pronunciation, told me the right word of the object I pointed to and listened with pleasure to my slow and hesitant reading of fairy tales.

Brian and I were the same age and soon became good friends. His shyness disappeared when we were alone. My English improved and we were able to discuss all kinds of topics, comparing our lives, parents and customs.

Most English people I met expressed surprise that I was not dressed in some national costume, that I used a knife and fork and spoon and was every bit as civilized as my English counterpart.

Every night in bed I conducted a one-sided conversation with my beloved family, the moon and stars being my messengers. In my mind I would walk through our old house, from room to room, and stroke the various pieces of furniture. I would gaze at the many paintings that hung on the walls and played such an important role in the stories I would weave around them when I was a child.

In spite of the general well-being afforded me by this kind and warm family, I was very homesick for my parents and sister. As Europe was gradually being swallowed by the German menace, my fears for the safety of my family grew. Mr Jones' efforts to bring my parents, or at least my sister, to England were all in vain.

When England stood alone, pathetically defenceless and the desperate evacuation of Dunkirk was uppermost in our minds, I too felt completely abandoned and frightened as if the end of the world was upon us. Mrs Jones comforted me, her words still ring in my ears! 'England will never surrender.' How right she was! Quiet courage, sense of humour, sacrifices and wonderful cameraderie enveloped me all through those dark years.

My best friend whom I met when we were both sixteen is still my best friend. Her mother, sister and aunt welcomed me into their home as naturally as if I always belonged there.

England will always be my second home. The Jones' clan have not only accepted me as a member of their extended family, but later also my sister, who survived the horrors of Nazi concentration camps, my husband and our children. We are forever connected and enriched. Our family members who perished and died during that dreadful era will go on living through us and our children.

Letter received by Marietta Ryba from her parents on her arrival in Birmingham, 1 July 1939

My dear sweet Marietta,
Yesterday we returned to Hodonin from Prague and as you can well imagine you have been constantly in our thoughts. We still see your face before us in that window of the railway carriage. You were so good and brave which made our parting so much easier. You are my clever and wise little girl. Everyone at home is asking about you and feel sure you will win everyone's heart over there the way you did here.

It is very lucky that such a nice family has enabled you to come over. Thank God for that. Continue to be good, grateful for everything, nice and decent to everyone. Be careful and diligent and I am sure you will make your way. I know we don't have to worry about your behaviour and manners. Did anyone else come with you from London? I await your letter anxiously and look forward to reading all about your trip, whether you are in need of anything, who was waiting for you, simply everything.

I have not yet seen Billy as I am writing rather early in the morning. I plan to visit him later in the day and will let you know. Edith stayed in Prague until Monday with the Tausik family.

Did you lose anything? Was the journey very tiring? Was the country beautiful? Were you able to sleep at night?

We hope Edith will be able to join you soon even though it would be a sacrifice for us. It would be better for you to have her close by.

Please write us everything, your impressions about your new surroundings, your family and don't forget to thank them for taking you in. I believe the school year is still in progress over there. Try hard from the very beginning so you may enjoy the holidays later. Should you need something please let us know. Keep your things neat and in good order. A young girl should be neat and well-groomed.

Susi Low is already in London and goes to school there. I understand another children's transport will be leaving in four weeks' time and Mrs Deutsch will try to get Evi on it. I would also be glad for Evi to join you.

Please write to us regularly. Your letter will ease the wounds caused by our parting. Lots of kisses and hugs from your ever loving Mama.

Everyone sends their love

My dearest Marietko.

Perhaps you have already written to us. We miss you and await your letter. Stay well my dearest child.

Kisses from your very homesick Papa.

*　　*　　*

Kurt Sachs

(Prague), Stourbridge, UK

AND I STILL HADN'T SEEN THE SEA

Judenblut – Schweineblut. . . a smear no bigger than a postage stamp on the wall of the school corridor, a graffito no bigger than the signature on a cheque . . . fifty years on, in the light of historical perspective, it is insignificant enough – what would the headline look like? 'Jewish blood – pig blood'. At the time it was portentous; it was frightening.

Strange how little memory remains of the others at school; a few names, very few faces. I can remember Schatzberger: if he survived he is a Wall Street tycoon. Schatzberger had useful contacts, useful to him, useful to me.

To get out of the Reich you needed two things: a passport and an entry visa to somewhere. The passport was easy: every resident was entitled to a passport, you only had to apply, filling in the proper form, supported by the proper supplementary documentation. This consisted of testimonials to the effect that there was no arrest warrant out against the applicant, that he had not committed a crime, that he did not owe income tax. So it was necessary to apply for these testimonials at the appropriate offices, the Magistrat, the Inland Revenue, the police, the Salzamt. I still have in my possession a '*steuerliche Unbedenklichkeitsbescheinigung*. As there were a lot of us wanting to leave, the appropriate offices were overrun by applicants, and long queues formed outside all the entrances of Kafka's Castle.

Unfortunately, all these testimonials only attested to good behaviour in the past and could not be extrapolated too far into the future. They were mostly valid for a month. Any testimonial in the portfolio that had outrun its 'sell-by' date had to be renewed, of course. This naturally extended the aggregate queueing time for the individual; the real time before the passport was secured.

Back to Schatzberger and his contacts. Aryans had priority access to the Castle; some of them would, for a consideration, take in a few documents from people in the queue and get them stamped. Schatzberger was a runner for one of these gentlemen. He gave me a free ride at one or two offices, especially valuable for those athwart the critical path. Why? For two reasons: he had copied my maths homework on occasions in the past, and he reckoned he might do more business with me in the future.

Getting an entry visa was much more difficult because no one wanted us. Schatzberger had a number of schemes and offered me two. Someone had 'rescued' a worn-out rubber stamp from the Czech embassy and this could, with skill, be made into a visa stamp. I rejected this option because the passport that had cost me so much effort was not going to be polluted by forgeries, thank you very much.

The alternative involved an arrangement, presumably made by Schatzberger's principals, with a Czech frontier guard, whom we could meet at a specified map location: he would allow us through and would slip us enough Czech money to get a train ticket to Prague. This scheme was rather expensive and was best financed and operated by a small ad-hoc cooperative. My task was to found or at least find one. It so happened that a small group of my grown-up sister's friends (well, she was twenty-one!) had just made an abortive attempt to jump the border into France. *Faute de mieux,* they were willing to try Czechoslovakia instead . . .

So one day in September 1938 a small group of *viertel-und-halbstarken* conspirators could be seen disembarking at the station of the Austro-Czechoslovakian half of a small country town. We had some hours before darkness fell and used it to reconnoitre the frontier area; especially the abandoned narrow-gauge railway line that crossed the border. It was at the intersection of rails and frontier that we were to meet 'our' frontier guard, under cover of darkness, an hour before the midnight train to Prague.

We were led along a field path until we saw the lights of the Czech town. We stumbled across the field, uncertain whether there was a friendly frontier guard at all, uncertain whether we should find him, uncertain whether another guard would pick us up . . .

At that point we heard a shout '*Rudolf*', – our password, – and made contact with our frontier guard, collected the money, sauntered into the town and caught the train to Prague.

I used to think it was more luck than judgement.

Now, fifty years on, I wonder . . . It all went so smoothly; perhaps Schatzberger's principals had a little arrangement with the frontier people on the Austrian side as well.

Meanwhile, in England, national and local committees organised a rescue operation. Families were asked to take refugee children into their homes.

Others provided funds for guarantee deposits to ensure that the children would not become a burden on public expenditure . . . In Birmingham the Goodman family had responded to Stanley Baldwin's radio appeal and had offered to take a child. The lady from the Quaker Committee said that there were not enough little girls around ten years old to meet the demand – fortunately for me the Goodmans were not infected with the Shirley Temple syndrome and did not lay down any rigid specifications. After some weeks a letter arrived from the committee to say that I would arrive in due course.

In Pilsen, I took up a new hobby; collecting the addresses of refugee committees, anywhere in the world, and writing letters of application. I guess I must have written over twenty. It was rather like sending a prospectus of my autobiography to publishers. There were no rejection slips, only silence.

Until March 1939. Early one day, walking to work, I met the German army walking towards me. Not with bands and flags and a cheering audience, but slinking along the housefronts, with hand grenades dangling from their belts.

Next day I had a letter from the Quaker refugee committee in Birmingham. They had found a family who would give me a home. They were making arrangements for a transport and would let me know further details soon. A few weeks later they wrote to say that I should be at the station in Prague one and a half hours before departure of the train on 11 May. There were about three weeks to go. Another visit to a Gestapo office, to get a travel permit for Vienna. I saw my parents for the last time, spent a week with them; my sister was still at home, she was organizing an affidavit to go to the USA and eventually left Vienna just after the official start of the war in Europe. I remember a taxi ride to the Ostbahnhof to return to Prague; and having to turn round and drive back because I had left my passport behind . . .

I remember very little of the journey itself. The compartments were very crowded and I was alone in the crowd. After a bit the older ones, the near teen-agers (I was fourteen at the time) congregated at one end of the corridor and we stood up all night and talked and talked. The train stopped for a long time in Osnabrück and eventually went on into Holland.

We arrived in Hoek late at night. I was very tired and lay down at once and did not wake up until Harwich. I had never seen the sea, and I missed it on the trip across the Channel.

We were put on the train to Liverpool Street station, London, and there each of us was collected by volunteers. My suitcase was missing, but I had a smaller one with me. Two young Quaker volunteers drove to Birmingham with me, and delivered me, with my hand luggage, to the Goodman family.

* * *

Inge Sadan

(Engelhard, Munich), Jerusalem, Israel

Even in those troubled times after the Kristallnacht, which had such a traumatic effect on every Jew who was caught up in it, to an optimistic nine-year-old life held its attractions. I had heard from a friend that she and her sister were being sent to England in a week or so, and I had run home to tell my parents, who had hastened round to my friend's parents to find out all the details. I also wanted to go to England – my brother would become a Lord and I would become a Lady, like all English people!

The exact details remain hazy, but within a week, on 4 January, my big sister of nearly sixteen and my brother of eleven and a half had gone, each with a suitcase and a lingering wave, as they made their way with a group of other children to the railway station. We were not allowed to accompany them to the station, so that they would not attract

The passport-like document hung around the children's necks for identification.

attention before the train left. So my parents and I returned home – a home now bereft of laughing, shouting, arguing, fighting children. On the other hand, for the first time in my life I had my mother all to myself, a very comforting feeling for a youngest child, and for the next six months a strange sort of limbo existed.

Every few weeks I expected to be accepted for the next Kindertransport, and I gradually witnessed the departure of friends to South America, Holland, England and other places, not fathomable to my skimpy geographical knowledge. My parents moved into the Jewish hospital which was considered a safe place, and worked there, and I was looked after by a half-Jewish family. I stayed with them for a month, spending the afternoons after school at the hospital, making friends with the patients, and being a pest to the staff.

And then, suddenly, it was my turn to be shipped off to study the ways of the aristocracy of England. I visited all the wards in the hospital to bid my farewells to my new friends, and left a huge cache of chocolates and other gifts with my mother, as I was only allowed one suitcase and one Mark in money. I parted from my parents quite cheerfully, expecting them to follow within a few weeks. My father had bought me a clockwork mouse at the railway station, which I kept for many years, and after blessing me and begging some big girls of sixteen to look after me, they watched the train move slowly out. It was midnight, 6 July 1939.

On the second morning we arrived in England; once again new impressions, green fields, and those amazing double-decker buses. At Liverpool Street station a waiting room was cordoned off as people came to claim their charges, and after a few hours only four of us remained, to be sent further, to the provinces. My destination was Coventry, to join my sister and brother.

My sister, after a few weeks at the reception camp at Dovercourt, had been picked as a maid, whilst my brother was chosen to be the playmate of a milkman's son. It seemed that shortly after that, the Provost of Coventry Cathedral, the Rev Bateman, had guaranteed £50 for me as well as for a large number of other children, and a committee of Jews and non-Jews in Coventry undertook to place these children in foster-homes.

My sister's 'family', being childless, took me, and a period of difficult adjustment followed. It was brought home to me rather drastically that the natives were not going to learn German and that I would have to make the supreme effort of learning English. At school, I was the object of great curiosity, especially wearing those foreign clothes – *dirndl* complete with little apron, etc. Some children were very kind, and I thought the title 'refugee' sounded most interesting. When the war broke out, two months later, I was not so popular, since I had come from Germany and was therefore classified by some children as a Nazi!

Since we were living with an English non-Jewish family, and I was forbidden to speak German with my sister, I soon learned English and began to accept their strange ways. On the Jewish festivals we were at first allowed to go to the Synagogue, and we spent the first night of *Chanuka* within the Jewish community, whilst soon afterwards being initiated into the rites of Christmas by our foster parents. The first *Pesach* we were invited by a Jewish family for the *Seder*, and it was bliss, almost like being at home again, as memories came flooding back.

My brother celebrated his *Bar Mitzvah* in the Coventry Synagogue. Our parents, who had in the meantime escaped to Yugoslavia, that day went to the Synagogue in Zagreb to mark the *Bar Mitzvah*; though we only found that out years later.

A very kind English lady who lived near us and was concerned that every child should drink the school half-pint of milk which cost a half-penny, which my foster family did not provide, insisted that I come to her house every morning to collect a penny and an apple. When I mentioned that the milk cost only a half-penny, she told me to spend the other half-penny on ice cream or sweets. Some saints come in the most unlikely forms, even as anonymous housewives!

Occasionally we received Red Cross messages from our parents, and eventually, when they reached neutral countries, they managed to write letters. On Christmas Day 1943, they reached England from Portugal, and after a month of stringent security clearance, were allowed to join us. It was a strange experience, getting to know our parents again. Nearly five years older than the last time we saw them, they were foreigners! They didn't speak English, my father wore a long, long coat and used a purse, and my mother counted the change she was given in the shops! They also wanted us to keep the Jewish customs which I had long since forgotten ... it was a difficult period of adjustment all over again; but we made it, and became a loving and loved family again.

My brother never became a Lord, and I never became a Lady, but as life doled out its fortunes and misfortunes, somehow we learned to take them as they came, and to thank those who saved us and helped us in so many ways.

* * *

Helga Samuel
(Kreiner, Leipzig), Northwood, Middlesex, UK

My story begins in Stettin, where I was born on 11 September 1927. My father held an excellent position as director of a large store.

In 1937, there was trouble at the firm, and my father was accused of making false entries in the accounts. He had to take the rap for something he had not done, merely because he was a Jew, and spent one agonizing month in prison, while the owner of the store fled to Switzerland.

I remember vividly the morning after Kristallnacht – the night on which all Jewish schools and Synagogues were burnt to the ground – I used to travel by tram and I remember well how everyone laughed and joked about it. The horror of it all, however, had not sunk in. When I arrived at the corner of the street in which the school was, one of the teachers came to meet me and told me to return home as quickly and as quietly as possible, as the school had been badly damaged and all our books had been burnt, many windows broken, and the headmaster had been arrested.

I remember many incidents of windows in our flat being broken by stones being thrown at them – of the Nazis marching through the streets in precise formation, and of everyone having to stand at the curbside and salute them. Anyone who disobeyed was marched off immediately ... I remember my fears of men in uniform and for many years after coming to England, I was afraid of policemen.

One night especially is vivid in my memory – when we heard the Nazi jackboots tramping along the street, stopping at the main front door of the block of flats where we lived, banging on the door – and my mother hurriedly putting out all the lights in our flat and hiding with us in the corner of a bedroom having to be as quiet as mice. The boots tramped up the stairs, there were gruff voices, while our hearts beat faster and faster, the boots still tramping, halting for a moment's agonizing silence outside our front door, and then going up to the next flight to the flat above. We heard the next morning that the gentleman who lived there, also a Jew, had been arrested. This time, they had passed us by. This was living in constant terror, degradation and suffering, and the fear of being marched off at any moment day or night.

I remember being very frightened at having to hide like this and having to be so quiet, sensing my mother's fears, but really at that time I was too young to appreciate the significance of the whole situation. This didn't really strike home, until the day my father was arrested on the street, taken to police headquarters and from there to the concentration camp at Buchenwald. I had gone that day to play with a schoolfriend. When my father did not return after a couple of hours, my mother fearing the worst, rang the police station, and was told that he was being held in custody. This went on for several days, until she received a printed card signed by my father, (address Buchenwald) asking for strong boots, warm underclothing, etc. This, we learned afterwards, he never received. I did not see my father again until several months after I had arrived in England.

My father was in the concentration camp for six terrible weeks, suffering many atrocities and severe hardships; however, this was 1938 and there was worse to come to so many innocent and peace-loving people. He returned from the concentration camp a broken man, with frozen toes, underweight and mentally distraught. He had existed during this time on inedible food, sleeping on wooden boards in freezing cold huts without blankets or any comfort; work consisted of breaking up stones, etc. However, he was one of the more fortunate, having been released after one month only because he had won the Iron Cross fighting for Germany in the 1914-18 war.

During the time my father was away, my mother was advised by a Jewish Committee to send my and sister and me to England with the first children's transport which was being organized in England. I was eleven years old at the time.

All the children from the different towns met at the Hauptbahnhof in Berlin. I was told to go into a compartment with several other children of my own age, my sister in the adjoining one. I recall vividly our arrival at the German-Dutch frontier, when the Nazis boarded the train for a last inspection before the train crossed into a 'free' country. One Nazi per compartment. The one in our compartment pulled down the blind, made us stand erect in the gangway, pulled down all the suitcases from the racks, opened them, threw everything on the floor, taking one or two items such as a gold necklace, watches, rings, and even a camera. He also asked each one of us to hand over our money, taking 9s. from each child. So we left the 'Fatherland' with 1s. in our pocket. Fear was in all of us, until the moment the Nazis disembarked, the whistle blew, and the train slowly moved out of the station and crossed the frontier into Holland. At this moment, we opened the windows, shouting abuse ... it was a terrible thing that we children should have undergone this and learning fast what hate was.

At the first stop in Holland, we were met by some wonderfully kind ladies of the organizing Committee, who stood waiting for us on the platform with big trolleys, laden with hot drinks, chocolate and sandwiches. Then came the journey by boat across the Channel at night.

On arrival at Harwich next morning, we were greeted by dozens of reporters and more Committee members. From there we were taken by coaches to a holiday camp at Dovercourt.

I was there for one month until one day I was told that I would be going to live with a family in Ealing, London. My sister unfortunately could not come to the same family – we would be split up – but she would also be living in London. I remember that when visitors came to the camp, it would usually be at mealtimes, and the visitors would walk up and down the rows of children, perhaps picking out this one or that one, rather like a cattle market.

The next event was my arrival at Liverpool Street station and my first encounter with my foster-parents, with whom I would spend the next months, perhaps years. An extremely kind-looking couple stood there, and a welcoming arm was placed around my shoulder. My sister had meantime also found her 'lady' – looking very smart – and it later turned out that she wanted my sister as nursemaid to her two-year old baby! (This was an unhappy story until eventually my wonderful foster-parents sorted it all out and found another happier home for my sister.) We then said goodbye – amidst more tears – an exchange of telephone numbers was made, and I was driven 'home' in a large car, complete with chauffeur.

On arrival at my new home, the maid opened the door. A lovely open coalfire was burning in the grate and a cup of tea and something to eat and more kind words helped me to bear it all. I cried all that first day – the strangeness of it all – the sadness of having first to part with my mother – then with my sister – now being all on my own – in a strange country – a strange house – strange people – but still with wonderfully kind faces.

So the days passed, difficult at first, mostly sign-language, as I had only learned a few English words by this time – gradually getting used to my new environment. I had acquired a new sister and brother – everyone doing their utmost to make me feel happy.

Time is a great healer and with so much kindness around me (I was also lucky enough to be 'adopted' by a wonderful school in the district) I settled in quite well. I wrote often to my parents (my father having meantime been released) and you can imagine their joy at knowing that we were safe. How truly wonderful this English Jewish family was to me. I was treated like their own, I lacked for nothing in either material things, comfort, love, understanding, protection and kindness.

This was even to be increased, when in May 1939, these people gave a guarantee for my parents and brought them to England and we were a united family once more. My mother was only allowed to leave as a domestic and worked for several years in a hostel as a cook for twenty refugee boys. My father helped with odd jobs in the hostel. Later, at the beginning of the war, my parents were interned on the Isle of Man for six months – again separated – but this could not be helped at that time.

When the war broke out we were on holiday in Devon and so stayed there because, like everyone else, we feared the air-raids. We lived there for two years and then returned to London, where I continued my education. I passed my matriculation in 1944. We took our exams in air-raid shelters, while bombs fell on London, and later I was lucky enough to be able to go to the 'Lycee Francais' in Kensington, where I took a shorthand-typewriting course in English and German. From there I entered my first employment in the foreign correspondence department of the Swiss Bank Corporation.

I had meantime gone back to live with my parents, as I was now earning money and could support myself adequately. My foster-mother had encouraged my return, in fact she never tried during all the time I lived in that happy house to take my mother's place, and I know her to this day as 'Aunty'.

I met my husband at a Youth Club – and even my wedding was arranged and paid for by my wonderful 'Aunt' and 'Uncle'. To them I owe much – it is impossible to tell of the many kindnesses they bestowed upon me and my family – but above all their great love and devotion which helped me through such a difficult time in my life.

Now that I have children of my own, I can appreciate how hard it must have been to take a strange child into one's home – not to expect anything from it in return – but to give it the love you give your own. I have now been married for fourteen years, have two sons and a wonderful husband.

*   *   *

NATIONALE MAHN- UND GEDENKSTÄTTE
- Historische Abteilung -   **BUCHENWALD**

Nationale Mahn- und Gedenkstätte Buchenwald
DDR · 5301 Weimar-Buchenwald

Frau
Helga Samuel

Northwood, Middx HA 6 3LX

England

DDR · 5301 Weimar-Buchenwald, den
20. Dez. 1988
rö-dü

Sehr geehrte Frau Samuel!

Wir möchten uns zunächst recht herzlich für die Kopie eines
Briefes Ihres Vaters aus dem Konzentrationslager Buchenwald
bedanken. Da wir unsere Recherchen zu Ihrer Anfrage noch nicht
abgeschlossen haben, hier zunächst ein Zwischenbescheid.

Ihr Vater wurde im November 1938 zusammen mit etwa 10 000 Juden
in ein Sonderlager auf dem Gebiet des KZ Buchenwald verschleppt.
In diesem Sonderlager standen fünf scheunenähnliche Notbaracken
mit der Bezeichnung 1a - 5a. Ihr Vater war in der Baracke 5a un-
tergebracht, im Verschlag (Block) 50.

Im Sonderlager herrschten furchtbarer Terror, Elend und primi-
tivste sanitäre Verhältnisse. Wir bereiten gegenwärtig eine Pu-
blikation über dieses Sonderlager vor. Außerdem besitzen wir die
Kopie einer Liste, auf der der Name Ihres Vaters erscheint. Einen Abzug davon werden wir Ihnen zusammen mit den weiteren Er-
gebnissen in Kürze übersenden.

Mit freundlichen Grüßen

Wolfgang Röll
Wolfgang Röll
Abteilungsleiter

Fernruf:
Weimar 67 481-483

Bankkonto:
IHB Weimar 4181-22-130412

Betriebsnummer
92734865

Lisl Saretzky

(Rubin, Vienna), New York, USA

It was the worst of days, but also the best of days ... My father was at
Vienna's Jewish Agency all night looking for my papers: 'Lisl Rubin
Kindertransport to London'. The Nazis had come in, and thrown all the

carefully arranged papers all over the room. He found mine at 5 am and
came running home: 'Quick, Lisl goes.' He had sewn me a cloth pocket to
wear next to my body, with all papers, passport, etc. He would not come to
the train; men were 'schlepped' away on sight. My mother, my suitcase and I
went to the Vienna train station. There was an ocean of humans everywhere
– panic, fear, confusion in the air. All of a sudden, as a Nazi shouted into a
bullhorn 'No talking or waving goodbye – or you'll be arrested', there was a
deadly silence.

I remember looking out of the open train window, my arms by my side,
looking at Mutti. She was so thin, so white, so shabby. I loved her so . . .
Someone handed me a baby through the window. The baby didn't cry.

I wore my thin gold *Magen David* around my neck, hidden under my
blouse. It was not allowed. It felt so loving on my skin. God was with us all,
no matter what the outcome.

The train pulled out. No waving – not a sound, just like that . . .

Next: Holland! Dutch women ran aside the train and handed us milk and
cakes – we grabbed hungrily and gratefully. Someone whispered: 'We are
free now.' I could not believe it. My parents and all the other Jews were not
free. I was connected to THEM ALL and not to freedom . . .

*   *   *

Anette Saville, A.R.C.M.

(Bankier, Vienna), London, UK

Coming with the second children's transport from Vienna, I landed in
England on 12 December 1938.

I had a shock when we boarded the train and waited to depart. There was a
W H Smith bookstall, full of copies of Hitler's *'Mein Kampf'*. We did not know
then that England was a free country and people could say and read
whatever they wanted, and that *'Mein Kampf'* was in fashion then.

There was plenty of musical talent amongst us youngsters, including
Jurgen Hess and his sister Marion. I also took part in the camp concerts. One
day a violin teacher, who had come over to England with Anna Essinger,
who had established a boarding school (Bunce Court), told me that an
English family was prepared to give a home to a musical boy or girl and give
him/her musical training. Would I like to go? Before I could say 'yes please',
she added: 'I would advise you not to go. You can't make a living with art or
music in England.' Do you know who went in my place? The late Peter
Schidlof of the Amadeus Quartet! I have never stopped kicking myself from
that day to this, regretting the only opportunity I had and lost.

We were then sent to The Beacon, Rusthall, Tunbridge Wells, for training as domestic servants. I worked in the kitchen and one day Lady Reading, who founded the WVS, came to our hostel in search of two kitchenmaids. She approached me and asked me if I would like to become her kitchenmaid. I was a brainy, promising youngster, *'Vorzugsschülerin'* in High School in Vienna and had been an advanced piano student. Fortunately the Austrian hostel warden came to my rescue and said: 'She prefairs playing ze piano.' Lady Reading lost interest in me and I did not become her kitchenmaid.

I had a bad nervous breakdown with all this unhappiness and wanted to join my parents in Shanghai. My mother warned me not to go because of the climate, etc., so I decided to wait until September to see if things were going to get better. The war broke out and Shanghai was out of the question. I later learnt from my parents that I could have become a teacher at Shanghai Conservatoire at fifteen, because they were so short of music teachers there.

At the age of eighteen, in my last year at school (yes, I did manage to get back to high school and get Matric, and a year's secretarial course) I passed Grade 8 Associated Board exam, and studied for the L.R.A.M. the following year in my first office job. It was impossible for me to take the examination as I had to leave the place where I was living due to circumstances outside my control and I began nursing.

At the age of thirty-six, with a broken neck and a broken marriage behind me, I finally managed to take, and pass, the A.R.C.M. for piano teaching, and wanted to become a music teacher, but was advised to stay in office work for financial security reasons. So I never became a professional.

I remarried nearly twenty-two years ago and we are still together.

*   *   *

Margot Schertz

(Heumann, Karlsruhe), New York, USA

My journey in the Kindertransport in April 1939 began in Karlsruhe where I was born. Some of my recollections are quite vivid, others vague; it was, after all, fifty years ago.

I lived through the terror of Kristallnacht and saw my father taken away to Dachau and so it seems strange to me now, that I was very excited by the prospect of going to England to live with strangers who had promised to care for me as one of their own. To leave the only home I had known, to say good-bye to my loving parents and grandmother (my brother had emigrated to the United States two years earlier), perhaps never to see them again, was not in my thoughts the day before I was to leave. The enormity of this situation began to hit me only when I had to bid farewell to my mother who had accompanied me to the city, where all the children gathered. The tears would not stop for many hours. I was desolate and was to remain so for a very long time.

I was taken in by a young family, a Rabbi and his wife and a beautiful little boy, to live in Southgate, a suburb of London. I was housed and fed but never loved. I was terribly homesick and despaired of ever seeing my folks again. I spent thirteen months in England, the unhappiest time of my life; my loneliness was at times unbearable and I worried constantly about my parents in Germany, and with the outbreak of the war there was no let-up in my concern for them. Fortunately I was able to keep in touch via friends in Switzerland, but after they were deported to Camp de Gurs, this became increasingly more difficult.

The ending of my story is a happy one. My parents survived and arrived in the United States in September 1941, two months before the US entered the war. I had preceded them in May of 1940 and was spared the blitz.

I married a wonderful man, have two equally wonderful children, one daughter with two little girls, living in Houston, Texas, a son – soon to be married – living in Wayne, New Jersey.

I recently returned to Karlsruhe by invitation from the city, and met many friends from all around the globe, who also survived through different channels, but we can never forget those who were less fortunate.

* * *

Irene Schmied

(Katzenstein, Berlin), New York, USA

Tied down by teaching assignments in New York, I was unable to attend the Kindertransport reunion. But the need to participate in the spirit of the reunion led me to dig out the diary that I wrote in German as a ten-year old. For 21 June 1939 I find a brief note about joining the Brownies at my new boarding school in Bexhill and a drawing of the Brownie uniform. Step by step, I was finding my way into a new world.

But the diary does not tell it all. It is more of a report, with a very Germanic touch to it. It records significant events and special occasions, never failing to mention the date, day of the week and time of day. Yet it makes no mention of the persistent gnawing of homesickness that could only be relieved by the free flowing of the tears that were continually pressing upon my eyes. Even later in life, I would taste again the bitter sadness of that time in moments of unhappiness or melancholy.

Yet, as the diary recounts, I was fortunate. I stayed with family friends in Hampstead for the first two months; I had relatives in London and above all my mother arrived some four weeks after I did. It was she who gave me the diary before leaving for her position as a domestic with a family in Kent.

Yet, despite my mother's arrival in England, I continued to feel wretched. I just could not feel happy where I was. It was so different from being at home with my parents. Trying to overcome this dejection, I turned to the diary and told it the story of leaving home, of the Kindertransport trip on board the *Manhattan* and of my LCC school and other experiences in *der neuen Heimat* up to my mother's arrival. The act of writing consoled me. It was as if I were back home in Berlin writing a composition for my mother on an *Ausflug* or special event – and drawing pictures to go along with my account.

By April, the diary begins to sound more cheerful. The writing loosened up a bit. I was now living with English people, in fact in the home of the octogenarian, Professor John Henry Muirhead, a distinguished philosopher, and his wife Pauline. I wrote about the countryside, and drew pictures of house and garden. Even now I can still feel how the heavy cloud of unhappiness began to dissolve a bit in the soft country air and in the warmth and kindness of the Muirhead home.

Yet, the dark shadows of the recent past did not melt into thin air very easily. Perhaps they were never really to go away. During my first months at boarding school that summer I would twist and turn anxiously in bed as sleep evaded me until late into the night.

Later, in August, I wrote in the diary about my father's arrival from Berlin, about his long conversations with Professor Muirhead in German (probably about their common experience at German universities) and his subsequent departure for South America. But it was different for me now. The poignancy of brief family reunions and uncertain partings barely seemed to touch me. The yearning to be with my mother had subsided. It is as if during that summer of 1939 she began to move away from the centre of the stage – at least for the time being. For me, the past was fading as I fitted myself into this new English world in which I was to grow up.

As the diary fails to dwell on the heart-aches, so it also leaves out the more amusing aspects of the times. In Berlin, I had been warned that English people never shake hands. The English were said to be so stiff and reserved. So, I learned not to extend a hand that would dangle – unshaken – in mid-air. Imagine my surprise when at the Muirheads in Rotherfield, I found that one kissed each other on meeting, on leaving and on saying 'goodnight' and on all sorts of other occasions. Even my mother was kissed when she came down to see us on her day off. I had never seen that much kissing in Germany – not even at home.

The diary closes with the statement: '*Ich spreche jetzt recht gut Englisch, und kaum noch Deutsch*'. In retrospect, how true this comment rings. Even if I was not to live my whole life in England, I would always draw sustenance and strength from my love of the English language and my ability to express myself in it. Only in moments of extreme despondency, would I turn again to German in an attempt to recapture the memory of the rich, sweet, comforting sights and sounds that had belonged to my childhood in a long vanished world.

* * *

Rabbi Dr Solomon Schonfeld

1912-1984
Educator, Innovator, Rescuer of thousands of Jewish lives

Following 'Kristallnacht', November 1938, the British Government declared its willingness to allow thousands of Jewish children into Great Britain.

Already involved in saving individuals from the Nazi terror, Dr Schonfeld formed himself into a one-man rescue operation. He organized two Kindertransports from Vienna in December 1938, and March 1939. This involved some 750 children.

Once on these shores, Dr Schonfeld made himself responsible for their welfare. He organized hostels in which they could live, *Yeshivot* (Talmudical Colleges) where they could study and families who would take them to their hearts.

During the war, Dr Schonfeld ministered to the spiritual needs of Jewish members of the Armed Forces.

Once the war was over however, he hastened to Poland and then to other centres of Europe, seeking out Jewish children who had survived the Holocaust.

Today, thousands of Jewish men and women – 'Schonfeld's children' are grateful to the man who brought them to safety and allowed them to flourish in the communities of the free world. Imposing of stature, eloquent of speech, and charming of manner, the late Dr Schonfeld opened doors which might otherwise have remained permanently closed.

Of this remarkable personality it can truly be said he was 'A LEGEND IN HIS LIFETIME'.

* * *

Harry Schramm

(Leipzig), Ramat Hasharon, Israel.

I arrived in England in June 1939 from Leipzig with my brother and small sister of four and a half years. I was ten and my brother eight and a half.

My Memories

1. First English school – Coolham, Sussex. Full day!! 9am-4pm!! Female teacher – strict discipline – raising hand – 'Can I be excused ma'am'!! Sandwich tin containing strange food. Lettuce/marmite sandwiches – cold fried sausages, cold pie!! But scones or cake!! Joy, oh joy!
   This was after two days in England – I was told there was another German boy at this school, already with some knowledge of English. The problem was I could not understand his German – he was from Vienna.

2. The second school was Billingshurst, where our foster father was headmaster. As a Quaker he was against corporal punishment. But in extreme cases (what could that have been in 1939?) the senior master gave out ten of the best. On one occasion a very large group of boys were found in an orchard next to the school eating apples. The next day at morning assembly the head asked all the culprits to step out and line up for caning – I was one. Later I was told when asked why I had gone through the hole in the fence, I said I followed the other boys. My English was still very weak, but I was congratulated on owning up and taking my punishment. It was my first caning at school but not the last.

3. Life with this very middle-class English family was very much different to what I had been used to at home. No doubt the addition of three foreign children to their daughter of eleven and a half had to be handled with skill. I had never done one chore at home. We had no servants, simply my mother did everything. Suddenly it was making my bed, helping to clean all shoes – but worse! What I thought was a female task – wiping the dishes.

4. Our adjustment to rural life in the country in England has very pleasant memories. Finding/searching for the first snowdrops in the snow of 1939 winter, later the first primroses, etc, wild strawberries, blackberry picking, cobnuts in the hedges, mushrooms, etc.

5. The English language. Due to the fact that we were thrown into the English-speaking society at once, I was even taken on my own to another family so as to stop speaking German to my brother and sister. We picked up

English quickly but also forgot to speak German.

The correct pronunciation was accomplished exercising after grace at mealtime, the 'th', why, who, etc.

6. Of course there are numerous other pleasant memories of those first years in England. Going to the seaside; picnicking in the rain; making tea with the black kettle full of smoke; singing songs where the words made no sense with our English, like, 'Ten green bottles hanging on the wall'; cross country walks in gumboots; tadpoles, etc.

7. As a normal boy of ten coming from Germany, the pacifist beliefs of our Quaker foster parents were more than strange to me. When our parents came to visit us once, my father was in British army uniform and I was very proud of him. Later my mother told me that they had asked him the next time to come in civvies!

When I did not come straight home from school one day and turned up late in the dark, due to participating in the school 'Scrap for the war effort' drive, I was scolded. My English was so poor at the time that I had learned parrot fashion what I had to say as I knocked at each door asking for 'old iron rails, kettles, silver paper, newspaper for the war effort' without knowing what each item was, let alone how they helped the war effort!

I was at a loss to understand that the problem for my getting scolded was not coming home late, but that they were against war!

*   *   *

Steffi Schwarcz

(Birnbaum, Berlin), Jerusalem, Israel

A notice in a Jewish newspaper drew our parents' attention to an advert which a Frau Kaufmann had inserted, selecting twelve children from good bourgeois (academic) Jewish homes, where there was only a slight possibility of the parents being able to get out. These twelve children were being guaranteed by Dr Bernard and Mrs Winifred Schlesinger of London, for residence and education in England. Dr Schlesinger was then paediatrician at University College and Great Ormond Street hospitals, London, and he and his wife were assimilated Jews of German parentage. Dr Schlesinger rose to a high position in the army and in the two hospitals and received the O.B.E.

I must stress the modesty, humanity and affection of the Schlesingers; their readiness to give without advertising themselves, their constant interest and the hospitality they gave to each one of their 'adopted' family until their death. Initially they saved our lives; they opened a hostel for us run by Jewish staff in Highgate, London, where we all landed via the Kindertransport on 16 March 1939. The hostel became our second home but unfortunately, due to Dr Schlesinger being called up, it dissolved and we were all evacuated with the local council school.

My sister and I were billeted with a young English Protestant couple, Albert and Margaret Kelly, who are now in their early eighties. After a period of disorientation, home-sickness, fright and unhappiness, we found ourselves taken care of, loved and being educated in a decent well-cared-for home.

For the Kellys we had been total strangers and unexpected Jewish refugee evacuees, but we left them, having received from them loving-kindness, the simplicity of a good family relationship, the early initiation into English customs – especially at Christmas, and motherly guidance. At no time did they try to change our belief or identity and we were encouraged to say the Hebrew *Brachot* at meals. To date we are part of their family and this relationship has been passed down to the second generation.

Unfortunately we did not stay with them, but were sent for higher education to Kingsley Boarding School in Tintagel, Cornwall, where in 1944 I gained my London University School Certificate. My sister left this school in 1947. Theoretically the education was good, but the spiritual environment was very poor. Worry and fear for our beloved mother – our father had 'luckily' died in our own home in October 1939 – grandmother, and aunts and uncles. The headmistress, emotionally unbalanced, started a vigorous campaign of conversion of the refugees, i.e.: enforced attendance at church, threats when she did not succeed, etc., etc.

There were many Jewish children at the school and we were terribly unhappy; especially the older ones of us, and outcasts if we did not conform. Rescue came from a determined Mrs Charles Waley-Cohen Singer, wife of the scientist, who lived in Cornwall and forthwith invited all the Jewish schoolgirls in the vicinity to her home for the festivals, initiated correspondence classes from the Liberal Jewish Synagogue in London, and stood up to the 'dragon'.

I left school in 1944 and then began a terrible period of fear for my family, self-doubt and searching. The school had not prepared us for life. The following three years passed with the revelation of the Holocaust and all it meant – the blessing of surviving relatives, such as our aunt and uncle in Holland, and my aunt and uncle in Berlin. All managed to survive except our beloved mother and grandmother and other dear relatives.

Our beloved mother was deported and sent to her death in 1943 and shortly before that, grandmother Jenny committed suicide so as not to go on the transport.

We had the great fortune of finding our aunt and uncle in Holland (and my aunt in Berlin – now aged ninety-one), who tried all in their power to give us love, affection and understanding. We were no longer children and I was independent and working. We paid yearly visits to my uncle's home in Amsterdam, where he still lives today, aged eighty-four, a widower.

My sister qualified as a nurse and later as a Health Visitor and still works in Hampstead for the London Authority.

I worked for thirteen years for the London County Council, qualified as a Social Worker, and emigrated to Israel in 1963, where I married and had a daughter who is now nineteen. For years I have been working at the Hebrew University in Jerusalem.

In this memoriam I think of a German-Jewish childhood, a cultural home imbued with deep love, harmony between our parents, a childhood so filled with beauty, guidance, and fullness. Remembrances of a country and landscape – the Silesian hills – of beauty and serenity, of our beloved parents who gave us so much and our two grandmothers.

I want to honour the following: the late Dr Bernard and Winifred Schlesinger who rescued us; Mrs Dora Segall who accompanied the children's transports to England and was a Social Worker at Bloomsbury House and is a beloved friend; Albert and Margaret Kelly of Torquay to whom we were evacuated and became part of their own family; to our surviving relatives who care for us still (my aunt Ilse Hamburg and my uncle Paul G Steinfeld), and to the many dear friends we made throughout the fifty years, in England and in Israel.

*   *   *

Dennis Schwarz

(Cologne), Los Angeles, USA

I was a member of a class of thirteen and fourteen year olds in the Jewish school *Jawne* in Cologne which was sponsored and brought to England by the congregation of Walm Lane Synagogue in north west London.

Our Kindertransport, approximately thirty girls and boys, left Cologne on 19 January 1939 and arrived in Harwich on the morning of 21 January. We were taken to London where the girls were distributed into private homes and the boys were lodged in the hostel at No. 1 Minster Road, Cricklewood.

With the outbreak of war in September 1939 we were evacuated to Bedford. I stayed there for about two months, then returned to London and the hostel at 243 Willesden Lane, where I remained until 1943. While there I met and, in 1944, married Regine Kampf who was from Vienna. My mother survived a concentration camp and joined us in 1946. She is alive and active to this day at age ninety-one.

We emigrated to the United States in 1947 and made our home in New York for the next twenty-seven years. Our son was born there in 1950. He now is married with two children of his own and practises medicine as an Intern, specializing in nephrology. They live on Long Island, NY.

In 1973 my wife and I moved to Los Angeles. After many years as Director of Purchasing for shoe manufacturers and in the leather manufacturing industry, I am now retired.

* * *

Gina Schwarz

(Kampf, Vienna), Los Angeles, USA

I left Vienna in August 1939 with a children's transport arranged by the *Kultusgemeinde,* for Eastbourne, England. There I stayed with an English couple who owned a boarding house and worked for them as a 'Girl Friday'. The man was a Canadian veteran and got a position in London to manage the Canadian Legion Club in Bower Street. I went to London with them and worked in the club as a kitchen maid – heating the stoves with coal, washing floors, peeling potatoes and the like. I was not supposed to mix with the soldiers for reasons of security and my protection, since I was both an alien and a young girl.

In 1941 my guarantee ended and I applied to Bloomsbury House for placement in a hostel with Jewish children. That done, I looked for work in London's garment centre. Starting as an apprentice, I went on to become a finisher, sewing machine operator and assistant cutter until I worked on my own as a dressmaker.

In the hostel we had a matron who took care of fifteen boys and girls, between sixteen and nineteen years old. There I met my future husband, Dennis. We married in 1944. I lost touch with my family and after the war found that none of them were alive. Dennis's mother survived a concentration camp and joined us in London.

In 1947 the three of us went to New York City – a new start! I worked in the garment trade and my husband went into the leather wholesale business. Our son was born in 1950.

* * *

Ruth B Schwarz

(Vogel, Dresden)

Poem written by her while in the cottage-camp, aged sixteen years, in January 1939

Allein in der Fremde
Oh, wie tut das weh!
Ob Sommer, ob Winter,
Ob Regen oder Schnee,
Man wird das Gefühl nicht los,
Allein in der Fremde
Und die Welt ist so gross.
Wie gut auch alle zu uns sind,
Ersatz für meine geliebten Eltern,
Ich nirgends find.
Nur einen Moment auf Mutti's Schoss
Und ich vergess, dass die Welt ist so gross.

Jetzt bin ich in England, jetzt bin ich hier
Und lieber G'tt, ich danke Dir,
Dass Du meinen Bruder und mich gerettet hast,
Für unsere Eltern in Deutschland ist es weniger Last,
Uns geht es hier gut
Das gibt mir Mut
Zu hoffen, dass unsere Eltern sich noch retten werden
Und wir alle zusammen ein Plätzchen finden auf dieser Erden.
Nur einen Moment auf Mutti's Schoss
Und ich vergess, dass dieWelt ist so gross.

Wir sind im Camp, soviele mit dem gleichen Schicksal
Wir hatten keine andere Wahl.
Man gibt uns alles, Essen, Betten und Freunde sind wir alle geworden
Entronnen der Gefahr von Hitler und seinen Morden.
Doch, immer denk ich, nur einen Moment auf Mutti's Schoss
Und ich vergess, dass die Welt ist so gross.

* * *

Ruth Schwiening

(Auerbach, Breslau), Warwicks., UK

THE HIDDEN STRENGTH

Hester was quiet, resigned. Her body flopped untidily onto the chair. She felt weak. There was no fight left in her. She eyed her brother. 'What now, what can we do?'

'Nothing,' came the slow reply, 'absolutely nothing.'

His face was drawn and sallow. His sunken, sad eyes said it all. 'She's dying.'

At last it was spoken. The unmentionable was spoken. He had said these few words quietly and slowly, but yet they seemed to echo loudly, gaining in momentum, as they rebounded from one wall to the other and eventually came to rest.

Hester looked at the man in the corner of the room. He must have heard but he showed no sign. He had spent the last sixty years bound to the woman. Yet he gave no sign. Hester could not see his eyes for they were cast downwards; down, down, down – pre-empting death – penetrating the woman's grave. So he had heard after all.

'Father, father.'

There was no reply. Hester wanted to go to the man; hug him, throw her arms around him, but she dared not intrude. Not even the intrusion of his child would have been acceptable to him; this she knew. She watched his every movement. Her eyes rested on his shoulders. These shoulders, which were so very strong and straight were now rounded, eroded by life.

The shoulders which transported her through forests and fields in times of peace, carried her to safety in times of war. When the sirens wailed he would tiptoe upstairs, pick her up in his strong arms and hold her close to him. Sometimes he would just sit there rocking and singing to her until the All Clear was sounded. At other times, when he knew that the bombs would drop nearer home, she remembered how she had clung to her father's strong neck with her bony legs, her dirty hands clutching his clammy forehead.

'Hold on, hold on, my little one, we will soon be in the warm,' he would whisper this as he crept along the ditch. Not once did he let her fall.

He had crept along with Hester on his back and had carried his woman in his arms. His body had paved the way for his sons, who held onto him, also seeking his warmth and reassurance.

The sky was spasmodically ablaze with light, just before the bombs fell. She then saw, in the red glow, the back of his full black hair – gleaming and shining. The strong smell of the damp earth and the sweetness of his fresh sweat penetrating her nostrils – a smell which she still retains. One hand would occasionally seek hers in the darkness, lovingly and protectively.

When they finally reached the shelter and relative safety – only then would he gently lower Hester down from his back or shoulders, cover her with his warm, damp coat and comfortingly stroke her hair until they both fell asleep. Other times he carried her to the shelter in the garden and left her in his big overcoat whilst he helped to extinguish one of the many fires. Sometimes she would not want him to go and clung to him, sensing the danger which he would not acknowledge. He promised her to return and he always did so.

He spent many years helping to build and farm the country which he considered to be his by birthright. He was in no doubt that he was one of the Chosen People. The strong sun beat down on him causing blistering of his youthful skin but this remained barely noticed as he went about his work cultivating the soil – bringing water to the deserts, crops to the barren land. He felt as strong as the earth itself not relenting until he was its master and he had forced and coaxed it to yield a harvest.

On his return to Europe he built his own farm. His now hardened skin had no trouble in lifting the planks, which he carried laden with bricks on his bare shoulders. he was now adept at climbing steep ladders and would laugh as he occasionally missed his footing. His was a happy life. His outer strength mirrored his inner strength. He thrived on physical hard work. This strength made him feel good and it also saved his life.

It was a cold winter's night when they came to fetch him. The wind whistled through the already broken windows. They had announced their arrival with bricks and stones.

'*Raus, raus, raus, Judenschwein*,' they had chanted.

At first the shouts were in the distance, then they came closer. As they approached, he did not run. He stood firm, not out of fear but because he knew that he had to go. He picked up his coat without fuss or panic. If he felt despair he did not show it and with a quiet '*Shalom*', he left.

The beatings he had to experience in the camps were tough but he was tougher. Whilst others collapsed with fatigue and disease he survived. Often during the *Appell* he would stand erect, head high, shoulders held well back supporting a weaker inmate. His strength of mind was not going to allow any weakness in body. He accepted the beatings, knowing full well that strength lay in silence. The whips made deep weals in his flesh. The number on his arm became infected and inflamed. The ugly weals carved into his back disfigured him, but yet he still managed to carry the burden of the 'Star' upon him without breaking – this he swore he would never do.

He had once said, many years later: 'I have seen humanity at its lowest ebb, something which I will never forget.'

It was only because he could show himself as being strong and well that he was eventually allowed his freedom.

England offered him a new home. It reunited him with his family. He had to learn and relearn but he was a willing pupil and he shirked no task. The work that followed helped to revitalize, broaden and rebuild his body and mind. He gained new confidence and his gratitude to the country which had adopted him without questioning his race and religion knew no bounds. He was determined once again to stand tall and broad for England as he had in his youth for Israel.

The years of unemployment and leanness did not discourage him. 'I've been through a living hell already. I'll get through this.' And he did. He, through his patience and tolerance, he, who had suffered so much because of the intolerance of others, taught Hester to be strong. Only once had she seen him sag under the pain inflicted by her upon him.

It was when she announced to him her intended marriage to a *Goy*. She did not look at his face as she told him.

'Father I am going to marry him. We love each other.' She watched his stance alter. He shuffled uncertainly from one foot to the other and then sat down heavily as if an invisible force had dragged him. Hester did not have the courage to face him to see his reaction – but there was no need for this. His back expressed all she needed to know. His neck muscles grew tense and she could feel the rising anger within him. Soon his shoulders dropped and his back rounded.

She did not need to look at his face to know that his eyes were full of tears. His shoulders spoke his thoughts louder than any voice. 'How could you do this to me? You are betraying yourself, your fathers and forefathers.' Hester had wanted to scream in reply,

'No father, you do me an injustice to accuse me.' She was now feeling his strength within her. 'What we are doing is good and right. We are betraying no one – least of all you, my father.' Hester however remained silent. She did not after all have the strength to hurt him. Time passed and with the passage of time his children bore him grandchildren. With the grandchildren came reconciliation. He played with his children's children and gave them rides on his back just as he had once done with Hester. Laughter, tears and happiness filled his days and years, but then came illness and sadness.

The one he loved even more than Hester, his life's companion was dying. During these hard years he nursed and tended her. He protected her until her despair infected him. Slowly he began to change. He began to weaken. His jackets no longer fitted squarely on his shoulders. It was not so much the obvious physical weakness; the narrowing of the shoulders, the wasting of the muscles and the hunching of the back that disturbed Hester but more the weakness that came from within him. She now noticed that his ability to make decisions and to take actions, to advise and even control had waned.

He began to falter in discussions and his arguments were no longer as sound.

Now as she observed him she could no longer fight her emotions. She rushed over to him, encircled his weak body with her strong arms and cradled him as he had so often cradled her. She was now his protector and his strength.

Dedicated to the memory of her father, whose courage, tenacity and love helped him through Dachau, internment and all adversities in life. He died in May 1989.

*   *   *

Margot Seewi
(Rapp, Weinheim), Israel

I suppose you are interested in children who came to the United Kingdom at the time. I might have been among those, but I was not. My parents had registered me for England, the Netherlands and Palestine (those were the possibilities we had), and they thought whatever would come first, there they would send me. It was 1939, the war had begun, and for many months (since November 1938) I was not allowed to go to school. Living conditions for Jews were getting worse every day and since there was no chance for the family to go away together, they wanted at least to save the children. My brother, alas, was too small for a children's transport, he was only three years old at the time, I was thirteen.

As it happened, the first possibility that turned up was Palestine; we had relatives there who guaranteed for me, so I left with a children's transport at the end of 1939, arrived in Palestine in January 1940. These were children twelve to fifteen years old who came to relatives; there were at the time also transports of fifteen to eighteen year olds, who went with *Youth Aliyah* straight to *Kibbutzim*. We went by train to Italy, which was not yet at war at the time, and from there by ship. The ship was called *Galilea*.

We had lived in Weinheim, a small town in southern Germany near Mannheim and Heidelberg, and all Jews from that area were deported in October 1940 to a concentration camp in southern France (Camp de Gurs). Many of them died there under terrible circumstances; those who didn't, were deported in 1942 to Auschwitz and killed there. My parents were among them. My little brother, who had been with my parents in Gurs, had become very ill there, was taken to a children's home in France of the OSE (*Oeuvre de secours aux enfants*) and was thus saved. Others of my family (grandmother, uncles and aunts) died in Gurs.

I know of three children of our town who came to England with a children's transport but I know nothing of their whereabouts. Their names were Lore and Beate Schloss (two sisters) and a boy called Werner Kassel.

Editors' Note: We found Werner Kassel, and they now correspond.

*   *   *

Yehudit Segal

(Batscha, Vienna), Nahalal, Israel

The Partingtons, an English Gentile family had answered my father's desperate plea by advertising in the *Manchester Guardian*, asking for home and shelter for his fourteen year old daughter until her parents could arrange to come themselves.

The date of my departure from Vienna was 12 February 1939. The train left and I was on my own. I felt completely grown up and capable of looking after myself.

I arrived in Bristol. There on the platform, waiting for me was Mrs Partington! We recognised each other as we had exchanged photographs. But I imagine she would have known me anywhere! I must have stuck out like a sore thumb, in my get-up of continental winter clothes, thick woollen stockings, high shoes (boots), that cap that had seemed so 'chic' when we had it made in Vienna and that heavy 'hand' luggage!

I learned a lot of new customs at the Partingtons and for a long time thought that every English household followed these. Of course some of them were just family rituals, though they stuck to them rigidly.

It took me some time to understand why, when I set the table, the jam I set out was invariably exchanged for a different kind! I found out that only orange jam was called marmalade and this was only eaten at breakfast. All other jams, but not marmalade, were suitable for the early evening meal called 'high tea'; apple jelly was served at dinner with certain kinds of meat!

My amazement at these customs was no greater than theirs at my ignorance of these basic rules of British life.

I began a new life in England where I stayed for over nine years. These were the formative years of my life, the impressionable years. They were difficult, hard times, with the war to come and the dreadful revelations of what had happened to all my family. England left its indelible mark on me, a beneficial mark. I liked the English people, whether Jews or Gentiles. I adjusted to the English mentality easily and I don't think only because I was young. I think it suited me and grafted on naturally to my Viennese background and upbringing. Most of all I appreciated the English sense of humour and do so to this day.

There is an emotional memory somehow connected with my stay with the Partingtons in Keynsham. I began a secret ritual of pretending to go for walks in the streets of Vienna; mainly where I used to go shopping with my mother, and with my mind's eye I would pass the shops and street names and so commit it all firmly to memory. I seemed to have a dread of forgetting. I visualized every place I knew and 'walked' along familiar routes. I rehearsed, often silently, songs, Viennese operas and songs learned in school with the exact text. I had a fear of one day not being able to visualize every smallest detail. I somehow knew I would not return, but wanted the memory to be alive always, and it is to this day.

Later of course, after war broke out and the hope of reunion became fainter, a second fear joined the first: the fear of forgetting what they all looked like. With no more letters to keep my mother's face and voice alive before me, I would look at her photograph and in that instant lose her real image in my mind's eye. This is an experience bordering on trauma; I believe it is harder to bear than being separated and certainly turns prolonged separation into endless agony.

As the years went by, the faces of my family became the faces of their photographs. For a long time I was able to screw up my eyes very tight and so conjure up the 'real' look of my father and mother, the screwing up excluded the photo image, but sadly, as year followed year, I lost their real look, as I had lost that of grandparents, uncles and aunts.

*   *   *

Steffi Segerman

(Bamberger, Leipzig), Kibbutz Kfar Blum, Israel

It's not easy to turn the clock back fifty years, but I have always wanted to tell my story, and now seems to be an ideal opportunity.

I cannot quite recall when we moved from our big house into an apartment, but it was from there that my father was taken on Kristallnacht. I remember that night very clearly. At 4 am there was a tremendous banging on the door. When we opened it (my room was right by the front door so I was the first to get up) four unshaven, frightening-looking Gestapo barged their way in. At gun point my mother had to show them where she kept her jewellery and where the money was kept. My father who had a paralysed leg from World War One was rushed out of bed and told to get dressed QUICKLY. At the bedside table were books for learning English; they spat on them and destroyed them, and the whole apartment was ransacked.

My mother put some sandwiches into my father's pocket and, while doing so, whispered into his ear to fall down the stairs and then maybe they wouldn't take him if he was hurt. No, my father wanted to go out of the house like a man, and at his own pace, and that is how we saw him entering this long, black, shining limousine. Their parting words to us were: 'Go and look at your business and at the Synagogue.'

We closed up the apartment and, penniless, got into a taxi (the driver knew us and was sympathetic and said that he would take us to wherever we wanted free of charge). We asked him to take us, via the business and

Synagogue, to our friends' house. He was the chief Professor of the Jewish hospital in Leipzig.

The sight of our business was unbelievable – just a skeleton of a building, everything inside burnt – hundreds of rolls of material, coats, shirts, sweaters and suits. I, as a little girl of nine, thought what a waste, it could have been given to the poor instead. I still had no idea what it was all about, never having experienced any anti-semitism at school or anywhere else. I remember we went into the burnt-out building to see if we could find the electric train my brother got for his *Bar Mitzvah*; we had stored it there when we moved from the big house. What was so unbelievable was that not a centimetre of the attached building was even charred, and not one window broken. The Synagogue was much the same picture.

We arrived at our friends and thought we would warn them and relate what had happened and what we had seen, and maybe they could still get out of the country. It was too late, and we all decided to go together to the Jewish hospital and see if we could be of any help there. We found chaos, the overnight staff seemed to have vanished, and patients who could stand on their two feet were taken away. We went to work. We were given white coats and both my mother and I worked very hard, sometimes two shifts! I did not work together with my mother, nor did we sleep in the same room, but all that we took in our stride. When I come to think of it now, the work I did there is done by a nurse in her second year of training. For example – after an operation I went into the theatre with the nurses and helped to clean up; the sight of blood did not disturb me. I helped sterilize the instruments. On the ward I would help the nurses dress wounds. I gave out meals, but I had to remember that this tray went to the patient that had half a stomach removed, and that tray went to a diabetic. I was known as '*Schwester Steffi*'. Every morning at 4 am the Gestapo came and took anyone who was able to stand up. Day after day the same procedure, and during all this time we were thinking about my father, where was he, and was he all right. One day, we got a note smuggled in from my father, saying that he was at the police station and was all right. With a lot of 'pull', we managed to get him into the hospital as a 'patient', so once again we were together as a family, and that made our work so much easier. I cannot remember how long this went on for, but when we finally returned to our apartment my parents told me that they were sending me to a wonderful family in England, and that in three months' time they would come and join me. It was difficult for me to understand, but I accepted it and when the time came, I packed all my special toys that I wanted to take with me. My mother came as far as Utrecht with me, and there we parted. So, with the Kindertransport, I went to England.

My parents had corresponded with the family in Liverpool to whom I was going, and sent them a photograph of me. My brother, who was at that time studying in Switzerland, wrote to them all about his little sister. He wrote that I had had all the children's illnesses – chickenpox, etc., and I remember he also wrote that I loved animals and that when I grew up I wanted to work with dogs. That letter exists to this day.

When I arrived in Liverpool, I was greeted by the whole family and made very welcome. In no time I felt very much at home and their daughter and I grew up just like sisters, very close. I was the older one of us two (there was a brother but he was in the Air Force) so if I wanted I could stay up later at night, but we always liked going up to bed at the same time. To this day we have a wonderful relationship, and I am in close contact with all the cousins and aunts and uncles.

I kept in touch with my parents as long as possible. They of course did not join me in England after three months as hoped. They were taken to Theresienstadt, and in 1942 we heard through the Red Cross that my father 'died', and in 1944, my mother.

*   *   *

Sidney Seide

(Elberfeld), London, UK

A TOOL STORY

When Winston Churchill, during one of his famous wartime speeches, proclaimed: 'Give us the tools and we will finish the job', everyone in Britain knew just what he meant.

Yet on the other hand, toolmaking was often interpreted too literally, by assuming that it consisted of crafting hammers and chisels, pliers, screwdrivers and the like. Perhaps that is what *I* imagined it to be, as a boy, when I said that I wanted one day to be – no, not a traindriver – but a toolmaker. I suppose that if I had understood then, that it meant painstakingly working to accuracies of one-tenth of a thousandth of an inch much of the time, so that the tools would enable machines to produce millions of identical components, it might have discouraged me. The German world for a toolmaker – *'Werkzeugschlosser'* – was itself rather off-putting, but much more serious were the words of the Nuremberg Laws in 1935 spelling out their anti-semitic edicts which eventually included among their restrictions the prohibition for Jews to engage in a trade or profession.

As things turned out, my taste of freedom in England, having arrived there just a few months before the war parentless, as a child refugee, was also burdened with restrictions. I was forbidden to work, paid or unpaid, and had to be wholly supported by the family with whom I had come to stay in London. The second time I arrived in England was in 1943. I had been shuffled around the other four continents of the world in the meantime. The situation workwise for me was completely the reverse: it was now compulsory to do work of national importance! So be it! Instead of being considered dangerous enough, barely sixteen years old in 1940, to put behind barbed wire, I could now contribute to the war effort of the Allies as a toolmaker. Well almost; after two years of experience working in India, I was only up to Improver standard in England.

As for the time I had spent in India, it really hadn't amounted to a full two years' work experience; you see, racial discrimination again provided an obstacle to the normal progress of my training for a skilled job. This time not the deprivation of citizenship and the 'racially inferior' classification of the Nuremberg Laws, but being a white European automatically put me into a superior category.

To the indigenous even at seventeen I was a pukka Sahib. It was rather ironic that I was frequently approached by beggars, addressing me as Sahib, whilst myself living on charity, in a refugee hostel, receiving minimal pocket money. How times had changed. I had certainly learned by then not to judge people at face value, certainly not by the colour of their skin. My opinion of the culture of the so-called Master race had certainly taken a bashing. How I wished my dear parents – I was an only child – had escaped the clutches of those blond-haired blue-eyed monsters. My mother worried a lot at the best of times; if only I could have let my parents know that I was OK.

Yes, I was well enough. Neither the climate, nor any other of the discomforts bothered me very much, but I was still without a job. There was certainly no shortage of British engineering companies in Bombay. Factories with familiar names like Metal Box and British Aluminium. The only snag was, that as a white man, it was considered undignified for me to make the tea, sweep the floor as well as work on machines or bench-vice, and generally getting my hands dirty. Anyway, after managing a year's training in a back-street workshop, coupled with evening classes, I did get employment with a reputable British company engaged in war-work. But in a supervisory capacity. At least from that time on, earning reasonable wages, I was able to live independently. No more the charity living in a Relief Association's hostel with the stigma of being a refugee. Nor that previous classification of being an Enemy Alien with the rigours of internment camps. I was in my own small way giving Mr Churchill the tools to finish the job – albeit without that time-served apprenticeship. The war had condensed everything to bare essentials and with it made the process of my growing-up a less lengthy procedure.

*   *   *

Refugee Children's Movement Ltd.

INTERNEE No.   Our Ref. 3922   Deported to AUSTRALIA (Bombay)

Children's Educational Permit No.   Passport issued at (Fremdenpass only)
or own visa No. 5441   No.   Valid till
                                                     Birth Certificate

NAME SEIDE   Forename Salomon   Nationality German (Stateless)

Date of Birth 3.4.24   Place and Country of Birth Elberfeld, Germany

Arrival in England 11.5.39   Guaranteed by Samuel Singer (cousin)
                                                 4 Median Road, London, E.5

Attained age of Sixteen on 3.4.1940

Registered with Police at   Date   Cert. No. 838352

Address at time of Reg.: 4 Median Road, Lower Clapton, E.5

ATTENDED TRIBUNAL AT   Date July 1940

  Address at time of Tribunal

  Result and remarks

INTERNED (Date)   At   Deported (Date)

Address and occupation at time of internment 4 Median Road, Lower Clapton, E.5

Remarks Release applied for by Region No.5 to Home Office, July 30,'40.
Boy released (see letter from New Scotland Yard, S.W.1
(79/S/5438(C 2 B). Returned to England on SS "Dunera", was stopped in
Bombay where he is now living at the hostel of the Jewish Relief
Organization. ~~(When Release Granted, Address 105, Bloomsbury House, dealing with this case)~~

Particulars of Parents

  Father Mendl   Mother Elsa

  Birth Date   Place   Nationality   Birth Date   Place   Nationality

  Present Address 26 Karlstrasse   Present Address same as for father
(W.=WUPPERTAL) W.-Elberfeld, Germany

Address of Responsible Committee in England Refugee Children's Movement, Ltd.,
                                            Bloomsbury House, Bloomsbury St., London, W.C.1

Corresponding Committees abroad   Jewish Relief Organization
                                         E.D.Sassoon,
                                         15 Dougall Road, Ballard Estate, Bombay.

EMIGRATION U.S.A

Registered at U.S.A. Consulate in Stuttgart   Date Sept.1938   No. 3710, Polish Quota

Registration verified by London Consulate

Affidavit   Sponsor's Name and Address

REMARKS : I know nothing of the details of this case since the guarantor
has consistently left letters unanswered.
The Consul might be asked if his case is a suitable one to be
transferred, i.e. if verified and affidavits submitted.

Walter Selinger

(Vienna), Arizona, USA

This is a tribute to my foster father, Mr Lazarus, a wonderful man, who saved three lives during the Hitler years.

When I was only twelve years old, he sponsored me to come from Vienna to London, England, he being only thirteen years older, newly wed only two years.

On Kristallnacht my father was arrested and sent to Dachau. My mother and I did not hear from him for six weeks. Two months later we received a letter from Mr Lazarus and his lovely wife Mary, telling us that he would sponsor me to come to London. He made all the arrangements and I left my mother behind and went to this wonderful young couple. After I arrived, I told them that my father was being held in Dachau. If my mother could show proof that he would leave the country, the Nazis would release him back to Vienna, in order that he may leave Austria. Mr Lazarus purchased a ship ticket, which cost him one month's wages. I sent the ticket to my mother who presented it to the Gestapo who then released my father. From Vienna my parents travelled to Italy and then on to Argentina, where they lived happily until their deaths in the late 1960s.

So God bless Mr Lazarus with good health and long life. Because of his unselfish generosity and love he saved the three of us from death, as befell the remainder of my family.

After forty years in America, my wife and I always keep in contact with my English foster family. I love him as my own father. He and his family will always be in my heart with gratitude.

Therefore, I request that his name 'Phineus Lazarus', known today as Phil Forman, is mentioned in the Kindertransports book.

*   *   *

Laura Selo

(Gumpel, Prague), London, UK

THANK YOU, MISS HARDER!

The following story was broadcast in 'Woman's Hour' and later published in AJR information. In it, Laura pays tribute to one of the many English people who gave hospitality to refugee children. Laura's parents, together with their three daughters, first fled from Germany to Prague. When the Germans invaded Czechoslovakia, her father escaped to Poland, and her mother decided she must somehow get her children to England. Laura, the eldest, was then fifteen.

There were children's transports coming to England, and the Czech Trust Fund in England and the Committee in Prague were finding families who would take refugee children like us. It was my mother's wish that we three children should not be separated, but the Committee could not find anybody willing to take all three of us into their homes. But, at last, one day we heard that we were finally leaving for England, and that a lady called Miss Harder would have all three of us.

We left in June 1939. I shall never forget the day when we arrived at drab Liverpool Street station, tired and slightly bedraggled. A lady dressed rather shabbily in old-fashioned clothes came towards us and into my hands she put a card on which the words '*Mother Love*' were written. I knew a little English, just enough to understand what she meant to convey, but at the time my sisters and I were rather bewildered and, quite frankly, disappointed. We were young and frightened, and I suppose we really had no idea what to expect, but we had certainly never thought that our new foster-mother would look quite so unattractive. We had even more of a shock when we saw her dingy home. It was a two-room flat in an old mansion block. She had given up her bedroom to the three of us and she slept in the sitting-room on the sofa. It all seemed very cramped and poor and the flat was dark.

I discovered later that Miss Harder had continuously offered her services to the Committee. She was a spinster, in her early fifties, who owned a small confectionery and tobacco shop just by the Archway Underground Station in Highgate. The Committee, although it had been touched by her desire to help, had never found a child who would have been suitable for her to take in. Probably they thought she was too poor. When, just by chance, someone mentioned the three of us and the fact that our mother did not wish us to be parted, Miss Harder offered to take us all, to the Committee's astonishment. She was asked to think the matter over carefully, taking into account her circumstances, lack of accommodation and the responsibility, but she had made her decision. She even turned down the Committee's offer of financial help because, as she put it, she did not want another child to be deprived of its chance of coming over to England because she had taken the money.

Those early weeks when we were miserable – we missed our mother and often cried – must have been very difficult for Miss Harder. She had to spend a good deal of her time in the shop and rush back to cook meals and care for us. Three tearful children who spoke very little of her own language could not have been easy to love. But she was patient and understanding and even treated us to a holiday in the Isle of Wight which, we found out later, she could barely afford. She was helped to pay for it by friends and customers who used to give her odd shillings towards it in the shop.

Gradually we learnt English and got to know Miss Harder and after the first few months, we managed to adjust ourselves to our new surroundings and began to settle down. Then came a telegram from a friend of my mother's in Prague saying that mother had disappeared. After that another message said that she had been arrested and imprisoned as a hostage for my father. Our foster-mother tried everything to console us and take our minds off our sorrow. Somehow her efforts to comfort us brought us even closer together.

Then the war came, and almost immediately, her business suffered. She had to do without her assistant and I helped out in the shop. We were too young to realize then that it must have been a most worrying time for Miss Harder. And we were certainly no angels. Sometimes we were naughty, as children inevitably are. On top of that her dog, Blackie, to whom she was devoted, died. Then she had an accident; in the blackout a cigarette machine fell on her. I do not quite know if it was this that caused her illness, but six months after our arrival in this country, Miss Harder died of consumption, and what she had tried to prevent, happened: my sisters and I were separated. They went to foster-parents and I got a job as a maid. Now, one of my sisters lives in San Francisco and the other one in New York, while I live in London. Our mother died in a concentration camp.

I think it is only now, after all these years later, that I understand what a truly kind, wonderful and courageous woman Miss Harder was. She was my second mother for those few months. My sisters and I owe our lives to her, but we can never repay her for her kindness, for having taken three unknown children into her home given them love and understanding and her compassion.

*　　　*　　　*

Erika Shotland

(Kirel, Vienna), Manchester, UK

I arrived in England in July 1939 with a children's transport from Vienna. I was fourteen years old at the time and I was allocated to live with an elderly, childless couple in Manchester, who were kind to me. They have long since died.

My own family, excepting my brother who lives in Israel and with whom I am very close, were sadly left behind in Vienna and when we said goodbye, I don't think any of us realized that this was the last time we would be together. They all perished in the Holocaust.

After fifty years in England, being happily married, bringing up lovely daughters and now being a grandmother myself, a feeling of loss still persists.

*　　　*　　　*

REFUGEE CHILDREN'S MOVEMENT, Ltd.

REGIONAL COMMITTEE No. 3.

30th August 1940.   24, PARK ROW,
                           NOTTINGHAM.

Dear Ernst,

TEL. Nottingham 3851.

I was glad to get your letter of the 25th August and to hear that you are now back with Mrs. Russell.

When Northampton became a protected area we sent you to a farm job in Weedon because we were quite sure that you would be safe from internment there. Unfortunately however, this did not prove to be the case and you were interned. But it was possible to apply for your release simply because under Government orders, if a boy was living with an English family in a non-protected area and in farm work, an application for his release could be made.

I therefore made the application for your release on the grounds that you were doing farm work and that your old job in Weedon was still open for you. You have been released solely on condition that you take up this work again and therefore it is out of the question to find you other work. In any case it is extremely difficult to find jobs in other trades and even farm jobs these days are not as plentiful as we should like.

You have been released on condition that you live and work for the Russells and therefore you must carry on with it. Later on I hope that things will improve and we shall be able to make other arrangements for you, but now you must carry on with your work and be very thankful that you have a job to do. I am surprised that you say you do not get paid - you are provided with board and lodging, don't you call that wages. Your pocket money you will get in the usual way as before.

I understand your position quite well but under present circumstances there is nothing we can do, for as I have said before your release is only due to the fact that Mrs. Russell offered you back your old job. Therefore repay them for their kindness to you by carrying out your work to the best of your ability and be happy that you

have work to do.

I do not know whether you have any re-emigration plans for overseas, but if not are you interested in the settlement scheme in San Domingo. I am enclosing you herewith a form which I shall be glad if you will fill out and return to me if you are interested - many of the boys have already entered their names for it.

With best wishes to you.

Yours very truly,

Irene Burnett

(Miss) Irene Burnett
Regional Secretary

Ernest Sicher

(Frankfurt), Israel

I came to England, aged fifteen and a half years, on 24 August 1939 on the last children's transport out of Frankfurt. On arrival at a gym hall near Liverpool Street station, it was found that the sponsoring family wanted a girl, i.e. my sister: so, but for the nearness of war, I would have been sent back. My sister perished in Auschwitz. This has been recorded in Karen Gershon's 'We Came as Children'. I was sent to a disused workhouse in Claydon near Ipswich. Our Housemaster, a Mr Percival, fixed our windows so that they could not be shut during the night, with the end result – in that cold winter of 1939 – one morning I could not move my legs – I had sciatica. However, everybody was kind to me and I recovered.

In the spring I moved to Northampton to work in a tanning factory where I contracted a chronic infection. When Northampton became a 'protected area' I was moved to a farm in nearby Weedon. I worked a sixteen hour day, seven days a week, except Sundays, when I finished after tea. I helped with the milking, cleaned out the cowshed, pigsty, horse stalls, chicken runs and did any other jobs going. I even helped the maid to serve lunch on occasions. All for my bed and food. The Refugee Committee sent me two and six pence spending money and fifteen shillings for the farmer's wife. When the farmer gave me a beating, I ran away. The local vicar helped me to get back to Northampton where I stayed in a refugee hostel. A Mr Marx in charge there was very kind and fatherly to me. I still have letters from the farmer's wife and Mr Marx.

I joined ORT in Leeds where I learned various skills. I worked for Maples in Tottenham Court Road, London, as a cabinet maker. I volunteered for the army, the Suffolk Regiment, later transferring to the Jewish Brigade.

I married an English-born Jewish girl. After demobilization I worked for numerous cabinet makers in the East End and further afield. During slack times I worked for J Lyons Teashops cleaning windows, lavatories and doing other duties. During these spells of unemployment, I worked in an iron foundry, a pickle factory, for Bryant and May making 'Gold Leaf' cigarettes and many others I have forgotten.

Together with my wife, we started a little part-time business. First we made toy furniture and tried to sell in the market. Then, more successfully, we obtained firewood from furniture manufacturers, resacked it and sold it at weekends from door to door. This eventually led to a DIY shop that we ran successfully for twenty-four years, when it was totally destroyed by fire, due to an explosion on the pavement outside. The thought of retirement was on our minds already. This was five years ago. Eventually we moved to Israel.

We have one son, who obtained a place at Oxford, and is now a lecturer at Ben Gurion University of the Negev. His wife also teaches there. They gave us five beautiful grandchildren. The youngest, David, is named after my grandfather, whose grave in the old cemetery in Munich I visited a few years ago. My father died in Camp de Gurs, France, my mother and sister in Auschwitz.

*   *   *

Siegmar Silber

(Koppold, Leipzig), New Jersey, USA

LEAVING IN STYLE: AN UNABASHED REMINISCENCE

After having arrived in England on a Kindertransport late in August 1939, almost nine years later I sailed for America on 22 May 1948. I was scheduled to arrive in New York on 28 May 1948. At eleven and a half years of age, my status was to change and instead of being under the Refugee Committee letterhead my affairs (or at least some of them) went under the 'Overseas Settlement Department' legend. While labels meant nothing to me then, looking back with the accuracy of forty years of hindsight, 'Settlement' seemed wonderfully final and terribly adventurous all at the same time.

The sense of adventure was heightened by the knowledge acquired about six weeks before departure that I was able to travel to the US aboard Cunard's liner, the *Queen Elizabeth.* The travel arrangements came about as Bertha and Arthur Staff of Norwich, who had cared for my cousin Vera Ribetsky, another Kindertransportee, were emigrating to Canada. The Staffs were asked to make one last contribution to the Refugee Movement and chaperone me on the trip across the Atlantic. Greta Burkill's rather innocuous request could not be refused as the Refugee Committee did so much for the children.

Although the Staffs had planned to make their trip to Toronto a romantic 'second' honeymoon, the care of an almost twelve year old boy would not be much trouble. I would be quartered in an adjoining first class cabin paid for by the Silbers, the family I was to join in the US. Besides, leaving the Mansfield household where I had been living, was quite an emotional wrench for me and, if the Staffs were to agree, they would be doing a great *Mitzvah* for the Committee. Fortunately, the Staffs did agree, and Bertha would later tease me, in her broadly humorous octagenarian manner, about having taken me on her 'honeymoon'.

Leaving England was no simple matter. In Cambridge, I was involved in scouting, camping, home and school. The scouts arranged a farewell party for me. The event was written up in the local Cambridge newspaper. I felt like quite a celebrity with such a fuss being made. The Cambridge scouts had also arranged a last camping trip for me in mid-May about a week before embarking for America.

School also changed for me just before leaving for America. While I was usually among the top few students in any given subject, the dislocation I anticipated severely shook my concentration. Mr Crapper was my French and geography instructor at Cambridgeshire High School for Boys. He entered remarks on the written report excusing my lapse in performance – instead of first or second in class, I was now sixth or seventh – and his report continued by wishing me well in my new life. Beneath the stern English schoolmaster's exterior, an unsuspecting warmth was demonstrated.

On the home front, Aunt Elsie and her brother, Uncle Len Mansfield were also more forgiving. While I was never spoiled in the modest life style of Eden Street, Cambridge, some extra leeway was provided during the last few weeks. There were extra trips with Aunt Elsie to W Heffer and Sons Ltd., Booksellers, so that I could add a few Arthur Ransome books to my collection and even a few volumes on English natural history. The Silbers were bemused by my coming to America with very few clothes and a 'ton' of books. Auntie also stretched the budget (she was a charlady and a spinster) to take me to the Red Lion Tea Room. Before I left Cambridge, Len, a butler at Trinity Hall College, brought home from his buttery extra ice cream and even an orange or two. These were simple statements of deep attachments.

My leaving brought forth warm, human qualities from schoolmasters, scout leaders, and others in my small universe. The style with which I was sent off and my experiences from 1939 to 1948 made me a staunch defender of the English. Later in life I would argue fiercely that the English people were emotional and loving, despite their reputation for detachment and stoicism. Understanding this as I did, I left England secure in my own self.

Time came for departure from Cambridge and everybody saw me off at the railay station with Aunt Elsie continuing on with me to London. Once there, it was Madame Tussaud's, the British Museum, and the Victoria and Albert Museum. Then, off to Southampton and the *Queen Elizabeth.*

The letter which follows was addressed to my cousin Vera Ribetsky in America, from Greta Burkhill of the Cambridge Refugee Comdmittee, a group with strong Quaker connections.

* * *

THE CAMBRIDGE REFUGEE COMMITTEE
(Recognised by the Central Committee for Refugees)

CHAIRMAN
Prof. D. WINTON THOMAS

HON. TREASURER
R . B. BRAITHWAITE

OFFICE: 55, HILLS ROAD, CAMBRIDGE
TEL. 3791

OFFICE HOURS
Monday-Friday 11-1, 2.30-5   Saturdays 11-1

HON. SECRETARIES
MISS HILDA STURGE
DR. H. A. SCHLOSSMANN

CHILDREN'S COMMITTEE
From   Mrs. BURKILL

In replying, please quote

13th January, 1947

Dear Vera,

Many thanks for your letter of the 17th December. I quite see that you are keen to have Siegmar with you in America; but you must, of course, understand that the parting for Miss Mansfield and for Siegmar will be very hard indeed.

I do not think that Miss Mansfield is quite as old a lady as you think, but I remember that at your age I thought everyone over 35 was ancient! Miss Mansfield, as you know, has not had an easy life, and Siegmar does mean a tremendous amount to her. I think you and the foster-parents whom you have found for Siegmar must understand all this, and you must go half-way to help Miss Mansfield to get over this great pain and sorry and make her feel that Siegmar is going to people who will love him as dearly as she has done, and who will care for him both physically and emotionally in the same way as he has been cared for in Cambridge.

/sorrow/

I would therefore be very grateful if you would ask the foster-parents to write to Miss Mansfield personally and tell her what sort of home they have got, and what sort of life they are going to give little Siegmar. You know, of course, that he is a very intelligent and very sensitive child, and he needs a very deep understanding.

I would very much like my cousin, Miss Hertha Vogelstein, 527 Riverside Drive, New York 2?, to go and visit your friends and let me have a personal report about her impressions. You met my cousin at the party, and she is now doing welfare work amongst Jewish foster homes, and even in her normal work in New York she would quite likely ultimately visit the home; but I do feel that if you could ask these people to let my cousin come and see them and talk to them, it would be not only a comfort to Miss Mansfield, but also a comfort to us.

What has worried me about all these arrangements is that we have never had a line from Paula since she went to Detroit. It is, after all, she who is responsible for the Koppold children, and she has never written and told us what she thinks of your plans. I am sure she agrees with them, but I nevertheless do feel that the children are our responsibility as long as they were handed over to the Movement by their parents, and we have always felt that Paula was the oldest of all of you and was the one who was really closely connected with the three Koppold children. This is not supposed to be a harsh letter, Vera, but you know very well that I have cared for the Koppold children since September 1939, and I want to be very sure indeed that they will grow up into happy and contented human beings with a good future. I know you want the same, but I must have all the assurances possible that no mistakes are made - and you see, I happen to be a "very old lady" !

Yours very sincerely,

Greta Burkill

Dorrith Sim

(Oppenheim, Kassel), Scotland, UK

PRECIOUS ROOTS

It was my son's first break away from home. With mixed feelings I waved goodbye to him from the deck of the ' *Caledonia*' as it left the Isle of Arran on the Firth of Clyde and headed back for the mainland. David at seven looked so much like myself at that age. I can remember so much of my early childhood in pre-war Germany and these memories came back so strongly to me as I sat on the deck watching the sun setting over Goat Fell.

My parents loved all forms of sport. We travelled everywhere on bikes. I had my own seat behind my father's saddle.

In the summer, with rucksacks on our backs and our walking sticks, we climbed the hills at weekends. At other times we sailed in our three seater canoe called *Der Fuchs – The Fox* on the river Fulda, the river of our town of Kassel. Occasionally we would camp on the banks of the Fulda, a great experience for a very small girl.

In the winter we skied. I hated climbing up hills but loved coming down them. There was skating too, with skates that you clipped onto your boots.

I had two 'Opas' and two 'Omas'. Opa and Oma Lindenfeld were my mother Trudi's parents. I remember only Oma Lindenfeld, a sweet gentle lady, but I think they must both have died when I was quite young.

My Opa Oppenheim was a doctor. I saw them most days. If I was ever ill, I would go and stay with my Oma. She would ignore Opa's fancy prescriptions and dispense old fashioned remedies like putting a stocking full of hot potatoes around your sore throat. She would let me play with a wonderful collection of lead soldiers, battleships and air balloons and my Opa would bring out his microscope or his stereoscopic viewer and cards.

I had an exciting first day at school. For weeks beforehand my mother had been collecting all sorts of different sweets for me, all the while pretending she was buying them for other children. When I was ready for school I was presented with a gigantic cardboard cone full of these confections and off I marched to school. Of course the other children all had their cones. I don't remember too much about the school except that we wrote on slates and besides the three Rs we studied Hebrew and learned games in the playground.

At one time I know we lived in a beautiful flat in a house with a flat roof and a balcony where my parents grew tomatoes and entertained their friends. I had my sandpit there and a wonderful chute which my father had made for me.

After we left there, our accommodation became more limited and my parents explained to me that being Jewish we had to be very careful about what we did and said and where we went. A suitcase was always kept ready and packed for my father in case he would be sent away.

Then came the morning I arrived at school to find it wrecked, and men removing and destroying all they could lay their hands on. A man said to me: 'You'd better go home. It will be a long time before you're back here again.'

It must have been about then that my Oma and Opa went off to Canada.

We were in another house again. This time living with two elderly Jewish brothers and their sister. They had a shop set up in one room because by this time we were banned from visiting the shops in town. People knew to expect trouble that night and my mother had brought some Jewish children out of a Home to stay with us. The Nazis came in that night and knocked the shop about, pulling down all the cupboards with their contents. They took away valuables from my mother and father, including the cup for swimming which my mother had been so proud of. They did not take my mother away because of the children, but they took away my father. I remember how relieved and happy my mother was when he walked back into the house in the afternoon.

Then there was the task of getting me out of Germany to England. Early each morning my mother and I went to the Town Hall to see an important man called Herr Schmidt. Each day we went away empty handed and I cannot remember how often we called there until the morning when he finally produced the documents which allowed me to leave.

My parents got me ready for the journey. They tried to teach me some English. All I succeeded in learning was 'I want to go to the WC' and 'I have a handkerchief in my pocket'. Among my clothes they packed a box full of precious family photographs, my own set of cutlery to which I still cling, and as a remembrance of them, the toilet case, cloth and soap which my father had taken with him to the First World War, where I knew, both my father and my Opa had won Iron Crosses.

I recall arriving at the railway station in Hamburg. I was carrying my toy dog Droll and my red leather shoulder-bag. I dropped Droll underneath the train and a man climbed down and rescued him. We children boarded the train to get our places. Then I was sent off again to say farewell to my mother and father. I can see them to this day. They were standing in a corridor behind a barrier. I said my goodbyes and then walked back up the long corridor away from them and into the train.

*   *   *

Ilse Sinclair

(Guttentag, Hamburg), Bristol, UK

I came over from Hamburg, Germany, in 1939 aged seventeen. I became a children's nanny, a Path Lab technician, a member of the National Fire Service in Guildford, and married a German-Jewish doctor, who had qualified in Germany in 1933.

I have been living in Bristol ever since 1945 and have three children – an optician, a medical social worker married to a reform Rabbi (with three children) and a consultant anaethetist.

My husband, who started a workshop for the elderly and other projects, died ten years ago.

I have been a marriage counsellor for over thirty years and helped to start a youth counselling service. I worked as a tutor-supervisor for the National Marriage Guidance Council for fifteen years and became a sex therapist.

* * *

Sam Smith

London, UK

THE BOYS' HOSTEL, 1 LINTON ROAD, OXFORD

In March 1942 my wife Judith and I were invited by the Oxford Refugee Committee to be joint wardens of the hostel.

It became our task to create and keep a Jewish atmosphere. Judith was responsible for all the duties of a house-mother; the kitchen, *kashrut,* general hygiene and so on. I became responsible for the religious and educational upbringing and also for budgeting, book-keeping and purchasing, as well as preparing and giving monthly reports to the Committee.

We always had between thirty and thirty-five boys, aged between six and sixteen in the hostel. During the period 1942-1948 about a hundred boys lived with us.

We also had our own son, Uri David, who was born in March 1940 who was soon accepted as the baby of the hostel by all the boys.

Every Friday evening we laid the tables with white tablecloths, we lit the *Shabbat* candles and made *Kiddush*; we had a nice *Shabbat* meal and sang *Zemirot.* On Saturday morning and on every holy day and at *Motza'e Shabbat* we always made *Havdalah.* This was usually followed by a meeting, when the weekly events were discussed and the house duties allocated. Each boy had his own initials or number sewn on his laundry. Socks had to be mended and buttons sewn on. Thus friends and other invited ladies came every week to a 'mending party'. These became social occasions for the boys to meet people of the town, and this in turn led to their being invited into the homes of local people.

Every *Shabbat* and also during the week, the boys received religious and Hebrew instruction given by Dr Wieder and Dr Ch Rabin and I helped with *Bar Mitzvah* preparation.

The *Pesach Seder* was always a special occasion to which many Jewish members of the Armed Forces were invited; amongst them many Americans who always brought additional food rations and also gifts for the boys. At these evenings, we had sixty to eighty people at the *Seder* table.

We also had our problems. Colds and influenza had their victims. Luckily, Judith, who is a trained nurse, knew how to cope with all this, in addition to her matron and cook duties.

We went through a very difficult period in 1943 when Judith, who was expecting our second son, became very ill with toxaemia and had to be hospitalized. We had one help in the hostel at that time. But the Committee and all the boys came to the rescue, and when Judith came home with our baby Gordon, both were received with great happiness. Gordon was the first baby born in the hostel. Everybody was on their best behaviour; everybody wanted to push the pram and Uri, who was then three and a half years old, took his brotherly responsibilities very seriously.

One of the boys, who had been referred to us by the Juvenile Court, needed additional help given by the Oxford Child Guidance Clinic. But his deep resentment against his parental background needed special help, and he was transferred to a special school.

Another boy, who was very pleasant and rather quiet and withdrawn, received a Red Cross letter saying that his father had died. With the help of our local Rabbi we arranged for him to attend prayers and to say *Kaddish,* which the boy did for a year.

Another boy developed osteomyelitis and after hospital treatment needed a lengthy convalescence at home.

We received Jewish boys not only from the Kindertransport but also from the general Jewish population.

When the boys passed school leaving age, they either started occupational training or went on to higher education. However, in 1945 we received five boys who had come after the war from concentration camps. This produced a testing period for all the boys for some time.

After the end of the war, it became our duty to help in the reunification of families with the help of the Red Cross and the various refugee organizations. There were many happy, but also some sad, situations. In one case in 1947, a mother arrived to meet her boy, whom she had not seen for more than eight years. She cried when I introduced her son, but she cried even more when she realized that she could not communicate with him. She could not speak English and the boy could not speak German any more. I had the difficult task of being the interpreter in such an emotional situation.

Slowly the boys were claimed by relatives and the hostel was closed in 1948.

From time to time in later years we met some of the boys, especially during our stay in Israel, or by correspondence from Australia. But the greatest pleasure was to meet some boys, now in their fifties, at the Fiftieth Anniversary Reunion at the Harrow Leisure Centre in June 1989.

*　　*　　*

Eve Soumerai

(Nussbaum, Berlin), West Hartford, USA

I was twelve years old, living in an apartment in Berlin with my mother, father, great-aunt and brother. I was accustomed to noises in the night, but those of 9 November were different. The sirens, sounds of smashing glass and drums and shouts, *'Stellt die Juden an die Wand'* (Put the Jews against the wall), frightened me.

The next morning the sun came up as though nothing special had happened and off I went to school.

Just around the corner was my family's Synagogue, which my great grandfather had helped to found. It lay in ruins: ugly, charred, blackened, with glass all over the pavement and people milling around, some laughing, some crying.

In front of me, on the ground, lay a particularly pretty piece of stained glass. I picked it up and held it in my hand. Suddenly I heard hysterical laughter behind me. I clasped the piece of glass and ran home as fast as I could.

'Eve,' called Mrs Müller, standing in the basement laundry of the apartment building where we lived. She was not Jewish. Maybe she would know what was happening.

'Drunks,' she said, assuring that it would not happen again. Germany was a civilized, Christian country. She took my hand, saw it was cut from the glass and washed and bandaged it.

Then Mrs Müller put a tray of apples in my hands, apples sitting on pieces of white bread, and told me to give them to my mother to bake in our oven.

I ran upstairs where my mother, great-aunt and brother were in varying stages of panic. Where had I been? I should have stayed home. I offered the apples by way of response.

During the night there were more terrible noises, shots and screams. What was going to happen next? Suddenly there was a knock at the door. My mother was sure it was the Nazis. My brother and I were frozen to the spot. But not my father. He was sure it was someone in need of shelter.

Outside stood a frightened young man, trying to get away from the Nazis. He had seen our name on the mailbox and decided to take a chance that we would help. My father fetched the French brandy reserved for special occasions. He poured the young man a glass and added a lump of sugar. The man sipped the drink slowly.

He told us his name was Adolf and asked how he might make an exit through the back alleys. My father explained and had him repeat the instruction. After one more sip of the brandy, Adolf prepared to leave, in much improved spirits. He thanked us and shook my father's hand.

We finished the last apple. We had a respite from the horrible happenings outside. The bluish-white light from the street lamp continued to shine on us – the little group huddled together waiting for the storm to subside.

I am the only survivor of that little group. Fifty years later I wonder what, if anything, the world has learned from Kristallnacht.

Have we learned that indifference to seemingly harmless acts of prejudice and discrimination – graffiti on the wall, an ethnic or racial joke – can lead to violence and destruction? Have we learned that one people's suffering cannot be viewed as just another special interest, but must be everyone's concern?

Eve Soumerai is director of the human-rights literacy project of the Connecticut-Western Massachusetts region of the National Conference of Christians and Jews.

Reprinted by kind permission from *The Hartford Courant*, USA.

*   *   *

Steven C Spronz

Los Angeles, USA

I am a child of a child of the children's transports. My father, Richard, died in 1981. I am left to tell his story and to the extent that it has been woven into the fabric of my family lore, which he transmitted to me, it is my story as well.

My father was born in Vienna, Austria on 4 October 1925 to working-class parents. My grandfather was a shoemaker, my grandmother a dressmaker. When word reached the community in late 1938 that unaccompanied children would be allowed to leave for England in the company of Rabbi Schonfeld, parents flooded the *Kultusgemeinde* with requests that their children be chosen. My grandfather came home from several visits to the council livid that he had to argue to have his son accepted on the transports. Since there were more children than places, the acceptance process must have involved a '*Selektion*' of Jewish children. My father was an active member of the *Agudath Israel* youth organization and he said that it might have been because of his active participation in the youth group that he was chosen.

My father left Vienna in December 1938, with one of the first transports. For the first couple of hours after the train left Vienna, he sat withdrawn and numb except for a few tearful bouts at the thought of leaving home. It had not yet occurred to him that he might never see his parents again. After a while, it became an adventure, he said, as the train crossed national boundaries and the Channel crossing drew nearer.

Almost immediately following my father's arrival in London, he was sent with a group to Portsmouth where he attended the Portsmouth Grammar School until the outbreak of the Second World War.

He had two categories of memories from his time at Portsmouth. First, he recalled the cameraderie among the other children of the transports, learning a new language from grammar texts, from interaction with Englishmen, and by reading an English translation of the Bible alongside the Hebrew original.

The second category relates to his repeatedly frustrated attempts to have school officials, the transport organizers, and officials of the British Jewish community arrange for native Englishmen to sponsor his parents so they could flee Hitler. On one occasion, my father and several of the other transport boys 'ran away' (my father's words) from the school to London to plead their case before officials of British Jewry. They had heard that transport children who remained in London were often able to locate English Jews (usually by going from shop to shop in London's East End) who would sponsor their families still on the Continent. Their pleas were to no avail. They were all thirteen years old at the time.

With the outbreak of war, the students at Portsmouth Grammar School were evacuated to Shefford, where they attended the relocated Jewish Secondary School and were billeted with non-Jewish English families.

From the years in Shefford, my father recalled the bucolic environment; the terrible fright the first time he unknowingly bumped against a cow in a field at night; soccer games; serious study; the observance of Jewish holidays with his classmates; excelling in mathematics and being offered a scholarship to study mathematics at university; turning down that opportunity because, in what must have been a period of adolescent rebellion, he wanted to be completely self-reliant and not accept scholarship assistance; and thinking about his parents left behind in Vienna and assuming that they had been killed in the Holocaust.

Of the staff at Shefford, my father mentioned only his mathematics teacher, whose name may have been Mr Levine and Mrs Grunfeld. In Mrs Grunfeld he found one of the few adults in whom he could confide and who provided comfort and understanding.

Around the time of high school graduation (I am guessing that this was 1942 or 1943), my father returned to London where he began working and studying architecture at the University of London (Northern Polytechnic).

During late May 1945 a soldier who had met my grandparents advised my father that his parents had survived Theresienstadt. He visited them in Vienna late in 1945 or early 1946 under a United Nations passport.

My grandparents emigrated to the United States at the beginning of 1947, and since my aunt had already settled there, my father reluctantly left England a few months later to be reunited with his family. My parents married in 1952 and my father practised architecture in New York until his death. My parents produced two healthy, upright, happy and successful children.

At about age five or six, I began to learn the history of my family in the context of the history of the Jewish people. I noticed that my grandfather spoke with an accent and I learned that he came from another country. I asked my father about it and he began telling me the history of our family. When I was eight or nine years old, I heard his story of the children's transports.

As I grew older, my father shared with me more and more of his experiences. He did not embellish his recollections in the least; however, as a child they seemed to me to be romantic and heroic exploits. It was not hard to commit his recollections to memory. When I strip away the romantic veneer which I once placed over my father's experiences, the rather harsh realities of having to flee from home as a child, of arriving in a strange country and the difficulties of growing up during the years of early adolescence, which are usually difficult under the best of circumstances, come into very clear focus. But even with the veneer gone, I am still amazed that there were Jews and non-Jews who cared enough to expend time, money and tremendous effort to save Jewish children, feed, clothe and house them, and provide them with secular and Jewish education. Transportees who are alive today are testimony to a great miracle. Like all miracles, it took much blood, sweat and tears to achieve, and it was not without its shortfalls and outright failures. However, this does not diminish the greatness of either the effort or the result.

Please tell your children the story and urge your fellow transportees to do the same. We read in the Passover *Haggadah* that one must see oneself as if one had personally participated in the Exodus from Egypt, and further, that one must teach the story of the Exodus to one's children. The reason is simple. Jewish history is a collective as well as an individual experience. To become part of our people's national consciousness, the story needs to be told again and again. To be imbued with it allows the recipient first to feel a part of that history and second, to take its lessons to heart.

*   *   *

Alice Staller

(Buchholz, Vienna), California, USA

I came to London in May 1939. My father, a freelance journalist, had persuaded several people to pledge support for me so that I could continue my education. I was met by one lady who acted as my guardian, while another assumed responsibility for room and board. I was entered for Michael Hall School for the remainder of the term.

As support dwindled, I was taken along with the school for the students' summer holidays to a farm near Combe Martin, where I worked as a maid. The school was later evacuated to Minehead and my activity as household help became full time, ending my schooling. I learned later that the school's headmaster had given his wife, who ran the 'dorm', an allowance of 2s. 6d. for me which she kept for herself. I was without means and recall phoning my mother in London, courtesy of a kind garage owner in the village. She forwarded some money to me for a rail ticket to come to London and join her. The family, where my mother was working as housekeeper, let me stay with her. I needed work, but no matter which job I aspired to, I had first to prove that there was no English worker available to fill the position.

Eventually, after a couple of jobs, the man for whom my mother worked, apprenticed me to his office book-keeper. Later I transferred to a big company, Spiers and Pond, where I worked for several years until my emigration to the United States.

Meanwhile, my father, who had gone to France to do some journalistic work, was picked up as an Austrian citizen, of all ironies, and ended up in a concentration camp in Vichy France. He survived and received permission to visit us in London, where my mother had undergone major surgery. When we saw this skeletal apparition we asked that he should be allowed to stay with us until we could all go to the USA. This was denied and he had to return to Vienna, where he shortly collapsed from a heart attack and died. My mother went ahead of me to America and I followed in 1949 when my quota came up.

*   *   *

Francis Steiner

(Vienna), Oxford, UK

My memories of the Kindertransport are patchy; I don't remember anything about my last day in Vienna, 10 December, except trying to catch a glimpse of my parents as the train drew out, and calling out of the window *'Ich komme wieder'* – which perhaps set me off a little from the others who were emigrating less reluctantly! Other memories are of the cold in the unheated chalets of the Pakefield Hall Holiday Camp near Lowestoft to which we were taken from Harwich. And of the first open coal fire I ever saw in my life, that in the study of the Catholic priest in Lowestoft, who took on the problems of our small group, when it became clear that the camp really would not do in that severe December.

All of which shows experiences different from the majority of the *Kinder,* not surprising in a boy from the perhaps ten per cent of 'non Aryan' *Kinder* of Catholic and Protestant faiths. I too was of course a potential victim of the *Shoah* and therefore had to leave, but I lacked experience of Jewish upbringing and, ungenerously, solidarity with all these others. I had been to a monastic school in Vienna where the staff had done their best for the non-Aryan boys, and to which I felt and still feel devoted. I felt essentially Austrian which made me regard the *Anschluss* as not merely the invasion by the Nazi enemy but as a foreign occupation. Which explains why it took me so long to realize that I too must save my life by emigration, but that I still resented having to do it. However, if I had to go, England was my favoured destination and I hoped to be allowed to stay, rather than be made to go on to an overseas destination.

The majority of the *Kinder* did not know anything about our background and problems and when the first Quaker mission came to call at Pakefield Hall Camp, and called for an assembly of the non-Jewish children, there was great surprise that there were any. When the camp was evacuated, our little group did not go to Dovercourt with the rest; we were sent to a boarding house in Felixstowe. After two months there I was taken in by a monastic boarding school, run by the same Benedictine order that had run my Viennese *Gymnasium* before the Nazis closed it down. It was the beginning of an education and career in England which took wholly unexpected turns.

With an English wife from an old-established farming background I have, on the surface, settled into English life and society, but some problems of identity remain. Fifty years ago I thought these involved the two strands of my country of origin and my country of adoption. Today I realize that there are three strands, and after 'fifty years among the Gentiles' I am more conscious of my Jewish background and of my long dead Jewish ancestors.

*　　*　　*

Marianne Schechter

Kibbutz Lavee, Israel

STORY BY SIDNEY L STERN

Marianne came to England with the Kindertransport in December 1938 from Germany, where all her family were lost. She stayed with my grandmother, Mrs Kate Simmons, who already had thirteen children of her own (nine girls and four boys) for four years, and was always regarded as the fourteenth child.

One incident vividly recalled by one of my aunts whilst Marianne was living with my grandmother is rather poignant. One of my uncles, who was in the Fire Service, came into the living room, and immediately Marianne burst into tears and ran from the room. It transpired that she had thought the blue uniform denoted an SS man!

Marianne went on *Hachsharah* to Thaxted in 1942, and then to South Wales, where she met and married her husband, Marcus Schechter. They went on *Aliyah* to Israel in 1948, and were founder members of *Kibbutz Lavee*, where they lived in tents for the first few years. They now have four children, two of whom live on *Lavee* with their families. Marianne and Marcus have twelve grandchildren.

Marcus was the manager of the guest house until fairly recently, when he retired, and Marianne was running the children's nursery until a year or so ago, when she took a course in needlecraft, which she now practises happily on the Kibbutz.

*　　*　　*

Robert Sugar

(Vienna), New York, USA

I left Vienna at the age of eight, arriving in London by way of Hook of Holland and Harwich on 1 December 1938. From London I went on to a hostel in Belfast, where there were already thirty or so other children, all older than I, some almost adults. I was tremendously unhappy in the hostel and would have run away, had I any idea where to run.

In the summer of 1939 we were all sent to a *Hachsharah* run by a group of German and Austrian *Chalutzim*. Conditions were primitive – but for us it was liberation. It was our farm, and to me it was almost our own country – our own houses, fields, animals, workshops. I tell the story in the brief article I attach, from *World Over*, a Jewish children's magazine. I did not intend to lie when I wrote the story, but I wrote it in reality for our children, who were then still quite young, and it's a protective story. It sounds like a great adventure. The facts are true, but as I read it now, it is not the truth. It does not deal with emotions. And that is what I'm hoping to get out of our reunion – finally some honest emotion. Because when I think of those days, which I do often lately, I am amazed at the lack of emotion shown to us, by those who saved us, and our own lack of emotion. We were all brave little soldiers. It was quite amazing how we accepted everything. I was eight then, am fifty-eight now and I think I am finally getting very upset. In my story, I tell that my parents did survive. But my grandmother, and her brother, a destitute war invalid, were deported and massacred in Minsk. As the years go by the pain in my heart for these dear old people only grows deeper. It will never heal.

A PLACE FOR JACOBI
by Robert Sugar

When I told my children of my childhood as a refugee I did not tell the story in one sitting, but in a series of short stories over many years. Individually each of the stories was quite true, but collectively they formed a sort of myth. I told them how I left Vienna in December 1938, alone, as a boy of eight; how I came to the dismal hostel in Belfast; and how we were miraculously rescued and sent to the farm. The farm was a Jewish refugee farm on the coast of County Down. There, about a dozen of us, all around ten years old, ran free for that first summer of 1939, on Jewish fields next to the Irish Sea. And there most of us stayed till well after the war. There most of us became orphans, except for Little Max, and myself, whose parents did survive. And the farm is the focus of most of these stories – some comic, some adventurous, all jaunty. In fact, I wrote these stories down some years ago and tried to publish them, but they were rejected. The most telling criticism was that they lacked emotion. It's true, they did. I had been so desolated by my separation from my parents, that in order to survive I had literally reinvented myself as a tough, adventurous kid, who had no emotions. And I formed the stories in my head at that time. Even though my fake toughness left me many years ago, the stories themselves have stayed the same.

Once, one of my children asked: 'Who took care of you on the farm?' And I answered immediately: 'No-one. We grew up by ourselves.' And this too is partly true, and partly myth. But here the fault is not only mine, it's also Jacobi's. He was so self-effacing, so elusive in real life, that even in memory he hid in my stories, skipping from one to the other as a minor character, never the hero of his own tale. But now I think it is time to give Jacobi his own story.

There were about thirty of us, in the Kindertransport group that came to the farm. More than half were adolescents and we, the dozen youngest, came to be called the children of the farm. And for the first year or so no-one

Kindertransport group, mixed with Chalutzim and some Irish visitors. The summer of victory, July 1945. (Robert Sugar)

actually took care of us. Somebody cooked meals, and others washed clothing, and someone made sure we were in bed. But there was no one person who stepped forward to be a mother or father to us, though there were a number of actual parents on the farm. Strange in retrospect, but at the time we took this for granted. But then Jacobi appeared. He was from Vienna, a bachelor, between thirty and forty years old. He was bald, less than five feet tall, immensely broad and very heavy, though he carried his weight well.

Jacobi, we found out, was the black sheep of a middle class family, most of whom were doctors. He played the saxophone in Vienna, was a night person and gambler, a maths genius and champion billiards and ping-pong player. He was put in charge of the medicine chest, because of his medical background, and in charge of the children, because no-one else would do the job. At first we barely acknowledged his presence. Who could take him seriously? But then, unnoticed at first, things began to change.

I had become deeply depressed. My mother, who had actually escaped to London, had returned to Vienna, to get my father and her mother to flee to Shanghai, and had been trapped by the war. I, who had thought my mother safe and had therefore felt special, was suddenly abandoned a second time.

As my tenth birthday approached my depression grew even deeper. Then a surprise! The children made me a party. There was a cake, Anni sang one of her beautiful, sad, Yiddish songs. I got a little notebook, and a leather wallet, made on the farm. I have the leather wallet still, my most prized possession. For years I thought the party had been my friends' idea. That's why I think it saved my life. I don't even remember Jacobi being there. And of course, from then on, everyone got a party.

Then came the great school revolt. We were sent to the public elementary school in Millisle, a little house of horrors presided over by a tyrannical headmaster. He caned the local kids, mercilessly and automatically, for the slighest infractions, for mis-spelled words, though to be fair, he spared us at first, as foreigners. Big Max made a miniature deck of cards with which he and I played under the desk. We were reciting the principal cities of England – Derby, Chesterfield, Buxton, Matlock. The headmaster approached unseen, snatched Big Max's text book and twenty-four little green cards fluttered to the floor. He hurled Max's book across the room: 'Throw your books into the sea,' he yelled. 'Hitler was right!' The whole class laughed. Even we. But it was friendly laughter. Our group had been popular with the other kids all along – this defiance of the common oppressor only increased our popularity.

We laughed but we didn't forget. It was winter 1939/40. We had grown out of the warm clothing in which we arrived and now wore thin blue English school coats. We had no gloves. It rained constantly. Waves broke over the sea wall along the road to school. We developed an idea. What if we start to walk to school, then turn back and say we can't go further. The waves are too high. It actually worked one day. But the second time we tried disaster befell us. Dr Kohner, a Prague lawyer, at this time one of the farm leaders, was enraged – 'You're acting like ghetto Jews, you're making a bad impression!' He lined us up, army style, and left, right, left marched us back to school. He asked the headmaster – in our interest of course – to clamp down on us. And the headmaster did. Instead of four sums homework, which was the regular dose, we got sixteen each. Not a joke at all. We could spend all night doing this. But the forces of collaboration and oppression did not reckon with Jacobi, our resistance hero. I don't want to lose you in the details, but Jacobi organized the group into copying teams so that each of us did only four sums as in the past, but we arrived in the morning with sixteen perfect answers. Perhaps a small thing, still, to have someone on your side is no small thing to a child.

It became clear to Jacobi that we were all miserable in the village school. Unknown to us at the time, each day the farm-cart went to a neighbouring town to deliver produce. Jacobi hitched a ride. In town, without directions, he walked around looking for what seemed to him a good school. A grammar school. And then he simply walked in, five foot tall, with his head cocked to one side, his shy but expectant smile (I imagine) and simply asked if there would be room for some refugee children. And he found places for all of us, and on top of that – he convinced the Belfast Jewish Refugee Committee to pay for our education. Not a little thing at all, to get good education for twelve children.

But the most vivid memory of Jacobi is of the winter of 1940/41. We, the younger boys, slept in an unheated dormitory in a wooden hut, among the older boys. Jacobi, as an adult was entitled to a small room, a cubicle. In this cubicle there was a single coil electric heater, an unheard of luxury. As it grew colder it suddenly occurred to Jacobi that he would change places with four of us. Two huge bunk beds were crammed into the tiny cubicle while Jacobi slept in the dormitory among the older boys. Also no small matter, because Jacobi was quite conscious of his odd appearance, and very private about his body. In his room four of us were warm for the first time since we came to Ireland. At bedtime, with the electric heater hissing, Jacobi would come into the room and read to us – not 'Little Bear' stories, but I remember precisely – 'The Ragged Trousered Philanthropists' by Robert Tressell. And so we fell asleep, pitying the poor workers of England. This was the winter that invasion seemed imminent. Outside our room the fields and coastline were totally unguarded. Nazi parachutists could have dropped down any minute, without opposition. We were not tested. But had they come I am certain Jacobi would have stayed with us.

Jacobi left the farm in 1946, quietly, with a shy smile. We didn't even give him a farewell party. I invited him a few times in New York, where, still a bachelor, he was selling window display signs to stores, door to door. The last time I saw him was in the sixties. I was married, and our first child was about one year old. It was awkward. I had so much more than he. Our roles were reversed. Then he went to Los Angeles, where he had a sister, and some years later I heard he had died. The children of the farm are now scattered in England, the Americas and Israel. Some of us have done very well. Among us are an architect, a professor of chemistry, an industrialist, a high-fashion dress designer, a *kibbutznik,* mother of many children and heroes of Israel. On the rare occasions when we meet, of course we talk about the old days, and sometimes about Jacobi. The truth is for most he has remained a figure of fun – a roly poly little man, who ran around the farm bringing cups of soup to the sick; who hurled his great weight around the ping pong table with amazing grace; a bachelor who was never seen with a woman, who took care of a dozen children, among them girls who were becoming women.

I think I was his favourite. But even to me it occurred only very recently, that in fact there *had* been someone who had taken care of us. And that in all the years on the farm, when most of my friends became orphans, there was only one person who loved the children of the farm, and that was Jacobi.

Were Jacobi still alive I would certainly have put his name forward to be invited as a guest of honour at our great reunion. As it is, I'd simply like a place for him in our collective memory. I promise he'll make no demands.

Gerda Svarny

(Polinecer, Vienna), London, UK

There I was, standing on a crowded platform, while friends and relations were reunited. Gradually the platform emptied and only a few children like me remained. In the end only I was left. Was there nobody to meet me? Perhaps it all was a ghastly mistake. Suddenly a flustered lady pulling a little girl behind her rushed up to me, peered at my label and said in German, 'Oh yes, you are Gerda. I nearly forgot you in my excitement. You see your people were unable to meet you here, so I am to take you with me to London, where they will pick you up.' My misery was made even greater by the journey to London. The little girl was the lady's own child and since they had just been reunited they were wrapped up in their own happiness.

Eventually we arrived in London and this time my 'new family' was there to meet me. I looked at them shyly. She was a thin tallish lady and her husband a rather chubby and jolly man. With them was a boy about my own age. The lady extended a limp hand to me, there was an awkward silence. I don't know what I expected, but I was disappointed, and I felt the lady was expecting someone quite different from this tear-stained miserable child facing her. So it was that after two months I was sent somewhere else and unfortunately I don't even recall the family's name.

Of course now I view the situation quite differently, for had it not been for the generosity of heart of these people, I would most certainly not be alive today.

*   *   *

Alfred Terry

(Tery, Vienna), Grantham, UK

This isn't the first time I've written my story, you know! It'll do you good to read it, dear stranger.

I was born at a very early age and soon became a precocious and cheeky little boy in my beautiful city of Vienna. At the age of eleven, being the only child of my parents Paul and Gisela Tery, I even managed to beat that criminal murderer Hitler and his gang of deranged followers, back there before the war, whilst many millions were soon to fall victim to his evil intent. The thought of having survived and beaten him is quite exhilarating at times, but it also leaves you with a certain guilt-feeling as well. Could I have helped others to escape death? Why didn't I manage to persuade my own parents to flee?

Recriminations at this late stage won't bring anybody back, that's for sure, and facing the facts now is the only way forward.

A very short time after the *Anschluss,* one of those thousands of despicable

This document of identity is issued with the approval of His Majesty's Government in the United Kingdom to young persons to be admitted to the United Kingdom for educational purposes under the care of the Inter-Aid Committee for children.

THIS DOCUMENT REQUIRES NO VISA.

PERSONAL PARTICULARS. ...

Name _TERY ALFRED_

Sex _MALE_ Date of Birth _20-7-27_

Place _VIENNA_

Full Names and Address of Parents

TERY PAUL + GISELA

73 5 LIECHTENSTEINSTRASSE

VIENNA IX

Germans who flocked into Vienna in the wake of the tanks, came and swindled us out of our little shop, which almost made my father explode with rage. If my mother and I hadn't dragged him away by force, he would have been arrested on the spot and probably never heard of again. My father was a private tutor in classical languages and all his private students (most of whom were Jewish and thus thrown out of their educational establishments, as indeed I was) had to leave him quite quickly, thus precipitating a complete nervous breakdown in this highly educated man, and leaving us as a family totally without any income at all. He used to spend his days roaming the streets and tearing his hair. There was such a change in my father; it was hard to believe, if one hadn't witnessed it. My mother went cleaning in the flat of Frau Professor Tedesco nearby. This nice lady's book collection now became my greatest fascination.

We heard about the possibility of children being sponsored in England, and in the summer of 1938 we applied. But that was just the start of it. We needed documents for me (much complicated by the fact that my father was stateless at the time) and there was no-one in my family to make the dozens of journeys from one office to another, and as most will know, all official offices were swamped with frightened people, all trying to obtain papers and documents. It took sheer determination, a lot of time and energy to run from one end of the city to the other (you were of course thwarted by officialdom at each and every opportunity) to try to get those papers, and I can assure you it wasn't easy. I did all this alone and without any help from an adult, weaving round the city on my bicycle in the summer heat of 1938, and after a lot of effort, had managed to obtain every single certification and document by the start of the winter. We had a small flat which was quite humble, and from which I set out each morning on my allotted task for that day. How exactly my father spent each day was a mystery to me, but with his nerves in the state they were in, you couldn't ask the simplest favour of him most of the time.

Now came the biggest hurdle of all and those of you who stood outside the passport office in the *Prinz Eugen Strasse* will know precisely what I mean. It was closely guarded by a German guard post at the entrance gate, who allowed just a certain number of shivering Jews, who had been queuing for many days and nights (in the cold and snow) into the building when they felt like it. The building itself was like an old palace, and contained on the first floor a large hall with about twenty-one different tables at which each and every one it was necessary to stop and present just one certain declaration or document. At the last desk you paid the passport fee, and usually about three weeks later you had to return (with a time-stamped pass) to collect your passport. Everything was made as awkward as possible, and the mile-long queue around the building was well known among the many who tried to get papers. You stood thus patiently, members of families taking turns until you finally were allowed in. There was no other way unless you knew of a miracle, but these were few. Fortunately I myself had such a miracle, and that is the reason why I can now sit writing this story.

When I arrived (clutching my thick folder of previous papers and documents obtained) on the very early morning tram in the *Prinz Eugen Strasse*, and the snow lay on the ground in November, I immediately saw the hopelessness of the situation, which my mother had already tried to impress upon me earlier. I did not even bother to join the immense queue, and just tramped up and down to get my feet warm. Shivering with cold at about 6 am in the greying damp of that November morning, I was suddenly approached by a complete stranger who was, I noticed, wearing the dreaded chromium-plated swastika badge and immediately my instinct was to run as fast as my legs could carry me.

I was clutching my precious papers with all my might (not a lot, because I was a very small boy really) as the man tried his best to reassure me. He invited me to a nearby café for some breakfast, and quickly thinking it over, I decided that I would probably be safer with him in there than out here in the street alone, and so reluctantly I followed. While I was eating my breakfast he started to question me, about what I was doing there and about my papers, which I would not let go on any account. He wanted to know if they were completely in order for the passport office routine, and I assured him of that fact. He seemed to know and understand the procedure so well, that I am convinced to this day, he might even have had inside knowledge through working in there. But it remains a mystery to me to this day, who he really was . . . A man who befriended a little boy, a total stranger, and to me, well I put it no higher, he saved my life . . .

Using as my cover the orphan school which arrived later that morning, with their time-stamped collective pass able to enter the building as a group, he arranged to mix me in quickly among them, as they stepped off the tram. We were not counted by the sentry, and in a flash I was up the stairs and in the hall. Everything turned out well, except for one over-zelaous official who looked me up and down and queried my age. Knowing full well that it was my parents' job to be here, and that a child of eleven cannot get his own passport, it was necessary for me to invent a plausible story quickly, which I did rather well. Consequently I managed to get right through (the man even helped me when he heard my tale) and was never happier than when I had paid my fee and left the building.

Returning home, I astounded my mother and Frau Prof Tedesco with the news they found almost impossible to believe, namely that I had succeeded that morning and that soon my passport would be available.

We will now move forward in time slightly, to the moment when the much awaited children's transport finally managed to get under way. If my hazy memory of that night of 10/11 January 1939 is not playing tricks, just before midnight we said our last farewells to our parents outside in the concourse of the railway station. Soon we were speeding through the blackness of the night to an unknown fate. I listened to the bitter crying of the many smaller ones, but the welfare workers soon managed to settle everybody. Daylight arrived once more, and we began approaching the frontier with Holland. It was now the turn of the uniformed SS and other frontier guards to attempt to frighten these hundreds of little children before we came to the border. It must be said that they succeeded. They threatened that, if anything were found during the search of the train which was shortly to take place, we would be turned round and sent back to Vienna.

I remember this episode well. We sat and shivered with fright, and most small children cried. But of course it was just another subterfuge, and there was no such search; and who would have been foolish enough to carry any money or valuables after all the regulations which turned everyone into vegetables overnight, and made frightened animals out of normal human beings?

If anything makes me angry about those times, it was the total arrogance and the Master-race attitude which was so flagrantly evidenced in every act by the Germans, which seems to be a national trait still to this day.

Holland soon came, and with it that welcome bun and cup of lemon tea which each and every one received. After that it was Hoek van Holland and the steamer to Harwich.

A day which will never be forgotten was 12 January 1939. This was the day I first stepped on British soil at Harwich. A new life full of surprises lay before me and it wasn't long before I had my very first. After we all underwent another medical examination, we boarded the train for London. It was towards evening when we finally arrived, and I remember a very boring hour or so, during which the various children were called over the loudspeaker and collected by their new 'parents'.

There was no-one who was remotely interested in me, so stepping outside the hall for a minute, I was astounded to find that everyone had completely melted away and I was left standing alone.

Later that evening (after I had been re-discovered at my overnight hostel) I was told that the whole of London's police force had been looking for me. I managed to enlist the help of a very rich-looking lady with a chauffeur driven car who finally delivered me (after a shopping expedition to the West End for madam) to my hostel where they welcomed me with open arms, and in amazement.

This, dear reader, is only the start of many an amazing adventure. There is a lot more to tell.

* * *

Ellen Thompson

(Cohn, Hamburg), Chorleywood, UK

I came to England in July 1939 from Hamburg to Southampton via the Kindertransport. After living in Grimsby for a few months, I went to Cambridge. Whilst there, I stayed with a non-Jewish family where I was very unhappy and badly treated. I was locked out of the house during the day and lingered around the playground. After many weeks, my class teacher, Mrs Hensher, noticed me and enquired why I was so unhappy and crying. She then asked me to write down everything I had had to eat for a week. Afterwards she asked me if I would like to live with her and very kindly took me back to her house that very day.

I was much happier living with her and her husband, who was studying to become a vicar. They always made sure that I attended Hebrew classes and lit the candles on *Chanukah*. I spent the rest of my school years with them until I went to London to study for my Nursery Nurse examinations.

Mrs Hensher is still alive and in her eighties and I am in touch with her and see her each year.

Further down the road there lived a family called Lipson who, on the festivals, invited me to join them for a meal at their home. They had three children – Judith, Anne and Stephen. Occasionally I took Judith, then two years old, out for walks in her pram. In October 1945 the Lipsons moved to Manchester and as a memento, they gave me a photograph of the three children. When I married and had a daughter of my own, I called her Judith.

Over the last twenty years I have often thought how nice it would be to contact the family again. Whenever I met anyone from Manchester I always enquired if they knew the Lipsons, but to no avail.

Last year I was invited to a *Bar Mitzvah* near to where I now live in Hertfordshire. During the meal I spoke to a gentleman from Manchester and he told me that a year or two before he had gone to Russia to trace his family. I asked him if he had heard of a family called Lipson and to my great amazement he told me I was sitting opposite a lady who was Judith Lipson before her marriage. After verifying that she was the daughter of the family I had been looking for, there was great excitement. I took her back to my house to show her the photograph that I still kept on my kitchen windowsill after all these years.

The story has a happy ending as both her parents are still alive and she was preparing to give them a golden wedding anniversary party at her home in Guildford. I was the surprise guest and we are still in contact.

*   *   *

Alfred Traum

(Vienna), Silver Spring, USA

I was born in Vienna, and came to England, along with my sister, in June 1939. We went directly to a pre-arranged home, a non-Jewish family, Mr and Mrs Charles Griggs, of London. We spent all the war years in their care, although for three of those years I was evacuated to the country.

When the war ended and the truth about the Holocaust became known, we were among the many who had lost all our family. The decision was now whether to remain living as we were, or to return to the Jewish fold. We decided to return to our roots and moved to Manchester where we made a new beginning. I became quite involved with *Habonim* and many other organizations.

In 1948, during the Israel War of Independence, I volunteered and served in the Israeli Army. At the completion of that service I returned to England to begin my two years national service with the British Army. Most of those two years were spent in Germany as a tank commander with the Royal Scots Greys.

On completion of my national service I began my studies for the Merchant Navy in radio and telecommunications. My goal was to serve as a radio officer in the newly formed Israeli Merchant Navy. Some years later that goal was reached. I was the chief radio officer on their newly commissioned passenger liner *ss Zion*. It was on that ship that I met Josiane, who later became my wife.

We lived for five years after our marriage in Haifa, Israel where I worked for IBM. In 1963 we moved to the United States where we still reside. We have three children, two boys and one girl. I am a communications engineer with Boeing.

*   *   *

Edith Unger

(Strauss), Melbourne, Australia.

Her contribution to this compilation of Kindertransportees' experiences is to be found as the dedication, at the beginning of this book.

The photograph of the Bergen-Belsen Memorial supplied by Lola Davies.

Frances Vanson

(Hirsch, Sportau), Jerusalem, Israel

Manfred Vanson

(Hamburg), Jerusalem, Israel

SUNSHINE HOSTEL

I understand that the Church of England Adoption Society wrote to the Jewish Refugees Committee at Bloomsbury House, London, and offered their building, known as 'The Old Vicarage' in Kingsbury, North West London for accommodating Jewish Refugee Children. They stipulated that they would like the building to be used for children from observant backgrounds. I am not sure how the selection was made, since we only came on the scene a year after the hostel was established, but twenty-five children aged between five and fourteen lived in the building like a family. The couple who were originally in charge were Mr and Mrs Gustav Erlebacher whom, unfortunately, we never met.

The building was a pleasant two-storey house, standing in its own grounds, part of which belonged to the church. The Erlebachers were due to leave for the United States in September 1940, and to take their place Mr and Mrs Schuster had been engaged. Along with so many refugees, Mr Schuster was interned, and Mrs Anna Schwab, the chairperson of the hostel, approached us with the request that we should take over the running of the hostel, at least temporarily. We were rather reluctant since we had only married ten days earlier, but Mrs Schwab talked us into agreeing, and after ten days of married life we had a family of twenty-five children!

As was not unusual in those days, we were delayed by an air raid and arrived at the hostel a few hours after the Erlebachers had left. A change in leadership always creates a feeling of tension and cautious reconnoitring but we were immediately impressed by the warm family feeling. Our predecessors had succeeded in welding the children into a lovely family, and the following two months were most enjoyable. Soon after we arrived, we celebrated the *Yamim Noraim* and *Succot.* The boys built the *Succah* and the singing of *Zemirot* is a happy memory.

We were fortunate in many ways. Next door to the hostel was the Oliver Goldsmith Primary School which had only been completed shortly before the outbreak of war. The headmaster, Mr Harris, was most welcoming to our children. The older girls went to Kingsbury School for Girls whose headmistress, Miss Nightingale, was equally positive towards our girls. The older boys attended a school in Burnt Oak, where I seem to remember there were problems. What was, to my mind, outstanding was how caring the children were towards each other in trying to overcome the feeling which most refugees must have experienced, at being separated at an early age from their parents. Some of the children had brothers and/or sisters at the hostel, others had a mother or father in the country.

Even today, there is a lot of contact between them and us. The equipment, furnishings and provisions were minimal, and from a financial point of view, I would have classified our hostel as one of the poorest. Pocket money was at the rate of one penny or two per week, depending on age. There was no money for clothing or entertainment. But on the whole, the children seemed to understand and accept the situation. I was fortunate in having full time employment during the day, and my remuneration consisted in free board and lodging. For the first two years, Frances did all the cooking as well as carrying out the duties of Matron. There were two girls to help with the housework, and they did not receive a princely wage, either.

The Jewish Community in Kingsbury was in its infancy. They owned a house, ten minutes' walk away, Eden Lodge, where the Rabbi lived and conducted Services, if and when a *Minyan* could be mustered, which was very seldom. We later usually walked to the *Adass Yisroel* Synagogue in Hendon where we made many friends.

Frances and I left the hostel in November 1940, after Mr Schuster was released from internment and could assume control, together with his wife. However, they found the task difficult and left the hostel at the beginning of February 1941. Mrs Schwab persuaded us to return to the hostel, and our association with it lasted until April 1945.

In 1942 the Church of England Adoption Society gave us notice because they needed the building for their own purposes. Due to the generosity of the Friedenheim family, we were able to move into their beautiful, though perhaps not over-suitable building in Rosecroft Avenue, Hampstead. This move entailed, amongst other things, re-schooling, mixing with a new Jewish Community, and new neighbours.

The war years were difficult for everybody. In Kingsbury we suffered from much bomb damage, and in particular from the famous 'Welsh Harp' incident which resulted in many persons being killed. Fortunately, our bomb damage usually only meant broken windows. Since the beginning of 1941, just before we returned to the hostel, the sleeping arrangements had been changed on the advice of the local authorities, and all children slept downstairs in double bunk beds. If, God forbid, a bomb had hit the hostel, it could have had devastating results. In Hampstead we were almost opposite the anti-aircraft guns situated on the Heath, and the nights were at times very noisy.

For the new neighbourhood, it took some time to absorb this strange community of refugee children. The only language spoken was English. This seems to have been a directive of the Erlebachers, and very beneficial it was. Neither Frances, nor I knew much about the English educational system and

I am not convinced that we always did the right thing regarding schooling and careers. There was no guidance whatsoever from the authorities at Bloomsbury House or anywhere else.

Our eldest daughter became the twenty-sixth hostel child in 1942.

Looking back on the five years we were there, we only know that we tried our best, as parents do, though doubtless we made mistakes.

The hostel was fortunate in attracting Ilse and the late Martin Purley to take over from us, and their relationship with the children was, and with many still is, very happy.

After the Purleys left for Israel, Mrs Else Grumer, assisted by Meir Engelhardt, had to preside over the disestablishment of the hostel – and with that an era came to an end.

How does one measure success? Those were not normal times. It is a tribute to the strength of our faith, in spite of having lost parents and siblings that, as far as we know, most of the children have done well and are useful citizens in whichever country they are now living. We are in contact with more than half of them – partly by way of correspondence, and in Israel several reunions have taken place of those who settled there. On a recent visit to England, we met with two of them. We know that three, living in Calfornia, meet from time to time.

On a sad note – most of them lost their parents in the Holocaust. After the end of the war some children from the camps came to live in the hostel, and the original children went all out to help absorb them within the community.

Mention should be made of the Hendon *Adass Yisroel* Synagogue in assisting the hostel to compensate for the absence of parental guidance.

Gratitude is due to the local authorities, especially those departments dealing with education. It was difficult for some of their officials to appreciate the special problems which these children experienced, and that especially manifested itself in relation to the efforts to obtain higher education. It was a real triumph when one of our hostel girls was the first of our children to be accepted by South Hampstead High School. She is now a well-established psychologist in the United States.

*   *   *

Bronya Veitch

(Schutz, Berlin), Baildon, UK

THE JEWS IN BELGIUM

Thirty thousand Jews – fifty-five per cent of the Jews registered in 1942 –were saved. All were hidden under assumed identities and cared for by non-Jewish people in Belgium, from the autumn of 1942 onwards. Through the actions of one woman in particular, Yvonne Nevejean, who was director of the National Institute for Child Welfare, financially responsible for independent children's homes, 4,000 children were, like me, taken into hiding. Three social workers who covertly belonged to the Committee for the Defence of Jews (CDJ), secreted them in over 7,000 non-Jewish families and 138 institutions, mainly convents, but also sanatoria, homes for blind and delicate children, and independent (non-state) children's homes. The communist Independence Front, its Committee for the Defence of Jews, the left wing *Poale Zion*, priests, nuns, the young Christian Workers Movement – all buried their ideological differences and made common cause. Two priests in Schaerbeck, Brussels, and in Lonvain, each saved over 3,000 children. The CDJ used the Jewish Council (Association of Jews of Belgium) set up in late 1941 by the Nazis to register all Jews and infiltrated it with two of its members as a cover to rescue Jews on the register.

The Belgian population was shocked when in June 1942 Jews were forced to wear yellow stars – many started to wear stars in the national colours in solidarity and many went out of their way to show their sympathy and their kindness.

Massive raids and deportations started in early August 1942. In the main cities, night after night for three months whole streets in the areas of Jewish residence were cordoned off and every house was searched and Jewish occupants taken to Casene Dorsin. People of Jewish appearance would also be picked up by a Gestapo vehicle in the daytime. From Casene Dorsin, in the three months from August to the end of October 1942, 17,000 men, women and children were sent to the death camps in seventeen convoys.

The two orphanages I was in, Rue des Patrides and Wezembrek, were official orphanages of the AJB (Jewish Council) and were controlled by the Gestapo. The latter had been opened in September 1942 to accommodate 'stray' children whose parents had been deported.

On the morning of 30 October 1942, the Gestapo raided my home. Wezembrek and all eighty-seven children and staff were forced onto trucks and taken to Casene Dorsin, from where a transport was to take us to Auschwitz the next day. The housekeeper, Mlle Dehaas, had the presence of mind to telephone Yvonne Nevejean who contacted the Queen Mother, Queen Elizabeth, who interceded with the German High Command (Belgium had a military administration) and we were all released during the night and taken back to Wezembrek. It was then that the CDJ put all its efforts into rescuing people and finding hiding places for children through three social workers employed by the AJB one of whom was Renée Goldstuck, who had brought me to my foster parents, and visited me in my foster home of St Niklaas in the late Spring of 1943. She died some five years ago.

It is a most miraculous and moving story – about which scarcely anything is known outside Belgium. After the war people picked up the pieces of their lives and did not wish to be reminded of it.

A young researcher, Jean Philippe Schreiber, at the Martin Buber Institute in Brussels told me: 'Everyone knows about Denmark, and about Holland because of Anne Frank's diary, but Belgium has been overlooked, although fifty-five per cent of Jews were saved through the help of the Belgian people, as against only twenty per cent in Holland.'

I asked my foster sister why, knowing the dangers, they had decided to rescue whom they could. 'We discussed it,' she said, 'but felt that we had to resist, that something had to be done for the children who were in danger of deportation, and there was no hesitation, no question of anything else but to do what we could.' Many, many people thought like that. I owe my life to the actions of so many, but mainly, of course, to my foster family. How can one be grateful enough for the self-sacrifice multiplied several thousand-fold?

The CDJ also posted ration stamps every month and money for people hidden in poor families – without which no-one could have survived in hiding, as well as false identity cards and birth certificates from towns like Ostend, as in my case, where the population registers had been destroyed in air raids. Eighty per cent of Jews in hiding had such cards.

On my return to London I spent a few days browsing through literature at the Wiener Library. On the last morning I was there, a phone call came through from a lady asking for the names of sixteen convents in the Liege area of Belgium. She and her sister had been hidden as toddlers in one of them. We met that evening and Leah told me her sad story. She was born in December 1938 in Antwerp and had lived with her parents and sister Sylvia, three years her senior. Her father had escaped to England before the war, her mother was deported to Auschwitz and she and Sylvia were hidden in a convent cell, very cold and with very little light.

After the war their father traced them and they arrived in England in February 1946. They were in a Jewish Refugee children's home and a year later Sylvia died of a brain tumour. Leah's father was brutal to her and she did badly at school. Her father died when she was eighteen. She resumed her education in English and Maths and became a very successful and attractive business woman. I have written for her to the Belgian Ministry of Public Health to see if they have any records.

This is a much sadder story than my own as I had two perfect years, from the liberation in September 1944 to coming here in September 1946 with my foster family, and my links were maintained.

Margot Velardo

(Deutsch, Berlin), London, UK

Until December 1938, Margot Velardo (nee Deutsch) was – as she styles herself – the Pedagogic Matron of the Berlin Jewish Children's Welfare Centre. This background made her eminently suitable to accompany the first Kindertransport from Berlin on 2 December 1938, on its way to England.

Apprehensive parents besought her to take care of their beloved offsprings. A task rendered only partially possible, due to the brutality of the Germans. Adult helpers were not permitted to travel with their charges beyond Osnabrück, the town where Germany and Holland meet.

Here the frightened group stood watching fierce looking black-clad SS officers, examining every piece of luggage, helping themselves to whatever they fancied.

Once through the Customs, the children walked unaccompanied over the border to be greeted by a party of Dutch Quakers. These good people fed them and led them on to the next stage of their journey – the Hook of Holland where they boarded the boat for England.

Soon afterwards Margot herself managed to obtain a visa for England, where she has lived ever since.

Subsequently, the organization of the Kindertransports became more sophisticated, with well-known personalities such as Norbert Wollheim and Dora Silbermann being permitted by the Germans to make several trips to England.

Norbert Wollheim survived and lives in America. Sadly Dora Silbermann, who Margot recalls was no longer young at that time, stayed behind and perished in the Holocaust.

Margot Velardo, now in her eightieth year, was interviewed by Paula Hill, in January 1990.

*   *   *

Dora and John Vernon

(Vienna), Herzlia, Israel

John and Dora Vernon are husband and wife who settled in Britain, but emigrated to Israel following their daughter. Today they are living in Herzlia.

They met through John's younger sister and married the day the Germans surrendered. John was already a soldier in the British Army.   The marriage date was set to coincide with John's first day of leave. Now they confess that they did not speak to each other about the Kindertransports. They did not want to remember the disappearing faces of their parents through the window of the trains, or the feeling of becoming orphans and their own journey to life and freedom.

Friends, whose parents did not bring themselves to send their children away, perished in the Holocaust. Dora remembered a close friend, whose mother was not able to part from her and who perished with her mother. Their daughter Susan decided to emigrate to Israel. Dora was then recovering after an operation and went to the train to see her off.

'At the railway station, when Susan was standing with the suitcase it all came back to me,' she tells. 'Suddenly I was my mother and my daughter was me in Vienna. Everything got mixed up and I cried, and cried and cried, when the train moved out. Only years later did I tell Susie. She was shocked. For years – I had not spoken about it. It does not mean that I forgot!

'My memory goes back to my age of fifteen, to the 11 July 1939,' says Dora. 'I will never forget the traumatic scene at the station. Children yelling and crying and parents fainting when realizing it was the last time they were seeing their children. I was travelling with a friend of my own age and her two younger brothers. During the journey there were no smiling children. The SS men continued to harass us in the compartments and took everything valuable they saw. We were allowed to leave with the clothes we were wearing and a set of change.

In the evening we arrived at the Dutch border and for the first time we again encountered kindness and generosity. The Dutch people smiled at us! Then we continued by ferry to England to a shelter for refugees.

After two months, when war broke out, I realized that I was separated from my parents for good and that I was quite alone. This feeling was common to many. A few children had nervous breakdowns and one committed suicide. One could not communicate properly. After the end of the war it came to my knowledge that my father tried to cross the border into Belgium and was caught and murdered in Buchenwald concentration camp. How my mother disappeared and where she died I do not know to this day.'

John was arrested on Kristallnacht, nearly seventeen years old, and appeared on a list to be sent to a concentration camp. Fortunately he was released after signing a form that he would leave the country within two months. His parents managed to place him on one of the Kindertransports.

'I remember the faces of my father and mother when the train left. The Nazis on the train pulling off a small golden chain from the neck of my thirteen year old sister,' he relates. 'In England I was taken first to a farmer's family in Oxfordshire, where I had a few happy weeks. After that I was sent to a reception camp for German and Austrian refugees, and from there to a family in Cornwall, and after the outbreak of war to a hostel in London. After the fall of Dunkirk, hysterical panic started in Britain fearing strangers.

Policemen knocked at the door and I was taken to an internment camp. After a while things calmed down, we were released and I was accepted into the British Army. I took part in the invasion of Normandy. I, one of the persecuted Jews, helped to defeat Hitler. At the end of the war I was amongst those who entered Bergen-Belsen and I remember myself announcing by loudspeaker: "The camp has just been taken over by the Allied Armies."'

Even if they did not speak about it, John and Dora's lives passed under the shadows of memories. John had to go back to Germany a few times in connection with work and Dora went with him only once. When she heard a woman speaking German at the bus stop she ran away and from that day onwards she never went back.

Not long ago they were flying back from Israel to England. On the way something went wrong and the plane landed in Germany. They stayed the night at the airport, Dora refusing to go into town to a hotel. They had few respites from running away from the past. A few years ago they tried to find the families, who took them in. They did not find them! People moved or had passed away. Most of all they are afraid of future generations forgetting the past. John and Dora promised themselves to continue to remember.

* * *

Walter Weg

(Leipzig), Ruislip, UK

With our parents both still in Germany, my two sisters came together on a Kindertransport about two months after I had come to England, early in January 1939. The younger, only three years old, was found a place at the Wellgarth Nursery Training School, while the eight year old was taken in by a family in Golders Green, north west London. I myself, then aged ten, was at a boarding school near Hastings. We had not been able to see each other since we arrived.

At the end of my first school term I had come to stay with a friend of my parents in London and I visited my sister in Golders Green. As the afternoon was fine, we went out for a walk.

Suddenly, my sister pointed across the road to a 'crocodile' of tiny children shepherded by two uniformed nurses. She had spotted our little sister and we both dashed across the road to speak to her in German. She was obviously delighted to see us and understood what we were saying, although she was no longer able to express herself in German. There were surprised and embarrassed looks on the faces of the nurses as they pulled their reluctant little charge away with them, to keep to their time schedule, while we followed for a few paces, trying to explain the situation in our not very good English.

This little incident was over in less than five minutes, but helped to sustain the three of us while we were anxiously waiting for our parents to join us in England. They eventually did escape from Germany – our father only three days before the outbreak of war.

*   *   *

Naftali Wertheim

(Fulda), Kibbutz Tirat Zvi, Israel

My first four school years were spent in the *Jüdische Volksschule* in Fulda. Then came Kristallnacht, the Kindertransport and nine more schools spread over the fair face of southern England. One of them was literally spread by a German bomb, luckily during the night, when no one was inside. The children were happy next morning – no school!

What I really want to tell about is a particular geography lesson given by Mr Dudlyke, who was a Welshman, a teacher at Parmiters Secondary School in Bethnal Green, and a hater of all things German.

Twice a week, first thing after Scripture, we had Geography. Two nights a week, immediately preceding our early morning Geography class, poor Mr Dudlyke spent on the roofs of London, fire watching for incendiary bombs, instead of in his warm bed at home. That's why he hated all things German. He wanted a German to take it out on, and there was one in his very first class. Kurt Wertheim, a Hun name if ever he heard one.

Instead of following what Mr Dudlyke was demonstrating on the blackboard, I was looking at my geography book. 'Come out here, you Prussian swine!' he shouted. Obviously he didn't know where I came from and therefore I cannot hold it against him, a geography master not knowing that Fulda is in Hessen, not Prussia.

'How long do you intend to stay in Britain?' he asked me. I told him that it didn't depend on me but on the British Government.

I received six stripes of the cane; three of the best on each palm, and was sent back to my desk with the admonition: 'You think this is Nazi Germany with a lot of Jerries doing what they bloody well like. Well, let me tell you this is a democracy and you do as you're bloody well told!'

*   *   *

Alan Westley

(Weisbard, Nuremberg), Solihull, UK

New Year's Day 1939 had not long gone when my mother was busy washing, ironing and packing two suitcases – one for my brother Heinrich, and one for me. I could not understand why she kept crying at irregular intervals, since we were only going on a short holiday. I was also mystified why so much clothing was necessary for a short time away.

All my most cherished treasures were to be packed up to take with me, my penknife, my stamp collection and my favourite books, and all the small paraphernalia of a ten year old boy. The time of departure came, we were wildly excited at the prospect of a train journey to a place only mother knew. My father could not see us off at the station as he had already been taken with my two sisters several months earlier, and deported to Poland.

It was cold that January morning. We were excited, apprehensive and a little afraid. It was after midnight when we left the house rather furtively and made our way to the railway station in Nuremberg. Various papers were thrust into our hands with strict instructions not to lose them. Parcels of food were given to us for the journey and lots of hugs and kisses and terms of endearment that are usually only heard on special occasions like birthdays and *Bar Mitzvahs*.

We were told not to make a noise as it would draw attention to our small band of people. What little noise we did make echoed round the almost empty station.

Suddenly, it all happened. The train appeared, doors opened, mothers cried uncontrollably, we were ordered to get into the coaches, last hugs, kisses and goodbyes – for ever.

* * *

Dorit B Whiteman, Ph.D.

(Vienna), New York, USA

What happened to those to whom 'Nothing happened at all'

Last summer, sitting at a dinner table in a pleasant house in a small town in England, my cousin talked about the fate of his parents. His father, he said, had died in Theresienstadt and his mother was deported to, and died in, Auschwitz. His wife then told about her mother, father and brother, all of whom perished in Auschwitz. My thoughts wandered to my parents, my sister, my cousins and myself. 'How lucky we were,' I reflected. 'We escaped from the Holocaust. Nothing happened to us at all.'

Suddenly my mind took a different turn. I began to think of the terror we all experienced after Hitler came, the frantic efforts my parents made to save us, the desperate attempts to be allowed to leave Vienna, and the more desperate attempts to be received somewhere else, the planning and scheming, the desperation, the wrenching good-byes. I recollected the veritable odyssey we experienced, the new countries, the endless resettlements, the many uncertain years before life assumed a semblance of normality. Nothing had happened to us at all? Did life really ever become ordinary again? Were we not for ever affected in our thinking, in our outlook on life, in our emotional reactions, in our family and professional relationships, in fact in every facet of our lives? Our experiences had paled when compared to the true Holocaust victims, so it had seemed presumptuous to consider that anything very untoward had actually happened to us. This reaction was a very general one. Recently a friend, who had escaped with her parents and her sister before the war broke out, was asked to talk to a high school class about her escape from Vienna. She replied that she would be happy to oblige, but recommended inviting someone to whom something noteworthy had happened, since she thought 'nothing had really happened' to her.

As another example: My mother wrote an autobiography covering her whole life until our arrival in New York. The pre-Hitler period and Hitler's arrival are covered in some detail. But when she wrote about our escape, all she said was: 'Now we are in America.' This is the short way of telling the story. Today, it is all too well known that no story of a lucky escape from Europe can actually be short if told in detail. But she did not go into detail. Why? Because it seemed to all of us grandiose, presumptuous to dwell on our escape when over six million had died.

And yet, the story of those of us who escaped before the war is one worth telling. Thousands of us were displaced in a migratory wave that changed the constellation of the population which we left and the one to which we came. But most of all, it changed all of us who were part of this wave and it changed every aspect of our lives. It changed us basically and it is a story that deserves to be remembered as a footnote to history – at least in the memory of our children.

* * *

Benny Winter
(Birmingham, UK), Netanya, Israel

Sometime, soon after Dunkirk and the fall of France, I was teaching in Birmingham when I received a phone call from the Rev A Cohen, informing me that the Bishop of Lichfield had telephoned to tell him that fifty-one German Jewish refugee boys had been 'dumped' as evacuees on the mining village of Chase Terrace in Staffordshire. These boys had originally been brought to England in 1939 and housed in a boarding school in Margate, Kent, until the bombing of the south east coast had begun.

I was asked to check up on these boys and their billeting accommodation and to make suitable arrangements for their Jewish welfare and education as far as I possibly could.

When I arrived, I found the billeting authorities very helpful. They provided me with a village hall where the boys could have Services and lessons from Friday afternoon to Sunday afternoon. During the rest of the week I was involved in teaching in Birmingham and in my duties as a Special Constable.

I found the boys, whose ages ranged from seven to fifteen, very pleased to see a Jewish face again (there were no Jews in Chase Terrace) and quite eager to have some contact with the Jewish community through me. The boys were all billeted in poor miners' cottages and were physically well looked after. Unfortunately they mostly ate non-kosher food except on *Shabbatot* and *Yamim Tovim,* when I brought them kosher food from Birmingham, provided by kind acquaintances.

The programme I mapped out for them was, of necessity, very elementary because most of them knew very little of Judaism, Hebrew or religious life. Therefore, on Friday afternoons we had a *Kabbalat Shabbat* Service (after a while this was conducted by the boys themselves, as some of the older ones learned or remembered), followed by a meal, after which the younger boys went home. The older boys then had an informal lesson when we spoke about some Jewish topic in history or ethics or ritual.

I rented a room in one of the houses and invited one of the older boys each *Shabbat* to eat with me. During this time we became better acquainted and they could unburden themselves of their innermost troubles and feelings about what had happened to them, and what had or might have happened to their families left behind in Germany.

Each *Shabbat* morning, we had a proper *Shacharit* Service, followed by a lesson for the younger boys. In the afternoons some of the older ones often walked with me around the village and then, after *Minchah,* had their second lesson and I also visited some of the foster parents.

On *Yamim Tovim* we gradually had more and more elderly men and women attending the Services – people who had evacuated themselves to the area from London and other cities. On these days I usually took one of my young sons with me to make friends with the Chase Terrace boys.

In the process of time the boys began to learn or remember more and more of their Judaism and their Jewish background, and I began to prepare the younger ones for their *Bar Mitzvah.* When the great day arrived, I arranged for the boy concerned to come to Birmingham (without the approval of the authorities, because Birmingham was a danger area), stay in my house and attend *Shul* where my brother-in-law was the Rabbi. My wife gave a party for the boy where he met sons of our friends and received presents.

Somehow, despite the shortage of petrol and difficulty in getting out of Birmingham after a heavy air raid, I never missed being with the boys any weekend. There were many problems, but somehow we managed. For instance, once my wife had arranged to fry 150 pieces of fish on a certain Thursday for the approaching *Seder* nights, but on that Wednesday night the bombing was particularly severe and all the gas mains were broken. So my wife had to fry all that fish on a small open coal fire – but it was done and the boys had kosher fish for *Yom Tov.*

This was the pattern for a long time, during which I was dissatisfied with the way the boys lived in non-Jewish surroundings, mostly eating non-kosher food and possibly being influenced, even unintentionally, by their very kind Christian foster parents. Eventually, with the help of my sister-in-law, the Rabbi's wife, and many good friends, a large house was rented in Walsall near Birmingham and converted into a hostel for the boys. A German refugee Rabbi and his wife were appointed as Master and Matron to supervise the establishment and look after the boys' education and welfare. From that date they were in a completely Jewish environment, and I was no longer worried. My job was finished.

Of all the fifty-one boys, I lost only one. He had become very fond of his foster parents and was content to remain with them, become a coal miner when he left school, and break off all ties with the Jewish people. From the hostel, the boys spread all over the world, some to Israel, some to families whom they remembered, some to various towns in England.

* * *

Margot Wohlman-Wertheim

(Frankfurt), Jerusalem, Israel

I came to England with a Kindertransport, which left from Frankfurt-am-Main on 2 February 1939. The children in this transport were of all ages and from many different places in South Germany. I was eleven years old at the time.

I particularly remember a boy who sat opposite me on the train to Emmerich on the Dutch border. He wore a tight-fitting beret which covered his hair completely and to me he looked like a very old man. Someone in the compartment asked him why he didn't take the uncomfortable headgear off, whereupon he lifted the beret for a second and I saw that he was completely bald. I realized immediately that he must have just been released from a concentration camp, as my father had returned home from Dachau with the same hairstyle.

On 3 September 1939, Lisa aged eleven, Kurt ten, and I, eleven, were evacuated with the rest of the pupils of Finsbury Park Council School to St Ives, Huntingdonshire. Gas masks hanging from our necks, name-tags on our chests, we were ready for war. Trouble started when about thirty cockney-speaking children, bored and miserable while waiting to be assigned to local families by the billeting officer, formed a circle around me, jumped up and down rhythmically and chanted in unison: 'Margaret loves Eidolf 'Itler, Margaret loves Eidolf 'Itler . . . ' My poor English, after only a few months in the country, was irrefutable proof of the fact that I was a German spy and the more I denied it, the more incriminating the evidence became to the ears of my torturers. Mrs Williams, a harried teacher who had accompanied us from London, put a stop to the proceedings.

Our assigned landlady was Mrs Noble, an impoverished, elderly widow, whose interest in us was confined to the few shillings she received from the Government for our upkeep. On our first evening we were served fried bacon with fried bread. Lisa had no English at all, having arrived a few weeks previously from Paris, and my brother Kurt was the youngest, so I naturally became the spokesman for the three of us.

'We can't eat that,' I said.

'Why not?' asked Mrs Noble.

'Because we're Jewish.'

'That's impossible!'

'Why?'

'Because you haven't got a tail!' And that was that, succinct and final. We sat and didn't eat. Mrs Noble sat and glared at us. I had an inspiration:

'We're vegetarians.'

'Why couldn't you say so right away – you can have cheese,' responded Mrs Noble.

A week later, we received a parcel of Frohwein's kosher sausages from London and my ingenuity was put to a severe test: How to hide this *corpus delecti* from Mrs Noble ... but that's another story.

*   *   *

Helga Wolff

(Cohn, Frankfurt), Wembley, Middlesex, UK

The 18 August 1938 is deeply engraved on my memory, for on that hot summer day I saw my parents for the last time. We said goodbye in the Hauptbahnhof in Frankfurt-on-Main. after my father had entrusted me to another passenger in the train bound for Paris.

'Would you be kind enough to look after our Helga? She has never been abroad before' ... My father's voice faltered as he noticed the swastika on the stranger's lapel.

'Don't worry, it will be my pleasure to see that your daughter gets to Paris safely. Will there be someone to meet her?'

'Oh yes, very good friends of ours who have always been fond of her and have promised to take care of her.' The guard closed the doors. The train pulled slowly out of the station. From the compartment window I looked at my mother and father. They made every effort to smile, yet they could not hide the unhappiness which shone out of their sad eyes.

I sat down opposite the tall dark-haired gentleman, my guardian for the duration of the journey.

'You will like Paris, it's a wonderful place. Do you speak French?' He obviously wanted to cheer me up.

'Yes, I've always had good marks in French. It's like music.'

'How old are you, Helga?'

'My birthday is next month. I'll be fifteen years old.'

Everything seemed completely unreal. Yesterday at the same time the four of us, my parents, my brother Kurt and I had been sitting together in our small top floor flat.

'I'm so relieved you are going to Tante Wally and Onkel Jas in Paris,' my mother had said. 'You were always Wally's favourite, the daughter she never had.' My mother gave herself courage thinking of the many times I had stayed in the elegant flat with the famous *Biedemeir Zimmer* when my parents had been invited to one of Tante Wally's fashionable social gatherings.

Now I sat forlorn, oblivious of the fact that all my tomorrows would be so different from my yesterdays.

My uncle was rarely at home. He travelled in grand style for his firm. Tante Wally worked day and night dealing with orders, staff and sometimes irate clients. That left me very much to my own devices. When I was not attending the course at the *Alliance Française*, the youngest student at the time, I wandered through the streets of Paris. '*Battre le pavé*' describes exactly what I did. My untiring legs carried me everywhere. The town seemed so beautiful, so big, I was enthralled by the magic. I soaked up everything French.

My dream ended abruptly. My visa had expired months before. I had to take matters into my own hands. With my student card and a letter confirming that Tante Wally would be entirely responsible for my upkeep I made my way to the Prefecture of Paris. An official insisted I had to leave France by 15 May.

On 30 May the police arrived at the flat with a search warrant. My aunt tried to find a solution. A letter from the *Comite Israelite* of 23 May had requested:

> *Would you be good enough to ensure that the child is ready to join, at short notice, the transport organized by us for the children due to be sent to England which is expected to leave within a few days.*

Once again I found myself at the Gare du Nord. The dream had become a nightmare. We were met by the leader of the *Sammeltransport*. Fifteen children stood assembled around him, clutching the hands of their relatives. The youngest of the party was not yet four years old. All of us were about to emigrate for the second time in our young lives. For the second time we said goodbye, most of us unable to understand why we were once again torn from our loved ones. The scene was heart-rending. We were led into our compartments. The train left, German, Czech and French children cried and uttered their grief in their native tongue. The leader of the party was equal to the formidable task expected of him. He counted his charges and made the older ones sit next to the little ones.

'Helga, take care of these two little ones,' he said to me.

'Lieschen and Hannchen, look what I have got for you.' He pulled out some delicious sweets and popped one in each mouth. Tears gradually gave way to smiles. Everyone was mentally and physically exhausted. I cannot even remember when or how our little flock was taken on board ship at Calais. As the train slowed down I recovered my faculties.

'Get yourselves ready. We have arrived.' On the sign I could read 'Victoria Station'.

*   *   *

Otto Wolffs

(Aurich), Germany

My home was in Aurich/Ostfriesland until June 1939. This little town which had a total population of six thousand when Hitler came to power, had a Jewish congregation which numbered almost four hundred persons. Our forefathers were very proud of the fact that Napoleon contributed monies to the construction of our Synagogue in 1811. It was destroyed by Nazi vandals on 10 November 1938. The Jews of Aurich were mostly religious and our Christian neighbours knew that the shops owned by Jews were not open on '*Schabbes*' and they did their shopping on other days.

A large number of the Jews in Aurich served in the First World War, but despite the fact that they were given medals for bravery, this did not save their lives. In fact the very nationalistic Jews in our town went so far as to participate in the elections in March 1933 – three months after Hitler came to power – and received several hundred votes.

Due to the constant pressure after our father had died at Buchenwald, my mother decided to bring her youngest children, my sister and myself, to safety. My sister went to England and spent several years in a youth hostel in Sunderland. She now lives in Stamford Hill, London, with her family. I was lucky, Mr and Mrs Morris, a Jewish family in Hackney, adopted me, although they already had eight grown-up children.

On 2 September 1939, all of the pupils of Lauriston Road School in London E9 were evacuated to Norfolk. The group that I was in arrived at a village called West Bradenham late that night. Mr and Mrs Moore, a very charming Methodist couple and their four grown-up children, were my family for the next two years. When I visited West Bradenham a few years ago, I renewed my contacts with the Moore clan. Unfortunately Mr and Mrs Moore are no longer alive; I had wanted to express my appreciation to them.

During the war, I was working in various positions to assist the war effort and in January 1946, I joined the American forces in Germany as a civilian employee. My first position was with the Civil Censorship Division of US Military Government in an area which is now Baden-Württemberg. From 1947 to 1979 I worked for various US agencies on the continent. In 1979 I gave up my position because of illness due to experiences in my younger days. My past had caught up with me.

My family now consists of three children and five grandchildren and my wife and I live in a little town only fifteen miles from Frankfurt/Main.

*   *   *

Betty Wolkenfeld

(Hauser), USA

I arrived in Liverpool, having boarded the '*Bodegraven*' in Scheveningen on 20 May 1940, the day the Nazis invaded Holland. I was part of that little group of children from the Wajsenhuis in Amsterdam, who were put on buses without being told where we were going. I thought we were on an excursion and left my clothes and special belongings behind. I remember riding down the long pier, passing long lines of people walking. Did they make it to safety? The boat, a former coal barge, had no cabins, only the floor with harsh blankets; tea with milk and ships' biscuits for food. Why did it take five days, including bombing at sea, for us to reach England?

I was sent to the girls' hostel at 42 Heaton Road, Withington, Manchester at the age of twelve to spend three and a half years of my life there. Before this, I remember being in a very old house with a cellar. When the air raid sirens sounded we were herded downstairs to sleep on mattresses on the cellar floor.

Heaton Road was not an orthodox hostel, but *kashrut* was kept and *Shabbat* observed, and I went to Synagogue. For Passover, I went to a distantly related family in Manchester and couldn't wait to get back to Heaton Road. One exciting Passover was spent in Wales.

My plans for *Hachshara* and eventual settlement in Israel changed when I learned in the summer of 1941 that my family was saved and on their way to the United States. They had lived in Belgium, France and Morocco for various periods of time.

Meanwhile, those in charge of our well-being, helped to plan my education. I took the entrance exam for the Junior Commercial School and qualified for a place. English, shorthand, typing, book-keeping and Spanish were the main courses. This education has stood me in good stead all my life, and I was happy going to school and not to work.

Our Jewish education was scanty. Twice a week lessons by Professor Dr Rabbi Papo were hardly enough, though at that time it seemed too much. We also had French lessons, went to the ballet, the movies and to concerts. We also went on vacations.

Strange that life was run so normally in war-time England. Radio was a different matter – you had to be invited into the kitchen to listen to it. Everyone was invited to hear Churchill's speeches, though. To this day I remember hearing some of his words ' ... Never in the field of human conflict was so much owed by so many to so few ... '

Sunday morning was clean-up day at the hostel. Every girl aged six and upwards had to do her own washing and was responsible for cleaning the house, dusting common use areas, and so on.

The boys' hostel was at 40 Heaton Road. Mr and Mrs Alexander and Mrs

Strauss were in charge. Some joint activities were planned and friendships developed.

I lived in England from May 1940 until November 1943. After leaving I continued to write to my hostel friends until the end of the war when they left. Life there was certainly regimented, and although I can understand the need for that now, it was difficult for me as a child. However, I knew we were with people who cared about us: Mrs Sawitz, Mrs Meta Brinkmann, and Miss Elja Baruch. As an adult, I applaud their dedication and commitment to the good and welfare of the children who were in their care.

* * *

Norbert Wollheim

(Berlin), Fresh Meadows, NY, USA

I became involved with the Kindertransports after the Kristallnacht. I was part of a group of social workers who did general work within the Jewish community, but worked especially with people who had been released from concentration camps. I was approached by my former youth leader who told me that Great Britain was prepared to accept up to ten thousand unaccompanied children from Germany, Austria and Czechoslovakia. The Central Board of Jews of Germany were handling this as far as Germany was concerned and needed help, especially with technical matters. I applied for the job and was accepted.

Everybody was trying to get out. We were overwhelmed by the tremendous amount of paperwork involved in processing those children who had been selected for emigration. The selection of the children was not my responsibility, but was done by social workers in each Jewish community. At the beginning the parents thought that they could leave together with their children, so it was not easy for us when we had to tell them that this was not so. Then came the parents' questions: Where would the children go? How long would they be separated? Would they be able to join their children later? We had no answers to these questions and many others.

The criteria for selecting children included their health, their parents' willingness to let them go etc. As time went on and the Nazis' atrocities increased, we were besieged by parents who wanted to get at least their children out. It was now our task to put the transports together, having regard to the permits having arrived from England, the availability of trains and many other factors. The parents had to be advised that their children had been selected for emigration and that they should bring their children to a certain railway station on a given day at a given time.

Then there were the German police requirements of course. At the beginning they were quite cooperative and were happy to rid themselves of so many Jewish children and accepted the British travel permits, so that passports were unnecessary. But they wanted lists containing full records and details of each child with several copies. This was certainly not easy because there were always last minute changes and we had to wait until the last moment. And so we worked through many a night to get the lists etc ready.

Apart from this we had to deal with a constant stream of parents in person and by telephone; with telephone calls from the various refugee committees in England, from prospective foster parents and of course from the central refugee committee at Bloomsbury House in London, who needed copies of lists of children arriving in order to place them in camps, hostels or with foster parents. We were aware that the situation was deteriorating rapidly and that we had to get the children out as fast as possible. We reckoned that we could reach the ten thousand limit by the end of 1939. The outbreak of war in early September halted the Kindertransports, leaving us some hundreds short of the target.

Our task was not only very demanding physically, but, perhaps even more so, mentally. Some parents became impatient and frantic to get their children out and many times we were accused of favouritism. Time and again we had to tell parents that the permits for their children had not yet arrived from London and we could only include those children for whom we had permits. This was a great emotional drain for us. I was twenty-six years old at that time and had worked in Jewish youth movements, so I was used to dealing with parents to some extent. What was even more difficult was to tell parents at the railway station to say goodbye to their children in the waiting room, as the police would not allow them on the platform in order not to have heart-rending scenes in public. The escorts took over and checked the children onto the trains, gave them numbers and helped them with their luggage. These escorts were youth leaders, teachers etc and had some experience in dealing with children. Nevertheless there were terrible scenes; many children were crying; in some cases there was an eerie silence; always there was tension. I never got used to it. At the beginning the escorts were only allowed to travel as far as the border, but later they were permitted to travel all the way to London on condition that they returned to Germany. If they did not return it would put future Kindertransports in jeopardy. Many escorts travelled several times. They were allowed to stay in London for two or three days only, during which time they discussed future arrangements with Bloomsbury House and of course tried to make plans for their own eventual emigration.

I was involved with every Kindertransport which left Berlin. On three occasions we managed to get some children on a ship sailing from Hamburg to New York. Needless to say, there were a number of mishaps with some of the transports, but we managed to overcome them. There were also some problems with the German customs. In many instances they opened the children's suitcases and threw everything on the floor and even stole some things. I understand that there were also some difficulties with the British customs, although not many.

I was supposed to escort a Kindertransport leaving Berlin on 1 September 1939, but events became so awesome that we tried to get an earlier date. I decided to get my own passport in order, but I then had a wife and daughter, my brother and sister and I did not want to be separated from them in case something happened. So the transport left without me on 30 August and still managed to get a boat which landed in England on the day the Germans invaded Poland. This was the last transport from Berlin. After the outbreak of war we managed to send some children on two transports to Sweden. They were sent on *Hachsharah* there and then to Israel (then Palestine).

I look back on this chapter of my life with great satisfaction and only regret that the outbreak of war prevented us from saving many more children. I was only a small cog in the machinery, but my co-workers and I made the machinery work.

Editors' note: Norbert Wollheim escorted several Kindertransports to England and had many opportunities to save himself. He considered it his duty to work right to the outbreak of war. He left it too late to save himself and his family. His wife and daughter perished in a concentration camp, while he was fortunate to survive one. He remarried after emigrating to the USA.

* * *

Susan Woolf

(Rosenthal, Göttingen), London, UK

I recall little of the events on landing until the moment of meeting my 'family', when my hostess (hence to be addressed as 'Auntie') uttered one of the very few words of English that I understood. She took one look at me and exclaimed: 'Isn't she LITTLE!' Poor lady, the head-and-shoulders photograph from which she had, no doubt with the greatest care, selected one particular child of the same age as her own daughter, did not give any indication that the nine year old she was expecting – and got – was an undersized shrimp who in Germany had had a five-year-old playmate taller than herself! (Did you grow up to be a giant, Margot S . . . , over there in the States?) Certainly I never attained the dizzy height of five feet!

Auntie was to suffer other disappointments too. I was, I must admit, a spoilt brat of an only child, and the transition from a position of prime importance in the family to one merely on the periphery was not an easy one. Then, the passably pretty face of the photograph was soon to be marred by ugly spectacles when it was discovered at school that I was extremely short-sighted – a condition which must have been present, undetected for years. But at least no time was lost in discarding the ankle boots and arch-supports with which I arrived.

My few words of English had been acquired from the worthy but unqualified Frau Wertheim who was engaged to give me lessons when my departure to England had become inevitable. 'Good day, Mrs Wertheim' she taught me, and the only other sentences that stuck, were: 'Do you speak English?' to which the answer was: 'Yes, a little.'

'Uncle' spoke some Yiddish in which he tried to converse with me but, like many German Jews I had never heard it.

Always a fussy eater, at breakfast on my first morning, I was horrified to see a mound of I know not what being poured from a large packet into a bowl in front of me. *'Weniger, weniger'* I squeaked in dismay and the Irish maid, clearly at a loss but trying to be helpful, shrugged her shoulders and obligingly produced the vinegar. I actually came to like cornflakes quite a lot. I could not stop crying, and could not understand why. Nothing was as bad I had feared – the people were not alarming; the daughter of the house was a much nicer child than myself and inclined to be kind to the stranger; the household was neither more grand nor more impoverished than I was accustomed to – and I had no foreboding that I was never to see my parents again. But cry I did, uncontrollably and continuously, and nobody knew what to do with me. Not an auspicious start.

I was thrown headlong into the local school, to get by as best I might. There were a few other refugees in the school, perhaps even in my class, and we spoke German together in the playground, which was my only opportunity to do so. All this immersion in the English language, at that age, meant that I learned to speak it very quickly and without an accent. For this I am grateful as it has saved me from having to recount my life-story to the curious, when I might not wish to do so. It also meant that I temporarily forgot all my German. I recall the day, shortly before the outbreak of war, when I was summoned to the radio that had been tuned to a German station, and urged to translate what was being said. I was unable to oblige, to the chagrin if not disbelief of the family.

In July 1940 Auntie and her daughter were evacuated to the States, and I was sent to a hostel. As most of the girls had been there since their arrival in England, the language they spoke was still German, mixed with a little English. *'Ich muss das Wasser changen'* is a choice phrase I heard early on which impaled itself on my memory. For a few days I could not understand anybody, but before long I was breaking the 'No German in the Dining Room' rule as enthusiastically as everybody else.

Auntie had provided me with a suitcase full of excellent clothes, some outgrown by her daughter and waiting for me to grow into. Unfortunately, she included a pink velvet party dress and white button shoes, and when told to put on my best dress on my first Friday night, I decked myself out in these! I also had a fairy cycle which I hated to allow much bigger girls to ride. To crown it all I possessed – and had been intiated in the use of – hair curlers! None of these things were destined to win me instant popularity with girls who had by that time outgrown their own original good clothes and were already wearing each other's hand-me-downs to destruction.

All the same, at the Beacon I made friends for life, and we regard each other almost as sisters. Our interests and lifestyles may differ, but however infrequently we meet we can always pick up where we left off.

* * *

Anne Woolf-Skinner

(Ansbach, Berlin), London, UK

Anne Woolf-Skinner was born Annette Brigitte Ansbach in Berlin and came to Britain aged twenty-two months on 13 July 1939. She came with her sister, Inez, two years older, and the children were accompanied by a German nanny. She has been told that she was the youngest child to come without an adult relative.

'I don't remember anything myself – I've been told everything by my sister, who now lives in Israel. We were taken by a Jewish family in North Finchley, and then we moved to Surrey. We think they wanted to take only one child, because they already had three children of their own. But eventually they took both of us.

Our mother died of pneumonia when I was six months old. Our father was a tuberculosis specialist at a Berlin hospital. Our aunt and grandparents looked after us, and it was our grandparents who insisted that we should come to England. We know that our father and grandparents died in Auschwitz.'

Anne's only surviving relatives are two cousins in South America, daughters of the aunt who looked after them. Once she was married, her husband discovered, through *Yad Vashem,* the Holocaust memorial authority in Jerusalem, a cousin of her father's who remembered the two little Ansbach girls. 'I was told that I'd just started talking and when we came here I stopped talking altogether for a month. My sister says that my father had asked, "Please show them the picture of their mother every night." But I think that our adoptive mother was a bit possessive and didn't want to tell us much about our background.'

SAVE THE CHILDREN FUND
INTER-AID COMMITTEE FOR CHILDREN FROM GERMANY
(AND AUSTRIA)

Chairman:
Brigadier-General SIR WYNDHAM DEEDES, C.M.G., D.S.O.

Jt. Hon. Secretaries:
MRS. G. SKELTON
FRANCIS E. BENDIT, Esq.

Hon. Case Secretaries :
MISS D'AVIGDOR
MRS. JAMES GERSTLEY

Hon. Treasurer :
L. G. MONTEFIORE, Esq.

Temporary Administrative Offices;
16, RUSSELL SQUARE,
LONDON, W.C.1.
Tel. Museum 3451

Head Office :
20, GORDON SQUARE,
LONDON, W.C.1

December 16ᵗʰ 1938

Dear Mrs Woolf

We wonder if you would consider taking two little girls, of two, and one. Their name is Ansbacher. Their grandfather is a doctor and was head of a famous clinic in Vienna. Their ~~father is in Dachau~~, the worst concentration camp in Germany, the mother is dead, & the children are at present with their grandmother's hands. Their great aunt is in London, and we could put you in touch with her; the whole family are very nice people, well known to us. I enclose a guarantee form and would you kindly fill it up & send it to us with your letter, if you can have them. We are so grateful for your kind offer.

Yours faithfully
H P Maher
(p. Miss B'd'Avigdor.)

Anne became very involved in the Wimbledon Synagogue, where she became the much respected musical director of a number of the congregation's theatrical events.

Reprinted by kind permission from the *Jewish Chronicle*

* * *

Sybil Wulwick
London, UK

On a cold winter's day – end of December 1938, the newly formed 'Refugee Committee' of the Middlesbrough Hebrew Congregation, received an urgent message from London to meet a boat arriving at Harwich with refugee children on board and to take our quota of them into our care for 'the duration'. The dedicated young *Chazan*, Gershon Wulwick, who spoke fluent German, was foremost in leading his committee in responding to the call. It had earlier been decided to open a hostel for orthodox girls as so many other communities were worried about providing exclusively for very orthodox children.

As the hostel was not ready by the time the children arrived, we put them up in our private homes for a few weeks, and then worked at full speed to provide loving homes for them. A very large house in The Avenue, Linthorpe, belonging to the Benjamin family was lent for the purpose of a hostel, and a committee of hard-working ladies joined the men's committee to furnish a comfortable home for these lovely young girls, so tragically separated from their parents.

Gifts of carpets, bedroom furniture, lounge suites, crockery, linen and cutlery were given with full hearts, and early in 1939 the Middlesbrough hostel was ready to receive twenty-five girls and a matron, Mrs Mahler with her husband, Professor Mahler and their young daughter. We even employed an orthodox continental lady who cooked and baked the food the children were used to. The men's committee undertook to collect funds to keep the hostel going. The children were very appreciative of all we tried to do for them and we in our turn became very affectionate uncles and aunts.

We were very grateful to the local education authorities who found places in the local schools for all the children and a non-Jewish language teacher offered her services free to teach the children English. The few senior girls were specially catered for in Further Education colleges and taught hairdressing and dressmaking – according to their preferences.

It is a source of great pride and pleasure to know that after fifty years have gone by, these young children have grown up into educated and responsible adults, taking their rightful place in the world in spite of the cruelties of the Nazis' hateful regime.

Eva Yachnes

(Steiner, Vienna), Bronx, NY, USA

I was screaming, hysterically clinging to my grandmother with all the strength of my six year old arms. I was beyond words; finally there was no choice but to detach me bodily and put me on the train with the other children. It was a night in late December 1938, and my family had at last found a way to get me out of Austria – I had a place on a Kindertransport. My mother was to meet me in England, where she had already been since April.

The next day the train was halted in Germany, and soldiers boarded to check our papers and search our luggage.

I clung to my coat. 'See where I've sewn Mummy's name and address into your coat. If you're lost, show it to a grown-up,' was one of my grandmother's parting reminders. The soldiers, however, were not very interested in us; the train soon moved on.

It was late at night when we passed through Holland, and boarded the ferry.   When the ferry docked in England, we were herded into a large customs shed. Here we were given brief physical examinations. It was my bad luck to be examined by a nun – I had always been afraid of nuns in their billowing black habits. And this one spoke only English, which made her even more frightening.

Our next stop was a children's summer camp, unheated except for one pot-bellied stove in the recreation hall. That night, we were put to bed in small chalets scattered around the main building. The warm glow from my bath soon faded, in spite of the thick flannel dressing gown I had been given.

'Move your legs quickly back and forth,' the woman minding us said as we lay shivering in our cold beds. 'That will warm up the sheets.' Dressing in the cold the next morning was misery. We bundled into our outer clothes and paired off for the walk to breakfast.

All that day people came to the camp to choose children to take home with them. Most of the children on the train were orphans or had left their parents behind in Austria. In the confusion and rush to get us to better quarters, no one had time to pay attention to one small girl claiming to have a mother in England. And, in the general muddle, no one had informed my mother that the train had arrived, or where we were.

Soon I, too, was claimed. A young Congregational Minister, wanting to adopt a little girl near his four year old son's age, chose me.

Christmas had just passed, and my new family had a present for me – a baby doll dressed in a blue crocheted outfit. I had had to leave my beloved dolls behind, so I was delighted with my present. I carried her everywhere, and slept with her that night.

Their little boy showed me his new electric train set. We communicated by gestures. My father had tried to teach me some English before he left Vienna, but that had been back in July. The only words that I could remember from those lessons were 'Yes' and 'No'. I used them – correctly when I understood the question – or more often than not, by guessing what was wanted.

The minister knew a little German, his wife none. I showed them my mother's name and address in my coat, and tried to tell them that this was my mother. They were convinced, however, that I was an orphan. They couldn't imagine whose name and address this might be, or how she was related to me, but they decided to write and find out. That letter was the first step in reuniting me with my mother.

'To whom it may concern,' the letter began. 'We have a little girl in our house with your name and address in her coat.'

*   *   *

Jesse Zierler

(Berlin), London, UK

It was June 1939. I lived in Berlin and had been picked with about twenty-five other children, aged thirteen to fifteen, to spend one week at a selection centre at Hamburg/Blankenese for emigration to Britain.

The girls had all been assigned to domestic duties, while we boys were taken to the huge orchards on the Warburg family estate for cherry harvesting. We soon became reasonably expert at clearing the trees of fruit without removing our hands from our pockets, which left our baskets only about half full.

One of the estate's Alsatians arrived on the scene and drawn to one particular boy, took a deep interest in Bernie's private parts. This left Bernie more or less transfixed, pleading with us to give the brute some alternative interest in life.

The next morning found the dog almost waiting for Bernie's arrival, immediately pushing his snout up Bernie's shorts and only occasionally coming up for air. Much to Bernie's despair, this turned into a daily routine. By Friday night all of us had gone down with stomach cramps. Except Bernie, who had lost his appetite for cherries.

Surprisingly we passed the selection. Now waiting to leave for home, we spent our last day at Blankenese interviewing some of the new arrivals. In the guise of an official reception committee, we took down such personal details as what they wished to be served for breakfast, their favourite filmstars, and did they possess the regulation number of legs. They answered our questions without exception, too nervous to object.

We arrived at Harwich on 23 August 1939, and on to Great Engeham Farm in Kent. There seemed nothing but tents, hundreds of them. And hundreds of children who all ignored our arrival. Ten of us boys were directed to a small tent with ample room to sleep six. Night-time brought the inevitable pillow fight.

The night patrol outside managed to bring our battle to an abrupt end, pulling out the groundpegs of our tent which then collapsed. We learned how to erect a tent at night in less than two hours, and too exhausted for further battle fell asleep.

The following night saw a repeat performance with very much the same result. On the third night, quite undeterred by punitive measures so far handed out, we planned our counteraction. At the first sign of tent walls slackening, we grabbed hold of the tentpole which now remained upright. After a good ten minutes it became quite clear that none of us was going to get any sleep standing squashed against the pole and by a majority vote decided to let go.

We had become quite expert at erecting our tent in the dark, and were badly in need of a change. Four days later we left the camp. 180 children belonging to *Mizrachi* made their arrival at Gwrych Castle in North Wales. This was to be our home for an indefinite period together with our six *Madrichim*. No more collapsing tents! Walls at least fourteen inches thick that had stood for centuries gave us a sense of reassurance. We had no beds, no sanitation, no electricity. But we did have a real castle. Its builders had clearly intended it to be occupied by 180 children who very quickly settled down to its comforts and facilities.

A flat-topped solid wood contraption, richly carved on all four sides, graced the first floor landing. It might well have been designed for resting the coffin of a recently departed member of the family. From our point of view it now served a far better purpose as ping-pong table, being of almost regulation height and size. It very soon became the venue for inter-group and inter-room tournaments, and greatly helped improve the overall standard of table-tennis, but not doing much to maintain the antique's appearance.

As winter approached, a large consignment of second-hand frayed clothes arrived on our doorstep. It had been donated by more affluent members of society and provided us with sufficient gents' suits and ladies' dresses to last until old age. None of it was of any immediate use except one rare item. An

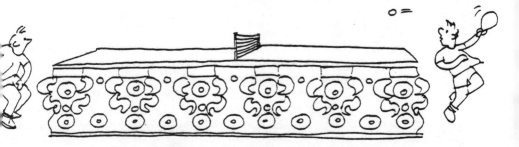

old bowler hat took a fancy to me. It fitted like a glove and we became virtually inseparable. I did take it off at night.

Romantic associations soon began to flourish. This generally took the form of 'serious' discussions on some quite idiotic subject. I had been approached by one pretty girl who, impressed no doubt with my bowler hat, insisted on my helping her studies of geography. I did know that Africa was to the South. In the afternoon she worked in the kitchen and had access to certain delicacies. She brought along two very large Spanish onions, a welcome feast for our ever-hungry stomachs. Romance however failed to blossom.

A fancy dress parade had been announced for *Purim*. The winner was to receive a giant box of chocolates some benevolent visitors had donated. The girls furiously prepared their costumes. Queens, princesses, pirates, you name it. Imaginations ran riot. Boys were less enthusiastic and on the whole were more concerned with pursuing their normal routine of advanced inactivity.

Herman Rothmann and I retreated to our room for a well-earned rest. I was fast asleep when our *Madrich* looked in, threw us out of bed accompanied by a lecture on such matters as failing to fall into the spirit of things, etc.

Given that kind of incentive we made for the old-clothes cupboard, and with less than ten minutes to go, selected two moth-eaten ladies' dresses, two enormous wide brimmed floral hats (once paraded at Ascot before Queen Victoria) and some other *shmattes* to form respectable bosoms. A heavy woollen sweater rolled into a bundle was to play the part of a mongrel. We somehow laid our hands on an old rusty bicycle without tyres, brakes or a seat. It did however have a bell that worked loud and clear.

Thus kitted out, we entered the packed auditorium which had just about finished applauding the last of the participants. With our appearance all hell broke loose. The outcome was never really in doubt. Waltzing off with our fully-deserved box of milk and plain assortment, our popularity with the opposite sex increased beyond belief.

One section of the castle's cellar had been well barricaded by the owner to discourage any unwelcome visitors. As it had also been placed out of bounds to us, the time had come for some investigation. Our labours through a long corridor revealed racks carrying hundreds of assorted bottles, covered in

thick dust and cobwebs. They had clearly been forgotten by the owner when he moved. The labels showed them containing wine, which by now could have gone off.

It made sound sense to sample some of them before getting rid of the lot, in case some of it was still all right. We must have tried dozens without finding one single bad drop. In fact the wine improved with continuous tasting. Further experimentations brought our judgement to a state of warm appreciation. The less sweet variety seemed fine to wash off the dirt and cobwebs we were all covered in.

Shortly after, in the summer of 1941 we were evicted. The owner had either planned to keep all the remaining wine for himself, or now intended turning the castle into a proper ruin. My very recent visit to Gwrych Castle proved the latter to have been the case. I was filled with nostalgia and sadness.

Gwrych Castle in 1989

Aufstellung über alle von der Kultusgemeinde, Wien, abgefertigten Kindertransporte vom 10.12.1938-22.8.1939

12. 12. 1938	England	400 Kinder	
	Holland	59	
17. 12.	England	132	
18. 12.	England	68	
19. 12.	Belgien	7	
20. 12.	England	134	
21. 12.	England	117	
26. 12.	Frankreich	6	923 Kinder
10. 1. 1939	England	83 Kinder	
	Holland	13	
11. 1.	Belgien	21	
	England	112	
12. 1.	Schweden	7	
31. 1.	Belgien	18	
	Holland	7	261 Kinder
19. 2. 1939	Holland	5 Kinder	
20. 2.	England	107	
21. 2.	Belgien	10	
22. 2.	Belgien	20	142 Kinder
6. 3. 1939	Belgien	70 Kinder	
13. 3.	England	140	
14. 3.	Frankreich	50	
22. 3.	Frankreich	53	
27. 3.	England	118	
	Holland	19	450 Kinder
17. 4. 1939	Belgien	17 Kinder	
23. 4.	Schweden	46	
25. 4.	England	124	187 Kinder
13. 5. 1939	England	84 Kinder	
21. 5.	Amerika	50	
22. 5.	Schweiz	5	139 Kinder
3. 6. 1939	England	78 Kinder	
7. 6.	Schweden	25	
13. 6.	England	69	
20. 6.	England	85	257 Kinder
4. 7. 1939	England	102 Kinder	
11. 7.	England	102	
16. 7.	England	38	
25. 7.	England	49	291 Kinder
1. 8. 1939	England	70 Kinder	
8. 8.	England	49	
15. 8.	England	40	
22. 8.	England	35	194 Kinder
			2844 Kinder

Editors Note

The following stories were received too late for alphabetical insertion in the main text.

Leo Bergman

(Ludwigshafen), Coseley, West Midlands, UK

In October 1938 I missed being deported to the Polish frontier because my father pretended that he did not have a passport.

On *Kristallnacht* I saw our Synagogue being burned down, and our home and shop ransacked and smashed.

On 5 January 1939 I left Ludwigshafen with my older brother, after our step-mother had arranged our departure with the *Jüdische Gemeinde*. We arrived in Harwich next day, after a journey through Germany and Holland, picking up more children at various stations. My brother and I stayed in Dovercourt until selected by a Jewish family from New Cross, London.

After a few months in London with this family, we were sent to a hostel in Margate. In June 1940, after the fall of France, we were evacuated to Chase Terrace near Walsall in the West Midlands.

We were again selected, this time to stay with an English family. After a few months we were once more transferred to another family, where we stayed until fourteen. During the latter part of the war a Jewish teacher from Birmingham visited us during weekends to give us Hebrew lessons, as well as tins of kosher meat. I was invited to stay in Birmingham for my *Bar Mitzvah*.

At age fourteen I left school and Chase Terrace, and obtained a job in Birmingham at £1 per week, and subsequently found lodgings in Birmingham.

In 1948, at the age of twenty, I volunteered for *Machal* to join the Israel Army. I left the Army in May 1949 and obtained work in Haifa at the oil refinery.

In 1950 I returned to England and did various kinds of work. In 1954 I met a young lady in Birmingham and married her in 1956. We settled in Coseley and have lived here ever since. We have two grown-up sons.

In 1957 I joined local government in the finance department and have been working in the public service for thirty-one years; the last six years as a finance officer for the Birmingham Polytechnic.

This is briefly what has happened to me since, by a miracle, I was saved from the horrible fate which befell most of my family.

*　　*　　*

Bertha Bracey, O.B.E.

A friend for Jewish Children

Bertha Bracey, a quaker who played a large part in the Society of Friends' efforts to rescue Jews and other victims of Nazism from Germany before the Second World War, died at the age of 95.

In early 1939 Bertha Bracey became the organizing secretary of the recently set up Inter-Church Committee to help Christians and others of Jewish origin who were trapped in Germany. The Friends at this time mounted a special operation which resulted in some thousands German-Jewish children getting to safety in Britain.

It was Bertha Bracey who, on behalf of the Quakers, went with Lord Samuel, the Liberal statesman, to persuade Sir Samuel Hoare, then Home Secretary, to secure Parliament's urgent consent. This was under the impact of the Nazis' *Kristallnacht* pogrom of November 1938.

The Quakers had responded to an appeal from a prominent Nuremberg Jew on behalf of German Jewish parents desperate to get their children to safety. A small group of English Quakers went to Germany to make the local arrangements because it was judged too dangerous for any English Jews to visit Hitler's Germany.

Bertha Bracey had lived in Germany during the 1920's doing youth work as a member of the Quakers' War Victims Relief Committee teams in Berlin and Nuremberg. This was part of the Society's efforts towards post-war reconciliation. She acquired a deep knowledge of German ways and spoke excellent German and after Hitler seized power in 1933 she became secretary of the Germany Emergency Committee set up by the Society in London.

Under her co-ordination, Quakers from England began working to help those of Jewish origin, and others persecuted by the regime, including inmates of the concentration camps, obtain the right emigration papers to overcome the bureaucratic hurdles in their way. Her team was often helped by German Quakers to identify those in need.

The Quakers had also to obtain guarantors in Britain who would take on financial responsibility for the refugees and their families.

In 1946 she left her work with the Quakers to join the Allied Control Commission in Germany, later supervising women's affairs in the British and American zones. Again, she sought to bridge the gulf between those who had recently been enemies.

She was appointed OBE in 1942.

Bertha Bracey was born in Bournville where her father worked for Cadburys and, after taking a degree at Birmingham University, was for a while a teacher. She never married.

* * *

Eva Brück

(Morgenstern, Vienna), East Berlin, German Democratic Republic

We were lucky. Without a series of coincidences we would have shared the fate of six million other Jews, whose lives rose to heaven as smoke from the chimneys of Auschwitz or Maidanek concentrations camps. Each of us has a story which should be told to those born after us.

Bert Brecht said: "Der Schoss ist fruchtbar noch
aus dem das kroch."
(The womb that brought forth those creatures is still fertile).

I think that Jews, driven from one country to the other throughout the long history of the Diaspora, frequently playing an important part at crossroads of the paths of human destiny, are predestined to make – even if, as in this case, only a modest – contribution to the great task of building bridges of understanding in the world.

The Nazis came in the night to search our flat. I was torn out of sleep; I thought I was still dreaming. Our room was a scene of wild chaos. Everything was scattered over the floor – linen, books, toys. Strange men in SA and SS uniforms were barking crudely at my mother, who was standing in the middle of the room in her nightdress with dishevelled hair, with my sleepy crying brother on her arm. A young man in the brown SA uniform held a smoking gun in his hand and said : 'We've just bumped off one red bastard, now we've come for the next one . . .' With a fright I was immediately wide awake and almost cried out with horror. Behind a blue curtain at the foot of my bed, which concealed dressing gowns and a laundry bag, I saw my father, pale and motionless like a wax figure. I was struck with terror; another moment and they would tear away the curtain and . . .

Noise from the street, rough bawling and cries interrupted my thoughts. And then, as though by a miracle, the Nazis had disappeared, as suddenly as they had come. For a few moments we all remained motionless in fear, waiting whether they would return. They did not come back that night. Before dawn my father was taken by his comrades across the German frontier.

My brother and I were strictly ordered not to reply to any questions by other people about my father and the family, except by the words: *My name is Rabbit; I know nothing!*

'Say only that – not a word more, do you hear? No matter what happens or who should ask – even if the auntie or uncle is ever so nice, gives you sweets, make promises. . .'

My brother and I were taken to Auntie Lotte for a time. Her husband, Uncle Fritz, still 'magnanimously' allowed his wife to receive her Jewish relations then. He was told that my mother was ill. My mother had warned us against uncle Fritz, with justification as it soon became evident – because dear uncle Fritz very quickly turned out to be a staunch Nazi. Not long after

Hitler came to power, he divorced his Jewish wife, and chased her and their little son out into the street without a penny. After a long ordeal they were able to emigrate thanks to the help of my mother. While we were staying with my aunt, my mother and our faithful maid Martha packed all our things, sent off boxes and books and some furniture and household accessories and prepared a damp lightless basement room in a different area of the city as emergency accommodation. We never went back to the *Feuerbachstrasse*.

Once again we had to move. This time to an even worse dungeon in a strange environment, where nobody knew us and we knew nobody. My mother managed to conjure up homely comfort even in this dreary place. With a few orange crates, covered with brightly coloured oilcloth, a bunch of flowers in empty bottling jars fished out of a rubbish bin, carefully rinsed and painted with cheerful colours, an old blanket cut up and transformed into a curtain – and the room had an almost homely atmosphere.

I had not been able to go to school for some time, The 'secular' school had ceased to exist, and we had, so to speak, gone 'underground'. For all the world we had disappeared.

And then, one day, I was so sick of spending my days in the dark dungeon when the sun was shining outside, I slipped out into the steet and played with my ball, when suddenly I heard screeching brakes close to me. Before I knew what was happening, I was squeezed in on the back seat of a car, between two strange men in leather coats, their hats drawn almost over their eyes. Generally a car drive was exciting and pleasant, but this time it was uncanny and I was stunned with fear. After a long drive the car stopped outside a tall brick building. The strange men took me across a long passage, then up some stairs, into a room with no furniture, except a heavy desk and a few chairs. Then a man came in wearing a white overall, who looked like doctor. He looked at me with a piercing glance, like a wild beast looks at its prey, and unpacked some instruments out of a bag. I was terribly frightened, but was unable to cry or shout, nor resist. There was only one thing I had in mind all the time: '*My name is Rabbit; I know nothing*'.

That was all these people got out of me, despite apparent kindness at first, despite painful blows later, despite vile abuses and threats, and despite horrible 'investigations', during which I was tied to a high chair, the purpose of which I could not understand. I cannot remember what actually happened; I only know that my legs were torn apart by beasts with angry faces, that I closed my eyes and felt great pain, and I heard them say again and again that I should answer their questions or it would hurt even more. Since that time I am overcome by uncontrollable fear every time I have to go to a gynaecologist. . . .

I have no idea how long I was kept in that room. I only remember that I was suddenly sitting on the cold damp pavement of an unknown street, leaning against a wall, without underpants, shoes or stockings, with my coat torn; a bleeding nose and the left eye so swollen that I could hardly open it. I tried to get up and walk, but walking was no less painful than sitting. Wherever I put my hand, I was full of sticky blood. I felt dizzy and did not know what to do. I did not even know the name of the street where we were living at that time. I crept into a house entrance, where it was not quite as cold as in the street where it was windy, wet and getting dark. I must have gone to sleep with exhaustion, as I was suddenly aware of a strange woman standing over me, asking what was wrong and to whom I belonged.

'To . . . to Frau Klawitter' I sobbed, as though I was thawing at the sound of a friendly human voice, evidently genuinely concerned and willing to help me. 'At the grocer's shop in the *Feuerbachstrasse* in Steglitz . . . *My name is Rabbit; I know nothing!*

The strange woman had a kind heart. She took me to Frau Klawitter. When we arrived there, it was late at night. Frau Klawitter came to the door in her nightdress. She looked at me and threw up her hands in dismay. 'My God, my God' she exclaimed, thanked the strange woman and took me into her large, soft and sweaty arms. The strange woman wanted to explain where and how she had found me, but Frau Klawitter only thanked her once more and then hastily pulled me inside the flat, as though I really belonged to her. My mother had been her customer for years, and evidently it had got around what happened to us that night, and that we had since disappeared.

'My name is Rabbit; I know nothing!' I kept repeating again and again. 'All right, all right, little girl,' said Frau Klawitter and asked no questions. She washed and bandaged me and packed me into bed already occupied by another little girl, who was fast asleep. I was so exhausted that I must have dropped off immediately. When I woke up, there was Martha, who took me to my mother. At the end of that day we left Berlin for Vienna to my father's mother, known to us as 'Oma Wien' (Grandma Vienna).

The five years in Vienna, from April 1933 to April 1938, seem to me a long and decisive period of my life; almost longer and no less decisive than the first seven years in Berlin. I cannot remember in detail how we travelled from Berlin to Vienna. I only retained the scene of our dear faithful maid Martha. A girl from the country, around twenty years of age, who had stood by my mother with courage and self-sacrifice in those days of hardship and became a reliable friend, stood on the platform, weeping desperately as our train started rolling away.

Only now can I fully appreciate how hard it must have been for my mother to travel into the uncertainty of a new life with two small children and hardly any money, not knowing the whereabouts of her husband or whether he was still at large and alive, and if and when she would see him again, and forced to leave behind so much that she had built up in years of hard work. But my mother was young, full of courage, energy and optimism.

On my desk before me today, as I write these lines more than half a century later, I have a photo of her when she was about my present age. She is sitting in a room of her house in Oxford, England; one of the many homes she had made cosy, attractive and comfortable with endless energy and persistence in the course of her eventful life. She radiates vitality, courage and confidence, even years after she found her last repose.

My father, who had managed to leave Germany earlier, was united with us again at Oma Wien's flat. She and our other relatives in Vienna selflessly helped and assisted us during the next five years until the Nazi invasion of Austria.

One day in March 1938 I was on my way home from school. When I turned into the Schottenring from the Herrengasse, I was suddenly swept forward amidst a crowd of pushing, shouting people. On the Kärntnerstrasse I heard terribly coarse, barking shouts of *'Sieg Heil! Sieg Heil!'* by hundreds of voices.

The Nazis were in power! Anyone in their way was knocked down. As a stimulant and outlet, Communists and Jews were thrown as prey to mob violence, in the same way as in Germany, five years earlier. Yet the scenes which had taken place in Germany when the Nazis seized power, abominable as they had been, could almost be described as 'mild' compared with the bestial excesss in which innumerable 'good natured' Austrians participated.

Apart from the charming and light-hearted cheerful side of that which is described as the 'Austrian national character', there is also another side which is extremely repugnant: gloating pleasure at the expense of others is its main feature. That quality is very frequently evident among a significant part of this generally musical and soft-hearted nation, above all in the incited mob. Things which normally ripple lightly on the edge of Austrian life as side phenomena in the form of gossip, gloating mockery or grousing, can very quickly result in the development of the most vile informers, brutal sadism and vicious aggression, if the green light is given to mob violence. *'A Hetz'*, *'a Gaudi'* – having fun, especially at the expense of others – has always been a favourite leisure occupation of the masses in Austria. The Nazis consciously whipped up all primitive instincts in that mass. Everything that was basically inadmissible and in violation of the principles of justice, law, religion and human civilization was suddenly permitted to everyone – children, adolescents and adults, men and women – provided it was directed against Jews, Negroes and Communists.

Howling de-humanized crowds with sadistically distorted faces relished in the destruction and pillage of Jewish shops as spectators and as actors. They watched with satisfaction as Jewish men and women, among them old and sick people who found it hard to move, we dragged by arrogant SA men out of their homes and forced with horse whips to wipe away slogans against the Nazis for the plebiscite planned for 13 March from the pavements. Jews were forced to dip floor cloths into buckets of hydrochloric acid with their bare hands and to scrub the pavements on their knees, surrounded by a crowd of bestial sadists, who were free to jeer and spit at them, to kick them and to throw stones and dirt at them. Jewish doctors were dragged from their surgeries, professors from the universities, musicians from their instruments and sick people from their beds. Orthodox Jews and Rabbis in their caftans were driven to the slaughterhouses and forced with blows and kicks to go down on their knees and to lick up the blood of pigs from the soiled floor. The transition from normal life to this indescribable horror came overnight. The Nazis began to rage as soon as they had set foot across the frontier. In schools the teachers were forced immediately to raise their hand for the Nazi salute as they entered the classroom. Jewish children had to sit on the back benches, and were ultimately thrown out.

One evening we were having supper, when there was frantic knocking on the door. When I opened it, Hedy Endress, the older sister of my friend Liesl stood there. In tears, shaking and trembling, and stammering in anxiety, she warned my parents not to turn on the light and not to show themselves at the window. The Nazis were going to fetch them for scrubbing the streets, because my father was a red swine and a dirty Jew, and the SS were combing all houses for Jews and Communists. When Hedy had left, we all stood in the dark, peeping through the window, concealed behind the curtains. Shuddering with horror we looked down at the men and women on their knees, scrubbing, groaning and weeping, assaulted, jeered, humiliated and tormented by the frenzied sadists around them. That evening we were spared.

Thumping boots and gruff voices tore me out of my sleep.

'Look at that! So the Communist swine want to go on a trip . . .,' I hear a jeering male voice next door.

'But those who have no passport have to stay at home, old boy, don't you know?'

'Where is your passport, you bastard?' asked the voice. Another short exchange of words, thumping steps, then the door was slammed.

Silence. All this happened so quickly that I only began to realize the situation after they had left.

The passports! I clearly remembered that my father had deposited a large envelope containing our passports and documents on the desk under a briefcase. I hopped out of bed and ran into the living room, where the light was still burning. The desk was strewn with boxes, bags and rucksack. I found the envelope with the passports under the briefcase. Meanwhile my brother had also woken up and began to cry. I stood in the living room, amidst crates, boxes and luggage, wondering what to do next, when I noticed the cut telephone wire. It make me think of that first night in Berlin, when I experienced a house search for the first time.

For several months our small room had been inhabited by one of my father's patients, a girl of fifteen, named Nelly Kraus. She had come for treatment, because she was afflicted by a severe neurosis. She could hadly eat anything and what she ate had to be mashed up. The doctors had not discovered any physical symptoms that might have been the cause. She had come to live with us for a time, and my mother had to prepare all her meals separately. She was a frail creature with dark hair, nervously blinking eyes which reminded me of a night owl caught in a beam of light. When my brother woke up that night and called for his mother, Nelly came out of her room and asked what was going on. When I told her, she took charge of my brother and suggested that I should try to find my parents at the police station. She had heard that Jews were rounded up and taken there to be deported. 'Surely they will let them go if you produce the passports!'

That sounded plausible enough and I was astonished that this shy and neurotic girl was suddenly so calm and grown up. I threw a coat over my pyjamas, slipped into my shoes and hurried to the police station. It was dark outside. I saw a crowd of people in front of the building; men and women, many of them wrapped in blankets, nightdresses or pyjamas, with tousled hair, frightened and agitated, some sobbing, others shouting and calling the names of their relatives. Some women held small children in their arms. It was cold and wet. Then I saw the trucks, covered with tarpaulin, hovering like bleak shadows in the dark. A beam of light was cast on the dreadful scene when an SA man stepped out of the door, followed by a group of others, bawling and slashing at those around them with rubber truncheons and loading them into the trucks. With all my might I battled my way towards the door and into an evil smelling and overcrowded room, where I spotted my parents sitting on a bench next to a door leading to another room. Suddenly an SA man pushed that door open and hit an old man in the face. The old man stood on the side of the door opposite the bench where my parents sat. The old man cried out with pain, whereupon he received another blow in the face, which was covered with blood. The SA man was about to raise his hand once more to hit the old man, who was hardly able to remaining standing. I saw my mother jump to shield him from the blow. My father also rose in an attempt to protect my mother, who stood before the old man and looked at the SA brute in calm and fearless dignity. My heart beat wildly as I expected him to hit my mother, but he suddenly let his arm drop, pushed the old man to one side and my parents to the other, and barked: 'The trucks are full; we'll collect all of you for the next transport!' At that point I managed to force my way through the crowd and get to my parents.

As though by a miracle we were saved once again.

That same night we left Vienna.

Editor's Note: Eva Brück kindly gave us permission to print extracts from her manuscript in this book. She has travelled around the world for many years and has written extensively. We gratefully acknowledge her valuable contribution.

* * *

Mary Bunn

Peterborough, UK

I was not a Jewish refugee, but one who had many friends amongst this group of children. I was twelve years old at the outbreak of war and living in the tiny village of Whipsnade, mainly known for its zoo.

We had no school in the village because there were not enough children to warrant one. Then came 1939 and evacuees came to our village from London. The group were from a school in the Hampstead area. A few children were English, but most were Jewish German refugees. Before the children were handed over to foster parents, the villagers were asked to volunteer to take the Jewish children. I did not think about this very much at that time, but much later it occurred to me that the foster parents who took in these children were practising Christian families.

My parents took into our home a brother and sister, making us then a family with four children. They were with us for just a few months, and were two of the most lucky ones, as their parents managed to get to England and later they all went to America. The rest of the group remained in the village right through their school days (now a school in the old village hall) and got jobs locally. Some boys joined the Army on reaching eighteen years.

Several of these children were my friends right through my adolescent years, and I could not have had better friends. I marvelled at the brave way they coped with life without parents and when they were waiting for the so rare letters from their parents. I really suffered with them, particularly when the time came that no more letters arrived.

I will never forget my wonderful friends of those war years. If anyone should contact you who had been at Whipsnade, I would love to hear from them.

*　　*　　*

Günther Cahn

(Düsseldorf), Scarborough, Ont., Canada

I came to England in March 1939 via the *USS Manhattan* from Hamburg to Southampton.

I was sent to Rowden Hall School in Margate and lived there until we were evacuated in 1940 to Cannock Chase, Staffordshire. After a few months at a secondary school, I started work in leather goods in Walsall.

In 1943 I joined the R.A.F. I was stationed in Germany from March 1945 to August 1950 and took part in the Berlin Airlift.

I married Renate in March 1952, and we left for Canada in September 1954. I worked in leather goods again until 1961, when we opend and owned children's wear stores for twenty-five years. I retired in July 1985.

* * *

Renate Cahn

(Herzog, Krefeld), Scarborough, Ont., Canada

I came to England on 19 June 1939 together with my brother Manfred and Helmuth Cahn (now Harry Curtis living in Ruislip, Middlesex, UK), who was to become my future brother-in-law, although of course I did not know this at the time.

At first I stayed in a boarding house in Margate. Just before the outbreak of war, I came to London and stayed in the Willesden Lane hostel. I worked in a factory making small leather goods, e.g.: belts etc. In 1941, during the Blitz, we were bombed out, and I was moved to another hostel in Belsize Park. I did war work as a lathe operator until after the war, when I went back to working in leather goods.

I got married in 1944, had a daughter in 1947 and was divorced in 1949. I married again in 1952, this time Günther Cahn, Helmuth's brother. My husband, daughter and I came to Canada in February 1955. In 1961 we opened children's wear stores, where I worked for twenty-five years. I am now retired.

My brother Manfred, joined the British Army and was killed on the last day of the war.

* * *

Stella Cooper

Leeds, UK

I was fifteen years old in 1938, and my family, consisting of my widowed mother, elder brother and myself, were part of the Jewish community in Harrogate, Yorkshire.

I remember a committee being formed to sponsor a hostel to house Jewish refugee girls from Germany. My mother worked on that committee. She and her friend Mrs Solk were the wardrobe ladies, providing and distributing all clothing for as long as the girls remained in residence in Harrogate. They also gave their love, friendship and a motherly ear. The matron was Mrs. Wolfe.

When my mother remarried in 1942, she was invited to dinner at the hostel and was presented with a hand embroidered table cloth. Each one of the girls had handstitched some part of the cloth. My mother treasured that table cloth and its story has been told many times.

My mother died in 1983, aged ninety years. She was a dear, sweet and caring lady.

The table cloth, which is getting rather worn now, is in my care now, and I continue to tell its story over and over again.

I hope that some of the ex Harrogate girls will read this, and that the years have dealt kindly with you all. Many of you will have children of your own. I hope they give you all much love, respect and a happy family life.

* * *

Hilda Francis

Oswestry, Shropshire, UK

Our Oswestry Fellowship of Reconciliation Group was concerned about what was happening in your countries in 1937 and wanted to help. We knew that the Quakers were bringing children over at their parents' request, so we decided to guarantee two children to be company for each other; i.e.: to be responsible for each child until fifteen years old. We felt that if we made a start, other local help would be forthcoming. It was!

That same week I saw an advert in the Church Times, asking for a home for one Czech child. I replied, saying that we would like two. Kathe Grünwald, an Austrian Jewess from Vienna working as a cook in London, replied. She was trying to find homes for the two daughters of a Czech friend. She put us in touch with their parents and we received a prompt reply from Wilhelm Neumann in English-German, thanking us and stating that he and his wife hoped to get here too. She did, but found English difficult to learn; so different from Czech. We asked the Quakers to bring the children over, and the two girls, Edith (ten) and Melitta (nine), arrived in England, but were sent to two different homes in Kent. Meanwhile we had rented a partly furnished house some three miles from Oswestry, with a big garden, two small fields, five bedrooms and out-buildings for the Neumann family and others we hoped would come.

Instead of the girls, we were asked to take twelve adults for a time. They arrived: Two doctors and their wives, three other couples and two single men; the former with luggage, but the latter eight without anything. Local people called on them, bringing much needed gifts. A week or so later I called and found that the gardener had organized the men to dig and plant the garden, using all the seeds which we had provided. It was a happy household until a letter arrived from H.Q., saying that the three couples and the two single men should have gone to a camp in Scotland en route for Canada. I shall never forget that day and the agony of having to ask them to leave. I do not remember

their names and would like to know what became of them.

That left Dr and Mrs Myers and Dr and Mrs Bergson. They did not think that the Neumann parents would succeed in coming to England, and so we made arrangements for two friends to share their homes with these two couples.

On Good Friday 1938 we received a card from Mr Neumann saying that he and his brother-in-law had crossed the frontier and hoped to arrive in Oswestry soon. He did arrive and, after visiting his daughters in Kent, was satisfied that they were happy, and would we guarantee his two nieces instead. He and his wife, when she arrived, would care for the four girls at Selattyn.

So we arranged two more guarantees for Liesl and Britta Neumann, aged eight and eleven. They duly arrived at Selattyn, as did Edith and Melitta and their parents.

When war broke out, Mr Neumann was interned, and Mrs Neumann coped with the four girls, who came to stay with me and my father during school holidays. The four girls went to the village school and got on very well with the villagers. Those who qualified went on to High School in Oswestry. When the war ended, Mr and Mrs Neumann obtained jobs at a Czech centre in London and so this period also ended. I would like to know what they are doing and where they are now.

There were also four other Czech children in Oswestry – Tommy Katz and a young girl, both of which were taken into Miss Morrell's school. Tommy's parents arrived, and Dr Katz, like Dr Myers, soon found a post in a hospital. Two girls of sixteen also came, but without guarantees. Miss Morrell had one, and we had Hana Bandler. Hana had been told by her parents that she was being sent to England to be educated, and she wanted to work in a laboratory. Hana lived with me and my old father during the daytime, but slept in the house of a friend, as we felt that it would be better for her to be with a family with children. Before long she was 'adopted' by a group of friends in Shrewsbury, and went to Priory School until the Czech school was opened in Llandrindod Wells.

Two other Czech couples, friends of those already mentioned, also found homes in Oswestry.

Emily Rogers was the stalwart of our group. She fetched most of these children from London in her old car. I would like to have her name mentioned.

Editors Note: Hilda Francis wrote this story in December 1988 at the age of 94 years!

Vera Gissing

(Diamant, Prague), London, UK

In June 1939, shortly before my eleventh birthday, I came to Britain from occupied Czechoslovakia with a children's transport, organized by Nicholas Winton. My sister Eva, four and a half years my senior, travelled with me, but I saw little of her during the war, as she was based in a different part of England.

The war started before I had a chance to settle down with my adoptive family in Liverpool, and I was evacuated. In the autumn of 1941 I joined the Czechoslovak school, first in Shropshire and then in Wales. The small colony of Czech refugee children and staff were like a large extended family, and the closeness which grew out of adversity has remained to this day.

By the time I returned to Prague in 1945, I knew that both my parents had perished in the Holocaust. In Prague I continued my studies, but the void which my parents' death had created, coupled with anti-semitism and antagonism towards those connected with Britain, which surfaced after the Communist coup in 1948, drove me back to Britain.

I married an Englishman, had three children, worked in the family import fashion business, and, as a hobby, translated books from Czech into English – then started writing my own – particularly for children. In recent years I divorced, and now share my life with a man of the same background, with whom I had shared a classroom forty-five years ago!

The memories and emotions rekindled by a reunion of the Czech school in 1985, prompted me to open the diaries I had kept throughout the war, and to find the strength to relive the past and tell my story. I am proud to say that *Pearls of Childhood* was published by Robson Books in September 1988, and that the reaction of the media and general public has been most rewarding. Although it is a book for adults, it is being introduced into schools and colleges as a piece of history in human form; the general feeling being that the diary extracts make it an authentic record, and that even youngsters will be able to understand and identify with the little girl who had to grow up under such extraordinary – but to us so common – circumstances.

At my publisher's request, I am now working on the continuation of the story.

*	*	*

Jeffrey Hammond

(Hammer, Hamburg), Edinburgh, Scotland, UK

My name was Jacob Hammer and I lived in Hamburg with my parents, who had a wholesale perfumery business. After my father's death in 1940, my mother, eldest sister Berta and her daughter Gisela, aged five years, were all deported to Auschwitz concentration camp on 11 June 1941 and there met their fate which befell so may of our fellow Jews.

My younger sister Toni managed to get to Portugal, and married Alfonso Cassuto, also from Hamburg. Unfortunately she died there soon after 1942. She left my brother-in-law and two children, who still live near Lisbon today.

I am married and have three sons and four grandchildren. I settled in Scotland some fifty years ago, after arriving from Hamburg with the unforgettable Kindertransport on 15 December 1938 at Lowestoft. I was seventeen years old then. For a short while I lived in the hostel in Stainbeck Lane, Leeds, and worked for an engineering firm. I was interned and sent to Australia on the infamous hell ship *Dunera*. In Australia I joined the Pioneer Corps and was returned to Scotland serving in the 137th Company in Dumfries and East Calder, where I met my wife Mary. Subsequently, after D-Day, I served in France, Belgium and Rendsburg in Germany. Unfortunately I have lost contact with most of my friends from that period.

*   *   *

Tosca Kempler

(Sussman, Berlin) Forest Hills, N.Y., USA

LIVING MEMORIES – BITTER REFLECTIONS

I was born in Berlin to a very orthodox Jewish-Polish family, consisting of my father Jacob, my mother Sima, my brother Aron and myself.

The war disrupted all our lives. My brother, a brilliant student, who at seventeen years was ready for higher education, was shut out from the university. When my parents sent him to art school, he gave every indication of having a talent that was well worth developing. But that was not to be. The war tore our lives, hopes and dreams to shreds.

While we all tried desperately to survive, I was the only one to do so, partly because I was the right age; my brother was seventeen and my sister too young at four. I was lucky enough to pass the process of selection for the children's transport. I left Berlin in August 1939 and was sent to the Great

Engham Farm, just two weeks before war broke out. My mother's courage at the time of our parting, is still with me today. This was the last Kindertransport leaving Berlin.

As we boarded the train, the Germans threatened the parents that if they went near it, their children would be taken off. My mother defied their threats to say goodbye to me. I still cry at that final goodbye.

On 1 September the war broke out in Europe. My father and brother were sent to Oranienburg concentration camp. My mother was able to buy them out in 1941, and they were given twenty-four hours to leave Germany. But no country would open its doors to them, so they went to Poland which proved to be a worse fate.

In 1942, at the 'Wannsee Conference' in Berlin, the 'Final Solution' was decided upon, and the extermination of the Jews began. My father was sent to Sokolow in Poland, where he was killed. My brother was sent to Stalowa Wolla in Poland, a working camp. In 1944 he tried to escape and was shot. Meanwhile my mother and little sister were in hiding, but they were betrayed and deported. Finally Berlin was *judenrein;* the only Jews who remained were in hiding for the remainder of the war.

I would like to mention that, before I left Berlin, I had to go for four weeks to a *Vorbereitungslager,* Rudnitz. There it was decided who would be accepted or rejected for the Kindertransport. About half the children were rejected – for whatever reason. The policy of the *Palestina Amt* was to take only the cream of the crop of children and reject the others. The *Palestina Amt* only had so many certificates and just so many permits. Because of the political situation at that time, Arab policy interests, etc., the rejected children were unknowingly condemned to death.

On 1 September I was sent to Gwrych Castle in Wales.

Before I conclude, I would like to point out that, when my mother defied the Germans by saying goodbye to me on the railway station platform, I suddenly realized from the depth of my being that this was the end. I would never see her or my family again. I was proved to be right.

Where was the world? What happened to their humanity – their fine sense of values and their lofty sentiments? England did give us refuge, as did Denmak, Sweden, China and Colombia.

I will always be grateful to England for they saved many Jewish children and, among them, myself.

*   *   *   *

Karoline Laib

(Frenkel, Frankfurt), Berkeley, California, USA

INTERVIEW FOR ORAL HISTORY CLASS, 1 MARCH 1984

Eva: I am talking with my friend Karoline, a nurse-practitioner at the Student Health Centre at the University of California at Berkeley, California. I first met Karoline in December 1947, when she immigrated to Berkeley from Frankfurt, Germany, via England. Karoline, I would like to ask you about the significant turning point in your life, which really changed the direction of your life.

Karoline: As you know, there have been a number of turning points in my life, but you want to hear about when I left Germany in 1939. My parents, brother and sister had already left Frankfurt in January, and after a long and anxious period of waiting, I was finally granted a permit to enter Great Britain. I was assigned to the children's transport, which left Frankfurt on 3 May 1939.

Eva: Tell me more about your family in Germany.

Karoline: My father was a physician; a paediatrician and internist in Frankfurt; a well respected citizen, who had earned the highest decorations for bravery during World War 1. My mother was a nurse, whom he had met at the army field hospital in Strasbourg, Alsace. My mother trained with the Red Cross and was an excellent nurse. My father was active in the Jewish Congregation, the Jewish Welfare Board, the orphanage and a number of scientific, medical and natural history organizations. I have a brother who is eighteen months older and a sister who is three and half years younger than I am.

Eva: What initial event happened to cause your parents to leave Germany?

Karoline: The persecution of the Nazis. Life became increasingly restricted. In 1938 father was no longer allowed to practice medicine at large, but was limited to Jewish patients only. We had to move from our flat. On 11 November 1938, the day after the infamous Kristallnacht, my father was deported to Buchenwald concentration camp. He was detained there until mid-December, when we miraculously obtained a permit to emigrate to what was then Palestine. My family left on 30 January 1939.

Eva: Who made the arrangements for you to join a children's transport?

Karoline: In Frankfurt, the Jewish Community Social Welfare Department, and in England, the Committee for the Aid of Children from Germany at Woburn House, London. I had no parents to see me off, as they had already left, but my legal guardian and his wife, who were friends of my parents, helped me with all the formalities which were required.

Eva: Did you have any friends?

Karoline: There was one boy whom I knew from school. He happened to sit across the aisle from me on the train. Rudy was younger than I and we did not know each other well. His sister was in my sister's class.

Eva: How was the journey?

Karoline: Our train left Frankfurt at 6 am and we crossed the border about noon. The customs inspection was very scary; the Gestapo were stern, rough and intimidating. Finally we continued and we knew that we had crossed into Holland, when we saw the friendly people who smiled and waved. In Rotterdam we were taken to a convent and given supper. We crossed the English Channel during the night and arrived in Harwich next morning.

Eva: How old were you?

Karoline: Sixteen.

Eva: What happened next?

Karoline: We continued to London, where the Refugee Committee ladies welcomed us. One of the ladies, Mrs Selma Heinemann, was a distant relative of ours. She took me to her home for the night and the following day I was sent to a hostel in Southport.

Eva: How long did you stay at the hostel?

Karoline: About four months. The hostel was funded and run by the Synagogue Ladies Guild. We had English, elocution and Hebrew lessons and religious instruction. On Saturdays we went to Synagogue. After the Service we were often invited to the home of one of the families. There were fourteen girls and four small sisters. We girls did all the housework and helped with meal preparation. I started school. At first I was a day pupil, but after a short time the headmistress asked me if I would like to live in. I was glad to become a boarder, as I wanted to become part of the British scene and shed my German past as fast as possible.

Eva: Where did you go after you left Southport?

Karoline: I lived at the Brentwood School for Girls and proudly wore school uniform. I was in charge of the youngest group's dormitory, the four to five year olds; getting them up and dressed in the morning, and bathed and into bed at night. I did my studies after they were asleep. At weekends I was in charge of the Jewish girls, taking them to Synagogue on Saturdays and to Hebrew school on Sundays.

Eva: How long did you stay there?

Karoline: I was very happy at Brentwood, preparing for my exams independently and attending the appropriate lessons. I became a prefect – a sort of senior monitor. In the spring of 1940 all aliens had to leave the coastal areas, and that included me, although by then I had been classified as 'a refugee from Nazi oppression'. So, reluctantly, I packed my belongings again and went to a hostel in Manchester. This was quite a different scene. There were boys and girls much older than I, who were working and paid for their room and board. There was no privacy at all. I shared a room with five other girls, and we had to keep our belongings in one suitcase under the bed. I was glad to put up with the situation however, as arrangements had been made for me to attend the local high school.

Eva: Did you have any language barriers when you came to England?

Karoline: I knew some English from high school in Germany and from a summer vacation at Ariye House School in Brighton in 1936, but in order to pass the exam, I had to enlarge my vocabulary, learn grammar and correct spelling.

Eva: You learned it very fast, because when I first met you I noticed that you were one of the few German-Jewish people I knew who had almost no accent, except for a British one.

Karoline: As I wanted to disassociate myself from everything German, I made a point of socialising mostly with English-speaking people and I refused to speak German unless I had to.

Eva: What about the rest of your education? You matriculated and what did you do after that?

Karoline: I looked for a job. I found a position with a physician, whose regular help had an appendectomy. It lasted about six weeks, but was pleasant, though not challenging. Next, I worked for a dressmaker, helping with the sewing. My mother's training came in handy, but this job, too, was short-lived; the business was bombed one night and that was the end. Within a week I landed a job in a factory, cutting loose threads of the army coats they were making there. All the employees were paid according to how many batches of parts they completed. It was called piece work and was very monotonous. Mercifully, I was soon promoted to do the book keeping and payroll. This was a new skill and not too difficult. Meanwhile I had been accepted by the local sick children's hospital and was cleared for 'national service by an alien' as they called it.

Eva: You were about nineteen then?

Karoline: No, I was still eighteen.

Eva: And you graduated from this nursing school?

Karoline: Yes, I graduated in 1945 with a RSCN and went on to study adult nursing and earned my SRN in 1947. I was then selected from my class to be the staff nurse in the operating room, and I enjoyed the challenge of assisting the surgeons and teaching the students theatre technique.

Eva: Since your schooling was interrupted in Germany, I wonder whether you could imagine if you did not have to leave Germany, would your professional life have taken a different direction, or did you always want to be a nurse?

Karoline: No, I did not always want to be a nurse. It was partly what was open to me, and partly necessity. I thought nursing would give me a skill that I could use after the war was over, whereas the Armed Services had duties and training that would probably not be as useful. Also I wanted to live in a more structured and less crowded environment, engage in goal-oriented work and become an informed, skilled professional. I think that medicine or teaching would have been my first choice, but, as you know, my work as a Nurse Practitioner involves teaching healthcare and examining and treating sick patients, which combines the two nicely and is very gratifying.

Eva: Let me touch on your social and religious life. Your father was a fairly orthodox Jew. Did you have any contact with any family members or the Jewish community in England?

Karoline: The hostel in Southport was orientated towards Synagogue and the Jewish congregation. While at boarding school I continued this link through attendance at religious Services and Hebrew school. My matriculation included the subjects of Old Testament and Hebrew and I received some help with my studies from the teachers there. After the move to Manchester, I made friends through the Synagogue youth group. During the nightly air-raids, we would shelter-hop between waves of overhead planes till we reached the social club, which was located in the cellar under the Synagogue, to meet there, play games and socialize and provide moral support to one another. I also enrolled in night school but we rarely had a complete lesson. The 'Jerries' were over Manchester at 7 pm sharp and we all had to go to the shelter.

At that time I was going with a Jewish young man. We met at the youth club, went to the Halle concerts each Sunday afternoon, did some hiking, went to the cinema and swimming. At the hospital, my association with Jewish things and people were very limited, and days off were scheduled without consideration for Jewish holidays or dietary preference. There was a war on and one worked when and where one was assigned and ate what was being served, as food was rationed and we were always hungry. At boarding school the Jewish pupils were served vegetarian meals. The hostels were of course kosher. Family contacts were few and far between, but included going home with some of my fellow student nurses, visiting friends from Germany and spending some days off with the family of a former colleague of my father's near Manchester.

Eva: You must have felt quite lonely and missed your family very much; they were so far away in Palestine at the time.

Karoline: We had quite an extensive correspondence. The many air raids and times spent in the shelter or taking cover under an overturned couch or armchair were often spent in writing letters to my parents and to my brother in the USA. Student nurses study very hard to pass the State Board Examinations, and there was little time to think about feeling lonely. Additionally, there were always the fire drills, the decontamination practice and evacuation exercises often held in the evenings. The worst days were of course birthdays and holidays and the time when on the nightshift some colleagues confronted me, telling me that, because of refugees like me, they had to suffer rationing and could not buy a new dress for a dance, or when my name on the door in the nurses residence was changed from Frenkel to Heinkel. Mail service from overseas was very erratic during the war. The aerograms were censored and photocopied in a reduced form and hard to decipher. They often arrived in twos and threes and then nothing for what seemed ages.

Eva: I imagine that your parents were worried about you in England, during the air raids and so forth.

Karoline: I am sure they were worried about me but they never told me so in their letters. They encouraged me to work hard, to study diligently, so that they could be proud of me. I somehow had the notion that a refugee had the duty to prove him or herself and do everything as perfectly as possible. Still, I went to the noon-time concerts at the National Gallery, the ballet or the theatre as often as my finances allowed on my days off.

After the war I saved all my money to finance a trip to Palestine to see my parents and prepared for emigration to America. I should explain that I petitioned for and received first papers for naturalization, but the British Government was slow to naturalize me, and I was anxious to get away from institutional living, from austerity and rationing and above all, my stateless status.

Eva: Thank you so much, Karoline, for sharing this fascinating part of your life.

*   *   *

Gabrielle Margules

(Salzburg), Cold Spring, N.Y., USA

A TEDDY BEAR'S SONG

Bear bear a teddy bear
hug hug a lovable mug
August Ella's bear
older Nina pulling Ella's hair

Nina wise teasing wise
sisters pushing pulling
Nina wise book wise
teddy loving Ella's eyes

Heil Hitler
black shirts brown shirts
Jude a Jew we hate
Jude a Jew we bait
up against a wall
shoot with a deadly ball

Visa visa we need a visa
lungs okay
Ella okay Nina okay
August okay

To England
the land of the free
friendly enemy aliens
come to tea

Tea tea tea and toast
sad Nina sad Ella
sad August
come to tea

Ella to school
Nina to work
words are odd
words are hard
all all is cold
bear bear a teddy bear
a cuddly bear to hold

'Biskuit fressende
Tee drinkende Engländer
ich werde sie ausradieren – Hitler

Fire fire everywhere
Heil Hitler
would come to England free
Nein no
Hitler never
come to tea

Tea tea tea and toast
glad Ella glad Nina
glad August
come to tea
in England
for ever free

Gabriele Margules

*   *   *

Liesl Munden

(Heilbronner, Düsseldorf), Sussex, UK

I was born in Germany in 1924. I lived with my parents in Düsseldorf and was an only child, but my parents had a daughter who died two years before I was born.

Hitler came to power in 1933, when I was nine years old. The first event that happened to make me aware that I was being singled out as a Jewish child was when I was ten and my parents told me that I would have to leave my school and attend another. The reason given to me then was that there were too many Jewish children in the school and that it had been decreed by Hitler that I should go to another school. Many other children of my age had to change schools, but the loss of my friends at that time was a great shock to me.

The new school was in fact very good; a big, well established girls school, and I soon made new friends. To this day I have a German Catholic girl-friend from that school.

So, at the age of ten, my life went on, having as much fun as I could going swimming and skating in my spare time. I mixed with Jewish and non-Jewish children and took little notice of what was going on in the world around me. My parents shielded me from many unpleasant experiences they had.

A little time later another incident took place. I was not allowed to continue having skating lessons, simply because I was Jewish. The teacher, who was giving me private lessons, telephoned my mother, saying that, as I did not look Jewish, she would like to continue teaching me, but my mother refused. It was against my parents' principles that I should capitalize on my non-Jewish appearance, and furthermore if it were discovered, the teacher would be in serious trouble.

Then came a worse experience. I loved swimming. One day a non-Jewish girlfriend and her parents took me to an open air pool where we had been many times before. Now there was a big notice in the entrance hall which said: 'Dogs and Jews are forbidden to enter'.

These were only small incidents, but to me – a child – it seemed that the world had come to an end. It hadn't of course. Worse, much worse was to come.

During most of my childhood we lived in a first floor flat. We had a lot of rooms and my father had his office in the flat, where he and his secretary worked. My mother had help with the housework. Because my father had business connections with Holland and Switzerland, he was able to continue earning a living, although many Jewish men and women lost their jobs and livelihoods during the mid-1930s. Then came a decree which forbade non-Jewish people working for Jews. We moved to a much smaller flat, where my mother could run the home on her own and my father had a desk for his office in the dining room, which also became my bedroom at night.

On the 9 November 1938 the Nazi Stormtroopers came into our flat and almost totally destroyed it. All Jewish homes were ransacked that night; all Synagogues were set alight and many Jews were deported to concentration camps. As the result of this unexpected outrage, Jews began trying to escpe in earnest; some committed suicide by jumping from windows.

The great amount of broken glass on that night, gave it a special name – *Kristallnacht.*

* * *

Vera Tann

Norwich, UK

When I read the note in the Harwich newspaper of your fiftieth Anniversary reunion, it brought the old days, when I lived in Dovercourt, back to me very vividly. My husband, Fred, was employed then as a railway shipping clerk at Parkston Quay continental office and witnessed the arrival of many Jewish children. As they had to identify their luggage and many of them were very young, the men worked overtime to help these young refugees. He was very upset on one occasion when he was told of one transport of orphans, who had been turned out in the middle of the night, as their orphanage had been burned down. I shall never forget their scared and bewildered faces.

My late friend, Eleanor Coombe, and myself, both school teachers, decided to offer our help and teach English at the Dovercourt Holiday Camp, where they were accommodated. We were amazed how quickly and eagerly they learned. It was like playing a game with them. We put every-day articles, such as spoons, forks, knives, sugar and milk, on a table and sat around it. We taught them to ask 'what is this?' (vot is dis?) at first, but not for long. When they watched the workmen, we went on to nails, screws, saw, hammer etc. This was great fun.

We wanted to adopt two little girls of about six and eight years, but the organizers explained to us that, being Jewish, they had to keep to their dietary laws.

I am really reliving those historical days again and wish you every success.

Editors' Note: Bertha Leverton met with Vera and Fred Tann, now in their eighties, when they made a special point to be present at the unveiling of the plaque erected by the Harwich Town Council on 3 June 1990 to commemorate our arrival in 1938/39. She also met with Betty Scott, who in 1988 had sent her the well-known photograph of the smiling policeman

The unveiling Ceremony. From left to right: Mr Eric Sotto, Councillor Clive Booth, Mrs Bertha Leverton and Mrs Margaret Olmer

Bertha Leverton and Margaret Olmer with the plaque

holding two little boys by the hand with the boat in the background. That policeman was her father.

Mrs Scott helped to organize the unique unveiling ceremony, which was graced by the attendance of the Deputy Mayor, Councillor Clive Booth and several council members. Among those present was Mr D Mann, who was a sailor on the boats we came on.

*   *   *

Alisa Tennenbaum

(Scherzer, Vienna), Kfar Vitkin, Israel

I arrived in England one week before the outbreak of war with a lot of other children. We were the last Kindertransport out of Austria.

From London I was sent to a children's hostel in Tynemouth near Newcastle. There we were twenty girls from Austria, Germany and Czechoslovakia. The youngest was three years old, and the oldest fourteen. Shortly after the war started, our two matrons, Mrs Sieber and Mrs Urbach, were sent inland to look for another house, as we had to be evacuated. After a few months we all moved to Windermere in the Lake District, where we lived together until the end of the war. We all went to the village school. When we reached the age of about fifteen, the refugee committee asked each of us to choose a trade or profession, because, they said very wisely, that we would have to stand on our own feet in the future. One of the girls went to the local hairdresser, another trained as a nurse, etc. I took up dressmaking, which I enjoy very much to this day as a hobby.

I was very lucky in that my father was also in Britain. He was taken to Dachau on 10 November 1938, released after two months and was one of the lucky ones to be accepted in the Kitchener Camp. At the outbreak of war he immediately joined the British Army. I was then the only one who had a father. Later one other girl heard from hers and he also came to England. I am still in touch with five other girls. Last year I was in Britain for my holiday, making a nostalgic journey, meeting with two of the girls and visiting the hostel in Windermere. It was wonderful. I have many loving memories from that period, in spite that there was a war on, we were not with our families and we had to get used to living for years together with twenty girls. Our childhood was a good one. The ladies of the Newcastle Committee took good care of us.

After the war the Red Cross informed me that my mother was thankfully still alive. She was taken from the concentration camp to Sweden to recuperate. After nine months there, my mother joined us. Daddy was discharged from the Army, and I left the hostel in January 1946. After a few months the hostel was closed; everybody going their own way. Most of the girls were in their teens, and the younger ones were sent to another hostel in Manchester

I came to Israel in 1949 together with my parents. My sister has been here since January 1939. She came with *Youth Aliya*.

I am now chief librarian in our regional high school. One of the girls from our hostel lives in Kibbutz Zikkim. The others live all over the world, but most of them stayed in England.

* * *

Norman Tuckman

(Tuchmann, Munich), Ashkelon, Israel

I am one of the Kinder who came to England from Munich at the end of 1938. We were sent to Butlins Dovercourt Bay Holiday Camp near Harwich, and after a short while to Kitchener Camp near Sandwich. After a short spell there, working in the post office, I was sent to a farm training centre near Nuffield, close to Oxford. Woburn House found me a job with an electrical contractor in Portsmouth. My employer was most helpful, provided me with a bicycle and paid for my evening classes at the Portsmouth Municipal College.

In 1940 I had to leave Portsmouth, as it was a prohibited zone for all aliens. I came to London and worked for a radio firm as a mechanic. I joined the RAF in 1941, reached the rank of Sergeant, and moved with the RAF or rather the TAF (Tactical Air Force) right through the European campaign from D-Day onwards, through France, Belgium, Holland and Germany into Denmark. G-d was kind; I came back. I was discharged in 1946, rather worse for wear, having spent the last three months prior to my discharge from Bomber Command, in the RAF hospital in Wroughton near Swindon.

After my discharge, I settled down to business, well endowed with my demob suit and the money I had saved from my Sergeant's pay. I married in 1952, and for some twenty years was principal of a busy estate office in South East London. On a voluntary basis I was National Treasurer of the Friends of Akim for twenty-four years, Chairman of the JIA (Joint Israel Appeal) Streatham, South West London, Committee for ten years, and a member of the Board of Management of the Streatham Synagogue for over twenty years, as well as Chairman of its Functions Committee.

We have two daughters and four grandchildren living in Israel, and decided to come on *Aliya* in December 1985. We have a cottage near the sea, small but beautiful.

I was indeed fortunate to find refuge, help, kindness and a new home in Britain, and I will always look upon England as my home.

*   *   *

Annie Wolfson
Manchester, UK

During 1938/39 I lived in London, and my late husband and I were very much involved with the refugee work.

We were originally approached by the late Rabbi Schonfeld, who, on his own, brought out orthodox children from Germany and Austria. Within a short period many more children were allowed to come, and my late husband and I organized through the Ministers of all the London Synagogues, working committees, who found homes in their areas and arranged all the after-care when children arrived in England.

In Hackney, where we lived at that time, I organized our own committee. We bought a house in Victoria Park Road with the funds we had collected and had it suitably adapted as a hostel for about twenty girls, who were cared for by a very loving refugee matron and a small staff. This hostel was used as a clearing house for children for whom suitable homes could not be found on arrival, but who were eventually housed and replaced by new arrivals. We were known as the 'Hackney Aid Committee for Refugee Children' and we worked with *Bnei Brith*.

When war was declared, all the children and staff were evacuated to Norfolk. Other children were evacuated with their schools. Our committee continued to keep a watchful eye on the children in Norfolk and provided whatever was necessary for them.

Unfortunately, owing to many unforseen circumstances and our move to Manchester, I lost complete touch with most of the work, but we were successful in bringing together a whole family of parents and three children, who subsequently emigrated to America. After a few letters, I lost contact with them.

*   *   *

MOVEMENT FOR THE CARE OF CHILDREN FROM GERMANY

BRITISH INTERAID COMMITTEE

In association with:

THE COUNCIL FOR GERMAN JEWRY
THE CHRISTIAN COUNCIL
SAVE THE CHILDREN FUND

69 GREAT RUSSELL STREET,
LONDON, W.C.1
Tel.: HOLborn 4512

Joint Chairmen:
VISCOUNT SAMUEL
SIR WYNDHAM DEEDES

Hon. Secretary:
Mrs. NORMAN BENTWICH

THE NEED

There are at least 50,000 children in Germany (including Austria and Sudetenland) who should be helped to come out. They are mostly Jewish, but a large proportion are " Non-Aryan " Christians. Their present conditions are intolerable. Every future prospect is closed to them. This country will be ready to join with other countries in their rescue.

To raise a great central fund for their support is not practicable. If each child cost only £25 a year and had to be maintained for an average period of four years, the total sum required would be £5,000,000. And the Central Funds are already faced by immense demands for relief of refugees, training, and emigration—far beyond their capacity.

THE PLAN

There are numbers of people in this country, and in other countries, who are ready to come to the rescue of these unhappy children. This movement has been set on foot to organise those efforts and bring them into one comprehensive scheme.

This involves taking responsibility for the maintenance and welfare of the children for some years—until they can rejoin their parents in happier circumstances, or until they are old enough to be self-supporting. The Central Committee cannot be in direct touch with all the people all over the country who would be acting as the children's guardians. There must be local bodies of a stable character, who will take responsibility.

GUARDIAN COMMITTEES

Such committees may be formed in connection with churches, synagogues, and philanthropic or social organisations. Any individual who is willing to take care of one or more children should, if possible, get into touch with such a local committee; or else communicate with this office, who will give the necessary information.

Where funds have to be provided in connection with the care of the children, **it is most important not to compete with the collections for the Central Funds.** Any subscriptions should be from persons who are willing to make a special contribution locally for this special purpose.

Jewish Committees will realise the importance of not cutting across the efforts of the Women's Appeal Committee for German-Jewish Women and Children (75 Great Russell Street, W.C.1) who have been at work for the last five years. Where there is a local committee for that appeal, those who are taking part in the present movement will no doubt desire to work in co-operation with it.

Similar considerations apply with reference to the Church of England Committee for non-Aryan Christians.

THE CENTRAL AND THE LOCAL COMMITTEES

The Central Committee will be responsible for bringing the children over, for maintaining them in hostels until they can be properly allocated, and for entrusting them to approved persons or committees. The Central Committee will maintain a system of inspection. They will guarantee the Home Office that the children will not become a public charge and will either be emigrated in due course or be absorbed in this country in ways approved by the Government. The arrangements for emigration or employment will be made, as a rule, by the Central Committee. The Local Committees will be expected to make themselves responsible for the maintenance of the children, whether in hostels, in private homes where hospitality is offered and which are ascertained to be suitable, or in private houses, where they may be received for payment. They will arrange co-operation, where possible, with the Local Authorities, for their education and agricultural or industrial training. In general, they will be the children's guardians and be responsible for their happiness and welfare. They will report to the Central Office on each child periodically.

ADMINISTRATION

It is important to allocate the children as a general rule to the care of persons of their own faith, and with an environment similar, as far as practicable, to that of their own homes. Children who do not know English should, if possible, be in constant touch with people who know German.

The availability of places in the local secondary and technical schools should be taken into account in allocating the older children.

Arrangements have been made by the Central Committee for the supply of clothing and other requirements on very favourable terms. Communications on this subject should be addressed to the Supplies Group at this office.

The maximum age of boys and girls accepted under this scheme is seventeen.

Further information will be circulated in due course.

December 7, 1938.

THE CENTRAL FUNDS referred to are those of :—
   Earl Baldwin's Appeal. (Cheques may be sent to any of the branches of the principal banks.)

   Council for German Jewry. (Bankers: Messrs. N. M. Rothschild & Sons, New Court, St. Swithin's Lane, London, E.C.4.)

   Christian Council, 2 Gordon Square, London, W.C.1.

London Caledonian Press Ltd. (T.U. all Depts.), 74 Swinton Street, W.C.1.—3760

REPORT OF THE ACTIVITIES OF
THE RUGBY (CHRISTADELPHIAN)
REFUGEE COMMITTEE WITH
ESPECIAL REFERENCE TO THE
JEWISH BOYS' HOSTEL AT RUGBY.

Early in 1939 The Nazi persecution of the Jews was being viciously extended across Greater Germany. Parents were suddenly wrenched from their children and thrown into Concentration Camps and Prisons, often never to see their loved ones again. Periodically Transports arrived in England with homeless Jewish Refugee Children on board, and heart-rending scenes were regularly to be seen at Liverpool Street Station in London when "The Movement for the Care of Children from Germany" accepted delivery of this tragic human freight.

A Christadelphian who became aware of the arrival of the first Transport from Germany, soon discovered the dire need of these pathetic children. He felt compelled, whenever he could make opportunity, and at every Ecclesia he visited, to spread the news of their unhappy plight and urge all who heard his appeal to offer hospitality and loving care to these little ones whose sorrow was so poignant, whose lot so pitiable, and whose need so great.

Some found difficulty in believing the horrors of Nazi persecution, and some advised great caution, pointing out the dangers and inconenviences of taking strangers into our homes, but to be present in The Reception Hall at Liverpool Street when these unhappy children arrived, was to witness scenes of human misery sad enough to soften hearts of stone. Even the hardened London Policemen and Railway Porters, who frequently saw sorrowful leave-takings, were often observed in tears as they assisted the small band of workers with their frightened homeless charges, each bearing around his or her neck—a number on a disc. Their individuality had been temporarily erased, they had become merely cargo. Their distress was pathetically evident ; their need, urgent.

Soon letters containing offers of homes came from towns as far from one another as Preston and Bournemouth and it became evident that little girls were especially welcomed and sought after. As an example of the generous offers received we remember with gratitude one, among others, which enabled us to arrange for three pathetic little sisters, all under seven, to live together in their new English home.

The finding of homes for Refugee Jewish boys, however, was a much greater problem. The Camps in England, set up to receive these boys, were full and until homes were found for them, others in Germany, waiting to take their places, were not allowed to enter the Country. This left them at the mercy of the Nazis and it was therefore imperative that they be brought out of Germany without delay.

About this time a refugee Jewish lady from Czechoslovakia, together with her two boys, was enjoying the hospitality of a Christadelphian home in Rugby, and the need for establishing them in a more permanent residence provided the germ of an idea for future activity on a more ambitious scale. It was thought that if a hostel for refugee boys could be established and maintained at a reasonable cost, with a refugee matron in charge, a similar project, under Christadelphian control and upon Christiadelphian aid, might be adopted in other parts of the country, and many more boys thus be saved from the horrors of Germany.

Consequently, in July 1939, "Little Thorn," Bilton Road, Rugby, opened its doors to the first small company of Jewish refugee boys and provided at once for them, a comfortable home, good food, a kindly matron, and a small company of Christadelphians to watch over their development and welfare. So much for the beginning of the Hostel, which by the end of July was in full operation and comfortably housing nine boys from Germany, Poland and Czecho-Solvakia. But the work of providing accommodation in private homes still persisted.

Space does not allow us to report in detail the offers of homes and material help which came, to mention a few, from Preston, Ormskirk, Bournemouth, Reading, Derby, Rugby, Burton, Birmingham, Leicester, Ashby, Coventry, Stratford-on-Avon, Nottingham, Halford Bridge, London, Leigh-on-Sea, Dudley, Rowley Regis, Wolverhampton, Romford, Nuneaton, Portsmouth, Kennilworth. The letters and practical help which came from these and many other towns were a constant source of encouragement and were greatly appreciated.

The Rugby Hostel has now been in operation for over three years, and in addition to providing a permanent home, for varying periods, for twenty-four different refugees, it has also served the further useful purpose of becoming a temporary home for very many more. Very quickly it became a centre at which Jewish refugee men and women have been able to gather to refresh themselves and enjoy social amenities with fellow Jews at week-ends and holidays. Those who have so generously and consistently contributed to the Refugee Fund would have found a real joy on many a Sunday afternoon during the summer months to see so happy a company collected in the garden behind " Little Thorn," having come from the surrounding district to share news of home and of friends who were still coming over from the Continent. From the Hostel, refugees have gone to America, Spain, Canada and to Australia, either to join parents once more or to start a new career in a new land.

On occasions the happy atmosphere of " Little Thorn " has been clouded over with difficulties and trouble—as for example when the boys of sixteen years of age and over were suddenly arrested for internment in the Isle of Man. But great was our joy and relief on one such occasion when, after a special appeal on behalf of two of the boys, The Aliens Tribunal of Birmingham, actually rescinded an earlier decision to intern the boys, and were agreeable to accept the Hostel and our personal supervision of the boys affected, as an adequate alternative to internment.

Boys who have resided in the Hostel have been given a sound training ; wherever possible, in accord with their own inclination and aptitude, and have already begun careers in Leather Manufacturing, Cabinet Making, Engineering. Commerce and Chemistry.

The Fund has also provided aid and support for other children in private homes, both boys and girls who are scattered in various parts of England, Scotland and Wales.

The creation of the Fund enabled friends of the refugees to come to their aid when financial help has been desperately and urgently needed, and the existence of the Hostel has provided food and a bed whenever a Jewish refugee has been stranded with nowhere else to go.

The deep felt appreciation of those behind the scenes in this small effort to help God's people, is now warmly expressed to all who in so many ways have made it possible. It has been a great privilege to be connected with a work of aid to Jacob's People in the time of their Trouble, and it is our prayer that the time may speedily come when they shall be saved out of it.

For the Committee,

R. A. OVERTON, Honorary Secretary,

The Grove in the Kindertransport Forest outside Jerusalem, planted on the occasion of our 50th Anniversary with money contributed by Kinder.

POSTSCRIPT

The stories which you have read, have come to an end. But in a way they are also a beginning. A beginning for you, the reader, to know what happened to us and hopefully to tell your children and others about the *Kinder*. Many of us did not find it easy to recall and tell the traumatic events which befell us. Many did not even tell their spouses and children the happenings recorded here. It was the need to let future generations know the role which we, as children, played in history, which made us put pen to paper.

We would have preferred to print all these stories in full but, due to limited space, we had to make some cuts, whilst trying our best to maintain continuity.

Some of us have tried to hide the fact that we were once refugees. It was something not quite acceptable. Even today some people, often prominent, deny their background. Most of us, however, now admit it and are proud of having achieved some measure of success in our countries of adoption. Unfortunately some of us were cut off from our roots, as we had to leave our homes and parents at a very tender age, but most of us have now returned to the fold. We were condemned for what we were, but we have retained our Jewish identity and are proud of our heritage.

One wonderful result of our reunion in June 1989 is the local meetings now being held all over the world, with friends and even relatives finding each other, not knowing that they had survived. Other researches are being conducted into our history now and we list overleaf those of which we are aware.

We wish to put on record our sincere gratitude to our publishers, The Book Guild Ltd., and their staff for the great interest and faith they have always shown in this book and for the way they coped with some manuscripts which were less than perfect.

Our final thanks, dear reader, go to you.

Bertha Leverton   Shmuel Lowensohn

*   *

Research projects on the subject of the Kindertransports are being conducted by:

Dr Tydor Baumel, Bar Ilan University, Israel

Melissa Hacker, New York, USA

Dr Vernon Hamilton, Reading University, UK

Paula Hill, M.A., London, UK

Ingrid Lomfors, Goteborg, Sweden

Prof Rabbi Dr Ya'acov Newman, Bar Ilan University, Israel

Linda Pakula, Texas, USA

Dr Dorit Whiteman, New York, USA

The Imperial War Museum, London, UK

The National Life Story Collection, British Library Sound Archives, London, UK

*   *   *

The Joint Editors Bertha Leverton and Shmuel Lowensohn. Photograph taken by Harvey Nyman at the Stanmore Jewish Book Week, May 1990.

INDEX